THE ECONOMICS OF CREATIVE DESTRUCTION

The Economics of Creative Destruction

New Research on Themes from Aghion and Howitt

UFUK AKCIGIT *and* JOHN VAN REENEN

HARVARD UNIVERSITY PRESS

Cambridge, Massachusetts & London, England

2023

First printing

Library of Congress Cataloging-in-Publication Data

Names: Akcigit, Ufuk, editor. | Van Reenen, John, editor.
Title: The economics of creative destruction : new research on themes from
    Aghion and Howitt / [edited by] Ufuk Akcigit, John Van Reenen.
Description: Cambridge, Massachusetts ; London, England : Harvard
    University Press, 2023. | Includes bibliographical references and index.
Identifiers: LCCN 2022056727 | ISBN 9780674270367 (cloth)
Subjects: LCSH: Aghion, Philippe. | Howitt, Peter, 1946– |
    Creative destruction. | Economic development.
Classification: LCC HD45 .E256 2023 | DDC 338.9—dc23/eng/20230306
LC record available at https://lccn.loc.gov/2022056727

We dedicate this book to Emmanuel Farhi, who began the journey with us in 2018 when we were in the planning stages. We sorely miss him, as does the wider community of scholars of which he was such an integral part.

Contents

Foreword

EMMANUEL MACRON

We are in a time that begs for a fundamental redefinition of economic doctrine. For more than forty years, most of the world's economies have been organized according to the same precepts, commonly referred to as the "Washington Consensus." This doctrine insists on openness, privatization, deregulation. It was probably appropriate for a historic moment at the end of the twentieth century, and it is undeniable that it has produced results, lifting hundreds of millions of people out of material poverty, especially in the least-developed countries. But now its shortcomings are glaring. It is too short-term. It finds itself very poorly equipped to face the challenges of our time: the threats to the environment, rising inequalities, demographic changes, technological revolutions, the weakening of our democracies—a weakening that is the direct and indirect consequence of the other revolutions.

The global pandemic has bluntly revealed the flaws that are eroding our societies, as Philippe Aghion and his coauthors rightly emphasize in their latest book. On one hand, in countries of "cutthroat capitalism," often Anglo-Saxon, we see the harms of inadequate social protection, and the harms of policies that have allowed inequalities to widen, in all their dimensions. On the other hand, in countries of "cuddly capitalism," often in continental Europe, the crisis has exposed the cost to society of research and innovation policies that are not ambitious or innovative enough.

We must therefore build a new way of thinking, a new consensus. And I think the Schumpeterian paradigm must be a key part of this new consensus. A renewed Schumpeterian paradigm, which dares to tackle the challenges of the twenty-first century head-on. This is why the work by Philippe Aghion and Peter Howitt is especially useful and relevant, including their seminal article written in 1987, "A Model of Growth through Creative Destruction."

Creative destruction is the vital energy of the "spirited horse" of capitalism. If we know how to tame it and steer its path, then it is possible to reconnect with shared prosperity while protecting our common goods.

The chapters in this volume address a large number of issues and economic enigmas on which the Schumpeterian dynamic sheds a new light, in areas as diverse as development, employment, competition, trade, the environment, business dynamism, and innovation. The breadth of these topics shows the extent to which it is a paradigm at the heart of economic life. I would like to highlight three strong messages from this work.

First, it reinstates a growth objective. We have given in too much to defeatism, by taking growth as exogenous and lamenting its slowdown. If we believe in creative destruction, we know we can influence the rate of growth, through more work and more innovation. We can also influence the course of innovation to make this growth inclusive and sustainable. This conviction also reinstates public policies, after forty years of dominant beliefs in a great automatic moderation.

Next, inequalities must be reduced while preserving the incentives to innovate. Professors Aghion's and Howitt's results, and the work that followed, clearly demonstrate that it is possible, and that it is highly desirable, because the two objectives are mutually reinforcing, contrary again to popular beliefs. The freedom to research and the freedom to *entreprendre,* if you allow me to use this French word, are critical drivers of social mobility. To combat inequalities effectively, we must combine a well-designed monetary redistribution scheme with other levers that act directly on equal access to opportunities, provide support to families since early childhood, enable access to good education, integrate through work and activity, enable access to good jobs, support training and retraining, and expose to innovation, given that exposure to innovation helps develop a taste for innovation itself. It is a very demanding multidimensional agenda. In my opinion, it is the only one that can fundamentally reform our economic models and prevent the gradual collapse of our liberal democracies.

Finally, and this my third remark, to achieve this dual objective of greater prosperity and greater equality through creative destruction, a strong ecosystem of innovation must emerge. This is certainly one of the major challenges that France and Europe must face in the aftermath of the pandemic. To go beyond an easy mantra, the work in this volume is crucial in characterizing what a "strong innovation ecosystem" means in practice, because it ventures behind the scenes of innovation. Innovations do not fall from the sky, they are not exogenous. We must act at each level of the long process of idea generation: from fundamental research, to which we must provide sufficient resources and the necessary academic freedom, to applied R&D, which must be encouraged in companies, funded, and for which healthy competition must be guaranteed. The public authorities have a major role to play in this process, and its exact positioning must be carefully chosen: It is up to the public authorities to identify the "major challenges" to which it is urgent to respond, and they must provide adequate means for maximizing the probability of breakthrough innovations. This is key, especially for France and Europe.

If I chose to emphasize these three powerful ideas, among the many threads to be drawn from the work undertaken by Philippe Aghion and Peter Howitt and the research that followed, it is because they strike me as central to building a new economic consensus, and yet they are far from being consensual today in our public debate. Indeed, the debate is often too polarized in quarrels filled with prejudice, for instance: "are we for or against capitalism." I am deeply convinced that we can make our societies fairer and more sustainable. I am convinced that this requires a policy of well-redesigned growth, and that this is how to generate real equality and social mobility, a growth based on ideas and permanent innovation. Creative destruction has never been so relevant to the challenges of our time. It is up to all of us to continue to unravel its mysteries, and to continue to apply its teachings.

THE ECONOMICS OF CREATIVE DESTRUCTION

Introduction

UFUK AKCIGIT *and* JOHN VAN REENEN

In 1992, Philippe Aghion and Peter Howitt published their seminal paper, "A Model of Growth through Creative Destruction." Citations are not the only metric of success, but it is striking that the paper has over 15,000 citations on Google Scholar,[1] a very impressive achievement. The paper fundamentally changed the way that economists thought about growth. It formalized the idea that to understand the success of modern economies, we must not only recognize that innovation is a deliberate choice of firms facing a changing and uncertain environment, but also that the process is highly disruptive. Innovating firms necessarily make older ideas, lines of business, and forms of organization obsolete. Research and Development (R&D) is by nature both creative and destructive.

This notion of growth owed much to Joseph Schumpeter (1942), but his insights were notoriously difficult to incorporate into formal economic models. Aghion and Howitt's endogenous growth framework elegantly showed how this could be done, combining insights from several fields of economics, above all by integrating industrial organization into macroeconomics.

The Aghion and Howitt (1992) paper created a new space for theoretical and empirical work that has reverberated through almost every field of economics and into other disciplines. Nearly three decades after the publication

---

[1] https://scholar.google.com/scholar?hl=en&as_sdt=0%2C5&q=philippe+aghion&btnG=.

1

of the paper, in June 2021, we brought together over a hundred scholars (including eleven Nobel Laureates) to present their views on how the creative destruction framework has influenced our discipline. We uncovered a strong narrative linking many of the papers, so we then commissioned chapters from many of these presenters to chart a course through modern economics. This book is the result.

Organization of the Book

We have organized the book to reflect the many areas where the Aghion-Howitt framework has had a major influence on scholarship. All chapters are original contributions by the authors. Some are analytical reviews of the literature; others offer novel theoretical or empirical contributions. We hope the reader finds all of them immensely stimulating.

In the overview of the book (Part I), Nobel Laureate Edmund Phelps (Chapter 1) reflects on how our thinking about growth policies has fundamentally changed due to Aghion and Howitt. He echoes the themes of several other chapters that innovation is not simply the product of scientists—it involves entrepreneurs, managers, and workers. Indeed, he views the wellspring of sustained innovation in a country as intimately tied to cultural values, especially of individualism and rewards to effort and talent. The importance of norms is stressed in many other chapters (e.g., by Besley and Persson in Chapter 14 and by Mokyr in Chapter 26). History and sociology are also increasingly being woven into models of creative destruction, and we expect much more exciting work along these lines in the future.

Next, in Chapter 2, Akcigit sketches out the essential elements of the Aghion-Howitt framework, how it built on the shoulders of giants, but also how its originality fundamentally advanced our understanding of growth. The chapter shows how the basic architecture of the model paved the way for new possibilities in many different areas of economic research.

The main body of the book consists of eight more parts: Part II, Competition and International Trade; Part III, Inequality and Labor Markets; Part IV, Growth Measurement and Growth Decline; Part V, The Environment: Green Innovation and Climate Change; Part VI, Development and Political Economy; Part VII, Finance; Part VIII, Taxation; and Part IX, Science.

The Conclusion, by Aghion and Howitt, reflects on our book as a whole.

Competition and International Trade

Creative destruction implies that the structure of product markets is critical for innovation. The existing frameworks, which abstracted away from the strategic interaction between firms, had no way to adequately integrate competition with growth. Griffith and Van Reenen (Chapter 3) discuss the intellectual history leading up to the famous "Inverted-U" paper, which used the creative destruction framework to argue that intermediate levels of competition would maximize an economy's total innovation. At high levels of competition, the marginal effect of further competitive intensity would be negative (as Schumpeter argued), but at lower levels of competition, an increase in competitive intensity would boost innovation (as Arrow argued).

Griffith and Van Reenen emphasize the dialectic between empirical findings and theoretical developments, and how modern structural industrial organization models have been influenced by creative destruction. An important point, often overlooked in policy debates, is that although the relationship is nonlinear, the average effect of competition on innovation tends to be positive (consistent with earlier work, such as by Blundell et al. 1999). Indeed, for the cases most often examined by antitrust authorities, competition is already low, so we are on the part of the Inverted-U where further reductions in competition are likely not only to put upward pressure on prices but also to chill innovation.

Chapter 4, by Gilbert, Riis, and Riis, focuses more squarely on one aspect of competition policy: mergers and acquisitions. It discusses how merger rules must be adapted to consider potential downward pressure on innovation. The current merger regimes focus on upward pricing pressure, which is important for static losses, but it misses the much more important dynamic changes to productivity. As more of the modern economy moves into high-tech industries and as so-called "superstar firms" (such as Facebook, Apple, and Google) increase their reach (see Autor et al. 2020), competition authorities need to take innovation more seriously in their enforcement activities. The authors of this chapter develop a new model used to address such issues around mergers.

Understanding competition requires thinking about the complex network of interactions, often deeply personal, that influence innovation. In Chapter 5, Jackson, Mayerowitz, and Tagade apply network theory insights to an empirical analysis of coauthorship in patenting. They find that patenting and the number of coauthors also follows an inverted-U. This reflects the trade-off between the benefits of collaboration and the threat that your presently friendly co-innovators may become your future rivals.

Trade can be a strong mechanism for increasing competition through the threat of entry from foreign firms. However, there are many other channels through which trade can influence innovation. These are thoroughly documented in Chapter 6 by Melitz and Redding, who look at theoretical and empirical work in this area. They emphasize that competition is only one mechanism through which trade matters. For example, global integration also increases market size, which increases the return to innovative investments (e.g., enabling the fixed costs of R&D to be spread over a larger revenue base). Furthermore, more sophisticated high-quality inputs can be sourced from overseas—often through global value chains—which will also stimulate innovation. Globalization can thus lead to dynamic gains in addition to the standard benefits from improved allocation of resources. Because of this, the recent tide of deglobalization and supply chain disruption caused by Brexit, Trump's trade wars, COVID-19, and the war in Ukraine are likely to be another headwind against global growth.

Inequality and Labor Markets

Many people, politicians especially, bristle at the notion of creative destruction—and perhaps for good reasons. Innovation is disruptive, not only for firms who lose market positions but also for their workers, who see their jobs, wages, and skills threatened. Because of this, the shaking up of labor markets by new technology may create more inequality and unemployment. In Chapter 7, Blundell, Jaravel, and Toivanen begin Part III by examining the relation between innovation and inequality. They argue against a monocausal approach. Although innovation can certainly raise inequality through, for example, monopoly rents or increasing the demand for the skilled who earn more, there are countervailing forces. New opportunities are created by innovation, and if new entrants rather than incumbents seize these chances, this process will foster social mobility and so reduce inequality. They emphasize the many policies that could both increase innovation and reduce inequality (or at least inequality of opportunity). Data from several countries and periods show that children born to the richest parents are more likely to grow up to be inventors than those born to parents in the bottom half of the distribution (Aghion et al. 2016, 2023; Akcigit et al. 2020). For example, US data show that children born to the richest 1 percent of parents are ten times more likely to grow up to be inventors than those born in the bottom half of the income distribution (Bell et al. 2019). The vast majority of this correlation is not due to lower intrinsic ability. Improving access to education and exposing "lost Einsteins and Marie Curies" to the possibility of becoming inventors (Bell et al. 2019) would both reduce inequality and raise the growth rate, with education having positive effects across generations (Aghion et al. 2023; Akcigit et al. 2020; Toivanen and Väänänen, 2016). Such policies would be good for growth and equity.

The next two chapters focus on labor markets and the main way in which rewards are distributed to individuals in a market economy. Chapter 8 by Bilal, Engbom, Mongey, and Violante takes a macroeconomic approach, focusing on the role of technological imitation in raising growth. Entrant firms creatively destroy incumbents by poaching their workers. These authors examine what happens when imitation becomes harder—consistent with the work of Bloom et al. (2020) that ideas have become harder to find. They show that this framework matches many trends in the US over the past three decades: lower firm entry, less employment response to productivity shocks, and falling job-to-job transitions. Despite this, the authors of Chapter 8 find that lower imitation does not produce much lower productivity growth through more misallocation, because the slower rate of obsolescence induces productive growing firms to invest more in costly hiring.

In Chapter 9, Skans, Choné, and Kramarz look at the very rich administrative data from Sweden to show that skill is highly multidimensional. They argue that recent innovations have tended to "unbundle" these skills, making it easier to outsource tasks to specialists. Rather than have a general manager in charge of scheduling, monitoring, organizing suppliers, finding buyers, and so forth, each of these skills is performed by a specialist sometimes inside the organization, but often outside it (or even automated by software). This specialization generates a much tighter sorting of workers in different firms and increases competition among specialists, driving down their wages. This leads to increased inequality, with generalists earning much higher market wages than specialists do. It also helps explain why the economy seems bifurcated into "good" firms, where all workers seem highly paid, and "bad" firms, where all workers are poorly paid (the so-called "McKinsey-McDonalds economy").

Growth Measurement and Growth Decline

One of the most worrying trends in recent years has been the decline in productivity growth, which occurred after the mid-1970s oil shocks. This was eventually reversed by the Information and Communications Technology-based productivity acceleration during 1995–2004. Unfortunately, productivity growth has again slowed since then and has remained lackluster for two decades. Chapter 8 by Bilal et al., discussed in the previous section, matched the falling business dynamism trends but could not account for the productivity slowdown. The chapters in this section take this issue head-on.

Chapter 10 by Boppart and Li examines ways of improving the measurement of growth to incorporate creative destruction. They document considerable mismeasurement problems that generally cause us to underestimate growth, which is good news. However, the measurement problems have always been there, and the mismeasurement has not increased so severely since the mid-2000s that it could account for the magnitude of the recent decline in growth. This is the bad news.

Next, Bergeaud, Cette, and Lecat (Chapter 11) examine the role of monetary policy, considering that interest rates could be both an effect and a cause of slower growth. Until recently, the slowdown of productivity growth has gone hand-in-hand with a decline in long-term real interest rates around the world. Conventionally, if long-term productivity growth declines, then the real return on capital investment has fallen, and therefore, so too will interest rates. However, the authors also consider how there may be a reverse channel from lower interest rates to growth through the lens of creative destruction. Lower interest rates may make it easier for low-productivity firms to survive (so-called "zombie firms"), and this will drag down the growth rate. The authors find evidence for these mutually reinforcing trends and argue that demographic aging is what has driven the shift. This is a rather pessimistic conclusion for our future productivity prospects.

Chapter 12, the final chapter in this section, is by Ates, who reviews the models of competition and step-by-step innovation introduced in Chapter 2. He then focuses on knowledge diffusion and shows that a decline in this margin does go a long way toward accounting for the broad trends of declining dynamism discussed by Bilal et al. in Chapter 8. The key mechanism that underlies these results is the combination of endogenous responses of firms to a decline in knowledge diffusion (incentive effect) and the ensuing shift in the sectoral composition of the economy (composition effect). Falls in diffusion weaken the incentives of laggards to innovate, which in turn reduces pressure on leaders. This leads to an increase in the relative size of sectors that are highly concentrated with high markups. These two forces reinforce the trends toward lower innovation and growth. This dynamic also potentially explains the low interest rates discussed by Bergeaud et al. in Chapter 11. Ates then links these forces with industrial policy and the importance of encouraging foreign competition between global firms.

The Environment: Green Innovation and Climate Change

Climate change is the biggest long-term challenge facing the human race. Tackling climate change will require innovation—reducing carbon consumption through higher prices and tougher regulation are unlikely to be successful without more frontier innovation and speedier adoption of clean technologies. Part V on the environment brings together four perspectives on the issue of green innovation as a form of directed technical change, leveraging the power of the Aghion-Howitt framework.

Lord Nicholas Stern wrote a landmark review on the importance of climate change (Stern, 2007). In Chapter 13, he opens this section with a policy-focused approach, emphasizing the need for urgent action on climate change and showing that this strategy easily passes a cost-benefit test. Part of this action is a requirement to invest heavily in subsidizing R&D to direct technologies away from dirty technologies and toward clean technologies.

Besley and Persson (Chapter 14) emphasize another mechanism for stimulating green innovation that operates through the social values and norms held by individuals. They show in the data that there is a shift in attitudes—particularly among the young—toward more pro-green preferences. This shift will affect demand, as consumers will prefer environmentally friendly products and services. These authors also show that the attitudinal shift has supply-side effects. First, as the expected market size for green products becomes larger, inventors direct more efforts toward this market. Besley and Persson then focus on a second channel: As scientists themselves are "motivated agents," concerned with their mission as well as with money, they will want to do more R&D in this area. This may help push technical change in a clean direction and implies that the battle for "hearts and minds" has direct economic and environmental implications.

Despite the optimism that can arise when we consider how technology can support the transition, there is a serious risk that it may be too little, too late. The COP-26 (Conference of the Parties) meetings in Glasgow in 2021 showed how difficult it is to get international climate change agreements. If global cooperation fails to produce the transition to net zero, humanity needs a Plan B. Fuglesang and Hassler (Chapter 15) take on this challenge, suggesting geoengineering solutions in case emissions are not cut sufficiently. They favor the approach of launching thousands of sunscreens ("solar kites") into space between the earth and the sun to divert dangerous solar emissions and keep global warming to manageable levels. They sketch the costs of this bold proposal and argue that it is both technically feasible and cost effective. They then analyze a game-theoretic model to deal with the objection that creating such a Plan B would undermine Plan A—a global agreement to cut emissions. They concede that this is a danger but argue that the greater risk is that we may end up with no way of preventing the earth from heating up dangerously.

In Chapter 16, Dechezleprêtre and Hémous show how Lord Stern's conclusion in Chapter 13 arises from an extension to the endogenous growth framework allowing for directed technical change. When there is an existing installed base of dirty technologies, the shift to clean technologies becomes a lot harder, because dirty innovation is locked in. For example, current innovators will tend to "build on the shoulders of giants" of past inventions, and since the current stock of ideas is mainly in fossil fuels, the natural evolution is to do more dirty innovation. Dechezleprêtre and Hémous show that shifting toward clean R&D requires not only a carbon tax but also direct subsidies with intense action early on. The good news is that as the installed base of clean technologies widens, the long-term costs are even lower. These authors illustrate this with several recent econometric studies, such as the move to electric/hybrid vehicle innovation and away from the internal combustion engine (see Aghion et al. 2016).

Development and Political Economy

The discussion of solutions to climate change in the previous section highlights the political constraints on economic analysis. Just as the creative destruction paradigm opens up the analytical space to consider issues like competition, inequality, and the environment, it also allows a reexamination of classical issues in Development and Political Economy. In Chapter 17, Peters and Zilibotti give a magisterial overview of the profound impact of the paradigm on development. They emphasize that the set of social and political institutions that help maximize growth during an initial catch-up period are quite different from those needed at a later stage. For example, catch-up institutions for diffusion are distinct from those required to push the technological frontier forward.

Roland (Chapter 18) takes on the big-picture question of what modes of industrial societies succeed in the long run. In the 1950s, there were fears that the Soviet Union would surpass the United States in technological prowess, as symbolized by the successful launch of Sputnik. Yet Communism failed to deliver sustained technological advance, collapsing under the weight of its own contradictions. Many suspect that despite China's current growth rates, it will go the same way as the USSR. Roland is less sanguine. He sees Russia's key economic failure as the suppression of entrepreneurialism that allows creative destruction to be the engine of growth. China, unlike the USSR, has a vibrant entrepreneurial sector, even though it has a politically repressive Communist regime. It is not obvious why this entrepreneurial culture will wane and hence, why China will not continue to pull away from the West in terms of its economic mass. This trend is having a profound effect on geopolitics.

In addition to studying the growth of China itself, an enormous body of work looks at the impact of the "China shock" on Western economies. As Griffith and Van Reenen discuss in Chapter 3 on competition and innovation, although the effects on jobs in domestic sectors of competing with Chinese imports is clearly negative, the impact on innovation is more heterogeneous, with many studies documenting strong positive effects of Chinese competition. Bombardini, Cutinelli-Rendina, and Trebbi (Chapter 19) investigate lobbying by US firms. They argue that although more productive firms respond positively in response to increased Chinese import competition by innovating (e.g., as found by Bloom et al. 2016), firms well below the productivity frontier will tend to respond instead by lobbying for protection and subsidies. This is because such firms both find it relatively hard to innovate to escape competition and more attractive to collude after the China shock.

Baslandze (Chapter 20) continues the theme of analyzing the tension between market entrants and incumbents. She discusses her model in Akcigit et al. (2023) where entrants try to replace incumbents through creative destruction and incumbent firms respond to this by investing in innovation or in political connections to maintain their market power. She uses rich data on Italian firms to show that market leaders are less innovation intensive and more politically connected. Political connection at the firm level is associated with higher employment growth but not productivity growth. Those sectors that have more politically connected incumbents feature lower business dynamism.

As a whole, this section shows how politics and economics are profoundly entwined and cannot be studied separately. The Aghion-Howitt framework enables a deeper understanding of these connections and offers a tractable way to build political economy into our models of growth and development.

Finance

Schumpeter emphasized the importance of imperfections in financial markets, which can hold back the ability of entrepreneurs and innovators to commercialize and develop their ideas. Chapter 21 by Kalemli-Özcan and Saffie reviews this literature. They show how firm heterogeneity is crucial for understanding the important role of finance in influencing innovation, as the financial system is meant to be allocating capital to its most profitable uses. When this system becomes impaired—such as after the Global Financial Crisis—it can have long-run effects through failing to channel resources toward innovative firms (e.g., new entrants, which are often found to be creators of the most radical inventors). The authors develop a tractable framework that allows for creative destruction and firm dynamics to be integrated into the workhorse quantitative models of international finance. The model generates the "hysteresis" effects of downturns (i.e., that the effect of recessions can persist a long time after the economy has started to recover) through financial markets and firms rather than the traditional labor market models focused on unemployment persistence. Celik (Chapter 22) takes a more micro approach, reviewing the literature on finance and firm dynamics, especially on how it relates to the discovery, reallocation, and implementation of new ideas. He presents a new endogenous growth model with collateral constraints to highlight the interaction of financial frictions with firm innovation.

Taxation

In Chapter 23, Jones emphasizes that three key factors have been important in understanding the modern analysis of growth. Creative destruction as emphasized by Aghion and Howitt (1992) is certainly important, but so is the nonrivalry of ideas and misallocation of talent. Drawing on all of these aspects, Jones takes a more macroeconomic perspective, focusing on the intense arguments about the top rate of taxation. These are often presented in quite a static framework that ends up focusing on how shifts in the top tax affects tax revenues collected. However, to the extent that those in the top income group have become rich through their entrepreneurial and innovative abilities, increasing the top rate will affect the incentives to innovate. Hence, the growth effects of taxation could be large, and such dynamic considerations will swamp the usual static public finance calculus.

In Chapter 24, Stantcheva gives a more detailed account of how taxation affects innovation and provides a detailed overview of this area, looking both at the corporate and individual sides. There is an extensive empirical literature on R&D tax credits (see the survey by Hall 2022), suggesting that they are an effective policy to raise R&D and innovation (e.g., Dechezleprêtre et al. 2023). In contrast, Stantcheva emphasizes a more recent literature suggesting that individual taxes (and the overall level of corporate taxation) also seem to play an important role. She provides a new theoretical framework for thinking about taxation and innovation and looks at her own empirical work (Akcigit et al. 2022), using rich data on a century of innovation in the United States that supports this framework. Although state-specific taxes generate much relocation, she argues that lower top rates of personal tax also have a positive effect on aggregate innovation.

In these two chapters, both Jones and Stantcheva show that the top tax rate plays an important role for innovation. Stantcheva also shows that the top tax rate could be a relatively blunt tool for fostering innovation. For instance, there are far fewer innovators in the top 1 percent of the income distribution than most people think. If people with inherited wealth made up a lot of this group, as is the case in many countries, the incentive effects of top tax rates are muted. Policies aimed at building up the research and human capital infrastructure of a country may be a much more effective innovation policy than getting involved in a beggar-thy-neighbor approach of cutting tax rates.

Science

The Aghion-Howitt framework focuses on the incentives for profit-maximizing firms to perform R&D, but there is also a science base behind this effort, often driven by other incentives (as emphasized in Chapter 14 by Besley and Persson on green innovation). The interaction between the academic science base and entrepreneurial startups is the focus of Chapter 25 by Kolev, Haughey, Murray, and Stern. They show that since 2000, top American university research has become increasingly important for startups. Analyzing a new database of patents from these top US universities shows that startups have a big advantage over incumbents in terms of the importance and originality of their innovations. Such firms are able to scale up more quickly than established firms. Given the general picture of declining dynamism discussed in other chapters, this is a more optimistic take that emphasizes the role of academia in helping stimulate growth, not just indirectly via the analysis in this volume, but also directly in terms of entrepreneurship.

In Chapter 26, Mokyr looks at these issues in a broader historical context, focusing on the Industrial Revolution as the case study par excellence of creative destruction. He distinguishes between culture (what people believe and think they know) and institutions (the rules and customs that determine their incentives) and shows how their coevolution affects one another in many complex ways. He argues forcefully that in the era of the Industrial Revolution, the central cultural tenet that drove creative destruction was a strong belief in progress. Perhaps the loss of confidence in progress in the West is what has retarded growth in recent decades.

Conclusions

The many contributions in this volume help give a flavor of the endurance and adaptability of the creative destruction paradigm launched three decades ago. The Conclusion by Aghion and Howitt themselves reflects on the history of their work and how its development has important implications for modern policy (e.g., Aghion et al. 2021; Bloom et al. 2019). Given the vibrancy of the literature, we expect a similar flourishing over the course of the next thirty years.

We thank many, many people for making this book possible. All chapters were read by a variety of students and researchers whose "referee reports" vastly improved the initial drafts. These individuals include Harun Alp, Jack Fisher, Santiago Franco, Furkan Kilic, Peter Lambert, Matthias Mertens, Jeremy Pearce, Marta Prato, Younghun Shim, Polly Simpson, Marcos Sora, Andreas Teichgraeber, Anna Valero, and Daria Zelenina. The support at College de France was also critical in enabling the complex production function to take shape: In particular, Emma Bursztejn has provided superb assistance throughout. The staff at Harvard University Press have also been fabulous in their support.

References

Aghion, Philippe, and Peter Howitt (1992) "A Model of Growth through Creative Destruction." *Econometrica* 60(2): 323–351.

Aghion, Philippe, Antoine Dechezleprêtre, David Hemous, Ralf Martin, and John Van Reenen (2016) "Carbon Taxes, Path Dependency and Directed Technical Change: Evidence from the Auto Industry." *Journal of Political Economy* 124(1): 1–51.

Aghion, Philippe, Céline Antonin, and Simon Bunel (2021) *The Power of Creative Destruction: Economic Upheaval and the Wealth of Nations.* Cambridge, MA: Harvard University Press.

Aghion, Philippe, Ufuk Akcigit, Otto Toivanen, and Ari Hyytinen (2023) "Parental Education and Invention: The Finnish Enigma." *International Economic Review,* forthcoming.

Akcigit, Ufuk, Jeremy Pearce, and Marta Prato (2020) "Tapping into Talent: Coupling Education and Innovation Policies for Economic Growth." National Bureau of Economic Research Working Paper 27862.

Akcigit, Ufuk, John Grigsby, Tom Nicholas, and Stefanie Stantcheva (2022) "Taxation and Innovation in the 20th Century." *Quarterly Journal of Economics* 137(1): 329–385.

Akcigit, Ufuk, Salome Baslandze, and Francesca Lotti (2023) "Connecting to Power: Political Connections, Innovation, and Firm Dynamics." *Econometrica* 91(2): 529–564.

Autor, David, David Dorn, Larry Katz, Christina Patterson, and John Van Reenen (2020) "The Fall of the Labor Share and the Rise of Superstar Firms." *Quarterly Journal of Economics* 135(2): 645–709.

Bell, Alex, Raj Chetty, Xavier Jaravel, Neviana Petkova, and John Van Reenen (2019) "Who Becomes an Inventor in America? The Importance of Exposure to Innovation." *Quarterly Journal of Economics* 134(2): 647–713.

Bloom, Nicholas, Mirko Draca, and John Van Reenen (2016) "Trade Induced Technical Change? The Impact of Chinese Imports on Innovation, IT and Productivity." *Review of Economic Studies* 83(1): 87–117.

Bloom, Nicholas, John Van Reenen, and Heidi Williams (2019) "A Toolkit of Policies to Promote Innovation." *Journal of Economic Perspectives* 33(3): 163–184.

Bloom, Nicholas, Chad Jones, John Van Reenen, and Michael Webb (2020) "Are Ideas Becoming Harder to Find?" *American Economic Review* 110(4): 1104–1144.

Blundell, Richard, Rachel Griffith, and John Van Reenen (1999) "Market Share, Market Value and Innovation in a Panel of British Manufacturing Firms." *Review of Economic Studies* 66(3): 529–554.

Dechezleprêtre, Antoine, Elias Einio, Ralf Martin, Kieu-Trang Nguyen, and John Van Reenen (2023) "Do Fiscal Incentives Increase Innovation? An RD Design for R&D." *American Economic Journal: Policy,* forthcoming.

Hall, Bronwyn (2022) "Tax Policy for Innovation." Chapter 5 in Ben Jones and Austan Goolsbee (eds.), *Innovation and Public Policy.* Chicago: University of Chicago Press.

Schumpeter, Joseph A. (1942) *Capitalism, Socialism, and Democracy.* New York: Harper & Bros.

Stern, Nicholas (2007) *The Economics of Climate Change: The Stern Review.* Cambridge: Cambridge University Press.

Toivanen, Otto, and Lotta Väänänen (2016) "Education and Invention." *Review of Economics and Statistics* 98(2): 382–396.

PART I

Overview

CHAPTER 1

Innovation and Growth Policy

EDMUND S. PHELPS

In the very early 1900s, the German Historical School, led by Arthur Spiethoff, celebrated the discoveries of "scientists and navigators," suggesting that they were the fundamental *Ursprung* of economic development. What Joseph Schumpeter made famous with his 1912 classic, *Theorie der Wirtschaftlichen Entwicklung* (Schumpeter, 1912)—in the 1934 translation, *The Theory of Economic Development* (Schumpeter, 1934)—is his thesis that the birth of new products and methods requires entrepreneurs to organize and to market the innovations made possible by new discoveries. (Ironically, subsequent models have usually abstracted from the entrepreneurial function or left it implicit.) I don't know of any further steps of Schumpeter's beyond that theory and certainly no departures from that theory.

In their book, *Endogenous Growth Theory* (Aghion and Howitt, 1997), Philippe Aghion and Peter Howitt relocated those "scientists and navigators," who were *exogenous* to the economy, to the operations research divisions in business corporations, where the results are heavily *endogenous* to the economy. "Philippe and Peter built and analyzed a model in which 'research activities,' with their probabilistic results, generate random sequences of quality-improving innovations," as my recent book (Phelps, 2023) describes their approach. (Philippe and Peter employed this model in Aghion and Howitt's *The Economics of Growth*, 2009.)

This was a major advance. Their econometric work indicates that much weight ought to be given to this "endogenous" theory of economic growth—

17

more than on the German School's exogenous theory. (I would note that the weights would surely depend on the relative size of the nation studied.)

I have built a quite different theory of innovation, one introduced nine years ago in my book *Mass Flourishing* (Phelps, 2013). In this theory, much innovation—I think most innovating—comes from the dynamism of the people. It's conceived by a wide range of people—from the grassroots on up—and sparked by a desire to create, meet challenges, and venture into the unknown. My thesis is that some "modern values" that reached full force in the nineteenth century over much of the West—values such as individualism, vitalism, and self-expression that came out of the Renaissance and the Enlightenment—were the wellspring of this dynamism. The imagining, creating, and venturing into the unknown of a great many people brought not only widespread prospering—prospering in the sense of improving terms for the sort of work one is doing—but also flourishing: the satisfactions of achieving and succeeding.

The new book, *Dynamism* (Phelps et al., 2020), by me, Raicho Bojilov, Hian Teck Hoon, and Gylfi Zoega, reports research supporting this theory. In fact, one of its econometric analyses finds that indigenous innovation is much more important than exogenous innovation deriving from scientific progress.

A discussion of growth policy could not be more timely. The semi-stagnation of the American economy that prevailed in the twenty years from the early 1970s to the early 1990s and—after the Internet Revolution—the resumption of that semi-stagnation for another almost twenty years has inflicted a severe slowdown of wage rates, a steep rise in housing prices, and a huge fall in the rate of return on saving. These developments and others brought social tensions, division, and resentment.

In America, many in the white working class appear to resent the rising competition for jobs and government support coming from the rise of non-whites. They also fear "losing what they have."

In much of the West, the working class in general may feel frustrated by the growing productivity of workers in much of Asia. As my frequent coauthor Hian Teck Hoon has argued, a continuation of the steep rise of productivity in Asia over an epoch when productivity in the West has grown slowly would continue to send the terms of trade between West and East on a strongly downward slide. This force would operate to drive down the pecuniary rewards of labor in the West.

A recovery of economic growth in the West—by which I mean growth of total factor productivity—could be expected to reduce these tensions and thus buoy up Western societies as a whole.

What steps could be taken in the West to regenerate adequate growth? The use of many of the familiar policy levers might be opposed—by some groups, at any rate—or they might do more harm than good.

Just as the massive gain of innovation over the nineteenth century in Britain, America, France, and Germany can be attributed to a massive rise of modern values, I propose that we could expect that public policies designed to restore those modern values could revive innovation. And if some of the loss of innovation in the national economies as a whole—some of the semi-stagnation—can be attributed to a loss of the necessary values, it will be all the more effective to boost those values. If the problem lies in the people, then the best solution lies in the people.

I could be wrong about this, of course. But I am afraid that if we in America, France, and elsewhere in the West fail to address this decline of modern values—a decline that has made room for other isms, notably the *corporatism* that was born in continental Europe and still has an iron grip in some parts of the world—none of the other reforms being discussed will succeed. The right stuff—the right values—may prove essential.

Similarly, it could very well be that no return to high innovation will be possible if governments do not address the corruption and dishonesty that has become so rampant across society in America and perhaps other nations in the West.

It may be that we will have to wage the battle for innovation on many fronts.

References

Aghion, Philippe, and Peter Howitt (1997) *Endogenous Growth Theory*. Cambridge, MA: MIT Press.

Aghion, Philippe, and Peter Howitt (2009) *Endogenous Growth Theory*. Cambridge, MA: MIT Press.

Phelps, Edmund S. (2013) *Mass Flourishing*. Princeton, NJ: Princeton University Press.

Phelps, Edmund S. (2023) *My Journeys in Economic Theory*. New York: Columbia University Press.

Phelps, Edmund S., Raicho Bojilov, Hian Teck Hoon, and Gylfi Zoega (2020) *Dynamism: The Values That Drive Innovation, Job Satisfaction, and Economic Growth.* Cambridge, MA: Harvard University Press.

Schumpeter, Joseph (1912) *Theorie der Wirtschaftlichen Entwicklung.* Berlin: Duneker & Humblot.

Schumpeter, Joseph (1934) *The Theory of Economic Development.* Cambridge, MA: Harvard University Press.

CHAPTER 2

Creative Destruction and Economic Growth

UFUK AKCIGIT

The most basic proposition of growth theory is that to sustain positive macroeconomic growth in the long run, there must be continuous technological progress through new innovations. However, innovations do not simply fall like manna from heaven; instead, firms or individuals incur costs to innovate. Therefore, to understand the "fundamental causes" of economic growth, one has to understand not only the macroeconomic structure of growth but also the many microeconomic issues regarding incentives, policies, and organizations that interact with growth (such as who the winners and losers are from innovations, and what the net rents are from innovation). This is exactly the reason behind the emergence of a new literature in the late 1980s and early 1990s: "innovation-based endogenous growth (IBEG) models."

The study of economic growth has evolved over time. Until the early 1990s, the neoclassical growth model constituted the primary framework in the literature. As is well known, the main ingredient of that model is its production function:

$$Y_t = AK_t^{\alpha} L_t^{1-\alpha},\tag{1}$$

where Y_t, K_t, and L_t represent the output, capital, and labor at time t, respectively. The productivity term A is assumed to be constant. In this expression, the capital share $\alpha < 1$ has generated *decreasing returns to scale*.

Therefore while this economy could grow in the short run, it could not do so in the long run.

Romer (1986) was one of the first attempts to introduce *increasing returns* by making the productivity term a direct function of the level of capital as follows:

$$A_t = \gamma K_t,$$

where γ is some constant. Romer introduced the idea that technology is a by-product of capital accumulation, which can also be interpreted as a form of learning-by-doing.[1]

The reader should note that the above structure was an attempt to generate long-run growth through capital accumulation; therefore, it was completely silent about the role of incentives for research and development (R&D) and innovation for economic growth. This omission is at odds with the fact that technological change is the result of intentional efforts by firms and humans and the empirical evidence that those economies that produced more innovations also grew faster over the twentieth century (e.g., Akcigit, Grigsby, and Nicholas, 2017).

Innovation-Based Endogenous Growth

Inventors spend countless hours to come up with new ideas. Firms spend millions of dollars to finance their implementation. These important decisions of inventors and firms were missing in the early attempts of generating endogenous growth through the neoclassical growth model. It wasn't until Romer (1990) that profit-driven agents were modeled as investing in R&D to produce a new variety of goods, or Aghion and Howitt (1992) that new entrants were modeled as replacing old incumbents through *creative destruction* by introducing a higher-quality version of an existing product.

The IBEG models have evolved along two main separate branches. These two branches were initiated by two revolutionary papers: Romer (1990) and Aghion and Howitt (1992). The tree in Figure 2.1 illustrates those two branches and the subbranches that emerged from them.

---

[1] Lucas (1988) introduced similar spillovers through human capital externalities.

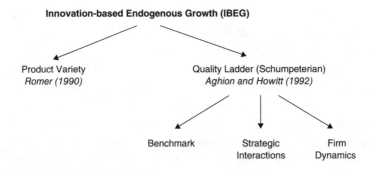

Figure 2.1. Innovation-based endogenous growth (IBEG)

Next, I describe the two main building blocks of today's modern IBEG models. Further details can be found in Akcigit (2017).

Romer (1990): Product Variety Model

Romer's model views each innovation as the introduction of a new product variety that becomes a permanent part of the economy and the inventor of which becomes its permanent producer. Since his model is based on product variety, the Romer model is also known as the "horizontal" model of IBEG. There are some important ideas in the widely celebrated paper by Romer (1990). Romer knew that having *increasing returns* was the essential ingredient for long-run growth. But he also realized that ideas are not simply a by-product of capital accumulation. Innovation was costly in real life, as firms and individuals spend time and invest money to produce them. Hence, the first important step in Romer (1990) was to introduce and make explicit the R&D production function.

Second, Romer recognized that ideas are *nonrival,* in the sense that the use of an idea by one user does not preclude its use by others. Therefore, if a society has already accumulated A_t amount of knowledge by period t through all preceding innovations, that society does not need to spend any additional resources in period t to replicate A_t since it is nonrival. That the society did not need to re-create nonrival A_t led to increasing returns in the production technology. Hence, Romer could naturally combine the nonrivalry of ideas with increasing returns in the production technology.

However, an important model ingredient was needed to incentivize costly R&D. This is where the third ingredient of his model came into play: Romer assumed that although the stock of ideas are nonrival, new ideas can be *excludable* through patent protection. As a result, new ideas were associated with monopoly rents (through imperfect competition), which is another new ingredient compared to the earlier models with perfect competition. This new structure made profit-seeking entrepreneurs engage in deliberate research activities aimed at creating new knowledge and thereby being compensated with monopoly rents for their costly idea production.

The Romer setup

More specifically, the Romer model employs the product variety theory of Dixit and Stiglitz. There is a continuum of intermediate goods x_i, indexed on the interval $i \in [0, A_t]$. Each good is produced by a monopolist. Final output Y_t is produced using labor L and the intermediate goods according to:

$$Y_t = L^{1-\alpha} \int_0^{A_t} x_i^\alpha \, di, \quad 0 < \alpha < 1. \tag{2}$$

The Romer model introduces a new idea production function where researchers (R) use existing knowledge stock at time t to produce new ideas $\dot{A}$:

$$\dot{A} = \delta A_t R, \tag{3}$$

where δ is some constant. In the Romer model, each innovation introduces a new variety i, and its owner has the perpetual patent rights over that intermediate good. If we denote the per-period profit by π and the discount rate by r, the value of innovating a new variety i can be simply expressed as

$$\textit{Romer Value Function: } V = \frac{\pi}{r}. \tag{4}$$

In this model, agents are profit-driven. They go into research if the expected value of a new idea exceeds the agent's outside option of earning a wage rate w by being a production worker. Therefore the occupational choice problem of the researchers simply boils down to the following arbitrage equation:

$$w_t = V \, \delta A_t.$$

This indifference condition pins down the fraction of labor force that work as researchers versus production workers.

Apart from generating a framework with long-run economic growth through endogenous innovation investment, Romer (1990) showed the importance of *market size* for innovation. Equation (2) makes it clear that each new innovation of A_t makes production workers L more productive. In other words, once an idea is discovered, it can be used by as many workers as needed (in this case, by every L in equation (2)). This is again due to the nonrival nature of ideas. This particular prediction was adopted by some of the work in the subsequent "directed technical change" literature. For instance, Acemoglu (2002) used this theoretical machinery to explain why the skill premium in the US has been rising despite the increase in the relative supply of skilled workers at the same time.

Normative implications of Romer (1990). An important goal of the endogenous growth literature has been to understand the role of policy for boosting economic growth. Romer (1990) had a one-directional prediction on this. Because of the knowledge spillovers introduced through the R&D production function (3), the equilibrium level of investment in new idea creation has always been below the efficient level. Entrepreneurs do not internalize the knowledge spillovers that they are producing when they invest in R&D. Hence, the most common policy prediction of this model has been to subsidize innovation.

Limitations of Romer (1990). Despite its brilliance in incorporating endogenous innovation decisions into a dynamic general equilibrium macro model, various important missing links between the Romer model and the data made it hard to create and sustain a productive interaction between theory and empirics. Romer's model views each innovation as the introduction of a new product variety that becomes a permanent part of the economy and the inventor of which becomes its permanent producer. This fundamental feature is also what makes this framework hard to extend and to build on in order to capture important real-world features and policy questions. As it stands, this structure abstracts from many important micro firm- and inventor-level aspects of innovation that we deeply care about.

First, a growing literature shows that reallocation of production inputs, broadly defined to include entry and exit, accounts for around 50 percent of manufacturing and 90 percent of US retail productivity growth (Foster, Haltiwanger, and Krizan, 2001, 2006). Similarly, Hsieh and Klenow (2009, 2014); Bartelsman, Haltiwanger, and Scarpetta (2013); and Syverson (2011) discuss how variations in reallocation across countries play a major role in explaining differences in productivity levels. Unfortunately, Romer (1990) does not have much to say about this important aspect of economic growth, because there is no notion of firm exit, turnover, or factor reallocation in his model.

Second, there is an important debate on the role of entry in the empirical growth literature. While Akcigit and Kerr (2018); Bartelsman and Doms (2000); and Foster, Haltiwanger, and Krizan (2001) argue that around 25 percent of aggregate productivity growth comes from new entry, Garcia-Macia, Hsieh, and Klenow (2016) find more modest impact of new entry on aggregate growth. Romer (1990) would say that the contribution of new entry to aggregate growth is 100 percent, because his model considers only innovation by new entrants as the source of innovation.

Third, the returns to innovation are not necessarily evenly distributed in society. As a result, inequality and innovation are likely to have a two-way relationship. A growing literature documents these links: For instance, using historical data, Akcigit, Grigsby, and Nicholas (2017) show that innovation has been negatively associated with inequality.[2] Similarly, Jones and Kim (2018) provide an analysis of innovation, inequality, and economic growth. Finally, Aghion, Akcigit, Bergeaud, Blundell, and Hémous (2019) show that top income inequality shows a strong positive association between innovation and inequality. Unfortunately, Romer (1990) is silent about the winners and losers of the growth process. To put it simply, when digital cameras were introduced, producers of traditional film cameras (most famously Kodak) went out of business, and their workers became unemployed. Hence, the growth process has important asymmetric effects on society, which are entirely absent in Romer's model.

Fourth, market competition comes with a tension between market leaders and their potential competitors (Krusell and Rios-Rull, 1996). While new entrants and small firms are trying to surpass the dominant market leader and to attract a larger share of customers by innovating better products or technologies, the market leader is trying hard to maintain its leadership, among other things, by adopting protective defensive strategies. These protective strategies include political connections, which can help maintain leadership or overcome certain regulatory barriers. For

---

[2] For additional readings on inventors, inequality, and innovation, see Aghion, Akcigit, Hyytinen, and Toivanen (2017); Akcigit, Pearce, and Prato (2020); Bell, Chetty, Jaravel, Petkova, and Van Reenen (2019); and Celik (2023).

instance, Akcigit, Baslandze, and Lotti (2023) show that firms start to hire more politicians and innovate less as they become the dominant market leader. Akcigit and Goldschlag (2023) document that when an inventor moves to a large incumbent compared to a young firm, his wage income increases but his innovativeness declines significantly. Similarly, Akcigit and Kerr (2018) show that young and small firms produce more radical innovations, whereas large and old incumbents produce more incremental innovations, mostly to build a patent thicket to make it harder for competitors to leapfrog them. These tensions among competing firms and the resultant changing innovation incentives of firms over their life cycle have first order implications for economic growth. Yet they are also absent from the Romer model.

Finally, as I highlighted above, the Romer model generates a trivial policy implication due to uninternalized knowledge spillovers. Thus under no circumstances can there be an equilibrium with an efficient or excessive level of R&D. This prediction is questionable, since market competition could make firms overinvest in R&D in order to push their rivals out of the market. Since competitive forces are missing in the Romer model, the resulting policy implications are also not satisfactory.

In conclusion, all these missing links between Romer's brilliant model and the data made it hard to create a productive dialogue between theory and empirics. This disconnect between the model and the data made it hard for researchers to ask positive and normative questions using his framework. As already mentioned, these limitations make Romer-style horizontal models much less frequently utilized in the current literature. Most of the current work utilizes Schumpeterian models, as I explain next.

Aghion and Howitt (1992): Quality-Ladder Model

The model by Aghion and Howitt (1992), also known as the *Schumpeterian* or *vertical* model, revolutionized the way we think about the innovation and growth process. The Aghion-Howitt framework became the main workhorse of most of the models that we use today in the endogenous growth literature. Aghion-Howitt's Schumpeterian model prioritized the *industrial organization* aspect of economic growth. As a result, Schumpeterian growth theory à la Aghion-Howitt has developed into an integrated framework for understanding not only the macroeconomic structure of growth, but also the many microeconomic issues regarding incentives, policies, and organizations that interact with growth. Who gains and who loses from innovations? What are the net rents from innovation? The answers to these questions ultimately depend on characteristics such as property right protection, competition and openness, education, and democracy. These traits also matter to a different extent in countries or sectors at different stages of development. Moreover, the recent years have witnessed a new generation of Schumpeterian growth models focusing on firm dynamics and reallocation of resources among incumbents and new entrants.

Through the notion of creative destruction, these Schumpeterian models introduced firm entry-exit and competition into the endogenous growth literature. This feature has been essential to map these IBEG models to the firm- and inventor-level micro data, and to estimate them. Moreover, these features enable Schumpeterian models to generate richer policy implications. Since the Romer-style product variety models feature uninternalized spillovers through equation (3), they generate major underinvestment in R&D and call for research subsidies. In contrast, Schumpeterian models brought in a competitive force through the so-called "business-stealing" effect, whereby new entrants try to replace incumbents through new innovations. If the spillovers associated with each innovation are not big enough, the social return from it would be less than the private return, which, in equilibrium, could make firms *overinvest* in R&D. Therefore Schumpeterian models call for empirical estimates of the innovation spillovers and the business-stealing externality to inform optimal policy.

Schumpeterian growth theory delivers distinctive theoretical predictions on many important issues, such as the relationship between (i) growth and industrial organization; (ii) growth and firm dynamics; (iii) growth and development and the notion of "appropriate" institutions; and (iv) growth and long-term technological waves, among many others. By generating directly testable predictions, the Schumpeterian approach also builds a very tight connection between theory and data.

The Aghion-Howitt setup

The Aghion-Howitt model is Schumpeterian in that: (i) it is about growth generated by innovations; (ii) innovations result from entrepreneurial investments that are themselves motivated by the prospects of monopoly rents; and (iii) new innovations leapfrog and replace old technologies: in other words, growth involves *creative destruction*.

There is a final good, which is also the numeraire. The final good at time t is produced competitively using an intermediate input, namely:

$$Y_t = A_t y_t^\alpha, \tag{5}$$

where α is between 0 and 1, y_t is the amount of the intermediate good currently used in the production of the final good, and A_t is the productivity (or quality) of the currently used intermediate input.

Growth in this model results from innovations that improve the quality of the intermediate input used in the production of the final good. More formally, if the previous state-of-the-art intermediate good was of quality A_t, then a new innovation will introduce a new intermediate input of quality

$$A_{t+1} = A_t + \underbrace{\gamma A_t}_{\substack{\text{int ertemporal} \\ \text{spillover}}},$$

where $\gamma > 0$. This immediately implies that growth will involve *creative destruction*, in the sense that Bertrand competition will allow the new innovator to drive the firm producing the intermediate good of quality A_t out of the market, since at the same labor cost, the innovator produces a better good than that of the incumbent firm.

If we denote the rate of creative destruction by τ, the Aghion-Howitt framework implies that the value of being a monopolist is

$$\textit{Aghion-Howitt Value Function: } V = \frac{\pi}{r+\tau}. \tag{6}$$

The reader should note that the key difference between this value function and the Romer's value function is the so-called "effective discount rate $r + \tau$" in the denominator, which implies that more creative destruction lowers the value of being an incumbent by shortening the expected monopoly duration. This key departure has led to many fundamentally distinct conclusions, both positive and normative, as I describe below.

Normative implications of Aghion and Howitt (1992). Growth in Aghion-Howitt's Schumpeterian model involves both *positive* and *negative externalities*. The positive externality is referred to by Aghion and Howitt as a "knowledge spillover effect": namely, any new innovation raises productivity A forever (i.e., the benchmark technology for any subsequent innovation). However, the current innovator captures the rents from her innovation only during the time interval until the next innovation occurs. This effect is also featured in Romer (1990), where it is referred to instead as "non-rivalry plus limited excludability." But in addition, in the Schumpeterian model, any new innovation has a negative externality, as it destroys the rents of the previous innovator: Following the theoretical industrial organization literature, Aghion and Howitt (1992) refer to this as the "business-stealing effect" of innovation. The welfare analysis in that paper derives sufficient conditions under which the intertemporal spillover effect dominates or is dominated by the business-stealing effect. The equilibrium growth rate under laissez-faire is correspondingly suboptimal or excessive compared to the socially optimal growth rate.[3]

Limitations of Aghion and Howitt (1992). As indicated in production function (5), the Aghion-Howitt model consists of only a single sector. Thus, innovation competition takes place at the economy level. A successful innovation improves the entire economy. Therefore, the economy features aggregate uncertainty, and the growth rate is not deterministic. Following the lead of Aghion-Howitt, Grossman and Helpman (1991) resolve this problem by introducing a continuum of products, each with its own quality ladder:

$$\ln Y_t = \int_0^1 \ln[A_{jt} y_{jt}]\, dj.$$

In Grossman and Helpman (1991), R&D races take place simultaneously in each product line j. This tractable extension to Aghion-Howitt utilizes the law of large numbers and generates smooth aggregate dynamics in the sense that the aggregate growth rate is deterministic.

This framework has been extended in two main directions. One of them is models with strategic interactions (see Griffith and Van Reenen, Chapter 3 of this volume for a more extensive discussion).

Application 1: Strategic interactions models based on Aghion and Howitt (1992)

An extensive literature has shown that competition can lead to higher economic growth (e.g., Nickell, 1996; Blundell, Griffith, and Van Reenen, 1995, 1999). Policymakers also try to promote growth through regulations that encourage competition among firms. In addition, recent data on the US economy have shown concerning trends. Total factor productivity growth

---

[3] Later work has tried to explicitly quantify these two offsetting effects. See Bloom, Schankerman, and Van Reenen (2013) for further details.

has slowed down dramatically since the 1980s, while business dynamism—the perpetual process of firms entering, growing, downsizing, and ultimately exiting the market—through which labor and capital are reallocated toward more productive uses, has weakened considerably since the 1980s, as evidenced by declines in firm entry rates and job reallocation rates. In their recent work, Akcigit and Ates (2021) summarize these trends, which have been documented by a large number of studies, as follows:[4]

- Market concentration has increased.
- Markups have increased.
- Profit share of GDP has increased.
- The labor share of output has declined.
- Market concentration and labor share are negatively correlated.
- The labor productivity gap between industry (technology) leaders and other competitors has widened.
- Firm entry rates and the economic share of young firms have both declined.
- Job reallocation and churn have receded.
- The dispersion of firm growth rates has decreased.

These facts show that competition in the United States has been weakening over the past several decades. A rich theoretical framework is needed to understand the underlying reasons behind these trends and study the role of industrial policy to restore dynamism and competition. How can we think about competition in Romer's framework? Unfortunately, that model doesn't lend itself easily to such a task, since it lacks an explicit treatment of competitive forces. However, the following reasoning could offer ways to think about this question: Given that more competition leads to lower profits, Romer's model would allow for such an observation by making different products more substitutable through the elasticity parameter (α in equation (2)). Yet making products more substitutable means lower rents for innovation and lower economic growth. Therefore the correlation between growth and competition could only be negative in Romer's framework. Moreover, many of the empirical facts above would remain unexplained by this model.

In contrast, the benchmark Schumpeterian model has a different take on competition. Rather than thinking about the substitutability of goods,

---

[4] Please see Akcigit and Ates (2021) for an extensive literature review and the relevant references for all trends.

competition can be interpreted as the additional pressure from new entrants on incumbent firms. To make things more concrete, let's consider the following example. Let's assume that there is more entry to the market by new entrepreneurs, which would shorten the average survival rate of incumbent firms and reduce the discounted sum of future profits that they earn as in equation (6). This would decrease the monopoly rents and therefore reduce the incentive for innovation.

It is possible to draw the conclusion that any policy that would intensify competition through entry would lead to lower innovation incentives. Hence the benchmark model by Aghion-Howitt cannot generate the desired positive link between competition and growth, because incumbents cannot react to the competitive pressure coming from entrants. However, a simple extension to the benchmark model does resolve this problem. Once incumbents are allowed to have different technology gaps relative to their rival firms and respond to their innovation outcomes, the link between competition and growth becomes drastically enriched, as described next.

Step-by-step innovation. An important assumption in the benchmark Aghion-Howitt model is that entrant firms leapfrog incumbents upon innovation, which removes the possibility of incumbent firms responding to entrant's innovation. Therefore, the so-called "step-by-step models," à la Aghion, Harris, and Vickers (1997) and Aghion, Harris, Howitt, and Vickers (2001), extend the baseline Aghion-Howitt model by allowing at least two incumbent firms to coexist in the market and compete strategically. Firms can have heterogeneous technology gaps, proxied by a positive integer $m \in \{0, 1, 2, \ldots\}$, indicating the number of cumulative innovation differences between them.

In this new structure, the degree of competition m (the proximity of firms in terms of their technologies) determines firms' incentives to improve their technologies. Unlike the previous models, innovation efforts intensify when the technological gap between the two firms decreases (i.e., when competition strengthens) as the incremental gain of innovating, which helps the innovating firm outpace its rival and escape competition, increases. This channel, dubbed the "escape-competition" effect, introduces an additional force through which competition can foster economic growth and distinguishes the model from other endogenous growth models. In contrast, firms that fall very much behind in the race get discouraged and stop investing as much in R&D. Those leaders that are very far ahead in the race also relax due to this decreased pressure from their rivals, hence they exert less innovation effort. Therefore, the overall performance of an economy depends on the composition of its sectors (i.e., the share of its sectors that are in neck-and-neck competition). This ladder force is referred to as the "composition effect." Without doubt, these novel features make the step-by-step innovation framework a fertile ground for the analysis of market competition, firm dynamics, and economic growth.

Using the step-by-step framework, Aghion, Bloom, Blundell, Griffith, and Howitt (2005) have shown theoretically that the relationship between competition and innovation follows an inverted-U pattern, and the average technological gap within a sector increases with competition. In addition, more intense competition enhances innovation in "frontier" firms but may discourage it in "nonfrontier" firms. Acemoglu and Akcigit (2012) used this framework to examine the optimal design of patent policy. Most recently, Akcigit and Ates (2021, 2023) have extended the step-by-step framework to study the declining business dynamism in the United States. In particular, Akcigit and Ates (2023) have shown that this class of models can be very powerful quantitatively and can help us understand the empirical trends described above.

An important feature of this class of models is that markups are determined endogenously as a function of the technology gap between two firms. Peters (2020) uses this feature to study the relationship between markups and misallocation. Acemoglu, Akcigit, Hanley, and Kerr (2016) interpret the two firms in every sector as two alternative technologies, clean versus dirty, to study the competition between clean and dirty technologies and the design of optimal environmental policy. Finally, Akcigit, Ates, and Impullitti (2018) use the step-by-step models to investigate the optimal trade and innovation policy in an open-economy framework.

Application 2: Firm dynamics models based on Aghion and Howitt (1992)

One of the main applications of the Schumpeterian theory has been the study of firm dynamics. The empirical literature has documented various stylized facts using micro firm-level data. Some of these facts are: (i) the firm size distribution is highly skewed; (ii) firm size and firm age are highly correlated; (iii) small firms exit more frequently, but the ones that survive tend to grow faster than at the average growth rate; (iv) a large fraction of R&D in the US is done by incumbents; and (v) reallocation of inputs between entrants and incumbents is an important source of productivity growth.

These are some of the well-known empirical facts that non-Schumpeterian growth models cannot account for. In particular, the first four facts listed require a new firm to enter, expand, then shrink over time, and eventually be replaced by new entrants. These and the last fact on the importance of reallocation are all embodied in the Schumpeterian idea of *creative destruction*.

What was missing in the early literature was firm- or individual-level heterogeneity that would provide a better connection between growth theory and micro-level data. Providing solid micro-level foundations would lead to stronger macro-growth models that generate more accurate positive predictions and relevant normative implications.

A major step in that direction was an important paper by Klette and Kortum (2004), which built a novel Schumpeterian growth model. The Romer model predicts that innovations come only from new entrants, that new entrants and young firms are the largest firms in the economy, and that exit rates would be uncorrelated with firm age or size. These predictions are at odds with the firm-level data. The Klette-Kortum model fixed these problems by defining a firm as a collection of production units, where each of these units go through Aghion-Howitt's creative destruction structure. In this framework, firms could grow by investing in "external innovation" to introduce better quality versions of the products of other firms and thus add those products to their portfolio. Therefore the value of each innovation is simply

$$\textit{Klette-Kortum Value Function: } V = \frac{\pi}{r + \tau} + v_{external}. \tag{7}$$

The main difference of this value function relative to the Aghion-Howitt's in equation (6) is the addition of $v_{external}$. The Klette-Kortum model allows firms to expand into new product lines through external innovation produced in their own existing lines. Therefore each product line comes with its franchise value of external innovation capacity. The Klette-Kortum model could thus map the benchmark Schumpeterian models to a more realistic firm dynamics setting.

Klette-Kortum's extension of Aghion and Howitt (1992) and the literature that followed this framework have produced various important predictions that are all supported by the empirical literature:

Prediction 1: *The distribution of firm size is highly skewed.*

Prediction 2: *Firm size and firm age are positively correlated.*

Prediction 3: *Small firms exit more frequently. The ones that survive tend to grow faster than average.*

Prediction 4: *A large fraction of R&D is done by incumbents.*

Prediction 5: *Both entrants and incumbents innovate. Moreover, the reallocation of resources among incumbents, as well as from incumbents to new entrants, is the major source of productivity growth.*

In a more recent article, Akcigit and Kerr (2018) extended the Klette-Kortum framework by allowing firms to improve not only other firms' products through "external innovations" but also their own products through "internal innovations":

$$\textit{Akcigit - Kerr Value Function: } V = \frac{\pi + v_{internal}}{r + \tau} + v_{external}. \tag{8}$$

Innovation and firm size heterogeneities allow the model to generate a close fit to the firm- and innovation-level data from the US Census Bureau and the US Patent Office. The estimated model shows that small firms are spending disproportionately more effort to do external innovations, and the spillovers associated with external innovations are significantly larger. These findings suggest that R&D policies that aim to correct for underinvestment in R&D should take into account the differential spillovers generated by different-sized firms in the economy. As exemplified by these papers, a close dialogue between Schumpeterian endogenous growth theory with heterogeneity and micro data allow researchers to quantify certain mechanisms and study the impact of counterfactual industrial policies.

A central feature of this model is that both incumbents and entrants innovate and contribute to productivity growth. Bartelsman and Doms (2000) and Foster, Haltiwanger, and Krizan (2001) have shown that 25 percent of productivity growth in the US is accounted for by new entry, and the remaining 75 percent is accounted for by continuing plants (incumbents). Moreover, Foster, Haltiwanger, and Krizan (2001, 2006) have shown that reallocation of resources through entry and exit accounts for around 50 percent of manufacturing and 90 percent of US retail productivity growth. In a recently growing cross-country literature, Hsieh and Klenow (2009, 2014); Bartelsman, Haltiwanger, and Scarpetta (2013); and Syverson (2011) describe how variations in reallocation across countries explain differences in productivity levels. Lentz and Mortensen (2008) estimate a variant of the baseline model in Klette and Kortum (2004) to quantify the importance of reallocation. Ates and Saffie (2021) add financial frictions to a similar framework to study productivity effects of financial crises.

In a recent work, Acemoglu, Akcigit, Alp, Bloom, and Kerr (2018, AAABK) introduced heterogeneous firm types into the Klette-Kortum framework to study the impact of industrial policy on firm selection, reallocation, and productivity growth. In this framework, "high-type" and "low-type" firms, which differ in terms of their innovative capacity, compete in a general equilibrium environment, and industrial policy influences the resulting selection in the economy. I find it useful to provide the expression of the AAABK value function to illustrate how this model builds on and extends the earlier models:

$$\text{AAABK Value Function: } V^{b,l} = \frac{\pi}{r+\tau} + v_{external}^{b,l}. \tag{9}$$

Among other things, the key difference now is the fact that franchise value of firms $\left(v_{external}^{b,l}\right)$ are type (l, h) dependent. AAABK estimate their model using US Census data and find that taxing incumbent fixed operations can lead to significant productivity gains by exploiting the resulting positive selection among firms.

Firm value functions are not only essential for solving growth models but also have pedagogical importance in terms of summarizing the key economic forces. Therefore Table 2.1 lists some of the significant iterations of the IBEG models and compares their value functions. As can be seen from this table, to carry the IBEG models to data and estimate them structurally, researchers have relied heavily on the notion of creative destruction, followed the Aghion-Howitt tradition, and added a new major component in every step.

Table 2.1. Evolution of the IBEG models and their value functions

Romer	Aghion-Howitt	Klette-Kortum	Akcigit-Kerr	AAABH
$V = \dfrac{\pi}{r}$	$V = \dfrac{\pi}{r+\tau}$	$V = \dfrac{\pi}{r+\tau} + v_{external}$	$V = \dfrac{\pi + v_{internal}}{r+\tau} + v_{external}$	$V^{b,l} = \dfrac{\pi}{r+\tau} + v_{external}^{b,l}$

Conclusion

It was the year of 1987 when Peter Howitt, a visiting professor on sabbatical from the University of Western Ontario, met Philippe Aghion, a first-year assistant professor at MIT. During that year they wrote their "model of growth through creative destruction," which ultimately came out as Aghion and Howitt (1992) in *Econometrica* and became one of the most influential papers in economics. Aghion and Howitt did not only thoroughly analyze the foundations of innovation-based endogenous growth models, but also incorporated industrial organizations into economic growth and macroeconomics. Aghion and Howitt (1992) provided us with a growth theory based on creative destruction that brought realistic innovation dynamics and sensible policy debates into innovation-based endogenous growth models, which also built a tight connection between growth theory and micro firm-level data. Their novel approach opened up a rich subsequent literature, which will be examined in each chapter of this book.

I have no doubt that Aghion and Howitt's contribution will continue to guide the literature and young researchers in the years to come.

References

ACEMOGLU, D. (2002): "Directed Technical Change," *Review of Economic Studies,* 69(4), 781–809.

ACEMOGLU, D., AND U. AKCIGIT (2012): "Intellectual Property Rights Policy, Competition and Innovation," *Journal of the European Economic Association,* 10(1), 1–42.

ACEMOGLU, D., U. AKCIGIT, H. ALP, N. BLOOM, AND W. KERR (2018): "Innovation, Reallocation, and Growth," *American Economic Review,* 108(11), 3450–3491.

ACEMOGLU, D., U. AKCIGIT, D. HANLEY, AND W. KERR (2016): "Transition to Clean Technology," *Journal of Political Economy,* 124(1), 52–104.

AGHION, P., U. AKCIGIT, A. BERGEAUD, R. BLUNDELL, AND D. HÉMOUS (2019): "Innovation and Top Income Inequality," *Review of Economic Studies,* 86(1), 1–45.

AGHION, P., U. AKCIGIT, A. HYYTINEN, AND O. TOIVANEN (2017): "The Social Origins of Inventors," National Bureau of Economic Research Working Paper No. 24110.

AGHION, P., N. BLOOM, R. BLUNDELL, R. GRIFFITH, AND P. HOWITT (2005): "Competition and Innovation: An Inverted-U Relationship," *Quarterly Journal of Economics,* 120(2), 701–728.

Aghion, P., C. Harris, P. Howitt, and J. Vickers (2001): "Competition, Imitation and Growth with Step-by-Step Innovation," *Review of Economic Studies*, 68(3), 467–492.

Aghion, P., C. Harris, and J. Vickers (1997): "Competition and Growth with Step-by-Step Innovation: An Example," *European Economic Review*, 41(3–5), 771–782.

Aghion, P., and P. Howitt (1992): "A Model of Growth through Creative Destruction," *Econometrica*, 60(2), 323–351.

Akcigit, U. (2017): "Economic Growth: The Past, the Present, and the Future," *Journal of Political Economy*, 125(6), 1736–1747.

Akcigit, U., and S. T. Ates (2021): "Ten Facts on Declining Business Dynamism and Lessons from Endogenous Growth Theory," *American Economic Journal: Macroeconomics*, 13(1), 257–298.

Akcigit, U., and S. T. Ates (2023): "What Happened to U.S. Business Dynamism?" *Journal of Political Economy*, forthcoming.

Akcigit, U., S. T. Ates, and G. Impullitti (2018): "Innovation and Trade Policy in a Globalized World," National Bureau of Economic Research Working Paper No. 24543.

Akcigit, U., S. Baslandze, and F. Lotti (2023): "Connecting to Power: Political Connections, Innovation, and Firm Dynamics," *Econometrica*, 91(2): 529–564.

Akcigit, U., and N. Goldschlag (2023): "Where Have All the 'Creative Talents' Gone? Employment Dynamics of US Inventors," University of Chicago Working Paper.

Akcigit, U., J. Grigsby, and T. Nicholas (2017): "The Rise of American Ingenuity: Innovation and Inventors of the Golden Age," National Bureau of Economic Research Working Paper No. 23047.

Akcigit, U., and W. R. Kerr (2018): "Growth through Heterogeneous Innovations," *Journal of Political Economy*, 126(4), 1374–1443.

Akcigit, U., J. G. Pearce, and M. Prato (2020): "Tapping into Talent: Coupling Education and Innovation Policies for Economic Growth," National Bureau of Economic Research Working Paper No. 27862.

Ates, S. T., and F. E. Saffie (2021): "Fewer but Better: Sudden Stops, Firm Entry, and Financial Selection," *American Economic Journal: Macroeconomics*, 13(3), 304–356.

Bartelsman, E., J. Haltiwanger, and S. Scarpetta (2013): "Cross-Country Differences in Productivity: The Role of Allocation and Selection," *American Economic Review*, 103(1), 305–334.

Bartelsman, E., and M. Doms (2000): "Understanding Productivity: Lessons from Longitudinal Microdata," *Journal of Economic Literature*, 38(3), 569–594.

Bell, A., R. Chetty, X. Jaravel, N. Petkova, and J. Van Reenen (2019): "Who Becomes an Inventor in America? The Importance of Exposure to Innovation," *Quarterly Journal of Economics*, 134(2), 647–713.

Bloom, N., M. Schankerman, and J. Van Reenen (2013): "Identifying Technology Spillovers and Product Market Rivalry," *Econometrica*, 81(4), 1347–1393.

BLUNDELL, R., R. GRIFFITH, AND J. VAN REENEN (1995): "Dynamic Count Data Models of Technological Innovation," *The Economic Journal*, 105(March), 333–344.

BLUNDELL, R., R. GRIFFITH, AND J. VAN REENEN (1999): "Market Share, Market Value and Innovation in a Panel of British Manufacturing Firms," *Review of Economic Studies*, 66(3), 529–554.

CELIK, M. A. (2023): "Does the Cream Always Rise to the Top? The Misallocation of Talent in Innovation," *Journal of Monetary Economics*, 133: 105–128.

FOSTER, L., J. C. HALTIWANGER, AND C. J. KRIZAN (2001): "Aggregate Productivity Growth: Lessons from Microeconomic Evidence," in *New Developments in Productivity Analysis*, 303–372. Chicago: University of Chicago Press.

FOSTER, L., J. HALTIWANGER, AND C. J. KRIZAN (2006): "Market Selection, Reallocation, and Restructuring in the US Retail Trade Sector in the 1990s," *Review of Economics and Statistics*, 88(4), 748–758.

GARCIA-MACIA, D., C.-T. HSIEH, AND P. J. KLENOW (2016): "How Destructive Is Innovation?" National Bureau of Economic Research Working Paper No. 22953.

GROSSMAN, G. M., AND E. HELPMAN (1991): "Quality Ladders in the Theory of Growth," *Review of Economic Studies*, 58(1), 43–61.

HSIEH, C.-T., AND P. J. KLENOW (2009): "Misallocation and Manufacturing TFP in China and India," *Quarterly Journal of Economics*, 124(4), 1403–1448.

HSIEH, C.-T., AND P. J. KLENOW (2014): "The Life Cycle of Plants in India and Mexico," *Quarterly Journal of Economics*, 129(3), 1035–1084.

JONES, C. I., AND J. KIM (2018): "A Schumpeterian Model of Top Income Inequality," *Journal of Political Economy*, 126(5), 1785–1826.

KLETTE, T. J., AND S. KORTUM (2004): "Innovating Firms and Aggregate Innovation," *Journal of Political Economy*, 112(5), 986–1018.

KRUSELL, P., AND J.-V. RIOS-RULL (1996): "Vested Interests in a Positive Theory of Stagnation and Growth," *Review of Economic Studies*, 63(2), 301–329.

LENTZ, R., AND D. T. MORTENSEN (2008): "An Empirical Model of Growth through Product Innovation," *Econometrica*, 76(6), 1317–1373.

LUCAS, JR., R. E. (1988): "On the Mechanics of Economic Development," *Journal of Monetary Economics*, 22(1), 3–42.

NICKELL, S. J. (1996): "Competition and Corporate Performance," *Journal of Political Economy*, 104(4), 724–746.

PETERS, M. (2020): "Heterogeneous Markups, Growth, and Endogenous Misallocation," *Econometrica*, 88(5), 2037–2073.

ROMER, P. M. (1986): "Increasing Returns and Long-Run Growth," *Journal of Political Economy*, 94(5), 1002–1037.

ROMER, P. M. (1990): "Endogenous Technological Change," *Journal of Political Economy*, 98(5, Part 2), S71–S102.

SYVERSON, C. (2011): "What Determines Productivity?" *Journal of Economic Literature*, 49(2), 326–365.

PART II

Competition and International Trade

CHAPTER 3

Product Market Competition, Creative Destruction, and Innovation

RACHEL GRIFFITH *and* JOHN VAN REENEN

Introduction

Is product market competition conducive to innovation and growth, or does it dampen incentives for research and development (R&D)? This is one of the longest-standing questions in social science and is a central feature of the legacy of Aghion and Howitt (1992), which brought key elements of industrial organization (IO) into modern macro growth models. Some prominent inventors and entrepreneurs (e.g., Thiel, 2014) have argued that tough competition discourages innovation and thus inhibits productivity growth by reducing the expected returns from innovation. This conclusion is often taken as the main message from Schumpeter (1943), who argued that the benefits of static efficiency gains (e.g., lower prices) from competition were outweighed by dynamic efficiency losses, as all innovation rents would be dissolved when price was equal to marginal cost. By contrast, competition authorities generally argue that competition is beneficial not just because of static gains of prices but also for innovation, because it encourages new entry and forces incumbent firms to innovate in order to stay ahead of rivals.

As we will see, there are theoretical arguments that predict both positive and negative effects of competition on innovation. The empirical evidence has also been mixed. So, what weight should policymakers place on rewarding successful innovation through allowing monopoly power vs.

43

enhancing the competitive pressures that markets place on firms to push forward the frontier? Is there a trade-off, or can these policies be used as complementary mechanisms?

One recurring theme is that competition can mean different things. Observable indicators of within-market competition (the number of firms, levels of concentration, price-cost margins, etc.) are endogenous outcomes of more primitive objects, such as elasticities of substitution (consumer preferences) and barriers to market entry. Of course, these primitive objects themselves can change through business strategies, technological innovation, and government policy.

We structure this chapter as follows. Section 1 gives an intellectual history of these issues, leading to Aghion and Howitt's development of endogenous growth theory. In Section 2, we then explain the key insights of the approach to "step-by-step" innovation models and the "inverted-U" relationship. Next, in Section 3, we examine some applications of the approach in competition policy, trade policy, and structural IO models. The final section offers some conclusions.

1 Intellectual History

1.1 Theoretical underpinnings

Smith to Arrow-Debreu

Economists since Adam Smith (1776) have generally seen competition as an important driver of growth and prosperity. Standard models, such as Arrow and Debreu (1954), formalize this result regarding the efficient allocation of finite resources in producing the first Welfare Theorem.

One extension of the idea of allocative efficiency is how aggregate productivity can be depressed by misallocation of output across firms. When firms have heterogeneous levels of productivity, for example, due to different levels of managerial capability (Bloom and Van Reenen, 2007), tougher competition results in a Darwinian process by which inefficient firms shrink and die, and high-productivity firms survive and grow. Market frictions that inhibit this process generally result in lower aggregate productivity. The importance of misallocation is at the center of modern macroeconomics (e.g., Hsieh and Klenow, 2009).

In addition to these between firm reallocation effects, a subterranean "folk wisdom" among economists is that competition improves productive efficiency *within* firms. Leibenstein (1966) labeled this idea "X-efficiency," and this was encapsulated by Sir John Hicks' quip that "the best of all monopoly profits is a quiet life." This idea has been formalized in various ways, perhaps most simply by recognizing that firms generally do not maximize shareholder value because of the principal-agent problem between the owners and managers of a firm. Firms are subject to agency problems, because it is not possible for the (usually dispersed) owners of corporations to fully observe managerial effort and performance, nor to implement first-best contracts to elicit this optimal effort. Competition can act to push managerial effort, not least because the CEO will be more fearful of the firm going bankrupt (Hart, 1983; Schmidt, 1997).[1]

Schumpeter

Schumpeter (1943) emphasized the importance of innovation and entrepreneurialism to capitalism and was skeptical of formal equilibrium models, which initially made his contributions hard to parse into modern economics. His emphasis was that competition can lower incentives to innovate, with the main mechanism through reducing the ex post profits of innovators.[2] Since there is a cost to performing R&D, the reward must be some temporary profit advantage. When competition immediately drives the innovation quasi-rents to zero—for example, from instant diffusion—there is no incentive to conduct R&D. In modern terms, the nonrivalrous and nonexcludability of R&D means that it will be under-supplied in a decentralized competitive economy.

---

[1] Another way may be through managerial career concerns and for the labor market to provide incentives (Holmstrom, 1982). Note that managerial incentives actually have an ambiguous relationship to product market competition. The Raith (2003) model shows this most clearly, measuring competition by consumer price sensitivity in the context of a Hotelling model. Greater competition means that an increase in marginal managerial effort shifts more market share to the high-effort firm, which increases effort incentives as some part of this will be linked to CEO pay. But competition also means less profits for any given level of effort, which has the opposite effect. This is exactly like the standard trade-off between competition lowering average innovation rents but increasing the marginal return to research effort.

[2] He also argued that competition cut the ability to invest in R&D ex ante through firms having less financial resources to invest. This assumes imperfect competition in the financial markets. Otherwise, a firm with a profitable idea could simply borrow the money to finance the innovation or allow a venture capitalist to take an equity stake. This theme was later pursued by Arrow (1962), but given space constraints, we will focus only on product market frictions in this chapter.

Policy makers have long recognized this problem. The patent system grants temporary monopoly property rights to an innovator precisely to enable her to obtain some stream of rewards (in return for publishing the patent to allow future inventors to build on the knowledge). There are often calls to abolish the patent on a particular product to restore competition—a recent example being around pharmaceuticals, such as vaccines. If we were to ignore dynamic incentives, then the first best policy would be to supply the new drug at marginal production costs. But this removes the profits from the R&D used to create the drug in the first place. Hence, abolishing intellectual property rights would clearly reduce innovation incentives.[3]

Arrow

A key contribution of Arrow (1962) was to show how Schumpeter's intuition could be overturned. Arrow compared innovation incentives for an industry characterized by monopoly to one with perfect competition. Who will invest the most in cost-reducing R&D? Agents' decisions depend on comparing the profits earned post-innovation to pre-innovation. Let us say that the competitive firm becomes a monopolist if she innovates, so that the post-innovation rents are the same in both cases. But the monopolist by definition is earning a stream of pre-innovation rents, so he will have less incrementally new profits than the competitive firm and so will have less incentive to invest in R&D.

The monopolist's disincentive to replace his own stream of rents by innovating has come to be called the "Arrow replacement effect" and works in direct opposition to the Schumpeterian incentive.

IO literature through the early 1990s

In the early 1990s, the IO literature started incorporating these incentives into formal models and examining new ones. One way to look at this is in models of entry with spatial competition. At Stage one, there is a decision to pay a sunk cost to enter. In Stage two, there is a game in the product

---

[3] Some argue (e.g., Boldrin and Levine, 2009) that there are many other ways to protect innovation without patents (e.g., secrecy, lead-times, holding on to key personnel) and their harms outweigh their benefits. These mechanisms are important—and much more important in some industries than in others (e.g., Cohen and Levin, 1989). We are skeptical, however, that wholesale abolition is called for. For example, it is hard to believe that the bio-pharmaceutical industry could flourish without any patents.

market, say, with product differentiation generating imperfect horizontal competition, such as Hotelling (1929) and Salop (1979). Competition depends on (i) the endogenous number of firms and (ii) the degree of product substitutability, which is governed by consumers' preferences (the actual or psychological transport costs). If consumers begin perceiving that products are more substitutable (increased competition), there are lower profit markups for any given number of firms in the market. If we regard the sum of sunk costs to enter as R&D, there will be lower aggregate R&D, because the market is less attractive. Dasgupta and Stiglitz (1980) described this effect by saying that "ex post competition drives out ex ante competition," and this is the essence of the Schumpeterian effect of competition.[4]

Gilbert and Newbery (1982) emphasize another reason why monopolists may innovate more. They consider R&D incentives for a nondrastic innovation—one where the successful innovator's costs are not so low that they can charge the monopoly price and still drive all other firms out of the market. They compare an incumbent monopolist with a potential new entrant. Arrow's replacement effect would give the entrant the strongest R&D incentives. However, if the monopolist innovates, he stays a monopolist. By contrast, if the entrant innovates, she enters the market and becomes a duopolist. Since joint profits under duopoly will be lower than monopoly profits (unless there is perfect collusion), the monopolist will invest more in innovation. This is a preemption incentive that Gilbert and Newbery (1982) labeled the (private) "efficiency effect." Several papers put the replacement and efficiency effects into more general IO theory models (see chapters 8 and 10 of Tirole, 1989).

Endogenous growth theory

In the late 1980s and early 1990s, these innovation models were firmly in the realm of micro-theory (see Reinganum (1989) for a good overview). The revolution of Aghion and Howitt (1992) was to bring some of their insights into macro growth models.

---

[4] Note that there will generally be an inefficiently high level of R&D in these models. There is actually inefficiently high entry as firms compete for market share through business-stealing and do not internalize the loss of rivals' profits from the sunk cost of entry. In more general models, these business-stealing effects need to be weighed against the knowledge externalities of R&D, which have been found to be empirically large. Most empirical assessments have found that the knowledge spillovers dominate, implying under-investment in innovation from society's perspective (e.g., Bloom, Schankerman, and Van Reenen, 2013).

One issue with early endogenous growth models was that they all pre-dicted that increases in competition discouraged innovation by reducing the returns to R&D. Some models, such as Romer (1990), had a relatively simple supply side—monopolistic competition with constant elasticity of substitution preferences and symmetric firms. Although this simplifies the analysis so that a representative agent approach could be used, it leaves no role for firm heterogeneity, creative destruction, and therefore the issue of strategic competition. The prediction that competition discourages innova-tion reflects Schumpeter's early intuition of competition reducing the rents from a sunk cost investment like R&D entry costs. The same effect is also at play in Aghion and Howitt (1992), but the paper did open a rich seam of em-pirical and theoretical work linking IO and growth through endogenous innovation.

2   Confronting Theory with Empirical Evidence

2.1 Empirical approaches to the innovation-market structure relationship

Initial attempts

The very early empirical evidence was based on case studies of particular firms or industries. As useful as these can be for developing theories and intuitions, it was not until after the Second World War that this area, along with the economic profession, turned to more systematic quantitative evidence. Scherer was an early pioneer in studying the empirical link between compe-tition and innovation, finding a positive cross-sectional relationship between concentration and patenting activity (Scherer, 1965a, 1965b). Cohen and Levin (1989) provide a comprehensive survey of this early econometric literature, concluding that although some factors, such as technological opportunity and appropriability, had clear positive effects on innovation, the role of market structure remained deeply ambiguous.

The modern literature

The advent of new panel data (following the same firms over time) on in-novation and market structure, new econometric methods, and more powerful computers allowed the burgeoning of a rich micro-empirical literature investigating the predictions of endogenous growth theory, heavily influenced by Aghion and Howitt's work.

Blundell, Griffith, and Van Reenen (1995, 1999; henceforth BGVR) were among the first to use firm-level panel data on innovations to advance this literature. They tackled two related issues—could the correlation between market structure and innovation be interpreted *causally*, and if so, *why* would market structure enable firms to be more innovative?

They found three main results. First, their measures of industrywide competition had a strong positive association with innovation (e.g., industries that became more open to imports and/or less concentrated subsequently had larger numbers of directly measured innovations and patents). Second, within an industry, firms with higher market shares also tended to be more innovative. These authors argued that this could be explained by the greater incentives that high market share firms have to innovate (as in Gilbert and Newbery, 1982). Their third result was testing this hypothesis by examining the heterogeneous response in the stock market (as a measure of the firm's value) to innovation events. They showed that changes in a firm's innovation or patenting boosted stock market values, especially if these were "surprise" innovations (an idea that has been taken up in the event studies of Kogan et al., 2017). Most importantly, they established that the magnitude of the innovation-induced increase in value was much greater for firms that already had high market share.

A crucial part of BGVR was assembling new firm-level panel data on innovation and new econometric methods—a fixed effects estimator that exploited pre-sample data to control for unobserved heterogeneity in dynamic count data models.

Innovation data

One key issue in this literature is how to measure innovative output. BGVR used data on commercialized innovations collected by the Science Policy Research Unit (SPRU, described by Pavitt et al., 1987) and linked it with accounting data on publicly listed firms. The SPRU data were based on expert surveys identifying over 4,000 of the most "technologically important and commercially successful" innovations in the UK since the Second World War, as well as the names of the firms who first produced and used them. These data provided a long time series and were instrumental in enabling the burgeoning of a new body of empirical innovation work (see Geroski, 1995).[5] In addition, BGVR matched in the more conventional patents data from the US Patent Office.

Patents data and R&D expenditure are the other main measures of innovation, in addition to total factor productivity (TFP)—a residual measure of the amount of growth that cannot be explained by other factors. Each of these measures has strengths and weaknesses.

R&D expenditure is an innovative input, not an output. In addition, it tends to focus on formal activities in labs rather than on the more informal search for innovations. Moreover, in many countries and time periods, it has not been mandatory for firms to report R&D spending. For example, in the UK prior to 1990, it was generally not reported, even by publicly listed firms. In the US, R&D is well reported for publicly listed firms, but not for privately listed ones. Administrative data sources are better in this respect, although they are typically only samples, and access is often hard for researchers to obtain (for exceptions see Dechezleprêtre et al., forthcoming, and Rao, 2016).

Patenting activity, innovation counts, and TFP are all output measures. Patents are a very heterogeneous measure of innovation (see Griliches, 1990); a patent can represent a fundamentally new technology worth billions or an incremental improvement in an existing technology worth little. The advantage of using R&D is that it is measured in dollars and so has a natural value attached to it. Various solutions to the problem of valuing patents have been implemented and include citation-weighting (assuming that more valuable patents are more often cited), family size (taking out protection in more countries signals greater value), and renewals and/or using stock market data (e.g., Pakes, 1986; Kogan et al., 2017).

TFP is a measure of technological progress (and thus of implemented innovative activity).[6] However, for most firms, TFP growth is not pushing

---

[5] The Community Innovation Survey (CIS, https://ec.europa.eu/eurostat/web/microdata/community -innovation-survey) run by Eurostat also attempts to measure innovations directly. However, survey questions are a mix between innovation that is "new to the firm" (diffusion) and "new to the economy" (our definition of innovation).

[6] TFP reflects the adoption of various technologies that are sometimes measured directly— information and communication technologies, robots, new drugs, artificial intelligence, etc. The "intangible capital" approach treats these as other forms of capital, which in principle can be measured in the same way as tangible capital through the Perpetual Inventory Method (see Haskel and Westlake, 2017). But these measures are mostly about diffusion rather than innovation per se, which is the focus of this chapter.

the technological frontier forward but rather reflects the diffusion of innovations that may be new to the firm but are not new to the world. In addition, TFP may reflect things other than technology, such as managerial efficiency improvement. Moreover, this assumes that TFP is well measured. In reality, there are a large number of problems with measuring outputs and inputs. The lack of firm-specific output price measures means that TFP typically reflects price-cost markups as well as technical efficiency (Hall, 1988; Klette and Griliches, 1996; de Loecker, 2011). Mismeasurement of input prices and quality also cause biases (e.g., Goldberg et al., 2016). Despite these issues, huge progress has been made in recent years toward better TFP measurement and production function estimation (see de Loecker and Syverson, 2021, for a review). And TFP has the advantage of being measured in principle on a cardinal scale, but it is more widely available across a wider spectrum of firms than R&D.

Econometrics of innovation

The modern empirical literature tried to tackle a number of empirical challenges. Prior work had largely used cross-sectional data to establish correlations between innovation on one hand and market structure on the other. However, this relationship is inherently dynamic and nonlinear. A successful innovation will likely lead to firm growth and an increase in the firm's market share (the fundamental endogeneity problem); this growth in market share will change a firm's ability and incentives to innovate.

BGVR introduce into the panel data econometrics literature a new method of estimating nonlinear count data models with firm fixed effects when such dynamic feedback effects are important. This was vital given the fact that innovation measures are fundamentally count data processes (e.g., patents). The firm fixed effects try to capture the unobserved heterogeneity, such as the vastly different technological opportunities and appropriability conditions facing firms. Failing to control for these firm capabilities could lead to spurious associations between firms' innovative performance and their market position. Richer panel data allowed researchers to control for other, potentially confounding, firm and industry characteristics that affect innovation and firm performance. Policy variation and better econometric methods helped identify the causal impact of competition on innovation. These "pre-sample mean scaling" methods were further developed in Blundell et al. (2002).

2.2 *Bringing the theory and empirical evidence closer together*

At the start of the twenty-first century, the advances in empirical evidence seemed at face value to contradict the theoretical literature. Theories of IO (e.g., Salop, 1979) and endogenous growth theories (e.g., Romer, 1990; and Aghion and Howitt, 1992) predicted that increased product market competition would reduce the returns to entry and innovation and so discourage it. However, the empirical literature, such as BGVR, pointed to net positive effects. In addition, although some theories also pointed in that direction, such as Arrow's replacement effect, these were not incorporated into canonical models.

The inverted-U model: Theory

In an attempt to reconcile this empirical evidence with standard theory, Aghion, Bloom, Blundell, Griffith, and Howitt (2005, henceforth, ABBGH) developed a model of the inverted-U relationship. This idea built on work by Harris and Vickers (1987), which developed the idea that competition can spur innovation by allowing both current technological leaders and their followers to innovate, which was fused with growth theory and further developed in Aghion, Harris, and Vickers (1997) and Aghion, Harris, Howitt, and Vickers (2001).

The novelty of the work by Harris and Vickers (1987) was to assume that innovations by leaders and followers all occur step-by-step, that is, an innovator cannot move too far ahead of the lagging firm, due for example, to knowledge spillovers. If a firm that is already at the technology frontier in an industry innovates, then the follower will learn to copy the leader's previous technology.[7]

This assumption means that there are two kinds of sectors in the economy: (i) *leveled* (or *neck-and-neck*) sectors, in which both firms are at technological par with one another, and (ii) *unleveled* sectors, in which the leader is one-step ahead of its competitor.[8] The model implies that innovation incentives depend

---

[7] The basic model has a duopoly structure, but it can be generalized in order to think of the follower as a group of firms.

[8] Aghion et al. (2001) analyze the more general case where the leader can move any number of steps ahead, but this case provides no closed-form solution for the equilibrium R&D levels and the steady-state industry structure. Thus it cannot formally establish qualitative results (e.g., the existence of an inverted-U relationship between competition and innovation) or charac-

not only on post-innovation rents (which is how they had previously been modeled in the endogenous growth models where all innovations are made by outsiders), but on the *difference* between post-innovation and pre-innovation rents. More competition will foster innovation and growth when it increases the *incremental profits* from innovating—i.e., when it reduces a firm's pre-innovation rents by more than its post-innovation rents.

The role of innovation in this model is that it allows firms to escape competition, to move one-step ahead in technology terms from its rival. This incentive to escape competition is likely to be most powerful when firms are operating at similar technological levels: in this case, firms have incentives to compete *for the market* to escape competition *in the market.*

By contrast, when innovation is made by firms that are using inferior technologies (laggard firms), their pre-innovation profits are low, and increased product market competition does not have much of an impact on these. What increased product market competition does is reduce their post-innovation rents—a rent dissipation effect—which disincentives them from innovating.

On average, an increase in competition thus has an ambiguous effect. The model captures the Arrow replacement effect (escape competition) as well as classical rent dissipation (Schumpeterian effect). The inverted-U arises because the fraction of sectors with neck-and-neck competitors is itself endogenous and depends on equilibrium innovation intensities in the different types of sectors. When competition (as measured by consumer price sensitivity) is low, a larger equilibrium fraction of sectors involves neck-and-neck competing incumbents, so that overall, the escape-competition effect is more likely to dominate the Schumpeterian effect. However, when competition is high, the Schumpeterian effect is more likely to dominate, because a larger fraction of sectors in equilibrium have innovation being performed by laggard firms with low initial profits.

Putting these results together with the effect of competition on the equilibrium industry structure, ABBGH establish an inverted-U relationship—if the degree of competition is very low to begin with, an increase in competition results in a faster average innovation rate, whereas if it is high to begin with, then an increase in competition results in a slower average innovation rate.

---

terize the relationship between competition and the distribution of technological gaps. More recent work has tackled this shortcoming by numerical simulation methods (e.g., Aghion, Bergeaud, and Van Reenen, 2021).

This dynamic arises because when there is not much competition, the incentive for neck-and-neck firms to innovate is low, so the industry will be slow to leave the leveled state (which happens when one of the neck-and-neck firms innovate). The overall innovation rate will be highest when the sector is unleveled, so the industry will be quick to leave the unleveled state (meaning that the lagging firm innovates). As a result, the industry will spend most of the time in the leveled state, where the escape-competition effect dominates, meaning that starting from a low degree of competition, an increase in competition should result in a faster average innovation rate.

In contrast, when competition is initially very high, there is relatively little incentive for the laggard in an unleveled state to innovate. Thus, the industry will be relatively slow to leave the unleveled state. Meanwhile, firms in the leveled state face a large incremental profit, giving them a relatively large incentive to innovate, so that the industry will be relatively quick to leave the leveled state. As a result, the industry will spend most of the time in the unleveled state, where the Schumpeterian effect is at work on the laggard, while the leader never innovates, so if the degree of competition is very high to begin with, an increase in competition should result in a slower average innovation rate.

The reason that the escape-competition effect dominates when competition is low, whereas the Schumpeterian effect on laggards dominates when competition is high, is this "composition effect" of competition on the steady-state distribution of technology gaps across sectors.

The inverted-U model: Evidence

ABBGH provided empirical support for these predictions using nonparametric estimates of the relationship between patents and the Lerner Index (the estimated price cost margin at the industry level) for UK firms. Figure 3.1 shows the basic relationship in the raw data, using both an exponential quadratic curve and a nonparametric spline fitted to the data. The horizontal axis is one minus the Lerner, so it is increasing in competition. A value of 0.9 implies a price-cost margin of 10 percent, whereas a value of one is when price equals marginal cost (perfect competition). These are based in industry by year observations. As industry competition rises from 0.87, cite-weighted patents increase, but eventually plateau at around 0.95 and then decreases when competition becomes very high.

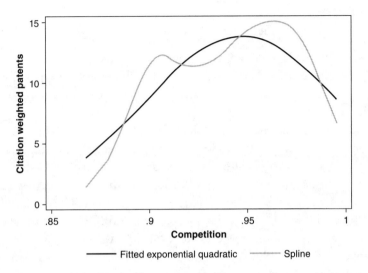

Reformatted with permission from Oxford University Press Journals from Aghion et al. (2005), figure II.

Figure 3.1. Empirical inverted-U relationship

A concern about this correlation is the endogeneity of the market power measure. Does this represent the effect of market power on innovation or of innovation on market power? To tackle this issue, ABBGH instrument the Lerner Index with three sets of policies: (i) the Thatcher-era privatizations, (ii) the EU Single Market Programme, and (iii) the Monopoly and Merger Commission investigations that resulted in structural or behavioral remedies being imposed on an industry. Since they include industry and time fixed effects, the instruments identify the impact of competition using the differential timing of the introduction of policy changes across industries. The basic relationship shown in Figure 3.1 in the raw data holds up to this extended analysis. Further, as predicted by the theory, more neck-and-neck industries show a higher level of innovation activity for any level of product market competition, and the inverted-U curve is steeper for more neck-and-neck industries. The authors show robustness of the results to alternative measures of innovation (e.g., R&D expenditure instead of patents) and competition (e.g., the Herfindahl Index instead of the inverse Lerner Index). We discuss some policy implications of these findings in Section 3.1 below.

Direct extensions of the inverted-U model

ABBGH spawned a literature that proposed both complementary and contradictory theoretical models and provided both empirical support for the inverted-U and evidence that seems to question the robustness of the relationship.

Papers that extend the approach include Aghion et al. (2009), who study the impact of foreign entry as a form of competition and show that the impact on domestic incumbent firms depends on the technology distance between the firms. Aghion et al. (2008) and Griffith and McCartney (2014) consider the mitigating impact of labor market institutions. Haruyama (2006) adds three additional reasons that complement ABBGH and reinforce the inverted-U; these reasons relate to cross-industry R&D spillovers, the cumulative aspects of technological progress, and rent protection activities by firms. Hashmi (2013) finds a negative relationship between competition and innovation using US data. The model in ABBGH uses the assumption that the technology gap between the leading firm and the laggard can be only one step. Hashmi relaxes that assumption and shows that this generates richer dynamics and means that the relationship between competition and innovation can be positive, negative, or an inverted-U, depending on how close or far competitors are in technology space (what AABGH call the "degree of neck-and-neckness" of the industry). To quote that article:

> The reconciliation of the empirical results between the U.K. and the U.S. samples depends on the assumption that the U.K. industries are more neck-and-neck than the U.S. industries. This is just one possible explanation for the different empirical results. The different results could also be attributed to differences in the data sets and the samples.

Beneito, Rochina-Barrachina, and Sanchis (2017) find a positive relationship between competition and innovation using Spanish data. They extend the ABBGH model to accommodate the possibility that inefficient firms face the threat of exit when competition intensifies, and this generates a model in which the effect can be positive or an inverted-U. In sectors where there is a laggard firm that uses nonfrontier technology (unleveled sectors in ABBGH), the threat of exit means that these laggard firms have an incentive to innovate to avoid bankruptcy, which offsets the negative Schumpeterian effects. De Bondt and Vandekerckhove (2012) provide an excellent discussion of the literature and highlight earlier work by Kamien and

Schwartz (1976) that showed an inverted-U relationship, which is not well acknowledged in the literature.[9]

In conclusion, some papers provide empirical support for the inverted-U,[10] and while others show empirical evidence that questions the robustness of the relationship,[11] our sense is that the inverted-U relationship has held up reasonably well. On average, though, the relationship between innovation and competition tends to be more positive than negative.

3 Some Applications and Developments

This body of work has wide-ranging implications for policy and future research in economics. We discuss three of these—competition policy, international trade, and structural models.

3.1 Competition Policy

Competition or antitrust policy refers to the set of laws, regulations, and policies that governments put in place to guard against the unnecessary creation and abuse of market power. Primary among these is merger policy, where competition authorities investigate whether a proposed merger and acquisition is against the public interest. However, policies concerning collusion and abuse of an existing dominant market position are also important.

Economic thinking is deeply embedded in competition policy, with consumer welfare having been generally adopted as the standard criteria for

---

[9] In that model, firms compete in R&D to win a patent. The firm trades off the cost of accelerating research effort with the payoff from successful innovation; increased competition increases the risk of someone else getting the patent first, leading to an inverted-U relationship.

[10] These papers include Aghion and Braun (2008) for South Africa; Lambertini et al. (2017); Peneder and Woerter (2014) with Swiss data; Polder and Veldhuizen (2012) for the Netherlands; and Askenazy, Cahn, and Irac (2013) using French data.

[11] These include Hashmi (2013), Tingvall and Poldahl (2006) with Swedish data, Michiyuki and Shunsuke (2013) for Japan, and Correa (2012), who provide an econometric investigation of the parametric version of the model estimated by ABBGH and show evidence of a structural break that coincides with the establishment of the US Court of Appeals for the Federal Circuit in 1982. They find a positive relationship between competition and innovation in the period prior to 1982 and no relationship after 1982, and they argue that the empirical results in ABBGH are driven by misspecification.

whether a merger is harmful. The standard test is whether a proposed merger is likely to lead to a significant reduction in competition, often interpreted as when there is likely to be an increase in (quality-adjusted) prices.

Innovation considerations are increasingly discussed in competition cases. For example, the European Commission initially blocked a merger of the agricultural chemicals division of Dow and DuPont largely on innovation grounds (European Commission, 2017). Gilbert and Greene (2015) surveyed US merger cases in high-tech sectors and found that since 2000, most challenges by US antitrust enforcers to mergers have included allegations of harm to innovation. The Department of Justice raised innovation concerns in US vs. Microsoft (as did the European Commission's Directorate General of Competition) and in its recent action against Google. The Federal Trade Commission (FTC) filed a complaint that Facebook harmed innovation by acquiring Instagram and WhatsApp. Gilbert, Riis, and Riis (2021) discuss these cases in more detail and show how elements of the "Inverted-U" approach can be generalized in merger analysis.

Nevertheless, judges frequently complain that standard economics is of limited practical use. Often in practice, Schumpeterian "dynamic considerations" are set against the traditional static considerations of antitrust. Under this view, a horizontal merger may create monopoly power and so generate static consumer losses, but a more concentrated market could support greater innovation. These results may be caused by the incentive effects discussed earlier, through relieving financial constraints that hold back R&D (which has high sunk/fixed costs and much uncertainty) or through reducing duplicative research. Thus, merging parties could in principle appeal to the dynamic efficiency benefits that will ultimately more than offset the static deadweight losses.

As we have seen, however, these arguments are likely to be fragile in a generic sense, as there are as many reasons why a more competitive market could stimulate greater innovation (e.g., Arrow's replacement effect). Indeed, the argument could be turned on its head. Even if a merger reduced prices due to (say, large short-run merger-related marginal cost synergies), the innovation losses in the longer run from a reduction in competition could outweigh these static gains.

What does the inverted-U model imply for policy? What it clearly does *not* imply is that competition policy should be lax on firms with market power. It does suggest that at high levels of competition, it might be important to weigh up potential dynamic efficiency losses vs. static efficiency gains from tough antitrust policy (i.e., focus more on competition *for the market* than competition *in the market*), although this range is not nearly as large as previous theory suggested.

The prior of most competition authorities, at least in Europe, is that competition is beneficial for innovation/dynamic efficiency. For example, Kai-Uwe Kuhn, the former chief economist of the EU's DG-COMP, has argued that the most controversial merger cases (those that go to Phase II after the Commission has issued a Statement of Objection) are by their nature in less competitive markets (Kuhn et al., 2012). Hence, they will usually be on the upward-sloping region of the inverted-U, meaning a negative innovation effect from the reduction in competition.

The empirical evidence on using natural experiments from antitrust policy changes on innovation is thin. Watzinger et al. (2020) find substantial increases in innovation following the US government's break-up of AT&T into the "Baby Bells." By contrast, a recent paper by Kang (2020) examining all prosecuted US cartel cases finds that innovation was higher when the cartels operated than when they were suppressed (but argues that the effects are via relaxing financial constraints rather than product market effects).

The Aghion-Howitt perspective also implies that it might be important to consider the impact of market liberalization and tough antitrust policy on industries that lag behind the technological frontier. This is not to suggest that these industries should be protected, but that complementary institutions and policies may be required to cope with the displacement of workers. The results also suggest that in industries where firms are currently well matched technologically, antitrust might be particularly effective at spurring innovation, as these firms seek to escape competition. In industries where firms lag behind the technological frontier, other policies might be needed to facilitate innovations aimed at catching up with the frontier. These policies could increase the fraction of industries where there is neck-and-neck competition and in this way encourage aggregate innovation.

A final implication is that patent policy is a necessary complement to competition policy. Patents ensure that an innovative firm is rewarded, while competition policies ensure that firms that do not innovate earn little profits. However, it is important that patent policies do not make it too easy for frontier firms to lock in their positions.

Although it has always been there, the issue of innovation is climbing up the agenda of competition authorities. This is primarily because of the growth of the importance of dynamic high-tech sectors where innovation (rather than price) is the key mode of competition. This is most obvious in digital sectors, which have become dominated by the GAFAMs (Google, Amazon, Facebook, Apple, and Microsoft). These multinationals have achieved stratospheric market valuations and have come to dominate increasing numbers of sectors. Part of the reason for their dominance are some powerful network effects, which give their core markets a "winner takes all" flavor. For example, Google dominates in search in large part because of data. When someone uses Google to search, it helps improve the quality of the underlying algorithm. In addition, the better this search algorithm is, the more people will use it. It is hard for rivals to break into this market because the data Google amasses on search means that other engines struggle to be as attractive, even if sponsored by deep financial pockets (e.g., Microsoft's Bing). The product itself is free, but the value is monetized through advertising.

There are many competition concerns with the GAFAMs. A major one is that the dominant platforms cement their power through reducing future competition by stifling rival innovation (see Tirole, 2020, for a comprehensive overview). One strategy may be to try to kill off a promising start-up through business strategies such as degrading interoperability between the dominant firm's platform and that of the entrant. This strategy was at the heart of the European Commission's landmark case against Microsoft in 2004 (see Kuhn and Van Reenen, 2009; Genakos et al., 2018). Ultimately, this is about degrading a rival's ability to innovate by restricting access to some essential facility, such as a platform or core data.

If a rival cannot be thwarted through raising its costs, an alternative tactic may simply be to buy up the competitor. In the 1990s, start-ups would aim to have an exit strategy by eventually doing an initial public offering. Today, venture capitalists are more likely to state that the "exit strategy" is not to become the next Amazon or Microsoft via an initial public offering, but rather to be acquired by a tech titan. This may have benefits to the smaller firm, but it deprives the consumer of competition with an alternative provider.

Such acquisitions can be even worse than simply reducing competition. Cunningham et al. (2021) describe the phenomenon of "killer acquisitions," where a dominant firm takes over a smaller firm and kills off its nascent technological innovation. They show this happens in parts of the pharmaceutical industry, where a new drug in a biotech's pipeline would threaten a drug maker's inferior current product. Rather than spend the additional

R&D resources to take the drug to market (e.g., Phase III trials or marketing), Big Pharma may prefer to simply continue enjoying their rents from the current branded product.

The key problem is that a dominant firm may use its power to reduce the ability and incentives of rivals to innovate. In principle, competition authorities could act on this behavior, but in practice, it is difficult. For example, consider a merger investigation. The standard practice is to look at the current market shares of the merging parties to assess the risk to competition. GAFAM acquisitions of start-ups are based on their future potential, not current size. When Facebook took over Instagram and WhatsApp, they were relatively small platforms, which did not add much to Facebook's market share, whatever the market definition. However, clearly Instagram and WhatsApp had the potential to grow and potentially threaten Facebook's dominance. Blocking the acquisition would have to be based on the risks to future competition. This is particularly difficult in the US, where the DOJ and FTC have to convince a judge that there is a greater than 50 percent chance of competition being harmed. The parties can easily argue that the empirical evidence for this is thin.

As Tirole (2020) and de Loecker, Obermeier, and Van Reenen (2021) argue, the standard of proof in such cases should be shifted more to the dominant firm to provide greater assurance that the takeover will *not* reduce innovation. The Furman Review (2019) suggests many similar reforms for the UK Competition and Markets Authority in judging mergers and acquisitions as well as the creation of a specialist regulator for the digital sector. The European Commission's Digital Markets Act is along similar lines.

All these considerations of competition policy are rooted in Aghion and Howitt's emphasis that future innovative incentives should be front and center of decision-making.

3.2 International Trade

Changes in the patterns of international trade offer some sharp changes to competition. However, the impact of trade is complex because it may operate on multiple margins (see Shu and Steinwender, 2019, and Melitz and Redding, Chapter 6, this volume, for a longer discussion). We briefly discuss the impact of trade competition on productivity levels (a static effect) and on productivity growth (i.e. innovation, a dynamic effect).

Static effects of trade on productivity

The survey by Van Reenen (2011) argues that on average, positive effects of competition on productivity have been found, although there is certainly a large degree of heterogeneity. Part of the impact is by reallocation on the extensive (less efficient firms exit) and intensive margins (less efficient firms lose some of their market share). Syverson (2004), for example, shows that productivity is higher in the concrete industry in locations with greater competition, because lower productivity establishments shrink and exit. However, part of the impact is also through changes within firms, whereby an increase in competition causes an incumbent firm to upgrade its productivity (Backus, 2020 showed this re-examining Syverson's concrete data). This is a theoretically more ambiguous effect, because like the inverted-U, there can be positive Arrow-like escape competition effects, as managers work harder to avoid losing rents, but negative Schumpeterian-like effects from lower rents. The empirical work suggests positive effects on average. Holmes and Schmitz (2010) survey the evidence and discuss many interesting case studies, such as the opening of the Great Lakes. They stress how competition forced many incumbents to move to more efficient management practices. The importance of competition for improving management has also been shown econometrically by Bloom and Van Reenen (2007); Bloom, Propper, Seiler, and Van Reenen (2015); and Bloom, Sadun, and Van Reenen (2016) using explicit measures of management.

This literature is fundamentally static, however, rather than examining innovation per se. We next turn to this issue.

Dynamic innovation effects

Much of the literature has focused on the positive impacts of exports on innovation. A reduction in the barriers to exporting effectively increases the effective market size faced by a firm, and a wide class of models implies that larger markets will encourage innovation. For example, if there are fixed costs of R&D, a larger market means that these fixed costs can be spread across a wider number of units. Several papers have shown the positive effects of growth of export market size on innovation (e.g., Aghion et al., 2018; Aghion, Bergeaud, and Van Reenen, 2021; Aw, Roberts, and Xu, 2011).

Direct product market shocks are more evident when barriers to imports (e.g., tariffs) in a firm's product market fall. In this case, a firm faces increased competition from foreign exporters. Although entry into a firm's input markets may have a clear benefit in terms of a wider variety, higher quality, and lower cost of inputs, the Aghion-Howitt perspective suggests that product market competition may have more ambiguous effects (e.g., the "inverted-U" discussed above).

The early firm-level work by Blundell et al. (1995, 1999) found positive correlations between innovation and import penetration in the firm's industry, even after controlling for fixed effects. Although suggestive, there could be other factors driving the relationship: An unobserved shock to domestic growth expectations could boost both innovation and imports, for example.

Much recent work has used the rise of China as a prospective exogenous quasi-experiment. The growth of China is clearly due to policy decisions, starting with Deng Xiaoping in the early 1980s, to open up China's economy and make the country the "workshop of the world." This accelerated with China's accession to the World Trade Organization in December 2001, causing an enormous growth in Chinese goods imports into Western countries.

The impact of the "China Shock" (Autor, Dorn, and Hanson, 2013) on US labor markets has been extensively discussed. Bloom, Draca, and Van Reenen (2016) examined the impact of Chinese imports on technical change in twelve European countries since the mid-1990s. They found that although firms more exposed to the China shock reduced employment, they increased their innovation as measured by raw or cite-weighted patent counts. These authors also found increases in the adoption of IT and in TFP. Moreover, the falls in jobs were much stronger in low-tech firms, implying that China stimulated technological upgrading both within firms and through reallocation to more innovative firms. This positive mean impact of import competition on innovation emerged from simple correlations of the long-differenced growth in patents and Chinese import penetration, as well as an identification strategy using the industry-specific removal of quotas as part of WTO accession (specifically, the abolition of the Multi-Fiber Agreement, which China gained access to when it joined the WTO).

By contrast, Autor, Dorn, Hanson, and Shu (2020) looked at US data and found negative effects of Chinese imports on US firm patents. The identification strategy of Autor et al. (2020) differed from that of Bloom et al. (2016) and used increases in Chinese imports in European industries as an exogenous shift to those in the US. Nevertheless, Bloom, Romer, Terry, and Van

Reenen (2021) show that replicating the same Autor et al. (2020) Instrumental Variable strategy on the European data continued to produce positive effects.[12]

Autor et al. (2020) and Bloom et al. (2021) both suggest that the inverted-U approach of ABBGH offers a reconciliation between the differing results in the EU compared to those for the US. European markets were generally less competitive than US manufacturing markets in the 1990s, due to greater regulation and fragmentation (e.g., the Single Market was still being built). Hence, the China shock moved countries along the upward-sloping part of the inverted-U. By contrast, in the more competitive markets of North America, we may be on the downward-sloping part of the inverted-U, so even higher competition causes the Schumpeterian effect to outweigh the "escape competition" effect.[13]

3.3 Structural IO approaches

Introduction to structural models

As noted earlier, an advantage of the Aghion-Howitt creative destruction approach to endogenous growth compared with Romer-style expanding variety approaches is that firm heterogeneity is at its center (e.g., in the decisions of entrants vs. incumbents). This makes it a natural framework for thinking about innovation and market structure.

The Aghion-Howitt framework is, in some ways, a marriage between IO (where imperfect competition and firm heterogeneity have always been central) and macro (which focuses on the need to explicitly aggregate in order to understand general equilibrium outcomes, such as growth).

There is a growing body of structural IO work, which has been influenced by Aghion-Howitt but draws more on modern IO approaches that explicitly estimate models of innovative conduct in specific industries. This contrasts with the more "reduced-form" work on innovation and market structure described above, which is less wedded to estimating structural parameters from a specific model of conduct.

---

[12] Bloom et al. (2021) develop the theoretical underpinnings through a "trapped factor" model, where the resources (like skilled labor) displaced in a firm by Chinese competition are redeployed into innovation activities. They embed this model in a macro endogenous growth model to show the large impacts of China on Western aggregate innovation. Quispe (2020) also finds positive effects of China's WTO accession on quality upgrading in Peru.

[13] This explanation chimes in with our contrast between the UK findings in ABBGH and the US work of Hashmi (2013) discussed earlier.

The advantages of taking a structural approach are that the behavior of players in the game can be characterized explicitly, and deep parameters are in principle identified. It is therefore possible to conduct more credible counterfactual exercises (e.g., what would have happened if a merger had been banned), explicitly examining changes in price and innovation. Importantly, it is also possible to explicitly quantify social welfare under different policies and changes in market structures.

The disadvantage of a structural approach is that one will usually have to take a narrower focus on a specific industry to institutionally justify the modeling assumptions. Thus, it is hard to generalize. In addition, stronger assumptions typically have to be made, particularly around functional forms, in order to recover parameters. And the models and estimation techniques are quite complex, making it harder to assess the credibility of the identifying assumptions.

Static structural IO models of short-run price and quantity games are common (for surveys, see Pakes, 2021, and Ackerberg et al., 2007). However, these mostly take as given the level of productivity and the number/ quality of brands and products. R&D investments are designed to explicitly enhance these primitives and are taken at an earlier stage. Structural dynamic models of investment will be strategic, given the imperfect competition in the later stage of the game. Estimating these dynamic games poses many tricky issues, especially since multiple equilibria are endemic.

SOME STRUCTURAL IO PAPERS ON INNOVATION AND COMPETITION[14]

Goettler and Gordon (2011) estimate a dynamic oligopoly game of the PC microprocessing industry, where there was competition between leader Intel and AMD over several decades. They incorporate the durable nature of the good by making demand and price-setting dynamic. They perform a counterfactual analysis of innovation under an Intel monopoly and find that Intel would innovate by about 4 percent more in the absence of AMD. Consumer surplus, however, is overall higher with AMD competing, because prices are

---

[14] Our review is partial by necessity, and we leave out many good papers. For example, Yang (2020) studies the incentives to innovate in a vertical relationship, such as System-on-a-Chip vendors selling technology to cell phone manufacturers. Empirically, the benefits of a hypothetical merger between Qualcomm and a smartphone manufacturer, who can then coordinate R&D incentives and reduce double marginalization, exceed the harms from foreclosing entry or increasing costs for other smartphone makers.

lower. These authors emphasize that their result depends crucially on the durable nature of the good. Product upgrades are necessary to stimulate demand, and they happen only if consumers highly value quality and are relatively price insensitive. Nonetheless, their bottom line is that they find that monopoly outperforms duopoly in terms of innovation.

Goettler and Gordon (2011) use a full solution concept, which requires explicitly characterizing the entire game.[15] Bajari, Benkard, and Levin (2007) propose a two-step approach to estimating dynamic investment models, which enables a researcher to relax some of the functional form assumptions (essentially, by taking a semi-parametric approach to estimating the R&D policy correspondence rule). This approach does not require solving for the full equilibrium. Hashmi and Van Biesebroeck (2016) implement this two-step approach in the global automobile industry. They model car quality for the average consumer, which is determined by the dynamic control variable, innovation (proxied by patents). Innovation as a function of market structure is not easy to characterize, but they do find that after entry, although incumbent innovation falls, aggregate innovation rises. Thus, their conclusions are consistent with Blundell et al. (1999) that although high market share is followed by more innovation, higher aggregate competition leads to higher aggregate innovation.

A disadvantage of the previous two papers is that they analyze the innovation decisions of a few incumbent firms. Igami (2017) goes beyond this to incorporate both incumbents and entrants (up to more than two dozen firms)[16] and focuses on the incumbent-entrant heterogeneity in innovation incentives.[17] His context is the hard-disk drive (HDD) manufacturing industry between 1981 and 1998. He finds that despite cost advantages and preemptive incentives, incumbents innovate less than entrants because of the Arrow replacement effect—they do not want to cannibalize their own products.

Igami and Uetake (2020) look again at the HDD industry using data that are more recent (1996–2016, which was a period of rapid consolidation, leading eventually to only three global players). Given this context, they focus

---

[15] This is also true in the approach of Benkard (2004) for aircraft.

[16] Aw, Roberts, and Xu (2011) study the Korean electric motor industry, which is characterized by many firms, and they apply a monopolistic competition framework. This mutes strategic interactions between incumbents and entrants.

[17] Methodologically, Igami builds on Aguirregabiria and Mira (2007), who study entry games (static and dynamic, respectively) with incomplete information.

on the impact of consolidation on innovation and whether competition authorities were too lax in allowing so many mergers. Unlike Igami (2017), they explicitly endogenize mergers and the evolution of technology at the frontier (i.e., Kryder's Law,[18] which was kept exogenous in the earlier paper). Their estimates suggest that innovation and competition are more like a rise to a plateau than an inverted-U. Their counterfactual analysis suggests aggregate innovation increases when the industry moves from monopoly to duopoly and from duopoly to triopoly. After this, it is less clear, with a lot of heterogeneity across time and space. Igami and Uetake conclude that the current competition authority's "rule of thumb," which is not to allow further consolidation beyond three players, is roughly right.

Another interesting recent paper is Bhattacharya (2021), who examined the US Navy's Small Business Innovation Research (SBIR) program. He considers this program as a three-stage game. Firms bid for R&D procurement contracts. The Navy puts out a request for solutions to an innovation problem. Firms compete, and a subset of them are awarded a Phase I contract to develop a white paper. Of those who innovate in this way, a subset of the players then progress to a Phase II, where they try to develop a workable prototype. Finally, the Navy selects no more than one of these to produce the new product in a Phase III military contract for production, which is where the serious money is.

Bhattacharya (2021) observes the Phase II and III contracts (the money paid by the Navy and some contract characteristics) and the identity of the successful firms at each stage. He builds a model in which firms must decide how much R&D effort to supply in Phase I and Phase II, motivated by the (small) prospect of a prize in the Phase III. Effort in Phase I increases the chances of stochastically discovering an innovation (of heterogeneous value) and progressing in the contest. Greater effort in Phase II will reduce the cost of producing the innovation. The Navy awards Phase III to the firm with the highest surplus (innovation value minus production costs) but pays only a fraction of this surplus to the firm. This generates the classic hold-up problem, which means that firms do "too little" R&D. The business-stealing effect, however, also generates the possibility that there may be "too much"

---

[18] Kryder's Law is an engineering regularity that states that the recording density (and therefore storage capacity) of HDDs doubles approximately every twelve months, just like Moore's Law, which states that the circuit density (and therefore processing speeds) of semiconductor chips doubles every eighteen to twenty-four months.

R&D. So there remains the classic Aghion-Howitt trade-off, and which effect dominates is an empirical issue.

Bhattacharya (2021) structurally estimates the dynamic sequential contest and then simulates counterfactual policies. He finds that increasing competition (for example, by allowing more firms to enter Phase II) would increase both the quality of innovation and social welfare, as would allowing the Phase III winner to keep more of the surplus. However, this does not happen in practice, and Bhattacharya argues that this is because the narrow interests of the Navy dictate a greater emphasis on cost containment than is socially optimal.[19]

CONCLUSIONS ON STRUCTURAL MODELS

Structural estimation of IO models of innovation and competition is a growing research area, but the complexity of the problem has meant that progress has not been speedy. Overall, our take on the current literature is that, although there are certainly many differences between industries, increasing entry from monopoly (i.e., very low competition) does seem to increase aggregate innovation. But at some point, these gains flatten out. This behavior is compatible with falling innovation for incumbents, which is compensated with the innovation of entrants. What is not clear is the point at which these aggregate gains may go into reverse (as in the downward part of the inverted-U).

These models, and the development of more structural dynamic IO models with endogenous investment, make up an exciting area of frontier research, and we expect to see many more papers in the next decade (see also the Pakes, 2021, survey). An issue here is to ground the complex models in institutional reality and well-identified causal parameters in a transparent way.

4 Conclusions

Aghion and Howitt's work combines the insights of the IO literature on market structure and innovation into macro growth theory. Thus, it became a powerful way to link micro insights into growth policies.

---

[19] See Howell et al. (2021) for a causal evaluation of a reform to the US Air Force's SBIR program.

The evolution of the work in this area is clear. By the start of the twenty-first century, the econometric and data tools for the analysis of innovation and market structure had become well developed, allowing for estimation of the dynamic, nonlinear effects of competition with unobserved heterogeneity. However, this work (e.g., Blundell et al., 1999) strongly suggested that the competition had a positive impact on innovation, rather than the negative impact highlighted by Schumpeter that operated through the dissipation of innovative rents. AAGBH incorporated the insight from Arrow that the preexisting rents of a monopolistic incumbent created a disincentive to innovate, because these would be replaced by a new stream of innovation rents. When both insights were combined, the impact was ambiguous. When put in an equilibrium step-by-step model, some clear predictions could be made relating to the inverted-U and the impact of competition in leveled and unleveled sectors. The relationship has held up reasonably well over time, although on average, we conclude from our survey that the positive effect of competition on innovation still seems to dominate empirically.

Where should the research go from here? One can never write the music of the future, because if one did so, it would already be written. However, here are some suggestions.

First, the weight of the economy has shifted toward high-tech, innovative sectors. Hence, understanding the dynamics of these sectors has become ever more important. Innovation requires ex post rewards, as this helps drive private sector incentives (i.e., we want firms to compete for the markets of the future). But as well as allowing deserved rewards for innovation, a wise policymaker should seek to reduce artificial barriers that protect dominant firms from reducing the ability of rivals to innovate to catch up or replace the leader, as this reduces dynamic competition for the market. Some of these barriers are created by the government through regulation, trade barriers, and so forth. But some may be created by the incumbents, who quite rationally wish to reduce their chance of being displaced (so they stifle competition for the market). Strategies such as takeovers of potential future rivals, raising rival costs through reducing interoperability or other business practices, and/or lobbying activities to protect market power are commonly used. We need to build institutions and develop policies (especially around competition authorities) that reduce the ability of incumbents to implement these strategies, even if they have achieved their success through legitimate innovation (see Van Reenen, 2018). This point is broader than just market structure. Increasing inequality is a feature of many modern capitalist societies, and we need to ensure that incumbents do not use their wealth and power to lock themselves and their descendants into elite positions (Case and Deaton, 2020).

Second, on a more methodological point, the use of quasi-experiments to better identify the impact of competition on innovation (and other outcomes) should be exploited more in this literature. One of the strengths of ABBGH was to pioneer this approach.

Finally, a critique of the general literature is that the models are relatively simple and applied to the economy as a whole. Focusing on more specific markets, as is accomplished in a typical structural IO paper, allows a richer description of the environment and institutions. This approach makes the modeling potentially more credible. Our sense is that this area will also grow in the coming decades.

References

Ackerberg, Daniel, Lanier Benkard, Stephen Berry, and Ariel Pakes (2007) "Econometric Tools for Analyzing Market Outcomes," in Edward Leamer and James Heckman, eds., *Handbook of Econometrics,* vol. 6, chap. 63. Amsterdam, Netherlands: Elsevier.

Aghion, Philippe, Antonin Bergeaud, Matthieu Lequien, and Marc Melitz (2018) "The Impact of Exports on Innovation: Theory and Evidence." NBER Working Paper 24600.

Aghion, Philippe, Antonin Bergeaud, and John Van Reenen (2021) "The Impact of Regulation on Innovation." NBER Working Paper 28381.

Aghion, Philippe, Nicholas Bloom, Richard Blundell, Rachel Griffith, and Peter Howitt (2005) "Competition and Innovation: An Inverted-U Relationship." *Quarterly Journal of Economics* 120(2): 701–728.

Aghion, Philippe, Richard Blundell, Rachel Griffith, Peter Howitt, and Susanne Prantl (2009) "The Effects of Entry on Incumbent Innovation and Productivity." *Review of Economics and Statistics* 91(February): 20–32.

Aghion, Philippe, and Matias Braun (2008) "Competition and Productivity Growth in South Africa." *Economics of Transition* 16(4): 741–768.

Aghion, Philippe, Robin Burgess, Stephen Redding, and Fabrizio Zilibotti (2008) "The Unequal Effects of Liberalization: Evidence from Dismantling the License Raj in India." *American Economic Review* 98(4): 1397–1412.

Aghion, Philippe, Christopher Harris, Peter Howitt, and John Vickers (2001) "Competition, Imitation and Growth with Step-by-Step Innovation." *Review of Economic Studies* 68: 467–492.

Aghion, Philippe, Christopher Harris, and John Vickers (1997) "Competition and Growth with Step-by-Step Innovation: An Example." *European Economic Review* 41: 771–782.

Aghion, Philippe, and Peter Howitt (1992) "A Model of Growth through Creative Destruction." *Econometrica* 60(2): 323–351.

Aghion, Philippe, and Jean Tirole (1994) "Opening the Black Box of Innovation." *European Economic Review* 38(3–4): 701–710. https://doi.org/10.1016/0014 -2921(94)90105-8.

Aguirregabiria, Victor, and Pedro Mira (2007) "Sequential Estimation of Dynamic Discrete Games." *Econometrica* 75(1): 1–53.

Arrow, Kenneth (1962) "Economic Welfare and the Allocation of Resources for Invention." In *The Rate and Direction of Inventive Activity*, 609–625. Princeton, NJ: Princeton University Press.

Arrow, Kenneth, and G. Debreu (1954) "Existence of an Equilibrium for a Competitive Economy." *Econometrica* 22(3): 265–290.

Askenazy, P., C. Cahn, and D. Irac (2013) "Competition, R&D, and the Cost of Innovation: Evidence for France." *Oxford Economic Papers* 65: 293–311.

Autor, David, David Dorn, and Gordon Hanson (2013) "The China Syndrome: Local Labor Market Effects of Import Competition in the United States." *American Economic Review* 103(6): 2121–2168.

Autor, David, David Dorn, Gordon Hanson, Gary Pisano, and Pian Shu (2020) "Foreign Competition and Domestic Innovation: Evidence from US Patents." *American Economic Review: Insights* 2(3): 357–374.

Aw, Bee Yan, Mark Roberts, and Daniel Xu (2011) "R&D Investment, Exporting and Productivity Dynamics." *American Economic Review* 101, 1312–1344.

Backus, Matthew (2020) "Why Is Productivity Correlated with Competition?" *Econometrica* 88(6): 2415–2444.

Bajari, Patrick C., Lanier Benkard, and Jonathan Levin (2007) "Estimating Dynamic Models of Imperfect Competition." *Econometrica* 75(5): 1331–1370.

Beneito, Pilar, María Engracia Rochina-Barrachina, and Amparo Sanchis (2017) "Competition and Innovation with Selective Exit: An Inverted-U Shape Relationship?" *Oxford Economic Papers* 69(4): 1032–1053. https://doi.org/10 .1093/oep/gpw080.

Benkard, Larnier (2004) "A Dynamic Analysis of the Market for Wide-Bodied Commercial Aircraft." *Review of Economic Studies* 71, 581–611.

Bhattacharya, Vivek (2021) "An Empirical Model of R&D Procurement Contests: An Analysis of the DOD SBIR Program." *Econometrica* 89(5): 2189–2224.

Bloom, Nicholas, Mirko Draca, and John Van Reenen (2016) "Trade Induced Technical Change? The Impact of Chinese Imports on Innovation, IT and Productivity." *Review of Economic Studies* 83(1): 87–117.

Bloom, Nicholas, Carol Propper, Stephan Seiler, and John Van Reenen (2015) "The Impact of Competition on Management Quality: Evidence from Public Hospitals." *Review of Economic Studies* 82: 457–489.

Bloom, Nicholas, Paul Romer, Stephen Terry, and John Van Reenen (2021) "Trapped Factors and China's Impact on Global Growth." *Economic Journal* 131(633): 156–191.

Bloom, Nicholas, Raffaella Sadun, and John Van Reenen (2016) "Management as a Technology." CEP Discussion Paper 1433.

Bloom, Nicholas, Mark Schankerman, and John Van Reenen (2013) "Identifying Technology Spillovers and Product Market Rivalry." *Econometrica* 81(4): 1347–1393.

Bloom, Nicholas, and John Van Reenen (2007) "Measuring and Explaining Management Practices across Firms and Nations." *Quarterly Journal of Economics* 122(4): 1351–1408.

Blundell, Richard, Rachel Griffith, and John Van Reenen (1995) "Dynamic Count Data Models of Technical Change." *Economic Journal* 105: 333–344.

Blundell, Richard, Rachel Griffith, and John Van Reenen (1999) "Market Share, Market Value and Innovation in a Panel of British Manufacturing Firms." *Review of Economic Studies* 66(3): 529–554.

Blundell, Richard, Rachel Griffith, and Frank Windmeijer (2002) "Individual Effects and Dynamics in Count Data Models." *Journal of Econometrics* 108(1): 113–131. https://doi.org/10.1016/S0304-4076(01)00108-7.

Boldrin, Michele, and David Levine (2009) *Against Intellectual Property.* Cambridge: Cambridge University Press.

Case, Ann, and Angus Deaton (2020) *Deaths of Despair.* Princeton, NJ: Princeton University Press.

Cohen, W., and R. Levin (1989) "Empirical Studies of Innovation and Market Structure." In *Handbook of Industrial Organization,* R. C. Schmalensee and R. Willig, eds. Amsterdam: Elsevier, 1059–1107.

Correa, Juan A. (2012) "Innovation and Competition: An Unstable Relationship." *Journal of Applied Econometrics* 27(1): 160–166. https://doi.org/10.1002/jae.1262.

Cunningham, Colleen, Florian Ederer, and Song Ma (2021) "Killer Acquisitions." *Journal of Political Economy* 129(3): 649–702.

Dasgupta, Partha, and Joseph Stiglitz (1980) "Industrial Structure and the Nature of Innovative Activity." *Economic Journal* 90(358): 266–293.

De Bondt, Raymond, and Jan Vandekerckhove (2012) "Reflections on the Relation between Competition and Innovation." *Journal of Industry, Competition and Trade* 12(1): 7–19. https://doi.org/10.1007/s10842-010-0084-z.

Dechezlepretre, Antoine, Elias Einio, Ralf Martin, Kieu-Trang Nguyen "Do Fiscal Incentives Increase Innovation? An RD Design for R&D." Forthcoming. CEP Discussion Paper 1413.

De Loecker, Jan (2011) "Product Differentiation, Multi-Product Firms and Estimating the Impact of Trade Liberalization on Productivity." *Econometrica* 79(5): 1407–1451.

De Loecker, Jan, Tim Obermeier, and John Van Reenen (2021) "Firms and Inequality." POID Working Paper 27.

De Loecker, Jan, and Chad Syverson (2021) "An Industrial Organization Perspective on Productivity." NBER Working Paper 29229.

Dixit, Avinash and Joseph Stiglitz (1977) "Monopolistic Competition and Optimum Product Diversity." *American Economic Review* 67(3): 297–308.

European Commission (2017) *CASE M.7932–Dow/DuPont*. https://ec.europa.eu
/competition/mergers/cases/decisions/m7932_13668_3.pdf.

Furman Review (2019) "Unlocking Digital Competition. Report of the Digital
Competition Expert Panel." London: HMSO. https://www.gov.uk
/government/publications/unlocking-digital-competition-report-of-the-digital
-competition-expert-panel.

Genakos, Christos, Kai Uwe Kuhn, and John Van Reenen (2018) "The Incentives
of a Monopolist to Degrade Interoperability." *Economica* 85: 873–902.

Geroski, Paul (1995) *Market Structure, Corporate Performance and Innovative
Activity*. Oxford: Oxford University Press.

Gilbert, Richard, and H. Greene (2015) "Merging Innovation into Antitrust
Agency Enforcement of the Clayton Act." *George Washington Law Review* 83:
1919–1947.

Gilbert, Richard, and David Newbery (1982) "Pre-emptive Patenting and the
Persistence of Monopoly." *American Economic Review* 72: 514–526.

Gilbert, Richard, Christian Riis, and Erlend Riis (2021) "Innovation, Antitrust
Enforcement and the Inverted U." University of California, Berkeley,
manuscript.

Goettler, R., and B. Gordon (2011) "Does AMD Spur Intel to Innovate More?"
Journal of Political Economy 119: 1141–1200.

Goldberg, Penny, Amit Khandelwal, Jan de Loecker, and Nina Pavcnik (2016)
"Prices, Markups and Trade Reform." *Econometrica* 84(2): 445–510.

Griffith, Rachel, and Gareth McCartney (2014) "Employment Protection
Legislation, Multinational Firms, and Innovation." *Review of Economics and
Statistics* 96(1): 135–150.

Griliches, Zvi (1990) "Patent Statistics as Economic Indicators: A Survey." *Journal
of Economic Literature* 28: 1661–1707.

Hall, R. (1988) "The Relation between Price and Marginal Cost in US Industry."
Journal of Political Economy 96: 921–947.

Harris, Christopher, and John Vickers (1987) "Racing with Uncertainty." *Review
of Economic Studies* 54(1): 1–21.

Hart, Oliver (1983) "The Market Mechanism as an Incentive Scheme." *Bell
Journal of Economics* 14(2): 366–382.

Haruyama, Tetsugen (2006) *An Inverted U Relationship between Competition and
Innovation: A Revisit*. Kobe University, manuscript.

Hashmi, Aamir Rafique (2013) "Competition and Innovation: The Inverted-U
Relationship Revisited." *Review of Economics and Statistics* 95(5): 1653–1668.

Hashmi, Aamir Rafique, and Johannes Van Biesebroeck (2016) "The Relationship
between Market Structure and Innovation in Industry Equilibrium: A Case
Study of the Global Automobile Industry." *Review of Economics and Statistics*
98(1): 192–208.

Haskel, Jonathan, and Stian Westlake (2017) *Capitalism without Capital*.
Princeton, NJ: Princeton University Press.

Holmes, Thomas, and James Schmitz (2010) "Competition and Productivity: A Review of Evidence." *Annual Review of Economics* 2: 619–642.

Holmstrom, Bengt (1982) "Moral Hazard in Teams." *Bell Journal of Economics* 13(2): 324–340.

Hotelling, Harold (1929) "Stability in Competition." *Economic Journal* 39(153): 41–57.

Howell, Sabrina, Jason Rathje, John Van Reenen, and Jun Wong (2021) "OPENing up Military Innovation: An Evaluation of Reforms to the U.S. Air Force SBIR Program." NBER Working Paper 28700.

Hsieh, Chiang-Tai and Pete Klenow (2009) "Misallocation and Manufacturing TFP in China and India." *Quarterly Journal of Economics* 124(4): 1403–1448.

Igami, Mitsuru (2017) "Estimating the Innovator's Dilemma: Structural Analysis of Creative Destruction in the Hard Disk Drive Industry, 1981–1998." *Journal of Political Economy* 125: 798–847.

Igami, Mitsuru, and Kosuke Uetake (2020) "Mergers, Innovation, and Entry-Exit Dynamics: Consolidation of the Hard Disk Drive Industry, 1996–2016." *Review of Economic Studies* 87: 2672–2702.

Kamien, Morton, and Nancy Schwartz (1976) "On the Degree of Rivalry for Maximum Innovative Activity." *Quarterly Journal of Economics* 90(2): 245–260.

Kang, Hyo (2020) "How Does Competition Affect Innovation? Evidence from U.S. Antitrust Cases." SSRN Scholarly Paper 3516974. Social Science Research Network: 34.

Klette, Tor, and Zvi Griliches (1996) "The Inconsistency of Common Scale Estimators When Output Prices Are Unobserved and Endogenous." *Journal of Applied Econometrics* 11(4): 343–361.

Kogan, Leonid, Dimitris Papanikolaou, Amit Seru, and Noah Stoffman (2017) "Technological Innovation, Resource Allocation, and Growth." *Quarterly Journal of Economics* 32(2): 665–712.

Kuhn, Kai-Uwe, Szabolcs Lorincz, Vincent Verouden, and Annemiek Wilpshaar (2012) "Economics at DG Competition, 2011–2012." *Review of Industrial Organization* 41: 251–270.

Kuhn, Kai-Uwe, and John Van Reenen (2009) "Interoperability and Market Foreclosure in the European Microsoft Case." In *The Economics of European Competition Cases,* Bruce Lyons, ed., 50–72. Cambridge: Cambridge University Press.

Lambertini, Luca, Joanna Poyago-Theotoky, and Alessandro Tampieri (2017) "Cournot Competition and 'Green' Innovation: An Inverted-U Relationship." *Energy Economics* 68 (October 1): 116–123. https://doi.org/10.1016/j.eneco.2017.09.022.

Leibenstein, Harvey (1966) "Allocative Efficiency vs. X-Efficiency." *American Economic Review* 56(3): 392–415.

Michiyuki, Yagi, and Managi Shunsuke (2013) "Competition and Innovation: An Inverted-U Relationship Using Japanese Industry Data." Discussion Papers.

Tokyo: Research Institute of Economy, Trade and Industry (RIETI), July 2013. https://ideas.repec.org/p/eti/dpaper/13062.html.

Pakes, Ariel (1986) "Patents Options: Some Estimates of the Value of Holding European Patent Stocks." *Econometrica* 54: 755–784.

Pakes, Ariel (2021) "A Helicopter Tour of Some Underlying Issues in Empirical Industrial Organization." Harvard University, manuscript.

Pavitt, Keith, Mark Robson, and John Townsend (1987) "The Size Distribution of Innovating Firms." *Journal of Industrial Economics* 35(3): 297–316.

Peneder, Michael, and Martin Woerter (2014) "Competition, R&D and Innovation: Testing the Inverted-U in a Simultaneous System." *Journal of Evolutionary Economics* 24(3): 653–87. https://doi.org/10.1007/s00191-013-0310-z.

Polder, Michael, and Erik Veldhuizen (2012) "Innovation and Competition in the Netherlands: Testing the Inverted-U for Industries and Firms." *Journal of Industry, Competition and Trade* 12(1): 67–91. https://doi.org/10.1007/s10842-011-0120-7.

Quispe, Pamela (2020) "Import Competition, Quality Upgrading and Exporting: Evidence from the Peruvian Apparel Industry." University of Toronto, manuscript.

Raith, Michael (2003) "Competition, Risk and Managerial Incentives." *American Economic Review* 93(4): 1424–1436.

Rao, Nirupama (2016) "Do Tax Credits Stimulate R&D Spending? Revisiting the Effect of the R&D Tax Credit in Its First Decade." *Journal of Public Economics* 140: 1–12.

Reinganum, Janet (1989) "The Timing of Innovation: Research, Development, and Diffusion." In *Handbook of Industrial Organization, Volume I,* Richard Schmalensee and Robert Willig, eds., 849–908. Amsterdam: Elsevier.

Romer, Paul (1990) "Endogenous Technological Change." *Journal of Political Economy* 98(5): S71–S102.

Salop, Steven C. (1979) "Monopolistic Competition with Outside Goods." *Bell Journal of Economics* 10(1): 141–156.

Scherer, F. M. (1965a) "Firm Size, Market Structure, Opportunity, and the Output of Patented Innovations." *American Economic Review* 55(5): 1097–1125.

Scherer, F. M. (1965b) "Corporate Inventive Output, Profits and Growth." *Journal of Political Economy* 73(3): 290–297.

Schmidt, Klaus (1997) "Managerial Incentives and Product Market Competition." *Review of Economic Studies* 64(2): 191–213.

Schumpeter, Joseph (1943) *Capitalism, Socialism and Democracy.* London: Allen Unwin.

Shu, Pian, and Claudia Steinwender (2019) "The Impact of Trade Liberalization on Firm Productivity and Innovation." *Innovation Policy and the Economy* 19: 39–69.

Smith, Adam (1776) *An Inquiry into the Nature and Causes of the Wealth of Nations.* London: Methuen and Co., Ltd.

Syverson, Chad (2004) "Market Structure and Productivity: A Concrete Example." *Journal of Political Economy* 112(6): 1181–1222.

Thiel, Peter (2014) "Competition Is for Losers." *Wall Street Journal,* September 12. https://www.wsj.com/articles/peter-thiel-competition-is-for-losers-1410535536.

Tingvall, Patrik Gustavsson, and Andreas Poldahl (2006) "Is There Really an Inverted U-Shaped Relation between Competition and R&D?" *Economics of Innovation and New Technology* 15(2): 101–118.

Tirole, Jean (1989) *The Theory of Industrial Organization.* Cambridge, MA: MIT Press.

Tirole, Jean (2020) "Competition and the Industrial Challenge for the Digital Age." IFS Deaton Review on Inequalities. https://www.tse-fr.eu/sites/default /files/TSE/documents/doc/by/tirole/competition_and_the_industrial _challenge_april_3_2020.pdf.

Van Reenen, John (2011) "Does Competition Raise Productivity through Improving Management Practices?" *International Journal of Industrial Organization* 9(3): 306–317.

Van Reenen, John (2018) "Increasing Difference between Firms: Market Power and the Macro Economy." In *Changing Market Structures and Implications for Monetary Policy.* Kansas City Federal Reserve: Jackson Hole Symposium, 19–65.

Watzinger, Martin, Thomas A. Fackler, Markus Nagler, and Monika Schnitzer (2020) "How Antitrust Enforcement Can Spur Innovation: Bell Labs and the 1956 Consent Decree." *American Economic Journal: Economic Policy* 12(4): 328–359.

Yang, Chenyu (2020) "Vertical Structure and Innovation: A Study of the SoC and Smartphone Industries." *RAND Journal of Economics* 51(3): 739–785.

CHAPTER 4

Innovation, Antitrust Enforcement, and the Inverted-U

RICHARD GILBERT, CHRISTIAN RIIS, *and* ERLEND RIIS

1 Introduction

The effect of competition on the pace of innovation evokes controversy despite being one of the most studied questions in economics. Joseph Schumpeter (1942) emphasized the importance of market power to appropriate the benefits from investments in research and development (R&D). For adherents of the Schumpeter school, innovation incentives can be a defense against otherwise anticompetitive conduct or mergers. Others believe that there is a negative relationship between market power and innovation incentives. They can be thought of as followers of the Arrow school, because Kenneth Arrow (1962) first developed a theoretical model that shows how competition increases the incentive to innovate.

Loury (1979), Lee and Wilde (1980), and Reinganum (1989) developed models of races to patent a discovery and show that competition for a discrete prize increases the probability of innovation. But many factors determine the returns to R&D, including competition between new products and the old products they displace. Philippe Aghion, Peter Howitt, and their coauthors developed and tested dynamic models in which firms in a duopoly can invest to improve their technologies but successful outcomes do not eliminate rivals (Aghion et al. 1997, 2001, 2005). These models of "stepwise" innovation reconcile opposing forces described by Schumpeter and Arrow and greatly advance our understanding of the economic determinants of innovation incentives. For some payoff functions, the authors identify an inverted-U relationship between competition and innovation, with the pace of innovation most intense at a moderate level of competition.

Consistent with the stepwise model, most empirical studies find a positive correlation between competition and innovation (measured by discoveries, or indirectly by R&D investment or patenting) for firms that are at or near the industry technological frontier and a negative correlation for firms that lag the frontier (Gilbert 2020, Ch. 6). Some studies, however, find a negative effect of competition on innovation for firms at or near the frontier (Autor et al. 2020) or, relatedly, a positive effect from market share (Blundell et al. 1999). These results can be explained by appropriability and economies of scale or by the incentive for firms with monopoly power to invest in R&D if by doing so, they can exclude rivals and maintain their monopoly (Gilbert and Newbery 1982).

Gilbert et al. (2018) extend the stepwise innovation duopoly model to an oligopoly. When consumers have constant cross-elasticity of substitution (CES) demand for products, increasing the number of rivals reduces the incremental profit from escaping competition and, to a lesser extent, reduces the profit from catching up to a technology leader. The net effect is that the steady-state industry growth rate can exhibit an inverted-U dependence on the number of rivals, but the quantitative effects for the pace of innovation from increasing the number of rivals are not the same as the effects from making products closer substitutes in a duopoly.

Antitrust enforcement historically has emphasized harm from higher prices, but innovation can have much larger consequences for consumer welfare (Solow 1957; Jones and Williams 1998; Gordon 2016). Section 2 discusses the role of innovation for antitrust enforcement that involves the acquisition or maintenance of monopoly. Economic research pioneered by Philippe Aghion, Peter Howitt, and their coauthors supports a rebuttable presumption of antitrust liability for conduct that acquires or maintains monopoly power in R&D. Additional support for this presumption is evidence that R&D would, if successful, jeopardize a firm's existing monopoly profits. This is "coincident market innovation" (Gilbert and Melamed 2021); the replacement effect described by Kenneth Arrow (1962) is a disincentive for investment in coincident market innovation.

Measured by the number of interventions, merger enforcement is by far the most active component of antitrust policy. In the United States, the Antitrust Division of the Department of Justice and the Federal Trade Commission annually review thousands of proposed mergers and challenge dozens of them, most of which are abandoned or resolved with consent decrees to remedy agency objections. The European Commission and its member states also review and challenge many proposed mergers each year.

Section 3 addresses merger policy for innovation. Some argue that the inverted-U relationship between competition and innovation identified in models of stepwise innovation has no application to mergers, because a merger is not the same as a reduction in the number of rivals. An industry with one less rival is an industry with one less innovator; a merger centralizes control of prices and R&D investments for the merging firms while leaving their R&D capabilities intact.

Under some conditions, mergers reduce industry R&D effort, because a merger eliminates the incentive of each merging party to profit at the expense of its merger partner. A key question is whether this disincentive also implies that mergers always reduce industry R&D incentives if they occur in industries that have an inverted-U relationship between the number of rivals and innovation. Section 4 explores this question. We employ a Poisson model of innovation that shares some features of stepwise models of innovation and assume that the pre-merger industry is in the region in which a reduction in the number of rivals would increase innovation. We show that this is not sufficient for a merger to increase total industry innovation if there are no merger-specific benefits, although there are industry payoffs from R&D for which a merger would promote innovation.

Section 5 examines the effects of merger efficiencies for innovation incentives in the Poisson model. Mergers can increase innovation if they facilitate transfers between the merging parties of information related to the production of recent discoveries or transfers of technologies to create new discoveries. In an example of an otherwise symmetric industry with CES demand, the Poisson model predicts that mergers harm innovation if there are no knowledge spillovers, but they promote innovation if a discovery by either party to the merger also benefits the other merger party. Section 6 concludes with a discussion of the implications of insights from these dynamic models for antitrust enforcement.

2 Innovation as a Determinant of Liability for Monopolization

Antitrust enforcers have increasingly raised innovation concerns in allegations of the abuse of monopoly power as well as in challenges to mergers (Hesse 2016). Antitrust cases that allege harm from unilateral conduct often challenge behavior that excludes rivals (Melamed 2006; Baker 2013). Such exclusionary conduct can raise prices and suppress innovation by denying rivals the scale necessary for them to compete (Whinston 1990; Segal and Whinston 2007; Baker 2016).

A complaint recently filed by the US Department of Justice and several states alleges that Google's payments for default search status on devices that access the Internet and its agreements that require Android mobile phone licensees to install Google search and other Google services thwart innovation by denying rivals scale to compete effectively. The complaint specifically alleges that "By restricting competition in general search services, Google's conduct has harmed consumers by reducing the quality of general search services (including dimensions such as privacy, data protection, and use of consumer data), lessening choice in general search services, and impeding innovation."[1]

A complaint recently filed by the US Federal Trade Commission challenges Facebook's pattern of acquiring startups such as Instagram and WhatsApp that are potential competitors for social networks. The Commission alleges that Facebook's acquisitions of potential competitors "deprives personal social networking users in the United States of the benefits of competition, including increased choice, quality, and innovation."[2]

Concerns about the effects of market power on innovation were also addressed in the report of the majority staff of a committee of the US House of Representatives, which called for heightened antitrust scrutiny of "products [that] appear to be 'free' but are monetized through people's attention or with their data," and in the President's recent Executive Order on Promoting Competition, which emphasized the role of antitrust in promoting "competition and innovation."[3]

---

[1] U.S. et al. v. Google LLC, Case 1:20-CV-03010, Complaint (October 20, 2020) at 53.

[2] U.S. Federal Trade Commission v. Facebook, Inc., First Amended Complaint (August 19, 2021) at 6.

[3] House Subcommittee on Antitrust, Commercial and Administrative Law of the Committee on the Judiciary, Majority Staff Report and Recommendations. Investigation of Competition

The Google and Facebook cases are not the first examples of antitrust mo-nopolization cases that raised innovation concerns. In *U.S. v. Microsoft*, the Department of Justice alleged that Microsoft harmed innovation by:

a. impairing the incentive of Microsoft's competitors and potential competitors to undertake research and development, because they know that Microsoft will be able to limit the rewards from any resulting innovation;

b. impairing the ability of Microsoft's competitors and potential competitors to obtain financing for research and development;

c. inhibiting Microsoft's competitors that nevertheless succeed in developing promising innovations from effectively marketing their improved products to customers;

d. reducing the incentive and ability of [original equipment manufac-turers] to innovate and differentiate their products in ways that would appeal to customers; and

e. reducing competition and the spur to innovation by Microsoft and others that only competition can provide.[4]

A district court held that Microsoft was liable for monopolizing the market for Intel-compatible personal computer operating systems. An appellate court sustained most of the district court's findings but gave little attention to the alleged innovation harms. The court of appeals noted that monopoly power may be temporary in technologically dynamic markets, and for support, the court cited Joseph Schumpeter, who wrote that economic progress is driven by "perennial gale[s] of creative destruction" by which technological advances supplant formerly dominant products or processes.[5]

Courts might give greater consideration to the innovation allegations in the Google and Facebook cases because the challenged conduct harms con-sumers that do not pay a monetary price for the services provided by these platforms but instead compensate the platforms by providing valuable data.[6] Alternatively, they might apply traditional price-theoretic tools to assess

---

in Digital Markets at 51 and Order on Promoting Competition in the American Economy (Presidential Actions, July 9, 2021) at 8.

[4] United States v. Microsoft Corp., Complaint ¶ 37, Civil Action No. 98–1232 (D.D.C. May 18, 1998).

[5] United States v. Microsoft Corp., 253 F. 3d 34, 49 (D.C. Cir. 2001) (en banc).

[6] The complaints also include allegations of harm to advertisers on the revenue side of the platforms.

allegations that Google's conduct reduced the quality of search or that Facebook's conduct reduced the quality of social networking services. The quality of the services that consumers obtain from the use of a search engine or a social network depends, for example, on the space reserved for advertisements in the display of search results or content from social network friends. All else equal, a reduction in quality is equivalent to an increase in price, even if the quality refers to a service that is offered at a zero monetary price.

If a plaintiff can demonstrate that a monopolist engages in conduct that reduces the quality of zero-price services with no offsetting efficiency benefits, it would not be necessary to determine that the conduct also harms innovation to reach a finding of unlawful monopolization. Although harm to innovation is not necessary to show a violation of the antitrust laws if conduct has a predictable adverse effect on quality-adjusted prices, evidence that conduct is likely to harm innovation can strengthen the case for antitrust enforcement by easing the concern that courts might otherwise have about the risk of false positives.

A determination of antitrust liability for innovation requires a means to identify market power in R&D and evidence that market power suppresses innovation incentives. Courts define markets as a tool to inform their evaluation of market power. Antitrust authorities have proposed the concept of an R&D market to identify potential innovators. According to the *Antitrust Guidelines for the Licensing of Intellectual Property* published by the US Department of Justice and Federal Trade Commission:

> A research and development market consists of the assets comprising research and development related to the identification of a commercializable product, or directed to particular new or improved goods or processes, and the close substitutes for that research and development. When research and development is directed to particular new or improved goods or processes, the close substitutes may include research and development efforts, technologies, and goods that significantly constrain the exercise of market power with respect to the relevant research and development, for example by limiting the ability and incentive of a hypothetical monopolist to reduce the pace of research and development.[7]

---

[7] U.S. Department of Justice and Federal Trade Commission (2017, 11–12).

Market power in R&D markets and market power in product markets have different consequences for the ability and incentive to suppress innovation. Highly concentrated ownership of the assets necessary to engage in R&D directed toward a new product or process gives a firm that controls these assets the ability to suppress innovation investment relative to a market in which control of the assets is more dispersed.[8] Market power in a product market can suppress incentives to invest in R&D if discoveries are likely to cannibalize existing profits. Coincident innovation refers to innovations that are likely to be commercialized in a product market in which the potential innovator or its customer or licensee for the innovation has profits at risk from the innovation. Market power in a coincident product market deters innovation investment, because it implies a significant replacement effect.

There is an exception to the principle that market power in a coincident product market suppresses innovation if a firm can protect that power by innovating or acquiring assets, such as intellectual property rights, that are necessary to compete (Gilbert and Newbery 1982). While a firm with market power might have an incentive to invest aggressively in R&D to preempt competition, that incentive is likely to exist only in special circumstances. Compared to a firm in a more competitive industry, a firm with product market power has no greater incentive to invest in R&D for a drastic innovation (defined as an innovation that eliminates competition) unless it can appropriate more value from a discovery (for example, by combining complementary assets). Moreover, aggressive R&D investment to preempt rivals is likely to be an unprofitable strategy for innovations that are not drastic if successful exclusion is uncertain (Reinganum 1983).

Just as antitrust enforcers employ presumptions concerning the likely effects of monopoly on prices, the economic literature offers sufficient learning to defend presumptions concerning the likely effects of monopoly on innovation. Antitrust liability for the suppression of innovation should be presumed if the defendant has market power in a product market and engages in conduct that creates or maintains monopoly power over R&D assets directed to innovation that is likely to cannibalize the defendant's profits in the product market (i.e., coincident innovation). These conditions imply that the conduct increases the defendant's ability to suppress innovation when it

---

[8] Firms in the same R&D market engage in activities that are close substitutes. An alternative approach to assess this condition is to examine technological overlaps in patenting. See, e.g., Bloom, Schankerman, and Van Reenen (2013).

also has the incentive to do so as a consequence of the replacement effect. A presumption of harm to innovation also should apply if the defendant controls assets necessary for R&D and engages in conduct that creates or maintains market power in a coincident product market. This scenario implies an increased incentive to suppress innovation from the replacement effect in a circumstance in which the defendant has the ability to suppress innovation (Gilbert and Melamed 2021).

Noncoincident innovation refers to innovations that are likely to be commercialized in a product market in which the potential innovator or its customer or licensee for the innovation does not have profits at risk from the innovation. For noncoincident innovation, a presumption of harm to innovation should apply if the defendant has engaged in conduct to acquire or maintain monopoly power in R&D (Gilbert and Melamed 2021).

These presumptions can be rebutted with evidence that the defendant's conduct promotes R&D or reduces industry incentives to suppress R&D, perhaps by increasing appropriation or allowing the defendant to improve the efficiency of its R&D expenditures. However, courts should not, without careful scrutiny, accept a Schumpeterian claim that monopoly power promotes innovation. The incremental benefit for innovation from increased monopoly power, if any, need not outweigh the harmful effect of higher prices.

Courts also should not presume that monopoly promotes innovation by easing constraints on the availability of funds for investing in R&D. In the words of a noted antitrust scholar, "[O]ne can always argue that a firm will use monopoly profits to innovate more, and that the gains from the resulting innovation might possibly far exceed the losses from short-run consumer injuries. But this argument proves too much and justifies monopoly no matter how created or maintained" (Hovenkamp 2008, 277). It also overlooks the availability of funding for prudent innovation projects in the capital markets of developed economies.

3 Do Mergers Suppress Innovation?

Economic theory and empirical evidence support a rebuttable presumption that monopoly power in R&D suppresses the incentive to innovate. Evidence of the effects of mergers on innovation is less clear when several firms with the ability and incentive to invest in R&D remain post-merger. After controlling for the determinants of merger activity, Danzon et al. (2007) find no average adverse effect on post-merger R&D investment from 165 large pharmaceutical mergers (transactions valued at more than $500 million or representing more than 20 percent of a firm's pre-merger enterprise value) over the period 1985–2001, although small firms experienced some reduction in R&D in the first year following a merger. Igami and Uetake (2020) estimate a dynamic model of pricing and R&D investment in the market for personal computer hard disk drives and use the estimated parameters to assess the consequences from hypothetical mergers. They conclude that mergers in the hard disk drive industry would have no significant adverse effect on R&D investment if more than three firms remain post-merger.

Others identify harm to innovation from mergers or acquisitions. In a study of twenty-seven large pharmaceutical mergers over the period 1988–2004, Ornaghi (2009) finds that the merging firms did less R&D and produced fewer important drug patents in the three years following the merger, relative to a comparison set of firms with comparable merger propensities. Haucap et al. (2019) examine sixty-five mergers reviewed by the European Commission between 1991 and 2007. They find a reduction in patenting by the merging firms and their competitors. Cunningham et al. (2021) find empirical evidence for the disincentive for coincident innovation that arises from the replacement effect. They show that acquired drug projects are less likely to be developed when the acquirer has an existing portfolio of drugs with profits that are at risk from the acquired projects.

A merger of firms that sell differentiated products that are close substitutes creates incentives to raise prices, because neither party to the merger has an incentive to compete for sales that it would obtain at the expense of its merger partner. This upward pricing pressure is proportional to the diversion ratio, which measures the fraction of the increase in demand from a price reduction by one division of the merged firm that occurs at the expense of sales by its merger partner (Farrell and Shapiro 2010). Similarly, neither party to a merger has an incentive to invest in R&D which, if successful, would merely take sales from its merger partner (Federico et al. 2017, 2018, 2020; Motta and Tarantino 2017; Salinger 2019).[9]

---

[9] These incentives do not describe total industry effects, which include reactions from non-merging firms. Moraga-González et al. (2019) and Johnson and Rhodes (2021) offer examples of responses by non-merging firms that can reverse innovation incentive effects from the merging parties.

Consistent with the view that mergers suppress innovation, antitrust authorities often allege harm to innovation from mergers in high-technology industries in addition to predictions of higher prices. Since 2000, most challenges by US antitrust enforcers to mergers in R&D-intensive industries have included allegations of harm to innovation (Gilbert and Greene 2015). The European Commission also has alleged harm to innovation in several proposed mergers. For example, the Commission conditioned approval of the merger of the agricultural chemicals divisions of Dow and Dupont on the divestiture of DuPont's R&D organization and other assets to address concerns that the combination would suppress innovation for pesticides.[10]

A merger that lowers output by raising prices also reduces the incentive for each merger party to invest in R&D if innovation only increases the margin that a firm can earn on its sales, for example, by lowering marginal production cost (Bourreau et al. 2021). In that case, the merger would suppress the incentive to invest in R&D by reducing the output that would benefit from a higher margin. The correspondence between upward pricing pressure from a merger and downward innovation pressure can fail, however, for mergers that increase demand. Jullien and Lefouili (2018a, 2018b) and Bourreau and Jullien (2018) offer examples of demand-increasing mergers that increase the incentive to innovate.[11] Mergers also can promote innovation by facilitating knowledge spillovers between the merging parties. López and Vives (2019) find that even mergers to monopoly can be socially optimal if R&D has sufficiently large knowledge spillovers.

Our focus in this chapter is to investigate whether mergers might suppress or promote innovation incentives when an industry exhibits an inverted-U relationship between innovation and the number of rivals. The inverted-U implies that there is a region in the competition space for which the elimination of a competitor would promote innovation. It is instructive to see whether predictions in the literature of harm to innovation from mergers differ from the inverted-U result because existing models that generate an

---

[10] European Commission Press release, March 27, 2017. See also European Commission (2016). Gilbert was retained by one of the parties to this transaction.

[11] Chen and Schwartz (2013) show that mergers can increase incentives to innovate by allowing the merged firm to coordinate prices for new and old products. See also Greenstein and Ramey (1998). Marshall and Parra (2018) describe a market in which firms compete to sell innovations to a downstream market. They show that mergers of firms that compete downstream and invest in R&D can increase innovation incentives under some circumstances. Denicolò and Polo (2018b) discuss conditions for which mergers might promote innovation.

inverted-U do not analyze mergers or because proponents of the concept of downward innovation pressure do not fully consider interactions that might give rise to an inverted-U.

In the next section, we consider the effects of mergers in a model described by Delbono and Denicolò (1991) for which discovery has a Poisson distribution and firms invest to accelerate its timing. The model predicts an inverted-U relationship between rivalry and innovation in a symmetric industry for some parameter values and can illustrate the effects of a merger on investment incentives. We show that mergers can increase R&D incentives under some circumstances. However, they also can suppress industry R&D investment even if they occur in an industry for which a reduction in rivalry would increase innovation incentives. This adverse effect can be reversed if there are sufficient technological spillovers between the merging parties.

4 Investment with Poisson Discovery

Consider a symmetric oligopoly with N firms. A firm that invests at rate x innovates with Poisson probability $h(x)$, with $h(0)=0$, $h'(x)>0$, and $h''(x)<0$. Let $\eta_i = \sum_{j \neq i} h(x_j)$. Competition ends when a firm innovates. The discount rate is r. Define the payoffs:

$\pi_W^N =$ a firm's flow profit if it innovates

$\pi_L^N =$ a firm's flow profit if another firm innovates

$\pi_0^N =$ a firm's flow profit if no firm innovates

Firm i chooses x_i^N to maximize its discounted present-value profit:

$$V_i^N = \int_0^\infty \exp\{-(r + h(x_i^N) + \eta_i)t\}\left[h(x_i^N)\frac{\pi_W^N}{r} + \eta_i \frac{\pi_L^N}{r} + \pi_0^N - x_i^N \right] dt$$

$$= \frac{h(x_i^N)\frac{\pi_W^N}{r} + \eta_i \frac{\pi_L^N}{r} + \pi_0^N - x_i^N}{r + h(x_i^N) + \eta_i}.$$

In a symmetric equilibrium, $x_i^N = x^N$, $V_i^N = V^N$, and each firm's profit-maximizing investment satisfies the first-order condition

$$h'(x^N)\left[\frac{\pi_W^N}{r} - V^N \right] = 1. \tag{1}$$

Expression (1) is sufficient for a local maximum, given that $h''(x) < 0$. We assume throughout that equilibria pre-merger and post-merger are unique.

Suppose firms 1 and 2 merge. Post-merger there are $N-1$ firms, one of which has two divisions with the ability to innovate. Assume that the merged firm's flow profit from discovery does not depend on the division that makes the discovery. Denote by "independent" a firm that does not merge, and to simplify the exposition, assume that the profit of an independent firm when another firm innovates does not depend on whether the innovator is the merged firm or another independent.[12] Define the following post-merger profit flows:

π_W^M = the merged firm's flow profit if one of its division's innovates

π_L^M = the merged firm's flow profit if an independent firm innovates

π_0^M = the merged firm's flow profit in no firm innovates

π_W^I = an independent firm's flow profit if it innovates

π_L^I = an independent firm's flow profit if another firm innovates

π_0^I = an independent firm's flow profit if no firm innovates.

Let $\eta_m = \sum\limits_{j \neq 1,2} h(x_j)$. The merged firm's expected profit is

$$V^M = \frac{[h(x_1^M) + h(x_2^M)]\dfrac{\pi_W^M}{r} + \eta_m \dfrac{\pi_L^M}{r} + \pi_0^M - x_1^M - x_2^M}{r + h(x_1^M) + h(x_2^M) + \eta_m}.$$

In equilibrium, $x_i^M = x^M$, and the necessary and sufficient condition for profit-maximizing investment by each division of the merged firm is

$$h'(x^M)\left[\frac{\pi_W^M}{r} - V^M\right] = 1. \tag{2}$$

Proposition 1 *Let $X^S(N)$ be total R&D investment by a symmetric industry with N firms, and let $X^M(N)$ be the total post-merger R&D investment when firms 1 and 2 merge. A necessary and sufficient condition for $X^M(N) > X^S(N)$ is*

$$\pi_W^M - \pi_W^N > r(V^M - V^N) \geq rV^N. \tag{3}$$

Proof. Comparing the first-order conditions for investment pre-merger and post-merger (Expressions (1) and (2)), given $h''(x) < 0$, each division of the merged firm would profitably invest more than it would invest as an independent firm pre-merger if $\dfrac{1}{r}\left[\pi_W^M - \pi_W^N\right] > V^M - V^N \geq V^N$, where the latter

---

[12] We do not make this assumption in simulations reported below.

inequality follows if the merger is profitable. This is a necessary and suffi-cient condition for $X^M(N) > X^S(N)$, because investments are strategic complements.[13]

We probe further to address whether a merger might promote innovation when the symmetric industry exhibits the inverted-U. Suppose that $X^S(N-1) > X^S(N)$; i.e., a reduction in rivalry increases total industry R&D investment.[14] Our approach compares $X^M(N)$ to total investment in the symmetric industry with $N-1$ firms. Given that $X^S(N-1) > X^S(N)$, the merger increases total industry R&D investment if $X^M(N) > X^S(N-1)$.

Define the incremental payoffs for the symmetric industry with $N-1$ firms:

$$\Delta_1^{N-1} = \pi_W^{N-1} - \pi_L^{N-1}$$
$$\Delta_2^{N-1} = \pi_W^{N-1} - \pi_0^{N-1}.$$

The first-order condition for equilibrium profit-maximizing investment by a firm in the symmetric industry with $N-1$ firms can be expressed as fol-lows using the incremental payoffs:

$$\varphi(x_i^{N-1}) + h'(x_i^{N-1})\left[(N-2)h(x)\frac{\Delta_1^{N-1}}{r} + \Delta_2^{N-1} \right] = r + (N-2)h(x), \quad (4)$$

where $\varphi(x_i^{N-1}) \equiv h'(x_i^{N-1})x_i^{N-1} - h(x_i^{N-1})$, and x is investment by other firms. The right-hand side of Expression (4) is independent of x_i^{N-1}, and the left-hand side is a decreasing function of x_i^{N-1}. Furthermore, investments are strategic complements. Therefore, each firm's investment is an in-creasing function of Δ_1^{N-1} and Δ_2^{N-1}.

Next, consider the post-merger industry. The assumed symmetry and con-cavity of $h(\bullet)$ implies that the merged firm would profitably split any total investment $y = x_1^M + x_2^M$ equally between its divisions. Moreover, in equi-librium, independent firms invest at the same rate, x^I. Therefore, we can write the merged firm's equilibrium discounted present-value profit as

$$V^M = \frac{\hat{h}(y)\dfrac{\pi_W^M}{r} + (N-2)h(x^I)\dfrac{\pi_L^M}{r} + \pi_0^M - y}{r + \hat{h}(y) + (N-2)h(x^I)},$$

---

[13] Strategic complementarity follows from the first-order conditions, because V^N, V^M, and the ex-pected profits of independent firms post-merger are declining functions of rival investments.

[14] We note that an increase in total R&D expenditure $X^S(N-1) \geq X^S(N)$ differs from an increase in the probability of discovery, which requires $(N-1)h(x^{N-1}) \geq Nh(x^N)$.

where

$$\hat{h}(y) \equiv 2h\left(\frac{y}{2}\right).$$

For the post-merger industry, define:

$$\Delta_1^M = \pi_W^M - \pi_L^M$$
$$\Delta_2^M = \pi_W^M - \pi_0^M$$
$$\Delta_1^I = \pi_W^I - \pi_L^I$$
$$\Delta_2^I = \pi_W^I - \pi_0^I.$$

The first-order condition for equilibrium profit-maximizing investment by the merged firm can be expressed as

$$\hat{\varphi}(y) + \hat{h}'(y)\left[(N-2)h(x^I)\frac{\Delta_1^M}{r} + \Delta_2^M\right] = r + (N-2)h(x^I), \qquad (5)$$

where $\hat{\varphi}(y) \equiv \hat{h}'(y)y - \hat{h}(y)$. The right-hand side of Expression (5) is independent of y, the left-hand side is decreasing in y, and investments are strategic complements. Thus, the merged firm's equilibrium investment is an increasing function of Δ_1^M and Δ_2^M.

The corresponding condition for equilibrium profit-maximizing investment post-merger by the independent firms is

$$\varphi(x_i^I) + h'(x_i^I)\left[\left[\hat{h}(y) + (N-3)h(x^I)\right]\frac{\Delta_1^I}{r} + \Delta_2^I\right]$$
$$= r + \hat{h}(y) + (N-3)h(x^I). \qquad (6)$$

Similarly, each independent firm's investment is an increasing function of Δ_1^I and Δ_2^I.

The net effect of a merger on innovation investment compared to an industry with $N-1$ symmetric firms depends on three factors in the Poisson model:

(i) The concavity of the investment function $h(x)$. Because $\hat{h}(x) > h(x)$ and $\hat{h}'(x) > h'(x)$, if payoffs were equal, the two divisions of the merged firm together would invest more in R&D than any single independent firm in a symmetric industry with $N-1$ firms.[15]

---

[15] This is not inconsistent with a possible negative effect on post-merger investment by each division compared to its pre-merger investment as an independent firm in a symmetric industry.

(ii) The incremental payoffs Δ_1^M, Δ_1^I, and Δ_1^{N-1}. The contribution of these payoffs to post-merger investment is ambiguous, because the signs of $\Delta_1^M - \Delta_1^{N-1}$ and $\Delta_1^I - \Delta_1^{N-1}$ generally depend on industry characteristics.

(iii) The incremental payoffs Δ_2^M, Δ_2^I, and Δ_2^{N-1}. Suppose a merger increases profits for existing products and consequently increases the profits at risk from innovation. If $\pi_W^{N-1} = \pi_W^M = \pi_W^I$, then $\Delta_2^M < \Delta_2^{N-1}$ and $\Delta_2^I < \Delta_2^{N-1}$. This would have a negative effect on post-merger investment incentives.

The net effect of a merger on the incentives to innovate depends on the balance of these three factors. If, hypothetically, they cancel, then total investment post-merger is equal to total investment in a symmetric industry with $N-1$ firms. In that event, whether a merger decreases or increases total industry R&D investment depends on whether total investment in a symmetric industry with N firms exceeds or is less than total investment in a symmetric industry with $N-1$ firms.

In this respect, the existence of the inverted-U for the symmetric industry is relevant to the effect of a merger on total industry R&D investment. Whether the symmetric industry exhibits the inverted-U does not, however, determine a merger's directional effect on industry R&D. For example, suppose a reduction in rivalry would increase industry R&D investment by a symmetric oligopoly. Nonetheless, a merger might suppress industry investment incentives by increasing the replacement effect from an innovation; that is, by making $\Delta_2^M < \Delta_2^{N-1}$ and $\Delta_2^I < \Delta_2^{N-1}$.

A special case involves post-merger incremental profit flows from investing that are not firm-specific. Then $\Delta_1^M = \Delta_1^I \equiv \Delta_1$ and $\Delta_2^M = \Delta_2^I \equiv \Delta_2$.

Proposition 2 *If post-merger payoffs are not firm-specific, a merger increases total industry investment if* (i) $min\left[\Delta_1 - \Delta_1^{N-1}; \Delta_2 - \Delta_2^{N-1}\right] \geq 0$ *and* (ii) $X^S(N-1) \geq X^S(N)$.

Proof. Let y^M be the merged firm's equilibrium investment and x^{N-1} the equilibrium investment by each firm in the pre-merger industry with $N-1$ symmetric firms. Assume that part (i) is satisfied, and suppose that $x = x^I = x^{N-1}$ on the right-hand sides of Expressions (4) and (5). The expressions would then imply that $y \geq x^{N-1}$. Furthermore, from Expression (6), $x^I > x^{N-1}$, and because investments are strategic complements, $y^M > x^{N-1}$.

Therefore, $X^M(N) > X^S(N-1)$ and $X^M(N) > X^S(N)$ if part (ii) is also satisfied.[16]

4.1 Mergers with CES demand

Next we simulate the effects of a merger in a symmetric industry when consumers have constant cross-elasticity of substitution (CES) demands and a discovery lowers the marginal cost (or increases the quality) of a product sold by one of the firms or a division of the merged firm. In this section, we assume that there are no spillover benefits; a discovery by one firm or division has no benefit for another firm or division.

Households maximize

$$f(q_1, \cdots, q_n) = (q_1^\sigma + , \cdots, + q_n^\sigma)^{\frac{1}{\sigma}},$$

where $\sigma \epsilon (0, 1]$, and q_j is the consumption of product j, subject to the budget constraint

$$\sum_{i=1}^{n} p_i q_i \leq Y.$$

This utility function gives rise to CES demands with the cross-elasticity of substitution equal to

$$\alpha = \frac{1}{1-\sigma}.$$

We simulate the Poisson model with CES demand when $\sigma = 0.50$, corresponding to $\alpha = 2$, and a discovery that reduces the constant marginal cost of production from c to $c/1.2$. We also assume that $h(x) = 0.02\sqrt{x}$ and $r = 0.05$. Under these assumptions, industry R&D expenditure is a maximum with three firms in the industry; the symmetric industry displays the inverted-U.

Suppose there are four symmetric firms pre-merger and firms 1 and 2 merge. In a symmetric industry, total industry R&D effort would increase if a rival is eliminated; $X^S(3) > X^S(4)$. By contrast, solving the system of first-order conditions given by Expressions (4–6) shows that a merger would have

---

[16] Nash-Cournot competition is a special case of Proposition 2, although we note that mergers, other than merger to monopoly, are not generally profitable for a static symmetric Nash-Cournot oligopoly.

Table 4.1. Profit flows (four firms pre-merger; no spillovers)

	Symmetric (N−1)	Merged firm	Independent firm
π_W	0.223	0.309	0.177
π_L	0.189	0.281	0.152
π_0	0.200	0.295	0.158
Δ_1	0.034	0.028	0.025
Δ_2	0.023	0.014	0.019

the opposite effect and reduce total industry R&D. Table 4.1 provides some insight into this result by comparing the equilibrium profit flows for a symmetric industry with three firms versus an industry with one merged firm and two independent firms. For our purpose, only the relative magnitudes are significant, not their absolute values.

The merger elevates the profit from discovery for the merged firm relative to a firm in symmetric industry with three firms. But the merger also elevates the merged firm's profit if an independent firm innovates or if no firm innovates. The net effect is a reduction in the incremental profits Δ_1^M and Δ_2^M relative to the symmetric industry with three firms. The merger also lowers Δ_1^I and Δ_2^I relative to the symmetric industry. These changes in the incremental payoffs have negative effects on post-merger investment incentives, which are compounded because investments are strategic complements.

Figure 4.1 illustrates the effects of a merger in a symmetric industry with the assumptions that correspond to the CES model. (We do not consider merger to monopoly.) The vertical axis is not labeled, because only relative values are significant for our purpose. A merger suppresses industry R&D investment significantly if it occurs in an industry with only a few firms, but the effects diminish for mergers with larger numbers of firms.

5 R&D Efficiencies, Licensing, and Knowledge Transfers

A merger can facilitate different types of efficiency benefits that promote innovation. Some of these benefits, such as eliminating duplicative R&D investments, are analogous to production efficiencies. Denicolò and Polo (2018a) show that by coordinating their investments, the merging firms can increase the effectiveness of their R&D spending while economizing on R&D costs under some circumstances. Régibeau and Rockett (2019)

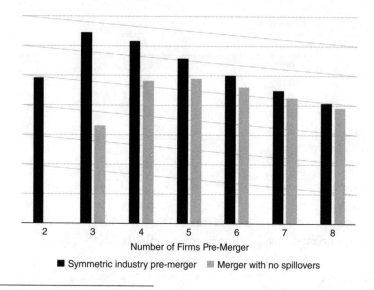

Figure 4.1. Industry investment pre-merger and post-merger with no spillovers

identify three other types of potential merger-specific efficiencies that are relevant to innovation incentives: licensing, spillovers, and intra-firm knowledge transfers.

5.1 Licensing

First consider licensing. A firm that makes an invention can exploit its value internally, license the invention for use by others, or employ a combination of both strategies. Optimal exploitation of an invention requires licensing if the inventor cannot supply the innovation at the lowest cost or if the inventor lacks complementary assets that add value to the innovation. However, licensing is not a profit-maximizing strategy unless the inventor can write and enforce contracts that compensate the licensor for the opportunity cost of lost sales (Gilbert and Kristiansen, 2018). Bargaining over the terms of a contract requires the licensor to communicate details of the invention, which the counterparty might exploit without compensating the inventor. Some jurisdictions have laws that constrain the profits an inventor can earn from licensing by limiting permitted contract terms (such as restrictions on the use of exclusive territories in the European Union). In addition, firms that license innovations might patent improvements that they withhold from the licensor or agree to license back to the original inventor only at a high royalty.

For these reasons, a firm might choose not to license an invention at all or might elect to negotiate licenses with a small subset of potential licensees. Prior to a merger of firms 1 and 2, suppose that neither term would license an invention to the other. A merger would eliminate market and regulatory impediments to licensing. Each firm would have an incentive to transfer knowledge about an invention to its merger partner, although the effectiveness of such transfers might be limited by bureaucracy or other internal rigidities. The next section explores the effects for post-merger R&D incentives when firms do not license innovations and there are knowledge spillovers between the divisions of the merged firm.

5.2 Spillovers and intra-firm knowledge transfers

Knowledge spillovers, both intra-firm and external, can have two effects. First, in the short run, a firm can profit by employing the information embodied in an innovation to improve or lower the cost of its own product. This benefit is similar to the benefit from licensing, although with no compensation to the innovator and possibly less complete transfer of technology. Some knowledge spillovers can be expected without a merger. It is difficult to keep knowledge private, and protection from imitation afforded by intellectual property rights is often imperfect. Jones and Williams (1998) review several empirical studies that compare estimates of the private and social returns to R&D. The studies report social returns (the change in output from an increase in R&D) that greatly exceed the private rate of return on R&D, which they attribute to benefits from knowledge spillovers.

Proximity, measured by geography or by technological or business overlaps, has a large impact on knowledge spillovers. Jaffe (1986), Bernstein and Nadiri (1989), Bloom et al. (2013), and Lucking et al. (2018) demonstrate the importance of technological overlaps by exploiting firm-level data on patenting in different technology classes and participation in lines of business to locate firms in a multidimensional technology or product space. They show that firms benefit more from R&D performed by other firms whose technology classes or products are closer to their own. Griffith et al. (2006) examine the importance of geographic proximity by comparing the R&D performance of UK firms that locate in the US against UK firms in the same industries that remained in the UK. They find that the US R&D stock had a much larger impact on the total factor productivity of UK firms that had more of their inventors located in the US.

Second, knowledge spillovers can have long-term effects by allowing a firm to invest in R&D with a greater expectation of success. If Firm A makes a discovery and Firm B learns something about how Firm A succeeded, then Firm B should be able to invest to make a subsequent discovery with a higher probability of success than it could have expected if it had learned nothing from Firm A. This suggests a multistage model to analyze the benefits of this R&D knowledge spillover.

We illustrate the effects of knowledge spillovers between merging parties by assuming that a discovery by one division is available at no cost to the merged firm's other division with probability $s \in (0, 1]$ and there are no knowledge spillovers pre-merger or between rival firms. Let π_{W1}^M be the merged firm's flow payoff if a single division innovates, and let π_{W2}^M be the merged firm's flow payoff if both divisions innovate. With spillovers, the merged firm's expected flow payoff if division 1 innovates is

$$\pi_W^M(s) = (1 - s)\pi_{W1}^M + s\pi_{W2}^M. \tag{7}$$

There is a similar expression if division 2 of the merged firm innovates.

As an upper bound to merger benefits attributable to knowledge spillovers, suppose that pre-merger, no innovator would license another firm and post-merger, either party to the merger would make a discovery available instantaneously and at no cost to the other merger party, corresponding to $s = 1$ in Expression (7). Table 4.2 reports equilibrium profit flows for the Poisson model with CES demand under these assumptions. Except for knowledge spillovers with $s = 1$, the parameter assumptions are the same as for Table 4.1.

Compared to the model with no spillovers, perfect spillovers increase the merged firm's flow profit from discovery and decrease the flow profit earned by an independent firm when the merged firm makes a discovery. With perfect spillovers, $\Delta_1^M > \Delta_1^{N-1}$ and $\Delta_2^M > \Delta_2^{N-1}$. These inequalities imply that the merged firm has a greater incentive to invest in R&D compared to the incentive of a firm in symmetric industry with $N-1$ firms.

Figure 4.2 illustrates the effects of perfect knowledge transfers within the merged firm for post-merger R&D incentives. The parameter values for Figure 4.2 are unchanged from Figure 4.1 with the exception that $s = 1$ in Expression (7). A merger increases industry R&D investment if there are

Table 4.2. Profit flows (four firms pre-merger; perfect spillovers in the merged firm)

	Symmetric (N − 1)	Merged firm	Independent firm
π_W	0.223	0.323	0.177
π_L	0.189	0.281	0.147
π_0	0.200	0.295	0.158
Δ_1	0.034	0.042	0.030
Δ_2	0.023	0.028	0.019

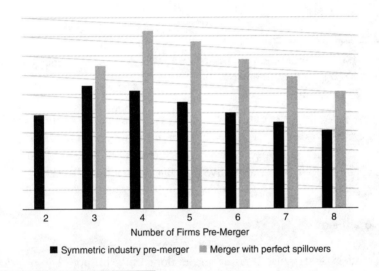

Figure 4.2. Industry investment pre-merger and post-merger with perfect spillovers

perfect spillovers between the divisions of the merged firm. As in Figure 4.1, we focus on relative values and do not label the vertical axis.

Parties to a proposed merger often allege efficiency benefits from merging. A question is: How large must such benefits be to offset likely adverse effects from the merger? Another way to explore this issue is to fix the spillover probability and ask whether it is sufficient to offset a merger's adverse effects. For the Poisson model with CES demand, Figure 4.3 shows the smallest number of firms pre-merger for which post-merger R&D investment exceeds pre-merger investment given discrete values of the spillover probability. We limit the inquiry to $N \geq 3$ and do not consider merger to

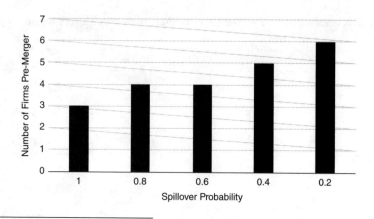

Figure 4.3. Minimum number of firms pre-merger for which a merger increases industry investment

monopoly. With perfect spillovers ($s = 1$), post-merger investment exceeds pre-merger investment for any $N \geq 3$. The minimum number of firms pre-merger for which post-merger investment exceeds pre-merger investment is four if $s \in [0.6, 0.8]$, increases to five if $s = 0.4$, and to six if $s = 0.2$.

6 Conclusions

The models of stepwise innovation developed by Philippe Aghion, Peter Howitt, and their coauthors demonstrate the harm to innovation from monopoly power and the benefits from modest levels of competition. A firm has the ability to suppress innovation if it has monopoly power over assets necessary to engage in R&D. A firm also has the incentive to suppress innovation if it has existing profits that an innovation would jeopardize. When innovation coincides with a market in which the firm has market power, there is a replacement effect that deters the firm's incentive to innovate. A rebuttable presumption of harm to innovation should apply if the defendant has monopoly power in R&D and engages in conduct that creates or maintains monopoly power in a coincident product market, because such conduct would reduce the incentive to invest in R&D by increasing the replacement effect.

A rebuttable presumption of harm to innovation also should apply to conduct that achieves or maintains monopoly power over relevant R&D

assets. However, such a presumption is not warranted if conduct reduces the number of R&D rivals and the industry is in a region of an inverted-U for which greater rivalry discourages industry investment. Antitrust enforcement should prevent conduct by a dominant firm that raises entry barriers when barriers are already high, so that the equilibrium number of rivals is small.

Merger policy is crucial for antitrust enforcement due to the large number of mergers that take place in the economy and their consequences for market structure and performance. We employ a Poisson model of discovery to analyze the effects of mergers on R&D investment in an industry for which the pre-merger relationship between industry investment and rivalry exhibits an inverted-U. Our results suggest that mergers in high-technology industries can promote innovation in some circumstances, but they are likely to suppress R&D investment incentives if the merging parties have significant profits that are at risk from innovation. This presumption can be rebutted with evidence of merger-specific benefits, such as spillovers between the merging parties of technical information from discoveries.

The US *Horizontal Merger Guidelines* impose a high bar for efficiency defenses related to R&D. These guidelines note that "[E]fficiencies, such as those relating to research and development, are potentially substantial but are generally less susceptible to verification and may be the result of anticompetitive output reductions" (U.S. Department of Justice and Federal Trade Commission 2010). Antitrust authorities should not accept efficiency defenses if they cannot be verified or if they can be realized in a different arrangement (such as an R&D joint venture) that does not have the merger's anticompetitive effects. But antitrust authorities also should not accept an innovation theory of harm from a merger without giving careful consideration to credible efficiency defenses.

References

Aghion, Philippe, Nick Bloom, Richard Blundell, et al. 2005. "Competition and Innovation: An Inverted-U Relationship." *Quarterly Journal of Economics* 120, no. 2: 701–728.

Aghion, Philippe, Christopher Harris, Peter Howitt, et al. 2001. "Competition, Imitation and Growth with Step-by-Step Innovation." *Review of Economic Studies* 68, no. 3: 467–492.

Aghion, Philippe, Christopher Harris, and John Vickers. 1997. "Competition and Growth with Step-by-Step Innovation: An Example." *European Economic Review* 41, no. 3–5: 771–782.

Arrow, Kenneth J. 1962. "Economic Welfare and the Allocation of Resources for Invention." In *The Rate and Direction of Inventive Activity*, ed. Richard R. Nelson. Princeton, NJ: Princeton University Press, pp. 609–626.

Autor, David, David Dorn, Gordon H. Hanson, et al. 2020. "Foreign Competition and Domestic Innovation: Evidence from U.S. Patents." *American Economic Review: Insights* 2, no. 3: 357–374.

Baker, Jonathan B. 2013. "Exclusion as a Core Competition Concern." *Antitrust Law Journal* 78, no. 3: 527–589.

Baker, Jonathan B. 2016. "Evaluating Appropriability Defenses for the Exclusionary Conduct of Dominant Firms in Innovative Industries." *Antitrust Law Journal* 80: 431–461.

Bernstein, Jeffrey I., and M. Ishaq Nadiri. 1989. "Research and Development and Intra-Industry Spillovers: An Empirical Application of Dynamic Duality." *Review of Economic Studies* 56: 249–269.

Bloom, Nicholas, Mark Schankerman, and John Van Reenen. 2013. "Identifying Technology Spillovers and Product Market Rivalry." *Econometrica* 81, no. 4: 1347–1393.

Blundell, Richard, Rachel Griffith, and John Van Reenen. 1999. "Market Share, Market Value and Innovation in a Panel of British Manufacturing Firms." *Review of Economic Studies* 66, no. 3: 529–554.

Bourreau, Marc, and Bruno Jullien. 2018. "Mergers, Investments and Demand Expansion." *Economics Letters* 167: 136–141.

Bourreau, Marc, Bruno Jullien, and Yassine Lefouili. 2021. "Mergers and Demand-Enhancing Innovation." Toulouse School of Economics Working Paper 18–907.

Chen, Yongmin, and Marius Schwartz. 2013. "Product Innovation Incentives: Monopoly vs. Competition." *Journal of Economics & Management Strategy* 22, no. 3: 513–528.

Cunningham, Colleen, Florian Ederer, and Song Ma. 2021. "Killer Acquisitions." *Journal of Political Economy* 129, no. 3: 649–702.

Danzon, Patricia M., Andrew Epstein, and Sean Nicholson. 2007. "Mergers and Acquisitions in the Pharmaceutical and Biotech Industries." *Managerial and Decision Economics* 28: 307–328.

Delbono, Flavio, and Vincenzo Denicolò. 1991. "Incentives to Innovate in a Cournot Oligopoly." *Quarterly Journal of Economics* 106, no. 3: 951–961.

Denicolò, Vincenzo, and Michele Polo. 2018a. "Duplicative Research, Mergers and Innovation." *Economics Letters* 166: 56–59.

Denicolò, Vincenzo, and Michele Polo. 2018b. "The Innovation Theory of Harm: An Appraisal." https://ssrn.com/abstract=3146731.

European Commission. 2016. "EU Merger Control and Innovation." *Competition Policy Brief*, April.

Farrell, Joseph, and Carl Shapiro. 2010. "Antitrust Evaluation of Horizontal Mergers: An Economic Alternative to Market Definition." *B.E. Journal of Theoretical Economics* 10, no. 1: 1–39.

Federico, Giulio, Gregor Langus, and Tommaso Valletti. 2017. "A Simple Model of Mergers and Innovation." *Economics Letters* 157(C): 136–140.

Federico, Giulio, Gregor Langus, and Tommaso Valletti. 2018. "Horizontal Mergers and Product Innovation: An Economic Framework." *International Journal of Industrial Organization* 59: 1–23.

Federico, Giulio, Fiona Scott-Morton, and Carl Shapiro. 2020. "Antitrust and Innovation: Welcoming and Protecting Disruption." In *Innovation Policy and the Economy* 20, ed. Josh Lerner and Scott Stern. Cambridge, MA: National Bureau of Economic Research.

Gilbert, Richard J. 2019. "Competition, Mergers, and R&D Diversity." *Review of Industrial Organization* 54, no. 3: 465–484.

Gilbert, Richard J. 2020. *Innovation Matters: Competition Policy for the High-Technology Economy*. Cambridge, MA: MIT Press.

Gilbert, Richard J., and Hillary Greene. 2015. "Merging Innovation into Antitrust Agency Enforcement of the Clayton Act." *George Washington Law Review* 83: 1919–1947.

Gilbert, Richard J., and Eirik Gaar Kristiansen. 2018. "Licensing and Innovation with Imperfect Contract Enforcement." *Journal of Economics and Management Strategy* 27, no. 2: 297–314.

Gilbert, Richard J., and A. Douglas Melamed. 2021. "Innovation under Section 2 of the Sherman Act." *Antitrust Law Journal* 84, no. 1: 1–54.

Gilbert, Richard, and David Newbery. 1982. "Preemptive Patenting and the Persistence of Monopoly." *American Economic Review* 72, no. 3: 514–526.

Gilbert, Richard, Christian Riis, and Erlend Riis. 2018. "Stepwise Innovation by an Oligopoly." *International Journal of Industrial Organization* 61: 413–438.

Gordon, Robert J. 2016. "Perspectives on the Rise and Fall of American Growth." *American Economic Review: Papers and Proceedings* 106, no. 5: 72–76.

Greenstein, Shane, and Garey Ramey. 1998. "Market Structure, Innovation and Vertical Product Differentiation." *International Journal of Industrial Organization* 16: 285–311.

Griffith, Rachel, Rupert Harrison, and John Van Reenen. 2006. "How Special Is the Special Relationship? Using the Impact of U.S. R&D Spillovers on U.K. Firms as a Test of Technology Sourcing." *American Economic Review* 96, no. 5: 1859–1875.

Haucap, Justus, Alexander Rasch, and Joel Stiebale. 2019. "How Mergers Affect Innovation: Theory and Evidence." *International Journal of Industrial Organization* 63: 283–325.

Hesse, Renata B. 2016. "Antitrust: Helping Drive the Innovation Economy." *Journal of Technology Law & Policy* 21, no. 1. https://scholarship.law.ufl.edu/jtlp/vol21/iss1/1.

Hovenkamp, Herbert. 2008. "Schumpeterian Competition and Antitrust." *Competition Policy International* 4, no. 2: 273–281.

Igami, Mitsuru, and Kosuke Uetake. 2020. "Mergers, Innovation, and Entry-Exit Dynamics: Consolidation of the Hard Disk Drive Industry, 1996–2016." *Review of Economic Studies* 87, no. 6: 2672–2702.

Jaffe, Adam B. 1986. "Technological Opportunity and Spillovers of R&D: Evidence from Firms' Patents, Profits, and Market Value." *American Economic Review* 76, no. 5: 884–1001.

Johnson, Justin P., and Andrew Rhodes. 2021. "Multiproduct Mergers and Quality Competition." CEPR Discussion Paper no. DP15830. https://ssrn.com/abstract=3795213.

Jones, Charles, and John Williams. 1998. "Measuring the Social Return to R&D." *Quarterly Journal of Economics* 113, no. 4: 1119–1135.

Jullien, Bruno, and Yassine Lefouili. 2018a. "Horizontal Mergers and Innovation." *Journal of Competition Law and Economics* 14, no. 3: 364–392.

Jullien, Bruno, and Yassine Lefouili. 2018b. "Mergers and Investments in New Products." Toulouse School of Economics Working Paper.

Lee, Tom, and Louis L. Wilde. 1980. "Market Structure and Innovation: A Reformulation." *Quarterly Journal of Economics* 94, no. 2: 429–436.

López, Ángel L., and Xavier Vives. 2019. "Overlapping Ownership, R&D Spillovers, and Antitrust Policy." *Journal of Political Economy* 127, no. 5: 2394–2437.

Loury, Glenn C. 1979. "Market Structure and Innovation." *Quarterly Journal of Economics* 93, no. 3: 395–410.

Lucking, Brian, Nicholas Bloom, and John Van Reenen. 2018. "Have R&D Spillovers Changed?" National Bureau of Economic Research Working Paper 24622.

Marshall, Guillermo, and Alvaro Parra. 2018. "Innovation and Competition: The Role of the Product Market." https://ssrn.com/abstract=3110042.

Melamed, A. Douglas. 2006. "Exclusive Dealing Agreements and Other Exclusionary Conduct—Are There Unifying Principles?" *Antitrust Law Journal* 73, no. 2: 375–412.

Moraga-González, José, Evgenia Motchenkova, and Saish Nevrekar. 2019. "Mergers and Innovation Portfolios." Tinbergen Institute Discussion Paper TI 2019–085.

Motta, Massimo, and Emanuele Tarantino. 2017. "The Effect of Horizontal Mergers When Firms Compete in Prices and Investments." Universitat Pompeu Fabra, Economics Working Paper Series no. 1579.

Ornaghi, Carmine. 2009. "Mergers and Innovation in Big Pharma." *International Journal of Industrial Organization* 27: 70–79.

Régibeau, Pierre, and Katharine E. Rockett. 2019. "Mergers and Innovation." *Antitrust Bulletin* 64, no. 1: 31–53.

Reinganum, Jennifer. 1983. "Uncertain Innovation and the Persistence of Monopoly." *American Economic Review* 73: 741–748.

Reinganum, Jennifer. 1989. "The Timing of Innovation: Research, Development, and Diffusion." In *Handbook of Industrial Organization,* ed. R. Schmalensee and R. Willig. Amsterdam: Elsevier Science, pp. 849–908.

Salinger, Michael A. 2019. "Net Innovation Pressure in Merger Analysis." https://ssrn.com/abstract=3051249.

Schumpeter, Joseph A. 1942. *Capitalism, Socialism, and Democracy.* New York: Harper.

Segal, Ilya, and Michael D. Whinston. 2007. "Antitrust in Innovative Industries." *American Economic Review* 97, no. 5: 1703–1730.

Shapiro, Carl. 2012. "Competition and Innovation: Did Arrow Hit the Bull's Eye?" In *The Rate and Direction of Inventive Activity Revisited,* ed. Josh Lerner and Scott Stern. Cambridge, MA: National Bureau of Economic Research, pp. 361–404.

Solow, Robert M. 1957. "Technical Change and the Aggregate Production Function." *Review of Economics and Statistics* 39, no. 3: 312–320.

U.S. Department of Justice and Federal Trade Commission. 2010. *Horizontal Merger Guidelines.* Washington, DC.

U.S. Department of Justice and Federal Trade Commission. 2017. *Antitrust Guidelines for the Licensing of Intellectual Property.* Washington, DC.

Whinston, Michael D. 1990. "Tying, Foreclosure, and Exclusion." *American Economic Review* 80, no. 4: 837–859.

CHAPTER 5

Innovation Networks and Business-Stealing

MATTHEW O. JACKSON, ANTOINE MAYEROWITZ,
and ABHIJIT V. TAGADE

1 Introduction

Research involves putting ideas together and building on knowledge held by different people and sources. There is substantial evidence that teams can be more effective than individuals and that connections between groups help spark new ideas (e.g., Walker et al. 1997; Burt 2004; Hong and Page 2004; Page 2007; Ozman 2009), with larger teams leading to more breakthroughs and creativity. Although such positive externalities and synergies offer incentives for researchers and inventors to collaborate, inventors also face forces that push in the opposite direction. In particular, they may face competition from their collaborators as well as broader leakage of information about their inventions. In this chapter, we examine the implications of these countervailing forces both empirically and theoretically.

For our empirical analysis, we use the universe of the U.S. Patent and Trademark Office (USPTO) data on granted patents and inventors from 1976 to 2017 to look at how inventors' potential concerns for business-stealing affects coauthorship on patents. First, we find an inverted-U relationship in the growth in coauthorship as a function of the number of other inventors working in an area: The rate per year at which inventors add new collaborators is highest at intermediate levels of competition in terms of the number of other inventors patenting in the same subject area. Second, we use an event study method to examine how networks are influenced by having major breakthroughs, which we measure as a patent in the top 2 percentile of citations over following years. We find that after a breakthrough, the fraction of coauthors who are new on the inventor's patents drops significantly below what it was before the breakthrough and does not recover to its pre-breakthrough value. Third, we examine how the extent to which an inventor stops working with new coauthors depends on two measures of potential losses from business-stealing: the average price markups by firms (aggregated at the level of National Bureau of Economic Research (NBER) technology sectors) and the number of other inventors in the area. In both cases, there is a significantly higher drop in the number of new coauthors after the breakthrough when there are greater potential losses from business-stealing, as measured by either the number of competitors or price markups.

We also provide a model that offers an explanation as to why these effects should be expected, and the simplicity of the model shows how robust these effects can be. The two forces in the model are countervailing: Having greater numbers of collaborators on a team increases the probability of having a successful invention, but having more new collaborators can lead to lower potential profits for the inventor from the breakthrough, both by spreading profits more thinly and by increasing the probability that information leaks to others in the field. Moreover, the potential loss in profits due to information leakage and spreading the profits among more total team members is greater with greater numbers of potential competitors and/or higher markups. The results from the model are consistent with the patterns that we discover in the data.

The implications of our findings are important for economic efficiency and growth. Fears of business-stealing and leakage of ideas lead to lower investment in collaborative research, and our analysis shows that these effects can be substantial and hold across patent areas, especially those with many inventors or high price markups.

Our chapter relates to several strands of literature. First, we add new insights into the literature on networks and how communication depends on worries about sharing information (e.g., Immorlica et al. 2014). Indeed, we are not the first to recognize that business-stealing can lead to inefficiencies. Stein (2008) shows how information exchange can be hampered when players are in competition with each other, and that can be exacerbated when information can diffuse. Dasaratha (2019) examines a game of network formation among competitors who can share ideas to innovate, but those might be then shared further in the network. Dasaratha finds that the network ends up being exactly at a critical threshold between sparse and dense networks, and he shows that welfare can be improved by having public innovators who freely share information. Our contribution is to provide evidence of the importance of business-stealing in the dynamics of research networks, and to show and model how the fear of business-stealing interacts with competition in the inventor's field.

Also related to our analysis is the literature on research teams and research output. For example, Akcigit et al. (2018) show how interacting with other researchers, particularly with top researchers, positively affects innovation. Azoulay et al. (2010) and Jaravel et al. (2018) show how the death of a top innovator negatively affects the subsequent productivity of their coauthors. We contribute to these literatures by pointing out the importance of business-stealing and competition in the dynamics of network building.

Our chapter also relates to the literature on competition and innovation. In particular, Aghion et al. (2005) describe an inverted-U relationship between innovation and competition. Our finding instead is about the formation of teams and the inverted-U between an inventor's fraction of new collaborators per year and the potential losses from business-stealing. Thus, our inverted-U is between different things and occurs for different reasons than that described by Aghion et al. (2005). Moreover, our event studies have no parallel in the previous literature. The patterns that we uncover on breakthrough patents leading to fewer than usual new collaborators, and more notably with more potential losses from business-stealing, are novel and provide interesting facts and questions for further research.

The remaining part of this chapter is organized as follows. Section 2 presents our data and measures, Section 3 discusses our empirical results, Section 4 describes our model, and Section 5 concludes.

2 Data, Measurement, and Empirical Strategy

2.1 Data description

We use the universe of USPTO data on inventors and utility patents that are filed from 1976 to 2017 and eventually granted. Throughout the chapter, the year of patent refers to its year of application, and a patent's citations are measured in its first five years of application.

Table 5.1. Descriptive statistics of coauthorship and citation networks of the full data

Coauthorship network	1976–1985	1986–1995	1996–2005	2006–2015
Number of inventors	522,279	845,907	1,396,121	1,481,191
Average number of coauthors	3.63	5.83	9.06	11.60
Giant component size	138,116	382,120	858,732	992,365
Overall clustering	0.76	0.77	0.76	0.77

Citation network	1976–1985	1986–1995	1996–2005	2006–2015
Number of patents	592,789	1,012,254	1,934,934	2,012,732
Average number of citations	1.95	3.22	5.66	4.14
Giant component size	548,503	988,623	1,914,253	1,873,129
Overall clustering	0.10	0.10	0.10	0.14

Notes: The table lists descriptive statistics over sequential periods of time using Patentsview data. *Giant component size* refers to the number of nodes in the largest connected component. *Overall clustering* examines situations in which one node is connected to two others and reports the fraction of those for which the two others are connected to each other.

We identify inventors and assignees using the disambiguation algorithm of Monath and McCallum (2015) on the Patentsview database (our data include assignees and inventors based both inside and outside the United States).

We use the coauthorship of inventors to build collaboration networks and track them over time. Similarly, patents are connected to one another through the citations that appear in the patents.

A statistical overview of these networks is presented in Table 5.1. Inventors in more recent years have more than three times as many coauthors as they did in the 1970s and 1980s. Similarly, on average, patents have become more interconnected over time.

Some coauthors on patents, such as intellectual property lawyers and management executives, may not contribute to the creative process of an invention. To filter out such individuals, we restrict our attention to those inventors who, within our data: (i) publish at least one patent alone, (ii) publish at least three patents, (iii) have a research career that lasted more than three years, and (iv) coauthor with at least three other people in our data.

We present the summary statistics for the selected and the full population of inventors in Table 5.2. Overall, our selected sample covers about 25 percent of the people in our data, and those in our sample tend to have a broader network of coauthors, longer experience, and more published patents than the full population.

Table 5.2. Cross-sectional summary statistics of the full and selected inventors' data

Year of application:	1985			1995			2005		
	All	Selected	Treated	All	Selected	Treated	All	Selected	Treated
Degree									
Mean	14	15	22	23	27	42	38	48	77
Median	6	8	10	10	12	20	16	24	42
Growth rate of degree	0.11	0.12	0.14	0.15	0.14	0.16	0.13	0.12	0.13
Fraction of new collaborators	0.79	0.74	0.72	0.73	0.69	0.64	0.69	0.65	0.59
Experience	5.98	6.77	6.92	8.7	10.2	10.9	10	13	14
Patents per inventor	0.47	0.55	0.74	0.64	0.77	1.10	0.69	0.88	1.26
Team size	2.59	2.47	2.64	3.19	2.93	3.20	3.71	3.08	3.33
Patenting inventors	32	33	39	38	39	48	38	44	53
CPC Section									
Chemistry and metallurgy	21	18	19	19	14	15	16	11	12
Electricity	16	19	19	19	22	23	24	26	27
Fixed constructions	3.1	2.8	2.2	2.4	2.3	1.9	2.0	2.0	1.9
Human necessities	11	9.5	8.5	12	10	9.7	12	9.9	9.5
Mechanical engineering	9.9	9.9	8.5	8.1	8.4	7.7	6.6	7.5	7.4
Performing ops.; Transporting	18	18	17	16	16	15	13	14	13
Physics	19	21	24	22	25	26	27	29	29
Textiles and paper	2.1	2.2	1.5	1.5	1.5	1.1	0.8	0.8	0.7
Country									
Other	50	48	47	51	51	46	51	54	46
United States	50	52	53	49	49	54	49	46	54

Assignee type									
Firm	89	94	96	92	95	97	95	97	97
Other	11	6.2	4.1	7.8	4.8	3.2	4.7	3.4	2.7
Number of inventors	167,989	41,863	7,382	309,519	74,980	13,574	446,534	93,514	17,244

Notes: Summary statistics are presented for three given years. All values are percentages except for entries in the row listing number of inventors. Our selected sample of inventors are those who have at least one single-authored patent and a career spanning at least three years, with three granted patents, and having at least three coauthors in our data. "Treated" inventors (in our event study) are the selected inventors that publish one breakthrough patent over their career. A breakthrough is a patent that is among the top 2 percent most-cited patents during the five years following its application, among the pool of all patents filed within two years of the patent in its CPC (Cooperative Patent Classification) subclass. We discuss this further in Section 2.4. *Degree* is defined as an inventor's cumulative number of unique coauthors up through a given year. *Growth rate of degree* is the growth rate of the inventor's degree. *Fraction of new collaborators* is the fraction of an inventor's coauthors of patents in a given year who are new. *Experience* is the number of years since the filing date of the inventor's first granted patent. *Patents per inventor* is the average number of patents filed per inventor in the given year (that were eventually granted). *Team size* is the number of coauthors on the last filed patent. *Patenting inventors* is the share of inventors applying for a patent in that year. *CPC Section* shows the distribution of inventors in each broad technology class as defined by the USPTO.

***p < 0.01; **p < 0.05; *p < 0.1

2.2 *Measuring changes in inventors' networks*

To analyze the evolution of an inventor's network, we build a panel of inventors and track their collaborations over time. We consider two measures of how inventors expand their networks.

Our first measure of the expansion of an inventor's network is based on the fraction of collaborators who are new in each year. Let $C_{i,t}$ denote the number of collaborators of an inventor i during year t, and $S_{i,t}$ be their stock of (unique) collaborators up through year t. The fraction of new collaborators is:

$$f_{i,t} = (S_{i,t} - S_{i,t-1}) / C_{i,t}. \tag{1}$$

This measure is normalized per number of collaborators in a given year to account for the fact that the stock is growing over time, and so we divide by C and not S. Since collaborators of an inventor are observed only in years during which they apply for a patent, the value of f is imputed to the last observed value during the years in which no patent was filed.

Our second measure of the expansion of an inventor's network is the growth rate of the stock of coauthors as measured by the log of the change:

$$\Delta \log(S_{i,t}) = \log(S_{i,t} / S_{i,t-1}). \tag{2}$$

Since $S_{i,t}$ does not change until an inventor collaborates with new coauthors on patents, this measure is 0 until the inventor collaborates with a new coauthor.

Given that our main focus is on inventors' willingness to expand their network subject to the threat of business-stealing, we consider the first measure to be preferable for our empirical exercises, since it is robust to the productivity of inventors. By contrast, although the growth rate of new coauthors allows us to estimate the impact on aggregate networks of inventors, it depends on research productivity. Nonetheless, it is a useful robustness check and alternative view of the evolution of the network.

2.3 *Measuring the potential concern for business-stealing*

We consider several measures of the potential concern for business-stealing, each capturing a different aspect of potential concerns.

First, areas with greater numbers of inventors reflect greater potential competition for profits from innovation than those areas with fewer inventors, and they can also reflect a greater potential possibility of leakage of information. Thus as our most basic measure of potential concerns of business-stealing, we consider the number of active inventors in a USPTO CPC subclass.[1] An inventor's CPC is defined by the technology they most frequently publish patents in. The number of active inventors in a given year and CPC subclass are counted as those who have patented at least once in that subclass by the end of the year and will patent again in the future in that subclass. The distribution of the number of inventors in CPC subclasses is presented in Figure 5.6 in Appendix A. Since inventive activity in technologies can change in the long run, we reclassify the CPC subclasses into high or low concern for business-stealing every year.

Second, we also consider the rate of entry of new inventors, classifying those technologies with more inventors entering per year as being ones with a higher level of competition. Entry rate is estimated as the ratio of the number of inventors who are patenting for the first time to the number of patenting inventors in a given year in each technology category. Because the number of new inventors patenting in various CPC subclasses each year may be too small to provide sufficient precision for our analysis, we use the broad NBER technology categories as our unit of aggregation for the entry rate of inventors.[2] We treat inventors patenting in the NBER categories with an above-median entry rate as those facing a higher-than-average concern of business-stealing.[3]

Third, we examine average size of price markups in the corresponding sector: Higher markups can lead to higher potential lost profits from business-stealing. We estimate markups for each NBER technology sector using a three-step process: first, we measure markups at the firm level using the method of De Loecker et al. (2020) using the Compustat database. Second, we match firm-level markups with patent assignees using the data of Dorn et al. (2020). Third, weighting by patent citations, we estimate the markups for each NBER technology sector using the matched firm-level markups, and we update its value every three years.[4]

---

[1] A subclass of a patent in our data is a four-character USPTO CPC classification. For example, *H04N* is a subclass that represents the technology of *Pictorial Communication*.

[2] See Marco et al. (2015) for details on patent classification by NBER technology categories.

[3] Replicating our empirical exercises by aggregating entry rate of inventors at the level of CPC class does not change the direction of our results.

[4] Repeating our estimations with alternative weightings—by patent applications and firm revenue—we find no significant changes in our results.

Fourth, we construct a localized measure of competition for each inventor based on how much competition each of their patents faces. For this purpose, we build a network of similar patents and estimate the density of this network. This captures how intensely researchers are working on similar problems. In particular, say that two patents are *similar* to one another if the patents they cite overlap. We estimate the Jaccard index (size of the intersection over union) of the backward citations between all pairs of patents, and consider that two patents (vertices) are connected by an undirected and unweighted edge if their similarity is greater than 5 percent.[5] Since two patents published many years apart are less likely to be in competition than if they are published within a few years of each other, we retain only those edges between similar patents that are published within three calendar years of each other. We also use this narrow time band to have a measure that is less likely to be contaminated by knowledge spillover.[6] Within this network of patents, we identify patent communities using the Louvain algorithm developed by Blondel et al. (2008) and estimate a community's density as its total number of connections normalized to the total possible connections within the community. More formally, we define the density measure of community C of similar parents as:

$$dens(C) = \left(\sum_{(p,q) \subset C,\, p \neq q} \mathbb{1}_{p,q} \right) \Big/ \binom{N(C)}{2},$$

where $N(C)$ is the number of patents in community C, and $\mathbb{1}_{p,q}$ is equal to one if the two patents p and q are connected, and is equal to zero otherwise. Since density can be correlated with the size of a community, we residualize the density measure $dens(C)$ by the size of C (i.e., by the number of patents in C). Note that some patents are isolated: without other patents in their community. In that case, we define their density as 0, meaning that such patents do not face any competition, given that no patent is similar to them.[7]

---

[5] For a pair of patents A and B, their respective set of backward citations (whom they cite) C_A, C_B and the set of technologies—measured by the CPCs—of their backward citations $T_i = T(C_i)$ $i \in \{A, B\}$, the similarity index is defined as $S(A, B) = S(B, A) = |T_A \cap T_B| / |T_A \cup T_B|$.

[6] Distinguishing business-stealing from knowledge spillovers is challenging (e.g., see the discussion in Bloom et al. 2013), and our results should be interpreted with corresponding caution.

[7] Some inventors patent in multiple research areas and may face different levels of competition in each of them. We define the degree of competition faced by an inventor to be the average of the level of competition faced by each of their patents in their corresponding communities.

2.4 Breakthrough inventions and event studies

We examine how a breakthrough invention impacts an inventor's collaboration, and how this effect depends on the measures for potential concern of business-stealing listed above.

We define a *breakthrough* as a patent that is among the top 2 percent most-cited patents within five years following its application, among the pool of all patents applied for within two years in its CPC subclass. The most recently granted patent in our dataset was applied for in 2015, and its citations are measured up to (and including) 2017. To minimize the chance that we misidentify a patent as a breakthrough, we only consider those CPC subclasses with at least one hundred patents in their comparison set.

The "event" we consider is the year of application of a patent that is a breakthrough, and our treated inventors are the ones who author them. We time the event by the year of the patent's application. We compare the changes in the inventor's network normalized to the stream of previous patents that were not breakthroughs, as a proxy for what would have happened if no breakthrough had occurred.

In our baseline event study exercise, we look at how a breakthrough patent affects the growth rate of inventor i's network at period t as captured by their fraction of coauthors who are new connections (i.e., $f_{i,t}$), as well as the growth rate of their stock of coauthors (i.e., $\log(S_{i,t} / S_{i,t-1})$). We then decompose the baseline by looking at how a breakthrough invention's impact on the dynamics of coauthorship depends on the threat of business-stealing.

We restrict our analysis to inventors who have only one breakthrough over their research career to capture the effect of business-stealing on networks in our event study. A statistical overview of inventors with a breakthrough is presented in the *Treated* columns in Table 5.2.

3 Empirical Analysis of the Dynamics of Collaborations

3.1 Cross-sectional analysis

Looking at all inventors, we first examine how our main measure of collaboration of inventors (the fraction of coauthors who are new connections in a given year) depends on our basic measure of concerns of business-stealing (the density of active inventors in a patent's subclass).

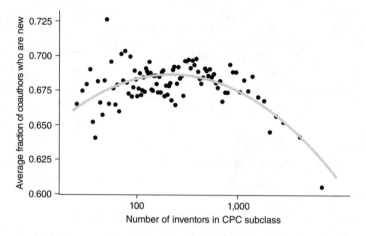

Notes: The figure plots the binned scatter relationship between the average fraction of coauthors in a given year who are new connections for its patenting inventors (along the vertical axis) and the log of the number of active inventors in a CPC subclass (along the horizontal axis) using one hundred bins. The unit of observation is a CPC subclass. The solid line is the least squares fit with a second order polynomial. Both variables are residualized by year and centered around the sample average.

Figure 5.1. Correlation between the density of inventors and new collaborations

Figure 5.1 and Table 5.3 show an inverted-U relationship between the density of the technological sector and the willingness of inventors to add new collaborators to their team. We find positive and significant regression coefficients on concerns of business-stealing (density), and negative and significant regression coefficients on the square term. Controlling for variation both by year and by technology classes within a year, the direction of their relationship remains stable. Controlling for technology subclass in addition to year, the fraction of new coauthorships is (weakly) negatively correlated with the density of inventors.

Intuitively, starting from zero density, higher density increases the scope for coauthorship as there are more researchers working in an area, hence the upward part of the inverted-U; however, too much density induces the inventor to reduce coauthorship so as to limit the risk of business / knowledge-stealing. Absent any risk of business-stealing, one would expect the relationship between new collaborations and people working in the area to be increasing or at least be nondecreasing.

Table 5.3. New collaborations as a function of the density of inventors

	Fraction of coauthors who are new			
	(1)	(2)	(3)	(4)
Variables				
(Intercept)	0.612***			
	(0.017)			
Log number of inventors	0.049***	0.054***	0.035***	−0.015***
	(0.006)	(0.005)	(0.005)	(0.008)
Log number of inventors squared	−0.005***	−0.005***	−0.003***	−0.002***
	(0.000)	(0.000)	(0.000)	(0.001)
Fixed-effects				
Year		✓		✓
Year × CPC class			✓	
CPC subclass				✓
Fit statistics				
Observations	17,842	17,842	17,842	17,842
R^2	0.02042	0.40238	0.62621	0.63106
Within R^2		0.01104	0.00507	0.02623

Notes: The table shows the estimates of the regression of the average fraction of coauthors who are new connections in a given year for patenting inventors within a CPC subclass, on the log number of inventors in the CPC subclass. Standard errors are in parenthesis. *CPC class* is one unit of patent classification above CPC subclass.
***$p < 0.01$; **$p < 0.05$; *$p < 0.1$

3.2 An event study of breakthrough patents

Next we measure the pattern of inventors' coauthorships during and after the filing of an application for a breakthrough patent. This gives us a different perspective and allows us to see whether inventors act differently once they make a big discovery.

The idea is that inventors should be more willing to collaborate when they are looking for breakthrough ideas than once they have one in hand. Once they have a breakthrough, there is less value from adding new collaborators and more potential risk in losing profits and leaking information.

Our identification strategy relies on a difference-in-differences design with staggered adoption. The empirical model for the outcome of interest for an inventor i on year t is:

$$Y_{i,t} = \alpha_i + \lambda_t + b_{i,t} \times Treated_{i,t} + \varepsilon_{i,t}, \tag{3}$$

where α_i and λ_t capture inventor and year fixed effects, respectively, on the dependent variable of inventor network measured by $Y_{i,t}$, and $Treated_{i,t} = 1[t \geq E_i]$ is a dummy variable indicating that the inventor is treated, where E_i is the year in which inventor i makes an application for her breakthrough patent. Finally, $b_{i,t}$ is the individual treatment effect, that is, the effect of having a breakthrough patent. Model (3) works from a parallel trends assumption: Had there been no breakthrough patent, the expected outcome of an inventor would be $\alpha_i + \lambda_t$.

The canonical method to estimate the treatment effect in this setting is an ordinary least squares (OLS) with two-way fixed effects (TWFE) and some leads to test for pre-trend along with lags to recover dynamic effect. However, recent literature has shown that this estimator is not reliable in the presence of treatment-effect heterogeneity.[8] We thus use the *imputation estimator* proposed by Borusyak et al. (2021) for its ease of interpretation, efficiency, and performance with large sample.

The estimation is a three-step procedure. First, inventor and year fixed-effects α_i, λ_t in (3) are estimated on not-yet-treated observations, that is, observations where $Treated_{i,t} = 0$. Second, we compute the treatment effect $\hat{b}_{i,t} = Y_{i,t} - \hat{\alpha}_i - \hat{\lambda}_t$ of each treated observation using the estimated fixed effect. Finally, averaging $\hat{b}_{i,t}$ gives a consistent estimate of the average treatment effect on the treated β. The procedure allows estimation of the dynamic effect $\hat{b}_h$ for each horizon h relative to the treatment year by averaging individual treatment effect $\hat{b}_{i,t}$ at each horizon. That is,

$$\hat{b}_h = \frac{1}{|I_h|} \sum_{i \in I_h} \hat{b}_{i,t}, \tag{4}$$

with I_h the set of inventors observed h periods after treatment. We focus on $h \in \{0, \ldots, 10\}$.

To provide support for our empirical analysis, we also test for parallel trends following Borusyak et al. (2021). We run a TWFE regression on not-yet-treated observations:

$$Y_{i,t|t<E_i} = \alpha_i + \lambda_t + \sum_{p=-P}^{-1} \gamma_p \, Treated[t = E_i + p] + \varepsilon_{i,t}, \tag{5}$$

---

[8] See De Chaisemartin and d'Haultfoeuille (2020), Borusyak et al. (2021), and Goodman-Bacon (2021).

where E_i is the year of treatment, and *Treated* $[t = E_i + p]$ is an indicator variable of being treated p years later. In our event study plots, we combine both treatment effect coefficients $\{\hat{b}_h\}$ and pre-trend coefficients $\{\hat{\gamma}_p\}$. In all subsequent analysis, we report the standard errors clustered at the inventor level.[9]

In our baseline regression, we adopt a richer model that allows time fixed effects to vary by technological field at the CPC subclass level and by the inventor's country of origin. We also control for a life-cycle effect by adding the experience of the inventor as measured by the number of years since the application of her first patent observed in our dataset:[10]

$$Y_{i,t} = \alpha_i + (Year \times CPC\ subclass \times Country)_{i,t} \\ + Experience_{i,t} + b_{i,t} \times Treated_{i,t} + \varepsilon_{i,t}. \tag{6}$$

We conduct event studies using this approach for each of our two network measurements, namely, fraction of new coauthors as well as the growth rate of the stock of coauthors.

3.3 Results

Figure 5.2 (see also Figure 5.7 in Appendix A) and Table 5.4 show the results of our baseline event study exercise. The bars in the figure are 95 percent confidence intervals.

We see a large and significant·drop in the fraction of new coauthors per year in the year of the event and subsequent years.[11] Treated inventors work

---

[9] While it would be even more desirable, clustering at team level is not tractable, because teams change over time.

[10] Since the fully tracked USPTO PatentsView data series begins in 1976, we are unable to retrieve the true years of experience for inventors active prior to 1976. Therefore, inventors with two years of observed experience as of 1978 might have more years of experience. This may bias our event study estimates, particularly for inventors observed early in their careers. However, we do not find reason to believe that they are differentially biased by concerns for business-stealing. Moreover, limiting our data to inventors who are first observed in years beginning 1986 onward, which keeps only those few inventors active prior to 1976 who did not receive a patent in over ten years, does not change our results.

[11] The drop in the year of the breakthrough is smaller than in subsequent years. There can be other patents in that year that come before the breakthrough, and it might also take some time to realize that one has a breakthrough. In Figure 5.7, we actually see a jump up at the time of a breakthrough. That reflects the fact that the year of a breakthrough has a selection bias to have more patents than usual and hence more new coauthors than in a typical year. That is controlled

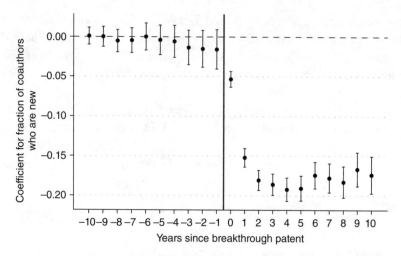

Notes: The figure plots the treatment effect of a breakthrough patent on inventor collaborations using the Borusyak et al. (2021) imputation estimator. The event is the application for a patent by an inventor that is among the 2 percent most-cited patents filed in its CPC subclass within a range of two years; the event is timed by the year of its application. The outcome is the fraction of new coauthors among all coauthors in a given year of an inventor. Pre-trends are estimated using OLS on not-yet-treated observations. For years with no patent, the value is imputed using the last observed value. Bars indicate the 95 percent confidence interval. The estimation controls for inventor, experience, and for year×CPC subclass×country-specific shocks.

Figure 5.2. Event study of an application for a breakthrough patent on fraction of coauthors on patents who are new connections

with fewer than usual new coauthors on research teams during and subsequent to a breakthrough, and they do not return to their previous level.

The baseline effect sizes summarized in Table 5.4 show that the measured change in coauthorship with new inventors is negative, and it is statistically significant, regardless of the granularity of controls.[12]

One alternative explanation for why successful inventors end up reducing coauthorship after a breakthrough is that they enter a different phase of

---

for in the fraction of new coauthors calculation, as that controls per patent, and so this effect is eliminated in Figure 5.2.

[12] Note that team members on a given breakthrough patent may differ in their measured effect size due to differences in baseline rates of new coauthorship, previous coauthorship with team members, and stage of the inventor's research career. Our results indicate that controlling for experience, as measured by years elapsed since the application of first patent, magnifies the effect size.

Table 5.4. Baseline effect of a breakthrough on subsequent inventor coauthorship

	Fraction of coauthors who are new				Growth rate in stock of coauthors			
	(1)	(2)	(3)	(4)	(5)	(6)	(7)	(8)
Treated	-0.194***	-0.081***	-0.072***	-0.152***	-0.123***	-0.058***	-0.052***	-0.071***
	(0.003)	(0.005)	(0.005)	(0.006)	(0.003)	(0.003)	(0.004)	(0.004)
Inventor		✓	✓	✓		✓	✓	✓
Year		✓				✓		
Year×CPC×country			✓				✓	
Experience				✓				✓
Wald statistic	137.139	10.470	4.305	1.055	127.816	4.346	1.591	2.030
Observations	349,130	343,816	326,066	326,066	349,130	343,816	326,066	326,066
Units	18,899	18,899	18,899	18,899	18,899	18,899	18,899	18,899

Notes: This table summarizes the change in the inventor networks, as measured by our two metrics, subsequent to the application of a breakthrough patent, relative to had they not. Note that the coefficients are negative regardless of the controls, and the effect size remains similar when controlling for year of application, the CPC subclass of the applied patent, and country of origin of the inventor. The coefficients for columns (1) to (4) are interpreted as the change in growth rate of stock of coauthors of an inventor, and for columns (5) to (8) as the percentage point change in team members that are new coauthors, subsequent to application of a breakthrough patent relative to inventors who have not yet applied for or published a breakthrough patent. Standard errors are clustered at the inventor level.

***$p<0.01$; **$p<0.05$; *$p<0.1$

production, where instead of inventing (exploring), they turn to developing the product (exploitation).

If that is the case, then the extent to which successful inventors reduce new collaborations would have no reason to vary as a function of potential business-stealing. To explore this idea, we interact the breakthrough event with the degree of concern for business-stealing faced by the inventor.

Following our previous notation, we define $b_{h,q}$ as the treatment effect of having a breakthrough during a time horizon h, and belonging to a level of concern for business-stealing $q \in \{q, \overline{q}\}$, which we denote as being above the median in $\overline{q}$. This is a natural extension of equation (4), and the treatment effect is given as the average value of $b_{i,t}$ for inventors in each group. That is,

$$\hat{b}_{h,q} = \frac{1}{|I_{h,q}|} \sum_{i \in I_{h,q}} \hat{b}_{i,t}, \tag{4'}$$

where $I_{h,q}$ is the set of inventors belonging to group q and observed h periods after treatment.

Table 5.5 presents the results of the event studies decomposed by concerns for business-stealing using our four different measures of potential business-stealing concerns (as defined in Section 2.3). The event studies for price markups and the entry rate of new inventors are presented in Figures 5.3a and 5.3b.

First, note that the baseline event study estimates hold for both high and low levels of concerns: Breakthroughs induce a decline both in the fraction of coauthors who are new and in growth rate of the stock of coauthors. Second, this decline is significantly larger among inventors who face a higher threat of business-stealing by every one of the measures. Moreover, the difference in the decline between above- and below-median measures is statistically significant for each specification. Depending on how we measure concern for business-stealing, this additional drop amounts to between 1.4 to about 10 percentage points in the fraction of coauthors who are new connections, and between 2.7 to about 6.8 percentage points in the growth rate of the stock of unique coauthors.

Our results are consistent with business-stealing playing an important role in inventors' decisions to (not) expand their coauthorship networks. The difference between the drop across these different measures could conceivably

Table 5.5. Drops in number of new coauthors as a function of measures of concerns for business-stealing

	Fraction of coauthors who are new				Growth rate in stock of coauthors			
	(1)	(2)	(3)	(4)	(5)	(6)	(7)	(8)
Density of inventors: <median	-0.135*** (0.009)				-0.051*** (0.006)			
Density of inventors: >median	-0.162*** (0.007)				-0.083*** (0.005)			
Sector markup: <median		-0.123*** (0.009)				-0.045*** (0.007)		
Sector markup: >median		-0.165*** (0.007)				-0.082*** (0.004)		
Entry rate: <median			-0.104*** (0.007)				-0.056*** (0.005)	
Entry rate: >median			-0.203*** (0.007)				-0.083*** (0.005)	
Similarity density: <median				-0.149*** (0.007)				-0.038*** (0.005)
Similarity density: >median				-0.163*** (0.008)				-0.106*** (0.005)
Inventor	✓	✓	✓	✓	✓	✓	✓	✓
Year×CPC×Country	✓	✓	✓	✓	✓	✓	✓	✓
Experience	✓	✓	✓	✓	✓	✓	✓	✓
Wald statistic	0.811	1.020	1.335	1.043	1.246	1.705	1.562	5.105
Z score	2.337	3.713	10.000	1.324	4.005	4.479	4.209	9.176
Observations	326,064	322,549	321,027	326,066	326,064	322,549	321,027	326,066
Units	18,899	18,872	18,803	18,899	18,899	18,872	18,803	18,899

Notes: This table summarizes the event study estimates for the effect of a breakthrough on inventor networks decomposed by the various measures of concerns for business-stealing discussed in Section 2.3. We estimate the coefficient for two levels of each measure: Above median reflects a higher concern for business-stealing over below median. Coefficients in columns (1) and (5) correspond to the density of inventors in their main CPC subclass; columns (2) and (6) to the entry rate of inventors in the different NBER categories; columns (3) and (7) to the measure of sector level markup faced by inventors; and columns (4) and (8) to our measure pertaining the density of patent similarity in inventors' areas of research. The Wald statistic is testing for nullity of 10 pre-trend coefficients using an OLS regression on not-yet-treated observations. The Z score is computed assuming the absence of covariance between the two parameter estimates. Standard errors are clustered at the inventor level.

***$p<0.01$; **$p<0.05$; *$p<0.1$

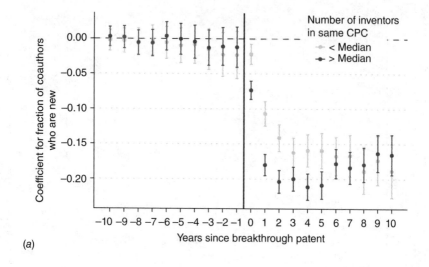

(a)

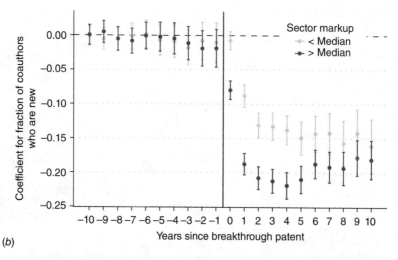

(b)

Notes: The figure plots the treatment effect of a breakthrough patent on inventor collaborations using the Borusyak et al. (2021) imputation estimator. The event is the application for a patent by an inventor that is among the 2 percent most-cited patents filed in its CPC subclass within a range of two years; the event is timed by the year of its application. The outcome is the fraction of new coauthors among all coauthors in a given year of an inventor. Figure 5.3a shows treatment effect decomposed by above and below median number of inventors in a CPC subclass. Figure 5.3b shows the treatment effect decomposed by above and below median price-markup in the NBER technology sector of the inventor. Pre-trends are estimated using OLS on not-yet-treated observations. For years with no patent, the value is imputed using the last observed value. Bars indicate the 95 percent confidence interval. The estimation controls for inventor, experience, and for year × CPC subclass × country specific shocks.

Figure 5.3a–b. Event study of the application of breakthrough patent on fraction of coauthors on patents who are new connections by concerns of business-stealing

be correlated with some other unmeasured variables that differ from business-stealing and cause team structures to diverge, but the fact that this holds for all four measures makes such alternatives less plausible.

4 A Business-Stealing Explanation for the Empirical Results

In this section, we propose a model that illuminates the empirical findings. It provides a direct explanation for: the inverted-U relationship; the fact that the growth rate in the number of collaborators drops after a breakthrough innovation; and the finding that the negative impact of the breakthrough invention on the subsequent growth in coauthorship becomes more pronounced as inventor concern for business-stealing increases. It is one possible model with these features, concentrating on the obvious trade-off between an increased probability of breakthroughs from adding more collaborators versus decreased profits for the inventor conditional on a breakthrough.

4.1 A base static model

We begin with a simple static model.

An inventor has access to up to n collaborators.

The inventor chooses a number d of collaborators.

The project has a probability of $P(d)$ of being successful, where d is the number of collaborators (beyond the inventor) who work on it. $P(0) > 0$ and $P(\cdot)$ is increasing and strictly concave in d.

If successful, the project yields profits $\pi_b(d)$. The subscript b refers to the level of the threat of business-stealing. We take $\pi_b(d)$ to be positive, decreasing, and strictly log-concave in d; and so that $-\pi_b'(d)/\pi_b(d)$ is positive and increasing in d. We also assume that $\pi_b(d)$ tends to 0 as d tends to infinity. Thus, increased numbers of collaborators lead to lower profits and eventually to full dissipation.

Finally, take $-\pi_b'(d)/\pi_b(d)$ to be increasing in b, so that inventors who see more threat of business-stealing see a greater marginal percentage loss in profits from a successful project from adding new collaborators.

We take all functions to be differentiable.

4.2 An inverted–U relationship between competition and collaboration

First, let us explain why this simple model leads to an inverted-U relationship between the potential for business-stealing and the number of new collaborators on a project.

The expected payoff to the inventor who has d collaborators is

$$P(d)\pi_b(d).$$

A necessary condition for an optimal d, when it lies strictly between zero and n and ignoring integer constraints, is

$$P'(d)/P(d) = -\pi_b'(d)/\pi_b(d). \tag{7}$$

This expression has a natural interpretation. The left-hand side is the elasticity of the probability of a breakthrough, and that has to offset the right-hand side, which is the elasticity of the loss in profits.

Given that P is positive, increasing, and strictly concave, it follows that $P'(d)/P(d)$ is positive and is decreasing in d. Given that $-\pi_b'(d)/\pi_b(d)$ is positive and increasing in d, it follows that there is at most one interior solution to Equation (7). Note also that expected profits are positive at $d=0$ and converge to 0 as d becomes too large, and so if there is no solution satisfying (7), then the solution is at $d=0$.

Let $d^*(b)$ denote the unconstrained optimum (ignoring the available n). Since the left-hand side of Equation (7) is independent of b and decreasing in d, and the right-hand side is increasing in b and d, it follows that $d^*(b)$ is decreasing in b (whenever nonzero), as pictured in Figure 5.4.[13]

This analysis shows the two competing effects. The benefits from new collaborations come through the elasticity in the probability of a breakthrough, while the fear of business-stealing is reflected in the potential lost profits (here shown by the upward shift of the elasticity of the lost profits).

The overall maximum is $\min[n, d^*(b)]$. As an example, if $P(d) = \min\{1, ad\}$ and $\pi_b(d) = \max\{0, \pi_0 bd\}$, then $d^*(b) = \pi_0/(2b)$, and the overall maximum given the constraints (ignoring integer constraints) is $\{n, \pi_0/(2b), 1/a\}$.

---

[13] The optimum is the intersection of a downward-sloping curve that does not depend on b, and an upward-sloping curve that shifts upward as b increases, so the equilibrium quantity $d^*(b)$ decreases as b increases, unless it was already 0. This is analogous to shifting up a supply curve intersecting a demand curve that is not shifting.

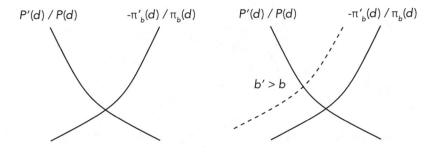

$P'(d) / P(d)$ $-\pi'_b(d) / \pi_b(d)$ $P'(d) / P(d)$ $-\pi'_b(d) / \pi_b(d)$

$b' > b$

Note: Higher levels of potential business-stealing reduce the rate at which profits decrease with collaboration, shifting the right-hand curve inward.

Figure 5.4. The optimal number of collaborators reflects two effects

Substituting n as one possible proxy for potential business-stealing b, the overall maximum becomes $\min[n, d^*(b)]$. If $d^*(n)$ is ever positive, then noting that $d^*(n)$ is decreasing in n, the overall function has an inverted-U shape with a maximum at the point at which $d^*(n) = n$, as it is initially constrained by the min function and eventually follows $d^*(n)$. Figure 5.5 pictures this for the example above in which the overall optimum is $\min\{n, \pi_0/(2n), 1/a\}$.

Although we have shown this without worrying about the integer constraints on d, the optima for the above functions will be an adjacent integer to the unconstrained solution, and so a similar result will hold, at least in some approximate sense, for most functions satisfying our assumptions.

This analysis establishes an inverted-U shape in the number of added collaborators to a promising project for a very simple example that trades off the probability of a breakthrough against potential lost profits.

4.3 The increase and subsequent decrease in added collaborators

We now discuss how to extend this model to cover the event study results, incorporating time and information.

There are three periods, $\{0, 1, 2\}$, and an inventor is working on a project. There are two states of the world, *High*, *Low*, which describe the project's potential. The prior probability of the *High* state is $\theta \in (0, 1)$. The project has the potential to lead to a profit in period 2 only if the state of nature is *High* and not if the state of nature is *Low*.

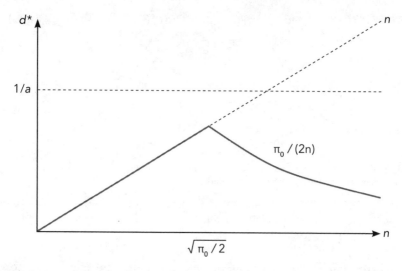

Notes: For probability of success, $P(d) = \min\{1, ad\}$, and profits as a function of the number of collaborators are $\pi_n(d) = \max\{0, \pi_0 nd\}$.

Figure 5.5. The optimal number of collaborators d^* as a function of the number of inventors n in the area

In period 1, the inventor gets a preliminary signal S_1 about the potential of the project, and the signal takes on one of two values: $\{H, L\}$. If the state of nature is *High*, there is a probability $p \in (0, 1)$ that the signal is $S_1 = H$ and probability $1 - p$ that the signal $S_1 = L$. If the state is *Low*, the probability is 1 that the signal is $S_1 = L$. Thus, conditional on seeing H, the inventor knows the state is *High*, while conditional on seeing L, the posterior that the state is *High* is

$$\theta \frac{1-p}{1-\theta p} < \theta. \tag{8}$$

After seeing the signal in period 0, in period 1, the inventor can choose a number of up to n collaborators to help with the project. Invited collaborators observe the signal and decide whether to join the project in period 1.

If the state of nature is *High*, then the project has a probability of $P(d)$ of being successful in period 2 (as above). If the state of nature is *Low*, the project leads to 0 profits no matter how many people work on it.

If successful, the project yields profits $\pi_b(d)$, where b is the level of potential business-stealing.

Take projects without an H signal to be nonbreakthrough projects. They do not attract new collaborators. A breakthrough project then attracts new collaborators, and in a way that matches the empirics: the maximal amount for intermediate levels of competition.

The post-phase empirical results—in which fewer new collaborators are added—can then be rationalized by adding an additional period to the model.

Suppose that in an additional period 3, a successful project can be further developed to result in additional profits by more efforts. So, the innovator can invite a new set of collaborators m to develop the product. The additional profits happen with probability $P^m(d)$ and then generate profits of $\pi_b^m(d)$, which have similar properties as $P(d)$, $\pi_b(d)$, but now in m. However, we presume that the product having already been successful is already known to have very high potential for additional profits, and so the additional gains from adding new team members does less to increase the probability but more to decrease the profits, and so the $m^*(d, b)$ is lower than before for all levels of competition and moreover is further decreasing in b. Thus, the additional period brings in fewer collaborators than during the first innovation stage.

Note that in this model, we have not distinguished between new and existing collaborators, which could be added with some complications of notation and analysis. Also note that we presume that projects with L signals that are not breakthroughs have no collaboration, which is counter to the data. This is easily accommodated by adding a medium signal, which is indicative of a positive- but lower-profit project that would attract fewer collaborators.

We present a further extension to endogenous competition in Appendix B.

5 Conclusions

In this chapter, we uncovered an inverted-U relationship between the extent to which inventors work with new coauthors and the potential business-stealing that they face. Second, we showed that breakthrough innovations lead to fewer new collaborators afterwards, with a bigger drop for bigger threats of business-stealing.

While business-stealing explains our observations, our event studies do not rule out alternative explanations. One alternative explanation for the basic event study finding is that inventors do not have incentives to share the pie, and consequently, do not expand their coauthorship network once they have a breakthrough. However, this mechanism fails to reconcile the finding that all four of our measures of potential business-stealing lead to a bigger decrease in the rate of collaboration.

A second possible explanation is that inventors on breakthrough projects plan multiple patents during their collaboration and apply for them in the years following the filing of the breakthrough. This explanation could mechanically reduce observed coauthorship in subsequent years, since we capture only those years where inventors do file a patent. However, our findings are that the pattern continues for many years.

A related potential explanation is that inventors might reduce their research efforts and prioritize to consume the monopoly rents earned from breakthrough inventions. Such inventors may choose to collaborate with existing coauthors rather than spend effort to further expand their network. While this explanation may hold for older researchers, subsequent to a breakthrough, younger team members may continue to become team leaders (e.g., Akcigit et al. 2018). Examining patterns of expanding coauthorship among younger researchers would be a natural next step to our analysis.

A third potential explanation is reputation. Having filed a breakthrough patent, inventors may enjoy the privilege of becoming selective about whom they work with and prioritize collaborating with other *high* type inventors. In such a case, we should similarly observe a decline in new coauthorships. High-competition areas may have higher gains from reputation due to larger prize pools, and therefore, inventors may set higher thresholds for whom they subsequently collaborate with. This is empirically difficult to disentangle from concerns for business-stealing.

Lastly, our analysis is limited to inventors who have at most one breakthrough patent. It would be interesting to examine how this analysis works for superstar inventors with many breakthroughs and whether there is any selection effect in our data.

Our analysis can also be extended in several other directions. One avenue is to continue to explore the implications of business-stealing for the structure of research networks and the conditions under which successful breakthrough innovators become central to the network rather than moving to the periphery. Another avenue is to explore policy implications: How and when should collaborative research be encouraged in fields, and how does that depend on competition? Which competitive environments maximize social welfare when endogenous research is taken into account as well as competition in the product markets? A third avenue is to look in more detail at past coauthorships: When are relationships continued rather than severed? It would also be interesting to directly measure knowledge spillovers and actual business-stealing when it does occur, and to see how they interact. Also, although we have focused on patents, there are much wider areas in which research is collaborative (across science generally), and where there are some competitive aspects to the process. It would be interesting to see whether similar results hold outside of patents. These and other extensions of the analysis in this chapter are left for future research (e.g., Aghion et al., 2021).

References

Aghion, Philippe, Nicholas Bloom, Richard Blundell, et al. 2005. "Competition and Innovation: An Inverted-U Relationship." *Quarterly Journal of Economics* 120.2, pp. 701–728.

Aghion, Philippe, Matthew O. Jackson, Antoine Mayerowitz, et al. 2021. "Innovation Networks and Business-Stealing." Available at SSRN 3917979.

Aghion, Philippe, and Jean Tirole. 1994. "The Management of Innovation." *Quarterly Journal of Economics* 109.4, pp. 1185–1209.

Akcigit, Ufuk, Santiago Caicedo, Ernest Miguelez, et al. 2018. "Dancing with the Stars: Innovation through Interactions." NBER Working Paper 24466.

Azoulay, Pierre, Zivin Graff, S. Joshua, and Jialan Wang. 2010. "Superstar Extinction." *Quarterly Journal of Economics* 125.2, pp. 549–589.

Blondel, Vincent D., Jean-Loup Guillaume, Renaud Lambiotte, et al. 2008. "Fast Unfolding of Communities in Large Networks." *Journal of Statistical Mechanics: Theory and Experiment* 2008.10, P10008.

Bloom, Nicholas, Mark Schankerman, and John Van Reenen. 2013. "Identifying Technology Spillovers and Product Market Rivalry." *Econometrica* 81.4, pp. 1347–1393.

Borusyak, Kirill, Xavier Jaravel, and Jann Spiess. 2021. "Revisiting Event Study Designs: Robust and Efficient Estimation." arXiv preprint arXiv:2108.12419.

Burt, Ronald S. 2004. "Structural Holes and Good Ideas." *American Journal of Sociology* 110.2, pp. 349–399.

Dasaratha, Krishna. 2019. "Innovation and Strategic Network Formation." arXiv preprint arXiv:1911.06872.

De Chaisemartin, Clément, and Xavier d'Haultfoeuille. 2020. "Two-Way Fixed Effects Estimators with Heterogeneous Treatment Effects." *American Economic Review* 110.9, pp. 2964–2996.

De Loecker, Jan, Jan Eeckhout, and Gabriel Unger. 2020. "The Rise of Market Power and the Macroeconomic Implications." *Quarterly Journal of Economics* 135.2, pp. 561–644.

Dorn, David, Gordon H. Hanson, Gary Pisano, et al. 2020. "Foreign Competition and Domestic Innovation: Evidence from US patents." *American Economic Review: Insights* 2.3, pp. 357–374.

Goodman-Bacon, Andrew, 2021. "Difference-in-Differences with Variation in Treatment Timing." *Journal of Econometrics* 225.2, pp. 254–277.

Hong, Lu, and Scott E. Page. 2004. "Groups of Diverse Problem Solvers Can Outperform Groups of High-Ability Problem Solvers." *Proceedings of the National Academy of Sciences* 101.46, pp. 16385–16389.

Immorlica, Nicole, Brendan Lucier, and Evan Sadler. 2014. "Sharing Rival Information." New York University Working Paper.

Jaravel, Xavier, Neviana Petkova, and Alex Bell. 2018. "Team-Specific Capital and Innovation." *American Economic Review* 108.4–5, pp. 1034–1073.

Marco, Alan C., Michael Carley, Steven Jackson, et al. 2015. "The USPTO Historical Patent Data Files: Two Centuries of Innovation." Available at SSRN 2616724.

Monath, Nicholas, and Andrew McCallum. 2015. "Discriminative Hierarchical Coreference for Inventor Disambiguation." PatentsView Inventor Disambiguation Technical Workshop, USPTO, Alexandria, VA. Vol. 122.

Ozman, Muge. 2009. "Inter-firm Networks and Innovation: A Survey of Literature." *Economics of Innovation and New Technology* 18.1, pp. 39–67.

Page, Scott E. 2007. *The Difference: How the Power of Diversity Creates Better Groups, Firms, Schools, and Societies.* Princeton, NJ: Princeton University Press.

Stein, Jeremy C. 2008. "Conversations among Competitors." *American Economic Review* 98.5, pp. 2150–2162.

Walker, Gordon, Bruce Kogut, and Weijian Shan. 1997. "Social Capital, Structural Holes and the Formation of an Industry Network." *Organization Science* 8.2, pp. 109–125.

Appendix A: Figures

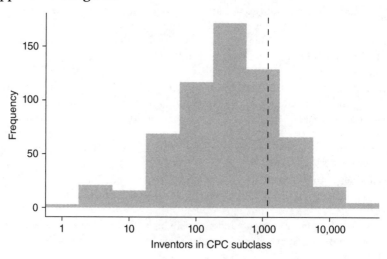

Notes: The figure plots the histogram of the total number of inventors per CPC subclasses using the USPTO Patentsview database from 1976 to 2015. The dashed vertical line represents the average number of inventors in CPC subclasses.

Figure 5.6. Distribution of the number of inventors in CPC subclasses

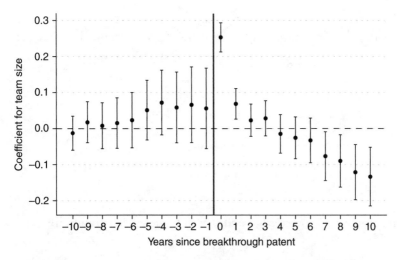

Notes: The figure plots the treatment effect of a breakthrough patent on inventor collaborations using the Borusyak et al. (2021) imputation estimator. The event is the application for a patent by an inventor that is among the 2 percent most-cited patents filed in its CPC subclass within a range of 2 years; the event is timed by the year of its application. The outcome is the fraction of new coauthors among all coauthors in a given year of an inventor. Pre-trends are estimated using OLS on not-yet-treated observations. For years with more than one patent, the value is the average team size. For years with no patent, the value is imputed using the last observed value. Bars indicate the 95 percent confidence interval. The estimates control for inventor, experience, and for year×CPC subclass×country-specific effects.

Figure 5.7. Event study of application for a breakthrough patent on team size

Appendix B: Extending the Model to Have Endogenous Competition

Further insights into business-stealing come from extending the model to allow for *endogenous* competition from collaborators, as developed here.

Let us return to the decision of the inventor at time 1 after seeing an H signal. Competition now is allowed to depend on the number of coauthors and not just on the size of the community (in line with Aghion and Tirole 1994).

For the sake of illustration, we look at a particular parametric form. Let

$$P(d) = \min\{1, ad\},$$

where $a > 0$, and

$$\pi_b(d) = \max\{1 - b, b(d, n), 0\}.$$

The threat of business-stealing, $b(d, n)$, is itself endogenous and depends on both n and d: some collaborators turn into competitors. In particular:

$$b(d, n) = c_0 + \delta n + \gamma d.$$

The innovator then solves

$$\max_d P(d) \pi_{b(d, n)}(d),$$

or

$$\max_{d \leq \frac{1}{a}, \frac{1 - c_0 - \delta n}{\gamma}} ad(1 - c_0 - \delta n - \gamma d),$$

presuming that $1 - c_0 - \delta n > 0$ and ignoring integer constraints. This yields:

$$d^* = \min\left[n, \frac{1 - c_0 - \delta n}{2\gamma}, \frac{1}{a} \right].$$

Here again, we see that d^* has an inverted-U shape in n and is decreasing in the base amount of competition $c_0 + \delta n$ after the cap on n is no longer binding (and for small enough β).

We also note that the greater the threat of endogenous competition—via larger γ—the lower the amount of collaboration there is. This shows the power of endogenous competition in reducing collaboration.

Again, this result can be extended to the post-breakthrough period by having a higher a, c_0, δ, γ, which then all work to reduce the size of the collaboration.

CHAPTER 6

Trade and Innovation

MARC J. MELITZ *and* STEPHEN J. REDDING

1 Introduction

One of the central insights of recent research on innovation and growth is that the pace of innovation is endogenously determined by the expectation of future profits. As international trade is a key determinant of firm profitability, through both the size of the market and the extent of product market competition, it is natural to expect it to play a key role in shaping innovation and growth. In this chapter, we review the theoretical and empirical literature on trade and innovation, focusing on insights from taking a Schumpeterian perspective. According to this view, growth occurs through a process of creative destruction, such that existing state-of-the-art technologies are progressively replaced by the next generation of technologies.[1] Through endogenizing the rate of innovation, these theories open up an entirely new channel for potential welfare gains from trade. In addition to the conventional static welfare gains from trade, these theories point toward the possibility of dynamic welfare gains from increases in the rate of innovation and growth. Determining the magnitude of these dynamic welfare gains from trade, the relative importance of different possible mechanisms for them, and

---

[1] For an earlier review of trade and technological change, see Grossman and Helpman (1995). For surveys of recent research on trade and innovation, see Shu and Steinwender (2018) and Akcigit and Melitz (2022). For syntheses of Schumpeterian growth theory in general, see Aghion and Howitt (1997) and Akcigit et al. (2014).

whether they involve a permanent change in economic growth (endogenous growth) or a temporary one along the transition path (semi-endogenous growth) remain exciting areas of ongoing research.

In the existing international trade literature, there is a good deal of consensus about the static welfare gains from trade, defined as the increase in the level of flow utility from country participation in international markets. Traditional theories of international trade following Ricardo (1817), Heckscher (1919), and Ohlin (1924) emphasize cross-country variation in the opportunity cost of production for different commodities as the source of comparative advantage and welfare gains from trade. Specialization to exploit these differences in opportunity cost gives rise to inter-industry trade, as countries export in industries of comparative advantage and import in those of comparative disadvantage. New theories of international trade following Krugman (1979a), Helpman (1981), and Helpman and Krugman (1985) highlight product differentiation and increasing returns to scale, which can generate welfare gains from trade through both an expansion of product variety and reductions in production costs. The resulting specialization to realize these economies of scale generates intra-industry trade, in which countries simultaneously export and import similar products within the same industry. Finally, theories of heterogeneous firms in differentiated product markets following Melitz (2003) and Bernard et al. (2003) point toward the nonrandom selection of the most productive firms into international trade and the resulting intra-industry reallocations of resources. The most productive firms expand into export markets, while increased competition induces the least productive firms to exit. This generates welfare gains through increased average industry productivity.

While theories of endogenous innovation and trade open up the possibility for dynamic welfare gains from trade, there is much less consensus about the existence and magnitude of such changes in countries' rates of innovation and growth. Four main mechanisms for these dynamic welfare gains from trade have been proposed. First, international trade expands the market size accessible to firms. To the extent that innovation involves fixed costs, this expansion of market size can raise the incentive to innovate, because these fixed costs can be spread over a larger number of units of production. Second, international trade increases product market competition as the producers from different countries enter one another's markets. To the extent that this increased product market competition reduces firm profits, this can depress the incentive to innovate, as in the classic trade-off in industrial organization between static and dynamic efficiency. However, an important contribution of the Schumpeterian approach has been to uncover a rich nexus of channels through which increased competition can have the opposite effect of raising the incentive to innovate, or generate a nonmonotonic relationship between innovation and competition.

Third, international trade induces specialization according to comparative advantage, as in the conventional theories of trade discussed above. In this context, the distinction between directed and undirected technological change becomes important, where technological change is directed if agents can target endogenous investments in innovation to particular sectors or types of economic activity. If sectors differ in their rates of innovation and growth, this specialization according to comparative advantage can affect aggregate rates of growth through a change in sectoral composition. However, the implications of this specialization for welfare are more subtle, since output and consumption growth are not equal to one another in the open economy. Even if a country specializes in sectors with slow output growth, it can enjoy the fruits of its trade partners' more rapid output growth through an ongoing improvement in the international terms of trade. Fourth, international knowledge spillovers can directly affect countries' rates of economic growth, and international trade in goods itself can be a conduit through which ideas spread around the world. These knowledge spillovers can facilitate catch-up to the world technology frontier and can accelerate the rate of advancement of this world technology frontier. Trade can influence knowledge spillovers through changing both the set of firms selling in a market and the set of firms producing in a country. Knowledge spillovers may occur serendipitously, or as a result of either direct investment in knowledge acquisition or more indirectly via imitation of more advanced products (leading to product cycle, in which products are first invented in some parts of the world and then imitated in others).

In exploring these different mechanisms through which international trade can affect innovation and growth, we distinguish between three key classes of models of endogenous innovation. First, there are models of endogenous innovation through the expansion of product variety (horizontal differentiation), which build on the closed economy framework of Romer (1990) and include Rivera-Batiz and Romer (1991) and Grossman and Helpman (1991a). Second, there is the Schumpeterian approach of endogenous innovation through the improvement of product quality (vertical differentiation), including Aghion and Howitt (1992), Grossman and Helpman (1991c), and

Grossman and Helpman (1991a). Third, more recently, models combining elements of both those approaches have been developed. In much of this recent literature, firms supply horizontally differentiated varieties, but these varieties differ systematically from one another in terms of productivity or quality.[2]

Some economic forces are common to variety- and quality-based models of endogenous innovation. In both approaches, innovations differ from conventional economic goods in two key respects. First, they are *nonrivalrous*, such that once an idea has been created, it can be used by anyone at zero marginal cost. Second, they are *partially excludable*, such that intellectual property rights or intangible knowledge about the implementation of innovations enable researchers to appropriate at least some of the economic return from them. Furthermore, many of the forces that influence the future profits from innovation are common to both groups of models, including the roles of both market size and product market competition.

Other economic forces are quite different between variety- and quality-based models of innovation. In particular, creative destruction features much more prominently in the Schumpeterian approach. Since products are vertically differentiated, all consumers agree about which product is preferred at given prices. Therefore, when innovation occurs, the existing state-of-the-art technology is displaced. This property has several economic implications. First, creative destruction affects the incentives for innovation for incumbent and entrant firms. In the basic Schumpeterian model, the fact that the existing stream of profits is destroyed by innovation (the replacement effect of Arrow 1962) implies higher incentives for innovation by entrants who then displace incumbents. Second, creative destruction affects the nature and magnitude of the externalities from innovation, and hence the divergence between private and social rates of return. When making their endogenous investments in innovation, new entrants do not internalize the externality from the destruction of existing firms' profits. Third, the vertical nature of innovation has important implications for the relationship between incentives to innovate and product market competition. Depending on the distance between firms in the technology space, increased product market competition can either depress incentives

---

[2] See Akcigit and Melitz (2022) for a more detailed review of this recent literature.

to innovate (through a discouragement effect) or enhance incentives to innovate (as firms try to escape competition).

The remainder of this chapter is structured as follows. In Section 2, we review the baseline Schumpeterian approach and use this framework to discuss the different potential mechanisms through which trade can affect innovation. The remaining four sections of the chapter consider each of the above four mechanisms in turn. In Section 3, we review the literature on trade, market size, and innovation. In Section 4, we focus more specifically on the nexus between trade and Schumpeterian competition, and its consequences for innovation. In Section 5, we consider comparative advantage as a channel through which trade affects aggregate innovation and growth. In Section 6, we examine mechanisms where knowledge spillovers play a key role in shaping the impact of trade on innovation. Section 7 summarizes our conclusions.

2 The Schumpeterian Approach

In this section, we introduce the baseline Schumpeterian approach to endogenous innovation and growth from Aghion and Howitt (1992). To highlight the key insights, we begin by considering a closed economy setting, before using this setting to highlight the potential mechanisms through which trade can affect innovation.

Preferences and technology. We consider the following economic environment. Time is continuous, and we suppress the time subscript to simplify notation. The economy is populated by a continuous mass L of workers. Workers have linear intertemporal preferences, such that the interest rate is equal to the subjective rate of time discount (r). Each worker is endowed with one unit of labor that is supplied inelastically. Output of a single final good (y) is produced using intermediate inputs (x) according to the following production technology:

$$y = Ax^{\alpha}, \qquad 0 < \alpha < 1, \tag{1}$$

where A corresponds to the quality or productivity of intermediate inputs; we choose the final good as the numeraire, such that its price is equal to one.

Intermediate inputs are produced one-for-one with labor according to a linear technology, such that employment in intermediate production equals output of intermediate inputs (x). Labor market clearing implies that employment in intermediate input production plus employment in research (n) equals the economy's total supply of labor:

$$L = x + n. \tag{2}$$

Innovations are assumed to arrive randomly in the research sector, with a Poisson arrival rate λn, where λ parameterizes the productivity of research. Each innovation is assumed to improve the quality or productivity of intermediate inputs by a constant proportion $\gamma > 1$, such that there is a productivity or quality ladder, with $A_{t+1} = \gamma A_t$, where t indexes innovations. An important feature of this specification is that each generation of researchers benefits from knowledge spillovers from previous generations, with each innovation standing on the shoulders of the previous state-of-the-art technology. A firm that successfully innovates can monopolize the intermediate sector until replaced by the next innovator. We assume that innovations are drastic, in the sense that quality increments are sufficiently large (sufficiently large γ) that final goods firms prefer to employ the state-of-the-art intermediate input at the profit-maximizing monopoly price rather than the next best technology at its marginal cost of production.

Research sector. Free entry into research implies that the wage in the intermediate sector (w_t) using technology t equals the probability of innovation (λ) times the value of the next technology $t+1$ (V_{t+1}):

$$w_t = \lambda V_{t+1}. \tag{3}$$

The value of a successful innovation (V_{t+1}) depends on the flow of profits from monopolizing the intermediate sector (π_{t+1}) and the probability of being subsequently replaced by the next best technology (λn_{t+1}) according to the following Bellman equation:

$$rV_{t+1} = \pi_{t+1} - \lambda n_{t+1} V_{t+1}. \tag{4}$$

In equilibrium, all research is undertaken by entrants rather than the incumbent monopolist of the current state-of-the-art technology, because of the "replacement effect": The incremental increase in profits for the incumbent from developing the next generation of technology is smaller than the total profits gained by an entrant from displacing an incumbent. Aghion et al. (1997, 2001) extend this framework with multiple ladder rungs (resulting from "step-by-step" innovation outcomes). In this version, incumbents still have an incentive to innovate, but the highest innovation effort is still exerted in anticipation of replacing the incumbent at the top of the ladder.

Intermediate sector. At each point in time, the monopolist of the state-of-the-art technology t chooses output (x) of intermediate inputs to maximize profits ($\pi_t(x)$):

$$x_t = \arg\max_{x}\{\pi_t(x) = p_t(x)x - w_t x\}, \tag{5}$$

where $p_t(x)$ is the price of the intermediate input. This price is determined from the downward-sloping demand curve from the final goods sector:

$$p_t(x) = A_t \alpha x^{\alpha-1}. \tag{6}$$

Profit maximization implies that the equilibrium price of the intermediate input is a constant mark-up over marginal cost:

$$p_t = \frac{1}{\alpha} w_t, \tag{7}$$

where this constant mark-up ($1/\alpha$) reflects the fact that the producer of the state-of-art intermediate input faces a constant elasticity derived demand function (6). Equilibrium output and profits in the intermediate sector can be written as the following functions of the productivity-adjusted wage ($\omega \equiv w_t / A_t$):

$$x_t = \left(\frac{\alpha^2}{w_t/A_t}\right)^{1/(1-\alpha)} = \left(\frac{\alpha^2}{\omega_t}\right)^{1/(1-\alpha)} \equiv \tilde{x}(\omega_t),$$

$$\pi_t = \left(\frac{1-\alpha}{\alpha}\right) w_t x_t \equiv A_t \tilde{\pi}(\omega_t). \tag{8}$$

General equilibrium. The general equilibrium of the model can be characterized by a no-arbitrage condition equating the returns to working in the intermediate and research sectors and the labor market clearing condition. From the free entry condition (3), the asset equation (4), and equilibrium profits (8), no-arbitrage between the intermediate and research sectors implies:

$$\omega_t = \lambda \frac{\gamma \tilde{\pi}(\omega_{t+1})}{r + \lambda n_{t+1}}. \tag{9}$$

Labor market clearing (2), together with equilibrium intermediate production (8) implies:

$$L = n_t + \tilde{x}(\omega_t). \tag{10}$$

The no-arbitrage condition (9) and the labor market clearing condition (10) determine the equilibrium productivity-adjusted wage (ω_t) and research employment (n_t) for technology t as a function of expectations of the equilibrium productivity-adjusted wage (ω_{t+1}) and research employment (n_{t+1}) for technology $t+1$.

Steady-state equilibrium. In a steady-state equilibrium, there is a constant productivity-adjusted wage ($\omega_{t+1} \equiv n_{t+1} = n$) and constant research employment ($n_t \equiv n_{t+1} = n$). Combining the no-arbitrage condition (9) and the labor market clearing (10), steady-state equilibrium research employment solves the following relationship:

$$1 = \lambda \frac{\gamma^{\frac{1-\alpha}{\alpha}}(L-n)}{r + \lambda n}. \tag{11}$$

The economy's steady-state rate of output growth in turn depends on this equilibrium research employment (n), the productivity of research (λ), and the size of innovations (γ):

$$g = \lambda n \ln \gamma. \tag{12}$$

Introducing trade and its impact on innovation and growth. This characterization of the closed economy equilibrium suggests four potential mechanisms for international trade to affect endogenous innovation and growth. First, the closed economy equilibrium features a scale effect, such that countries with a larger supply of labor (L) experience higher rates of innovation and output growth. To the extent that international trade operates like an increase in the supply of labor, this suggests a first mechanism for trade to affect innovation and growth through larger market size.

Second, the rate of innovation and output growth in the closed economy depends on the profits from successful innovation. In this baseline Schumpeterian specification with drastic innovation, the mark-up from successful innovation is completely determined by the parameter α. More generally, the profits from successful innovation depend on market structure and the degree of product market competition. To the extent that international trade affects market structure, this points to a second mechanism for trade to affect innovation and growth through product market competition.

Third, this baseline Schumpeterian model features a single final good sector. More generally, one could envision multiple final goods sectors that differ in the productivity of innovation (λ), the step size for each quality improvement (γ), and equilibrium investments in innovation (n). To the extent that international trade changes the composition of economic activity across sectors that differ in rates of innovation and growth, this highlights a third mechanism for trade to affect innovation and growth through specialization according to comparative advantage.

Fourth, a key feature of this closed economy specification is that there are knowledge spillovers, such that each generation of researchers builds on the discoveries of previous generations of researchers. In an open economy, these knowledge spillovers can occur not only domestically but also internationally, revealing a fourth mechanism for trade to affect innovation and growth through international knowledge spillovers. The magnitude of these knowledge spillovers is likely to depend on the extent to which there is duplication in research, whether a country is close to or far from the global technological frontier, and whether international knowledge spillovers occur through international trade in goods (embodied) or occur independently of those flows of goods (disembodied).

In this baseline Schumpeterian model, there is a single intermediate input producer of the state-of-the-art technology in equilibrium, because of the vertical differentiation of technology. Additionally, all innovation is undertaken by entrants rather than incumbent firms, because of the "replacement effect" discussed above. More generally, technologies can be both horizontally and vertically differentiated, such that a range of technologies operates in equilibrium, and incumbents as well as entrants can invest in innovation. In such settings, international trade can also affect innovation and growth through reallocations of resources across heterogeneous producers. In much of the existing heterogeneous-firm literature in international trade following Melitz (2003), these reallocations affect the level of productivity rather than innovation and growth. In dynamic models of innovation and producer heterogeneity, they can also affect endogenous rates of innovation and growth through the four mechanisms discussed above.

Efficiency. Models of endogenous innovation typically feature a number of externalities, such that the private rate of return to research and development (R&D) differs from its social rate of return. Furthermore, these externalities in general differ between variety- and quality-based models of endogenous innovation. First, researchers typically only appropriate part of the return to innovation, because they capture only the profits from the innovation and not the associated consumer surplus. This "appropriability effect" acts to reduce private investments in innovation relative to the socially optimal level. Second, researchers typically do not take into account that their discovery can be used as an input into research by subsequent generations of researchers. This "knowledge spillovers" effect again works to reduce private investments in innovation relative to the socially optimal level.

Third, in the standard Schumpeterian model of innovation discussed above, all innovation is undertaken by entrants rather than incumbents, because of the replacement effect. As a result, the current generation of researchers does not internalize the destruction of the flow of profits from the existing state-of-the-art technology. This "business stealing" or "creative destruction" effect works to increase private investments in innovation relative to the socially optimal level. Fourth, in these Schumpeterian models in which incumbents are replaced by new entrants, the private and social discount rates differ. The current generation of researchers internalizes the expected flow of profits from innovation over the interval of time until they are displaced by a subsequent generation of researchers, whereas the social planner internalizes that the increase in quality from the innovation persists forever. Again this "discounting effect" acts to reduce private investments in innovation relative to the socially optimal level.

Even in the closed economy, these divergences between private and social rates of return to innovation can provide a rationale for policy interventions to either promote or retard investments in innovation. In the open economy, these domestic distortions can interact with trade frictions to influence the welfare gains from trade, as discussed further below. Akcigit et al. (2021) develop an open economy model of Schumpeterian growth that quantitatively examines those interactions. We discuss this contribution in the following section.

3 Market Size, Trade, and Innovation

The idea that market size is an important determinant of economic development dates back to at least Adam Smith. In the third chapter of the first book of the *Wealth of Nations*, Smith (1776) argued: "As it is the power of exchanging that gives occasion to the division of labour, so the extent of this division must always be limited by the extent of that power, or, in other words, by the extent of the market." We begin by discussing the role of market size in static models of international trade. We next turn to consider the impact of market size on innovation in dynamic trade models and the debate about scale effects. Finally, we close this section by considering the effect of market size on innovation in models of firm heterogeneity.

Market size in static trade models. In static models of international trade, this idea that market size influences the extent of specialization and the division of labor was formalized in Krugman (1979a, 1980). In the presence of horizontal product differentiation and increasing returns to scale from fixed production costs, each firm specializes in producing a distinct variety, and in the closed economy, the measure of varieties produced depends on the size of the economy's labor force. In Krugman (1979a), with a variable elasticity of demand system and firms competing under conditions of monopolistic competition, the opening of international trade both expands the measure of varieties available to consumers and increases output of each variety, which increases average productivity because of the economies of scale. Both forces imply welfare gains from trade, even for trade between countries with identical preferences and production technologies. In Krugman (1980), the assumption of constant elasticity of substitution (CES) preferences and monopolistic competition implies that there is no effect of the opening of trade on average firm size, and hence the sole source of welfare gains from trade is an expansion of the measure of varieties available to consumers.

Market size in dynamic trade models. Whereas in these static trade models, the creation of new varieties requires firms to incur a fixed cost, in dynamic models of endogenous growth through the expansion of product variety, such as Romer (1990), the stock of varieties expands gradually over time through flow investments in R&D. These flow investments again have the feature of a fixed cost: Once the blueprint for a new variety has been created, it can be used at zero marginal cost, leaving only production costs to be incurred. As a result, basic models of endogenous innovation and growth feature a powerful scale effect, such that larger economies have higher rates of endogenous growth.

Whether these scale effects are consistent with the data has been a lively source of debate. An influential series of papers (Jones 1995a,b, 1999) argues that this prediction of scale effects is inconsistent with the empirical evidence.

In particular, an implication of these scale effects is that an increase in resources devoted to R&D should lead to a proportionate increase in a country's long-run rate of economic growth. In contrast to this prediction, the number of scientists engaged in R&D in advanced countries grew dramatically in the second half of the twentieth century, but country growth rates either exhibited a constant mean or declined on average. More recently, combining these macro trends with micro firm data and industry case studies, Bloom et al. (2020) provide strong evidence of declining research productivity across a range of different research fields.

Motivated by the early empirical evidence of absence of scale effects, Jones (1995a) develops a semi-endogenous growth model, in which endogenous innovation shapes the economy's rate of growth in the transition to steady-state, but the economy's long-run rate of growth is exogenously determined by population growth. Young (1993) also develops a model in which scale effects show up in the level of economic activity through a proliferation of product variety but not in changes in the economy's long-run rate of growth. In practice, transition dynamics can be slow, and hence empirically distinguishing between endogenous and semi-endogenous growth models can be challenging. Furthermore, given these slow transition dynamics and discounting, whether policies affect the growth rate permanently or over a long transition period may be of relatively little consequence.

Although international trade expands market size and hence increases incentives to invest in innovation, its effect on the rate of growth is more subtle than an increase in an economy's supply of labor in the closed economy. The reason is that international trade also increases product market competition between firms, which decreases incentives to invest in innovation in the simplest models of endogenous growth. Paralleling the result discussed above for static models of international trade, if the horizontal differentiation of varieties takes a CES form, these market access and competition effects exactly offset one another in models of endogenous growth through product variety. In particular, suppose that countries open to trade in goods alone, with no knowledge spillovers between them and no duplication in research. In these circumstances, trade raises the level of countries' welfare through the increased range of varieties available to consumers, but it has no effect on countries' long-run rates of growth because of the offsetting market size and competition effects, as shown in Rivera-Batiz and Romer (1991) and Grossman and Helpman (1991a). Instead, international openness affects countries' rates of growth in these models through international knowledge spillovers and the elimination of duplication in research. As for static models of international trade, this result is specific to CES preferences, and the impact of trade in goods alone would be more subtle for the general additive preferences considered by Krugman (1979a) and Zhelobodko et al. (2012).

This interaction between countervailing market size and competition effects also occurs in Ricardian models of technology and trade with Bertrand competition between firms, as studied in Eaton and Kortum (2001). Additionally, if some factors of production are fixed at the firm-level and sunk costs to accumulate these factors have already been incurred, then changes in product market competition can affect the opportunity cost of using these "trapped factors." Bloom et al. (2021) explore this additional market size channel: Exposure to import competition reduces the opportunity cost of those "trapped factors" and induces the exposed firms to reallocate those factors from production to innovative activities.

Market size in heterogeneous firm trade models. Much of the recent literature on firm heterogeneity in international trade following Melitz (2003) has focused on models that are largely static. In these frameworks, trade affects the range of varieties available for consumption and reallocates resources across firms of heterogeneous productivity, but it does not influence innovation and growth. In the open economy equilibrium of these models, only the most productive firms self-select into exporting, because of the fixed costs of serving export markets. Symmetric reductions in international trade costs induce within-industry reallocations, in which high-productivity exporters expand; intermediate productivity firms enter export markets; lower-productivity firms that serve only the domestic market contract; and the lowest-productivity firms exit. Each of these responses reallocates resources within the industry to more productive firms, raising average industry productivity.[3] More recently, some studies have incorporated endogenous technology adoption or innovation into environments with heterogeneous producers, and we now consider the implications of this heterogeneity for the impact of international trade on technology adoption, innovation, and growth.

---

[3] For reviews of this literature on firm heterogeneity, see, for example, Bernard et al. (2007, 2018), Melitz and Trefler (2012), and Melitz and Redding (2014). For research on selection into importing and global value chains, see Antràs et al. (2017) and Antràs and de Gortari (2020).

In models of firm heterogeneity and endogenous technology choice, the effects of market size also play an important role in determining whether a more advanced technology is adopted. In this theoretical and empirical literature, trade liberalization is often used as a source of variation in market access, by reducing the cost of accessing foreign export markets. Bustos (2011) considers a version of the Melitz (2003) model, in which heterogeneous firms make endogenous decisions over both whether to incur a fixed cost of exporting and whether to incur the fixed cost of adopting a more advanced technology.[4] A key prediction of the model is that the increase in firm revenues from exporting can induce firms to upgrade technology. Consistent with the predictions of the model, the effect of tariff reductions from MERCOSUR on technology upgrading by Argentinian firms is greatest for firms in the upper-middle range of the firm-size distribution. Costantini and Melitz (2008) develop a dynamic model of the decisions of heterogeneous firms to adopt a new technology that features transition dynamics in response to trade liberalization. In this framework, the distributional effects of trade liberalization across firms depend on whether trade liberalization is anticipated or unexpected, and whether it occurs gradually or abruptly. In particular, the anticipation of future trade liberalization, or a more gradual path of trade liberalization once implemented, can induce firms to innovate ahead of export market entry.

Further evidence of the importance of market size for incentives to innovate is provided by Lileeva and Trefler (2010) using the Canada–US Free Trade Agreement. Canadian plants that were induced by the tariff cuts to start exporting or to export more increased their labor productivity, engaged in more product innovation, and had higher rates of adoption of manufacturing technology. Furthermore, the paper shows that the empirical finding that the productivity gains from exporting are largest for the plants that are initially small and less productive can be explained by allowing for two forms of heterogeneity: in productivity and the return to investment. The intuition can be seen by considering two firms that are initially just indifferent between either (i) exporting and investing and (ii) doing neither. The initially higher-productivity firm will perform well in export markets, and so its indifference must be due to low expected productivity gains from investing. In contrast, the initially lower-productivity firm will perform poorly in ex-

---

[4] This key trade-off involving exports and technology adoption was first analyzed by Yeaple (2005).

port markets, and hence its indifference must be due to large expected productivity gains from investment. As a result, when trade barriers fall, and both firms start to export and invest, the initially less productive firm will experience the greater productivity growth.

While the previous three studies focus on technology adoption, Atkeson and Burstein (2010) develop a model of firm heterogeneity with both product innovation (the entry of new firms) and process innovation (investments to increase firm productivity). The model features endogenous decisions over exit, exporting, product innovation, and process innovation. The paper decomposes the change in aggregate productivity from a reduction in trade costs into the direct effect (holding constant firms' decisions on exit, exporting, product innovation, and process innovation) and the indirect effect that arises from changes in firms' exit, exporting, process innovation, and product innovation decisions. The free entry condition that equates the expected value of entry with the sunk entry cost disciplines the overall magnitude of this indirect effect. The paper finds that, in the steady state, the magnitude of this indirect effect is not affected by the introduction of firm heterogeneity. Even though exporters respond to trade liberalization by raising their innovation rates relative to nonexporters (under heterogeneity), those differences do not translate into higher aggregate productivity relative to a model where all firms export and share a common innovation rate. Impullitti and Licandro (2018) introduce oligopolistic competition into a similar dynamic framework. They find that the endogenous mark-ups induced by this competition break that equivalence result highlighted by Atkeson and Burstein (2010), leading to a first-order impact of trade liberalization on welfare via firm selection with heterogeneous firms. Tougher selection reduces mark-ups and triggers higher productivity growth. In a calibrated version of this model, Impullitti and Licandro (2018) find that those additional welfare gains are substantial: They are roughly doubled relative to a model without the firm-selection channel.[5]

Using firm-level production, trade, and patenting data, Aghion et al. (2020) provide theory and evidence on the role of market size and competition effects in influencing incentives for firms to invest in ongoing innovation. To disentangle the direction of causality between export demand and

---

[5] Long et al. (2011) also incorporate oligopoly into a static model of trade and innovation. They find that the relative magnitude of the positive market size effect and negative competition effect critically depend on the level of the trade costs.

innovation, their paper constructs a firm-level export demand shock that captures demand conditions in a firm's export destinations but is exogenous to the firm's decisions. Using data for French manufacturing, the paper shows that French firms respond to exogenous growth shocks in their export destinations by patenting more, and that this response is entirely driven by the initially more productive firms. The paper shows that this pattern of results emerges naturally in a model of firm heterogeneity with endogenous innovation. The positive market demand shock induces all firms to innovate more because of the expansion in market size, but it also increases market entry and product market competition, which discourages innovation by the less productive firms.

4 Product Market Competition, Trade, and Innovation

As discussed in the previous section, the relative magnitude of market size and competition effects plays a key role in shaping the effect of international trade on rates of innovation and growth. In this section, we explore competition effects in further detail. We begin by discussing the negative effect of competition on innovation in conventional models of endogenous innovation and growth. We next discuss three novel mechanisms through which competition can have positive effects on innovation in Schumpeterian models.[6] Finally, we end this section by considering the empirical evidence on these mechanisms and discussing ongoing work on their role in shaping the effects of international trade in general equilibrium.

Competition effects in conventional innovation models. In conventional models of endogenous innovation, whether variety- or quality-based, greater product market competition depresses the incentive to innovate by lowering the expected future profits from innovation, as in the classic trade-off between static and dynamic efficiency under monopoly in industrial organization. In contrast to these theoretical predictions, there is empirical evidence that greater product market competition can in fact spur firms to greater innovative efforts. Using panel data for UK manufacturing companies, Nickell (1996) finds that increased product market competition leads to increased productivity, using both measures of domestic market competi-

---

[6] For a review of the evidence on competition and productivity, see Holmes and Schmitz (2010).

tion and import penetration. Using direct measures of innovation, such as patents, Blundell et al. (1995, 1999) find that increases in both domestic and international competition stimulate greater innovation, as discussed further in Chapter 3 by Griffith and Van Reenen in this volume. A distinctive feature of Schumpeterian models of innovation through product quality is that they provide microfoundations for this idea that greater product market competition can enhance incentives to innovate. We next discuss three different mechanisms for this positive effect of competition on innovation in Schumpeterian models.

Schumpeterian models of step-by-step innovation. Aghion et al. (2001) develop a model of endogenous growth with "step-by-step" innovation, in which technological laggards must first catch up with the leading-edge technology before battling for technological leadership in the future. Such a specification changes the incremental incentives that firms face when deciding on their innovative investments. In particular, when firms are "neck-and-neck" with similar levels of technology, each firm may have a strong incentive to innovate to escape competition. In contrast, if a firm is far behind the technological frontier, increased product market competition may reduce the incremental return to innovation, because the firm has to first catch up with the leader before advancing the frontier, leading to a "discouragement effect." Therefore, the effect of competition on the overall aggregate rate of innovation can be subtle and potentially non-monotonic, because it depends on the entire probability distribution of firms across alternative states of technology, which is itself endogenous to the intensity of product market competition.

Schumpeterian models of agency concerns. Aghion et al. (1999) develop a model of agency concerns, in which increased product market competition affects the incentives for technology adoption by non-profit-maximizing managers. In particular, the paper considers a setting in which managers enjoy private benefits of control and face private costs of technology adoption, but only appropriate some of the monetary returns from technology adoption, because the firm is dependent on outside finance. In such a setting, if the private benefits of remaining solvent are sufficiently large, a deterioration of profitability from an increase in product market competition can raise managers' incentives to adopt new technologies. This allows the firm to remain solvent and the manager to continue to benefit from the private benefits of control. Therefore, agency considerations from a separation of ownership and control can provide another route through which increased product market competition can spur greater innovative efforts. In this framework, debt contracts can provide an alternative mechanism to discipline managers to exert effort in order to continue to enjoy the private benefits of control.

Schumpeterian models of R&D. Aghion and Howitt (1996) consider a richer specification of technology and innovation that provides another channel through which greater product market competition can raise innovation and growth. In the basic quality ladder model of growth, technology is one dimensional, such that each generation of technology improves on the previous state-of-the-art technology by a proportion $\gamma > 1$. In contrast, Aghion and Howitt (1996) allow technology to be multi-dimensional by drawing a distinction between "research" and "development." Research produces fundamental knowledge, which by itself may not be useful, but which opens up windows of opportunity, which are modeled as new product lines. In contrast, "development" generates secondary knowledge, which allows these opportunities to be realized, by filling up the new product lines. In this specification, more competition between new and old product lines, as parameterized by increased substitutability between them, can induce developers to switch from old to new product lines more rapidly, thereby leading to more research and a higher rate of growth.[7]

Empirical evidence. Although Schumpeterian models highlight these three different channels through which increased product market competition can raise incentives to innovation, there is scope for more empirical research to discriminate between these three mechanisms. In an influential empirical study, Aghion et al. (2005) provide evidence of an inverted-U shaped relationship between competition and innovation using company accounts data on a panel of firms listed on the London Stock Exchange. This inverted U-shaped relationship is rationalized using a model of "step-by-step" innovation along the lines discussed above, in which competition encourages neck-and-neck firms to innovate but discourages laggard firms from innovating. Together these two effects generate the inverted-U shaped rela-

---

[7] Such models of multi-dimensional technological change create the potential for path dependence, hysteresis, and technological lock-in, in which historical patterns of technological development can influence long-run levels of economic activity, as discussed in Brezis et al. (1993) and Redding (2002).

tionship. When competition is low, a larger equilibrium fraction of sectors involves neck-and-neck competition, so that overall, the escape competition effect dominates, and greater product market competition increases incentives to innovate. In contrast, when competition is high, a large fraction of sectors has innovation being performed by laggard firms, so that the discouragement effect is more powerful, and greater product market competition decreases incentives to innovate. Additionally, two other properties of the data provide further support for the mechanisms in the model. First, the average technological distance between leaders and followers increases with competition, and second, the inverted-U shape is steeper when industries are more neck-and-neck.

International trade and the Schumpeterian mechanisms. International trade provides a natural empirical setting for examining the consequences of increased competition on innovation. As we previously discussed, international trade in general induces changes to both the market size and competition channels for innovation. However, asymmetric changes that predominantly affect import competition provide a way of assessing the competition channel for the domestic incumbent firms. Aghion et al. (2004, 2009) examine the impact of increased foreign competition on the innovation activities and outcomes of UK firms. They find that sectors in the United Kingdom that were more exposed to increased foreign competition exhibited higher rates of productivity growth—thus highlighting the importance of the escape competition channel. When restricting the measure of competition more narrowly to "greenfield" foreign entry (foreign direct investment), they find evidence supporting both the escape competition as well as the discouragement channel—leading to an inverted-U relationship between competition and innovation similar to that described by Aghion et al. (2005).

Another large asymmetric import competition shock that has hit advanced economies has been the so-called "China Shock," following that country's entry into the World Trade Organization (WTO) in 2001. Autor et al. (2020) examine the impact on the innovation response of US firms, and they find evidence mostly supporting the discouragement channel: US firms in sectors most impacted by the increase in Chinese import competition respond by reducing R&D expenditures and new patent introductions. However, Bloom et al. (2016) find that increased Chinese competition induced European firms to increase their rates of innovation, highlighting the escape competition channel. Returning to the case of the United States,

Hombert and Matray (2018) find evidence for both the discouragement and escape competition channels. More specifically, they find that this escape competition channel works through firm investments in more differentiated products. Yang et al. (2021) also find similar evidence for Canadian firms; and Fieler and Harrison (2018) find that this type of escape competition directed at product differentiation is also exhibited by Chinese firms that face increased competition by foreign firms entering the Chinese market following its accession to the WTO.[8]

Aghion et al. (2021b) offer a different explanation for the evidence of both positive and negative innovation responses to increased Chinese competition: They show that there are two very distinct components to this increased competition that induced adjustments in opposite directions for French firms exposed to Chinese exports. One component is horizontal: The exposed firms produce a good that competes with similar imported Chinese goods. The other component is vertical: The exposed firms use intermediate goods similar to the imported Chinese goods. Aghion et al. (2021b) find that the horizontal component of the China shock induces a strong negative innovation response for the affected French firms, whereas the response to the vertical component is positive.

On the theoretical side, there has been relatively little research introducing these Schumpeterian mechanisms into general equilibrium models of international trade—even though international trade plays a key role in shaping product market competition. In a notable exception, Akcigit et al. (2021) develop a general equilibrium model of step-by-step innovation and trade, which is used to study the welfare implications of country trade and innovation policies. An R&D tax credit is found to generate substantial welfare gains over medium and long horizons. The optimal value of this tax credit decreases with the level of trade openness. They also find that protectionist policies can generate welfare gains in the short run by shielding domestic firms from foreign competition. But they subsequently engender substantially larger losses in the long run, because they distort innovation incentives, leading to slower growth.

---

[8] Bombardini et al. (2017) find that a positive escape competition innovation response is exhibited by relatively more productive Chinese firms. In a broader sample of twenty-seven emerging markets, Gorodnichenko et al. (2010) find evidence supporting mainly the escape competition response.

5 Comparative Advantage, Trade, and Innovation

In models of endogenous innovation and trade, comparative advantage plays an important role, both in shaping the effects of economic growth and in determining the pace of innovation and growth. We first discuss how comparative advantage influences the effects of economic growth in the open economy. We next consider comparative advantage as determinant of innovation and growth. Finally, we consider potential implications for public policy in the open economy.

Comparative advantage and the effects of economic growth. In the open economy, comparative advantage plays a key role in shaping the effects of economic growth. Matsuyama (1992) and Uy et al. (2012) show that the effect of sectoral productivity growth on structural transformation and economic development hinges critically on whether the economy is closed or open to international trade. In a closed economy, higher productivity growth in agriculture induces structural transformation away from that sector in the presence of inelastic demand between sectors, as in the classic model of unbalanced growth of Baumol (1967). In contrast, in an open economy, higher productivity growth in agriculture can have the opposite effect, reallocating employment to that sector through specialization according to comparative advantage.

More generally, comparative advantage and international trade are important in determining the relative price implications of economic growth. For example, Ventura (1997) develops a Ramsey model of capital accumulation in which rates of economic growth decline with capital accumulation in the closed economy because of the conventional force of diminishing marginal returns to capital accumulation. In contrast, in the open economy, countries can continue to grow rapidly without any decline in the rate of return to capital accumulation, as long as their endowments remain within the factor price equalization set. This framework thus provides a neoclassical rationalization of "economic miracles," such as the rapid economic growth of South Korea beginning in 1960. In Acemoglu and Ventura (2002), international trade leads to a stable world income distribution even in the absence of diminishing marginal returns to capital accumulation. This is because specialization and trade introduce de facto diminishing returns, as countries that accumulate capital faster than average experience declining export prices, thereby depressing the rate of return to capital and discouraging further accumulation.

Comparative advantage as a determinant of economic growth. We now turn to comparative advantage as a determinant of economic growth. If sectors differ in terms of rates of innovation and growth, specialization across these sectors according to comparative advantage naturally affects aggregate economic growth through a composition effect. Therefore, specialization according to comparative advantage not only generates static welfare gains as in neoclassical trade theories, but it also has dynamic welfare effects through the rate of economic growth. As part of a broader analysis of human capital accumulation and economic growth, Lucas (1988) develops a two-sector model in which the two sectors differ in terms of their rates of learning by doing. Depending on patterns of comparative advantage, the opening of international trade can lead an economy to specialize in the sector with a lower rate of learning by doing, slowing its aggregate rate of economic growth. Relatedly, Young (1991) develops a Ricardian model with a continuum of goods, in which learning by doing in each good is bounded. When a less-developed country trades with a developed country with a higher level of technology, it specializes in lower-technology goods, in which more of the potential for learning by doing has already been exhausted. As a result, the less-developed country experiences static welfare gains from specialization according to comparative advantage but dynamic welfare losses, as specialization in these lower-technology goods reduces its rate of growth relative to the closed economy. In Lucas (1993), spillovers of such learning by doing across goods are shown to provide an alternative explanation for "economic miracles," such as the rapid economic growth of South Korea beginning in 1960.

While the three papers just discussed focus on learning by doing, Grossman and Helpman (1990, 1991a) develop R&D-based models of endogenous innovation, in which specialization according to comparative advantage can again affect aggregate economic growth. Consider an environment with two countries, two production sectors (low and high technology), and one factor of production (labor). In the low-technology sector, a homogeneous good is produced using a constant returns-to-scale technology under conditions of perfect competition. In the high-technology sector, horizontally differentiated goods are produced under conditions of monopolistic competition. In addition to these two production sectors, there is a research sector that produces designs for new horizontally differentiated varieties for the high-technology sector. Therefore, the low-technology sector is technologically stagnant, whereas there is endogenous innovation from an expansion of product variety in the high-technology sector. To focus on the role of these endogenous investments in technological capabilities, the two countries are assumed to be identical in all respects, except for the initial stock of technological knowledge (captured by the initial mass of blueprints for varieties in the high-technology sector).[9]

In this environment, the effect of international trade on economic growth and welfare depends critically on whether knowledge spillovers are international or national in scope. With international knowledge spillovers, research firms in both countries have access to the same stock of knowledge, as determined by the worldwide stock of designs for differentiated varieties in the high-technology sector. In this case, there is a continuum of equilibrium trajectories that are consistent with given initial conditions in the two countries. All of them lead to different steady-state patterns of production and trade. The two countries' rates of growth of output differ across these steady-state equilibria, because they involve different patterns of specialization between the low- and high-technology sectors. However, the two countries' rates of growth of consumption and welfare are equal and identical across all these steady-state equilibria. Even if one country experiences a slower rate of output growth than the other because it specializes in the low-technology sector, it nonetheless experiences the same rate of consumption growth as its trade partner, because it enjoys a terms-of-trade gain from the higher rate of output growth in its trade partner. Therefore, this prediction highlights the importance of distinguishing between output and consumption growth in the open economy, and the role of the international terms of trade in shaping the incidence of productivity growth between countries in the open economy.

With national knowledge spillovers, research firms in each country have access to different stocks of knowledge, as determined by the national stock of designs for differentiated varieties in the high-technology sector. In this case, initial conditions in the form of the initial stock of designs in each country play a central role in determining steady-state patterns of production and trade. In general, several different types of steady-state equilibria

---

[9] For Ricardian models of international trade that incorporate Schumpeterian models of innovation, see Scott Taylor (1992, 1994) and Somale (2021).

are possible, with different patterns of specialization across sectors and with different trajectories for relative wages in the two countries. However, a key property of the model with national knowledge spillovers is that it becomes possible for an initial technological lead in research to become self-perpetuating (hysteresis). Furthermore, in some of these steady-state equilibria, relative wages and welfare can differ between the two countries. The country with the higher initial stock of designs for differentiated varieties is characterized by a higher steady-state level of wages and welfare. In these circumstances, there is a potential for an R&D subsidy in the initially more technologically backward country to be welfare improving, depending on the assumptions regarding retaliation by its trade partner.

Another mechanism through which comparative advantage can influence long-run growth and income distribution is directed technological change. Acemoglu (2003) considers a setting where agents make profit-seeking investments in innovation that can be directed either to skilled or unskilled labor-intensive goods. An increase in the supply of skills, holding technology constant, reduces the skill premium, as in conventional neoclassical models of trade. However, an increase in the supply of skills also induces an endogenous change in technology, which raises the demand for skills. Through this mechanism of endogenous directed technological change, trade liberalization can induce rising wage inequality in both skill-abundant and skill-scarce countries. In contrast, in conventional neoclassical models of trade, trade liberalization raises wage inequality in skill-abundant countries but reduces it in skill-scarce countries.

Comparative advantage and public policy interventions. This property that national public policy interventions can, in some circumstances, be welfare improving is a common characteristic of models of comparative advantage and endogenous technological change. Krugman (1987) considers a Ricardian model of a continuum of goods following Dornbusch et al. (1977), in which learning by doing is specific to each sector. In this environment, comparative advantage evolves endogenously over time, because current patterns of comparative advantage determine current production and the rate of learning by doing, which in turn determines future patterns of comparative advantage. As a result, temporary shocks, such as real exchange rate appreciations or protectionist trade policies, can have permanent effects on long-run patterns of comparative advantage and trade.

Redding (1999) explores the idea that developing countries may face a trade-off between (i) specialization according to existing comparative advantage (in low-technology goods) and (ii) entering sectors in which they currently lack a comparative advantage but may acquire such a comparative advantage in the future as a result of the potential for productivity growth (in high-technology goods). Learning by doing occurs as an externality at the industry level and hence is not internalized by individual firms when making their production decisions. As a result, specialization according to current comparative advantage under free trade can be welfare reducing. Furthermore, public policy intervention to promote specialization in the high-technology sector can be welfare improving, not only for the country undertaking the intervention, but more surprisingly, also for its trade partner.

Melitz (2005) develops a welfare-maximizing model of infant industry protection, in which the domestic infant industry is competitive and experiences dynamic learning effects that are external to firms. The competitive foreign industry is mature and produces a good that is an imperfect substitute for the domestic good. A government planner can protect the infant industry by using domestic production subsidies, tariffs, or quotas in order to maximize domestic welfare over time. As protection is not always optimal (although the domestic industry experiences a learning externality), the paper shows how the decision to protect the industry should depend on the industry's learning potential, the shape of the learning curve, and the degree of substitutability between domestic and foreign goods.

In the three papers just discussed, learning by doing is modeled as occurring serendipitously through an externality. In contrast, in R&D-based models of innovation and growth, agents investing in R&D internalize the future profits to be derived from successful innovation. Nevertheless, there is in general a difference between private and social rates of return in these R&D-based models, as discussed above. This domestic distortion can interact with trade frictions to influence the welfare gains from trade and provide a rationale for public policy interventions, as discussed for the open economy models of R&D-based innovation in Grossman and Helpman (1990, 1991a). In these open-economy models, there is typically a difference between the decisions of national social planners and those of a world social planner, and the case for intervention for a national social planner typically depends heavily on whether retaliation occurs.

6 Knowledge Spillovers, Trade, and Innovation

Another key mechanism through which the international economy affects domestic economic activity is international knowledge spillovers. Such spillovers directly affect rates of innovation and growth, because they determine the growth rate of the world technological frontier and promote catch-up or convergence to this world technology frontier. As discussed in the previous section, these knowledge spillovers can also play an important role in shaping the effects of international trade in goods, depending, for example, on whether they are national or international in scope. These knowledge spillovers can occur serendipitously and independently from the flow of goods (e.g., through research publications); they can be promoted through flows of goods (as in the reverse-engineering of products); or they can be the result of investments in knowledge acquisition directly or in imitation (as in models of the product lifecycle). In the remainder of this section, we first review models of innovation and technology diffusion. We next examine the role of international trade as a conduit for knowledge spillovers. Finally, we consider models of the product cycle.

Innovation and technology diffusion. Eaton and Kortum (1999) develop a quantitative model of the invention of new technologies and their diffusion across countries. In equilibrium, all countries grow at the same steady-state rate, with each country's productivity ranking determined by how rapidly it adopts ideas. Research effort is determined by the economic return to idea generation at home and abroad. Patents affect the return to ideas. The decision to patent an invention depends on the cost of patenting in a country and the expected value of patent protection in that country. Using data on international patenting, productivity, and research, the paper shows how to infer the direction and magnitude of the international diffusion of technology. Using data from the five leading research economies, the paper finds that the world lies about two-thirds of the way from the extreme of technological autarky to free trade in ideas—in the sense that research performed abroad is about two-thirds as potent as domestic research. As a result, the United States and Japan together drive about two-thirds of the growth in each of the countries in the sample.

Acemoglu et al. (2006) develop a model in which firms undertake both innovation and adoption of technologies from the world technology frontier. The selection of high-skill managers and firms is more important for innovation than for adoption. As the economy approaches the frontier, selection becomes more important. Countries at early stages of development pursue an investment-based strategy, which relies on existing firms and managers to maximize investment but sacrifices selection. Closer to the world technology frontier, economies switch to an innovation-based strategy with short-term relationships, younger firms, less investment, and better selection of firms and managers. The paper shows that relatively backward economies may switch out of the investment-based strategy too soon. Therefore, policy interventions to encourage the investment-based strategy, such as limits on product market competition or investment subsidies, can be beneficial. However, these policies can have long-run costs, because they make it more likely that a society will be trapped in the investment-based strategy and fail to converge to the world technology frontier.

Trade as a conduit for knowledge spillovers. Using data on twenty-one OECD countries plus Israel during the period 1971–1990, Coe and Helpman (1995) provide empirical evidence on the role of international trade as a conduit for knowledge spillovers.[10] For each country, a domestic knowledge stock is created using cumulative domestic R&D expenditure. Similarly, a foreign knowledge stock is created using foreign cumulative R&D expenditure, weighted by bilateral import shares. Using a panel data regression specification, domestic total factor productivity growth is found to be statistically significantly related to both domestic and foreign R&D knowledge stocks. More open countries with higher shares of imports in GDP are found to benefit more strongly from foreign R&D capital stock than do more closed countries. For some of the smaller countries, foreign R&D capital stocks are more important as sources of domestic productivity growth than domestic R&D capital stocks. The rates of return to both domestic and foreign R&D are high, with an average rate of return from investment in R&D of 123 percent in G7 countries and 85 percent in the remaining fifteen countries being studied. Around one-quarter of the total benefits of R&D investment in a G7 country are found to accrue to its trade partners through international knowledge spillovers. In subsequent work, Coe et al. (2009) find that domestic institutions are an important determinant of the rate of return to R&D. Countries where the ease of doing business and the quality

---

[10] For a review of the literature on international technology spillovers, see Keller (2004).

of tertiary education systems are relatively high tend to benefit more from their own R&D efforts, from international R&D spillovers, and from human capital formation.[11]

Aghion et al. (2021a) find strong evidence for this knowledge spillover channel via international trade links. They find that a French firm's entry into a new export market induces (after a few years lag) a substantial innovation response in that export market. This innovation response takes the form of new patents that refer back to the technology developed by the French exporter, measured as a citation link from the new patent to the patents held by the French exporter.

Creative destruction. Hsieh et al. (2020) develop a Schumpeterian model of innovation, trade, and growth that builds on the closed economy model of Klette and Kortum (2004). Innovation is undertaken by both incumbent and entrants in a domestic and a foreign economy. Creative destruction occurs when innovators take over the market for an existing product. This creative destruction can occur both domestically and internationally, where domestic firms take over foreign markets for a product, or foreign firms take over the domestic market for a product. The arrival rates of innovation both at home and abroad are treated as exogenous and calibrated to match moments in the data. In the baseline version of the model, innovators build on the technology of sellers in a market, such that international trade in goods facilitates the flow of ideas. The diffusion of ideas between the two countries generates a constant reallocation of products and implies that the two economies grow at the same rate in the long run. In the baseline version of the model, in which flows of goods facilitate idea diffusion, lower tariffs boost trade and the long-run rate of export reallocation as well as growth. For the calibrated parameters of the model, these dynamic welfare gains from trade are larger than the conventional static welfare gains.

Dynamic selection. Sampson (2016) develops a dynamic model of heterogeneous firm selection that features elements of both variety- and quality-based models of growth. Firms supply horizontally differentiated varieties, but these varieties differ in terms of productivity or quality. As in the existing literature on firm heterogeneity following Melitz (2003), firms pay a sunk

---

[11] For evidence on the role of R&D and human capital as sources of absorptive capacity that facilitate catch up to the technological frontier, see Griffith et al. (2004).

entry cost to draw productivity from a distribution. However, the key new feature of the model is that the distribution from which this productivity is drawn upon entry depends on the productivity distribution of incumbent firms. This dependence captures a learning spillover from incumbents to entrants across the entire distribution of productivity. Because only a subset of relatively more productive entrants produces (and transitions to incumbent status), the productivity distribution shifts upward over time. This dynamic selection process induces technology diffusion that in turn generates endogenous growth without scale effects. On the balanced growth path, the lower bound of the support of the productivity distribution increases over time. The free entry condition implies that trade liberalization must increase the dynamic selection rate to offset the increase in profits from new export opportunities. As a result, trade integration raises long-run growth. This dynamic selection is a new source of welfare gains from trade that is driven by producer heterogeneity. For the calibrated parameters of the model, these dynamic welfare gains from trade are around three times larger than the conventional static welfare gains from trade.

Endogenous technology adoption. Perla et al. (2021) develop an alternative dynamic model of heterogenous firm selection in which incumbent firms (rather than entrants) choose whether to invest in upgrading technology. As in Melitz (2003), firms supply differentiated varieties under conditions of monopolistic competition with free entry. Firms choose whether to incur a fixed cost in order to export. Firms also choose to either upgrade their technology or to continue to produce with their existing technology. The productivity of the existing technology evolves stochastically according to a geometric Brownian motion. If a firm decides to upgrade its technology, it pays a fixed cost in return for a random productivity draw from the equilibrium distribution of firms that produce in the domestic economy. This upgrading process is interpreted as technology diffusion, because firms upgrade by adopting technologies already used elsewhere. A firm's incentive to upgrade depends on the expected benefit of a new productivity draw and the opportunity cost of taking that draw. In equilibrium, lower productivity firms find it profitable to upgrade technology, because they have both lower opportunity costs and higher expected benefits of a new productivity draw.

Reductions in iceberg trade costs increase the rate of technology adoption and economic growth, because they widen the ratio of profits between the average and the marginal adopting firm. As trade costs decline, low-productivity firms that serve only the domestic market contract, as foreign competition reduces their profits. In contrast, high-productivity firms expand and export, increasing their profits. For low-productivity firms, this reallocation process both reduces the opportunity cost and increases the benefit of a new technology. Therefore, trade liberalization leads to more frequent firm technology adoption, which in turn raises the economy's aggregate rate of growth. In equilibrium, the privately-optimal rate of technology adoption is lower than the socially-optimal rate of technology adoption, because firms only appropriate part of the return from technology adoption. As a result, the acceleration of technology adoption induced by trade liberalization generates dynamic welfare gains from trade that are again large relative to the conventional static welfare gains from trade.

Knowledge spillovers. Buera and Oberfield (2020) develop a quantitative model of innovation and technology diffusion between heterogeneous producers. Innovation and diffusion are modeled as a process involving the combination of new ideas with insights from other industries and countries. In a first specification, insights are drawn from those that sell goods to a country, following Alvarez et al. (2013). In a second specification, insights are drawn from technologies used domestically, as in Sampson (2016) and Perla et al. (2021). Openness to trade affects the quality of the insights drawn by producers, because it determines the set of sellers to a country and the set of technologies used domestically. Starting from autarky, opening to trade results in a higher temporary growth rate and a permanently higher level of the stock of knowledge, as producers are exposed to more productive ideas.

The overall welfare gains from trade can be decomposed into static and dynamic components. The static component consists of the gains from increased specialization and comparative advantage. The dynamic component consists of the gains that operate through the flow of ideas. The magnitude of the dynamic welfare gains from trade relative to its static counterpart depends on the rate of diffusion of ideas (the relative importance of insights from others) and whether insights are drawn from those that sell goods to a country or from the technologies used domestically. For the preferred calibration of the model, both the overall welfare gains from trade and the fraction of productivity growth explained by changes in trade costs are more than double those in a model without technology diffusion.

Product cycle. An influential idea in international trade dating back at least to Vernon (1966) is the idea of the product cycle. According to this view, products are typically first produced where they are invented in developed countries. As products mature, they become more standardized and can be produced in countries at lower levels of development. Eventually, products become completely standardized and can be produced in the lowest cost location in less-developed countries. As a result of this product cycle, the developed country where the product is invented transitions from being an exporter of the product in the early stages of its lifecycle to being an importer of the product in the late stages of its lifecycle.

This product cycle was first formalized in a general equilibrium model of international trade in Krugman (1979b). The world consists of two countries: an innovating North and a non-innovating South. Innovation is modeled as the exogenous rate of arrival of new products, which at first can only be produced in the North. Imitation also occurs at an exogenous rate, after which these products can be produced in the South. This lag in technological diffusion gives rise to international trade, with the North exporting new products and importing old products. In equilibrium, the North enjoys higher per capita income, because of the quasi-rents from the Northern monopoly of new products. The North must continually innovate, not only to maintain its relative income per capita but also to maintain its real income in absolute terms.

In Krugman (1979b), the rates of arrival of innovation and imitation are exogenous. Using a Schumpeterian approach, Segerstrom et al. (1990) develop a general equilibrium model of the product cycle, in which innovation is the result of endogenous investments in innovation. Again using a Schumpeterian approach, Grossman and Helpman (1991b) consider a richer specification in which the rates of both innovation and imitation are endogenous.[12] In the steady-state equilibrium of the model, the average rates of imitation and innovation are constant, as are the fraction of products manufactured in the North and the South, the North-South terms of trade, and the average length of the product cycle. The model features a rich set of interactions between innovation policies in the two countries. In particular, subsidies to innovation in the North can either cause the steady-state rate at which

---

[12] For a model in which a product cycle emerges endogenously as a result of contractural incompleteness, see Antràs (2005).

products flow from the North to the South to decline or increase, depending on the magnitude of the productivity advantage that Northern innovators enjoy over the next-best technology.

Extending this model of endogenous product cycles, Helpman (1993) explores the welfare implications of stricter intellectual property rights protection (IPR). On one hand, proponents of stricter IPR argue that it encourages innovation in advanced countries from which all regions of the world benefit. On the other hand, critics of stricter IPR argue that it only strengthens the monopoly power of companies based in developed countries to the detriment of less-developed countries. One of the key results of the paper is to show that stricter IPR necessarily reduces welfare in the South for economies that begin in steady state. In contrast, the effect of stricter IPR on welfare in the North depends on the rate of imitation. For sufficiently low rates of imitation, stricter IPR necessarily reduces welfare in the North. Although this stricter IPR raises rates of innovation in the North, it also increases monopoly power, which reduces consumer welfare through higher prices.

7 Conclusions

Research on endogenous innovation and growth has delivered fundamental new insights about the nature of economic growth and the role played by international trade. In the Schumpeterian approach, the pace of innovation is endogenously determined by the expectation of future profits, and growth is inherently a process of creative destruction. As international trade is a key determinant of both firm profitability and survival, it is natural to expect it to play a key role in shaping incentives to innovate and the rate of creative destruction. In this chapter, we review the theoretical and empirical literature on trade and innovation.

In the existing international trade literature, there is a good deal of consensus about the static welfare gains from trade, defined as the increase in the level of flow utility from country participation in international markets. Traditional theories of international trade emphasize variation in the opportunity cost of production across countries and sectors. New theories of international trade incorporate product differentiation and increasing returns to scale. More recent models of heterogeneous firms in differentiated product markets point toward within-industry reallocations of resources across firms with different productivities.

In contrast, theories of endogenous innovation and growth open up the possibility for dynamic welfare gains from trade through changes in the rate of growth. However, there is much less consensus about the existence and magnitude of these dynamic welfare gains, the mechanisms through which they occur, and whether they correspond to permanent differences in long-run growth (endogenous growth) or differences in growth along the transition to steady state (semi-endogenous growth).

Four main mechanisms for these dynamic welfare gains from trade have been proposed. First, international trade expands the market size accessible to firms, thereby raising the incentive to incur the fixed costs of innovation. Second, international trade increases product market competition. While this heightened competition reduces the incentive to innovate in conventional economic theory, Schumpeterian models have highlighted channels through which it may instead raise the incentive to innovate, including the motive to "escape competition." Third, international trade induces specialization according to comparative advantage, which can change aggregate rates of innovation and growth through changes in sectoral competition. Fourth, international knowledge spillovers can directly affect countries' rates of economic growth, and international trade in goods itself can influence technology diffusion, where knowledge spillovers can depend on either the set of firms selling in a market or the set of firms producing in a market.

While there is a commonly used framework for quantifying the welfare gains from trade in a class of trade models that uses observed domestic trade shares and estimates of the elasticity of trade flows with respect to trade costs, the quantification of these dynamic welfare gains from trade is much more dependent on model structure. Going forward, discriminating between alternative mechanisms for dynamic welfare gains from trade and developing robust approaches to quantifying their magnitude remain exciting areas for further research.

References

ACEMOGLU, D., AND J. VENTURA (2002): "The World Income Distribution." *Quarterly Journal of Economics* 117, 659–694.

ACEMOGLU, D. (2003): "Patterns of Skill Premia." *Review of Economic Studies* 70, 199–230.

ACEMOGLU, D., P. AGHION, AND F. ZILIBOTTI (2006): "Distance to Frontier, Selection and Economic Growth." *Journal of the European Economic Association* 4, 37–74.

AGHION, P., AND P. HOWITT (1992): "A Model of Growth through Creative Destruction." *Econometrica* 60, 323–351.

AGHION, P., AND P. HOWITT (1996): "Research and Development in the Growth Process." *Journal of Economic Growth* 1, 49–73.

AGHION, P., C. HARRIS, AND J. VICKERS (1997): "Competition and Growth with Step-by-Step Innovation: An Example." *European Economic Review* 41, 771–782.

AGHION, P., AND P. HOWITT (1997): *Endogenous Growth Theory.* Cambridge, MA: MIT Press.

AGHION, P., M. DEWATRIPONT, AND P. REY (1999): "Competition, Financial Discipline and Growth." *Review of Economic Studies* 66, 825–852.

AGHION, P., C. HARRIS, P. HOWITT, AND J. VICKERS (2001): "Competition, Imitation and Growth with Step-by-Step Innovation." *Review of Economic Studies* 68, 467–492.

AGHION, P., R. BLUNDELL, R. GRIFFITH, P. HOWITT, AND S. PRANTL (2004): "Entry and Productivity Growth: Evidence from Microlevel Panel Data." *Journal of the European Economic Association* 2, 265–276.

AGHION, P., N. BLOOM, R. BLUNDELL, R. GRIFFITH, AND P. HOWITT (2005): "Competition and Innovation: An Inverted-U Relationship." *Quarterly Journal of Economics* 120, 701–728.

AGHION, P., R. BLUNDELL, R. GRIFFITH, P. HOWITT, AND S. PRANTL (2009): "The Effects of Entry on Incumbent Innovation and Productivity." *Review of Economics and Statistics* 91, 20–32.

AGHION, P., A. BERGEAUD, M. LEQIEN, AND M. J. MELITZ (2020): "The Heterogeneous Impact of Market Size on Innovation: Evidence from French Firm-Level Exports." Harvard University, manuscript.

AGHION, P., A. BERGEAUD, T. GIGOUT, M. LEQIEN, AND M. MELITZ (2021a): "Exporting Ideas: Knowledge Flows from Expanding Trade in Goods." Manuscript.

AGHION, P., A. BERGEAUD, M. LEQIEN, M. MELITZ, AND T. ZUBER (2021b): "Opposing Firm Level Responses to the Chinashock: Downstream Competition Versus Upstream Relationship?" Manuscript.

AKCIGIT, U., P. AGHION, AND P. HOWITT (2014): "What Do We Learn from Schumpeterian Growth Theory?" in *Handbook of Economic Growth*, P. Aghion and S. N. Durlauf (eds.). Amsterdam: Elsevier, North Holland, 609–625.

AKCIGIT, U., S. T. ATES, AND G. IMPULLITTI (2021): "Innovation and Trade Policy in a Globalized World." University of Chicago, mimeograph.

AKCIGIT, U., AND M. J. MELITZ (2022): "International Trade and Innovation," in *Handbook of International Economics*, G. Gopinath, E. Helpman, and K. Rogoff (eds.). Amsterdam: Elsevier, North Holland, vol. 5, 377–404.

ALVAREZ, F. E., F. L. BUERA, AND R. E. LUCAS (2013): "Idea Flows, Economic Growth, and Trade." NBER Working Paper 19667.

ANTRÀS, P. (2005): "Incomplete Contracts and the Product Cycle." *American Economic Review* 95, 1054–1073.

ANTRÀS, P., T. FORT, AND F. TINTELNOT (2017): "The Margins of Global Sourcing: Theory and Evidence from US Firms." *American Economic Review* 107, 2514–2564.

ANTRÀS, P., AND A. DE GORTARI (2020): "On the Geography of Global Value Chains." *Econometrica* 88, 1553–1598.

ARROW, K. (1962): "Economic Welfare and the Allocation of Resources for Invention," in *The Rate and Direction of Inventive Activity: Economic and Social Factors,* R. R. Nelson (ed.). Chicago: Chicago University Press, 609–625.

ATKESON, A., AND A. BURSTEIN (2010): "Innovation, Firm Dynamics, and International Trade." *Journal of Political Economy* 118, 433–484.

AUTOR, D., D. DORN, G. H. HANSON, G. PISANO, AND P. SHU (2020): "Foreign Competition and Domestic Innovation: Evidence from US Patents." *American Economic Review: Insights* 2, 357–374.

BAUMOL, W. J. (1967): "Macroeconomics of Unbalanced Growth: The Anatomy of Urban Crisis." *American Economic Review* 57, 415–426.

BERNARD, A. B., J. EATON, J. B. JENSEN, AND S. KORTUM (2003): "Plants and Productivity in International Trade." *American Economic Review* 93, 1268–1290.

BERNARD, A. B., J. B. JENSEN, P. K. SCHOTT, AND S. J. REDDING (2007): "Firms in International Trade." *Journal of Economic Perspectives* 21, 105–130.

BERNARD, A. B., J. B. JENSEN, P. K. SCHOTT, AND S. J. REDDING (2018): "Global Firms." *Journal of Economic Literature* 56, 565–619.

BLOOM, N., M. DRACA, AND J. VAN REENEN (2016): "Trade Induced Technical Change? The Impact of Chinese Imports on Innovation, IT and Productivity." *Review of Economic Studies* 83, 87–117.

BLOOM, N., C. I. JONES, J. VAN REENEN, AND M. WEBB (2020): "Are Ideas Getting Harder to Find?" *American Economic Review* 110, 1104–1144.

BLOOM, N., P. ROMER, S. J. TERRY, AND J. VAN REENEN (2021): "Trapped Factors and China's Impact on Global Growth." *Economic Journal* 131, 156–191.

BLUNDELL, R., R. GRIFFITH, AND J. VAN REENEN (1995): "Dynamic Count Data Models of Technical Change." *Economic Journal* 105, 333–344.

BLUNDELL, R., R. GRIFFITH, AND J. VAN REENEN (1999): "Market Share, Market Value and Innovation in a Panel of British Manufacturing Firms." *Review of Economic Studies* 66, 529–554.

BOMBARDINI, M., B. LI, AND R. WANG (2017): "Import Competition and Innovation: Evidence from China." Manuscript.

BREZIS, E., P. KRUGMAN, AND D. TSIDDON (1993): "Leapfrogging in International Competition: A Theory of Cycles in National Technological Leadership." *American Economic Review* 83, 1211–1219.

BUERA, F. J., AND E. OBERFIELD (2020): "The Global Diffusion of Ideas." *Econometrica* 88, 83–114.

BUSTOS, P. (2011): "Trade Liberalization, Exports and Technology Upgrading: Evidence on the Impact of MERCOSUR on Argentinean Firms." *American Economic Review* 101, 304–340.

COE, D. T., AND E. HELPMAN (1995): "International R&D Spillovers." *European Economic Review* 39, 859–887.

COE, D. T., E. HELPMAN, AND A. W. HOFFMAISTER (2009): "International R&D Spillovers and Institutions." *European Economic Review* 53, 723–741.

COSTANTINI, J., AND M. MELITZ (2008): "The Dynamics of Firm-Level Adjustment to Trade Liberalization," in *The Organization of Firms in a Global Economy*, E. Helpman, D. Marin, and T. Verdier (eds.). Cambridge, MA: Harvard University Press.

DORNBUSCH, R., S. FISCHER, AND P. A. SAMUELSON (1977): "Comparative Advantage, Trade and Payments in a Ricardian Model with a Continuum of Goods." *American Economic Review* 67, 823–839.

EATON, J., AND S. KORTUM (1999): "International Technology Diffusion: Theory and Measurement." *International Economic Review* 40, 537–570.

EATON, J., AND S. KORTUM (2001): "Technology, Trade and Growth: A Unified Framework." *European Economic Review* 45, 742–755.

FIELER, A. C., AND A. HARRISON (2018): "Escaping Import Competition in China." Tech. Rep. w24527. Cambridge, MA: National Bureau of Economic Research.

GORODNICHENKO, Y., J. SVEJNAR, AND K. TERRELL (2010): "Globalization and Innovation in Emerging Markets." *American Economic Journal: Macroeconomics* 2(2), 194–226.

GRIFFITH, R., S. REDDING, AND J. VAN REENEN (2004): "Mapping the Two Faces of R&D: Productivity Growth in a Panel of OECD Industries." *Review of Economics and Statistics* 86, 883–895.

GROSSMAN, G., AND E. HELPMAN (1990): "Comparative Advantage and Long-Run Growth." *American Economic Review* 80, 796–815.

GROSSMAN, G., AND E. HELPMAN (1991a): *Innovation and Growth in the Global Economy*. Cambridge, MA: MIT Press.

GROSSMAN, G., AND E. HELPMAN (1991b): "Quality Ladders and Product Cycles." *Quarterly Journal of Economics* 106, 557–586.

GROSSMAN, G., AND E. HELPMAN (1991c): "Quality Ladders in the Theory of Growth." *Review of Economic Studies* 58, 43–61.

GROSSMAN, G., AND E. HELPMAN (1995): "Technology and Trade," in *Handbook of International Economics*, G. Grossman and K. Rogoff (eds.). Amsterdam: Elsevier, North Holland, vol. 3, chap. 25, 1279–1337.

HECKSCHER, E. F. (1919): "The Effect of Foreign Trade on the Distribution of Income," in *Heckscher-Ohlin Trade Theory*, H. Flam and M. J. Flanders (eds.). Cambridge, MA: MIT Press.

HELPMAN, E. (1981): "International trade in the Presence of Product Differentiation, Economies of Scale and Monopolistic Competition: A Chamberlin-Heckscher-Ohlin Approach." *Journal of International Economics* 11, 305–340.

HELPMAN, E., AND P. KRUGMAN (1985): *Market Structure and Foreign Trade.* Cambridge, MA: MIT Press.

HELPMAN, E. (1993): "Innovation, Imitation and Intellectual Property Rights." *Econometrica* 61, 1247–1280.

HOLMES, T. J., AND J. A. SCHMITZ (2010): "Competition and Productivity: A Review of the Evidence." *Annual Review of Economics* 2, 619–642.

HOMBERT, J., AND A. MATRAY (2018): "Can Innovation Help U.S. Manufacturing Firms Escape Import Competition from China?" *Journal of Finance* 73, 2003–2039.

HSIEH, C.-T., P. J. KLENOW, AND I. NATH (2020): "A Global View of Creative Destruction." Stanford University, manuscript.

IMPULLITTI, G., AND O. LICANDRO (2018): "Trade, Firm Selection and Innovation: The Competition Channel." *Economic Journal* 128, 189–229.

JONES, C. (1995a): "R&D-Based Models of Economic Growth." *Journal of Political Economy* 103, 759–784.

JONES, C. (1995b): "Time Series Tests of Endogenous Growth Models." *Quarterly Journal of Economics* 110, 495–525.

JONES, C. (1999): "Growth: With or Without Scale Effects?" *American Economic Review* 89, 139–144, Papers and Proceedings.

KELLER, W. (2004): "International Technology Diffusion." *Journal of Economic Literature* 42, 752–782.

KLETTE, T. J., AND SAMUEL J. KORTUM (2004): "Innovating Firms and Aggregation Innovation." *Journal of Political Economy* 112, 986–1018.

KRUGMAN, P. (1979a): "Increasing Returns, Monopolistic Competition, and International Trade." *Journal of International Economics* 9, 469–479.

KRUGMAN, P. (1979b): "A Model of Innovation, Technology Transfer and the World Distribution of Income." *Journal of Political Economy* 87, 253–256.

KRUGMAN, P. (1980): "Scale Economies, Product Differentiation, and the Pattern of Trade." *American Economic Review* 70, 950–959.

KRUGMAN, P. (1987): "The Narrow Moving Band, the Dutch Disease and the Competitive Consequences of Mrs Thatcher." *Journal of Development Economics* 27, 41–55.

LILEEVA, A., AND D. TREFLER (2010): "Improved Access to Foreign Markets Raises Plant-Level Productivity . . . For Some Plants." *Quarterly Journal of Economics* 125, 1051–1099.

LONG, N. V., H. RAFF, AND F. STÄHLER (2011): "Innovation and Trade with Heterogeneous Firms." *Journal of International Economics* 84, 149–159.

LUCAS, R. E. (1988): "On the Mechanics of Economic Development." *Journal of Monetary Economics* 22, 3–42.

LUCAS, R. E. (1993): "Making a Miracle." *Econometrica* 61, 151–272.

MATSUYAMA, K. (1992): "Agricultural Productivity, Comparative Advantage and Economic Growth." *Journal of Economic Theory* 58, 317–334.

MELITZ, M. J. (2003): "The Impact of Trade on Intra-Industry Reallocations and Aggregate Industry Productivity." *Econometrica* 71, 1695–1725.

MELITZ, M. J. (2005): "When and How Should Infant Industries Be Protected?" *Journal of International Economics* 66, 177–196.

MELITZ, M. J., AND D. TREFLER (2012): "Gains from Trade When Firms Matter." *Journal of Economic Perspectives* 26, 91–118.

MELITZ, M. J., AND S. J. REDDING (2014): "Heterogeneous Firms and Trade," in *Handbook of International Economics*, G. Gopinath, E. Helpman, and K. Rogoff (eds.). Amsterdam: Elsevier, North Holland, vol. 4, chap. 1, 1–54.

NICKELL, S. J. (1996): "Competition and Corporate Performance." *Journal of Political Economy* 104, 724–746.

OHLIN, B. (1924): "The Theory of Trade," in *Heckscher-Ohlin Trade Theory*, H. Flam and M. J. Flanders (eds.). Cambridge, MA: MIT Press.

PERLA, J., C. TONETTI, AND M. E. WAUGH (2021): "Equilibrium Technology Diffusion, Trade and Growth." *American Economic Review* 111, 73–128.

REDDING, S. J. (1999): "Dynamic Comparative Advantage." *Oxford Economic Papers* 51, 15–39.

REDDING, S. J. (2002): "Path Dependence, Endogenous Innovation and Growth." *International Economic Review* 43, 1215–1248.

RICARDO, D. (1817): *On the Principles of Political Economy and Taxation.* London: John Murray.

RIVERA-BATIZ, L., AND P. ROMER (1991): "Economic Integration and Endogenous Growth." *Quarterly Journal of Economics* 106, 531–555.

ROMER, P. (1990): "Endogenous Technical Change." *Journal of Political Economy* 98, 71–102.

SAMPSON, T. (2016): "Dynamic Selection: An Idea Flows Theory of Entry, Trade and Growth." *Quarterly Journal of Economics* 131, 315–380.

SCOTT TAYLOR, M. (1992): "Quality Ladders and Ricardian Trade." *Journal of International Economics* 34, 225–243.

SCOTT TAYLOR, M. (1994): "Once-off and Continuing Gains from Trade." *Review of Economic Studies* 61, 589–601.

SEGERSTROM, P. S., T. ANANT, AND E. DINOPOUIOS (1990): "A Schumpeterian Model of the Product Life Cycle." *American Economic Review* 80, 1077–1092.

SHU, P., AND C. STEINWENDER (2018): "The Impact of Trade Liberalization on Firm Productivity and Innovation." *Innovation Policy and the Economy* 19, 39–68.

SMITH, A. (1776): *An Inquiry into the Nature and Causes of the Wealth of Nations.* London: W. Strahan and T. Cadell.

SOMALE, M. (2021): "Comparative Advantage in Innovation and Production." *American Economic Journal: Macroeconomics* 13(3), 357–396.

UY, T., K.-M. YI, AND J. ZHANG (2012): "Structural Change in an Open Economy." *Journal of Monetary Economics* 60, 667–682.

VENTURA, J. (1997): "Growth and Interdependence." *Quarterly Journal of Economics* 112, 57–84.

VERNON, R. (1966): "International Investment and International Trade in the Product Cycle." *Quarterly Journal of Economics* 80, 190–207.

YANG, M.-J., N. LI, AND K. LORENZ (2021): "The Impact of Emerging Market Competition on Innovation and Business Strategy: Evidence from Canada." *Journal of Economic Behavior & Organization* 181, 117–134.

YEAPLE, S. R. (2005): "A Simple Model of Firm Heterogeneity, International Trade, and Wages." *Journal of International Economics* 65, 1–20.

YOUNG, A. (1991): "Learning by Doing and the Dynamic Effects of International Trade." *Quarterly Journal of Economics* 106, 396–406.

YOUNG, A. (1993): "Growth without Scale Effects." *Journal of Political Economy* 106, 41–63.

ZHELOBODKO, E., S. KOKOVIN, M. PARENTI, AND J. THISSE (2012): "Monopolistic Competition: Beyond the Constant Elasticity of Substitution." *Econometrica* 80, 2765–2784.

PART III

Inequality and Labor Markets

CHAPTER 7

Inequality and Creative Destruction

RICHARD BLUNDELL, XAVIER JARAVEL,
and OTTO TOIVANEN

1 Introduction

The creative destruction paradigm developed by Philippe Aghion and Peter Howitt provides an enormously attractive way of looking at the role of incumbents and entrants and the balance of policies toward innovation, inequality, social mobility, and growth. As can be seen from the string of high-profile empirical papers referenced in this volume, the increasing interplay between theory, data, and policy is reaping returns, uncovering key relationships in the dynamics of innovation, growth, and inequality.

Creative destruction generates inequality between the winners and losers from innovation. The Aghion-Howitt framework posits that this inequality will be concentrated at the top and is largely temporary, with mobility driven by entry and imitation. There is a balance though, and the incumbent beneficiaries of innovation have an incentive to protect their position and restrict the entry of competitors. The resulting inequality can be too high and too persistent, eventually reducing innovation and restricting social mobility and growth. Some inequality may be required to provide incentives to innovate, but there is evidence that the balance is getting worse, with incumbent firms, and wealthy families, gaining a stranglehold on entry and on upward mobility. In this survey chapter, we ask: How can we achieve a better outcome for innovation *and* inequality?

The impact of innovation on inequality will differ, depending on the economic and social institutions in place. The empirical studies we discuss have shown us how the relationship between inequality and innovation depends on the share of higher educated workers and scientists, the level of basic research, the bargaining power of workers, competition policy, patent law, the degree of globalization, the distribution of cognitive and noncognitive skills, the distribution of wealth and access to liquidity, the effective tax rates on rents, and the overall progressivity of the tax and social insurance system. These empirical findings on creative destruction can help inform policy design in a way that maintains, even enhances, the level of innovation with lower levels of inequality and increased social mobility. We argue that judicious choices concerning competition policy and education policy have great potential to achieve this goal.

We present our analysis of inequality and creative destruction in three parts. We begin in Section 2 by uncovering the key pathways from creative destruction to inequality. We review evidence showing that several groups are among the winners of creative destruction; that skills and bargaining power play an important role, as does geography; that especially among those who are not lucky enough to be counted among the winners, the adverse effects can be wider than just monetary (e.g., health); and that the mechanisms through which creative destruction affects individuals include prices and new goods. In Section 3, we examine how inequality can impact innovation. We pay special attention to market size effects, to unequal access to inventive careers (including entrepreneurship), and the role of financial incentives and taxes. And in Section 4, we explore potential policy interventions and highlight the central role of education and competition policy.[1] The former is key to (potentially) providing a level playing field for all individuals capable of invention; the latter plays a central role in keeping in check the forces through which inequality, achieved through invention, may become (too) persistent.

---

[1] For a recent overview of open policy questions related to the economics of innovation, see Bryan and Williams (2021).

2 From Creative Destruction to Inequality and Social Mobility

2.1 Conceptual framework: The winners and losers from creative destruction

2.1.1 The roles of the labor market, business ownership, and the product market

The winners from creative destruction include a wide range of individuals associated with innovation. These include business owners, managers, and stockholders as well as innovators, development scientists, and owners of the innovation. Inequality can also be generated post-innovation from the skill complementarity of the specific innovation. The skill distribution and the degree of bargaining power of workers will also play a key role, with the less-educated workers typically among the losers.

The impact of creative destruction may also be geographically dispersed, generating regional inequality. Firms that are adversely impacted may lie in specific geographical areas, resulting in pockets of deprivation and little local demand for managerial and scientific skills, or frontier firms. The impacts on the individuals and the families in the adversely affected communities can go well beyond income inequalities, exacerbating health inequalities and other social and economic inequalities more broadly. As Aghion et al. (2016) note, job destruction from innovation-led growth can have serious adverse impacts on well-being, the severity of which depends on, among other things, the generosity of social insurance policies.

There can be other important mechanisms that enhance the real incomes of those who have benefited from innovation. For example, recent evidence suggests that the relative price of the goods purchased by richer households has been falling in recent years in the United States, relative to goods purchased by lower-income households, which we discuss further in Section 3.1.[2]

---

[2] The bias of technological change in favor of higher-income consumers could stem from various sources, including skill-biased technological change if income-elastic goods have higher skill intensity.

2.1.2 Persistent inequality? The balance between entry and market power

Persistence in the inequality generated from creative destruction will be a central theme in this chapter. Persistent inequality has the potential to reduce opportunities for future innovators and adversely impact social mobility. The Aghion-Howitt framework recognizes this but suggests that inequality will be concentrated at the top and is largely temporary, with mobility driven by entry and imitation. As Aghion et al. (2021a, 13) put it: "in the short-term, innovation benefits those who generated or enabled it, in the long run innovation rents dissipate due to imitation and creative destruction. In other words, the inequality generated by innovation is temporary." However, the dissipation of rents is not guaranteed. The winners from creative destruction will have every incentive to protect their winning position by preventing new entrants. The winners may also use any political power, generated by their winning position, to lobby for a change in tax policies, patent laws, or competition policy to further protect their position. Incumbent innovators will have an incentive to increase the persistence of inequality, thereby reducing social mobility. Indeed, the winners may choose to use the rents that flow to them to enhance the position of their offspring, thereby prolonging the persistence of inequality across generations. Those adversely impacted could thus face persistent disadvantage.

The standard creative destruction model has a trade-off that determines the degree of inequality and persistence at its heart: A balance between entry and market power. Incumbents can have too much market power, but there can also be too much competition relative to the levels that would maximize innovation. Some market power may be needed to provide incentives for creative entry by new owners, managers, and innovators. But "too much" power in the hands of the incumbents can be used to deter new entrants and reduce innovation in the future. In the inverted-U framework of Aghion et al. (2005), this can be thought of as the wrong side of the inverted-U. In terms of inequality, some inequality may be needed to provide incentives for the owners, managers, and innovators. But the subsequent inequality can be too high and persistent or bring too much power and influence, as the owners of the rents use their income and wealth to keep out new entrants and reduce social mobility, eventually reducing future innovation and growth.

2.1.3 The role of institutions

The impact of innovation on inequality will differ, depending on the economic and social institutions in place. For example, Aghion and Griffith

(2022) note that innovation that takes place in the public sector may be more pro-equality—possibly more likely to foster health innovations and green technologies. Aghion et al. (2021a) note: "The problem with established firms is not solely that they try to prevent the entry of new, innovative firms. There is another problem relating to their conservatism regarding innovation and technical progress." The impact of innovation on inequality will therefore depend on the institutional setting in which the innovation takes place. It will depend on the type of innovation undertaken, the patent law, degree of globalization, the share of higher educated workers and scientists, the distribution of vocational skills, the effective tax rates on rents from innovation, and the overall progressivity of the tax system. Thus, we can ask how to design policy interventions that change the institutional setting toward one where the level of creativity is maintained while innovation results in lower levels of inequality and more social mobility.

In examining the impact of creative destruction on inequality in the remainder of this section, we begin with the impact of innovation on the top incomes and upward mobility. We then look at the impact of innovation on the skill premium and wage inequality, noting the role of frontier versus laggard firms and of the bargaining power of workers. We note that some less-educated workers appear to benefit from technology and innovation. We ask whether there are some skills among such workers that are valued by innovating firms—for these less-educated workers, innovative firms can act as a lever of social mobility. We also look at the impact on the demand for the goods produced by the highly skilled and on the prices of the good purchased by the rich. Finally, we note the potential impact on family incomes at the top and potential impact on the persistence of inequality across generations and on social mobility.

2.2 The impact of innovation on incomes

2.2.1 Innovation and top incomes

Innovators and entrepreneurs certainly show up among top income earners. Using deidentified US tax records including novel linked firm-owner–worker data, Smith et al. (2019, p. 1677) find "a striking world of business owners who prevail at the top of the income distribution." In every top income group and income definition, they find that entrepreneurial income rivals or exceeds both non-owner wage income and non-pass-through capital income. Not all entrepreneurs are innovators; nonetheless, the authors argue that top earners are predominantly "human-capital rich" and that the majority of top income in the United States accrues to the human capital of wage earners and entrepreneurs, not financial capital. Figure 7.1, taken from that study, plots the share of people by their majority income source in the United States. It shows the strongly increasing share of business income in the top share, dominating wage income and income from interest, rents, royalties, estates, and trusts, at the very top. Similar, although less strong, findings have been documented for the United Kingdom in Delestre et al. (2021).

Looking specifically at innovators and top incomes, Aghion et al. (2017) note that in a list of the wealthiest individuals per US state, eleven out of fifty are listed as inventors of a US patent, and many more manage or own firms that patent. Supporting this finding, *Forbes Magazine* reports that eight of the top ten innovators are US based, and a large majority of the top twenty-five richest individuals in the United States are first generation innovators. Germany also has a preponderance of innovators at the top. Figure 7.2, from Aghion et al. (2019) examines the correlation between innovation and the

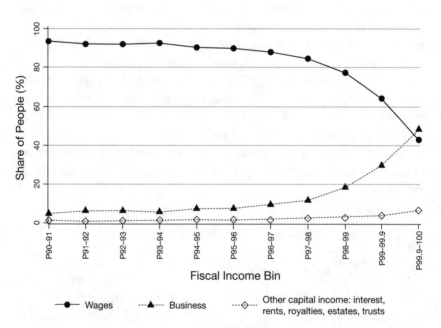

Extracted and reformatted with permission from Oxford University Press Journals from Smith et al. (2019), figure I(A).

Figure 7.1. Entrepreneurial income is a large portion of top incomes

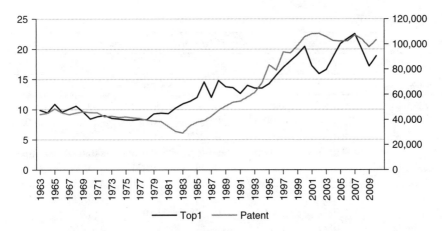

Figure 7.2. Innovation and top 1 percent income share in the United States, 1963–2010

top 1 percent income share in the United States over time. It shows that measures of innovation and top incomes share have also been found to be significantly correlated in the aggregate time series.

To address confounders that could be responsible for the time series relationship between innovation and top incomes displayed in Figure 7.2, Aghion et al. (2019) develop a state-level analysis, reported in Table 7.1. The analysis uses a state level panel to examine the dynamic relationship between top income inequality and innovation. State-level top 1 percent income shares from 1976 (Frank and Goyal, 2009) and patents data from the United States Patent and Trademark Office. Using a number of alternative measures of innovation, the robustness of the effect of innovation of the top income share measure is clear. A long list of control variables are included and the potential endogeneity of patents is allowed for using an instrument that measures the composition of specific appropriation committees. The study also builds a second instrument for state innovation which relies on knowledge spillovers from other states. The results are robust and show a positive and significant causal effect from innovation to top income shares.

Table 7.1. Top 1 percent income share and innovation

Dependent variable	Log of top 1 percent income share					
Measure of innovation	(1) Patents	(2) Cit5	(3) Claims	(4) Generality	(5) Top5	(6) Top1
Innovation	0.031***	0.049***	0.017*	0.024**	0.026***	0.020***
	(0.011)	(0.009)	(0.009)	(0.010)	(0.005)	(0.004)
GDP per capita	0.089**	0.063	0.096**	0.093**	0.074*	0.087**
	(0.043)	(0.044)	(0.045)	(0.043)	(0.043)	(0.043)
Population growth	0.943	1.089	0.943	0.934	0.990	1.074
	(0.654)	(0.700)	(0.651)	(0.647)	(0.690)	(0.685)
Finance	0.080**	0.109***	0.072**	0.078**	0.098***	0.094***
	(0.035)	(0.036)	(0.035)	(0.035)	(0.035)	(0.035)
Government	−0.018	−0.019*	−0.018	−0.018	−0.018	−0.016
	(0.011)	(0.011)	(0.011)	(0.011)	(0.011)	(0.011)
Unemployment	−0.006**	−0.006*	−0.005*	−0.006*	−0.006*	−0.005
	(0.003)	(0.003)	(0.003)	(0.003)	(0.003)	(0.003)
Capital taxes	−0.038***	−0.039***	−0.038***	−0.038***	−0.038***	−0.037***
	(0.004)	(0.004)	(0.004)	(0.004)	(0.004)	(0.004)
Labor taxes	0.017***	0.014**	0.017***	0.018***	0.013**	0.013**
	(0.006)	(0.006)	(0.006)	(0.006)	(0.006)	(0.006)
R^2	0.889	0.896	0.889	0.889	0.895	0.895
Observations	1734	1581	1734	1734	1581	1581

Notes: Innovation is taken in logs and lagged by two years. The dependent variable is the log of the top 1 percent income share. Panel data ordinary least square regressions with state and year fixed effects. Time span for innovation: 1976–2009 (columns 1, 3, and 4) and 1976–2006 (columns 2, 5, and 6). Autocorrelation and heteroskedasticity robust standard errors using the Newey-West variance estimator are presented in parentheses. Respectively, ***, **, and * indicate 0.01, 0.05, and 0.1 levels of significance.

Source: Aghion et al. (2019).

Digging deeper into the mechanism, Aghion et al. (2019) develop a simple extension of the Aghion-Howitt Schumpeterian framework. They derive five main predictions: (i) innovation by both entrants and incumbents increases top income inequality; (ii) the effect of innovation on income inequality is stronger in higher income brackets; (iii) innovation by entrants increases social mobility; (iv) entry barriers lower the positive effect of entrants' innovation on social mobility; and (v) national income shifts away from labor toward firm owners as innovation intensifies. We return to the importance of entrants and the impact on social mobility in Section 2.4. We first examine the distribution of innovation rents within and between firms.

2.2.2 Innovation and wage inequality

Van Reenen (1996) was the first to rigorously establish the positive effect of firm-level innovation on firm-level wages resulting in wage inequality between firms as firms become more dispersed. The distribution of these "innovation rents" across workers in the firm is also likely to increase within-firm wage inequality. To understand some of the key mechanisms involved, Kline et al. (2019) use a careful research design to look at who profits from patents within the firm. The analysis examines how patent-induced shocks to labor productivity propagate into worker earnings. They use linkages between patent applications with business and worker tax records. The results of this work highlight the role of skill complementarities, ownership, and bargaining power. Panel A of Figure 7.3 presents the difference-in-differences estimates of the effect of initial patent allowances on *within-firm* inequality measures. The results imply that the largest earnings effects are concentrated among men and workers in the top half of the earnings distribution. This is paired with corresponding improvements in worker retention among these groups. The authors interpret these earnings responses as reflecting the capture of economic rents by senior workers, who are most costly for innovative firms to replace. Indeed, panel B in Figure 7.3, from the Aghion et al. (2018) study of returns to invention within firms in Finland shows that by far the largest slice of returns to invention go to the entrepreneurs. Also using Finnish data, Aghion et al. (2022a) find that the level of education increases the innovation rents of non-inventing co-workers, but the "distance to human capital frontier," measured as time since obtaining the last degree, reduces innovation rents by some half a percentage point per year.

These findings suggest that separations of key personnel can be extremely costly to innovative firms, even when these employees are not themselves inventors. The fact that seniority appears to mediate the propagation of firm shocks into worker earnings suggests an important role for relationship-specific investments in the generation of labor market rents. More broadly, these results suggest that the influence of firm conditions on worker wages depends critically on the workers' degree of replaceability. This work confirms earlier analyses of the impact of patent applications or patent grants on inventor wages, for example, Toivanen and Väänänen (2016), Depalo and Di Addario (2014), Aghion et al. (2018), and Bell et al. (2019a). In general, inventor earnings are found to be more responsive to patent allowance decisions than are the earnings of non-inventors.

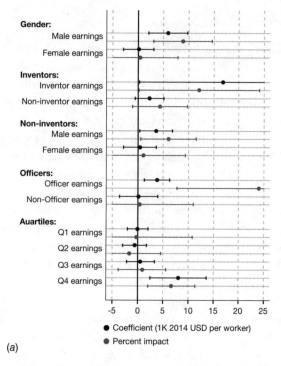

(a)

Reformatted with permission Oxford University Press from Kline et al. (2019), figure VII.

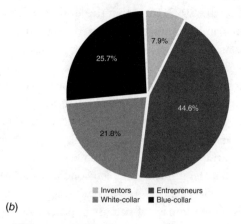

(b)

Reformatted from Aghion et al. (2018), figure 2.

Figure 7.3a–b. Distributional effects of patents: (*a*) The within-firm distribution of profits from patents in the United States, (*b*) Distribution of innovation returns among different workers in the firm in Finland

The impact of technology on task displacement and task replacement is a key idea underlying the task-based approach to inequality of Acemoglu and Restrepo (2021). They argue that when automation displaces unskilled labor from the tasks in which they used to specialize (which has been the modal impact so far), it increases inequality and the demand for skills. New tasks may or may not limit the increase in the demand for skills, depending on whether they mostly targeted at skilled workers. Replacement may be influenced by the duration of the relationship between the worker and firm and a worker's position in the firm hierarchy, issues emphasized in recent empirical studies of wage setting at European firms by Buhai et al. (2014), Jäger and Heining (2019), and Garin and Silverio (2018).

The impact on top income shares and the distributional outcomes within firms paints a rather depressing picture for less-educated workers and those not directly involved with the innovation. However, innovation may not always be bad for the outcomes of lower-educated workers, at least if they have the right skills and are matched with "good" firms. In a study of workers linked to firms and occupational tasks in the United Kingdom, Aghion et al. (2021b) find that less-educated workers engaged in soft skill tasks display, on average, higher wage progression. Figure 7.4 shows the relationship between workers in occupations with high levels of soft skills and wage progression. Drilling down further into this finding, the authors establish that innovating firms, and firms with larger shares of educated workers, value less-educated workers with soft skills. These are skills that complement innovation. Note that this does not mean that cognitive skills do not matter—far from it—rather that soft skills can be an important dimension of the skill set for less-educated workers that is complementary to other firm assets, such as the share of educated workers and the intensity of research and development (R&D).

The impact of innovation will also depend on the impact on the size of the innovating firm, the impact on their costs, and the impact on the prices of consumer products they produce. Using French data, Aghion et al. (2020) examine the impact of automation technologies on employment, wages, prices, and profits. The estimated impact of automation on employment is positive, even for unskilled industrial workers, which suggests that the productivity effects of automation outweigh its potential displacement effects. These authors also find that automation leads to higher profits, lower consumer prices, and higher sales. They note that the industry-level employment response to automation is positive and significant only in industries that face

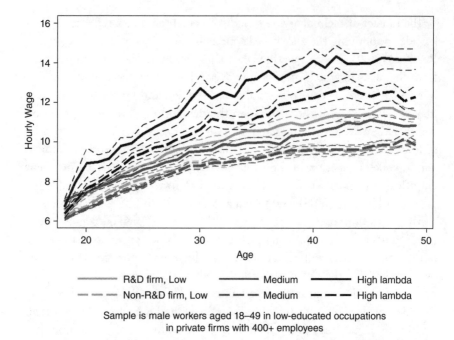

Figure 7.4. Soft skills and wage progression for less-educated workers

international competition. The key mechanism they suggest is via the pass-through of some of the productivity gains to consumers, inducing higher scale and higher employment. The results indicate that automation can increase labor demand and can generate productivity gains that are broadly shared across workers, consumers, and firm owners. This suggests that to measure the full impact on inequality requires the study of the impact on product markets and consumer prices, a theme we return to in the next section.

2.3 Innovation and between-firm inequality

Technological innovation is also associated with the growing inequality between "superstar" firms, reflecting a growing dispersion across firms in productivity, wages, mark-ups, firm size, and labor shares (see Van Reenen, 2018, and de Loecker et al., 2021). These firms appear to exploit increased productivity from innovation and the rents in the product market not only to generate higher profits but sometimes also to pay their workers better. Nonetheless, De Loecker et al. (2020) argue that there is an inverse relation between the firm's mark-up and the labor share. In general, firms that have higher mark-ups spend less on labor. Gabaix et al. (2016) argue that the returns to new technologies accrue not only to innovators, scientists, and owners but also to owners of capital in the form of higher capital incomes, changing the capital income and wealth distribution as well as the balance of power in the product and the labor market.

Eeckhout (2022) notes that in addition to the split of output between profits and labor income, market power also affects labor income inequality between workers. He distinguishes two routes for how market power affects between-worker inequality: profits sharing and monopsony. Market power tilts the split of output toward profits and away from wages. If the worker wage contains a share in profits, then wage inequality will in part be driven by profits. Therefore, an increase in market power leads to an increase in wage inequality. This is obviously the case for managers who get paid in stock options. There is also a positive correlation between a firm's mark-up and the executive pay, indicating that market power drives profits and hence also compensation. But this correlation holds not only for managers: Those in positions with responsibility and who supervise other workers often get paid based on performance and therefore share in the profits of the firm. Market power is not exclusive to the goods market. In the labor market, monopsony power arises when a firm with market power can affect the individual wages of workers in the firm. This leads to a mark-down (equivalent to a mark-up) that drives a wedge between the worker's marginal revenue product and their wage. The higher the monopsony power, the higher the wage mark-down.

Creative destruction can work by knocking out low-productivity firms. Aghion et al. (2008) show that the threat of technologically advanced entry encourages incumbent innovation and productivity growth in sectors that are initially close to the technological frontier, whereas it may discourage incumbents in sectors further behind the frontier; see Figure 7.5. Laggard firms are likely to be geographically concentrated in low-growth/low-wage areas. Creative destruction stimulates growth in firms in thriving areas with higher-skilled workers, increasing top incomes and geographical inequality.

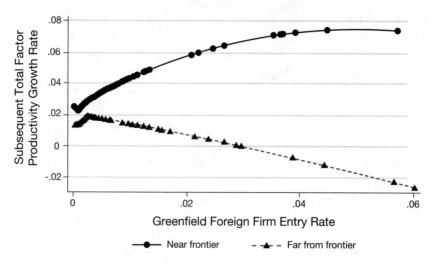

Reformatted from Aghion et al. (2008), figure 1.

Figure 7.5. Reactions to entry in incumbents near and far from the technology frontier

2.4 Creative destruction, social mobility, and persistent inequality

In the short-term, innovation benefits those who generated and enabled it. In the long run, we might hope that more innovation will raise macro-growth, reducing prices and raising equilibrium productivity and wages. Indeed, the theory of creative destruction predicts that rents will be dissipated through imitation and that innovation by entrants increases social mobility. As Aghion et al. (2021a, 13) put it: "in the short-term, innovation benefits those who generated or enabled it, in the long run innovation rents dissipate due to imitation and creative destruction. In other words, the inequality generated by innovation is temporary." However, creative destruction also predicts that entry barriers lower the positive effect of entrants' innovation on social mobility, increasing the persistence of inequality.

Social mobility and the dissipation of rents are not guaranteed. The winners from creative destruction will have every incentive to protect their winning position by preventing new entrants of competitors and shielding their rents (e.g., lobbying for a change in tax policies, in patent laws or competition policy, in labor laws, in social insurance, and in education policies). The reduced social mobility and restrictions on access eventually reduce innovation, further limiting opportunities for the losers and holding back general productivity.

Empirical results suggest that innovation is positively associated with social mobility, but lobbying is shown to dampen the impact of innovation on social mobility by reducing entry. Table 7.2, taken from Aghion et al. (2019), examines the impact of various innovation measures on social mobility, in which social mobility measures are taken when a person is 30 years old between 2011 and 2012 compared to his or her parents during 1996–2000. A comparison of the first two columns of results shows a stronger effect of entrants. The final columns show that this impact is driven by entrants when there are lower levels of lobbying by incumbents.

Persistent inequality is equivalent to inequality with low social mobility. Reducing persistence of inequality and enhancing social mobility while maintaining creative innovation is central to the policy implications of the creative destruction framework—encouraging new ideas and new innovations while preventing persistence and stagnation.

Many factors can impact the persistence of inequality following an innovation, for example, low competition, poor patent design, excessive entry barriers or harmful business lobbying. Are there changes in policy and institutional reforms that can change the balance, reducing inequality while encouraging innovation and social mobility—changing institutions and incentives?

The key therefore is to get the skill-firm match right. Warehouse jobs may be bad jobs, in terms of wage progression and career prospects, for less-educated workers. Skills policy for the less educated should go hand in hand with technology and innovation. By focusing on skills that are complementary to innovation and to higher-educated workers, a carefully chosen skills policy can mediate the impact of creative destruction on less-educated workers.

There is a parallel to the discussion of creative destruction and social mobility in the parenting and education "meritocracy" debate. In the first round of meritocracy, starting from an equal opportunity initial condition, the "more able" do best and earn more income. Assortative mating concentrates success in parents who invest in their kids and begin to undo the equal initial conditions for the next generation, reducing social mobility. Parents invest in schools, peers, neighborhoods, etc., deterring the "entry" and the social mobility of children whose parents are less advantaged.

Table 7.2. Top 1 percent income share, innovation, and the role of lobbying intensity

Dependent variable	Log of top 1 percent income share					
	(1)	(2)	(3)	(4)	(5)	(6)
Measure of innovation	Patents	Cit5	Claims	Patents	Cit5	Claims
Innovation						
by entrants	0.905***	0.527**	0.837***			
	(0.000)	(0.014)	(0.000)			
by incumbents				0.246	0.196	0.307*
				(0.172)	(0.312)	(0.091)
Lobbying × innovaton						
by entrants	−0.051***	−0.030**	−0.048***			
	(0.000)	(0.015)	(0.000)			
by incumbents				−0.016	−0.011	−0.019*
				(0.132)	(0.320)	(0.073)
Lobbying	−0.305	−0.151	−0.095	−0.053	−0.100	−0.079
	(0.245)	(0.468)	(0.683)	(0.813)	(0.631)	(0.707)
GDP per capita	0.107	0.014	0.105	0.095	−0.013	0.091
	(0.384)	(0.924)	(0.397)	(0.473)	(0.929)	(0.482)
Population growth	0.401	−0.146	0.379	0.640	0.150	0.622
	(0.738)	(0.897)	(0.754)	(0.613)	(0.902)	(0.622)
Finance	−0.021	−0.062	−0.027	−0.019	−0.057	−0.018
	(0.726)	(0.326)	(0.663)	(0.749)	(0.348)	(0.754)
Government	−0.107*	−0.189***	−0.108*	−0.117*	−0.221***	−0.115*
	(0.085)	(0.006)	(0.086)	(0.066)	(0.001)	(0.064)
Unemployment	−0.010**	−0.022***	−0.010**	−0.011**	−0.023***	−0.011**
	(0.026)	(0.000)	(0.023)	(0.016)	(0.000)	(0.015)
Capital taxes	−0.013**	−0.014**	−0.012**	−0.013**	−0.015***	−0.013**
	(0.025)	(0.012)	(0.028)	(0.023)	(0.010)	(0.022)
Labor taxes	−0.002	0.003	−0.003	−0.002	0.003	−0.002
	(0.840)	(0.815)	(0.815)	(0.844)	(0.811)	(0.884)
R^2	0.684	0.739	0.685	0.678	0.734	0.677
Observations	714	561	714	714	561	714

Notes: Other variable descriptions are given in Table 7.1. Innovation is taken in logs and lagged by two years. Columns 1–3 consider entrant innovation, whereas columns 4–6 consider incumbent innovations. The dependent variable is taken in logs. Panel data ordinary least square regressions with state and year fixed effects. Time span for innovation: 1996–2009 (columns 1, 3, 4, and 6) and 1996–2005 (columns 2 and 5). Autocorrelation and heteroskedasticity robust standard errors using the Newey-West variance estimator are presented in parentheses. Respectively, ***, **, and * indicate 0.01, 0.05, and 0.1 levels of significance.

Source: Aghion et al. (2019).

It seems indisputable that any society would want parents to invest in their children's education but would also want to develop the skills of the most able children, whatever their background. Increased inequality in a winner-takes-all society and skill-biased technological change increase the returns to education, and child investments more generally, providing further incentives for successful parents to invest in their own kids' success. At the same time, the overall productive quality of labor may decline due to increasing mismatch. Society can change the equilibrium by investing in subsidized/public education provision directed at skills that can produce the next generation of innovators. Redistribution also can help by providing the resources for less-privileged parents. By increasing the pool of potential innovators, such policies can increase social mobility and enhance overall productivity. We return to this idea below in Section 4.

3 From Inequality to Creative Destruction

Recent work characterizes the impact of several types of inequality on the rate and direction of creative destruction. Two main channels have been investigated: (i) how inequality in disposable income affects the direction of innovation; and (ii) how unequal access to careers in entrepreneurship and innovation across socio-demographic groups affects both the rate and the direction of innovation. Moreover, recent work shows that the impact of financial incentives and top tax rates on creative destruction is nuanced.

3.1 Due to market size effects, rising income inequality endogenously leads to "pro-rich" product innovations

A longstanding literature on endogenous innovation shows that market size creates incentives for innovation and entry (e.g., Aghion and Howitt, 1996). Growing markets make it worthwhile to pay the fixed costs necessary to innovate, reduce marginal costs, and enter new markets. The idea that larger market size leads to endogenous productivity gains goes back to the seminal work of Linder (1961) and Schmookler (1957). However, it is only recently that the literature has examined the implications of increasing returns and the market size channel for inequality.

Jaravel (2019) estimates the causal relationship between market size and consumer prices, links changes in market size across product categories to changes in the (nominal) income distribution, and quantifies the implications for purchasing power inequality. The starting point of this analysis is that many product markets target different populations of consumers. For example, scotch and tobacco have very different income elasticities. In the context of economic growth and rising income inequality, for example in a country like the United States, demand grows faster for premium (income-elastic) products. Consequently, there are financial incentives for innovation and entry to occur primarily for income-elastic products. These dynamics have the potential to reduce prices for existing products in these fast-growing premium categories, which are predominantly consumed by high-income households. Jaravel (2019) conducts several empirical tests showing the relevance of these mechanisms, primarily by using barcode-level scanner data covering the US retail sector between 2004 and 2015.

Figure 7.6 shows that higher-income households experienced a faster increase in product variety (panel A) and lower inflation in the US retail sector (panel B) from 2004 to 2015. Consistent with these findings, in related work using national accounts data covering the entire US economy, Boppart and Weiss (2013) show that total factor productivity growth is higher in more income-elastic sectors.

Can the equilibrium response of innovation to faster growth in demand from high-income consumers explain the patterns of differential inflation and increase in product variety? It is well documented that in recent decades, the share of US national income accruing to high-income consumers has steadily increased. As a result, the relative demand for income-elastic goods has increased. To estimate the causal effect of growing demand on product entry and equilibrium prices, Jaravel (2019) develops a shift-share research design. This design combines two components: (i) predetermined spending shares across the product space and various socio-demographic groups, and (ii) heterogeneity in the population growth rates for these various groups during the sample period. As age groups, education groups, racial groups, and regional populations have different spending shares across products, variation in the size of these groups over time generates changes in demand.

Figure 7.7 reports the reduced-form specification of this instrumental variable (IV), which draws out a downward-sloping supply curve. The IV estimate shows that increases in demand lead to a large fall in prices and increases in product variety. In Figure 7.7, the constant elasticity of substitution (CES) price index accounts for changes in product variety and measures the change in welfare stemming both from product variety and from price

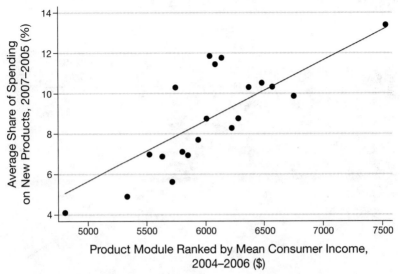

Coeff. 3.044*** s.e. (1.103)
Standard error clustered at the level of 1014 product modules

(a)

Reformatted from Jaravel (2019), figure 2, panel A.

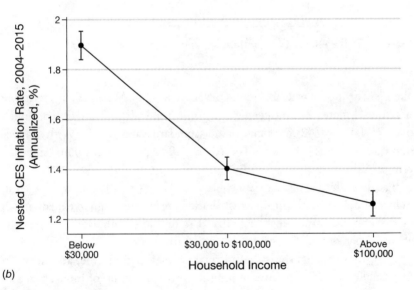

(b)

Reformatted from Jaravel (2019), figure 1, panel A.

Figure 7.6a–b. High-income consumers benefit from a faster increase in product variety and lower inflation: (*a*) Household income and increase in product variety, (*b*) Household income and inflation

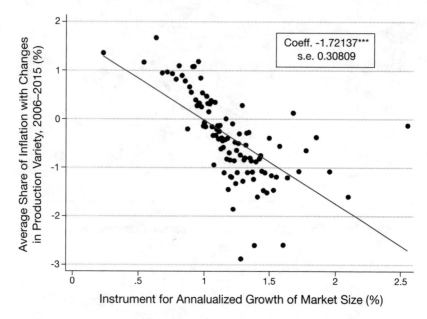

Reformatted from Jaravel (2019), figure V(C).

Figure 7.7. The effect of changes in demand on inflation and product variety

changes for products available in consecutive years. When the growth rate of demand increases by 1 percentage point, the inflation rate for continued products falls by 0.42 percentage points (standard error = 0.139). With changes in product variety, inflation falls further, by 0.62 percentage points (standard error = 0.258).

Based on the IV estimates, a calibration shows that changes in demand induced by shifts in the income distribution are large enough to explain much of the observed inflation inequality. The predicted inflation difference is about 70 percent of the observed inflation difference.

Thus, these results show that inequality in earned income, and hence in disposable income, can have an impact on the direction of innovation and lead to an amplification of inequality in purchasing power and welfare. These findings stand in contrast with a long tradition that emphasized the idea that all consumers benefit from innovation thanks to the "product cycle," the idea that high-income consumers may be targeted first but that the new products are soon brought to the mass market (e.g., Hayek, 1931; Schumpeter, 1942;

Vernon, 1966). In fact, the product cycle is not the only important force at play. Certain markets are clearly segmented such that there is no product cycle between them (e.g., scotch and tobacco), and they cater to households with different income levels. In the context of rising inequality, the segmentation of product markets leads to a feedback loop between income inequality and purchasing power inequality through market size and the endogenous direction of product innovations.

3.2 The choice of a science or innovation career is largely influenced by social backgrounds, which affects both the rate and direction of innovation

3.2.1 Who becomes an inventor?

Career choice is another important channel whereby inequality shapes the rate and direction of innovation. A recent and rapidly growing strand of literature documents the social origins of individuals who contribute to economic growth by pursuing careers in science, entrepreneurship, or innovation. The literature to date has studied a large number of countries and proxies that measure innovation, and it delivers a consistent message: There is a large pool of untapped talent, individuals who could have contributed to raising economic growth but did not choose an innovator's career. Although this research agenda has only recently used large-scale data sets, its roots go to the 1950s, when Schmookler (1957) laid out the main research questions and even back to the 1930s, when Rossman (1931) studied the motivations of inventors.

Figure 7.8 reports some of the key stylized facts from this recent literature. Panel A reports the key finding of Agarwal and Gaule (2020), who use data from the International Mathematical Olympiad (IMO) and show that talented students born in poorer countries are systematically less likely to enter a research career, as measured by the share getting a PhD in mathematics. IMO participants from low-income countries produce 34 percent fewer publications and 56 percent fewer citations than equally talented youth from high-income countries. Policies that can help talented youth from low-income countries to pursue scientific careers could have a large impact on knowledge creation.

The idea that there is untapped potential is also confirmed by country-specific studies. Panel B of Figure 7.8 examines the United States, reporting the propensity to become a patent inventor depending on parents' income

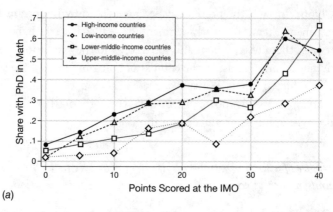

(a)

Reformatted from Agarwal and Gaule (2020), figure 3. Copyright American Economic Association; reproduced with permission of the *American Economic Review: Insights*.

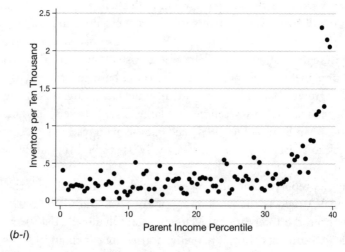

(b-i)

Reformatted from Akcigit et al. (2017), figure 21.

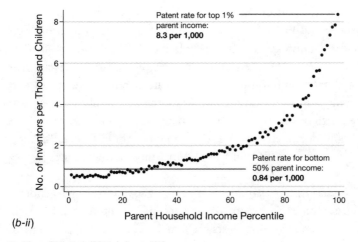

(b-ii)

Reformatted from Bell et al. (2019a), figure I(A).

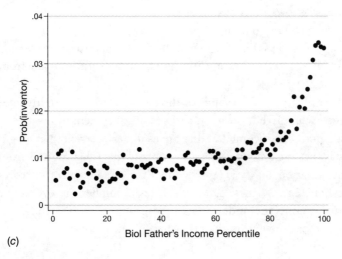

(c)

Reformatted from Aghion et al. (2017), figure 1C.

Figure 7.8a–c. Unequal access to science and innovation careers around the world and over time: (*a*) Share getting a PhD in mathematics across country income groups depending on rank at the International Mathematical Olympiad (IMO), (*bi–bii*) Evidence from patent inventors in the United States, (*c*) Evidence from patent inventors in Finland

percentiles. The patterns are very similar both using historical records, as in Akcigit et al. (2019), who study the United States over the period 1880–1940, and modern administrative data, as in Bell et al. (2019a) who study the United States after 1980. There is a strong convex relationship between parent income and patent innovation: Children with parents in the top 1 percent of the income distribution are ten times more likely to become inventors than children with below-median-income parents. As shown on panel C, Aghion et al. (2018) document a very similar relationship in Finland using data on men born between 1961 and 1984, with most parents born in the 1940s and 1950s.

Bell et al. (2019a) also document large gaps by race and gender: White children are three times more likely to become inventors than Black children, and only 18 percent of inventors are female. They show that the gender gap in innovation is shrinking gradually over time. However, at the current rate, it would take another 118 years to reach gender parity.

Figure 7.9 shows that unequal access to innovation in the United States persists even conditional on test scores and for the most impactful innovations. Panel A shows that children at the top of their third-grade math class are much more likely to become inventors, but only if they come from high-income families.

Panel B of Figure 7.9 examines the social origins of highly cited "star inventors," who drive innovation and growth. Women, minorities, and individuals from low-income families are as underrepresented among star inventors as they are among average inventors. Given the findings from panel A that innovation ability (as proxied by third-grade math test scores) does not vary much across these groups, this result implies there are many "lost Einsteins" among the underrepresented groups—people who could have had high-impact inventions had they become inventors.

3.2.2 How large are the implications for aggregate innovation and long-run growth?

To assess the amount of lost innovation due to unequal access to innovation careers, Bell et al. (2019a) carry out a simple reweighting exercise. If women, minorities, and children from low-income (bottom 80 percent) families invented at the same rate as white men from high-income (top 20 percent) families, there would be 4.04 times as many inventors in the United States as there are today. This simple calculation illustrates that leveraging the pool

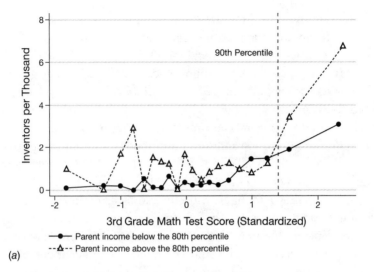

(a)

Reformatted from Bell et al. (2019a), figure IV(A).

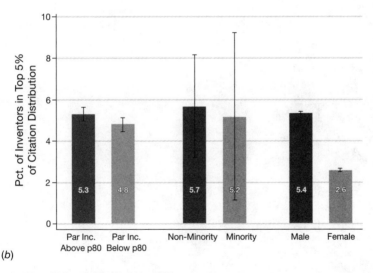

(b)

Reformatted from Bell et al. (2019a), figure XI(B).

Figure 7.9a–b. Unequal access to innovation conditional on test scores and for the most impactful innovations: (*a*) Third-grade math test scores and propensity to become a patent inventor, (*b*) Citations of inventors by characteristics at birth

of untapped talent—the "extensive margin" of the supply of inventors—could be a powerful approach to increase aggregate innovation.

Is this conclusion robust to general equilibrium effects? Einiö et al. (2022) build a dynamic general equilibrium model with endogenous growth, in which a part of the population (called the "minority" group) is subject to barriers to access innovation. The model features many sectors, heterogeneity in research productivity and consumer tastes, entry barriers that vary across socio-demographic groups, and social interactions between groups that can alleviate these barriers. Calibrating the model to the US economy, they find a large impact of reducing unequal access to innovation on the steady-state growth rate. As shown in Figure 7.10, eliminating completely the access barriers would lead to an increase in the long-run growth rates from 2 percent (in the current equilibrium) to about 4 percent (in the counterfactual equilibrium with no access barriers). Thus, misallocation of talent in the innovation sector can affect long-run growth rates. These results complement those of Hsieh et al. (2019), who quantify the impact on welfare of misallocation of talent.

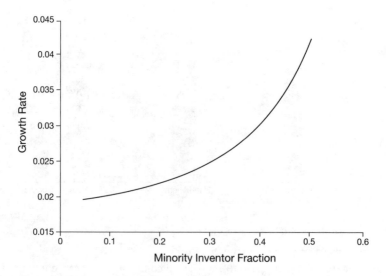

Reformatted from Einiö et al. (2022), figure 8, panel A left.

Figure 7.10. Predicted impact of equalizing access to innovation on the long-run growth rate in an endogenous growth model

Together, these results highlight the importance of a set of policies that can harness the underutilized talent, both within and across countries. Targeting exposure programs to children from underrepresented groups who excel in math and science at early ages is likely to maximize their impacts.

3.2.3 Implications for the direction of innovation

Recent work shows that the social environment influences not just whether a child grows up to become an inventor but also the types of inventions they produce and the types of customers they target. Figure 7.11 reports these findings. As shown in panel A, Bell et al. (2019a) find that children whose parents hold patents in a certain technology class (e.g., amplifiers) are more likely to patent in exactly that field themselves rather than in other closely related fields (e.g., antennas).

Einiö et al. (2022) examine whether innovators' social backgrounds have an impact on the target markets they pursue, which in turn could affect welfare inequality through purchasing power. An individual's background and social experiences may affect the types of problems and customer needs they are familiar with, and thus the kinds of innovations they might bring to market. Indeed, the discovery of entrepreneurial opportunities depends on the distribution of information in society (Hayek, 1945) and often requires engagement with specific real-world problems and users (Von Hippel, 1986).

To assess the empirical relevant of this hypothesis, Einiö et al. (2022) build a data set linking consumer characteristics to innovators' parental income, age, and gender. They find that innovators from a high-income family are more likely to create products purchased by high-income consumers. As shown in Panel B of Figure 7.11, entrepreneurs from high-income families are less likely to get a patent or start a firm in a "necessity" industry (like food) but are more likely to do so in a "luxury" industry (like finance). Moreover, they find that female consumers are significantly more likely to purchase products from startups that were founded by female entrepreneurs. For example, Panel C considers phone applications: female-founded phone applications-startups have an 8.2 percentage points higher female market share relative to their male counterparts, on a baseline of about 54 percent. Thus, there are clear homophily patterns between innovators and their consumers both across and within industries.

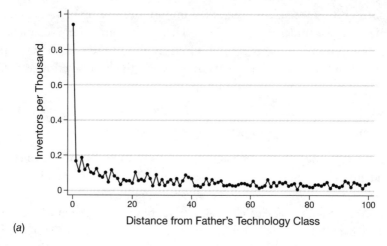

(a)

Reformatted from Bell (2019a), figure VII(A).

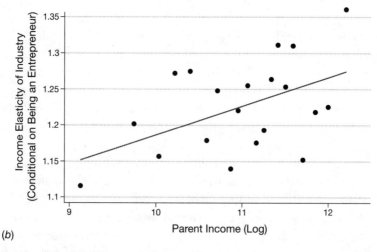

(b)

Reformatted from Einiö et al. (2022), figure 1, panel B.

Einiö et al. (2022) also document that innovators' characteristics may affect the rate of "green innovations." As shown in Table 7.3, female inventors as well as young inventors are more likely to invent "green" patents (using the classifications of Aghion et al., 2016), that is, to have positive environmental externalities: 6.5 percent of inventors of clean patents are female, as opposed to 2.8 percent for dirty patents. Younger inventors are also more likely to

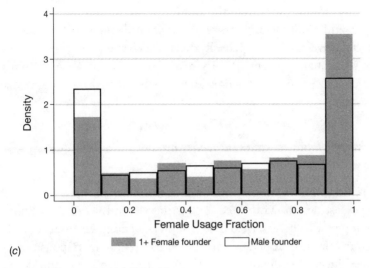

(c)

Reformatted from Einiö et al. (2022), figure 3A.

Figure 7.11a–c. Innovators' backgrounds and the direction of innovation in the United States: (*a*) Patent rates by distance from father's technology class for children of inventors, (*b*) Entrepreneur's parental income and industry income elasticity, (*c*) Female user fraction versus founder gender for phone applications

Table 7.3. Green innovations are more frequent for female and younger inventors

	Clean patent	
	(1)	*(2)*
Female inventor	0.326***	−0.001*
	(0.014)	(0.0006)
Mean	0.286	0.132
N	53,984	1,243

Respectively, ***, **, and * indicate 0.01, 0.05, and 0.1 levels of significance.
Source: Einiö et al. (2022).

patent in clean energy technologies, with a 0.1 percentage point decrease in the propensity to work on clean patents for one year's increase in age.

Similarly, Koning et al. (2020) study biomedical patents and find that increasing the share of female inventors shifts the supply of inventions toward the needs of women. According to their estimates, moving a disease-technology area from the average (10 percent female-led) to gender parity would result in 23.4 percent of inventions being female focused. Relative to the average of 18.5 percent, this is a 25 percent increase.

Thus, inequality of opportunity may play a crucial role in shaping the direction of creative destruction and who benefits from product-market innovation.

3.3 Are high levels of income inequality necessary to incentivize innovators?

There is an active debate about the role of top income inequality in spurring creative destruction, with three contrasting views: Low marginal tax rates at the top may be necessary to induce sufficient entrepreneurial effort; however, intrinsic motivation and career choices may not be responsive to such financial incentives; finally, the rate and direction of innovation depends more broadly on the entire structure of the tax system and not merely on top tax rates.

3.3.1 Low marginal tax rates on top incomes create financial incentives for entrepreneurs

A large literature highlights that creating financial incentives for entrepreneurs may be necessary to induce entrepreneurial effort and spur creative destruction. According to this view, since entrepreneurs and innovators are typically at the very top of the earnings distribution, low marginal tax rates on top incomes may be necessary to sustain innovation and growth, implying lower redistribution and higher disposable income inequality. For example, Jones (2022) considers an optimal taxation model based on this channel. He finds that this channel sharply reduces the optimal tax rate on top incomes. For this mechanism to operate, it should not be possible to target innovation with a separate research subsidy.

3.3.2 Intrinsic motivation and the choice to become an innovator appear to be largely responsive to marginal tax rates on top incomes

Another line of work suggests that high top income shares may not be necessary to sustain innovation. Indeed, innovators often have an "intrinsic motivation" to advance the knowledge frontier rather than being led by financial motives alone. This idea is not new to the literature: Rossman (1931) studied the motivation of inventors by surveying US (patent) inventors: "Love of inventing" gained 193 (22 percent) mentions from the 710 responding inventors "most active and important in this country" (p. 522), with an average of 39.3 patents. The second-most often mentioned motivation was "Desire to improve" with 189 (21 percent) mentions. "Financial gain" came third, among nine active choices, with 167 (19 percent) mentions.

Recent studies have deepened our understanding of the relevance of this channel. For example, Stern (2004) shows empirically that scientists accept lower salaries to work in research labs that give them more freedom over the choice of their research agenda. From a related theoretical perspective, Lockwood et al. (2017) study how taxation affects the allocation of talented individuals across professions. They show that, by blunting material incentives to enter high-paying occupations, high taxation magnifies the nonpecuniary incentives of pursuing a "calling." From that perspective, high marginal tax rates on top incomes may help direct the most talented toward careers promoting creativity, research, and innovation.

Standard neoclassical models of career choice deliver the same message: Changes in marginal tax rates on top incomes appear to have a limited impact on the decision to become an innovator. Indeed, if the returns to innovation are forecastable at the point of career choice, tax policies would only induce inventors of marginal quality to enter the field rather than star inventors, who are responsible for most innovations. Jaimovich and Rebelo (2017) establish this result in a neoclassical model of career choice with heterogeneous and known innovation abilities. Furthermore, Bell et al. (2019b) show that, even when innovation abilities are heterogeneous and unknown at the time of career choice, the elasticity of innovation with respect to top income tax rates is likely to be small in a standard expected utility model. Indeed, top income tax changes only affect payouts when inventors have very high incomes and low marginal utility.

Figure 7.12, taken from Bell et al. (2019b), focuses on the case where heterogeneity in inventors' incomes is unknown. In this setting, as the skewness of stochastic shocks rises, both the elasticities of the number of inventors and quality-weighted innovation with respect to tax rates converge to zero if agents are risk averse. To illustrate the logic underlying this result, consider an example with two states of the world: a bad state in which innovation has zero return and a good state in which innovation has a large payoff (e.g., $10 million). In the bad state, taxes have no impact on utility. In the good state, a smaller payout (e.g., $9 million instead of $10 million) would not significantly

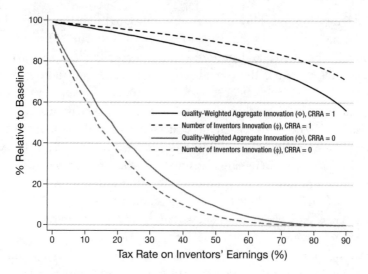

Reformatted from Bell et al. (2019b), figure IV(B).

Figure 7.12. Predicted impact of tax rates on innovation in a neoclassical model of career choice

reduce an agent's incentive to become an inventor, because the marginal utility of consumption is already low. Intuitively, when returns are very skewed, taxes only affect inventors' payoffs when they are very rich and are not sensitive to financial incentives, resulting in small behavioral responses. Put another way, when innovation has very risky payoffs, inventors must enter innovation partly because of its nonmonetary benefits and due to intrinsic motivation, making their behavior less sensitive to financial incentives.

Thus, low taxes on top income may not be necessary to attract talented individuals into innovators' careers, both when heterogeneous abilities are known or are uncertain. Although empirical evidence supporting these model-based predictions remains scant to date, these results call for a cautious assessment of the impacts of financial incentives and a greater focus on alternative policies to increase the supply of inventors, for example, through education and mentorship.

3.3.3 Due to market size effects, the rate and direction of innovation depends on the entire tax system, not only on top tax rates

Because innovators are typically at the top of the income distribution, the debate on financial incentives and innovation often focuses on top tax rates.

However, recent work highlights that the incentives to innovate depend more broadly on the entire tax system. Tax rates along the income distribution and the amount of redistribution change the relative market size of necessities and luxuries, which governs the financial incentives to innovate toward luxuries or necessities. Jaravel and Olivi (2021) study this channel in a model of optimal redistribution taxation à la Mirrlees (1971) with non-homothetic preferences, segmented markets, and increasing returns to scale consistent with empirical evidence (i.e., an increase in market size leads to a fall in the price index through endogenous innovation and entry). They show that endogenous innovations and price changes affect the marginal utility of disposable income and generate income effects such that it is optimal to increase redistribution toward households with a higher marginal propensity to spend on goods with falling relative prices. For example, an increase in redistribution to low-income households increases the market size of necessity products, whose prices fall because of endogenous innovations targeting necessities. As a result, the social marginal utility of redistributing an additional dollar to low-income groups increases, because they face lower prices and therefore a larger utility increase from additional spending. This endogenous increase in the value of redistribution at the bottom leads to more redistribution, which amplifies the endogenous innovation reducing the costs of necessities, hence the value of further redistribution toward low-income groups, and so on. This channel shows that the relationship between income inequality and creative destruction is nuanced—more redistributive tax systems may redirect innovation toward necessities and thus promote inclusive growth.

4 Innovation Policies and Inequality

The previous sections have highlighted how a variety of channels may affect both innovation and inequality. We now examine which policies have the most potential to achieve better outcomes for both innovation and inequality.

4.1 Broadening the toolkit of innovation policies

Any analysis of how innovation policies may affect not only innovation but also inequality necessitates that one defines what is meant by "innovation policies" and clearly delineates what types of inequality are taken into consideration. Traditionally, economists have viewed innovation policy to consist mostly of public funding of private R&D in one way or another, and intellectual property protection. Current practice is one justification for this view, as other potential tools (e.g., prizes and contests, public procurement, and promotion of research joint ventures) have largely played a secondary role.

The traditional approach is however unnecessarily narrow: A broader view considers any policy that has an impact on the innovative potential of an economy as part of innovation policy.[3] This approach brings into consideration education policy; basic research, taxation, competition policy; immigration rules; trade policy; and potentially other policies, too. We argue that, especially when the attention is aimed at the effects of innovation on inequality, the emphasis should be on indirect policies, and on education and competition policy in particular. This argument rests partly on the view that the two most important dimensions of inequality that one should consider when designing innovation policy are income inequality and inequality in market outcomes (i.e., the possibility that even those incumbents who rose to prominence on the strength of their innovativeness may over time become entrenched, at the expense of potential newcomers and thereby the society at large).[4] The latter dimension is important primarily as it eventually may feed into the first dimension.

Given this choice, we do not discuss direct innovation policies but instead concentrate on the role of education and the role of competition policy.[5] In the next section, we discuss the role of education before turning to competition policy in the following one.

---

[3] Takalo and Toivanen (2016) make a distinction between direct (government funding of private R&D, intellectual property protection, etc.) and indirect innovation policies. Without making such a clear categorization, Bloom et al. (2019) also consider a broader array of policies than the direct or traditional ones when discussing a "toolkit" for innovation policy (see also Van Reenen, 2021). They, too, point out that (certain) education policies improve innovation and reduce inequality.

[4] This choice obviously can be criticized. An obvious criticism is that with this choice, we sidestep the important question of gender inequality in invention. It is well documented that women are badly underrepresented in invention. An emerging literature tackles both the challenges along the educational path (Hoisl et al., 2020) as well as in research (Kim and Moser, 2021) that women face. Toivanen and Väänänen (2016) find that once they control for (endogenous) education, there are no gender differences in the probability of becoming an inventor, even though less than 10 percent of inventors in their data are female.

[5] Bloom et al. (2019) and Takalo and Toivanen (2016) are two recent surveys of the academic literature related to innovation policy widely defined. A distinction between them is that the latter authors discuss the differences between a large (closed) economy and a small open economy.

4.2 Education and invention

4.2.1 The causal effect of access to education on innovation

There are several interlinked arguments that suggest that one should view education as part of innovation policy. The most important one is that the advances in technology notwithstanding, invention is still a human activity. The second argument is that data strongly suggest that modern-day innovation requires specific training and human capital. The final argument has to do with our emphasis on the effects of innovation and policy on inequality: The educational system plays an important role in enabling or hindering social mobility.[6]

At least since the late nineteenth century, inventors have been highly educated (though not necessarily so earlier; see Khan and Sokoloff, 2004). Modern data show irrefutably that invention is to a large extent the prerogative of those with the right education. Giuri et al. (2007), using data from the European-wide PatVal survey, document that 77 percent of inventors have at least a master's degree and 26 percent a PhD. Similar descriptive statistics have been reported for non-European countries (e.g., Onishi and Nagaoka, 2012). Toivanen and Väänänen (2016) find that in late twentieth-century Finland, engineers dominate patenting. Figure 7.13 from Aghion et al. (2017) displays how the probability of becoming an inventor is related to one's own education in Finland. What emerges strongly from the figure is that having a STEM education in general (the lighter bars), and a high STEM education in particular is strongly associated with the probability of becoming an inventor.

The relation between STEM (or more narrowly, engineering) education and invention has not gone unnoticed by policymakers. Developing countries, India and China in the vanguard, have invested heavily in engineering education in the past few decades; and a perennial worry in the United States is that the drawing power of STEM studies is waning (e.g., Task Force on the Future of American Innovation).

A key question regarding the undisputed positive association between education and invention is whether there is a causal relationship. This is of first-order importance for policy: If the relationship is purely an association,

---

[6] In line with most of the literature, we mean inventors of patented inventions when we talk about inventors. This is an obvious limitation of the literature, this chapter included.

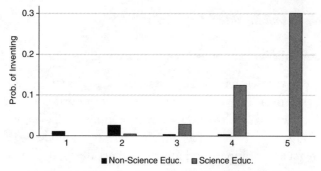

NOTE: 1 = base educ. 2 = secondary 3 = college 4 = master 5 = PhD

Notes: The figure displays the probability of inventing conditional on the education of the individual. We divide education into five groups by level of education (up to nine years, depending on age of parent): secondary, tertiary, MSc, and PhD. We also condition all other levels of education but base education on a parent having a STEM education. A STEM base education does not exist. We measure education at age 35.

Reformatted from Aghion et al. (2017), figure 10.

Figure 7.13. Own education and the probability of inventing

it would imply that the role of (STEM/engineering) education is to act as a sieve, catching as many individuals as possible who possess the capacity to become inventors. If the relationship is causal, it opens the door for a potentially large improvement in the inventive capacity of a society as the number of inventors can be increased much more.

Toivanen and Väänänen (2016) provide the first evidence that the relationship may be causal. Using the distance to the nearest (technical) university at the age of nineteen years as an instrument and leveraging the expansion of the Finnish university system in the 1950s and 1960s, they find that obtaining a university (MSc) engineering education increases the probability of becoming an inventor by 5 percentage points. Compared to the share of inventors in the population at large, which is about 1 percent (see Aghion et al., 2022b), this effect is obviously very large.

A related stylized fact is the relationship between parental education and invention, which is illustrated in Figure 7.14 (Aghion et al., 2018; see also Aghion et al., 2022b). This figure shows how the probability of becoming an inventor grows steeply with both maternal and paternal education, and in particular, with the STEM education of the parents.

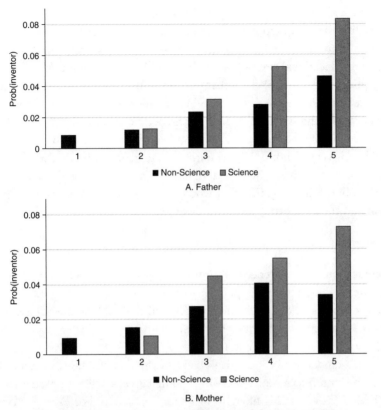

NOTE: 1 = base educ. 2 = secondary 3 = college 4 = master 5 = PhD

Notes: The figure displays the probability of inventing conditional on the education of the father (A) and mother (B). We divide parents into five groups by level of education: base education (up to nine years, depending on age of parent), secondary, tertiary, MSc, and PhD. We also condition all other levels of education but base education on a parent having a STEM education. A STEM base education does not exist. Parental education is measured in 1975 unless unavailable, in which case 1985 data is used.

Reformatted from Aghion et al. (2017), figure 5.

Figure 7.14. Parental education status and becoming an inventor

There is thus evidence supporting the view that increasing the number of individuals who obtain a STEM/engineering degree will increase invention. There is also evidence that invention increases both the inventing individuals' income (see Toivanen and Väänänen, 2012; Bell et al., 2019b), and that of their coworkers (Van Reenen, 1996; Aghion et al., 2018; Kline et al., 2019;

Aghion et al., 2022a). Regarding the relation between invention and income inequality, the key question then becomes access to education. From the point of view of invention and that of enhancing intergenerational mobility, equal access to educational tracks that lead to a STEM education is key.[7]

Aghion et al. (2022b) show that parental university education has a large positive causal impact on the probability of children becoming inventors; this further raises the stakes regarding intergenerational mobility. If the education system is biased in favor of, for example, those with a high income, one may lose inventors not only in the immediate generation but also in subsequent ones as talented young individuals from less privileged backgrounds do not obtain the education that would have raised the probability of both them and their offspring becoming inventors.

4.2.2 The importance of policies promoting exposure to innovation

There is mounting evidence that promoting innovation requires moving beyond general human capital policies to provide specific exposure to innovation careers. As we discussed in section 3, Bell et al. (2019a) provide evidence that the proximity to inventors in childhood has a causal effect on the probability of becoming an inventor.

Recent randomized control trials have shown the importance of mentoring programs and role-model effects in shaping career choice, in particular for STEM fields and fields likely to promote innovation. For example, Breda et al. (2021) show that a brief exposure to female role models working in scientific fields affects high school students' perceptions and choice of undergraduate major. The intervention caused a significant 2.4-percentage-point increase in STEM undergraduate enrollment among girls in grade 12 (i.e., an increase of 8 percent over the baseline rate of 29 percent). As shown in Figure 7.15, the effects on educational choices are concentrated among high-achieving girls in grade 12, who are more likely to enroll in selective and male-dominated STEM programs in college. In contrast, the effect for boys was negligible.

Relying on rich survey data, Breda et al. (2021) distinguish between various potential mechanisms that could explain the large effects of role models. In

---

[7] It may also be that providing equal access requires more than just the right education policies: There is evidence (see, e.g., figures 6 and 7 in UNESCO, 2017) that in more developed countries, gender segregation in higher education regarding STEM education is increasing (i.e., young talented females choose other educational paths).

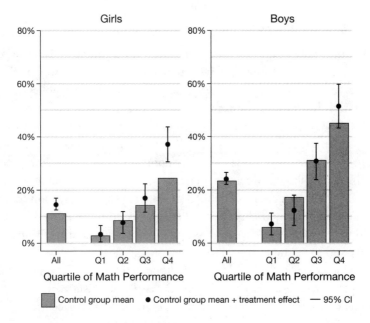

Reformatted from Breda et al. (2021), figure 3(a).

Figure 7.15. Role models and becoming an inventor

principle, role models could (i) affect students' preferences by increasing their taste for science; (ii) change their expectations by modifying their beliefs regarding careers in science, in particular with respect to the place of women in those careers; and (iii) counteract the effects of gender norms on students' social identity. The authors find evidence supporting primarily the second and third of these mechanisms. They also show that the most impactful role model interventions are those that did not overemphasize women's underrepresentation in science.

In related work, Falk et al. (2020) estimate the causal effect of mentoring on schooling decisions in Germany. They find that children from an underprivileged background, who were randomly assigned to a mentor for one year, are 20 percent more likely to enter a "high track" program more likely to lead to high-skill jobs (i.e., with more potential for the creation and diffusion of innovations). Scaling-up such interventions should be a priority for policymakers going forward, with the potential to increase long-run growth by mobilizing the pool of untapped talent (as discussed in Section 3).

4.3 Competition policy and innovation

Competition policy is an important arena of government decision-making that affects both the forms creative destruction may take as well as the effects creative destruction may have on society. Competition policy may affect creative destruction, for example, by removing restrictions that impede entry of new firms that are created either through mergers among the incumbents, through acquisition of small entrants by dominant incumbents, or by restricting other abusive practices of dominant players. Notwithstanding that the relationship between competition policy is discussed in other chapters in this volume (notably Chapter 3 by Rachel Griffith and John Van Reenen and Chapter 4 by Richard Gilbert et al.), it is worth devoting some space here to this topic as well, because competition policy may directly affect inequality and social mobility, which concerns this chapter.

It has long been understood that the rather static approach typically taken by competition authorities toward mergers may be unsatisfactory. Recent development in several markets, online markets and pharmaceuticals being two prominent examples, suggest that incumbent firms may be engaging in "killer acquisitions," where the economic logic rests on reducing future competition more than on improving one's own productivity.

In a recent paper, Cunningham et al. (2021) provide a model for and find evidence of the phenomenon of killer acquisitions. Using data from the pharmaceutical industry on 16,000 drug projects and 4,000 companies, between 5 and 7 percent of acquisitions are killer acquisitions, where the R&D project of the acquired firm is discontinued after the deal has been consummated. Importantly for policy purposes, such acquisitions happen below the antitrust intervention thresholds.

The relationship between market consolidation and innovation has also attracted the interest of theorists. Federico et al. (2017) find that in their model, merging parties always reduce their R&D investments whereas rivals increase them. Denicolo and Polo (2018), however, note that in the model of Federico et al., innovation may be spurred through the elimination of wasteful duplication.

Federico et al. (2020) provide a wide-ranging analysis of different types of mergers and how innovation would be impacted through them; they accompany these types with case analyses. They also point out the misplaced use of the existing evidence on the (inverted-U) relationship between competition and innovation in terms of antitrust policy. They summarize their view as follows (p. 127): "innovation is best promoted when market leaders are allowed to exploit their competitive advantages while also facing pressure to perform coming from both conventional rivals and from disruptive entrants."

Thus, it is crucial to design competition policies that safeguard the entry of new ventures and put limits on the ability of entrenched (dominant) incumbents to buy out their future rivals. To do so, competition policy needs to balance two forces: (i) the need to provide successful innovators rents, and (ii) the need to disallow incumbents to use their financial strength and market power to solidify their position against innovative and more productive entrants. Developing such policies is an important direction for researchers and policymakers going forward, as it has the potential to both increase innovation and reduce inequality in the long run.

5 Conclusions: How to Achieve Better Outcomes for Both Innovation and Inequality

In this chapter, we have reviewed recent evidence characterizing how market forces and policies shape the rate and direction of innovation. Innovation policies can have a first order impact on inequality, both in the short and in the long run. A standard view highlights that policymakers may face a dilemma between increasing innovation and reducing inequality. Indeed, enhancing innovation may lead to increased inequality through various market mechanisms, which we reviewed in Section 2. Taking these market mechanisms as given, policymakers may have to tolerate increasing inequality to achieve higher rates of innovation, while at the same time ensuring that inequality does not increase to the extent that it would stifle innovation through endogenous entry barriers.

Notwithstanding the prevalence and empirical relevance of the traditional view, recent work characterizes several market and social mechanisms whereby inequality acts as an important determinant of the rate and direction of innovation, such that there is little trade-off between innovation and inequality, as we discussed in Section 3. Recent findings on how the direction of innovation differentially affects different socioeconomic groups, how social background affects the prospects of becoming an inventor, and whether and how the tax system affects incentives to invent all call for a holistic yet nuanced approach to policy. Leveraging these mechanisms is an important direction for policy to achieve better outcomes for both innovation and inequality.

In Section 4, we argued that two policies, which are not traditionally viewed as part of innovation policy, play a key role in achieving the goal of increasing innovation while reducing inequality: education and competition policy. An *educational policy* that enables individuals to pursue an education that leads to the possibility of becoming an inventor, irrespective of the individual's social and financial background, is likely to lead to both more innovation and less inequality. Such policies would ensure that (i) all children (in particular, those from less privileged backgrounds) have the possibility of obtaining an education that matches their talents; and (ii) all children are encouraged to pursue careers in science and innovation, especially when they are unlikely to have role models in these careers, for example due to their family background or because of gender norms. *Competition policy,* by creating incentives to displace incumbents through innovation, both by facilitating entry and by restricting the ability of incumbents to abusively exploit their position, also has the potential to simultaneously increase innovation and reduce inequality.

References

Acemoglu, D. (2002) "Technical change, inequality, and the labor market," *Journal of Economic Literature,* 40(1), 7–72.

Acemoglu, D., and D. H. Autor (2011) "Skills, tasks and technologies: Implications for employment and earnings," in Orley Ashenfelter and David E. Card (eds.), *Handbook of Labor Economics* 4. Amsterdam: Elsevier, 1043–1171.

Acemoglu, D., and P. Restrepo (2021) "Technology and inequality," *IFS Deaton Review,* manuscript.

Agarwal, R., and P. Gaule (2020) "Invisible geniuses: Could the knowledge frontier advance faster?" *American Economic Review: Insights,* 2(4), 409–424.

Aghion, P., and P. Howitt (1996) "Research and development in the growth process," *Journal of Economic Growth,* 1(1), 49–73.

Aghion, P., N. Bloom, R. Blundell, R. Griffith, and P. Howitt (2005) "Competition and innovation: An inverted U relationship," *Quarterly Journal of Economics,* 120(2), 701–728.

Aghion, P., R. Blundell, R. Griffith, P. Howitt, and S. Prantl (2008) "The effects of entry on incumbent innovation and productivity," *Review of Economics and Statistics,* 91(1), 20–32.

Aghion, P., U. Akcigit, A. Deaton, and A. Roulet (2016) "Creative destruction and subjective well-being," *American Economic Review,* 106(12), 3869–3897.

Aghion, P., U. Akcigit, A. Hyytinen, and O. Toivanen (2017) "The social origins of inventors," NBER Working Paper 24110.

Aghion, P., U. Akcigit, A. Hyytinen, and O. Toivanen (2018) "On the returns to invention within firms: Evidence from Finland," *American Economic Association, Papers & Proceedings*, 108, 208–212.

Aghion, P., U. Akcigit, A. Bergeaud, R. Blundell, and D. Hemous (2019) "Innovation and top income inequality," *Review of Economic Studies*, 86, 1–45.

Aghion, P., C. Antonin, S. Bunel, and X. Jaravel (2020) "What are the labor and product market effects of automation? New evidence from France," LSE manuscript.

Aghion, P., C. Antonin, and S. Bunel (2021a) *The Power of Creative Destruction*. Princeton, NJ: Princeton University Press.

Aghion, P., A. Bergeaud, R. Blundell, and R. Griffith (2021b) "Soft skills and the wage progression of low-educated workers," Working Paper.

Aghion, P., U. Akcigit, A. Hyytinen, and O. Toivanen (2022a) "A year older, a year wiser (and farther from frontier): Invention rents and human capital depreciation," *Review of Economics and Statistics*. NBER Working Paper 29863.

Aghion, P., U. Akcigit, A. Hyytinen, and O. Toivanen (2022b) "Parental education and invention: The Finnish enigma." Manuscript.

Aghion, P., and R. Griffith (2022) "Innovation and inequalities," *IFS-Deaton Review of Inequalities*, IFS https://ifs.org.uk/inequality/innovation-and -inequalities/.

Akcigit, U., J. Grigsby, and T. Nicholas (2017) "The rise of American ingenuity: Innovation and inventors of the golden age." NBER Working Paper No 23047.

Autor, D., D. Dorn, L. Katz, C. Patterson, and J. Van Reenen (2020) "The fall of the labor share and the rise of superstar firms," *Quarterly Journal of Economics*, 135(2), 645–709.

Bell, A., R. Chetty, X. Jaravel, N. Petkova, and J. Van Reenen (2019a) "Who becomes an investor in America? The importance of exposure to innovation," *Quarterly Journal of Economics*, 134(2), 647–713.

Bell, A., R. Chetty, X. Jaravel, N. Petkova, and J. Van Reenen (2019b) "Do tax cuts produce more Einsteins? The impacts of financial incentives versus exposure to innovation on the supply of inventors," *Journal of European Economic Association*, 17(3), 651–677.

Bloom, N., J. Van Reenen, and W. Williams (2019) "Toolkit for policies to promote innovation," *Journal of Economic Perspectives*, 33(3), 163–184.

Boppart, T., and F. Weiss (2013) "Non-homothetic preferences and industry directed technical change," SSRN 2277547.

Breda, T., J. Grenet, M. Monnet, and C. van Effenterre (2021) "Do female role models reduce the gender gap in science? Evidence from French high schools," PSE Working Papers halshs-01713068, HAL.

Bryan, K., and H. Williams (2021). "Innovation: Market failures and public policies," in Mark Armstrong and Robert Porter (eds.), *Handbook of Industrial Organization*, 3rd edition. Amsterdam: North Holland, 281–388.

Buhai, I. S., M. A. Portela, C. N. Teulings, and A. van Vuuren (2014) "Returns to tenure or seniority?" *Econometrica*, 82(2), 705–730.

Cunningham, C., F. Ederer, and S. Ma (2021) "Killer acquisitions," *Journal of Political Economy*, 129(3), 649–702.

Delestre, A., H. Miller, and K. Smith (2021) "Taxation and top income inequality," *Deaton Review*, IFS, May.

De Loecker, J., J. Eeckhout, and G. Unger (2020) "The rise of market power and the macroeconomic implications," *Quarterly Journal of Economics*, 135(2), 561–644.

De Loecker, J., T., Obermeier, and J. Van Reenen (2021) "Firms and inequality," *Deaton Review*, IFS, May.

Denicolo, V., and M. Polo (2018) "Duplicative research, mergers and innovation," *Economics Letters*, 166, 56–59.

Depalo, D., and S. Di Addario (2014) "Inventors' returns to patents Domenico," Bank of Italy, January.

Eeckhout, Jan (2022) "Market power and inequality," *IFS Deaton Review*, IFS, March, https://ifs.org.uk/inequality/market-power-and-labour-market-inequality.

Einiö, E., J. Feng, and X. Jaravel (2022) "Social push and the direction of innovation," Centre for Economic Performance Discussion Paper 1861.

Falk, A., F. Kosse, and P. Pinger (2020) "Mentoring and schooling decisions: Causal evidence," IZA Institute for Labor Economics DP13387.

Federico, G., G. Langus, and T. Valletti (2017) "A simple model of mergers and innovation," *Economics Letters*, 157, 136–140.

Federico, G., F. Scott Morton, and C. Shapiro (2020) "Antitrust and innovation: Welcoming and protecting disruption," *Innovation Policy and the Economy*, vol. 20.

Frank, M., and V. K. Goyal (2009) "Capital structure decisions: Which factors are reliably important?" *Financial Management*, 38(1), 1–37.

Gabaix, X., J.-M. Lasry, P.-L. Lions, and B. Moll (2016) "The dynamics of inequality," *Econometrica*, 84(6), 2071–2111.

Garin, A., and F. Silverio (2018) "How responsive are wages to demand within the firm? Evidence from idiosyncratic export demand shocks," NBER, November.

Giuri, P., M. Mariani, S. Brusoni, G. Crespi, D. Francoz, A. Gambardella, W. Garcia-Fontes, A. Geuna, R. Gonzales, D. Harhoff, et al. (2007) "Inventors and invention processes in Europe: Results from the PatVal-EU Survey," *Research Policy*, 36(8), 1107–1127.

Griffith, R., S. Redding, and J. Van Reenen (2004) "Mapping the two faces of R&D: Productivity growth in a panel of OECD industries," *Review of Economics and Statistics*, 86(4), 883–895.

Hayek, F. (1931) *Prices and Production*. New York: August Kelly.

Hayek, F. (1945) "The use of knowledge in society," *American Economic Review*, 35(4), 519–530.

Hoisl, K., H.-C. Kongsted, and M. Mariani (2020) "Lost Marie Curies: Parental impact on the probability of becoming an inventor," Copenhagen Business School, manuscript.

Hsieh, Chang-Tai, E. Hurst, C. I. Jones, and Peter Klenow (2019) "The allocation of talent and U.S. economic growth," *Econometrica*, 87(5), 1439–1474.

Jäger, S., and J. Heining (2019) "How substitutable are workers? Evidence from worker deaths," Massachusetts Institute of Technology, manuscript.

Jaimovich, N. and S. Rebelo (2017) "Nonlinear effects of taxation on growth," *Journal of Political Economy*, 125(1), 265–291.

Jaravel, X. (2019) "The unequal gains from product innovations: Evidence from the U.S. retail sector," *Quarterly Journal of Economics*, 134(2), 715–783.

Jaravel, X., and A. Olivi (2021) "Prices, non-homotheticities, and optimal taxation," LSE manuscript.

Jones, C. I. (2022) "Taxing top incomes in a world of ideas," *Journal of Political Economy*, 130(9), 2227–2274.

Khan, Z., and K. Sokoloff (2004) "Institutions and democratic invention in 19th-century America: Evidence from 'great inventors,' 1790–1930," *American Economic Review Papers and Proceedings*, 94(2), 395–401.

Kim, S., and P. Moser (2021) "Women in science. Lessons from the baby boom." Manuscript.

Kline, P., N. Petkova, H. Williams, and O. Zidar (2019) "Who profits from patents? Rent-sharing at innovative firms," *Quarterly Journal of Economics*, 1343–1404.

Koning, R., S. Samila, and J. P. Ferguson (2020) "Inventor gender and the direction of invention," *AER Papers and Proceedings*, 110, 250–254.

Linder, S. (1961) *An Essay on Trade and Transformation*. New York: John Wiley and Sons.

Lockwood, B. B., C. G. Nathanson, and E. G. Weyl (2017) "Taxation and the allocation of talent," *Journal of Political Economy*, 125(5), 1635–1682.

Mirrlees, J.A. (1971) "An exploration in the theory of optimum income taxation," *Review of Economic Studies*, 38(2), 175–208.

Onishi, K., and S. Nagaoka (2012) "Life-cycle productivity of industrial inventors: Education and other determinants," manuscript.

Rossman, J. (1931) "The motives of inventors," *Quarterly Journal of Economics*, 45, 522–528.

Schmookler, J. (1957) "Inventors past and present," *Review of Economics and Statistics*, 39(3), 321–333.

Schumpeter, J. (1942) *Capitalism, Socialism and Democracy*. New York: Harper and Bros.

Smith, M., D. Yagan, O. Zidar, and E. Zwick (2019) "Capitalists in the twenty-first century," *Quarterly Journal of Economics*, 134(4), 1675–1745.

Stern, S. (2004) "Do scientists pay to be scientists?" *Management Science*, 50(6), 835–853.

Takalo, T., and O. Toivanen (2016) "Economics of innovation policy," *Nordic Economic Policy Review*, 2, 65–90.

Toivanen, O., and L. Väänänen (2012) "Returns to inventors," *Review of Economics and Statistics*, 94(4), 1173–1190.

Toivanen, O., and L. Väänänen (2016) "Education and invention," *Review of Economics and Statistics*, 98(2), 382–396.

UNESCO (2017) "Cracking the code: Girls' and women's education in science, technology, engineering and mathematics," ISBN 978-92-3-100233-5, https://unesdoc.unesco.org/ark:/48223/pf0000253479.

Van Reenen, J. (1996) "The creation and capture of rents: Wages and innovation in a panel of U.K. companies," *Quarterly Journal of Economics*, 111(1), 195–226.

Van Reenen, J. (2018) "Increasing difference between firms: Market power and the macro economy" in *Changing Market Structures and Implications for Monetary Policy*. Kansas City Federal Reserve: Jackson Hole Symposium.

Van Reenen, J. (2021) "Innovation and human capital policy," in A. Goolsbee and B. Jones (eds.), *Handbook of Innovation and Public Policy*. Chicago: NBER and University of Chicago Press, 61–83.

Vernon, R. (1966) "International investment and international trade in the product cycle," *Quarterly Journal of Economics*, 190–207.

Von Hippel, E. (1986) "Lead users: A source of novel product concepts," *Management Science*, 32(7), 791–806.

CHAPTER 8

Labor Market Dynamics When Ideas Are Harder to Find

ADRIEN BILAL, NIKLAS ENGBOM, SIMON MONGEY, *and* GIOVANNI L. VIOLANTE

1 Introduction

Economic growth has slowed down in the United States. One prominent explanation is that *ideas are getting harder to find* (Bloom, Jones, van Reenen, and Webb 2020) and, as a result, aggregate productivity growth is now weaker (Gordon 2016; Fernald 2016). At the same time, business and labor market dynamism have declined along a host of margins. Firm entry has fallen, firm employment has become less responsive to productivity shocks, job reallocation has decreased (Decker, Haltiwanger, Jarmin, and Miranda 2020), and job-to-job transitions have declined (Fujita, Moscarini, and Postel-Vinay 2019). In this chapter, we connect these two macroeconomic trends. We study the effects of a productivity slowdown on firm and worker dynamics in an economy with endogenous growth where the reallocation of labor between old obsolescing firms and new productive firms is intermediated by a frictional labor market. We show that a growth slowdown that originates from weaker imitation—an interpretation of "ideas getting harder to find"—predicts the above facts. Surprisingly, however, it also generates a countervailing *decline* in labor misallocation.

Our model extends Bilal, Engbom, Mongey, and Violante (2022) (hereafter cited as BEMV) to study the impact of economic growth on the labor market via creative destruction in the spirit of the seminal contribution by Aghion and Howitt (1994). The BEMV framework is a steady-state model of firm and worker dynamics in frictional labor markets that accommodates both firm turnover via entry and exit in the tradition of Hopenhayn (1992) and worker turnover via job-to-job transitions in the tradition of Postel-Vinay and Robin (2002).

Conceptually, creative destruction occurs along two margins. This first margin is that newly created businesses replace obsolete incumbents. This channel forms the backbone of models in the creative destruction literature and requires well-defined boundaries of the firm. Once firms innovate, they establish a monopolistic position in producing a variety, and face a firm-level marginal revenue function that is strictly decreasing in output, and hence in employment. Firms then hire an optimal amount of labor and firms of different productivities and sizes coexist.

The second margin of creative destruction is that key factors of production such as labor take time to reallocate to productive newcomers. This channel is mediated by labor market frictions that have remained largely absent from the creative destruction literature. Similarly, the deviation from constant marginal revenue that is common in growth models is extremely rare in search models. The reason is that it creates conceptual challenges, unresolved until now, in the determination of surplus sharing. The source of the problem is on-the-job search, which implies heterogeneity in outside options for workers, depending on their labor market history. As a consequence, solving for firms' decisions requires keeping track of the entire distribution of firm wages, a daunting task.

In BEMV we propose a contractual environment that solves this conundrum and so allows for a proper theory of the firm—where firm boundaries are determined by either diminishing returns in technology or consumers' taste for variety—alongside a frictional model of the labor market.[1] We show that all allocations can be derived from the maximization of the *joint surplus* of the firm and its incumbent workers, technically a simple problem, which leads to the emergence of an equilibrium *job ladder in marginal surplus*. In this chapter we add growth via imitation in the spirit of Luttmer (2007) and study a balanced growth path equilibrium. Good ideas are easier to find when entrants are better able to imitate ideas in the right tail of in-

---

[1] In BEMV, we write the model with DRS technology. Here we adapt it to a monopolistically competitive environment where decreasing returns is in revenue.

cumbent productivity, and harder to find when entrants draw them from the left of the incumbent distribution. In sum, the framework accommodates multi-worker firms, endogenous entry and exit, endogenous productivity growth with creative destruction, job reallocation, churning (excess worker turnover), and unemployment.

We calibrate the model to US data, matching moments on worker and firm dynamics. The process of economic growth requires new, productive firms to hire workers away from large, less productive incumbents, and job losses to unemployment as incumbents slowly fall behind the frontier. We therefore ensure that the model replicates statistics on such job-to-job quits, and employment-to-unemployment separations. The process of economic growth also requires firm entry, to replace incumbents, with stochastic growth of new firms toward their optimal size. We therefore ensure that the model replicates statistics on the entry and exit rates of firms, the distribution of employment across firms by age and size, and the rate of average firm growth over the life cycle.[2]

We use the calibrated model to assess the impact of worsening in entrants' ability to imitate. Four results stand out. First, growth slows down. Second, the implications of a growth slowdown via this mechanism are consistent with facts related to *firm dynamics*. Employment reallocation falls, as entrants are relatively lower productivity and poach less from incumbents, while incumbents obsolesce at a slower rate. The firm entry rate declines, and the share of employment in old firms increases. Following productivity shocks, firms also hire fewer workers, consistent with Decker, Haltiwanger, Jarmin, and Miranda (2020). As we discuss below, a lower rate of obsolescence reduces misallocation, with workers more efficiently sorted across the productivity distribution of firms. Poaching a worker from another firm to fill a new job is more difficult in a less misallocated labor market, so firms expand more slowly following a shock to their productivity.

Third, we document the implications for *worker dynamics*. We find that on all dimensions, labor market flows slow down: employment-to-unemployment (EU), unemployment-to-employment (UE), and employment-to-employment (EE) transition rates decrease. *Ceteris parabus,* the decline in the UE rate would lead to an increase in unemployment, but the decline

---

[2] A key step in our analysis is to provide a mapping between the equilibrium conditions of (i) the detrended steady state of the balanced growth path in our economy with growth and (ii) the steady state of BEMV. This result allows us to directly use the calibration of BEMV.

in the rate of obsolescence reduces the rate of layoffs. On net, the second force is stronger, such that unemployment declines. Compared to canonical matching models without on-the-job search, we find that unemployment is subject to weaker creative-destruction effects associated with faster growth. One important reason is that in our environment, as in the real economy, half of job separations are EE transitions that do not involve a spell of unemployment.

Fourth, these observations, combined with a decline in job-to-job mobility, may suggest that misallocation is worse when growth is slower, due to a lower intensity of imitation. Interestingly, however, we find the opposite. As growth slows, the misallocation that exists in the economy improves. This is observed in a decline in the dispersion of the marginal product of labor across firms and an increase in the correlation between firm size and productivity. This leads to a higher *level* of output, despite slower growth. We find that this difference in level is quantitatively significant, in the sense that it has the potential to offset the negative growth effects of lower imitation.

What is behind this last result? Our model is unique in the class of growth models in that firms operate a single product, start small, and then grow via costly hiring of workers. When the rate of economic growth is high, firms' productivity is quickly slipping behind the productivity of the economy as a whole, and so high-productivity firms are *less ambitious* with respect to these expansion plans. High-productivity firms no longer grow as large, which aggregates up as a misallocation of labor in the economy.

Our model generically encompasses the three standard channels by which higher growth can affect equilibrium outcomes: (i) higher growth increases the equilibrium *interest rate,* which reduces firm values and firm entry; (ii) higher growth has a *capitalization effect* that increases the incentives to firm entry and vacancy creation, due to streams of output being discounted at a lower rate; (iii) because higher growth comes about through higher productivity of new entrants relative to the incumbents, it leads to Schumpeterian *creative destruction*—the hallmark of the Aghion-Howitt approach—which leads to the obsolescence of incumbent firms, as their costs grow faster than their revenues.[3] In addition our model features the new *misallocation* channel that operates via firms being farther away from their optimal size when

---

[3] Because of our preference specification with unitary intertemporal elasticity of substitution, interest rate and capitalization effects exactly cancel out in our calibration.

growth is faster. The necessary ingredients for this mechanism to emerge are unique to our model of economic growth: frictional adjustment and a well-defined firm life cycle. We regard this as a novel economic force, and believe it may be important to study in the future.

1.1 Related literature

Our paper contributes to a large literature on growth, firm dynamics, and worker flows in frictional labor markets.

Imitation and growth. Our economy falls into the class of growth economies in which the set of varieties produced remains fixed, but the productivity of the technology used in production of these varieties increases over time. The particular way we model imitation is reminiscent of Lucas and Moll (2014) and Perla and Tonetti (2014). Rather than microfounding the process of entrants bumping into and imitating incumbents, as in these papers, we take a reduced form approach. An exogenous parameter links the thickness of the tail of entrant productivity draws to the distribution of incumbent productivity, as discussed in Luttmer (2010). We model ideas being harder to find as a comparative static in which this parameter skews entrants' draws away from the tail of incumbent productivities. Future work may adapt our framework to include expanding varieties, or endogenize this reduced form process via meetings of entrants and incumbents or as spin-offs from incumbent firms. We return on this point in the conclusions.

In this chapter we also abstract from horizontal innovation and endogenous improvements in productivity. Both have been combined with imitation in recent papers (Konig, Lorenz, and Zilibotti 2016; Acemoglu, Aghion, Griffith, and Zilibotti 2010; Benhabib, Perla, and Tonetti 2021). The new misallocation channel that we identify will carry over to such models of economic growth. Consider a setup where firms can invest in improving their productivity (as in, for example, Akcigit and Kerr 2018) and then grow via costly accumulation of labor through frictional labor markets toward their larger optimal size. With lower growth, firms are more ambitious in these expansions plans, and hence invest more in innovation. The same force should, in principle, apply to horizontal innovation. The key ingredient in both cases is that innovation is followed by costly growth of the firm, which is the empirically realistic case.

Growth models with frictionless adjustment. In this class of models (e.g. Garcia-Macia, Hsieh, and Klenow 2019), firms instantaneously grow to their optimal size and labor is reallocated through a frictionless labor market. Moreover, all changes in employment are due only to creative destruction. Our result that slower growth leads to declining dynamism is reminiscent of Akcigit and Ates (2021), where a frictionless model of step-by-step innovation shows that a decline in a parameter that governs exogenous diffusion of technology from leaders to followers can generate falls in productivity growth, entry, and job reallocation. Akcigit and Ates (2023) also compute the transition path between balanced growth paths and feature a horse race between alternative explanations. They find that a slowdown of knowledge diffusion from frontier to laggard firms (and indirectly, entrants) can explain a large portion of the observed facts. Relative to this work, we introduce labor market frictions, and hence unemployment and the distinction between worker and job turnover, and uncover the new misallocation channel.

Costless adjustment—i.e., abstracting away from convex or nonconvex adjustment costs or costs microfounded through labor market frictions—maintains tractability in all these models by making employment decisions static. In our model, firms receive shocks to productivity—or isomorphically, demand—that cause changes in employment, and experience obsolescence due to the creative destruction from entrants that leads them to drift toward exiting the economy. In this sense our model introduces into the creative destruction literature, in the tradition of Aghion and Howitt (1992, 1994), features of firm dynamics models with costly adjustment, in the tradition of Hopenhayn and Rogerson (1993), where the costly adjustment in response to demand or productivity shocks occurs through frictional labor markets, in the tradition of Postel-Vinay and Robin (2002).

Search models without growth. We build on the random search setup developed by Postel-Vinay and Robin (2002), which has become a workhorse of the literature: Bertrand competition between employers for workers and wage renegotiation under mutual consent. Our contribution is to generalize this *sequential auction* protocol to multi-worker firms with diminishing returns in technology and show how one can still solve the model's equilibrium through the notion of joint surplus, which yields a dramatic simplification and analytical tractability. In traditional versions of random search models with linear technology, the size distribution of firms is either indeterminate or nondegenerate only because of the existence of search frictions:

as frictions disappear, all workers become employed at the most productive firm, an implausible limiting behavior. Our approach, instead, goes back to (Lucas 1978): the dominant force that delivers a nondegenerate firm-size distribution is the combination of diminishing returns in production and heterogeneity in productivity.[4] The frictionless limit of our model is, therefore, a version of the competitive firm dynamics model of Hopenhayn (1992).

Growth models with frictional adjustment. Recent papers have microfounded this adjustment process by combining search and growth. Engbom (2017) integrates economic growth into a model with job-to-job mobility as in Postel-Vinay and Robin (2002). As in other search models with constant returns to scale in production, the unit of analysis is not a firm, but a job. As explained, our model is closer to the tradition in the firm dynamics literature where the unit of analysis is a firm, and its boundaries are naturally determined by decreasing returns, here due to monopolistic competition. Martellini and Menzio (2020) show that exogenously declining search frictions in a Diamond-Mortensen-Pissarides model generates a unique balanced growth path equilibrium when productivity is match specific and matches are inspection goods. We keep search frictions constant, and study a balanced growth path that emerges from imitation and creative destruction: newcomers with the best ideas replace obsolete incumbents in the production of one of the varieties consumed by households.

Outline. The rest of the paper is organized as follows. Section 2 describes the model. Section 3 discusses its parameterization. Section 4 presents the results. Section 5 concludes.

2 Model

In this section we first describe the household, government, and production sector. Next, we obtain the surplus representation from which all allocations are derived, and illustrate the contractual environment that underlies it. Finally, we explain how to construct a balanced growth path (BGP), and define an equilibrium. The model is written in continuous time.

---

[4] See also Elsby and Gottfries (2022) for a related framework.

2.1 Household

The representative household is composed of $\bar{n}$ individuals who supply inelastically one unit of time to the labor market. The size of the population is constant. A share u_t of individuals is unemployed and the remaining $n_t = \bar{n} - u_t$ are employed. Employed workers receive wage payments from their firm and unemployed workers receive unemployment benefits from the government. There is full insurance within the family, and thus the household problem can be split into a choice of aggregate consumption and a second stage where the consumption is distributed across household members. This second stage is irrelevant for labor market dynamics, so we abstract from it and focus on the former.

The household discounts the future at rate ρ and is endowed with one unit of a fixed factor each period. It may rent $X_t \leq 1$ units of this factor at rate p_t^X to firms who need it for production. The household gets utility out of consumption C_t, which we assume is log, and linear utility from the unrented stock of the fixed factor.[5] Flow utility is therefore:

$$U(C_t, X_t) = \log C_t + \eta (1 - X_t)$$

Utility from consumption C_t owes to consuming a fixed measure m of varieties of goods. We assume that C_t is a CES aggregator over these goods with elasticity of substitution $1/(1 - \alpha)$:

$$C_t = \left[\int_0^m c_{it}^\alpha \, di \right]^{\frac{1}{\alpha}}.$$

Given a set of prices p_{it} for each good, the household demand for each good can be characterized by the usual demand system:

$$c_{it} = \left(\frac{p_{it}}{P_t} \right)^{-\frac{1}{1-\alpha}} C_t, \quad P_t = \left[\int_0^m p_{it}^{-\frac{\alpha}{1-\alpha}} \, di \right]^{-\frac{1-\alpha}{\alpha}}. \tag{1}$$

The first-order conditions with respect to C_t and H_t yield the equilibrium price $p_t^X = \eta P_t C_t$. We assume that the household trades shares of the mu-

---

[5] This fixed factor can be interpreted in different ways. One example is managerial time needed by the firm to perform certain activities (i.e., entry, operating, and recruiting). Another example is land, also needed for the same activities.

tual fund that owns all firms in the economy, and trades a risk-free bond in zero net supply. As is standard, this implies that in equilibrium on a BGP, firms discount future payoffs with a constant risk-free rate $r = \rho + g$.

2.2 Government

Unemployed workers receive benefits b_t from the government that are funded by a constant tax on sales τ. Hence, the government budget constraint is:

$$u_t b_t = \tau \int_0^m p_{it} y_{it} \, di = \tau P_t Y_t. \tag{2}$$

Define $\tilde{b} = b_t / P_t Y_t$, constant along the BGP, and note that $\tilde{b} = \tilde{b}(\tau, u) = \tau / u$, since also u is invariant on the BGP.

2.3 Incumbent firms

Each incumbent firm is a monopolist in producing one of the m varieties. Firms operate with a linear production function $y_{it} = \bar{z}_{it} n_{it}$. Firm-level productivity $\bar{z}_{it}$ follows a geometric Brownian motion:

$$d \log \bar{z}_{it} = - \bar{\mu} dt + \bar{\sigma} dW_t.$$

In order to remain in operation, a firm incurs a flow fixed cost c_f, and in order to hire workers it has to spend vacancy costs c_v (v, n). Both costs are assumed to be denominated in the fixed factor that the firm rents from the household sector.

Invoking the theoretical results in BEMV, which we summarize in Section 2.5 below, we can solve for the equilibrium allocation of the economy by focusing on the surplus of a coalition between a firm and its n incumbent workers. The flow surplus of such organization is

$$\pi_{it} = (1 - \tau) p_{it} \bar{z}_{it} n_{it} - b_t n_{it} - p_t^X c_f - p_t^X c_v(v_{it}, n_{it}),$$

where the term $b_t n_{it}$ captures the flow outside options of the incumbent workers. The demand function implies that the price a firm gets for its output of variety i is

$$p_{it} = \left(\frac{y_{it}}{Y_t} \right)^{-(1-\alpha)} P_t.$$

Exploiting the fact that $Y_t = Y_0 e^{gt}$ on the BGP, the post-tax revenues of the firm are

$$(1-\tau)p_{it}y_{it} = P_t Y_t \times (1-\tau)\left(\frac{y_{it}}{Y_t}\right)^{\alpha} = P_t Y_t \times Y_0^{-\alpha}\underbrace{(1-\tau)\bar{z}_{it}^{\alpha}\,e^{-\alpha gt}}_{=\,z_{it}}\,n_{it}^{\alpha}$$

where the firm's *relative productivity* $z_{it} = (1-\tau)\bar{z}_{it}^{\alpha}e^{-\alpha gt}$ follows

$$d\log z_{it} = \mu dt + \sigma dW_t \tag{3}$$

where $\mu = -\alpha(\bar{\mu}+g)$ and $\sigma = \alpha\bar{\sigma}$.

Using the government budget constraint, the first-order condition $p_t^X = \eta P_t Y_t$, and the equilibrium condition $C_t = Y_t$, flow post-tax surplus can be written:

$$\pi_{it} = P_t Y_t \times \left[Y_0^{-\alpha}(z_{it}n_{it}^{\alpha}) - \tilde{b}(\tau,u)n_{it} - \eta c_f - \eta c(v_{it}, n_{it})\right]. \tag{4}$$

2.4 The labor market

Unemployed and employed workers search in a common, single labor market. Unemployed workers search with an intensity that, without loss of generality, we can normalize to one. Employed workers also search for jobs, but with relative search efficiency χ. Hiring firms and job seekers meet in a common, single, frictional labor market. Search is random.

The total number of meetings is given by the CRS aggregate matching technology $m(s_t, v_t)$. Inputs to this function are total vacancies v_t and total units of search efficiency $s_t = u_t + \chi n_t$. Thus, an unemployed worker meets a firm at rate $\lambda^U(s_t, v_t) = m(s_t, v_t)/s_t$. An employed worker meets a firm at rate $\lambda^E(s_t, v_t) = \chi\lambda^U(s_t, v_t)$. A vacancy meets workers at rate $qt = m(s_t, v_t)/v_t$. The rates q_t and λ_t^U can be expressed in terms of *market tightness* $\theta_t = (v_t/s_t)$. The employed workers can become unemployed because they choose to quit, or because the firm lays them off, or exogenously at the constant rate δ.

2.5 Contractual environment

As we explain in detail in BEMV, the contemporaneous presence of random search, on-the-job search, and a revenue function decreasing in employment makes the firm problem intractable—i.e., computing optimal layoff, retention, and vacancy policies requires keeping track of the entire wage distribution (possibly hundreds or thousands of states).

We propose a minimal set of assumptions on the contractual environment such that the state vector becomes manageable. Three assumptions on bargaining and surplus sharing are common to many single-worker firm environments: (i) lack of commitment; (ii) wage contract renegotiation by mutual consent (i.e., only when one of the parties has a credible threat, or an outside option more valuable than the current contract); (iii) Bertrand competition among employers for employed jobseekers with take-it-or-leave-it offers. For example, these are the assumptions in Postel-Vinay and Robin (2002). Two further assumptions are required in our new multi-worker firm environment: (iv) no value is lost in internal wage renegotiations between a firm and its incumbent workers; and (v) vacancy policies maximize combined firm and worker value—for which in BEMV we offer an explicit microfoundation. Under these assumptions, firm and workers' decisions are privately efficient, as if the firm and incumbent workers maximize their total joint value. The state variables of the joint value (or surplus) function are only two: firm size n and productivity z.

We note that this joint surplus representation uniquely pins down allocations (firm and worker dynamics), but is consistent with multiple wage-setting mechanisms that determine how this joint value is split between the parties. Wages, therefore, are not allocative. In order to study the model's implication for wage dynamics, one would have to make additional assumptions. Since the subject of this chapter is labor reallocation, we refrain from making extra assumptions and abstract from discussing implications for the wage distribution. For additional details on the contractual environment, we refer directly to BEMV.

2.6 Surplus representation

Let $S(z, n, t)$ denote the joint surplus of an organization composed by a firm—the owner of the technology with productivity z— and by its n workers at time t. Using our expression for the flow surplus (4), the joint surplus is given by the Hamilton-Jacobi-Bellman (HJB) equation

$$rS(z,n,t) - \frac{\partial S(z,n,t)}{\partial t} = \max_{v \geq 0} P_t Y_t \times \left[Y_0^{-\alpha}(zn^\alpha) - \tilde{b}(\tau, u)n - \eta c_f - \eta c_v(v, n) \right]$$
$$- \delta S_n(z,n,t) + qv(\theta)\phi S_n(z,n,t)$$
$$+ qv(\theta)(1-\phi)\int_0^{S_n(z,n,t)} S_n(z,n,t) \tag{5}$$
$$- S_n(z',n',t)dH_t(z',n')$$
$$+ \mu(z)S_z(z,n,t) + \frac{\sigma(z)^2}{2} S_{zz}(z,n,t)$$

where $\phi = u/s$ is the share of unemployed job seekers and H_t is the employment distribution.

The first line of this equation is the flow surplus. The other lines represent events that can occur to the organization. In the second line, the firm exogenously loses one of its n workers to unemployment at rate J and as a result it loses the marginal surplus contributed by the lost worker. In the third line, the firm is hiring and meets an unemployed worker who brings marginal surplus $S_n(z, n, t)$ to the coalition. The firm also hires from other firms by poaching (fourth line). Workers at other firms are met according to the employment-weighted distribution of productivity and size, H_n. Upon hiring, total surplus increases by $S_n(z, n, t) - S_n(z', n', t)$. The first term is the gain in value to the firm and incumbent workers due to the new hire. The second term is the value pledged to the new worker, which is equal to the highest value its former employer would pay to retain them. Poaching is successful if this difference is positive and workers flow to the highest marginal surplus firm. Thus, the model implies a job ladder in *endogenous marginal surplus*, as opposed to exogenous productivity z as in the canonical Postel-Vinay and Robin (2002) model. Conversely, an incumbent worker may quit to a higher marginal surplus firm. The firm and remaining workers will lose $S_n(z, n, t)$ and so are prepared to increase the worker's surplus by at most $S_n(z, n, t)$ to retain them. Knowing this, the external firm hires the worker by offering them exactly $S_n(z, n, t)$. The joint surplus of the firm, remaining workers and poached worker are therefore unchanged and, as in Postel-Vinay and Robin (2002); no "*EE Quit*" term appears in (5).

The first-order condition for the firm's vacancy decision gives

$$c_v(v; z, n) = q(\theta_t)[\phi_t S_n(z, n, t) + (1 - \phi_t) \int_0^{S_n(z, n, t)} (S_n(z, n, t) - S_n(z', n', t)) dH_n(S_n(z', n', t))] \tag{6}$$

or the marginal cost of hiring (left-hand side) equals the expected return from hiring (right-hand side). On the *intensive margin*, an increase in S_n increases the return to hiring an unemployed or employed worker one-for-one. On the *extensive margin*, an increase in S_n widens the set of firms from which the firm will poach, increasing the probability of a hire by $(1-\phi)h_n(S_n)$, but hiring from these additional firms yields zero additional value because the target firm's marginal surplus associated with the worker is close to that of the poaching firm.

Finally, at every t, the operation of the firm requires (z, n) to be interior to an *exit boundary*, and an additional *layoff boundary* determines when separations occur:

$$\text{Exit boundary: } S(z, n, t) \geq 0, \quad \text{Layoff boundary: } S_n(z, n, t) \geq 0. \quad (7)$$

The exit boundary states that the joint surplus of the organization must be weakly positive to continue operations. The layoff boundary requires the surplus of the marginal worker to be weakly positive. If it is negative, the firm will instantaneously shed enough workers to restore equality.

2.7 Balanced growth path

We are interested in constructing a balanced growth path equilibrium of an economy in which output Y_t and consumption C_t grow at a constant rate g, and unemployment u_t is constant. We normalize the aggregate price level P_t in each period to 1. With constant population $\bar{n}$, employment $n = \bar{n} - u$ is constant on the BGP, and thus average firm size n/m is also constant.[6]

It is straightforward to guess and verify that $S(z, n, t) = P_t Y_t S(z, n)$. Because, without loss of generality, we normalize $P_t = 1$ and $Y_t = Y_0 e^{gt}$, then $S(z, n, t) = Y_0 e^{gt} S(z, n)$. Hence, $\partial S(z, n, t/\partial t) = gS(z, n, t)$. Using this, along with $r = \rho + g$, we obtain:

$$\rho S(z, n) = \max_v \left\{ Y_0^{-\alpha} z n^\alpha - \tilde{b}(\tau, u)n - \eta c_f - \eta c(v, n) - \delta S_n(z, n) \right.$$
$$+ qv \left(\phi S_n(z, n) + (1 - \phi) \int_0^{S_n(z, n)} (S_n(z, n) - S(z', n')) dH(z', n') \right) \right\}$$
$$+ \mu(z) S_z(z, n) + \frac{\sigma(z)^2}{2} S_{zz}(z, n). \quad (8)$$

The surplus (8) is exactly that in BEMV, with the following two additions: (i) an endogenous constant $Y_0^{-\alpha}$, and (ii) an endogenous equilibrium flow value of unemployment $\tilde{b} = \tau/u$.

Note that the drift in relative productivity $\mu(z) = -[\alpha(\bar{\mu} + g) + \sigma^2/2]z$ encodes the fact that growth leads the costs of inputs relative to sales to

---

[6] As in Luttmer (2007) we could include population growth at a constant rate, which would require the number of firms, and varieties, m, to also grow at a constant rate, since average firm size must be constant on any BGP.

increase—an *obsolescence (or creative destruction) effect*.[7] As we explain next, the endogenous growth rate of the economy g is determined by the free-entry condition.

2.8 Entry

To close the model, it remains to specify a process for firm entry. An entrant firm replaces one of the exiting incumbents in producing one of the m varieties.

We assume that new firms enter with a relative productivity z that is drawn from a Pareto distribution with some endogenous tail index ζ. Given the productivity distribution of entrants and the law of motion for incumbent productivity (3), it follows from standard arguments (see, e.g. Luttmer 2007) that the distribution of incumbent productivity is asymptotically Pareto with tail index $2\mu/\sigma^2$. Let the parameter ψ govern how well entrants can replicate the tail of the distribution of incumbent firms: $\zeta = \psi(2\mu/\sigma^2)$. A *lower value* of ψ means that entrants draw productivities that are further into the tail of the distribution of incumbent firm productivities (i.e., *better imitation*). This is the key parameter that we will vary in our counterfactual experiments.

Entrants are assumed to pay an entry cost c_0, again denoted in units of the fixed factor as all other operating costs, in order to make a productivity draw and start producing with n_0 initial employees. Free-entry then implies the equilibrium condition[8]

$$\eta c_0 = \int S(n_0, z) dF(z; \zeta) \tag{9}$$

where F is the endogenous productivity distribution of entrants. This condition uniquely determines the equilibrium growth rate of the economy. Surplus (8) is decreasing in g, since higher growth increases the rate at which the price of the fixed factor increases relative to the price of the varieties produced. Intuitively, consider a scenario where at a given growth rate, the free-entry condition did not hold—i.e., there was a positive expected surplus (net of the entry cost) from entering. More firms would choose to pay

---

[7] Because of log utility, interest rate and capitalization effects offset each other exactly and g does not show up in discounting.

[8] Specifically, $p_t^X c_0 = \int S(n_0, z, t) dF(z; \zeta)$, which implies $\eta P_t Y_t c_0 = \int P_t Y_t S(n_0, z) dF(z; \zeta)$, and condition (9).

the cost and draw new values of productivity. Through imitation, this would generate additional economic growth via an increase in average productivity. Higher growth causes the value of entry to fall until the free-entry condition holds.

2.9 Equilibrium

The equilibrium of the model determines the rate of growth g, and the level of output $Y0$ and benefits $\tilde{b}(\tau, u)$, which enter the detrended HJB equation (8).

First, the free-entry condition (9) uniquely determines the equilibrium growth rate of the economy. Second, the level of output Y_0 must be consistent with the production of the heterogeneous firms in the economy. Aggregation implies that $\int_0^m p_{it} y_{it} di = P_t Y_t$. Using our expression for relative sales:

$$1 = \int_0^m \frac{p_{it} y_{it}}{P_t Y_t} di = \int_0^m (z_{it} n_{it}^\alpha) \times (Y_0^{-\alpha}) di, \quad Y_0^\alpha = m \int_{N \times Z} z n^\alpha dH(z, n).$$

This pins down the initial level of output, which then grows at rate g: $Y_t = e^{gt} Y_0$. Third, we also require $\tilde{b}(\tau, u) = \tau / u$.

Finally, given an optimal employment policy of firms and the stochastic process for relative productivity, a standard Kolmogorov forward equation characterizes the distribution of firms over size and relative productivity. We provide the complete definition of the BGP equilibrium in the Appendix, Section A.1. Most of the definition follows directly from BEMV with the additional features to accommodate growth, such as those just described.

3 Calibration

The model period is set to a month.[9] For calibration, we use 2011–2016 as our reference period to construct all the empirical counterparts of the model's moments. We make the same functional form assumptions as in BEMV. The matching function is Cobb-Douglas with vacancy elasticity

---

[9] Because the model is written in continuous time, we can accommodate any observed data frequency with the appropriate time aggregation within the model.

β and match efficiency A; i.e., $Av^{\beta} s^{1-\beta}$. The vacancy cost function is

$$c_v(v_{it}, n_{it}) = \frac{\bar{c}_v}{1+\gamma}\left(\frac{v_{it}}{n_{it}}\right)^{\gamma} v_{it}.$$

Some parameters can be set externally. As we discuss in BEMV, the parameters $\bar{c}_v$ and c_f can be normalized. Because the preference parameter η multiplies all costs in the model, we can also normalize η. We also set the number of workers at new firm n_0 to 1 (the entrepreneur), and β, the elasticity of the matching function with respect to vacancies, to 0.5.

Moreover, we can estimate some of the model parameters outside the model. The measure of varieties and firms in the economy M is fixed on the balanced growth path. We choose an entry cost c_0 to deliver a value of M that is consistent with an average firm size of 23, which is fairly stable over time in the United States.[10]

To estimate the elasticity of the vacancy cost function γ, we build on the empirical finding of Davis, Faberman, and Haltiwanger (2013), who, from JOLTS microdata, document a nearly log-linear empirical relationship between the vacancy rate and the vacancy filling rate. We show that our model has a similar prediction. Starting from the firm's optimal vacancy policy and using a log-linear approximation, we obtain:

$$\log\frac{v(z, n)}{n} \approx \kappa_0 + \kappa_1 \log\left(\frac{h(z, n)}{v} - \kappa_2\right), \quad \text{with} \quad \gamma = \frac{1}{\kappa_1} \qquad (10)$$

where k's are combinations of structural parameters, and h denotes hires. Firms with high marginal surplus post more vacancies per worker, and fill them more quickly, as they can poach labor from more firms. We compute these objects in JOLTS microdata in narrow monthly growth-rate bins, then estimate (10) by nonlinear least squares.[11] Our estimates imply $\gamma = 3.45$.

Finally, we add to the model a rate of exogenous firm exit d, to match the exit of large firms in the data.

This approach leaves the following parameters to calibrate internally: $\theta_{BEMV} = \{\mu, \sigma, \zeta, \alpha, A, \chi, \delta, \tilde{b}\}$. These parameters are estimated jointly by

---

[10] When calibrating the model, note that one can compute the value of entry under any fixed number of firms m and then set c_0 ex-post appropriately such that the free-entry condition holds. Therefore, assuming the calibration hits the target for the employment rate (0.90), m can be chosen offline to match the average firm size. When computing comparative static exercises, we fix m and c_0. The firm size distribution, and average size, endogenously change.

[11] We use updated estimates of this relationship from BLS microdata from Mongey and Violante (2019).

minimum distance. Although the estimation is joint, we heuristically discuss what moments particularly inform what parameter. The overall drift, μ, is informed by the rate of firm exit. The standard deviation of productivity shocks, σ, is informed by the standard deviation of annual log employment growth. The thickness of the tail of entrant productivity draws, ζ, is informed by job creation among young firms. The diminishing return parameter α is informed by the share of large firms. Matching efficiency, A, is informed by the nonemployment rate, and relative search efficiency of employed workers χ and exogenous separation rate δ are informed by EE and EN rates.[12]

Finally, the flow value of nonemployment $\check{b}$—which in BEMV is a preference parameter instead of being financed by taxes—is informed by the rate of job destruction of incumbent firms. Once $\check{b}$ is set, we determine τ that balances the government budget. We keep τ constant across comparative statics. Table 8.1 summarizes these moments and shows that the model does well in matching them. We note that our estimate of α implies an elasticity of substitution across varieties of 5.46. This value would imply a markup of about 20 percent in a standard monopolistically competitive model.

The underlying parameters of our new endogenous growth model are $\theta_{\text{Growth}} = \{\bar{\mu}, \bar{\sigma}, \psi, \varphi\}$. Given the estimated parameters of θ_{BEMV} in Table 8.1, we can obtain θ_{Growth} as follows. First, we set a growth rate of the economy of 1.75 percent annually, which delivers g. Second, we back out $(\bar{\mu}, \bar{\sigma})$ via the mapping

$$\bar{\mu} = -\left(\frac{\mu}{\alpha} + g\right), \quad \bar{\sigma} = \frac{\sigma}{\alpha}.$$

Third, given $\{\mu, \sigma, \zeta\}$ we back out the implied ψ given our model of imitation: $\psi = \zeta\sigma^2/^2\mu = 1.24$. Fourth, given α we back out the elasticity of

---

[12] As in BEMV, we use a broader definition of the pool of nonemployed job-seekers than in the standard unemployment definition of the BLS. This accounts for the fact that a significant number of hires come directly from out of the labor force and some of our data sources (JOLTS and Census J2J) do not identify whether the origin of hires or destination of separations is unemployment or nonparticipation. In particular, our definition of the nonemployment rate is constructed as follows. The numerator equals the sum of the unemployed (FRED series UNEMPLOY) plus those out-of-the-labor-force who answer that they "currently want a job" in the CPS (NILFWJN). The denominator equals the sum of the civilian labor force (CLF16OV) plus the same subgroup of those out-of-the-labor-force (NILFWJN). For the period 2011–2016 this ratio is, on average, just above 10 percent.

Table 8.1. Estimated parameters and targeted moments

		Value	Moment	Data	Model
A. Externally set/Normalized parameters					
ρ	Discount rate	0.004	5% annual real interest rate		
c_f	Fixed cost of operation	1	Normalization		
$Cv/(1+\gamma)$	Scalar in the cost of vacancies	100	Normalization		
H	Preference parameter	1	Normalization		
n_0	Size of entrants	1	Normalization		
β	Elasticity of matches w.r.t. vacancies	0.5	Petrongolo and Pissarides (2001)		
B. Estimated offline					
m	Number of active firms	0.043	Average firm size (BDS)	23.340	20.851
γ	Vacancy cost elasticity	3.450	Vacancy filling rate vs. hiring rate	3.450	3.450
d	Exogenous exit rate	0.002	Exit rate, 1000–2499 empl. firms	0.002	0.002
C. Internally by minimum distance					
μ	Drift of productivity	−0.001	Exit rate (annual)	0.076	0.076
σ	St.d. of productivity shocks	0.016	St.d. of log empl. growth (annual)	0.420	0.354
α	Curvature of production	0.817	Empl. share of 500+ firms	0.518	0.527
ζ	Shape of entry distribution	11.844	JC rate, age 1 firms (annual)	0.247	0.255
A	Matching efficiency	0.195	Nonemployment rate	0.100	0.100
ξ	Relative search efficiency of employed	0.151	EE rate (quarterly)	0.048	0.041
δ	Exogenous separation rate	0.017	EN rate (quarterly)	0.056	0.055
$\bar{b}$	Transformed flow value of leisure	1.029	JD rate of incumbents (annual)	0.092	0.093

Notes: Annual firm dynamics moments are from HP-filtered Census BDS data for 2011–2016, with the exception of the standard deviation of annual growth rates, which is from Elsby and Michaels (2013). Quarterly worker flows are from HP-filtered Census J2J data for 2011–2016.

substitution $\phi = (1-\alpha)/\alpha$, which delivers $\phi = 4.46$. This value would imply a markup of about 30 percent in a standard monopolistically competitive model.

Summary and nontargeted moments. In summary, we have calibrated a model of endogenous growth at rate g that matches key facts regarding firm and worker dynamics in the US economy over the period 2011–2016.

In BEMV we show that the model matches a wide array of nontargeted moments. Here we focus on life-cycle firm dynamics, which are key to our results regarding misallocation and economic growth. First, Figure 8.1 verifies that the model matches the empirical distribution of firms and employment by firm age and firm size. Most firms are small, but most employment is at large firms. Most firms are old and most employment is at old firms. Second, Figure 8.2 reveals the dynamics of the distribution of firm size and productivity over the life cycle that deliver the empirical marginal distributions in Figure 8.1. The figure shows how misallocation is partially resolved over the life cycle, with employment and productivity becoming increasingly correlated as firms age. A key feature of the model, which we highlight in BEMV, is that the model can generate small, productive, young firms. Young firms with high productivity are small because they are young and yet to accumulate workers through the frictional labor market. This is a key source of misallocation in the economy, due to search frictions, to which we will return when we discuss our results.

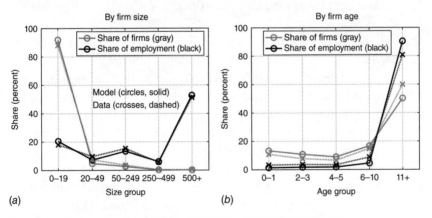

Data source: Business Dynamics Statistics (BDS), United States Census Bureau.

Figure 8.1a–b. Distribution of firms and employment by firm size and age in data and model

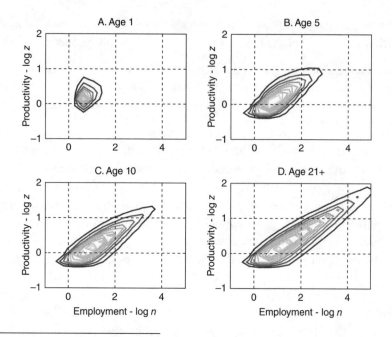

Figure 8.2. The model's firm distribution in the space of productivity z and size n at different points of the life cycle

4 Implications of Slower Growth for Business Dynamism, Labor Market Dynamics, and Misallocation

Our key counterfactual exercise is a comparative static change in the imitation parameter ψ across BGPs, holding all other parameters fixed.[13] Figure 8.3 plots the rate of growth as we vary ψ. We plot the relative imitation strength, which we define as ψ/ψ' because smaller values of ψ' imply draws of productivity that are further skewed toward the right of the incumbent productivity distribution. As we would expect, a lower ψ' raises the aggregate growth rate.

In the rest of this section, we analyze the implications of a change in the growth rate of the economy for business dynamism, labor market dynamics, and misallocation. Since we estimated the model to 2011–2016, our thought

---

[13] In the Appendix, we discuss how to solve such a counterfactual economy.

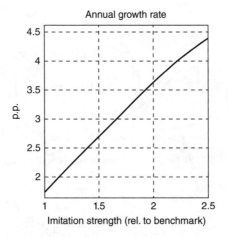

Notes: The baseline value of the imitation parameter is $\psi_0 = 1.24$, and the baseline rate of growth is $g_0 = 1.75$ percent. A lower value of ψ implies that the tail of the entrant productivity distribution is *fatter*. Relative imitation strength is therefore measured as ψ_0/ψ'.

Figure 8.3. Imitation strength iii and growth rate g

experiment is going backward in time or making ideas easier to find relative to the present (a fall in ψ and a rise in g).

4.1 Business dynamism

Figure 8.4 shows firm dynamics outcomes as we vary the underlying imitation parameter ψ. Because the parameter is not of direct interest, we plot these key outcomes as a function of the resulting endogenous growth rate.

Not surprisingly, a fall in ψ (i.e., moving to the right in these figures) is associated with an increase in firm creation (panel A). As imitation from the incumbents is easier, entrants are relatively more productive and firm creation is encouraged. As more entrants attempt to enter and there is more competition for inputs, the price of inputs rises faster. Consequently, incumbent firms exit at a faster pace and the rate of obsolescence increases. This is our counterpart of the *creative-destruction effect* of Aghion and Howitt (1994). Quantitatively, a fall in the aggregate growth rate of one percentage point annually—broadly consistent with the US experience over the past decades—is associated with a decline in firm entry of about 30 percent. For comparison, the United States has experienced a reduction in firm entry of over

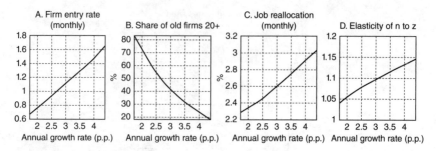

Notes: This figure plots moments from counterfactual BGP equilibria. We plot each moment against the growth rate of the economy, where variation in the growth rate is due to changes in the strength of imitation (Figure 8.3).

Figure 8.4. Business dynamism as ideas get harder to find

40 percent from the early 1980s to now (Pugsley and Sahin 2019; Akcigit and Ates 2021).

Also consistent with the US data over the past 40 years, a larger share of firms are old when growth is slower (panel B). This outcome arises naturally in our model in response to a fall in the rate of obsolescence—firms remain in the market longer, extending the firm life-cycle. The overall job reallocation rate falls with the aggregate growth rate (panel C). The reason is that as the rate of obsolescence declines, firms do not fall behind the market as quickly. Consequently, there is less need to reallocate employment across production units. Quantitatively, as the aggregate growth rate declines by one percentage point annually, the job reallocation rate decreases by around 10 percent. For comparison, the United States has experienced a decline in job reallocation of roughly 30 percent from the early 1980s to now (Akcigit and Ates 2021).

As pointed out by Decker, Haltiwanger, Jarmin, and Miranda (2020), reallocation can decline due either to lower dispersion of idiosyncratic shocks faced by businesses, or to weaker marginal responsiveness of firms to shocks. They show that it is the responsiveness of business-level employment to productivity that has weakened. Panel D of Figure 8.4 shows that the model predicts a decline in the elasticity of employment to productivity, as growth slows down. Quantitatively, the decline is smaller than its empirical counterpart, but the pattern is qualitatively consistent. A key result, which we discuss below, is that workers are better allocated across firms at lower levels of economic growth, despite lower rates of job reallocation. This makes growing following a positive productivity shock more costly, as it becomes less likely that a posted vacancy will be matched with a worker at a lower productivity firm. This novel mechanism links job-to-job mobility, growth, and the responsiveness of firm-level employment to idiosyncratic shocks.

4.2 Labor market flows

Figure 8.5 plots worker flows as a function of the aggregate growth rate, which in turn differs across BGPs due to differences in the imitation parameter ψ. As ideas get harder to find—moving from right to left in these figures—worker reallocation rates fall. As the rate of obsolescence decelerates, firms turn over more slowly in the relative productivity distribution. Consequently, there is less need to reallocate employment, which shows up as lower worker flows.

The pattern of lower worker flows is particularly evident in the EN rate and less pronounced for the EE rate. In our model, firms shrink either through quits or layoffs. When a firms' relative productivity is high, it shrinks only via quits. As its relative productivity falls, due to negative drift and obsolescence, the rate of quits increases. Finally, the firm starts to lay off workers in addition to quits, as the marginal value of a worker $S_n(z, n)$ hits the value of unemployment. With a lower rate of obsolescence, relative productivity drifts downward more slowly, extending the duration of time the firm is away from the layoff boundary. This significantly reduces EN layoffs.

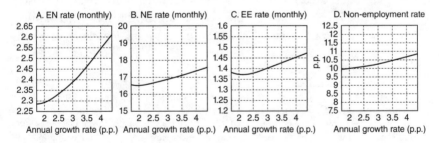

Notes: This figure plots moments from counterfactual BGP equilibria. We plot each moment against the growth rate of the economy, where variation in the growth rate is due to changes in the strength of imitation (Figure 8.3).

Figure 8.5. Labor market flows as ideas get harder to find

The NE rate also falls with slower growth, but by less than the separation (EN) rate, and as a result the nonemployment rate falls slightly. This is not surprising, since the capitalization effect is neutralized by the interest rate effect in general equilibrium with log utility (see, e.g., Aghion and Howitt 1994).[14] Note, however, how stable the nonemployment rate is in our model as the growth rate in the model almost triples. This result stands in sharp contrast with the predictions of plausibly calibrated canonical matching models featuring one-worker one-job matches and linear utility, where the effect of creative destruction on the unemployment rate is very strong (Pissarides and Vallanti 2007).

A first departure of our exercise from that in Pissarides and Vallanti (2007) is that in our case the increase in g is *endogenous*, caused by an increase in entrant imitation. With more imitation, firms are more productive and grow more quickly, and this reduces unemployment. A second departure is the inclusion of job-to-job transitions (as in Michau 2013). With job-to-job flows, the reallocation due to creative destruction can occur without generating the same amount of unemployment. Hence, the mechanism underlying the change in g in a search-and-matching model, as well as the model environment, affect the sensitivity of unemployment to growth.

4.3 Misallocation

Figure 8.6 illustrates a surprising result. As growth slows, the misallocation that exists in the economy improves, despite there being less firm and worker turnover. The dispersion of the marginal product of labor across firms falls (panel A) and the correlation between size and productivity increases (panel B). This is consistent with the well-documented reallocation of sales in the economy toward larger firms (Autor, Dorn, Katz, Patterson, and Van

---

[14] With log utility, the equilibrium discount rate in the detrended HJB equation (8) is ρ. If we had instead assumed CRRA preferences with a relative risk aversion γ, then the effective discount rate in (8) would be $\rho + (\gamma - 1)g$. If $\gamma < 1$, then the capitalization effect would resurface and would increase the relative value of future payoffs, increasing investment in creating jobs in terms of both the extensive margin of entry and intensive margin of vacancy creation by incumbents. Hence, higher g would lead to lower unemployment. An interesting avenue for future research would be understanding the strength of this capitalization effect in models like ours where firms, rather than matches, are the relevant unit. Individual job matches are relatively short-lived (4–5 years), which leads to a weak capitalization effect in existing work (Pissarides and Vallanti 2007), whereas the average age of a firm in the United States is closer to 20 years.

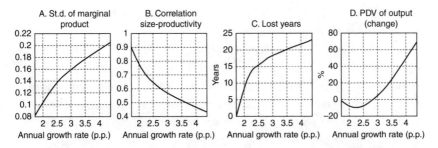

Notes: This figure plots moments from counterfactual BGP equilibria. We plot each moment against the growth rate of the economy, where variation in the growth rate is due to changes in the strength of imitation (Figure 8.3).

Figure 8.6. Improving misallocation as ideas get harder to find

Reenen 2020), and leads to a higher *level* of output, despite slower long-run growth.

What explains this finding? Our model is unique in the class of growth models in that firms operate a single product, start small, and then grow via costly hiring of workers. When the rate of economic growth is high, firms' productivity is quickly slipping behind the productivity of the economy as a whole. Therefore, the horizon of firms shrinks. All firms become *less ambitious* with respect to their expansion plans. Hiring is costly and takes time, and has a lower benefit when the incumbent firm will be swiftly replaced by better firms. A given reduction in firms' expected horizon of operations is, however, relatively more costly for high-productivity firms, who forgo a higher stream of profits when they exit. Thus, high-productivity firms no longer grow as large, which shows up as increased misallocation of labor in the economy.

We find that this output loss from misallocation can be quantitatively important. Panel C computes a measure of "lost years" caused by this level effect. It asks how many years, at the baseline annual growth rate of 1.75 percent, it would take to compensate the downward shift in the level of output caused by misallocation. For example, the additional misallocation that occurs at a growth rate of 4 percent would be offset by 22 years of economic growth at 1.75 percent. The relation is highly nonlinear: When the economy grows fast, the growth-induced misallocation is weak. Starting from low growth rates, however, a rise in the growth rate of one percentage point per year would require over 15 years of baseline growth to make up for the productivity loss from misallocation.

Panel D shows that in terms of the present discounted value of output, an improvement in imitation that increases the growth rate to at least 2.9 percent is required to offset the misallocation effects from higher growth. Admittedly, here we do not compute the transition between one balanced growth path and the other, and ψ is an exogenous parameter. Nonetheless, these calculations suggest that computing the misallocation costs of higher growth may be an important consideration in the formulation of pro-growth economic policies that could be implemented to change objects related to diffusion of ideas in the economy.

Taking stock, while a growth slowdown can have severe implications for business dynamism, the silver lining is that it can limit the degree of misallocation induced by labor market frictions. To the best of our knowledge this is a new mechanism, with the necessary ingredients being the frictional adjustment of small entering firms toward their optimal size. Our model has these features and also quantitatively replicates the joint age and size distribution of firms in the US economy, giving us some confidence in our conclusion that this force may be quantitatively relevant.

5 Conclusions

This chapter has evaluated the impact of slowing economic growth on labor market dynamism and misallocation. To that end, we have proposed a tractable extension of the rich framework of firm and worker dynamics in Bilal, Engbom, Mongey, and Violante (2022), which incorporates endogenous growth via creative destruction. Entrants imitate incumbents, gradually pushing out the technological frontier. Employment reallocates from old, obsolescing incumbents to new, more productive entrants. Although this process takes time, owing to labor market frictions, it does not necessitate workers spending time in unemployment. Instead, a large share of this reallocation takes the form of direct job-to-job moves, consistent with recent empirical evidence.

We apply the framework to show that a fall in entrants' ability to imitate incumbents, which captures the view that "ideas are getting harder to find" (Bloom, Jones, van Reenen, and Webb 2020) accounts for a range of US labor market patterns over the past 40 years. Firm creation naturally declines, as potential entrants are discouraged by the fact that coming up with good business ideas is more difficult. As fewer firms enter, less competition for inputs reduces the rate at which prices of factors of production rise. Consequently, incumbent firms become obsolete at a slower pace. Firm exit falls, the firm life-cycle lengthens, job reallocation declines, as do rates of job loss and job-to-job mobility, all consistent with secular trends in the United States. The lower entry rate and the lower productivity of entrants both contribute to lower the aggregate growth rate. At the same time, because growth is creative-destructive, allocative efficiency *improves*.

As a framework that links growth and labor market outcomes in a micro-founded theory of firm and worker dynamics, our model offers several promising directions for future research. For instance, it would be valuable to incorporate endogenous incumbent innovation, given recent evidence of the importance of such innovation for growth (Akcigit and Kerr 2018): our model only features (a reduced form of) exogenous incumbent innovation through improvements in productivity. Such an expanded framework may provide a richer understanding of how different sources of growth impact the labor market. Moreover, it would be interesting to further endogenize the process through which entrants learn about and build upon incumbent firms' technologies, along the lines of Chatterjee and Rossi-Hansberg (2012) or Akcigit, Celik, and Greenwood (2016), where new ideas occur to individual people, not organizations. A natural hypothesis is that this process involves the founder working at established firms, before spinning off to start a new firm. Under this view, the working of the labor market may affect the flow of knowledge in the economy.

A full policy analysis would require a characterization of constrained efficient allocations, which is beyond the scope of this chapter. Our results, however, do suggest that any macro or industrial policies that promote faster growth must take into account the "unintended consequence" of the higher labor misallocation and its impact on productivity. In addition, the faster labor reallocation, and the implied higher earnings volatility, could have adverse effects on workers' welfare in the presence of risk aversion and imperfect risk sharing. Interestingly, though, our model with on-the-job-search also indicates that workers' ability to move directly from one job to another may mitigate such unfavorable effects of creative-destructive growth on workers' welfare, since reallocation does not necessarily require workers to become unemployed in the process, as happens in the first generation of "growth and unemployment" models. A richer assessment of the welfare consequences of growth across the distribution of workers is best left for future work.

References

ACEMOGLU, D., P. AGHION, R. GRIFFITH, AND F. ZILIBOTTI (2010): "Vertical Integration and Technology: Theory and Evidence," *Journal of the European Economic Association*, 8(5), 989–1033.

AGHION, P., AND P. HOWITT (1992): "A Model of Growth through Creative Destruction," *Econometrica*, 60(2), 323–351.

AGHION, P., AND P. HOWITT (1994): "Growth and Unemployment," *Review of Economic Studies*, 61(3), 477–494.

AKCIGIT, U., AND S. T. ATES (2021): "Ten Facts on Declining Business Dynamism and Lessons from Endogenous Growth Theory," *American Economic Journal: Macroeconomics*, 13(1), 257–98.

AKCIGIT, U., AND S. T. ATES (2023): "What Happened to U.S. Business Dynamism?," *Journal of Political Economy*, forthcoming.

AKCIGIT, U., M. A. CELIK, AND J. GREENWOOD (2016): "Buy, Keep, or Sell: Economic Growth and the Market for Ideas," *Econometrica*, 84, 943–984.

AKCIGIT, U., AND W. R. KERR (2018): "Growth through Heterogeneous Innovations," *Journal of Political Economy*, 126(4), 1374–1443.

AUTOR, D., D. DORN, L. F. KATZ, C. PATTERSON, AND J. VAN REENEN (2020): "The Fall of the Labor Share and the Rise of Superstar Firms," *Quarterly Journal of Economics*, 135(2), 645–709.

BENHABIB, J., J. PERLA, AND C. TONETTI (2021): "Reconciling Models of Diffusion and Innovation: A Theory of the Productivity Distribution and Technology Frontier," *Econometrica*, 89(5), 2261–2301.

BILAL, A., N. ENGBOM, S. MONGEY, AND G. L. VIOLANTE (2022): "Firm and Worker Dynamics in a Frictional Labor Market," *Econometrica*, 90(4), 1425–1462.

BLOOM, N., C. JONES, J. VAN REENEN, AND M. WEBB (2020): "Are Ideas Getting Harder to Find?," *American Economic Review*, 110(4), 1104–1144.

CHATTERJEE, S., AND E. ROSSI-HANSBERG (2012): "Spinoffs and the Market for Ideas," *International Economic Review*, 53(1), 53–93.

DAVIS, S. J., R. J. FABERMAN, AND J. C. HALTIWANGER (2013): "The Establishment-Level Behavior of Vacancies and Hiring," *Quarterly Journal of Economics*, 128(2), 581–622.

DECKER, R. A., J. C. HALTIWANGER, R. S. JARMIN, AND J. MIRANDA (2020): "Changing Business Dynamism and Productivity: Shocks vs. Responsiveness," *American Economic Review*, 110(24236), 3952–3990.

ELSBY, M., AND A. GOTTFRIES (2022): "Firm Dynamics, On-the-Job Search, and Labor Market Fluctuations," *Review of Economic Studies*, 89(3), 1370–1419.

ELSBY, M. W. L., AND R. MICHAELS (2013): "Marginal Jobs, Heterogeneous Firms, and Unemployment Flows," *American Economic Journal: Macroeconomics*, 5(1), 1–48.

ENGBOM, N. (2017): "Firm and Worker Dynamics in an Aging Labor Market," discussion paper, New York University.

FERNALD, J. G. (2016): "Reassessing Longer-Run U.S. Growth: How Low?," Working Paper Series 2016–18, Federal Reserve Bank of San Francisco.

FUJITA, S., G. MOSCARINI, AND F. POSTEL-VINAY (2019): "Measuring Employer-to-Employer Reallocation," discussion paper, Yale University.

GARCIA-MACIA, D., C.-T. HSIEH, AND P. J. KLENOW (2019): "How Destructive Is Innovation?," *Econometrica*, 87(5), 1507–1541.

GORDON, R. (2016): *The Rise and Fall of American Growth: The U.S. Standard of Living since the Civil War*. Princeton, NJ: Princeton University Press.

HOPENHAYN, H., AND R. ROGERSON (1993): "Job Turnover and Policy Evaluation: A General Equilibrium Analysis," *Journal of Political Economy*, 101(5), 915–938.

HOPENHAYN, H. A. (1992): "Entry, Exit, and Firm Dynamics in Long Run Equilibrium," *Econometrica*, 60(5), 1127–1150.

KONIG, M., J. LORENZ, AND F. ZILIBOTTI (2016): "Innovation vs. Imitation and the Evolution of Productivity Distributions," *Theoretical Economics*, 11(3), 1053–1102.

LUCAS, R. E. (1978): "On the Size Distribution of Business Firms," *Bell Journal of Economics*, 9(2), 508.

LUCAS, R. E., AND B. MOLL (2014): "Knowledge Growth and the Allocation of Time," *Journal of Political Economy*, 122(1), 1–51.

LUTTMER, E. G. (2007): "Selection, Growth, and the Size Distribution of Firms," *Quarterly Journal of Economics*, 122(3), 1103–1144.

LUTTMER, E. G. (2010): "Models of Growth and Firm Heterogeneity," *Annual Review of Economics*, 2(1), 547–576.

MARTELLINI, P., AND G. MENZIO (2020): "Declining Search Frictions, Unemployment, and Growth," *Journal of Political Economy*, 128(12), 4387–4437.

MICHAU, J.-B. (2013): "Creative Destruction with On-the-Job Search," *Review of Economic Dynamics*, 16(4), 691–707.

MONGEY, S., AND G. L. VIOLANTE (2019): "Macro Recruiting Intensity from Micro Data," NBER Working Papers 26231, National Bureau of Economic Research, Inc.

PERLA, J., AND C. TONETTI (2014): "Equilibrium Imitation and Growth," *Journal of Political Economy*, 122(1), 52–76.

PETRONGOLO, B., AND C. PISSARIDES (2001): "Looking into the Black Box: A Survey of the Matching Function," *Journal of Economic Literature*, 39(2), 390–431.

PISSARIDES, C. A., AND G. VALLANTI (2007): "The Impact of TFP Growth on Steady-State Unemployment," *International Economic Review*, 48(2), 607–640.

POSTEL-VINAY, F., AND J.-M. ROBIN (2002): "Equilibrium Wage Dispersion with Worker and Employer Heterogeneity," *Econometrica*, 70(6), 2295–2350.

PUGSLEY, B. W., AND A. SAHIN (2019): "Grown-Up Business Cycles," *Review of Financial Studies*, 32(3), 1102–1147.

APPENDIX

A.1 Equilibrium

A *balanced growth path equilibrium* with positive entry consists of: (i) a de-trended joint surplus function $S(z, n)$; (ii) a vacancy policy $v(z, n)$; (iii) a law of motion for firm-level employment $\frac{dn}{dt}(z, n)$; (iv) a stationary distribution of firms $H(z, n)$; (v) vacancy- and employment-weighted distributions of marginal surplus $H_v(S_n)$ and $H_n(S_n)$; (vi) a positive mass of entrants m_0; (vii) a vacancy meeting rate $q(\theta)$ and conditional probability of meeting an un-employed worker ϕ; (viii) an initial level of output Y_0, unemployment rate u, rate of growth g, rate of return r, and price of the fixed factor p_t^X; and (ix) prices p_{it} and quantities of goods y_{it}. Under the normalization $P_t = 1$, these objects satisfy:

(i) Total surplus $S(z, n)$ satisfies the detrended HJB equation (8) under (Y_0, u, g)—and associated boundary conditions. That is, $\mu(z) = -[\alpha(\bar{\mu} + g) + \sigma^2/2]z$, the discount rate is $r = \rho + g$, the detrended rate of benefits is $\tilde{b} = \tau/u$, and detrended revenue is $Y_0^{-\alpha}zn^\alpha$.

(ii) The vacancy policy $v(z, n)$ satisfies the first-order condition:

$$c_v(v(z, n); z, n) = q(\theta)\left[\phi S_n(z, n) + (1 - \phi)\int_0^{S_n(z, n)}(S_n(z, n) - S_n')dH_n(S_n')\right].$$

(iii) The law of motion for firm-level employment is

$$\frac{dn}{dt}(z, n) = \begin{cases} -\frac{n}{dt} \\ q(\theta)v(z, n)\left[\phi + (1 - \phi)H_n\big(S_n(z, n)\big)\right] \\ \frac{n_L^*(z) - n}{dt} \\ \\ -n\left[\delta + \lambda^E(\theta)\big(1 - H_v(S_n(z, n))\big)\right] \end{cases} \begin{array}{l} \\ n < n_E^*(z) \\ \\ n \in \left[n_E^*(z), n_L^*(z)\right] \\ n \geq n_L^*(z) \end{array}$$

where the notation $\frac{n}{dt}$ denotes a jump of size n, and where the exit threshold satisfies value-matching, and the exit and layoff boundaries satisfy smooth-pasting conditions in productivity and employment:

$$S(z, n_E^*(z)) = \vartheta \, , \underbrace{}_{\text{Value-matching from (8)}}$$

$$\underbrace{S_z(z, n_E^*(z)) = 0, \, S_n(z, n_E^*(z)) = 0 \quad \text{if } \frac{dn}{dt}(z, n_E^*(z)) < 0, \, S_n(z, n_L^*(z)) = 0.}_{\text{Smooth-pasting conditions from (8)}}$$

(iv) Vacancy- and employment-weighted distributions of marginal surplus are consistent:

$$H_v(S_n) = \int 1_{[S_n(z, n) \leq S_n]} \frac{v(z, n)}{v} dH(z, n), \quad v = \int v(z, n) dH(z, n)$$

$$H_n(S_n) = \int 1_{[S_n(z, n) \leq S_n]} \frac{n}{n} dH(z, n), \quad n = \int n \, dH(z, n).$$

(v) The measure of firms $H(z, n)$ is stationary, and admits a density function $h(z, n)$ that satisfies:

$$0 = -\frac{\partial}{\partial n}\left(\frac{dn}{dt}(z, n)h(z, n)\right) - \frac{\partial}{\partial z}(\mu(z)h(z, n))$$
$$+ \frac{\partial^2}{\partial z^2}\left(\frac{\sigma(z)^2}{2} h(z, n)\right) + m_0 \pi_0(z)\Delta(n)$$

where Δ is the Dirac delta "function," which is zero everywhere except $n = n_0$, where it is infinite.

(vi) Entry m_0 is such that the expected value of a new entrant is zero:

$$\eta c_0 = \int S(z, n_0) dF(z; \zeta),$$

where F is a Pareto distribution with tail parameter, and ζ is determined by imitation: $\zeta = \psi(2\mu / \sigma^2)$, with $\mu = -\alpha[(\bar{\mu} + g) + \sigma^2 / 2]z$.

(vii) Vacancy meeting rate $q(\theta)$ and conditional probability of meeting an unemployed worker ϕ are consistent with the aggregate matching function given employment n, unemployment $(u = \bar{n} - n)$, and vacancies v.

(viii) The initial level of output in (8) is consistent with output of all firms in the economy under $H(z, n)$:

$$Y_0^\alpha = m \int_{N \times Z} z n^\alpha dH(z, n)$$

and the rate of benefits $\tilde{b}(\tau, u)$ is consistent with government budget balance $\tilde{b}(\tau, u) = \tau / u$, and the interest rate is consistent with the household Euler equation $r = \rho + g$.

(ix) The market for the fixed factor clears. This requires $p_t^X = \eta Y_t = e^{gt} Y_0$. Under this condition the fixed factor is perfectly elastically supplied by households, and hence the market for H_t clears at the quantity of the input demanded by firms.

(x) Prices p_{it} and quantities y_{it} are consistent with household demand (1) under $c_{it} = y_{it}$ for each good, which implies $C_t = Y_t$.

A.2 Methodology

Consider an alternative value ψ'. The equilibrium variables that enter the HJB for surplus (8) are: (i) growth g', via the drift in firm relative productivity $\mu' = -\alpha(\bar{\mu} + g')$, (ii) unemployment u', via the value of nonemployment to workers $\tilde{b}' = \tau / u'$, as well as the share of potential hires who are unemployed, and (iii) the level of output Y_0', via the shifter in revenue. Given a guess of these three objects (g', u', Y_0'), we can solve the detrended HJB equation (8) to obtain $S(z, n; g', \tilde{b}', Y_0')$ and the associated stationary equilibrium of firms $H(z, n)$ following the approach in BEMV. We then check whether (i) the guess of unemployment is consistent with worker flows in the stationary equilibrium, (ii) the guess of Y_0' is consistent with the aggregation condition under the stationary distribution of firms $H(z, n)$: $Y_0'^{\alpha} = m \int z n^{\alpha} dH(z, n)$, and (iii) the free-entry condition holds under the implied distribution of entrant productivity, which depends on ψ' and the distribution of incumbents via $\zeta' = \psi' (2\mu' / \sigma^2)$:

$$c_0 = \int S(z, n; g', \tilde{b}', Y_0') dF(z, \zeta').$$

The key observation is that the free-entry condition under fixed m is used to solve for g' in the new BGP equilibrium. The following argument makes this clear. As we decrease ψ, entrants draw from a distribution that is skewed further toward the tail of incumbent productivities. This makes entry more valuable. As more entrants attempt to enter, and entrants are better on average, costs of inputs are bid up, inducing more incumbent firms to exit. That is, the rate of obsolescence accelerates, increasing g. As relative productivity declines more quickly, however, the value of entry falls. The rate of growth g increases until the value of entry falls such that the free-entry condition is satisfied.

CHAPTER 9

When Workers' Skills Become Unbundled

Some Empirical Consequences for Sorting and Wages

OSKAR NORDSTRÖM SKANS, PHILIPPE CHONÉ,
and FRANCIS KRAMARZ

1 Introduction

This chapter studies how workers are sorted across establishments based on workers' attributes and firms' characteristics. This classic question in labor economics has a long tradition (e.g., assignment models à la Sattinger 1975). Recently the literature has started to focus on the multidimensional nature of workers' skills—that is, workers come equipped with *bundles* of skills, with no access to markets where skills can be traded separately. On the theory side, recent work of Choné and Kramarz (2021) and Edmond and Mongey (2020) has expanded the pathbreaking work of Heckman and Scheinkman (1987) and Lindenlaub (2017). On the empirical side, several papers have approached related questions on sorting and skills. In particular, Fredriksson et al. (2018) explore how workers are sorted across heterogeneous jobs whereas Guvenen et al. (2020) study sorting across occupations.

This chapter attempts to bring the empirical and theoretical strands closer together by providing reduced-form evidence using the model adopted by Choné and Kramarz (2021). In Choné and Kramarz (2021), following Heckman and Scheinkman (1987), *each worker is equipped with a set of skills that needs to be sold as a bundle to a single employer.* Firms have heterogeneous production technologies and, in equilibrium, use different types of workers. The model clearly outlines how the supply and demand for different types of skills determine the structure of sorting and of market wages across worker types. In addition, the model describes how sorting patterns and the wage structure change when innovations to technology and/or markets *unbundle* the skills so that they can be sold separately.

In this chapter we examine the empirical counterpart of the above theoretical structure. We contrast key predictions of the Choné and Kramarz (2021) model (CK, hereafter) with Swedish register data on cognitive and noncognitive skills, when bundled and when unbundled. Skills are measured for nearly all Swedish males who entered into adulthood during three decades starting in the early 1970s. We use these data to track the distribution of workers' sorting and the relationship to wages during the period 1996–2013.

Some of our empirical analyses have closely related predecessors, many of which used the same data sources. Fredriksson et al. (2018) used the same data to study how skill sorting at the job level evolves with tenure among new matches, in particular, when inexperienced workers search for a suitable job, but the theoretical motivations are entirely different. Our analysis of the evolution of labor market sorting is related to that contained in Card et al. (2013), Song et al. (2019), or Skans et al. (2009) for Sweden. Even more related is, however, Håkanson et al. (2021), which uses the same data as this chapter. Again, our objective differs, hence some of their results are connected to ours but with a different interpretation. Hensvik and Skans (2020) describe the association between skill content trends in labor demand at the occupational level (rather than at the job level). Recent work by Böhm et al. (2020) complements our analysis by relating sorting to wages using the same data source. However, their analysis identifies the effects of interest from workers' movements in the tradition of Abowd et al. (1999), when we show that this has no theoretical foundation in our approach. Their analysis is, in this sense, similar in spirit to Fredriksson et al. (2018), as both identify their effects from noncompetitive frictions across firms or jobs. More generally, our wage analysis focuses on the *market returns,* in the spirit of the Chicago school, by studying the impact of bundling constraints on wages, abstracting from search frictions and other market imperfections.

Our results clearly demonstrate that workers are nonrandomly sorted across establishments. Indeed, establishments specialize both in the horizontal (mix of skill types), as CK predicts, and vertical (quality of each skill type) dimensions, as assortative matching predicts. However, the horizontal dimension seems to dominate, in particular at the top of the ability distribution. For instance, high-skilled workers with more cognitive than noncognitive skills are much more likely to work with workers sharing these exact traits. In addition, as CK predicts, such workers are more likely to work with "middle skilled" workers whose skills are also "specialized" in this cognitive dimension. *But,* again in line with CK, they are *less* likely to work with high-skilled workers who hold *noncognitive* skills. Importantly, this tendency of specialists to work with others specialized in the same skill has increased progressively across cohorts and over time, regardless of the age at which we evaluate the patterns.

Furthermore, market wages have properties that are well in line with CK's predictions. In particular, wage returns to each specific skill is higher in the segments that are dominated by firms that rely more heavily on workers of that type. Finally, in parallel with the increase in sorting through time, wages of generalists have grown more rapidly than those of specialists as predicted by CK's analysis of skills' unbundling (due to innovations such as outsourcing or platform markets à la Uber).

This chapter is structured as follows. Section 2 presents the main elements of the theory contained in Choné and Kramarz (2021). Section 3 presents the data. Section 4 shows results on sorting. Sections 5 and 6 present results on wages. Section 7 concludes.

2 The CK Model of Skill Bundling and Unbundling

We start by presenting some useful elements of the theory in Choné and Kramarz (2021). We outline the nature of the theoretical problem and the essence of its mathematical solution. This solution will constitute the basis of the empirical elements presented in the subsequent sections.

2.1 *The setting: An economy with skill bundling*

CK models the matching between heterogeneous workers, endowed with multidimensional skills, and firms, heterogeneous in their production functions.

Formally, a worker's skill endowment is a vector $x = (x_1, \ldots, x_j, \ldots, x_k)$, where each element x_j represents worker's endowment level of skill type j. We may refer to $\lambda = |x|$ as the overall quality of a worker of type x. Similarly, we refer to $\tilde{x} = x / |x|$ as her skill profile. The skill profile represents a *horizontal* dimension of heterogeneity, or the comparative advantage of the worker. It is natural to think of some workers as generalists when they have a balanced skills set, whereas others are specialized, with a skills endowment that is large in some dimension but small in another. Similarly, heterogeneity in $\lambda = |x|$ represents *vertical* heterogeneity—i.e., some workers have larger skill absolute endowments but an identical skill profile. Throughout, we assume that the supply of skills is exogenously fixed, before the matching takes place.[1]

The multidimensional nature of workers' skills matters because firms are heterogeneous in their needs for these skills. CK models an economy where each firm's production process involves $k \geq 2$ tasks. Task $j, j = 1, \ldots, k$, is produced through a linear aggregation of the employees' endowments in skill j:

$$X_j = \int x_j \, dN^d(x; \phi), \tag{1}$$

where $dN^d(x; \phi)$ is the number of workers of type x hired by the firm of type ϕ.

All firms' production functions $F(X; \phi)$ are concave in the firm-level aggregate skill vector X. As mentioned above, firms differ in both their vertical and their horizontal dimensions. In the vertical dimensions, firms are endowed with a total factor productivity (denoted by z). In the horizontal dimension, firms differ in their need to use different tasks (and thus, skills) in the production process. Horizontal differences are captured by the parameter α. Firm-level heterogeneity thus takes the form $\phi = (\alpha, z)$, where $F(X; \alpha, z) = zF(X; \alpha, 1)$. It is natural to assume that firm heterogeneity and worker heterogeneity have the same dimension: that is, S $k - 1$.[2]

The output in equation (1) is an aggregation of workers' skills for each skill-type j used to produce an intermediary input, task j, that enters the firm's production function $F(X; \alpha, z)$. Hence, we use the terms "tasks" (both an input of the firm's production function and an output of skill aggregation) and "skills" (an input to produce tasks) interchangeably in what follows.

---

[1] Skills are distributed according to a positive probability measure $dH^w(x)$ on $X = R_+^k$.

[2] Firm types are distributed according to a probability measure $dH^f(\phi)$ on a set Φ. We normalize the numbers of firms and workers to one w.l.o.g.

A matching between workers and firms is characterized by a coupling $\pi(x, \phi)$ of the measures H^w and H^f—i.e., a measure on $X \times \Phi$ that admits H^w and H^f as marginals on X and Φ, respectively. The surplus to be shared between firms and workers is the total output in the economy:

$$\text{Total Output} = \int F\left(\int x \, d\pi(x \mid \phi); \phi\right) dH^f(\phi), \tag{2}$$

which differs from $\iint F(x; \phi) \, d\pi(x; \phi)$, the grand sum of firm-specific tasks, because F is nonlinear in X. To fix ideas, CK often makes use of the constant elasticity of substitution (CES) production function with constant elasticity of substitution and decreasing returns to scale:

$$F(X; z, \alpha) = (z/\eta) \left[\sum_{j=1}^{k} \alpha_j X_j^\sigma \right]^{\eta/\sigma}, \tag{3}$$

with $\Sigma_{j=1}^{k} \alpha_j = 1, \eta < 1, \sigma \neq 0$, and $\sigma < 1$. The parameter α_j reflects the intensity of the firm's demand for skill-type j.

Competitive bundling equilibria. Under bundling, *the workers' sets of skills cannot be untied* because there are no separate markets for each skill. Firms and workers are restricted to trade in packages of skills $x = (x_1, \ldots, x_k)$. The worker skills are observed by the firm and are contractible. We rule out agency problems: a firm that pays $w(x)$ for x gets exactly x. Apart from the bundling friction, we abstract from all labor market frictions. CK shows that there is a market wage for a worker of type x, denoted by $w(x)$.

Given the wage schedule $w(x)$, the skill demand of a firm of type ϕ is a positive measure $dN^d(x; \phi)$ that maximizes its profit

$$\Pi(\phi; w) = \max_{dN^d} F\left(\int x \, dN^d(x; \phi)\right) - \int w(x) \, dN^d(x). \tag{4}$$

The objective function of the firm depends only on its aggregate skill $X^d(\phi) = \int x \, dN^d(x)$ and on the associated wage bill $\int w(x) \, dN^d(x)$. The wage schedule in equilibrium must be such that the sum of all firms' skill demands $N^d(x; \phi)$ and supply of skills coincide for all worker types. The existence of equilibria as well as the equilibrium properties are presented in CK. In particular, in equilibrium, the wage schedule is shown to be convex and homogeneous of degree one.

At the firm ϕ's aggregate skill X^d demand, the productivity of each skill equals its marginal price:

$$F_j(X^d(\phi);\phi) = w_j(X^d(\phi)). \tag{5}$$

This first-order condition (5) generalizes the standard condition that wage equals marginal productivity at a competitive equilibrium. That is, when the wage schedule is locally linear, price equals marginal productivity. Otherwise, the *implicit* price of skill i in the neighborhood of the aggregate skill X^d is the partial derivative $w_i = \partial w / \partial x_i$ evaluated at that point.

The case with two skills and tasks. When $k = 2$, we may parameterize skill profiles as $\tilde{X} = (\cos\theta, \sin\theta)$ and represent the aggregate demand $X^d = (\Lambda^d \cos\theta^d, \Lambda^d \sin\theta^d)$ in polar coordinates, where Λ^d is the total quality of workers employed at firm ϕ.

The strict convexity of the wage schedule implies that it is cheaper for firms to purchase the bundle $(x_1(\theta), x_2(\theta))$ from a generalist worker (a worker endowed with both skills in sufficient quantities) than to purchase $x_1(\theta)$ units of skill 1 and $x_2(\theta)$ units of skill 2 separately from specialist workers.

Furthermore, when the production function is CES with two skills:

$$F(X_1, X_2; \alpha_1, \alpha_2, z) = \frac{z}{\eta}(\alpha_1 X_1^\sigma + \alpha_2 X_2^\sigma)^{\eta/\sigma},$$

CK shows that a sorting condition holds in equilibrium.

The sorting between workers and firms is represented by the increasing function, ensuring that firms with a technology that is efficient in the use of skill j also employ more j-specialists. Furthermore, CK shows that the total level of skills (quality) of the workers employed by firm, $\Lambda^d(\alpha_2, z)$, increases with firm's total factor productivity z. Thus, in this sense the model exhibits positive assortative matching (PAM). Overall, and in contrast to alternative models such as Lindenlaub (2017), the sorting pattern highlighted here pertains to both the horizontal and the vertical dimensions of workers' skills (skill profile and total quality) rather than to each of the two skills separately.

As is essential for labor economists, an equilibrium wage exists. Furthermore, for any strictly convex wage schedule $w(x)$, for any homogeneous production function $F(.; \phi)$ satisfying a classic single-crossing assumption, and for any workers' distribution H^w, there exist distributions of the firms' technological parameters ϕ for which w is the equilibrium wage.

When the equilibrium wage schedule includes linear parts (facets). Until now, we focused on the case when the equilibrium wage schedule we studied was *strictly* convex. But there is also a possibility that the equilibrium wage schedule includes linear parts. This can happen when the market demand for (local) generalists is sufficiently high that it starts to be profitable for firms to instead hire and combine, or "bunch," (local) specialists of different kinds instead of only hiring the generalists.

The equilibrium wage schedule typically has strictly convex parts together with linear parts. In the case where $k = 2$ it is useful to envision the space of skills as represented in a positive quadrant. We can consider workers at the extreme left and extreme right of the angle that defines a linear segment of the convex wage schedule. Workers in the middle of the angle are local "generalists"; workers on each side are local specialists. Essentially adding the price for the skills of a specialist worker at the extreme left to that for the skills of a specialist worker at the extreme right will yield the price for the skills of the (appropriately selected) generalist workers in the middle if the wage schedule is linear. Put differently, the sum of the wages for two (local) specialists is equal to the sum of the wages for two (local) generalists.

Hence, in the case of bunching, the firm will obtain its optimal mix by hiring workers with different skill profiles rather than focusing on a unique skill profile as in the case of strictly convex parts of the equilibrium wage schedule. But even when this happens, there remains a perfect separation in the sense that each firm's aggregate skill mix θ always increases with α. Thus, we still have full sorting in terms of the *skill mix* of the workers in relation to the technology of the firm.

2.2 Unbundling

CK discusses in detail what happens when new technologies (Uber being a prominent example) or changes in market institutions (such as the Hartz reforms that facilitated the use of temp agencies in Germany in the 2000s) enable unbundling of skills—workers and firms become able/allowed to trade skills as separate commodities. In a first step, CK discusses the case when this unbundling technology is costless for all market participants. In a second stage they assume that it entails some costs incurred by workers and/or firms.

Costless unbundling. In this case, full efficiency prevails when competitive markets for individual skills do exist. This unconstrained efficiency therefore requires that the marginal productivities are constant across firms, i.e., for any $j = 1, \ldots, k$, there exists μ_j such that

$$F_j(X^*(\phi); \phi) = \mu_j$$

for all firms ϕ. Because there are k markets, one for each skill, there are k prices. On the supply side, the total supply of skills is unchanged. However, each worker can split her entire supply of skills between an employing firm and the market, making individual labor supply *endogenous* (in contrast to the bundling case where workers were "forced" by the technology to sell all their skills to a unique firm, which used them in full).

Assuming two tasks and a CES technology, CK characterizes those workers benefiting from full unbundling and those harmed in the process. More precisely, CK shows that, when the production function is given by (3) with $k = 2$, and except in the case where the wage schedule is linear under bundling (i.e., there is full bunching), at least some generalist workers are strictly better off after unbundling. Furthermore, if skills are complements ($\sigma < \eta$), at least one type of specialist worker ($\theta = 0$ and / or $\theta = \pi/2$) is strictly worse off. The extent to which generalists benefit from unbundling and specialists are harmed by the process is an empirical question, partly addressed in the following empirical analysis.

CK characterizes this unbundling process further and shows that after unbundling, specialized firms tend to specialize further, with their skill mixes being better aligned with their technologies. So specialization is an outcome, a result of the opening of markets rather than an assumption embedded in unbundling.

Costly unbundling. So far, we have assumed that the unbundling of skills is a costless process. However, if unbundling comes from an innovation (such as Uber, which creates a market for driving skills), workers are likely to have to pay a fee or, more generally, incur a cost to have their skills unbundled. This creates wedges between the market wages paid to workers and prices paid by firms. Two interpretations for these wedges are possible:

1. There is one market price p_i^f for skill i, but workers incur a cost c_i per unit of unbundled skill i.
2. The platform(s) purchase(s) skill i from workers at price p_i^w and resell(s) it to firms at price p_i^f, with a margin c_i.

Furthermore, the range of implicit prices for each skill satisfies:

$$\max w_i^u - \min w_i^u \leq c_i, \tag{6}$$

where c_i is the cost incurred per unit of unbundled skill i. If a positive amount of skill i is traded on the market, then equality prevails in (6), with $p_i^f = \max w_i^u$ and $p_i^w = \min w_i^u$ being, respectively, the firm price and the worker price for that skill.

The presence of wedges between firm price and worker price implies that contracted workers—those who supply one of their skills through the market—and employed workers—those who supply their skills bundle to a firm—are paid different prices for the same skill used at the same firm.

3 Data and Empirical Strategies

3.1 Data overview

We use a broad data set covering Swedish male workers' multidimensional skills. The data originates from the Swedish military conscription tests taken by most males born between 1952 and 1981.[3] The tests were taken at age 18 and the data should therefore be understood as capturing premarket abilities. There are two main components; *cognitive abilities*, henceforth denoted as C, which are measured through a written test; and *noncognitive abilities*, henceforth denoted as N, which are measured during a structured interview with a specialized psychologist. As noted in the introduction, the data have been used to assess labor market sorting in previous work, most notably in Fredriksson et al. (2018) and Håkanson et al. (2021). Our definitions and setup draw heavily on Fredriksson et al. (2018) in several dimensions.

Our used data on employment cover 1996 to 2013, and we include all workers (aged 20 to 64) with reported test results. An important component of the analysis is that the cross-worker heterogeneity in skill types that is being measured at age 18 remains relevant for understanding worker heterogeneity later in life. Previous work (and our own results presented below) has shown that this is a plausible assumption. Skill types are related both to

---

[3] See Mood et al. (2012) for details on the data collection. Although the share of test takers is somewhat lower in the final years, we have no reason to believe that this will interfere with our analysis.

wages and to the type of work people perform throughout their careers; see, e.g., Fredriksson et al. (2018), Håkanson et al. (2021), and Lindqvist and Vestman (2011).

We include all workers in their main job in November as long as we can identify their establishment.[4] When studying the link between skills and wages, we use wage data from the Structure of Earnings Statistics. These data come from a firm-level survey that heavily over-samples large firms. The data cover 30 percent of private sector employees and all public sector workers. We can verify that our main wage results are insensitive to the sampling by using average monthly earnings, which we observe for all. For the same set of workers, we observe occupations. For all our analyses, we only include one job per worker and year.[5]

Our main target for the sorting analysis concerns how workers are sorted across *establishments*. We include all establishments with between 6 and 600 workers with measured skills. But we also present results for *jobs*, defined as the intersection of the occupation (at the three-digit level), and establishment of the worker, as in Fredriksson et al. (2018). All results are stable across these two definitions.

3.1.1 Defining generalists and specialists

The skill data are measured on an ordinal discrete (integer) scale ranging from 1 to 9. Standard practice in the literature is to treat these data as if continuous and cardinal after standardizing them to mean zero and standard deviation one within each birth cohort; see e.g., Lindqvist and Vestman (2011). We proceed differently and, whenever we can, instead strive to build our empirical strategies to account for the fact that the data are reported on a discrete ordinal scale. We assume that the ordinal scales have monotonic relationships to the underlying productive abilities they represent.

We use as our main empirical tool a classification of workers as *generalists* or *specialists* depending on the relationship between the two reported scores. This corresponds to the concept of x_1/x_2 in the theory section. Because we are unable to precisely compare the two scales, we allow the data to "wiggle"

---

[4] An establishment is a physical place of work within one firm. About 10 percent of all workers do not have a fixed physical place of work, and these workers are therefore not included.

[5] The preference order is to first use observations where the wage can be observed. Wages are sampled in October or November. If there is no (unique) such observation, we select the observation with the highest earnings.

one step before referring to workers as specialists and therefore count workers with less than a one-step difference between the scores as generalists. We thus heuristically define workers as *Generalists* if $abs\,(C_i - N_i) < 2$ and consequently define workers as *C-Specialists* if $C_i > N_i + 1$ and *N*-Specialists if $N_i > C_i + 1$.

These definitions force us to assume that there is some shared relationship between the two scales (the measures C_i vs. N_i) for each given worker i. On the other hand, the computation does not rely on any cardinal interpretation of differences along each of the scales.

Building on this worker-level classification, we classify the skill-type environment each worker has in his establishment. The classification relies on (between 5 and 599) coworkers with measured skills, and we need to assume that these coworkers' skills reflect the overall skill environment of the establishment. We define establishment types as follows: *Generalist establishments* have a share of generalists that exceeds 50 percent.[6] Other establishments are classified as either *C-establishments* or *N-establishments* depending on which type of specialist dominates among the employees. This classification does, according to the theory, inform us about α—the type of production function used by the establishment. To ensure that we do not generate any mechanical relationship between the worker's own skills and the measure of establishment types, we only use the *coworkers* when classifying establishments.[7]

For some of our analyses it is also useful to classify workers in terms of overall ability levels. Here we define workers as *low-skilled* if the "sum" of (measured) cognitive and noncognitive ability falls below 9, and *high-skilled* if the same sum is above 11, whereas the *mid-skilled* are those where the sum is in between. This classification is obviously more cardinal in nature, as the base is an accumulation of high and low values on to the inherently ordinal scale. This caveat should obviously be kept in mind when interpreting the results, but a mitigating factor may be that we use this classification only in contexts where we simultaneously account for the workers' specializations in the C/N dimension.

---

[6] Establishments with an exactly equal share of N-specialists and C-specialists are also considered "generalist." This is obviously relevant only to the smallest establishments.

[7] This means that the same establishment, in principle, can be classified differently for different workers within the same establishment (because the excluded worker is different). This empirical curiosity does not have any impact on our conclusions.

3.2 Descriptive statistics

Figure 9.1 depicts the joint distributions of the skills as reported on their 1–9 scale. The lower panels show the joint distributions, and, as is evident, the skills are correlated (correlation f 0.37 in the used data) but also contain independent information.

Table 9.1 shows descriptive statistics for the used sample. The first column shows the full used data. As is evident, average test scores are marginally above 5 in both dimensions. About half of the sample are classified as generalists (i.e., being on the diagonal of the joint distribution depicted in Figure 9.1) and about one-quarter of each are specialists in the cognitive or the noncognitive dimension.

The next columns split the data in these three groups (generalists, C- vs. N-specialists). The table shows, as expected, that the groups are equally distributed across years, ages, and birth cohorts. Cognitive skills are "twice" as

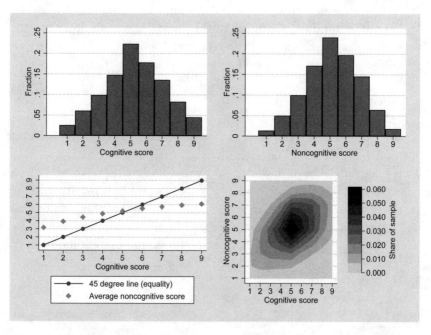

Notes: The figure shows the test score results in our used data. See restrictions in the text. The bottom panels illustrate the joint distributions.

Figure 9.1. Measured ability scores

Table 9.1. Descriptive statistics of used data

	(1)	(2)	(3)	(4)	(5)
	All	Generalist	C-specialist	N-specialist	Wage obs
Year	2004.8	2004.8	2004.9	2004.7	2005.1
Cohort	1965.8	1966.0	1965.4	1965.8	1965.1
Age	39.0	38.8	39.5	39.0	40.0
Worker skills:					
Cognitive (C=1–9)	5.252	5.190	6.914	3.643	5.366
Noncognitive (N=1–9)	5.179	5.206	4.090	6.267	5.239
C+N low (<9)	0.252	0.237	0.207	0.339	0.233
C+N mid (9–11)	0.376	0.422	0.316	0.325	0.371
C+N high (>11)	0.371	0.341	0.476	0.336	0.396
Establishment size	82.1	81.9	88.2	76.0	118.4
Generalist establishment	0.767	0.777	0.722	0.787	0.782
Cognitive establishment	0.136	0.125	0.209	0.087	0.141
Noncognitive est.	0.097	0.098	0.069	0.126	0.077
Matched	0.504	0.777	0.209	0.126	0.507
Observed occupation	0.517	0.514	0.539	0.503	0.978
Observed wage	0.529	0.526	0.551	0.513	1.000
ln(wage)	10.182	10.182	10.227	10.131	10.182
ln(earnings)	10.102	10.104	10.138	10.059	10.157
N	12,627,401	6,964,632	2,744,810	2,917,959	6,682,011

Note: Descriptive statistics for the used data covering 1996–2013. Establishments are restricted to size 6 (i.e., 5 coworkers) to 600. In columns 2–4 we split the sample, based on whether the worker is a generalist, defined as $abs(C-N)<2$, or a specialist in C or N. Column 5 uses only workers for whom we have information on wages. Generalist establishments have a majority of employees as generalists, or an exactly equal share of specialists of the two types. Nongeneralist establishments are classified according to the dominating type of specialists among employees. These classifications use only *coworkers,* not the subject himself. "Matched" workers are C-specialists in cognitive establishments, and so forth. Monthly earnings are recorded for all observations.

high (6.9 vs. 3.6) for cognitive specialists compared to noncognitive specialists, but as discussed above, these scales do not have a natural interpretation in terms of the productive content of these scores. The differences in terms of noncognitive skills are also clearly visible in the natural direction (6.3 vs. 4.1). There is a tendency for C-specialists to be overrepresented in the group of "high-skilled," but, as is evident, all ability levels are well represented among generalists and both types of specialists.

Since most workers are classified as generalists, most establishments are also dominated by generalists. And this also makes it more common for the generalists to be working in an establishment dominated by its own group (in that sense, "matched").

The final column presents statistics for the half of the overall sample where we can observe wages. As is shown, this sample is nearly identical to the sample where we can observe occupations. The most important aspect of this column is that the data are very similar to the first column (All) in all aspects (such as skill levels and composition), except for establishment size. The latter arises mechanically from an oversampling of large firms. Fortunately, we are able to verify the stability of our wage results by estimating the same models using monthly earnings data (that we observe for all) instead.

4 Sorting

We are interested in analyzing how workers' skills are related to the skill requirements. In the spirit of Fredriksson et al. (2018), we will classify the establishments based on coworker skill set as explained above. We then regress the worker skill type on the type of workers they are working together with. As a starting point, we only use one year (2005) and defer to later the analysis for trends over time. Thus, we estimate models of the following form:

$$Y_{ij}^{\tau} = a + b^{C,\tau} * C_j^{-i} + b^{N,\tau} * N_j^{-i} + \dot{o}_{ij} \tag{7}$$

where Y_{ij}^{τ} represents the type of worker i, employed at workplace j. Types will be indicators for being a specialist of type $\tau = C, N$, or a generalist. C_{jt}^{-i} and N_{jt}^{-i} measure the share of coworkers that are C-specialists and N-specialists (the residual type is generalists). If workers are sorted into contexts where other workers are of a similar type (arguably, because this is what the firm-level technology asks for), we expect positive values on $b^{C,C}$, but negative values on $b^{C,N}$ and so forth.

4.1 Simulating assignment principles

We contrast the real sorting patterns with corresponding estimates that we derive from a simulated allocation of observations across the actual establishment size distribution. In practice, we first sort the establishments at random, preserving their size. We then sort the workers and assign them to establishments. We start by randomly sorting workers before matching them to the establishments. The second simulated assignment ranks workers on *absolute ability* as proxied by C + N before allocating them to establishments, thus placing all the highest-skilled workers in the (randomly sized) first establishment, and so forth. This assignment captures the idea that better workers are assigned to more-productive firms, and it is therefore closely related to the concept of positive assortative matching (PAM). Third, we rank workers according to *relative abilities* as proxied by C/N, thus placing all workers with the strongest C-specialization in the (randomly sized) first establishment, and so forth.[8] This generates four different allocations (actual, random, absolute ranking, and relative ranking), all of which have the identical number of workers per ability type, and an identical establishment-size distribution.

The results presented in Table 9.2 show that workers indeed are systematically sorted across establishments, although not as strongly or one-dimensionally as suggested by the extreme absolute and relative sorting scenarios. Each type of worker is more prevalent if there are more coworkers of the same type. The table also illustrates that the empirical approach "works" in the sense that the random allocations indeed do generate an independence between the worker's type and coworker types (i.e., all estimates are insignificant if workers are allocated at random). Strikingly, the actual allocation is such that there are fewer C-specialists in establishments with many N-specialists, and conversely (remember, generalists are the omitted category). In terms of signs (although not magnitudes) this is exactly as implied by the relative sorting scenario emphasized by CK.

In Section 4.3 we will analyze how these patterns change over time, and there we also present robustness tests that show that these general sorting patterns are robust to a number of variations of the empirical model and data.

4.2 Two-dimensional types

Next we define a more detailed set of worker and establishment types by also accounting for ability levels. As discussed above, we define workers as low-skilled if the sum of cognitive and noncognitive ability falls below 9 and high-skilled if the sum is above 11, whereas the mid-skilled are those in between. By combining these categories with the indicators for generalists

---

[8] The collected data is discrete, but it is natural to think about the actual abilities as being continuous. We therefore first generate simulated raw continuous skills data that exactly aggregate up to our actual data in terms of number of workers with each combination of skills *and* that ensures that the correlations across skill types also are replicated within these types. We then allocate the workers according to these continuous scores. This process is inconsequential for the analyses presented here.

Table 9.2. Leave-out mean regressions on worker types

	(1)	(2)	(3)	(4)
	Actual sorting	Random sorting	Sorting on C+N	Sorting on C/N
Panel A dep. var.: Being N-specialist				
Coworker share of N-specialists	0.224	0.009	0.283	0.987
	(0.006)	(0.007)	(0.006)	(0.000)
Coworker share of C-specialists	−0.263	0.004	0.124	−0.005
	(0.004)	(0.005)	(0.005)	(0.000)
Constant	0.229	0.215	0.127	0.004
	(0.002)	(0.002)	(0.002)	(0.000)
Panel B dep. var.: Generalist				
Coworker share of N-specialists	−0.023	−0.010	−0.417	−0.980
	(0.008)	(0.008)	(0.008)	(0.000)
Coworker share of C-specialists	−0.155	−0.003	−0.423	−0.974
	(0.007)	(0.008)	(0.008)	(0.000)
Constant	0.593	0.555	0.740	0.990
	(0.003)	(0.003)	(0.003)	(0.000)
Panel C dep. var.: Being C-specialist				
Coworker share of N-specialists	−0.201	0.001	0.134	−0.008
	(0.004)	(0.005)	(0.005)	(0.000)
Coworker share of C-specialists	0.418	−0.001	0.299	0.978
	(0.007)	(0.007)	(0.006)	(0.000)
Constant	0.178	0.230	0.132	0.007
	(0.002)	(0.002)	(0.002)	(0.000)
Observations (all panels)	731,946	731,946	731,946	731,946

Notes: Dependent variable is own type, estimates are for the share of coworkers of different types. Reference is the share of generalists. Data are for 2005. At least 6 workers and at most 600 workers with measured skills are employed in each establishment. Three last columns show regression on simulated allocations across the actual establishment size distribution; see text for details. Standard errors are clustered at the establishment level.

and C- vs. N-specialists, we get 9 types of workers. We then run regressions based on equation (7) where we let each of these 9 types be the outcomes in separate regressions. The explanatory variables are the coworker (leave-out) mean levels of these attributes. We start by estimating the impact of horizontal (specialists) and vertical (high/low) attributes separately, and then present estimates from fully interacted models.

Table 9.3 shows the first set of estimates. The table highlights in **bold** the estimates that should be interpreted as indicating similarity between

Table 9.3. Leave-out mean regressions on two-dimensional worker types

	(1)	(2)	(3)
	N-specialists	*Generalists*	*C-specialists*
Panel A (high total ability)	*High*	*High*	*High*
Dep. var. types:	*N-specialist*	*generalist*	*C-specialist*
Estimates:			
Coworkers N-specialists	**0.075******	−0.055***	−0.105***
	(0.004)	(0.004)	(0.003)
Coworkers C-specialists	−0.098***	−0.027***	**0.223******
	(0.004)	(0.006)	(0.006)
(Reference: generalists)			
Coworkers high-ability	**0.075******	**0.329******	**0.184******
	(0.004)	(0.006)	(0.004)
(Reference: mid-ability)			
Coworkers low-ability	−0.078***	−0.127***	−0.039***
	(0.003)	(0.004)	(0.003)
Constant	0.072***	0.117***	0.023***
	(0.002)	(0.002)	(0.002)
Observations	731,946	731,946	731,946
Panel B (mid total ability)	*Mid*	*Mid*	*Mid*
Dep. var. types:	*N-specialist*	*generalist*	*C-specialist*
Estimates:			
Coworkers N-specialists	**0.083******	0.029***	−0.049***
	(0.004)	(0.005)	(0.003)
(Reference: generalists)			
Coworkers C-specialists	−0.063***	−0.079***	**0.096******
	(0.003)	(0.005)	(0.004)
Coworkers high-ability	−0.078***	−0.211***	−0.027***
	(0.002)	(0.005)	(0.003)
(Reference: mid-ability)			
Coworkers low-ability	−0.039***	−0.129***	−0.030***
	(0.003)	(0.005)	(0.003)
Constant	0.106***	0.355***	0.079***
	(0.002)	(0.004)	(0.002)
Observations	731,946	731,946	731,946
Panel C (low total ability)	*Low*	*Low*	*Low*
Dep. var. types:	*N-specialist*	*generalist*	*C-specialist*
Estimates:			
Coworkers N-specialists	**0.042******	−0.005	−0.016***
	(0.003)	(0.004)	(0.002)
Coworkers C-specialists	−0.051***	−0.034***	**0.032******
	(0.003)	(0.003)	(0.003)

(continued)

Table 9.3. *(continued)*

	(1)	(2)	(3)
	N-specialists	*Generalists*	*C-specialists*
Panel C (low total ability)	*Low*	*Low*	*Low*
Dep. var. types:	*N-specialist*	*generalist*	*C-specialist*
(Reference: generalists)			
Coworkers high-ability	−0.085***	−0.141***	−0.045***
	(0.002)	(0.003)	(0.002)
Coworkers low-ability	**0.126***	**0.263***	**0.053***
	(0.003)	(0.004)	(0.002)
Constant	0.076***	0.126***	0.047***
	(0.002)	(0.002)	(0.001)
Observations	731,946	731,946	731,946
R-squared	0.030	0.053	0.006

Note: Results from nine different regressions where the worker types are dependent variables. Types are defined from the combination of indicators for C/N-specialists vs. generalist, combined with indicators for total ability being low, mid, or high. Explanatory variables are coworker averages of the C/N-specialists (generalists as the reference) and low/high ability (mid-ability as the reference). Estimates in **bold** are for the same type. Data are for 2005. At least 6 workers and at most 600 workers with measured skills are employed in each establishment. Standard errors are clustered at the establishment level.

* $p < 0.10$; ** $p < 0.05$; *** $p < 0.01$

subject and coworkers. As is evident from column 1 of panel A, *high-level N-specialists* are found among other high-ability workers and other N-specialists; all other estimates are negative. The pattern repeats itself for *high-level generalists* in column 2 of the same panel and for *high-level C-specialists* in column 3.

The next panels reiterate the same patterns for mid- and low-level workers, and the patterns are qualitatively very similar—workers at all levels are more likely to have coworkers with a similar specialization and a similar ability level. Overall, the horizontal sorting does, however, appear to be stronger higher up in the ability ladder. The one estimate that deviates from the overall pattern is that there appears to be a positive association between N-specialists and mid-level generalists.

4.3 Sorting over time

In this section we document how labor market sorting has changed over time. The purpose is to illustrate the extent to which the general time trends are consistent with a process of *unbundling* as outlined by CK. Because our data do not cover all cohorts, changes over time will also generate changes in the age composition. To ensure that this does not generate spurious patterns, we follow Håkanson et al. (2021) and zoom in on a specific age group that we can follow consistently over time (ages 40 to 45) for the baseline analysis.

We estimate a version of equation (7) where the covariates of interest are interacted with time trends covering our 1996–2013 data period. The model accounts for year dummies and, for robustness tests, other plant-level controls. The model can thus be written as:

$$Y_{ijt}^{\tau} = a + g^{C,\tau} * t * C_{jt}^{-i} + g^{N,\tau} * t * N_{jt}^{-i} + b^{C,\tau} * C_{jt}^{-i}$$
$$+ b^{N,\tau} * N_{jt}^{-i} + D_{t} + X_{ijt}\beta^{\tau} + \partial_{ijt}^{\tau}$$

where Y_{ijt}^{τ} represents the type of worker i, in year $t = Year - 2005$ employed at workplace j. Types will be indicators for being a specialist of type $\tau = C, N,$ or a generalist. C_{jt}^{-i} and N_{jt}^{-i} measure the share of coworkers that are C-specialists and N-specialists (the residual type is generalists). D_{t} is a time dummy, and X_{ijt} reflects additional controls. If concentration has increased, we expect positive estimates for $g^{C,C}$ (i.e., a growing positive impact of coworker C on Y_{ijt}^{C}) and $g^{N,N}$, but negative estimates for $g^{N,C}$ and $g^{C,N}$.

The estimates are displayed in Table 9.4. Panel A shows the estimates for the outcome Y_{ijt}^{C} and panel B for Y_{ijt}^{N}. Column 1 is the baseline specification without any controls except for time dummies. The estimates suggest that sorting has increased over time, as C-specialists increasingly work with C-specialists and less with N-specialists. The converse is true for N-specialists. In column 2 we add controls for occupations. The sample here is somewhat smaller, as we do not observe occupations for all workers. The picture is, however, very similar. In column 3 we change the concept of coworkers and instead focus on other workers in the same *job* defined as occupation by establishment as in Fredriksson et al. (2018). Here the sample is reduced even further as we require that there are at least five other employees in the same job, but the estimated time-trends show a similar pattern as in the main specification. In column 4 we return to the baseline model, but add controls for establishment size (8 groups) and for the share of low- and high-skilled workers in the establishment. The results remain robust. In column 5 we remove low-tenured workers as in Fredriksson et al. (2018) without much change in results. Finally, in column 6 we widen the age span to also include workers aged 35 to 50, which makes the estimates more modest, although the qualitative results remain.

Table 9.4. Specialist coworkers increasingly predict same-type specialists

	(1)	(2)	(3)	(4)	(5)	(6)
	Base	Control for occupation	Coworkers in job	Additional controls	Only tenured	Broader age span
Panel A outcome: C-specialist						
Time*C-spec.	0.008***	0.008***	0.006***	0.008***	0.009***	0.003***
	(0.001)	(0.001)	(0.001)	(0.001)	(0.001)	(0.001)
Time*N-spec.	−0.003***	−0.002	−0.003***	−0.003***	−0.003***	−0.001**
	(0.001)	(0.001)	(0.001)	(0.001)	(0.001)	(0.000)
C-specialists	0.415***	0.269***	0.455***	0.345***	0.349***	0.361***
	(0.006)	(0.008)	(0.008)	(0.006)	(0.007)	(0.005)
N-specialists	−0.203***	−0.122***	−0.241***	−0.168***	−0.171***	−0.170***
	(0.004)	(0.007)	(0.006)	(0.004)	(0.005)	(0.003)
Low-skilled cow.				−0.025***	−0.023***	−0.022***
				(0.004)	(0.005)	(0.002)
High-skilled cow.				0.109***	0.121***	0.114***
				(0.005)	(0.005)	(0.003)
N	2,317,898	1,255,003	896,931	2,317,898	1,656,627	8,787,016
Panel B outcome: N-specialist						
Time*N-spec.	0.004***	0.002	0.003**	0.004***	0.004***	0.001*
	(0.001)	(0.001)	(0.001)	(0.001)	(0.001)	(0.001)
Time*C-spec.	−0.003***	−0.004***	−0.002*	−0.003***	−0.003***	−0.002***
	(0.001)	(0.001)	(0.001)	(0.001)	(0.001)	(0.000)
N-specialists	0.227***	0.144***	0.264***	0.200***	0.203***	0.208***
	(0.005)	(0.008)	(0.008)	(0.006)	(0.007)	(0.004)
C-specialists	−0.251***	−0.147***	−0.261***	−0.198***	−0.198***	−0.207***
	(0.004)	(0.006)	(0.005)	(0.004)	(0.005)	(0.003)
Low-skilled cow.				0.019***	0.019***	0.014***
				(0.004)	(0.005)	(0.003)
High-skilled cow.				−0.080***	−0.085***	−0.085***
				(0.004)	(0.004)	(0.003)
N	2,317,898	1,255,003	896,931	2,317,898	1,656,627	8,787,016

Note: Dependent variable is an indicator for being a C-specialist in panel A (N-specialist in panel B). Subjects are 40–45 years old. Explanatory variables are share of coworkers that are C/N-specialists interacted with time. Normalized so that main effects of coworkers reflect 2005. All specifications include year dummies. Column 2 also controls for occupation dummies at the three-digit level (sample requires that occupations are observed). Column 3 measures coworkers in job (occupation times establishment) instead (sample requires at least 5 coworkers in job). Columns 4–6 control for eight plant size dummies and the share of high-/low-skilled among coworkers. Column 5 includes only workers with at least three years of tenure. Column 6 widens the age span to 35–50. Standard errors clustered at the establishment level. Data cover 1996–2013.

  * $p < 0.10$; ** $p < 0.05$; *** $p < 0.01$

5 Skills and Wages

In this section we use our data to document how sorting is related to wages. In particular, we are interested in the extent to which market returns to each skill are higher in settings where the technology is likely to be more intensively using that particular skill.[9] We define employer from coworker skill specializations as explained in the data section. In terms of theory, our data aspire to represent the set of firms where the α-parameter in the production function makes the firm want to specialize in either one or the other type of worker—i.e., C- and N-establishments. We then interact the establishment type with the specialization of the worker and estimate if the returns to being a C-intensive worker are higher if the employment pattern is such that the firm appears to be using a C-intensive technology (and conversely for N). As we are interested in the sorting of specialists, we exclude generalist establishments at this stage. The model controls for the overall impact of level of skills in each dimension through dummies for each score on the discrete 1–9 scale:

$$ln\,W_{ijt} = \gamma^{C}_{C(i)} + \gamma^{N}_{N(i)} + D^{N-plant}_{jt} + b^{N}_{j} * D^{N-in-N}_{ijt}$$
$$+ b^{C}_{j} * D^{C-in-C}_{ijt} + X_{ijt}\beta + \partial_{ijt} \tag{8}$$

where $ln\,W_{it}$ represents the wage of worker i in establishment j in year t and where the γs are dummies for each value of C and N skills. The two key variables of interest are the interaction terms D^{N-in-N} (for N-specialists in N-establishments) and D^{C-in-C}, which capture the additional returns to N-skills in N-intensive employers, and C-skills in C-intensive employers, respectively. The vector of control variables will always include time dummies, plant size dummies, and an age polynomial.

The results are presented in Table 9.5. Throughout, the results suggest that the wages in the market sections where employers rely intensively on C-skills also pay higher returns to these skills. Similarly, the results suggest a premium for N-skills in market segments dominated by N-intensive firms. These patterns are robust to controls for occupations, analyzing data at the job level, controlling for very detailed skills, focusing on tenured workers, or zooming

---

[9] Some evidence in this direction at the *job*-level is presented in Fredriksson et al. (2018), with a focus on new hires, but here we revisit the issue at the *establishment* level for the *stock* of employees.

Table 9.5. Returns to specific skills are higher when coworkers are specialists in those skills

	(1)	(2)	(3)	(4)	(5)	(6)
	Base	Control for occupation	Coworkers in job	Interacted skills	Only tenured	Only 2005
Panel A: Wages						
C-sp. in C-est.	0.027***	0.009***	0.040***	0.027***	0.028***	0.020***
	(0.003)	(0.002)	(0.003)	(0.003)	(0.004)	(0.007)
N-sp. in N-est.	0.016***	0.005*	0.023***	0.021***	0.017***	0.009
	(0.004)	(0.003)	(0.004)	(0.004)	(0.004)	(0.007)
C-establishment	0.087***	0.020***	0.126***	0.089***	0.092***	0.075***
	(0.004)	(0.003)	(0.005)	(0.004)	(0.005)	(0.006)
N	1,458,790	1,432,159	1,259,521	1,458,790	961,640	85,291
Panel B: Earnings						
C-sp. in C-est.	0.036***	0.009***	0.044***	0.036***	0.032***	0.033***
	(0.003)	(0.003)	(0.004)	(0.003)	(0.004)	(0.007)
N-sp. in N-est.	0.023***	0.005*	0.026***	0.029***	0.025***	0.019***
	(0.003)	(0.003)	(0.004)	(0.003)	(0.004)	(0.007)
C-establishment	0.081***	−0.002	0.108***	0.083***	0.082***	0.067***
	(0.003)	(0.003)	(0.005)	(0.003)	(0.004)	(0.006)
N	2,945,409	1,432,159	1,259,521	2,945,409	1,899,162	168,815
Panel C: Specialized						
C-sp. in C-est.	0.038***	0.014***	0.129***	0.038***	0.035***	0.038***
	(0.004)	(0.005)	(0.007)	(0.004)	(0.005)	(0.010)
N-sp. in N-est.	0.024***	0.009*	−0.067***	0.031***	0.028***	0.006
	(0.005)	(0.005)	(0.008)	(0.005)	(0.006)	(0.011)
C-establishment	0.103***	−0.010**	0.026***	0.104***	0.103***	0.084***
	(0.004)	(0.004)	(0.009)	(0.004)	(0.005)	(0.008)
N	1,297,390	556,605	616,218	1,297,390	824,400	73,423

Note: Dependent variable is log wages. Control variables are the dummies for C-skills (1 to 9) and N-skills (1 to 9), dummies for being a C- or an N-specialist, as well as year dummies, an age polynomial, and eight plant size dummies. Displayed estimates are for C-specialists in C-establishments (and conversely for N-specialists). Sample excludes establishments where the majority of workers are generalists. Specialization of establishment is based on the specialization among coworkers. Column 2 adds controls for occupations. Column 3 performs the analysis at the job (occupation times establishment) level instead. Column 4 interacts the skills controls (C, N) into 81 groups. Column 5 includes only workers with at least three years of tenure. Column 6 zooms in on data for 2005. Panel A uses wages, whereas panels B and C use monthly earnings. Wage data are only collected for a 50 percent sample, but earnings data are available for all workers. Panel C only includes highly specialized establishments where C- or N-specialists are the most common type of worker. Samples in panels A and B overlap when conditioning on observed occupations (columns 2 and 3). Standard errors clustered at the establishment level. Data cover 1996–2013.

* $p < 0.10$; ** $p < 0.05$; *** $p < 0.01$

in on the center year of 2005. In panel B, we show that the message is identical as we instead use monthly earnings, which allows us to expand the data to include all observations instead of just the half where we observe wages. Panel C zooms in on establishments that are highly specialized (the most common worker type is either C or N-specialists). All establishment-level results are robust.[10]

6 The Growing Wages of Generalists

According to Choné and Kramarz (2021), a process of "unbundling" should lead to increased market wages of generalists relative to specialists. The reason is that the bundling constraint depresses the market wages of the generalists. In order to test if the evolution of the overall wage structure concurs with this prediction, we estimate wage regressions where our variable of interest is the interaction between time and a dummy for being a generalist (defined as above). The model controls for overall wage growth through year dummies and include a fixed effect for each "detailed type" of worker defined as the interaction of raw cognitive and noncognitive scores (thus, 81 types). Our identification thus comes from the relative wage changes among workers on the generalist skill-diagonal relative to other workers. The model can be written as:

$$ln\, W_{it} = \gamma_{CN(i)} + b^G * G_i * t + D_t + X_{ijt}\beta + \partial_{it} \tag{9}$$

where $ln\, W_{it}$ represents the wage of worker i in year t, and where $\gamma_{CN(i)}$ is the fixed effect for the worker type. We estimate the model for workers 40 to 45 years old, as above, and allow for a set of control variables X_{ijt} that will vary across specifications. We provide separate estimates for the sample of workers who are "well matched" (or, not bunched) in the sense that the type of worker corresponds to the type of firm (e.g., C-specialists working in C-establishments; see data section for definitions).

The estimates are displayed in Table 9.6. Panel A shows the estimates for the overall population, and panel B zooms in on the "well-matched" sample. Column 1 is the baseline specification without any controls except for time dummies and the type-specific fixed effects. The estimates suggest that wages

---

[10] The one deviating estimate in the table is for N-specialists in the job-level analysis.

Table 9.6. Generalists' relative wages grow over time

	(1)	(2)	(3)	(4)	(5)	(6)
	Base	Control for occupation	Additional controls	Only mid-skilled	Only tenured	Broader age span
Panel A: All workers						
Generalist × time	0.0012***	0.0007***	0.0006***	0.0005**	0.0011***	0.0009***
	(0.0002)	(0.0001)	(0.0001)	(0.0003)	(0.0002)	(0.0001)
N	1,281,151	1,255,003	1,255,003	476,822	928,127	4,723,064
Panel B: Well-matched sample only						
Generalist × time	0.0031***	0.0020***	0.0014***	0.0019***	0.0024***	0.0019***
	(0.0006)	(0.0004)	(0.0004)	(0.0006)	(0.0007)	(0.0006)
N	654,687	641,005	641,005	266,173	476,688	2,415,481

Note: Dependent variable is log wages. Subjects are 40–45 years old. Estimates are for interaction between year and a generalist dummy. All specifications include year dummies and control for 81 fixed effects for interactions between measured C (1 to 9) and N (1 to 9). Columns 2 and 3 have more-detailed fixed effects that also interact with occupation dummies at the three-digit level (sample requires that occupations are observed). Column 3 controls for eight plant size dummies and 18 additional time trends, each interacted with one of the possible nine values of C and N. Column 4 only includes workers with C + N between 9 and 11. Column 5 only includes workers with at least three years of tenure. Column 6 widens the age span to 35–50. Standard errors clustered at the establishment level. Data cover 1996–2013.
 * $p < 0.10$; ** $p < 0.05$; *** $p < 0.01$

of generalists have grown more than wages for workers in general. The magnitudes suggest a modest 1.2 percent additional wage increase across one decade.

The next columns establish that the qualitative conclusion is very robust. In column 2 we add controls for occupations interacted with the worker type. In column 3 we keep the controls for occupations and also introduce a set of controls for time trends that interact each possible value of N and C with time (thus, 18 trends) as well as controls for establishment size (8 groups). To ensure that the results are not driven by ceiling effects at the top, we let column 4 show results for the baseline model but where we only include "mid-skilled" workers that all have total skills (C + N) in the range 9 to 11. In column 5 we instead remove low-tenured workers, and in column 6 we widen the age span to include all workers aged 35 to 50.

For panel B we use the same set of specifications but include only those workers who are employed in establishments where the majority of other workers are of the same broad type (generalist, C-specialist, N-specialist). Estimates are unchanged in qualitative terms, but the magnitudes are much larger, suggesting that wages of well-matched generalists have grown by

2–3 percent more across a decade than wages of well-matched specialists. This amounts to around one-tenth of the average real wage growth during the period.[11]

7 Conclusions

This empirical chapter has illustrated patterns of worker sorting and the relationship between sorting and wages, with Choné and Kramarz (2021) as the theoretical foundation. The results show that workers are sorted across establishments in both the vertical dimension (skill intensity) and the horizontal dimension (specialization). Horizontal sorting dominates at the top of the ability distribution. High-level specialists are *less likely* to work with the opposing type of specialists than under random sorting, but *more likely* to work with mid-level specialists of the same type.

Furthermore, the chapter shows that sorting has increased over time. Every cohort of specialists is more likely to work with specialists of the same type, and less likely to work with specialists of the opposing type, than the previous cohort evaluated at the same age. In terms of wages, we show that the wage returns to specific skills is higher in the more specialized market segments. Furthermore, the results document a secular trend of growing relative wages for generalists relative to specialists. The two trends we document (increased sorting on relative skills, and growing wages of generalists) are both fully in line with a process of "unbundling" as outlined by Choné and Kramarz (2021). If new markets open up that allow workers to sell their skills separately, generalist wages will be less under pressure from competing specialist workers, thus allowing their wages to increase.

Some (but far from all) of our results mimic conclusions drawn in earlier or parallel work using similar data, most notably Fredriksson et al. (2018), Håkanson et al. (2021), and Böhm et al. (2020). But we add to the literature by compiling the results in one unified empirical setting, by adding a set of

---

[11] It is possible that we find larger estimates for well-matched workers because this sample is better at capturing the true worker types, and therefore also better reflects the market valuations. This could be owing to, for instance, deviations between our measured worker-level skills and the true skills of the workers (because of the aggregation into the integer scale, or measurement errors). Workers that are misclassified should be more likely to turn up as poorly matched (and hence excluded in panel B) if errors are uncorrelated across workers within establishments.

important missing pieces, and by setting the results in context by relating them to what we believe to be a more comprehensive theoretical framework.

The presented results are of a distinctively reduced form in nature, and the analysis is purely descriptive. A natural next step is to incorporate more detailed data on the firm side and use these data to estimate a structural model of worker–firm matching and to assess the performance of the model in settings where we can observe clear cases of "unbundling." This is the direction of our ongoing work.

References

ABOWD, J. M., F. KRAMARZ, AND D. N. MARGOLIS (1999): "High Wage Workers and High Wage Firms," *Econometrica*, 67, 251–333.

BÖHM, M., K. ESMKHANI, AND G. GALLIPOLI (2020): "Firm Heterogeneity in Skill Returns," CEPR Discussion Paper 15480.

CARD, D., J. HEINING, AND P. KLINE (2013): "Workplace Heterogeneity and the Rise of West German Wage Inequality," *Quarterly Journal of Economics*, 128, 967–1015.

CHONÉ, P. AND F. KRAMARZ (2021): "Matching Workers' Skills and Firms' Technologies: From Bundling to Unbundling," CREST Working Paper 202110.

EDMOND, C. AND S. MONGEY (2020): "Unbundling labor," unpublished paper.

FREDRIKSSON, P., L. HENSVIK, AND O. NORDSTROM SKANS (2018): "Mismatch of Talent: Evidence on Match Quality, Entry Wages, and Job Mobility," *American Economic Review*, 108(11), 3303–3338.

GUVENEN, F., B. KURUSCU, S. TANAKA, AND D. WICZER (2020): "Multidimensional Skill Mismatch," *American Economic Journal: Macroeconomics*, 12, 210–244.

HÅKANSON, C., E. LINDQVIST, AND J. VLACHOS (2021): "Firms and Skills: The Evolution of Worker Sorting," *Journal of Human Resources*, 56, 512–538.

HECKMAN, J. AND J. SCHEINKMAN (1987): "The Importance of Bundling in a Gorman-Lancaster Model of Earnings," *Review of Economic Studies*, 54, 243–255.

HENSVIK, L. AND O. N. SKANS (2020): "The Skill-Specific Impact of Past and Projected Occupational Decline," IZA Discussion Paper 12931.

LINDENLAUB, I. (2017): "Sorting Multidimensional Types: Theory and Application," *Review of Economic Studies*, 84, 718–789.

LINDQVIST, E. AND R. VESTMAN (2011): "The Labor Market Returns to Cognitive and Noncognitive Ability: Evidence from the Swedish Enlistment," *American Economic Journal: Applied Economics*, 3, 101–28.

MOOD, C., J. O. JONSSON, AND E. BIHAGEN (2012): "Socioeconomic Persistence across Generations: The Role of Cognitive and Non-cognitive Processes," in *From Parents to Children: The Intergenerational Transmission of Advantage*, ed. by J. Ermisch, M. Jäntti, and T. M. Smeeding, Russell Sage Foundation, chap. 3.

SATTINGER, M. (1975): "Comparative Advantage and the Distribution of Earnings and Abilities," *Econometrica*, 43, 455–468.

SKANS, O. N., P.-A. EDIN, AND B. HOLMLUND (2009): *Wage Dispersion between and within Plants: Sweden 1985–2000*. NBER, 217–260.

SONG, J., D. J. PRICE, F. GUVENEN, N. BLOOM, AND T. VON WACHTER (2019): "Firming Up Inequality," *Quarterly Journal of Economics*, 134, 1–50.

PART IV

Growth Measurement and Growth Decline

CHAPTER 10

Productivity Slowdown

Reducing the Measure of Our Ignorance

TIMO BOPPART *and* HUIYU LI

1 Introduction

This short chapter is motivated by the recurring discussion about "secular stagnation." This discussion is due to disappointingly low observed growth rates of GDP, labor productivity, or TFP in advanced economies since the early 2000s. Figure 10.1 illustrates this observation for the four countries Japan, the United States, Germany, and France. In the recovery phase of World War II, in particular the German, Japanese, and French economies had remarkably high growth rates. Subsequently, growth rates came down and labor productivity growth stabilized—with some bigger swings—at around 2 percent per year. However, since the early 2000s growth rates clearly fell short of this long-run average and did so in all four of the selected countries.

The recently reported growth rates look indeed grim well beyond the four countries. Figure 10.2 shows the slowdown in the club of OECD countries.[1] Will we in the future no longer see the same steady growth rates? Have the

---

[1] Figure 10.A1 in the Appendix shows that the productivity slowdown in non-OECD countries is not as clearly visible, possibly due to these economies being in transition of development. The online appendix can be found at https://drive.google.com/file/d/1RCC_JYPqxUfd2Z0pGyUwU -m39tu_NSq1/view?usp=drivesdk.

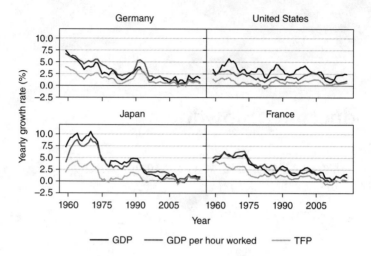

Notes: GDP = "rgdpna," TFP = "rtfpna," hours = "avh" times "emp," GDP per hours = "rgdpna" divided by hours. Five-year trailing moving averages.

Data source: Penn World Tables 10.0. 1960–2019.

Figure 10.1. Annual growth rates of GDP, labor productivity, and TFP in four advanced economies

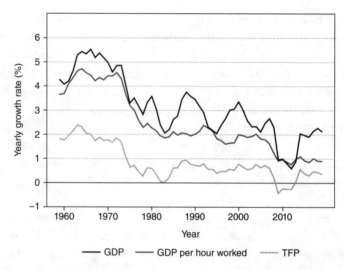

Notes: GDP = "rgdpna," TFP = "rtfpna," hours = "avh" times "emp," GDP per hours = "rgdpna" divided by hours. Five-year trailing moving averages. Average across countries is weighted by real GDP.

Data source: Penn World Tables 10.0. 1960–2019.

Figure 10.2. OECD averages

advanced economies run out of their growth potential? And if so, why? Can policy do something about it? The welfare consequences of questions like these are simply *staggering* (Lucas 1988), and they also have far-reaching implications for areas such as the sustainability of pension systems or levels of debt in advanced economies.

In this short chapter we take a closer look at the productivity slowdown in the United States. We show with a simple growth decomposition that the clear majority of the growth slowdown since the mid-1990s cannot be accounted for by a slowdown in factor accumulation (labor quality, capital deepening) and therefore remains "unexplained" (i.e., is attributed to a residual). We then provide a simple accounting framework to shed theoretical light on this unexplained "measure of our ignorance," called total factor productivity (TFP). We argue that rich dynamics across firms and products determine aggregate TFP and that these forces consist of both *growth rate* and *level* effects on productivity. We use our simple accounting framework to comment on potential measurement issues and discuss different mechanisms of the productivity slowdown stressed in the literature. This analysis leads us to the conclusion that the creative destruction paradigm originating in Aghion and Howitt (1992) is a key theoretical framework to foster our understanding of the observed growth slowdown.

2 Empirical Facts

Before returning to the productivity slowdown and studying the case of the United States more carefully, we take a step back and more generally motivate what is really *needed: a theory of total factor productivity* (Prescott 1998).

The macroeconomic data strongly suggest that simple factor-accumulation-based theories are not sufficient to account for output differences either in the cross-section of countries or in the time series. An often studied and tested prediction of the neoclassical growth model is its "convergence" property due to the diminishing marginal product of capital. Suppose all countries are identical except for their initial capital stock. Then the growth rates of all countries are expected to converge to the same level; for instance, a country that starts with a low initial capital stock is expected to subsequently show above-average output growth as the (detrended) capital stock increases along the transition toward its balanced-growth level. As a consequence, one expects a strong negative relationship between initial income levels (in, say, 1960) and the subsequent growth (1960–2019). Figure 10.3 shows that there is a lack of such "unconditional convergence" across countries post 1960. This finding has been used as a general motivation for endogenous growth theories. Interestingly, if one restricts the sample to OECD countries (Baumol 1986), or the post-2000 period as shown in Figure 10.A2 in the appendix (see also Kremer, Willis, and You 2021), there emerges a clearer convergence pattern. Furthermore, Rodrik (2013) shows that there is more evidence for convergence in labor productivity within manufacturing. Nevertheless, because the neoclassical theory predicts a very fast speed of convergence, even in cases where convergence is documented—e.g., across US states (see Barro, Sala-i-Martin, Blanchard, and Hall 1991)—there seems to be more than pure physical capital accumulation behind the phenomenon.

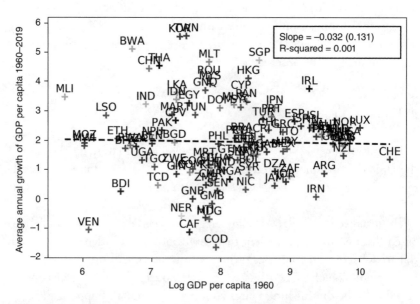

Notes: Real GDP per capita = "rgdpna" divided by "pop." The *x*-axis plots the natural log of real GDP per capita in 1960. The *y*-axis plots the average annual growth rate of real GDP per capita over 1960–2019.

Data source: Penn World Tables 10.0.

Figure 10.3. Convergence across countries, 1960–2019

Another powerful argument against purely factor accumulation based explanations of income differences across countries is the so called development accounting exercise as pioneered by Klenow and Rodriguez-Clare (1997) and Hall and Jones (1999). To fix ideas, let us assume that aggregate output, Y, is produced according to a Cobb-Douglas production function

$$Y = K^{\alpha} (\Gamma h L)^{1-\alpha}, \tag{1}$$

with the factors capital K, labor L, and human capital per worker h. The term Γ captures TFP expressed in labor-augmenting units. All variables should be thought of as potentially being time variant as well as differing across countries. From a balanced-growth perspective a country with a higher level of h or Γ is endogenously expected to end up with a higher long-run capital stock. To see this, let Γ and L grow at exogenous gross rates γ and η (where we normalize the initial level of L to one) and for simplicity consider h to be constant over time. Furthermore, we assume the following Solow-type capital accumulation equation

$$K_{t+1} = K_t (1 - \delta) + \Theta_t s K_t^{\alpha} (\Gamma_0 \gamma^t h \eta^t)^{1-\alpha}, \tag{2}$$

where $0 < s < 1$ denotes the constant fraction of output being saved, and $0 < \delta < 0$ the depreciation rate. The term Θ_t captures an investment-specific technology term that is assumed to grow at constant rate, i.e., $\Theta_t = \Theta_0 \theta^t$. With $\theta > 1$ this captures investment-specific technical change (Greenwood, Hercowitz, and Krusell 1997). In a competitive framework the price of investment relative to output is given by Θ_t^{-1} and therefore shrinks over time at gross rate $\theta^{-1} < 1$. Along a balanced-growth path we have $\dfrac{K_{t+1}}{K_t} = \eta\gamma\,\theta^{\frac{1}{1-\alpha}}$ and $\dfrac{Y_{t+1}}{Y_t} = \eta\gamma\,\theta^{\frac{\alpha}{1-\alpha}} \equiv g$. We can then reformulate the production function in (1) to express output per worker as

$$\frac{Y_t}{L_t} = \left(\frac{g}{\eta}\right)^t \cdot \underbrace{\Gamma_0 \Theta_0^{\frac{\alpha}{1-\alpha}}}_{=A} \cdot h \cdot \left(\frac{\Theta_t^{-1} K_t}{Y_t}\right)^{\frac{\alpha}{1-\alpha}}. \tag{3}$$

Consider all countries as being along their balanced-growth path and differing only in their saving rate s, the initial level of technology $A = \Gamma_0 \Theta_0^{\frac{\alpha}{1-\alpha}}$, and the level of human capital h. From the capital accumulation equation, we have $\dfrac{\Theta_t^{-1} K_t}{Y_t} = \dfrac{s}{g\theta - 1 + \delta}$ along the balanced-growth path, which is constant over time and just depends on s but is independent of h and A. Hence, from a balanced-growth perspective, (3) is a theory-consistent way to decompose GDP per worker differences across countries into differences in physical and human capital as well as a residual TFP level term A. Note that the thought experiment underlying the development accounting exercise assumes that countries share the same growth rate g/η. This assumption is typically justified by the lack of absolute divergence/convergence in Figure 10.3.

The standard development accounting exercise abstracts from investment-specific technological change (i.e., assumes $\Theta_0 = \theta = 1$). In this case output per worker in a country i in (3) simplifies to

$$\frac{Y_{i,t}}{L_{i,t}} = (g/\eta)^t A_i h_i \left(\frac{K_{i,t}}{Y_{i,t}} \right)^{\frac{\alpha}{1-\alpha}}. \tag{4}$$

Human capital in terms of efficiency units h can be quantified in a standard way using years of education of the labor force plus Mincerian returns (this relies on an assumption of competitive labor markets, perfect substitutability, and no externalities). Output per worker is readily available from the Penn World Tables (PWT), and K/Y can be quantified by the measure of the real capital stock relative to real GDP.[2] Then, together with a estimate for a (which can be set to $1/3$ to match the US capital income share), accounting equation (4) can be used to decompose income differences into differences in human capital h, physical capital $(K/Y)^{\frac{\alpha}{1-\alpha}}$, and a residual A that we can call TFP.

Table 10.1 shows the decomposition for some selected countries with recent data from the year 2018.[3] Multiplying the numbers of the last three columns by each other gives by construction the value of the second column. Furthermore, the entries of all columns are normalized to one in the United States; i.e., the numbers can be interpreted as relatives to the United States. Take the example of Nigeria, which is one-tenth as rich as the United States: What accounts for this income difference? It is not physical capital accumulation, as K/Y is roughly as big as in the United States. There is a clear

---

[2] We remove resource rents from output using resource shares calculated by Julieta Caunedo from the World Development Index, which is available until 2018.

[3] We provide the results of the full list of countries in the online appendix at https://drive.google.com/file/d/1RCC_JYPqxUfd2Z0pGyUwU-m39tu_NSq1/view?usp=drivesdk.

Table 10.1. Development accounting

Country	Y/L	$(K/Y)^{\frac{\alpha}{1-\alpha}}$	h	A
United States	1.000	1.000	1.000	1.000
Switzerland	1.002	1.214	0.987	0.836
France	0.806	1.342	0.857	0.701
Germany	0.753	1.194	0.981	0.642
Sweden	0.805	1.248	0.915	0.705
Japan	0.565	1.236	0.957	0.477
Republic of Korea	0.624	1.229	0.996	0.510
Russian Federation	0.379	1.277	0.913	0.325
Mexico	0.341	1.165	0.736	0.397
Argentina	0.388	0.995	0.819	0.476
Brazil	0.247	1.173	0.806	0.261
China	0.190	1.189	0.714	0.224
India	0.139	1.065	0.574	0.227
Nigeria	0.099	1.007	0.521	0.188
Kenya	0.068	0.852	0.621	0.128
Zimbabwe	0.048	0.703	0.716	0.095

Source: Penn World Tables 10.0. 2018 data.

Note: $\tilde{Y}$ = "rgdpo," s = natural resource shares from World Development Index, $Y = \tilde{Y}(1-s)$, L = "emp," K = "cn," h = "hc." $A = \dfrac{Y}{(K/Y)^{\frac{\alpha}{1-\alpha}} hL}$ with $\alpha = 1/3$.

difference in the average level of human capital between Nigeria and the United States, but only by a factor of about two. Hence, the majority of the observed income difference of a factor of ten remains unaccounted for by production factors differences and is consequently absorbed by the residual term A. This is indeed the general take-away message from development accounting exercises.

Figure 10.4 illustrates the relationship between the logarithm of output per worker and the logarithm of the residual TFP. If differences in physical and human capital did not account for any of the observed income differences, we would expect the data points to cluster around the 45-degree line. If in contrast all income differences were accounted for by differences in physical and human capital, we would expect a completely flat relationship (and all TFP observations would cluster around a value of zero). The implied TFP levels in Figure 10.4 show an elasticity in output per worker of 0.72 and are therefore relatively close to the 45-degree line. We therefore conclude that

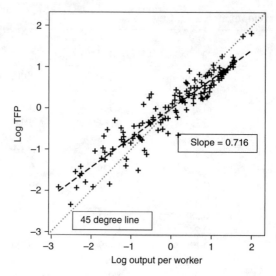

Notes: 2018 data $\tilde{Y}$ = "rgdpo," s = natural resource shares from World Development Index, $Y = \tilde{Y}$
$(1-s)$, L = "emp," K = "cn," h = "hc." $A = \dfrac{Y}{(K/Y)^{\frac{\alpha}{1-\alpha}} hL}$ with $\alpha = 1/3$. Each point is a country in 2018. The
x-axis (y-axis) is deviation of a country's log Y/L (log TFP) from the mean across countries. The
slope is the coefficient on log Y/L when regressing the y-axis values on the x-axis values.

Data source: Penn World Tables 10.0.

Figure 10.4. Development accounting: Implied TFP terms

the majority of observed cross-country income differences remain "unexplained" by differences in physical and human capital.

How would this standard result of development accounting change through the lens of a theory that allows for differences in the investment-specific technology term (over time and across countries)? In this case there are two goods: an investment and a consumption good with a relative price between them captured by the term Θ_t^{-1}. The left-hand side of equation (3) expresses output per worker in consumption units and can be measured as such by deflating nominal output by PPP-adjusted consumption prices. Furthermore, the theory in (3) adjusts the ratio of real capital to real output in (4) by the relative price Θ_t^{-1}. To make this adjustment we multiply the real capital–output ratio by the price of investment relative to the consumption. Figure 10.5 shows the scatter plot between log output per worker and the resulting log TFP if this adjusted capital–output ratio is

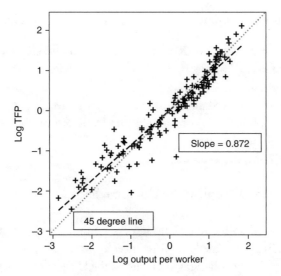

Notes: $\tilde{Y}$="rgdpo," s=natural resource shares from World Development Index, $Y = \tilde{Y}(1-s)$ times "pl_gdpo" divided by "pl_con," L="emp," K="rnna"/"pl_n," h="hc," Θ^{-1}="pl_i" divided by "pl_con."
$A = \dfrac{Y}{(\Theta^{-1}K/Y)^{\frac{\alpha}{1-\alpha}}hL}$ with $a=1/3$. Each point is a country in 2018. The x-axis (y-axis) is deviation of a country's log Y/L (log TFP) from the mean across countries. The slope is the coefficient on log Y/L when regressing the y-axis values on the x-axis values.

Data source: Penn World Tables 10.0.

Figure 10.5. Development accounting with investment-specific technology

used.[4] Because the relative price of investment is higher in poor countries (Hsieh and Klenow 2007), the adjusted capital–output ratio results in higher measures of physical capital in poor countries (compared to the rich) and therefore in an even larger "unexplained" part of the income differences. As a consequence, the slope of the fitted line in Figure 10.5 is steeper than the fitted line in Figure 10.4 (0.87 vs. 0.72).

Using the relative price of investment, we can use (3) to further decompose the differences in the TFP term A across countries into difference in Γ_0 and $\Theta_0^{\frac{\alpha}{1-\alpha}}$. For the countries in Figure 10.5, the elasticity of the relative price

---

[4] In the online appendix at https://drive.google.com/file/d/1RCC_JYPqxUfd2Z0pGyUwU -m39tu_NSq1/view?usp=drivesdk, we show the complete breakdown into physical and human capital differences as well as the residual for all the countries.

of investment to consumption goods with respect to real GDP per worker in consumption units is -0.170.[5] This implies that the elasticity of $\Theta_0^{\frac{\alpha}{1-\alpha}}$ with respect to GDP per worker is about 0.085, which is one order of magnitude smaller than the 0.87 elasticity of residual TFP in Figure 10.5. Hence, according to this quantification, differences in the investment-specific technology term explains only a relatively small fraction of the residual TFP differences across countries.

3 Taking a Closer Look at the US Time Series

In Section 2 we documented that factor-accumulation-based theories fall short of explaining income level differences across countries; i.e., a theory of TFP is needed. In the following we focus on the US economy and do a Solow growth decomposition to see to what extent factor-based explanations can account for the observed slowdown in output growth. Suppose again that output is produced according to the production function in equation (1), which we can rewrite in per-worker terms as

$$\frac{Y_t}{L_t} = \Gamma_t^{1-\alpha} \left(\frac{K_t}{h_t L_t} \right)^\alpha h_t. \tag{5}$$

Taking time differences of the logarithm of both sides of (5) allows us to do a growth decomposition and back out $g_{TFP,t} = (1-\alpha) \log(\Gamma_{t+1}/\Gamma_t)$ as

$$g_{TFP} = g_y - \alpha \cdot g_k - g_h, \tag{6}$$

where g_y denotes the growth rate in labor productivity, $y = Y/L$, g_k the growth rate in the capital intensity $k = K/(hL)$, and g_h the growth rate in human capital. Figure 10.6 and Table 10.2 perform this decomposition for the US economy using the FRBSF TFP data. Figure 10.6 shows the growth rate of labor productivity and its components for each year. Table 10.2 displays the growth rates averaged over high- and low-growth periods. Following the

---

[5] The elasticity is the coefficient on log GDP per worker when we regress log relative price of investment to consumption on log GDP per worker in consumption units and a constant. The relative price of investment equals pl_i/pl_con, where pl_i is the price level of capital formation and pl_con is the price level of real consumption of households and government (PPP/XR). See the footnote to Figure 10.5 for the construction of real GDP per worker in consumption units.

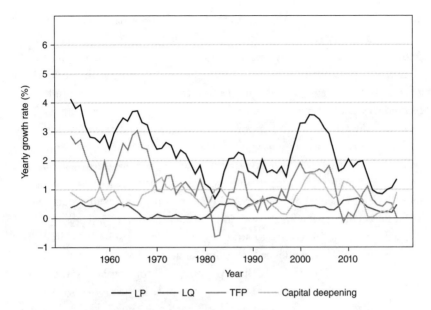

Note: The figure decomposes labor productivity growth (LP) into growth in labor quality (LQ), TFP, and capital labor ratio. Five-year trailing averages of annual growth rates.

Data source: Fernald et al. (2021), figure 1.

Figure 10.6. Sources of US labor productivity growth

Table 10.2. Sources of U.S. labor productivity growth

	Labor productivity	TFP	Capital deepening	Labor quality
1996–2004	3.32	1.82	1.13	0.36
2005–2019	1.39	0.45	0.54	0.40
Change	−1.93	−1.37	−0.59	0.03
% of LP change		71	30	−2

Source: Fernald et al. (2021), FRBSF TFP database version: June 7, 2021.

Notes: The first and second rows are average annualized growth rates in percentage points over 1996Q1–2004Q4 and 2005Q1–2019Q4, respectively. The third row equals row 2 minus row 1. The last row is the values in the third row divided by the change in labor productivity, expressed as a percent. TFP equals labor productivity growth minus capital deepening and labor quality.

literature on the US growth decline, Table 10.2 compares average annual growth rates over the two periods 1996–2004 and 2005–2019.[6] The second column shows the slowdown in labor productivity growth. Over the decade after the mid-1990s the US economy experienced a burst in productivity growth at an average annual rate of more than 3 percent. This number decreased by about 1.9 percentage points to only 1.4 percent for the post-2004 period. Columns (3)–(5) decompose this slowdown in labor productivity into TFP, g_{TFP}, capital deepening $a \cdot g_k$, and labor quality g_h. Comparing the two periods shows that capital deepening did slow down but only by about half a percentage point, whereas the improvement of labor quality actually slightly accelerated. Hence, about three-fourths of the slowdown is unaccounted for by factor accumulation and absorbed by a slowdown in residual TFP.

Therefore, when it comes to studying the observed slowdown in output growth, there is clear evidence that a simple factor-accumulation-based story is not sufficient. Consequently there is a potential role to play for theories of endogenous growth in explaining the slowdown. In Section 4 we sketch a theoretical accounting framework. We then use this framework to comment on measurement issues and to shed some theoretical light on what might be behind the change in residual TFP growth.

4 An Accounting Framework with Heterogeneous Firms and Products

Suppose final output in the economy is a Cobb-Douglas composite defined over N varieties

$$Y = \exp\left[\frac{1}{N}\int_0^N \log[N^{1+v}q(i)y(i)]di\right] \tag{7}$$

and produced competitively. The term N^{1+v} is added to introduce a separate parameter v that controlled the taste for variety. Product varieties come at quality $q(i)$ and are produced according to

$$y(i) = \varphi(i) \cdot k(i)^\alpha \cdot (hl(i))^{1-\alpha}, \tag{8}$$

---

[6] Using statistical break tests, Fernald (2015) find a high-growth regime from the mid-1990s to early 2000 and a slowdown after 2004. We do not use data post 2019 because of large cyclical fluctuations during the COVID pandemic.

where $\varphi(i)$ denotes a variety-specific productivity term. Firms producing intermediate products are assumed to charge a price $p(i)$ equal to a markup $\mu(i)$ over marginal cost

$$p(i) = \frac{\mu(i)}{\varphi(i)} \bullet r^{\alpha} \bullet w^{1-\alpha} \bullet \alpha^{-\alpha}(1-\alpha)^{-(1-\alpha)}. \tag{9}$$

All variables and parameters here could be thought of as being time-varying. We simply assume some exogenous levels of markup and do not micro-found the industry structure in detail. We do not embed this framework in general equilibrium either but instead simply close the production side by capital and labor market clearing. $K_t = \int_0^N k_t(i)\,di$ and $L_t = \int_0^N l_t(i)\,di$ assume perfectly mobile production factors and competitive factor markets and then determine the level of aggregate output.

Aggregate output. With a perfectly competitive final output market, the Cobb-Douglas structure implies as demand for each variety $y(i) = \dfrac{YP}{p(i)}$, where P denotes the aggregate price index $P \equiv N^{-v} \exp\left(\dfrac{1}{N}\int_0^N \log[p(i)/q(i)]\,di\right)$. The capital intensity, $\dfrac{k(i)}{hl(i)}$, is equalized across all firms. By aggregating up we then obtain for the level of real output

$$Y = \underbrace{N^v \cdot Q \cdot \Phi \cdot M}_{= TFP} \cdot K^{\alpha} \cdot (hL)^{1-\alpha}, \tag{10}$$

where Q denotes the geometric average of the quality levels $q(i)$,

$$Q = \exp\left(\frac{1}{N}\int_0^N \log(q(i))\,di\right),$$

Φ denotes the geometric average of the process efficiency levels $\varphi(i)$,

$$\Phi = \exp\left(\frac{1}{N}\int_0^N \log(\varphi(i))\,di\right),$$

and M is a measure of markup dispersion

$$M = \frac{\exp\left(\dfrac{1}{N}\int_0^N \log\dfrac{1}{\mu(i)}\,di\right)}{\dfrac{1}{N}\int_0^N \dfrac{1}{\mu(i)}\,di}.$$

The measure M can be viewed as the ratio of the geometric and arithmetic average of the inverse markup and is therefore smaller (or equal) to one. Without markup dispersion we would have $M=1$.

Interestingly, the aggregate production function boils down to the same overall structure as in (1). As a consequence, in a reduced form the same growth decomposition as in (6) can be obtained from this framework. But (10) further theoretically decomposed the TFP term into the effect of the gains from variety, the level of product quality, the level of process efficiency, and the markup dispersion.[7] This allows us to further speak to the underlying sources of a slowdown in TFP growth as emphasized by theories of endogenous growth and firm heterogeneity. Some, like the changes in the allocative efficiency M (or sometimes also the level of process efficiency Φ), are typically thought of as *level* effects that materialize over a transitional period. Others, like the effect of variety expansion N or quality Q, are typically thought of as showing long-run trends in *growth* rate. Modern theory of endogenous growth typically offers a rich set of micro-founded theories of markup and productivity dispersion across firms as well as quality upgrading and therefore speak to the terms behind residual TFP as highlighted in (10). The original framework in Aghion and Howitt (1992) directly speaks to the terms Φ and Q, whereas a step-by-step model of innovation as in Aghion, Harris, Howitt, and Vickers (2001) also speaks to M. In Section 6 we will highlight some examples from the literature that address the productivity slowdown. Before we turn to this, we first discuss how measurement error may influence the quantification of Solow's residual and whether the measured productivity slowdown could simply come from increasing measurement issues.

5 Growth Decline Due to Measurement Error?

As shown in Table 10.2, the decline in measured TFP growth accounts for the bulk of decline in output growth in the United States since the mid-2000s. Furthermore, the accounting framework of Section 4 sheds some light on what might be behind changes in residual TFP. But is this slowdown in productivity growth real or a figment of increasing measurement

---

[7] Due to the Cobb-Douglas structure these different components enter log additively. Under a more general CES specification the interactions of quality, process efficiency, and markups would matter too.

error? In this section, we discuss possible sources of understatement of growth ("missing growth"), relate them to our accounting, and then survey recent measurement literature. We find that the bulk of the slowdown cannot be explained by an increase in "missing growth."

5.1 True vs. measured growth

Let us first lay down some equations to clarify the relationship between measurement and growth decline. For concreteness, consider the accounting framework from the previous section. From equation (10) in the framework, true TFP growth coincides with equation (6) or

$$g_{TFP} = g_Y - g_L - \alpha \cdot g_k - g_h. \tag{11}$$

Measured TFP growth is given by

$$\hat{g}_{TFP} = \hat{g}_Y - \hat{g}_L - \hat{\alpha} \cdot \hat{g}_k - \hat{g}_h, \tag{12}$$

where $\hat{x}$ denotes the measured value of variable x.

For simplicity, suppose the growth in the number of workers is measured well, so that $g_L = \hat{g}_L$. Then, missing TFP growth arises from understating output growth or overstating input growth. That is, the difference between true and measured productivity growth is given by

$$g_{TFP} - \hat{g}_{TFP} = g_Y - \hat{g}_Y \tag{13}$$
$$+ \alpha \cdot (\hat{g}_k - g_k) + (\hat{g}_h - g_h) \tag{14}$$
$$+ (\hat{\alpha} - \alpha) \cdot \hat{g}_k \tag{15}$$

where (13) is missing output growth, (14) is an overstatement of capital input and labor quality growth, and (15) is a mismeasurement in the production elasticity of capital. When there are rents or quasi-rents, standard measures of TFP growth tend to overstate the production elasticity ($\hat{\alpha} > \alpha$) because standard measurements use one minus the value-added share of labor to estimate a. In our accounting framework of Section 4, this estimate corresponds to $\hat{\alpha} = (rK + \Pi)/(rK + wL + \Pi)$, where Π is the sum of firm profits. However, the capital production elasticity in our framework is equal to one minus the cost share of labor, or $\alpha = rK/(rK + wL)$, and is smaller than $\hat{\alpha}$ when $\Pi > 0$. Because there is usually capital deepening in the data (i.e., $\hat{g}_k > 0$), overstating a results in understating TFP growth.[8]

---

[8] See Fernald and Neiman (2011) for an application to Singapore.

There are many studies of measurement errors in terms of equations (13)–(15). For example, on missing output growth, there is large and long-standing literature since the Boskin Commission (Boskin, Dullberger, Gordon, Grilliches, and Jorgenson 1996) that finds significant *levels* of missing output growth due to measured output deflators not fully capturing substitution, new goods, and quality improvements. However, (13)–(15) are about biases in the *level* of growth, whereas the discussion of decline in growth is about the *change* in the growth rate. The time difference between changes in the true growth rate and the measured growth rate is

$$\Delta g_{TFP} - \Delta \hat{g}_{TFP} = \Delta (g_Y - \hat{g}_Y) \tag{16}$$
$$+ \Delta \alpha (\hat{g}_k - g_k) + \Delta (\hat{g}_h - g_h) \tag{17}$$
$$+ \Delta (\hat{\alpha} - \alpha) \hat{g}_k \tag{18}$$

where Δx denotes the change in x over time. The decline in measured TFP growth correctly captures the decline in true growth ($\Delta g_{TFP} = \Delta \hat{g}_{TFP}$) if measurement errors stayed constant over time, even if these errors are large on average. Hence, for true TFP growth to decline less than measured TFP growth ($\Delta g_{TFP} > \Delta \hat{g}_{TFP}$), one needs to show that understatements of output growth *increased* over time.

5.2 Has missing growth increased?

First, let us consider whether missing output growth (16) has increased. For the US private business sector, recent research has not found a significant increase in missing output growth. Moulton (2018) argues that inflation measurement error has not gotten worse since the Boskin Commission, whereas Aghion, Bergeaud, Boppart, Klenow, and Li (2019) find that missing growth from unmeasured creative-destruction innovation and new varieties are significant in levels but have not increased since the early 1980s. Furthermore, Fernald (2015), Byrne, Fernald, and Reinsdorf (2016), and Syverson (2017) argue that more missing growth in the ICT sector cannot account for post-2005 slowdown in US productivity growth. Similarly, Guvenen, Mataloni, Rassier, and Ruhl (2017) did not find offshore profit shifting contributing significantly to the measured slowdown in output growth.[9] One important

---

[9] Some studies, such as Brynjolfsson, Collis, Diewert, Eggers, and Fox (2019) and Hulten and Nakamura (2019), however, argue that missing output growth in non-market economy may have increased due to the rising prevalence of free goods.

margin that can potentially lead to large revisions of the level of output is the capitalization of intangible and R&D expenditures (Koh, Santaeulàlia-Llopis, and Zheng 2020). However, Brynjolfsson, Rock, and Syverson (2021) find that mismeasurement of intangible investments does not explain the productivity slowdown, because correcting the measurement error raised productivity growth before and after mid-2000s. Recent work by Crouzet and Eberly (2021) argues that the rise in intangible investments may have contributed to the slowdown in measured TFP growth post-1997 compared to pre-1997.

Even if missing output growth has not increased, measured TFP growth may have declined because we are becoming better at measuring inputs. For example, TFP growth is overstated if quality improvements in inputs are understated. Hence, measured TFP growth can decline if we have become better at measuring quality improvements in inputs. However, we are not aware of studies that find input measurement errors contributing significantly to the recent slowdown in TFP growth in the United States.

Lastly, various studies have documented rising markups for the US economy. If this trend reflects a rise in the share of rents or quasi-rents, then equation (18) may have increased and contributed to a slowdown in measured TFP growth. On the other hand, the effect of this measurement error may have been dampened by a significant slowdown in capital deepening. In Table 10.2, capital deepening $\hat{\alpha} \cdot \hat{g}k$ halved. Within this component, the measured capital share $\hat{\alpha}$ increased from an average of 0.33 to 0.38, while $\hat{g}k$ slowed from 3.53 to 1.51 percent per year. If true α stayed relatively constant over time at around 0.30 (which implies that the rent share of GDP increased from 4 percent to 11 percent of GDP), then the third component (18) has not increased.[10] In this back-of-the envelope calculation, the increasing measurement error in α does not contribute significantly to the decline in measured TFP growth, because capital deepening has slowed down.

Overall, our survey of the measurement literature suggests that individual changes in measurement error do not contribute significantly to the decline in TFP growth.

---

[10] This is equal to $(0.38 - 0.30) \times 1.51 - (0.33 - 0.30) \times 3.53 = -0.14$. Crouzet and Eberly (2021) also find small effects from this markup measurement channel.

6 Concluding Remarks and Outlook

Output growth has slowed down in the United States and other advanced economies, with a large part of the slowdown coming from a decline in TFP growth. This paper provides an accounting framework that links TFP growth to innovation and allocative efficiency and clarifies the relationship between true TFP growth and measured TFP growth. Surveying the measurement literature, we find that it is likely that a large part of the decline in measured TFP growth is in fact real.

There are several strands of explanation in the literature for what caused the decline in true TFP growth. One major strand investigates forces that changed the competitive environment, which in turn affects innovation and allocative efficiency—for example, Aghion, Bergeaud, Boppart, Klenow, and Li (2022); Akcigit and Ates (2023); Akcigit and Ates (2021); Autor, Dorn, Katz, Patterson, and Van Reenen (2020); Edmond, Midrigan, and Xu (2018); De Loecker, Eeckhout, and Unger (2020); Gutierrez and Philippon (2017); and De Ridder (2019). Other possible explanations are slowing population growth (Peters and Walsh 2020; Hopenhayn, Neira, and Singhania 2020), ideas getting harder to find (Gordon 2016; Bloom, Jones, Van Reenen, and Webb 2020), and declining discount rate (Farhi and Gourio 2018; Liu, Mian, and Sufi 2022; Chikis, Goldberg and López-Salido 2021). Finally, Baqaee and Farhi (2020) and Bils, Klenow, and Ruane (2020) suggest that allocative efficiency may have declined in the United States.

Through the lens of our framework, these theories operate through one or several of the channels Φ, Q, N, M in equation (10). We believe that the Schumpeterian growth theory à la Aghion and Howitt (1992) is a key approach to understanding the productivity slowdown because it offers rich testable predictions for quality, process efficiency, and markup dispersion as well as rich policy implications such as for antitrust. How quantitatively important are the different channels in explaining the productivity slowdown? Garcia-Macia, Hsieh, and Klenow (2019) and Klenow and Li (2020) provide quantification-based data on job creation and destruction. These papers find that about 90 percent of the slowdown is due to incumbent own innovation and creative destruction (which map into the terms Φ and Q) whereas the variety creation, N, accounts for 10 percent of the decline.

Finding the source of the decline in TFP growth, however, is ultimately a quantitative question because theoretical prediction can be ambiguous—for instance, the effect of competition has both positive (escape from competition) and negative (discouragement) effects on innovation (Aghion, Bloom, Blundell, Griffith, and Howitt 2005). Our view is that structural models disciplined by micro moments is a promising approach. Hence, we hope that in the future there will be more available micro data, such as product-level prices and quantities of output, or plant- and firm-level measures of inputs and R&D (especially outside of manufacturing), to make headway on this important question.

References

Aghion, Philippe, Antonin Bergeaud, Timo Boppart, Peter J. Klenow, and Huiyu Li. (2019). "Missing growth from creative destruction." *American Economic Review, 109* (8), 2795–2822.

Aghion, Philippe, Antonin Bergeaud, Timo Boppart, Peter J. Klenow, and Huiyu Li. (2022). "A theory of falling growth and rising rents." NBER Working Paper 26448.

Aghion, Philippe, Nick Bloom, Richard Blundell, Rachel Griffith, and Peter Howitt. (2005). "Competition and innovation: An inverted-U relationship." *Quarterly Journal of Economics, 120* (2), 701–728.

Aghion, Philippe, Christopher Harris, Peter Howitt, and John Vickers. (2001). "Competition, imitation and growth with step-by-step innovation." *Review of Economic Studies, 68* (3), 467–492.

Aghion, Philippe, and Peter Howitt. (1992). "A model of growth through creative destruction." *Econometrica, 60* (2), 323–351.

Akcigit, Ufuk, and Sina T. Ates. (2021). "Ten facts on declining business dynamism and lessons from endogenous growth theory." *American Economic Journal: Macroeconomics, 13* (1), 257–298.

Akcigit, Ufuk, and Sina T. Ates. (2023). "What happened to US business dynamism?" *Journal of Political Economy*, forthcoming.

Autor, David, David Dorn, Lawrence F. Katz, Christina Patterson, and John Van Reenen. (2020). "The fall of the labor share and the rise of superstar firms." *Quarterly Journal of Economics, 135* (2), 645–709.

Baqaee, David Rezza, and Emmanuel Farhi. (2020). "Productivity and misallocation in general equilibrium." *Quarterly Journal of Economics, 135* (1), 105–163.

Barro, Robert J., Xavier Sala-i-Martin, Olivier Jean Blanchard, and Robert E. Hall. (1991). "Convergence across states and regions." *Brookings Papers on Economic Activity*, (1), 107–182.

Baumol, William J. (1986). "Productivity growth, convergence, and welfare: What the long-run data show." *American Economic Review*, 1072–1085.

Bils, Mark, Peter J. Klenow, and Cian Ruane. (2020). "Misallocation or mismeasurement?" NBER Working Paper 26711.

Bloom, Nicholas, Charles I. Jones, John Van Reenen, and Michael Webb. (2020). "Are ideas getting harder to find?" *American Economic Review, 110* (4), 1104–1144.

Boskin, Michael, Ellen Dullberger, Robert J. Gordon, Zvi Grilliches, and Dale Jorgenson. (1996). "Toward a more accurate measure of the cost of living: Final report of the Senate Finance Committee from the Advisory Commission to Study the Consumer Price Index." *Advisory Commission to Study the Consumer Price Index.* US Department of Commerce, National Technical Report 199723.

Brynjolfsson, Erik, Avinash Collis, W. Erwin Diewert, Felix Eggers, and Kevin J. Fox. (2019). "GDP-B: Accounting for the value of new and free goods in the digital economy." NBER Working Paper 25695.

Brynjolfsson, Erik, Daniel Rock, and Chad Syverson. (2021). "The productivity J-curve: How intangibles complement general purpose technologies." *American Economic Journal: Macroeconomics, 13* (1), 333–372.

Byrne, David M., John G. Fernald, and Marshall B. Reinsdorf. (2016). "Does the United States have a productivity slowdown or a measurement problem?" *Brookings Papers on Economic Activity,* (1), 109–182.

Chikis, Craig, Jonathan E. Goldberg, and J. David López-Salido. (2021). "Do low interest rates harm innovation, competition, and productivity growth?" CEPR Discussion Papers 16184.

Crouzet, Nicolas, and Janice C. Eberly. (2021). "Intangibles, markups, and the measurement of productivity growth." NBER Working Paper 29109.

Edmond, Chris, Virgiliu Midrigan, and Daniel Yi Xu. (2018). "How costly are markups?" NBER Working Paper 24800.

Farhi, Emmanuel, and Francois Gourio. (2018). "Accounting for macro-finance trends: Market power, intangibles, and risk premia." *Brookings Papers on Economic Activity, 2,* 147–250.

Fernald, John G. (2015). "Productivity and potential output before, during, and after the Great Recession." *NBER Macroeconomics Annual, 29* (1), 1–51.

Fernald, John, Huiyu Li, and Mitchell Ochse. (2021). "Labor productivity in a pandemic." *FRBSF Economic Letter.*

Fernald, John, and Brent Neiman. (2011). "Growth accounting with misallocation: Or, doing less with more in Singapore." *American Economic Journal: Macroeconomics, 3* (2), 29–74.

Garcia-Macia, Daniel, Chang-Tai Hsieh, and Peter J. Klenow. (2019). "How destructive is innovation?" *Econometrica, 87* (5), 1507–1541.

Gordon, Robert J. (2016). "Perspectives on the rise and fall of American growth." *American Economic Review, 106* (5), 72–76.

Greenwood, Jeremy, Zvi Hercowitz, and Per Krusell. (1997). "Long-run implications of investment-specific technological change." *American Economic Review, 87* (3), 342–362.

Gutierrez, German, and Thomas Philippon. (2017). "Declining competition and investment in the U.S." NBER Working Paper 23583.

Guvenen, Fatih, Raymond J. Mataloni, Dylan G. Rassier, and Kim J. Ruhl. (2017). "Offshore profit shifting and domestic productivity measurement." NBER Working Paper 23324.

Hall, Robert E., and Charles I. Jones. (1999). "Why do some countries produce so much more output per worker than others?" *Quarterly Journal of Economics, 114* (1), 83–116.

Hopenhayn, Hugo, Julian Neira, and Rish Singhania. (2020). "From population growth to firm demographics: Implications for concentration, entrepreneurship and the labor share." NBER Working Paper 25382.

Hsieh, Chang-Tai, and Peter J. Klenow. (2007). "Relative prices and relative prosperity." *American Economic Review, 97* (3), 562–585.

Hulten, Charles, and Leonard I. Nakamura. (2019). "Expanded GDP for welfare measurement in the 21st century." In *Measuring and Accounting for Innovation in the 21st Century*, ed. Carol Corrado, Jonathan Haskel, Javier Miranda, and Daniel Sichel. University of Chicago Press.

Klenow, Peter J., and Huiyu Li. (2020). "Innovative growth accounting." *NBER Macroeconomics Annual, 35*, 245–295.

Klenow, Peter J., and Andres Rodriguez-Clare. (1997). "The neoclassical revival in growth economics: Has it gone too far?" *NBER Macroeconomics Annual, 12*, 73–103.

Koh, Dongya, Raul Santaeulàlia-Llopis, and Yu Zheng. (2020). "Labor share decline and intellectual property products capital." *Econometrica, 88* (6), 2609–2628.

Kremer, Michael, Jack Willis, and Yang You. (2021). "Converging to convergence." *NBER Macroeconomics Annual, 36*, 245–295.

Liu, Ernest, Atif Mian, and Amir Sufi. (2022). "Low interest rates, market power, and productivity growth." *Econometrica, 90* (1), 193–221.

Loecker, Jan De, Jan Eeckhout, and Gabriel Unger. (2020). "The rise of market power and the macroeconomic implications." *Quarterly Journal of Economics, 135* (2), 561–644.

Lucas, Robert E., Jr. (1988). "On the mechanics of economic development." *Journal of Monetary Economics, 22* (1), 3–42.

Moulton, Brent. (2018). "The measurement of output, prices, and productivity: What's changed since the Boskin Commission?" Technical Report, Hutchins Center on Fiscal and Monetary Policy, Brookings Institution.

Peters, Michael, and Conor Walsh. (2020). "Population growth and firm dynamics." NBER Working Paper 29424.

Prescott, Edward C. (1998). "Lawrence R. Klein lecture 1997: Needed: A theory of total factor productivity." *International Economic Review*, 525–551.

Ridder, Maarten De. (2019). "Market power and innovation in the intangible economy." http://www.maartenderidder.com/uploads/6/2/2/3/6223410/maarten_de_ridder_jmp.pdf.

Rodrik, Dani. (2013). "Unconditional convergence in manufacturing." *Quarterly Journal of Economics, 128* (1), 165–204.

Syverson, Chad. (2017). "Challenges to mismeasurement explanations for the U.S. productivity slowdown." *Journal of Economic Perspectives, 31* (2), 165–186.

APPENDIX: ADDITIONAL
FIGURES AND TABLES

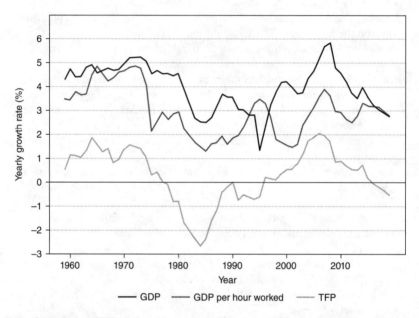

Notes: GDP = "rgdpna," TFP = "rtfpna," hours = "avh" times "emp," GDP per hours = "rgdpna" divided by hours. Five-year trailing moving averages. Average across countries is weighted by real GDP.

Data source: Penn World Tables 10.0. 1960–2019.

Figure 10.A1. Growth rate of GDP, labor productivity, and TFP in non-OECD countries

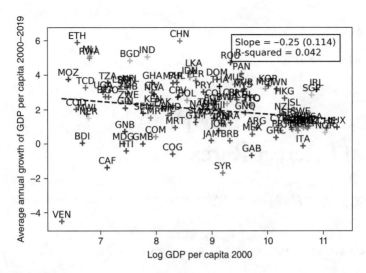

Notes: Real GDP per capita = "rgdpna" divided by "pop." The x-axis plots the natural log of real GDP per capita in 2000. The y-axis plots the average annual growth rate of real GDP per capita over 2000–2019.

Data source: Penn World Tables 10.0.

Figure 10.A2. Convergence for 2000–2019

Table 10.A1. Development accounting with investment-specific technology

Country	Y/L	$(\Theta^{-1}K/Y)^{\frac{\alpha}{1-\alpha}}$	h	A
United States	1.000	1.000	1.000	1.000
Switzerland	0.849	1.182	0.987	0.728
France	0.793	1.522	0.857	0.608
Germany	0.741	1.320	0.981	0.572
Sweden	0.831	1.250	0.915	0.726
Japan	0.561	1.290	0.957	0.454
Republic of Korea	0.589	1.626	0.996	0.364
Russian Federation	0.425	2.331	0.913	0.200
Mexico	0.364	1.972	0.736	0.251
Argentina	0.409	1.858	0.819	0.269
Brazil	0.243	1.906	0.806	0.158
China	0.184	1.806	0.714	0.142
India	0.141	2.606	0.574	0.094
Nigeria	0.112	2.018	0.521	0.106
Kenya	0.068	1.802	0.621	0.061
Zimbabwe	0.049	1.230	0.716	0.056

Source: Penn World Tables 10.0.

Note: $\bar{Y}$ = "rgdpo," s = natural resource shares from World Development Index, $Y = \bar{Y}(1-s)$ times "pl_gdpo" divided by "pl_con," L = "emp," K = "rnna"/"pl_n," h = "hc," Θ^{-1} = "pl_i" divided by "pl_con." $A = \dfrac{Y}{(\Theta^{-1}K/Y)^{\frac{\alpha}{1-\alpha}}hL}$ with $a = 1/3$.

CHAPTER 11

Productivity Growth and Real Interest Rates

A Circular Relationship

ANTONIN BERGEAUD, GILBERT CETTE, *and* RÉMY LECAT

1 Introduction

Economic growth in all advanced countries has slowed continuously since the 1970s and has fallen to a historical low since the Great Recession (at least compared to twentieth-century standards; see Bergeaud, Cette, and Lecat 2016, 2017). This secular slowdown is mainly the result of weaker growth in total factor productivity, which is difficult to interpret with a standard growth framework. The picture becomes even more puzzling if we consider the diversity of productivity levels, of new technology diffusion, of average human capital, and of openness to trade across advanced countries, all of which are affected by a slowdown. Such a shared TFP trend in a context of significant structural heterogeneity suggests that common global factors could be at play.

In this chapter we investigate one possible global factor: the decline in long-term real interest rates observed since the early 1990s in all developed countries. Specifically, we discuss and test the existence of a circular relationship between interest rates and productivity growth. It is, of course, well known that productivity is a long-term determinant of return on capital and thereby of interest rates, which explains a positive correlation between these two quantities. But we argue that this is only one side of the coin, as interest rates are also a determinant of the minimum expected return from invest-ment projects, and therefore of the productivity level required for such an investment. The decline in long-term real interest rates, notably due to neg-ative demographic pressures, may have led to a slowdown in productivity by making an increasing number of weakly productive companies and projects profitable (we refer to this mechanism as the "cleansing effect"). This two-way causality is what we coin the circular relationship between interest rates and productivity growth.

The first causal relationship, from potential growth to long-term real in-terest rates, is standard in the literature. Even if other factors have been shown to influence the equilibrium level of long-term interest rates, the decline in productivity gains, and hence in potential growth, appears to be an impor-tant contributing factor behind the fall in real interest rates since the early 1980s. (For an empirical analysis of this relationship and a summary of the existing literature, see Teulings and Baldwin 2014; Bean 2016; Eggertsson et al. 2016; Marx, Mojon, and Velde 2017.)

The reverse causal relationship, from long-term real interest rates to productivity, and consequently GDP growth, has recently received wide at-tention, with contrasted conclusions. Some authors document a negative impact of higher interest rates on productivity growth, which arises from tougher financial conditions when interest rates are too high and dampen investments in R&D. Different theoretical models show how lower credit constraints can foster innovation-led growth by reducing the costs of screening promising projects (e.g., see King and Levine 1993; Aghion, Bacchetta, et al. 2009). Empirically, this relation has been confirmed by numerous papers, such as Levine (1997), Rajan and Zingales (1998), Aghion, Angeletos, et al. (2010), and Aghion, Askenazy, et al. (2012). Using indi-vidual firm datasets in the context of the financial crisis, recent empirical contributions highlight similar results (see, for instance, Duval, Hong, and Y. Timmer 2017, and Manaresi and Pierri 2017, respectively, for US and Italian firms) and show that financial constraints have a detrimental impact on productivity growth.[1] But on the other side, the fall in real interest rates from the mid-1980s could have reduced mortality rates for less productive firms (a decline in the "cleansing effect") and could thus have hampered the

---

[1] In this chapter we study solely interest rates and not a direct measure of financial constraints. High financial constraints may not arise solely in a high interest rates environment, but high interest rates lead to tougher financial constraints, *ceteris paribus*.

reallocation of production factors toward firms at the frontier. Lower rates could also have made it possible to finance less efficient projects, and this could in turn have reduced productivity gains. Several studies have provided support for this explanation (see, for example, Reis 2013; Gopinath et al. 2017; Gorton and Ordonez 2016; Cette, Fernald, and Mojon 2016; Linarello, Petrella, and Sette 2019). In this chapter we focus on testing this latter explanation, which appears to be dominant over the period of estimation due to the overall level of real interest rates.

If the second channel (negative reallocation effect) dominates the first (positive relation from real interest rates to productivity growth), then a negative permanent shock on interest rates—due, for example, to population aging—would indeed lead to a secular fall in productivity growth. This fall would in turn lead to a decline in interest rates and create a circular relationship between these two quantities that ultimately would converge to a steady state characterized by low growth and low interest rates. When real interest rates are low (as it has been the case for several decades), it is likely that this second channel will dominate the first one. A recent paper from Aghion, Bergeaud, Cette, et al. (2019) proposes a Schumpeterian framework that combines these two channels in an inverted-U relationship between interest rates and productivity, with a positive relationship at low interest rate levels. Using French microdata, the authors confirm that, at least over the last two decades, the second channel has been active and has weighed on productivity. In this case, only a technology shock could disrupt this downward spiral.

In order to test this mechanism, and in particular the existence of a circular relationship between real interest rates and TFP growth, we take a long-run view. We first rely on the Long Term Productivity Database built by Bergeaud, Cette, and Lecat (2016), which provides comparable cross-country TFP estimates from the end of the nineteenth century; and on the work of Jordà, Schularick, and Taylor (2017) and in particular their Macrohistory Database, which provides yearly average values for long-term interest rates. We estimate this circular relationship by cross-country panel regressions using annual data on a sample of 17 advanced countries over the period 1950–2017. We jointly estimate the two relationships (from real interest rates to productivity growth, and from productivity growth to real interest rates) using different methods, and use the point estimates to look at the past and the future. To the best of our knowledge, our work here is the first to propose estimates of such circular relationship between real interest rates and TFP growth.

Our results hint at the existence of a circular relationship that results in a secular stagnation equilibrium: a situation where productivity grows slowly and where real interest rates are low. Between the two subperiods 1984–1995 and 2005–2016, TFP annual growth declined by about 0.66pp in the United States and 1.51pp in the euro area, and the contribution of real interest rates that we estimate fell by 0.6pp and 0.56pp, respectively. While, of course, other factors are at play during this period—particularly, in the case of the euro area, a slowdown in human capital stock—such contributions suggest that real interest rates could account for a significant share of the productivity slowdown.

One way to break out of this circular relationship is via a new technological revolution linked to the digital economy, or, in countries where there is still room for convergence, via structural reforms to improve the diffusion of new technologies. While having potential scarring effects on potential growth, the COVID-19 shock may as well accelerate the diffusion of information and communication technologies (ICT). Using our estimate results, we propose some simulations to test the impact of such shocks in the frontier economy. The results from these simulations confirm the intuition. We assess the impact of a negative shock on relative equipment prices with a magnitude that could be comparable to the "ICT shock" in the United States between 1985 and 2007. This shock would be enough to escape the secular stagnation trap, with TFP growth higher than the baseline rate by 0.6pp at the peak. This technology shock in the United States would spread to other countries through the catching-up process and lead to a slow but lasting acceleration in TFP, as its level converges with that of the United States. In the euro area, TFP growth relative to the baseline reaches a peak of 0.2pp, about ten years after the US peak. The digital revolution and its substantial effect on productivity that some economists have forecast could correspond to, or could have even been larger than, such a shock over the next decades (see, for instance, Van Ark 2016; Brynjolfsson, Rock, and Syverson 2017; Brynjolfsson, Rock, and Syverson 2018; or Branstetter and D. Sichel 2017).

The remainder of this chapter is organized as follows: Section 2 motivates our analysis and describes the data, Section 3 details and estimates the empirical model. Finally, Section 4 shows our model's response to a technology shock in the productivity leader.

2 Background and Descriptive Evidence

Before turning to the estimation of the circular relationship between interest rates and TFP growth, we first consider some descriptive evidence. As briefly explained in the introduction, we draw our data from two different sources. First, we rely on the long-term productivity database built by Bergeaud, Cette, and Lecat (2016), which provides comparable TFP estimates over a very long time dimension and for a large panel of countries. Second, we complete and backdate long-term real interest rate data provided by the OECD using the work of Jordà, Schularick, and Taylor (2017). Our final dataset includes 17 countries over a period of 68 years (from 1950 to 2017).[2]

Figures 11.1a-b show the median and confidence intervals, over the period 1950–2017 for our set of 17 developed countries, respectively, for TFP growth and for long-term real interest rates. We can make the following observations.

TFP growth trends. We distinguish three subperiods. First, up to the first oil shock at the beginning of the 1970s, TFP growth fluctuated around a stable rate of around 3 percent as European countries and Japan benefited from the big wave of productivity that the United States[3] had experienced decades earlier. Second, from the first oil shock to the mid-2000s, TFP growth declined by steps, and its level at the end of the period varied between 0.5 percent and 1 percent. After 1995 and until 2004, productivity growth in the United States overtook that of other countries, benefiting from a new productivity wave, albeit much lower than what was observed in the 1930s, 1940s, and 1950s. As documented in numerous papers, this productivity growth wave corresponds to the third industrial revolution, linked to ICT (see Jorgenson 2001; Jorgenson, Ho, and Stiroh 2008; Van Ark, O'Mahoney, and M. P. Timmer 2008; M. P. Timmer et al. 2011; Bergeaud, Cette, and Lecat 2016; and Cette 2014 for a survey). Apart from the very short second productivity wave, observed mostly in the United States (and

---

[2] These 17 advanced countries are: Australia, Belgium, Canada, Denmark, Finland, France, Germany, Italy, Japan, the Netherlands, Norway, Portugal, Spain, Sweden, Switzerland, the United Kingdom, and the United States.

[3] Throughout, we will refer to the United States as the technology leader (or frontier), even if some countries may have a higher level of TFP over some subperiods for particular reasons—as is the case, for instance, with Norway, due to the importance of its oil sector.

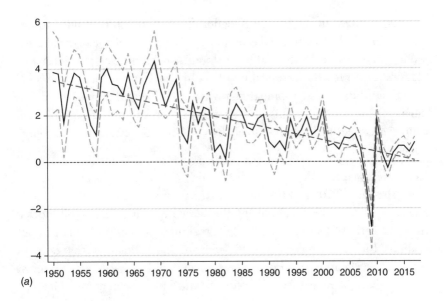

(a)

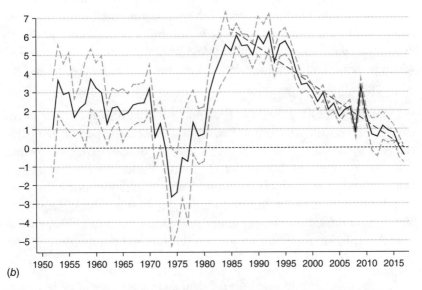

(b)

Notes: This figure reports the yearly median growth rate of TFP growth (a) and real interest rate (b) in 17 OECD countries (in %) and trends (dotted black line). The dotted gray lines around the median are confidence intervals, defined as the median + and – 2 standard errors across the 17 OECD countries of the sample.

Figure 11.1a–b. Trends of TFP growth and real interest rates

to a lesser extent in the United Kingdom), TFP growth continued to decline dramatically in advanced economies, irrespective of the original TFP level. Finally, from the mid-2000s, before the beginning of the Great Recession, TFP growth decreased in all countries. The current pace of TFP growth appears very low compared to what was observed previously, except during the world wars. This low growth performance for most advanced countries cannot be explained solely by the Great Recession and its consequences (Fernald et al. 2017).

Real interest rates. We mainly distinguish between three subperiods: (i) Until the early 1970s and first oil shock, real interest rates remained stable and close to 2.5 percent. (ii) During the decade covering the two oil shocks, from the early 1970s to the early 1980s, real interest rates posted large fluctuations. First a sharp decrease—fueled by high inflation rates that resulted from the acceleration in oil prices—which even led to negative real interest rates. A sharp increase then followed, explained by a rise in nominal interest rates and a decline in inflation. Real interest rates grew beyond 5.5 percent. (iii) From the mid-1980s to the end of the period, real interest rates declined dramatically by at least 5pp; this decline is observed simultaneously in all developed countries; their standard deviation across countries decreases, which points to an increasing role of international determinants for real interest rates.

Co-movement. TFP growth and real interest rates display periods of co-movements (1950s to the early 1970s; 1990s to the current period) and of divergence (from the mid-1970s to the 1980s). TFP has, indeed, slowed down from the 1970s as the benefits of the second industrial revolution were exhausted while the average duration of education slowed down (see Bergeaud, Cette, and Lecat 2018 for a survey and estimations).[4] Regarding real interest rates, their sharp fluctuations in the 1970s and 1980s were due to both the inflationary impact of the oil shock and the monetary policy counterreaction.

Yet the long-term decline in real interest rates, which can be related to structural factors such as demographic developments, could be a common

---

[4] On top of the declining returns of education, many alternative explanations for the slowdown have been put forward and studied extensively: e.g., declining productivity in R&D activities (Bloom et al. 2020); mismeasurement (Aghion et al. 2019b; Syverson 2017); inadequate competition policies leading to declining dynamism (Aghion et al. 2019a; Akcigit and Ates 2019).

factor behind the universal decline in TFP growth since the early 1990s in all developed countries. This would be a plausible explanation if the fall in real interest rates from the mid-1980s had slowed default rates in less productive firms (decline in the "cleansing effect"), thereby hampering the reallocation of factors of production to more cutting-edge firms. Lower rates could also have made it easier to finance less efficient projects, and this combination of factors could in turn have reduced productivity gains. Aghion, Bergeaud, Cette, et al. (2019) have illustrated this phenomenon on firm-level data using a quasi-experiment: the 2012 Eurosystem's Additional Credit Claims program, which generated an exogenous extra supply of credits for a subset of incumbent firms. Incumbent firms with easier access to credit experience higher productivity growth, but they also experience lower exit rates, particularly the least productive firms among them.

Theoretical mechanism. We know from the literature that potential growth affects long-term real interest rates directly, and that, at the same time, decreasing real interest rates can negatively impact productivity growth. Different theoretical mechanisms can explain this finding.

Aghion, Bergeaud, Cette, et al. (2019) extend the Klette and Kortum (2004) framework and include a parameter that limits the maximum amount that a firm can invest based on its value. This parameter, therefore, captures the idea that firms are constrained in their capacity to finance, and it also measures the level of credit constraints in the economy. This extension changes the dynamics of firms compared to the standard model (see Aghion, Akcigit, and Howitt 2015). In particular, if this parameter is too low, incumbent firms will invest more and deter the entry of new and more productive firms. To the extent that the level of credit constraints is correlated with real interest rates, their model shows how decreasing real interest rates (reducing credit constraints) can negatively impact growth through a negative effect on resources reallocation, especially if the level of credit constraints is already low enough.[5] The model also shows that if the level of constraint is large enough, a fall in real interest rates reduces the cost of capital and spurs corporate investment (see, e.g., Mazet-Sonilhac and Mésonnier 2016;

---

[5] Like most models of reallocation of resources, this mechanism makes the assumption that production factors are easily transferable across firms. In practice, both capital and labor are characterized by important adjustment costs that could be an obstacle to the reallocation process (see, e.g., Cooper and Haltiwanger 2006; Gavazza 2011; Bergeaud and Ray 2021).

Carluccio, Mazet-Sonilhac, and Mésonnier 2018) with a positive impact on growth. This inverted-U link between real interest rates and growth is at the heart of our empirical work and is corroborated by the existence of a non-linear relationship measured at the sector level (see Aghion, Bergeaud, Cette, et al. 2019). These dynamics are reinforced by the reverse relationship: the decline in productivity gains and hence in potential growth is itself a contributing factor behind the fall in real interest rates. (For an empirical analysis of this relationship and a summary of the existing literature, see Teulings and Baldwin 2014; Bean 2016; or Marx, Mojon, and Velde 2017.)

Other models have also considered the link between growth and real interest rates. In particular, they show how low interest rates can negatively impact productivity growth if they distort competition by giving a comparative advantage to the market leaders or larger firms, as emphasized by Liu, Mian, and Sufi (2019).[6] That paper, though, does not consider the dynamics of firm entry / exit and the impact of reallocation, which is the central mechanism at play in Aghion, Bergeaud, Cette, et al. (2019), both from a theoretical and an empirical point of view and regardless of the intensity of competition within a sector.

3   Estimations

In this section we present an empirical model to account for the complex relationship between real interest rates and productivity growth.

3.1   Econometric model

We consider the following system of simultaneous equations where countries are indexed by $i \in \{1 \ldots N\}$ and year by $t \in \{1 \ldots T\}$:

$$\begin{cases} g_{i,t} = a g_{i,t-1} + b r_{i,t-1} + C' X_{i,t} + \varepsilon_{i,t} \\ r_{i,t} = \alpha g_{i,t} + \beta r_{i,t-1} + \Gamma' Z_{i,t} + \eta_{i,t} \end{cases} \tag{1}$$

where g is the growth rate of total factor productivity and r the level of real interest rate. X and Z are two vectors of time-varying and time-unvarying exogenous covariates, and ε and η are error terms. In both equations, we add

---

[6] See also Chatterjee and Eyigungor (2020); Ruiz-Garcia (2019).

an autoregressive term that captures the persistence of both productivity growth and interest rates. In terms of timing, we assume that there is no direct contemporaneous effects of r on g in contrast with the effects of g on r.[7]

We are interested in the values of α and b and their long-term counterparts $\alpha/(1-\beta)$ and $b/(1-\alpha)$. b corresponds to the marginal effect of a change in past interest rates on the contemporaneous growth rate of TFP. In the other equation, we are mostly interested in the value of α, which corresponds to the marginal effect of a change in productivity growth rate on the level of contemporaneous interest rates. In line with the discussed mechanisms, we expect both α and b to be positive.

We first estimate model (1) equation by equation.[8] We do this using the GMM estimator to correct for endogeneity. We then turn to an estimation of the full model, taking into account the complete data-generating process as described in (1). More specifically, we relax the assumption implicitly made in the previous estimation procedures that errors ε and η are fully independent. We consider that the system of equation (1) displays contemporaneous cross-equation error correlation and is therefore a seemingly unrelated regression system (see Zellner 1962). We estimate this system using an iterative GLS method.

We estimate equation (1) for our set of 17 OECD countries and over the period 1950–2017. Although we have information on interest rates and productivity before 1950, we prefer not to consider pre–World War II data because during this period interest rates cover a very different reality across countries and time (see Levy-Garboua and Monnet 2016, in the case of France) and because the war periods yield fragile data.

3.2 Choice of exogenous variables

In selecting covariates to include in vector C and Γ, we need to bear in mind various criteria. First, we want these variables to explain part of the dynamics

---

[7] Because changes in factor allocation take time, the impact of interest rates on TFP growth is delayed, which is not the case for the impact of TFP growth on interest rates, changes in financial capital allocation being possibly fast.

[8] We have also experimented with slight variations around this model. Namely, we have allowed interest rates to have a contemporaneous effect on TFP growth and have used more lags of the main regressors. The results remain qualitatively unchanged and quantitatively similar. We keep this simple model because it makes the simulation exercise of Section 4.2 more transparent.

of growth or interest rates; and second, we want these variables to be as exogenous as possible; and third, we need these variables to be available for all our 17 countries and to be consistently measured since 1950.

As regards the first point, we know from the vast growth literature that the two main contributors to long-term TFP growth are improvement in human capital and technological progress. For most countries, the latter factor evolves following a catching-up process with the frontier economy (since World War II, this would be the United States; see Bergeaud, Cette, and Lecat 2016; Bergeaud, Cette, and Lecat 2018 for a review). We shall therefore control for the variation in human capital, measured both as the change in the average duration of education among the population and as life expectancy. Both the average duration of education and life expectancy are slowly varying series whose dynamics are mostly driven by historical policy decisions, demographics, and long-term technological change in the health system, and we consider that they are essentially unaffected by the contemporaneous growth rate of TFP.

For worldwide technological progress, we use the relative price of investment in the United States (i.e., the ratio of the price of investment over the price of GDP)[9] and we model its diffusion using the relative distance to the TFP level of the United States. All these variables are included in vector C and are available from 1950 for all our 17 countries. Data source, description, and measurement are detailed in Bergeaud, Cette, and Lecat (2019).

For the second equation, we control for the volatility of inflation in the past three years, for the age structure of the population, more precisely by the ratio of dependent population (i.e., below 16 or above 65; see Ang and Madsen 2016) to total population, and by a measure of the stability of economic policy—i.e., the number of changes in finance ministers in the past three years. We expect inflation volatility to capture the risk premium that stems from changes in expected inflation, the age-dependency ratio to proxy the supply of savings, which weighs on real interest rates, and changes in finance ministers to capture economic political uncertainty.

---

[9] Quality improvement in investment leading to increases in productive performances is partly incorporated into national accounts through investment prices, especially for ICTs. This incorporation is deeper in the US national accounts than in those of other countries. (For a summary on these aspects, see Byrne, Oliner, and D. E. Sichel 2013; Cette 2014.)

3.3 Results

As discussed above, we start to show results when each equation of system (1) is estimated separately, using the GMM. Indeed, in the likely case that errors are serially correlated in each equation of (1), we can have $E[\varepsilon_{i,t}\ r_{i,t-1}] \neq 0$, violating the identification assumptions of the first equation. We therefore instrument $r_{i,t-1}$ by its past value in nominal terms so as to also correct for inflation shocks.

3.3.1 From real-interest rates to growth

Results obtained from the estimation of the first equation of (1) are shown in columns 1, 2, and 3 of Table 11.1. The columns differ by the measure of the relative price of investment. Column 1 uses the variation in the price of equipment divided by the variation in the price of GDP for the United States applied to all countries. Indeed, as mentioned above, US national accounts are the most advanced in incorporating quality adjustment resulting from technological progress into investment prices. As this technological progress should be common to all countries, we use this measure as a proxy for the pace of global innovation. Column 2 uses the same measure but only set to 0 for countries that are farther than 1 percent from the productivity level of the frontier.[10] The underlying idea is that only countries that are close enough to the technological frontier directly benefit from an innovation shock, whereas other countries indirectly benefit from the shock through the catching-up dynamics. Finally, column 3 uses the same measure as column 2, but considers the price of all investment assets instead of focusing solely on equipment.[11]

In all instances, we see that the marginal effect of $r_{i,t-1}$ on $g_{i,t}$ is positive, significant, and of similar magnitude, showing a positive correlation between the previous year's level of interest rates and current productivity growth. Education has the expected magnitude: a one-year increase in the average

---

[10] Formally the variable is set to 0 for observation $(i,\ t)$ such that: $\frac{1}{5}\sum_{k=1}^{5}(\text{tfp}_{i,t-k} - \text{tfp}_{us,t-k}) > 0.01$, where tfp is the logarithm of the level of TFP.

[11] We extend our investment price measure as some technological assets might be included in structure investment series, although these are likely to be limited. The US national accounts also report price indices for specific IT assets such as computers. However, such series may suffer from imprecise price measurements; despite the efforts of the BEA and BLS, they remain imperfectly captured, as underlined by Byrne, Oliner, and Sichel (2013).

Table 11.1. Estimation results

Estimator	GMM (1)	GMM (2)	GMM (3)	SURE (4)	SURE (5)	SURE (6)
Panel A: Dependent variable: $g_{i,t}$						
$g_{i,t-1}$	0.204***	0.202***	0.206***	0.228***	0.223***	0.226***
	(0.036)	(0.036)	(0.037)	(0.028)	(0.028)	(0.028)
$r_{i,t-1}$	0.123**	0.118*	0.113*	0.035*	0.051**	0.050**
	(0.061)	(0.062)	(0.066)	(0.021)	(0.021)	(0.021)
Catch-up	−5.945***	−5.446***	−5.395***	−5.657***	−5.025***	−4.961***
	(0.601)	(0.578)	(0.563)	(0.476)	(0.453)	(0.447)
Variation in relat. price	−0.134**	−0.059	−0.128	−0.188***	−0.087*	−0.187*
	(0.056)	(0.044)	(0.118)	(0.041)	(0.046)	(0.103)
Variation in educ.	8.013***	7.432***	7.292***	8.147***	7.430***	7.252***
	(1.364)	(1.300)	(1.276)	(1.296)	(1.299)	(1.287)
Variation in life exp.	0.337	0.321	0.328	0.184	0.181	0.196
	(0.291)	(0.292)	(0.291)	(0.181)	(0.183)	(0.183)
Panel B: Dependent variable: $r_{i,t}$						
$r_{i,t-1}$	0.691***			0.705***	0.704***	0.704***
	(0.039)			(0.021)	(0.021)	(0.021)
$g_{i,t}$	0.121*			0.055**	0.064**	0.068**
	(0.070)			(0.027)	(0.027)	(0.027)
Age-dep. ratio	−0.050***			−0.043***	−0.043***	−0.043***
	(0.014)			(0.011)	(0.011)	(0.011)
Inflation volat.	0.105			0.022***	0.022***	0.022***
	(0.076)			(0.005)	(0.005)	(0.005)
Policy instability	0.083			0.076	0.077	0.077
	(0.067)			(0.052)	(0.052)	(0.052)

Notes: Number of observations: 1,122. This table presents regression results from estimating equation (1). g is the growth rate of TFP and r is the value of real interest rates (both in %). Columns 1 to 3 in the top panel and column 1 in the bottom panel use the GMM to estimate separately the two parts of equation (1). Column 1 measures relative investment price of investment using its current value for equipment in the United States for all countries, column 2 uses this value for countries with a TFP level at least 1 percent below that of the United States, and column 3 does the same as column 2 but considers relative investment price for total investment (instead of focusing only on equipment). Column 1 of the bottom panel uses two instruments for g: the logarithm of electricity consumption divided by population in $t-1$, and the ratio of ICT capital stock over GDP in value taken at $t-1$. Coefficients and standard errors (in parentheses) are obtained using the GMM using past realization of the nominal interest rate as an instrument. Autocorrelation and heteroskedasticity robust standard errors have been estimated using the Newey-West variance estimator with a bandwidth of 5 years. The p-value of the Kleibergen-Paap statistic of under-identification is always below 1 percent, and the F-statistics of the Kleibergen-Paap Wald test of weak instruments is larger than 45 in all cases (Kleibergen and Paap 2006). In column 1 of panel B, the Hansen J p-value is equal to 0.842. Columns 4 to 6 consider the model as SURE (seemingly unrelated regression). Columns 4, 5, and 6 differ by the way relative price of investment is measured, which is the same as for columns 1, 2, and 3 of the top panel. Heteroskedasticity robust standard errors are reported in parentheses. R-squared value: panel A: 0.263, 0.258, and 0.259 (columns 1, 2, and 3); panel B: 0.527 (column 1); SURE model: 0.255, 0.24 and 0.245 (columns 4, 5, and 6).
    *$p < 0.1$; **$p < 0.05$; ***$p < 0.001$

level of education of the population raises productivity by around 7–8 percentage points, in line with the literature (see Psacharopoulos and Patrinos 2004 and Bergeaud, Cette, and Lecat 2018 for a review). Life expectancy, which proxies the general health of the labor force, is also positively correlated (although not significantly) with growth, one additional year of life expectancy increasing TFP by about 0.3 percent. The catching-up coefficient implies that countries that are far from the productivity frontier tend to grow faster. The coefficient suggests that the speed of convergence is about 5 percent per year. Finally, relative investment price coefficients are negative and precisely estimated. Our preferred estimate is column 2, which takes into account potential endogeneity of nominal interest rates and allows all countries to benefit directly from technological progress. In this estimate, a 1 percent decrease in the investment price increases TFP by about 0.13 percent.

3.3.2 From growth to real interest rate

As regards the second equation of (1), results are shown in column 1 of panel B of Table 11.1. We instrument the TFP growth rate using one-year lagged values of the intensive margin of two technologies: information technologies, which are measured by the ratio of ICT capital stock to GDP, in value; and electricity, which is measured by the logarithm of electricity consumption per capita (both variables are taken from Bergeaud, Cette, and Lecat 2018, where more details on these two measures and their impact on TFP are given).

The correlation between TFP growth and real interest rates is positive and usually significant. Given a 0.7 autoregressive coefficient and a 0.1 TFP coefficient, the long-run impact of a 1pp increase in TFP on the level of interest rates is about 0.3. We may note that, according to the model in Aghion, Bergeaud, Cette, et al. (2019), this positive correlation is valid only in a low interest rates environment. If interest rates were significantly higher, the economy would stand on the other side of the "inverted-U" and an increase in TFP could in fact lead to a reduction of real interest rates. This may have been the case in the beginning of the 1980s, when real interest rates were particularly high; however, empirical results from Aghion, Bergeaud, Cette, et al. (2019) show that, at least in the recent period, this is not the case.[12]

---

[12] While we are not directly testing the cleansing effect as a channel through which credit and productivity could be positively correlated, we refer to Aghion, Bergeaud, Cette, et al. (2019)

A higher age-dependency ratio, which could lead to an increased supply of savings, weighs on interest rates, with a negative significant coefficient of similar amplitude across estimates: a 1pp increase in the age dependency decreases TFP by about 0.07pp in the long run. This relationship is important for the future: demography may exert a continuous downward pressure on long-term real interest rates as this ratio is expected to increase in the next decades (see Basso and Jimeno 2018). Inflation volatility may increase the risk premium on interest rates and has a positive coefficient, albeit not always significant. Policy instability, as proxied by changes in finance ministers, pushes up interest rates as expected, although the standard errors remain too large to make any precise conclusions.

3.4 Simultaneous estimations

We now turn to an estimation of the full system (1), assuming that it is a seemingly unrelated regression system, which supposes that error terms across equations are related. Results are presented in columns 4, 5, and 6 of Table 11.1. Like for columns 1, 2, and 3, these columns differ by how we measure relative investment prices. These results are qualitatively similar to the ones obtained using separate within estimations of the system—that is, the coefficient of interest rates is positive and significant, estimated at around 0.04, while the autoregressive coefficient of TFP growth is estimated at around 0.23, suggesting a 0.05pp long-run impact on TFP growth of a 1pp increase in interest rates. From these results, 0.3 point of the decline in TFP growth, or 15 percent of the slowdown, could be attributed to the decrease in interest rates *ceteris paribus*. Changes in education, life expectancy, and distance to the productivity frontier have the expected signs, although the life expectancy coefficient is not significant. Turning to interest rate estimates in panel B, results are qualitatively similar to the separate estimates, with a lower magnitude for the TFP coefficient. A one-point increase in the TFP growth rate leads to a long-term impact of 0.2 point on the level of interest rates, with a 0.06 short-term coefficient of TFP growth and a 0.7 autoregressive term. The age-dependency ratio, inflation volatility, and political instability have the expected signs and remain close to the within estimates.

---

for formal evidence that this channel is at play (in particular, they look at the exit rate of low-productivity firms following a credit shock).

4 Simulations

In this section we use our estimation results and conduct two exercises. First, we use the first line of the equation (1) to decompose the impact of r on g over different subperiods, and similarly we use the second line of the same system to decompose the impact of g on r. These two decompositions will indicate the contribution of the decline in real interest rates to the decrease in TFP growth and, similarly, the contribution of the decline in TFP growth to the decrease in real interest rates. Second, we simulate the full model and look at the impact on TFP growth and on real interest rates of a negative shock in the US relative investment price considered as resulting from a technology shock.

4.1 Long-run evolution breakdown

Table 11.2 uses point estimates of column 1 of Table 11.1 to estimate the long-run effects of interest rates on the evolution of TFP over different subperiods. We then use the point estimates to look at the average contribution of TFP growth to real interest rates. Results are shown in Table 11.3. We select five subperiods that correspond to the overall evolution of real interest rates as documented in Section 2—1950–1973, 1973–1984, 1984–1995, 1995–2005, and 2005–2017—and compare the United States with the euro area.

Table 11.2. Decomposition of TFP growth

USA	1950–1973	1973–1984	1984–1995	1995–2005	2005–2017
TFP growth	2.00	0.79	1.29	1.75	0.63
Contribution of real interest rates	0.28	0.22	0.78	0.50	0.18
Euro Area	*1950–1973*	*1973–1984*	*1984–1995*	*1995–2005*	*2005–2017*
TFP growth	3.92	1.60	1.84	0.80	0.33
Contribution of real interest rates	0.44	0.22	0.84	0.58	0.26

Notes: This table shows the average value of TFP growth and the long-run contribution of interest rates using estimates from column (1) in Table 11.1 from the first equation of model (1). Long-run contributions are defined as $\hat{x}/(1-a)\bar{X}$, where $\hat{x}$ is the estimated coefficient associated with variable X and $\bar{X}$ its average value over the subperiod (a is the autoregressive coefficient; see equation (1)).

Table 11.3. Decomposition of real interest rates

USA	1950–1973	1973–1984	1984–1995	1995–2005	2005–2017
Interest rates	1.84	1.42	5.07	3.25	1.17
Contribution of TFP growth	0.78	0.31	0.51	0.69	0.25

Euro area	1950–1973	1973–1984	1984–1995	1995–2005	2005–2017
Interest rates	2.85	1.45	5.45	3.78	1.70
Contribution of TFP growth	1.53	0.63	0.72	0.31	0.13

Notes: This table shows the average value of real interest rates and the long-run contribution of TFP growth using estimates from column (1) in Table 11.1 from the second equation of model (1). Long-run contributions are defined as $\hat{x}/(1-a)\bar{X}$ where $\hat{x}$ is the estimated coefficient associated with variable X and $\bar{X}$ its average value over the subperiod (a is the autoregressive coefficient; see equation (1)).

The contribution of real interest rates to TFP growth reaches a maximum in the subperiod 1984–1995 both in the United States and in the euro area. Between the two subperiods 1984–1995 and 2005–2017, the decline in TFP annual growth was about 0.66pp in the United States and 1.51pp in the euro area. The contribution of the decrease in interest rates to the decline in TFP growth in the euro area is similar to that in the United States, but TFP decelerates more in the euro area, as other factors have contributed more to the decline. Of these factors, the slowdown in the average level of education plays the biggest role: the level of education in the euro area was still in a rapid catching-up process with the United States during the 1984–1995 subperiod; this was no longer the case during the 2005–2017 subperiod, when convergence was almost achieved.

The contribution of TFP growth to real interest rates reaches a maximum in the subperiod 1995–2005 in the United States and in the subperiod 1984–1995 in the euro area. Between these subperiods and the final subperiod 2005–2017, the decline in real interest rates was about 2.08pp in the United States and 3.75pp in the euro area. The decrease in TFP growth explains 0.44pp (21 percent) of this decline in the United States and 0.59pp (16 percent) in the euro area. This small contribution of the decrease in TFP growth to the decline in real interest rates, for both the United States and the euro area, is due to the fact that many other factors have contributed to the dynamics of interest rates. Of these factors, the increase in age dependency plays an important role in the two areas. Because age dependency is expected to continue to increase in the future, interest rates growth could continue to decrease without a positive technology shock.

Without any positive technology or education shocks, the equation system converges toward a low TFP growth/low real interest rate equilibrium, which corresponds to the description of secular stagnation, although the mechanism at play differs partly from that of Hansen in 1939 or more recently Summers (2014) and Summers (2015), which relies mainly on a low-demand environment. Here, a low cleansing intensity leads to the survival of low-productivity firms thanks to low real interest rates. Real interest rates are maintained at a low and even declining level by the projected increase in the age-dependency ratio. Indeed, according to United Nations forecasts, the age-dependency ratio would increase from around 50 percent in 2016 to 62 percent in 2050. According to our estimates, this corresponds to a 0.5pp decline in real interest rates, and twice as much in a country such as Japan where the age-dependency ratio is expected to reach 90 percent in 2050.

An increase in average years of education of the working-age population can be foreseen only for a limited number of countries that still haven't converged to the maximum observed level, or at a very high cost in many advanced countries, such as the United States, where the expansion of tertiary education has been largely achieved (in the United States, the average number of years of schooling was over 13 toward the end of the period). Yet, improvement in the quality of education or on-the-job training could significantly increase the contribution of human capital to TFP.

4.2 Simulations

We now simulate the model (1) using estimates presented in Table 11.1. The dynamics of this model allows us to consider the long-term impact of a shock in any covariate or in the error terms. To see this formally, it is useful at this stage to rewrite the model (1) as a moving average representation. This can be done easily and results in the following equivalent equation system:

$$\begin{cases} g_{i,t} = a g_{i,t-1} + b r_{i,t-1} + C'X_{i,t} + \varepsilon_{i,t} \\ r_{i,t} = \alpha a g_{i,t-1} + (\alpha b + \beta) r_{i,t-1} + (\alpha C'X_{i,t} + \Gamma'Z_{i,t}) + (\alpha \varepsilon_{i,t} + \eta_{i,t}) \end{cases} \quad (2)$$

To simulate a shock in relative investment prices,[13] we use the coefficients as estimated in column 1 of Table 11.1 and consider a negative shock in

---

[13] For more details on the simulation, see Bergeaud, Cette, and Lecat (2019).

relative investment prices of equipment that has the same magnitude and duration as the one corresponding to the "ICT shock" in the United States between 1985 and 2007. We then plot the evolution of the TFP growth rate and of real interest rates over time, measuring the difference between a simulation with this technology shock and a simulation without any shock.

The shock in relative investment prices directly impacts TFP growth rate in the United States and therefore its contemporaneous level of real interest rates, which in turn will impact the TFP growth rate in the next period, and so on. For other countries, the impact of the shock depends on their relative TFP level compared to the United States: countries that are close or above the TFP level of the United States also directly benefit from the shock; other countries are only indirectly affected through the catching-up process. This is the case of the euro area, which, taken as a whole, is too far below the US TFP level at the time of the shock to be directly impacted.[14]

For the United States, most of the resulting effect is essentially homothetic to the shock, as real interest rates are too low to play a significant role at the time of the shock. Consequently, when the technology shock is over and relative investment prices do not change anymore, we expect the effect on TFP growth to quickly vanish. For the euro area, on the contrary, most of the effect stems from the catching-up with the frontier, as differences in TFP levels relative to that of the United States increase after the shock kicks in. We thus expect the effect to last longer (as long as it takes for the euro area to converge toward the US productivity level), but to be lower in magnitude. This is indeed what we see in Figure 11.2a. A similar pattern emerges when looking at the evolution of real interest rates in Figure 11.2b, whose dynamics are dictated by the growth rate of TFP.

The simulated shock is a small shock in terms of amplitude, as it has a limited impact on TFP growth compared to other shocks in the twentieth century. This shock could stem from a second wave linked to ICT, which could be due to the contribution of AI or robots to production processes. Still, this shock would be enough to escape the secular stagnation trap, with TFP growth higher than the very low baseline rate by 0.6pp at peak. This

---

[14] As in Bergeaud, Cette, and Lecat (2017), we aggregate data from eight euro-area countries (Germany, France, Italy, Spain, Netherlands, Belgium, Austria, and Portugal), which we consider as the whole euro area. More specifically, in the years following 2017, we measure TFP growth and real interest rates as the sum of each of the eight countries, weighted by their average population between 2000 and 2015.

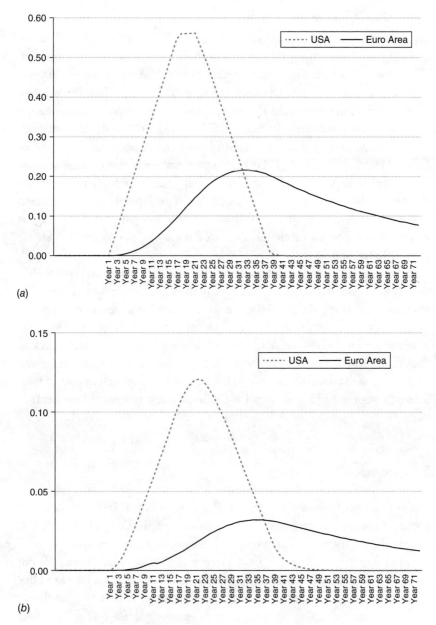

(a)

(b)

Notes: Simulation results in the Euro area and in the United States for a shock in the United States. Response of the growth rate of TFP *g* (a) and of the real interest rate *r* (b).

Figure 11.2a–b. Simulation results

technology shock in the United States would spread to other countries through the catching-up process and lead to a slow but lasting acceleration in TFP, as its level converges with that of the United States. In the euro area, TFP growth relative to the baseline reaches a peak of 0.2pp, about ten years after the peak in the United States (see Figure 11.2a). All other things being equal, the gain in terms of TFP level is, at the end of the process, about 25pp in the two economic areas. In terms of GDP, the gain would be larger, from the capital-deepening channel activated by the investment price decrease (see Cette, Mairesse, and Kocoglu 2005 for a presentation of these different types of channels). As TFP growth and hence real returns are higher than in the baseline, real interest rates increase by 0.12pp in the United States and 0.05pp in the euro area (see Figure 11.2b). This increase in interest rates would trigger a mutually reinforcing mechanism with TFP growth, due to the circular relationship framework.

As shown in Aghion, Bergeaud, Cette, et al. (2019), the relationship between real interest rates and TFP growth is positive in low interest rate environments when the cleansing effect dominates the negative impact of financial constraints on innovation, but negative in high interest rate environments. Hence, this simulation is valid for a limited technology shock at the current low interest rate juncture. If the shock were stronger, its impact on TFP growth would be dampened by the negative feedback impact of high interest rates on TFP. This negative feedback is not estimated here because our estimation period covers mostly a low real interest rate period.

5 Conclusion

The circular relationship between TFP growth and real interest rates contributes to the understanding of the slowdown in productivity since the 1980s. It contributes to the secular stagnation debate, and provides an alternative secular stagnation explanation from Hansen (1939), and more recently from, for instance, Summers (2014, 2015), which are mainly based on demand dynamics. Indeed, a combined low interest rate/low productivity growth environment can be explained by a Schumpeterian channel: a weak cleansing mechanism, whereby low interest rates support the survival of low-profitable firms and investment projects. The decrease in real interest rates since the early 1990s can therefore help to explain the slowdown in productivity over that period.

We provide supporting evidence for this explanation and estimate over a panel of advanced countries of the circular relationship between interest rates and TFP growth, taking into account endogeneity issues and simultaneous estimates of the TFP and interest rate equations. We show that the decrease in real interest rates since the early 1990s, which relies both on an increase in the age-dependency ratio and lower inflation volatility, explains a large part of the slowdown in TFP. Looking forward, simulations show that a new technology shock would be necessary to escape the current secular stagnation situation of low interest rates/low TFP growth, which could be entrenched in the foreseeable future by the negative impact of the increase in the age-dependency ratio on interest rates. A technology shock, even modest in amplitude, would push up TFP growth and, through higher expected returns on investments, real interest rates. In turn, high interest rates would free resources from weakly productive firms and foster TFP growth, leading to mutually reinforcing dynamics between interest rates and productivity.[15]

In the context of the COVID-19 pandemic, financial constraints have dramatically decreased in all advanced countries, both via more expansive monetary policies (lower real interest rate and easier credit access) and via large fiscal support to firms. This could contribute to accentuating the previous productivity slowdown, from lower cleansing of low-productivity firms, which adds to the other potential causes of productivity slowdown (in particular, the falling R&D productivity described in Bloom et al. 2020). At the same time, while this impact on financial constraints may cease with the end of the exceptional pandemic measures, the use of digital technologies by firms has accelerated during the pandemic, which should have a positive impact on productivity growth. The net medium-term impact of these two opposite mechanisms is still unknown. The global economy will face several headwinds in the foreseeable future (see Gordon 2010). In particular, significant productivity growth would be required to finance the energy transition toward a more sustainable growth, to lead to an ordered decrease in the crisis-inherited high debt level, and to face the consequences of an aging population. This technological shock would therefore be necessary to be able to face these headwinds with confidence. The debate on its emergence is still

---

[15] Our mechanism also highlights that without a large technological shock, suitable competition policies aimed at favoring the cleansing mechanism—i.e., the reallocation of workers toward more productive firms—could help circumvent, at least temporarily, the convergence toward a secular stagnation equilibrium when credit constraints are too low.

highly controversial among economists, but as the aftereffects of the crisis on productivity growth vanish, a clearer view of what we can expect in the coming years should be visible.

References

Aghion, Philippe, Ufuk Akcigit, and Peter Howitt (2015). "Lessons from Schumpeterian growth theory." *American Economic Review* 105(5), 94–99.

Aghion, Philippe, George-Marios Angeletos, et al. (2010). "Volatility and growth: Credit constraints and the composition of investment." *Journal of Monetary Economics* 57(3), 246–265.

Aghion, Philippe, Philippe Askenazy, et al. (2012). "Credit constraints and the cyclicality of R&D investment: Evidence from France." *Journal of the European Economic Association* 10(5), 1001–1024.

Aghion, Philippe, Philippe Bacchetta, et al. (2009). "Exchange rate volatility and productivity growth: The role of financial development." *Journal of Monetary Economics* 56(4), 494–513.

Aghion, Philippe, Antonin Bergeaud, Gilbert Cette, et al. (2019). "Coase Lecture—The Inverted-U relationship between credit access and productivity growth." *Economica* 86(341), 1–31.

Aghion, Philippe, et al. (2019a). "A theory of falling growth and rising rents." Federal Reserve Bank of San Francisco Working Paper 2019-11.

——— (2019b). "Missing growth from creative destruction." *American Economic Review* 109(8), 2795–2822.

Akcigit, Ufuk, and Sina T. Ates (2019). "What happened to US business dynamism?" NBER Working Paper 25756.

Ang, James B., and Jakob B. Madsen (2016). "Finance-led growth in the OECD since the nineteenth century: How does financial development transmit to growth?" *Review of Economics and Statistics* 98(3), 552–572.

Basso, Henrique S., and Juan F. Jimeno (2018). "From secular stagnation to robocalypse? Implications of demographic and technological changes." ECB/CEPR Labour Market Workshop.

Bean, Charles (2016). "Living with low for long." *Economic Journal* 126(592), 507–522.

Bergeaud, Antonin, Gilbert Cette, and Rémy Lecat (2016). "Productivity trends in advanced countries between 1890 and 2012." *Review of Income and Wealth* 62(3), 420–444.

——— (2017). "Total factor productivity in advanced countries: A long-term perspective." *International Productivity Monitor* 32, 6–24.

——— (2018). "The role of production factor quality and technology diffusion in twentieth-century productivity growth." *Cliometrica, Journal of Historical Economics and Econometric History* 12(1), 61–97.

—— (2019). "The circular relationship between productivity growth and real interest rates." Working Paper wp734. Banque de France.

Bergeaud, Antonin, and Simon Ray (2021). "Adjustment costs and factor demand: New evidence from firms' real estate." *Economic Journal* 131(633), 70–100.

Bloom, Nicholas, et al. (2020). "Are ideas getting harder to find?" *American Economic Review* 110(4), 1104–1144.

Branstetter, Lee, and Daniel Sichel (2017). "The case for an American productivity revival." Peterson Institute for International Economics Policy Briefs 17-26.

Brynjolfsson, Erik, Daniel Rock, and Chad Syverson (2017). "Artificial intelligence and the modern productivity paradox: A clash of expectations and statistics." NBER Working Paper 24001.

—— (2018). "The productivity J-curve: How intangibles complement general purpose technologies." NBER Working Paper 25148.

Byrne, David M., Stephen D. Oliner, and Daniel E. Sichel (2013). "Is the information technology revolution over?" *International Productivity Monitor* 25, 20–36.

Carluccio, Juan, Clément Mazet-Sonilhac, and Jean-Stéphane Mésonnier (2018). "Investment and the WACC: New micro evidence for France." Working Paper 710. Banque de France.

Cette, Gilbert (2014). "Presidential Conference: Does ICT remain a powerful engine of growth?" *Revue d'économie politique* 124(4), 473–492.

Cette, Gilbert, John Fernald, and Benoit Mojon (2016). "The pre-Great Recession slowdown in productivity." *European Economic Review* 88, 3–20.

Cette, Gilbert, Jacques Mairesse, and Yusuf Kocoglu (2005). "ICT diffusion and potential output growth." *Economics Letters* 87(2), 231–234.

Chatterjee, Satyajit, and Burcu Eyigungor (2020). "The firm size and leverage relationship and its implications for entry and concentration in a low interest rate world." Federal Reserve Bank of Philadelphia Working Paper 20–29.

Cooper, Russell W., and John C. Haltiwanger (2006). "On the nature of capital adjustment costs." *Review of Economic Studies* 73(3), 611–633.

Duval, Romain, Gee Hee Hong, and Yannick Timmer (2017). "Financial frictions and the great productivity slowdown." IMF Working Paper 17/129.

Eggertsson, Gauti B., et al. (2016). "A contagious malady? Open economy dimensions of secular stagnation." *IMF Economic Review* 64(4), 581–634.

Fernald, John G., et al. (2017). "The disappointing recovery of output after 2009." NBER Working Paper 23543.

Gavazza, Alessandro (2011). "The role of trading frictions in real asset markets." *American Economic Review* 101(4), 1106–1143.

Gopinath, Gita, et al. (2017). "Capital allocation and productivity in South Europe." *Quarterly Journal of Economics* 132(4), 1915–1967.

Gordon, Robert J. (2010). "Revisiting U.S. productivity growth over the past century with a view of the future." NBER Working Paper 15834.

Gorton, Gary, and Guillermo Ordonez (2016). "Good booms, bad booms." NBER Working Paper 22008.

Hansen, Alvin (1939). "Economic progress and declining population growth." *American Economic Review* 29(1), 1–39.

Jordà, Òscar, Moritz Schularick, and Alan M. Taylor (2017). "Macrofinancial history and the new business cycle facts." *NBER Macroeconomics Annual* 31(1), 213–263.

Jorgenson, Dale W. (2001). "Information technology and the US economy." *American Economic Review* 91(1), 1–32.

Jorgenson, Dale W., Mun S. Ho, and Kevin J. Stiroh (2008). "A retrospective look at the US productivity growth resurgence." *Journal of Economic Perspectives* 22(1), 3–24.

King, R. G. and Levine, R. (1993) "Finance and growth: Schumpeter might be right." *Quarterly Journal of Economics* 108, 717–737.

Kleibergen, Frank, and Richard Paap (2006). "Generalized reduced rank tests using the singular value decomposition." *Journal of Econometrics* 133(1), 97–126.

Klette, Tor Jakob, and Samuel Kortum (2004). "Innovating firms and aggregate innovation." *Journal of Political Economy* 112(5), 986–1018.

Levine, Ross (1997). "Financial development and economic growth: Views and agenda." *Journal of Economic Literature* 35(2), 688–726.

Levy-Garboua, Vivien, and Eric Monnet (2016). "Les taux d'intérêt en France: Une perspective historique." *Revue d'économie financière* 1, 35–58.

Linarello, Andrea, Andrea Petrella, and Enrico Sette (2019). "Allocative efficiency and finance." Questioni di Economia e Finanza (Occasional Papers) 487. Bank of Italy, Economic Research and International Relations Area.

Liu, Ernest, Atif Mian, and Amir Sufi (2019). "Low interest rates, market power, and productivity growth." NBER Working Paper 25505.

Manaresi, Francesco, and Nicola Pierri (2017). "Credit constraints and firm productivity: Evidence from Italy." Mo.Fi.R. Working Papers 137. Money, Finance Research group (Mo.Fi.R.)—Univ. Politecnica Marche—Dept. Economic, and Social Sciences. https://ideas.repec.org/p/anc/wmofir/137.html.

Marx, Magali, Benoit Mojon, and Francois R. Velde (2017). "Why have interest rates fallen far below the return on capital?" Working Paper 630. Banque de France.

Mazet-Sonilhac, Clément, and Jean-Stéphane Mésonnier (2016). "The cost of equity for large non-financial companies in the euro area: An estimation over the last decade." *Quarterly Selection of Articles—Bulletin de la Banque de France* 44, 28–39.

Psacharopoulos, George, and Harry Anthony Patrinos (2004). "Returns to investment in education: a further update." *Education Economics* 12(2), 111–134.

Rajan, Raghuram G., and Luigi Zingales (1998). "Financial dependence and growth." *American Economic Review* 88(3), 559–586.

Reis, Ricardo (2013). "The Portuguese slump and crash and the euro crisis." *Brookings Papers on Economic Activity* 44(1) (Spring), 143–210.

Ruiz-Garcia, Juan Carlos (2019). "Financial frictions, firm dynamics and the aggregate economy: Insights from richer productivity processes." Cambridge Working Papers in Economics 2157, Faculty of Economics, University of Cambridge.

Summers, Lawrence H. (2014). "US economic prospects: Secular stagnation, hysteresis, and the zero lower bound." *Business Economics* 49(2), 65–73.

——— (2015). "Demand side secular stagnation." *American Economic Review: Papers and Proceedings* 105(5), 60–65.

Syverson, Chad (2017). "Challenges to mismeasurement explanations for the US productivity slowdown." *Journal of Economic Perspectives* 31(2), 165–186.

Teulings, Coen, and Richard Baldwin (2014). *Secular stagnation: Facts, causes, and cures–A new Vox eBook.* Vol. 15. Voxeu.

Timmer, Marcel P., et al. (2011). "Productivity and economic growth in Europe: A comparative industry perspective." *International Productivity Monitor* 21, 3.

Van Ark, Bart (2016). "The productivity paradox of the new digital economy." *International Productivity Monitor* 31, 3.

Van Ark, Bart, Mary O'Mahoney, and Marcel P. Timmer (2008). "The productivity gap between Europe and the United States: Trends and causes." *Journal of Economic Perspectives* 22(1), 25–44.

Zellner, Arnold (1962). "An efficient method of estimating seemingly unrelated regressions and tests for aggregation bias." *Journal of the American Statistical Association* 57(298), 348–368.

CHAPTER 12

The Depth and Breadth of the Step-by-Step Innovation Framework

SINA T. ATES

1 Introduction

Looking back at the past thirty years, one can comfortably conclude that Aghion and Howitt (1992), with the tremendous body of work that followed, was a "big bang" in the literature of economic growth. The way the theory operationalized the Schumpeterian paradigm and the process of creative destruction did not just reshape how economists think about economic growth but also contributed to the analysis of a vast range of topics, from intellectual property rights policies to international trade to environmental issues. One such fundamental topic is the relationship between competition between firms and economic growth, and the authors contributed to it with another groundbreaking framework that extends the Schumpeterian paradigm in substantial ways: the step-by-step innovation model. In this chapter I will discuss the significance of this—arguably underutilized—framework, along with some recent applications.

Notwithstanding its numerous merits, the first-generation model of Schumpeterian creative destruction laid out in Aghion and Howitt (1992) did not truly capture the essence of competition between firms. While innovations are still competitive in that framework—the entrepreneur with an invention replaces the incumbent—it is not the case that firms respond to each other's actions in a forward-looking fashion.[1] Only the outsiders (potential entrants) innovate in equilibrium, whereas incumbents did not, reflecting Arrow's replacement effect. Moreover, the first-generation models predicted only a negative relationship between competition and economic growth predicated on the appropriability effect. Yet, subsequent empirical evidence pointed in the other direction, showing that competition can, in fact, boost economic growth and innovation in various environments.

Faced with these challenges, Philippe Aghion, Peter Howitt, and coauthors strove to build a more flexible framework that can speak to the nature of competition between firms and matches the relevant empirical evidence better. Crucially, they relaxed the assumption of a linear R&D production function and introduced decreasing returns to R&D at the firm level.[2] This small but fundamental change implies that incumbent firms find it optimal to invest in R&D. As introduced and analyzed extensively in a series of pathbreaking papers (Aghion et al. 1997, 2001, 2005), this new feature altered the dynamics of the model greatly while still retaining the core of the Schumpeterian creative destruction.[3]

To begin, the key agents in an industry are two forward-looking incumbent firms in a constant competitive race, as opposed to outside entrepreneurs

---

[1] Still, the concept of competitive innovations and Schumpeterian creative destruction distinguishes these first-generation models from contemporary work on endogenous growth theory. For instance, another milestone in this literature, Romer (1990), conceptualizes the endogenous nature of economic growth through the expansion of varieties in an economy enabled by the creation of nonrivalrous ideas. In this setting, each variety is produced by a monopolist that owns the blueprint for production of that specific variety, and once the monopolist gets that blueprint, it does not face any competitive pressure from other firms, be it potential entrants with newer blueprints or other incumbents.

[2] The assumption of a linear R&D production function in the earlier vintages of the Schumpeterian creative destruction models is the key reason incumbent firms refrain from engaging in R&D.

[3] Innovation by incumbent firms is an equilibrium outcome also in another pathbreaking contribution to the literature on firm dynamics, Klette and Kortum (2004), which itself builds on Aghion and Howitt (1992). Yet the nature of incumbent innovation in this setting is horizontal, akin to the expanding-varieties models. Randomly landing on the product of another firm, incumbent innovations are still competitive and generate creative destruction, in a fashion similar to the entrant innovations in Aghion and Howitt (1992). However, this undirected nature of innovations prevents firms from competing against rivals in their respective sectors. In this respect, the Klette and Kortum (2004) framework, like the Aghion and Howitt (1992) model, does not capture the strategic interaction between rival incumbent firms, and therefore is not a model of firm competition per se.

in the benchmark model. As such, the model captures the strategic interaction between a market leader and its competitors succinctly and explicitly. In this regard, the model has the essence of earlier R&D-race frameworks in the industrial organization literature (Harris and Vickers 1985, 1987; Grossman and Shapiro 1987; Budd et al. 1993) and embeds it into a dynamic macro general equilibrium setting. Second, the benefit of innovation is the incremental gain in profits as opposed to the absolute level in the benchmark model, and the size of the increment depends on the relative position of the rivals in the competitive race. Consequently, variables such as markups and market concentration become endogenous outcomes of the model, making the framework very suitable for the analysis of widely debated economic issues such as market competition and business dynamism. In addition, the model generates a nonlinear relationship between competition and economic growth. Again, as in Harris and Vickers (1987) and Budd et al. (1993), firms intensify their R&D efforts when the technological gap between them decreases in the model; i.e., when competition strengthens—as the incremental gain of innovating, helping firms escape competition, increases. This channel, dubbed the "escape-competition" effect (Aghion et al. 2001), introduces an additional force through which competition can foster economic growth and, thus, provides greater flexibility to the model when confronted with micro-level evidence (Aghion et al. 2005). Without doubt, these novel features of the step-by-step innovation framework opened up various new avenues in the analysis of market competition, firm dynamics, and economic growth.

In this chapter, I review two recent applications of the step-by-step innovation framework. First, I discuss how this model sheds light on the heated debate over increased market concentration and slowing business dynamism, which have been ailing the US economy in the past several decades (Akcigit and Ates 2021, 2023). Following Akcigit and Ates (2021), this section presents a basic setup, which also helps highlight the key mechanisms of the step-by-step innovation framework. Importantly, the analysis focuses on a specific channel—namely, the *knowledge diffusion*—and shows that a decline in this margin is able to go a long way in replicating some prominent trends in the data. The key mechanism underlying these results is the combination of endogenous responses of firms to a decline in *knowledge diffusion* (incentive effect) and the ensuing shift in the sectoral composition of the economy (composition effect). I also discuss how an extended version of the model à la Akcigit and Ates (2023) can capture other significant aspects of slowing business dynamism.

Next, I discuss how a rare application of this framework in an open-economy setting contributes to our understanding of industrial policy and its growth and welfare implications in the face of international technological competition. In this setting, market competition gains an international aspect, and firms' innovation incentives peak when faced with foreign competitors having similar technological capacities; i.e., when foreign competition stiffens. Ergo, the growth and welfare effects of industrial or trade policies crucially depend on how these policies alter the strength of foreign competition that domestic firms face, and, consequently, on the dynamic gains from trade they create. I recount some prominent policy implications that follow from this mechanism in light of the analysis by Akcigit et al. (2018).

Other applications of the step-by-step innovation framework include, first and foremost, the groundbreaking work by Aghion et al. (2005) documenting an inverted-U relationship between competition and innovation using data on British industries. The step-by-step innovation theory helps rationalize this inverted-U relationship with the two opposing forces it admits through which competition can affect firms' incentive to innovate: the negative Schumpeterian effect versus the positive escape-competition effect. The former is the dominating force when the initial level of competition is weak—i.e., an increase in competition induces firms to innovate more—whereas the latter effect dominates when competition is fierce to begin with.[4] Acemoglu and Akcigit (2012) employ this framework to examine the interaction between intellectual property rights (IPR) policies and competition. In particular, they focus on state-dependent policies and find that the optimal policy favors incumbents with a large lead over their rivals, providing them with greater IPR protection. The reason is that this asymmetric policy creates a trickle-down effect, increasing the incremental gain from innovating for leaders with smaller technology advantage over their rivals, thereby boosting their innovation efforts. More recent examples include Akcigit et al. (2018) and Akcigit and Ates (2021, 2023), which I review in this

---

[4] This result follows from a composition effect that the initial level of competition exerts on the distribution of sectors across technology gaps. For instance, if the product market competition is initially low, even when firms have similar technologies—e.g., if firms can collude to share the rents—then the incentive for firms to innovate and escape competition is also low, implying that the share of sectors with neck-and-neck firms is high to begin with. In this case, an increase in competition pushes up overall innovation as the escape-competition effect kicks in more forcefully in those neck-and-neck sectors.

chapter. Liu et al. (2019) use the step-by-step framework to explore the effect of falling interest rates on competition, whereas Chikis et al. (2021) investigate the robustness of this relationship in an extended version of the model. Another recent example that focuses on the recent dynamics in market concentration and competition is Olmstead-Rumsey (2020). In contemporaneous work on this topic, Cavenaile et al. (2019) generalize the step-by-step innovation framework to Cournot equilibrium at the product level, allowing for oligopolistic competition between rival firms. Cavenaile et al. (2021a) and Cavenaile et al. (2021b) apply similar frameworks to analyze the growth and welfare effects of advertisement activity and mergers and acquisitions, respectively.

The rest of the chapter is structured as follows. Section 2 discusses some lessons from the step-by-step innovation theory on slowing business dynamism. Section 3 explores the framework in an open-economy setting. Section 4 concludes.

2 A Basic Model to Study Slowing Business Dynamism

An extensive set of empirical regularities suggests that business dynamism and market competition have been slowing in the United States since the early 1980s.[5] By design, the step-by-step innovation framework provides an excellent ground to investigate these changes as it speaks to the essence of competition between firms and the resulting firm dynamics. In this section I discuss how a basic setup based on step-by-step innovation can help rationalize several prominent symptoms of slowing business dynamism.[6]

A few crucial features of the model are worth emphasizing: (i) Firms make strategic investment decisions that are key to understanding declining business dynamism, (ii) productivity-enhancing innovation decisions are endogenous, (iii) thus, markups are endogenous, depending on the technology gap between competitors, and (iv) a reduced-form parameter governs the pro-

---

[5] This slowdown is a crucial shift, because a healthy degree of business dynamism in an economy—the perpetual process of entry, growth, downsizing, and exiting of firms—ensures the reallocation of factors toward more-productive units, which is, in turn, the key source of aggregate productivity and thus long-run economic growth (Foster et al. 2000).

[6] This analysis follows the steps of Akcigit and Ates (2021).

cess of *knowledge diffusion*. This last feature reflects the exogenous flow of knowledge from the frontier firms to the followers, which allows the follower to close the productivity gap with the leader, bringing them to a neck-and-neck position. The rate of this knowledge diffusion will be crucial in my analysis; in particular, I show that a weakening in this margin can generate some of the observed changes in the economy.

2.1 Fundamentals

The model economy is in continuous time. Final-good firms produce the final output Y_t in a perfectly competitive market according to the following production technology:

$$\ln Y_t = \int_0^1 \ln y_{jt} \, dj, \tag{1}$$

where y_{jt} denotes the amount of intermediate variety $j \in [0, 1]$ used at time t. The final good provides the resources for consumption and R&D investment.

Turning to the intermediate-good production, in each product line j, there are two incumbent firms $i \in \{1, 2\}$ that can produce a perfectly substitutable variety of good j. Total output of variety j is given by

$$y_{jt} = y_{ijt} + y_{-ijt},$$

where $-i$ denotes the competitor of firm i, such that $-i \in \{1, 2\}$ and $-i \neq i$. Each firm produces using labor l_{ijt} according to the following linear production technology:

$$y_{ijt} = q_{ijt} l_{ijt}.$$

Here, q_{ijt} denotes the labor productivity of firm i. These firms compete for market leadership à la Bertrand. Higher labor productivity gives a firm a cost advantage over its rival, allowing it to supply good j to the entire market. Accordingly, firm i is the market leader and $-i$ is the follower in j if $q^{ijt} > q_{-ijy}$. The two firms are neck-and-neck if $q_{ijt} = q_{-ijt}$.

Firms invest in innovative activity to improve their productivity. An innovation increases the innovating firm's productivity level proportionally by a factor $\lambda > 1$ such that $q_{ij(t+\Delta t)} = \lambda q_{ijt}$. We set the initial value $q_{ij0} = 1$. Then, the productivity levels at time t becomes $q_{ijt} = \lambda^{n_{ijt}}$, where n_{ijt} captures the number of productivity improvements that firm i generated since time 0. Thus, the productivity difference between two firms reflects the difference between the total number of rungs these firms' production technologies build on. The productivity level of a firm relative to its rival is given by

$$\frac{q_{ijt}}{q_{-ijt}} = \frac{\lambda^{n_{ijt}}}{\lambda^{n_{-ijt}}} = \lambda^{n_{ijt} - n_{-ijt}} \equiv \lambda^{m_{ijt}},$$

where $m_{ijt} \in \{-1, 0, 1\}$ defines the technology gap between the firm i and $-i$ in sector j. For simplicity, we set the maximum size of this difference to one; therefore, the economy admits two types of product lines: leveled and unleveled. The technology gap between firms in a product line is a sufficient statistic to describe firm-specific payoffs. Hence, we will drop industry subscript j and use the notation $m_{it} \in \{-1, 0, 1\}$ whenever m is specified to denote a firm-specific value. Likewise, we will use $m_{jt} \in \{0, 1\}$ to index sectors that are leveled or unleveled.

Firms choose the arrival rate of an innovation x_{ijt}. We take the associated cost of generating x_{ijt} to be of quadratic shape such that

$$R_{ijt} = \alpha \frac{x_{ijt}^2}{2} Y_t,$$

with R_{ijt} denoting the R&D spending. The scale parameter is given by α, and we assume that the cost scales with aggregate output.

An additional feature of the model is that knowledge diffuses from the leader to the follower at an exogenous Poisson flow rate δ. Knowledge diffusion enables the follower to catch up with the leader's productivity level, bringing both firms to a neck-and-neck position. In this sense, δ is a reduced-form representation of spillovers from the leaders to the followers: It captures the mechanisms through which technologically laggard firms learn from products and processes at the technology frontier (Bloom et al. 2013).[7] Notice that this margin is different from the endogenous R&D decisions of firms in that it occurs exogenously and is independent of firms' R&D investments.[8]

---

[7] An alternative interpretation is that this margin captures *intellectual property rights (IPR) protection* (see Acemoglu and Akcigit 2012). A leader's patent expires with the flow rate δ, allowing the follower to replicate the frontier technology and catch up with the leader. Then, a lower value of δ implies higher protection and lower catch-up.

[8] This margin also helps the economy maintain a competitive environment at the industry level, preventing firms from falling too far behind the technology frontier. This effect is more evident in a richer setting where the technology gap between firms can grow beyond one step (see Akcigit and Ates 2019).

Closing the model, a unit measure of representative households consume the final good admitting log-utility preferences and supply a unit of labor inelastically at the competitive wage rate w_t. They also own the firms in the economy and earn interest on their assets at rate r_t.

2.2 Balanced growth path

In the remainder of our theoretical analysis, we focus on a balanced growth path equilibrium. The equilibrium is Markov perfect, with strategies depending only on the payoff-relevant state variable $m \in \{-1, 0, 1\}$, and on the balanced growth path (BGP), all aggregate variables grow at the same rate g. In this section, we will list the objects that are most relevant to our analysis and defer the full set of equilibrium relationships to Appendix A. Henceforth, we will drop the indices i, j, and t except where doing so might cause confusion.

The optimization of the representative final-good producer results in a unit-elastic demand for good $j \in [0, 1]$:

$$y_{ij} p_{ij} = Y, \tag{2}$$

where p_{ij} is the price of intermediate j charged by the producing monopolist i. Under the linearity of the production function, an intermediate producer's marginal cost is

$$MC_{ij} = \frac{w}{q_{ij}}. \tag{3}$$

The marginal cost of production increases in the unit labor cost w and decreases in labor productivity q_{ij}. Faced with a unit-elastic demand from the final-good producer and engaging in price competition with its rival, the intermediate producer follows a limit pricing rule in equilibrium. More precisely, it sets its price to the marginal cost of the competitor:

$$p_{ij} = \frac{w}{q_{-ij}}. \tag{4}$$

Consequently, the equilibrium quantity of intermediate good j is simply

$$y_{ij} = \frac{q_{-ij}}{\omega} \text{ for } q_{ij} \geq q_{-ij} \tag{5}$$

and $y_{ij} = 0$ otherwise.[9] Here, ω is the normalized wage rate in the economy as defined as $\omega \equiv \dfrac{w}{Y}$. It also measures the aggregate labor share of output.

The operating profits of an intermediate firm exclusive of its R&D expenditures is

$$\pi(m_i) = \begin{cases} \left(1 - \dfrac{1}{\lambda}\right)Y & \text{if} \quad m_i = 1 \\ 0 & \text{if} \quad m_i \in \{0, -1\} \end{cases}.$$

Similarly, the markups in leveled ($m_j = 0$) and unleveled ($m_j = 1$) sectors are given as

$$Markup_j = \dfrac{p_{ij}}{MC_{ij}} - 1 = \begin{cases} \lambda - 1 & \text{if} \quad m_j = 1 \\ 0 & \text{if} \quad m_j = 0 \end{cases}.$$

Notice that only leaders can charge a positive level of markup and earn profits. Therefore, aggregate levels of profits and markups are determined by the distribution of intermediate lines across leveled and unleveled ones, whose evolution depends crucially on endogenous innovation decisions of firms. As such, these objects become endogenous to firms' strategic decisions taking each other's responses into account, and therefore, this setting provides a convenient starting point to analyze their dynamics.

We now define two more endogenous objects that prove useful in characterizing key aggregate variables in equilibrium. First, the aggregate productivity index of the economy is given by

$$Q \equiv \exp\left(\int_0^1 \ln q_j \, dj\right).$$

Next, the share of unleveled industries, which also acts as a proxy for the level of *market concentration*, is denoted by

$$\mu \equiv \int_0^1 I(q_{ij} \neq q_{-ij}) \, dj.$$

The aggregate wage rate follows from the final good production function (1) and the equilibrium intermediate goods (5):

$$w = \dfrac{Q}{\lambda^\mu}. \tag{6}$$

---

[9] We assume that production in an industry is randomly distributed when firms are neck-and-neck.

Then, the labor market clearing condition, $\int_0^1 l_{jt}\, dj = 1,$ implies the following labor share ω:

$$\omega = 1 - \mu \frac{(\lambda - 1)}{\lambda}. \tag{7}$$

The labor share decreases in the level of market concentration μ and the markup parameter λ. Therefore, the market concentration and the labor share are negatively correlated (Autor et al. 2017b).

Finally, equations (6) and (7) yield the level of final output as

$$Y = \frac{Q}{\lambda^\mu \left[1 - \mu \frac{(\lambda - 1)}{\lambda}\right]}. \tag{8}$$

Notice that, along the BGP, final output scales with the aggregate productivity. Consequently, the long-run growth rate of aggregate productivity also determines the growth rate of output and consumption. Moreover, equation (8) implies that the distribution of markups leads to static efficiency losses. In fact, at the minimum ($\mu = 0$) or maximum ($\mu = 1$) level of concentration we have $Y = Q$. However, additional efficiency losses arise in the economy when markups are unevenly distributed across the sectors.

Firm values and innovation. We denote the stock market value of a firm that is in state $m_i \in \{-1, 0, 1\}$ by V_{m_i} and define $v_{m_i} \equiv V_{m_i}/Y$. Then, the normalized value function of an incumbent firm that is one step ahead, i.e., $m_i = 1$, is given by

$$\rho v_1 = \max_{x_1} \left\{ \left(1 - \frac{1}{\lambda}\right) - \frac{x_1^2}{2} + x_1[v_1 - v_1] + (x_{-1} + \delta)[v_0 - v_1] \right\},$$

where x_{m_i} for $m_i \in \{-1, 0, 1\}$ denotes the innovation rate of a follower, neck-and-neck firm, and a leader, respectively. The first two terms on the right-hand side define the profits net of R&D expenditures. The third term captures the result of a successful innovation by the leader. When the one-step-ahead leader innovates, the gap difference does not increase, because an upper limit is imposed on the potential size of gaps. Therefore, the one-step-ahead leader will optimally avoid investing in R&D; i.e., $x_1 = 0$ holds in equilibrium. The fourth term reflects the result of an innovation by the follower or the exogenous knowledge diffusion happening at rate δ. In these cases, the leader loses its productivity advantage and becomes neck-and-neck with the competitor.

Reciprocally, the value of function of a follower is defined as

$$\rho v_{-1} = \max_{x_{-1}} \left\{ -\frac{x_{-1}^2}{2} + (x_{-1} + \delta)[v_0 - v_{-1}] \right\}. \tag{9}$$

The follower does not produce and, therefore, does not earn any profits. Yet, the forward-looking firm invests in R&D with the prospect of taking over the leader through successive (step-by-step) innovations. The catch-up can also happen at the exogenous flow rate δ. Finally, the value of a neck-and-neck incumbent is given by

$$\rho v_0 = \max_{x_0} \left\{ -\frac{x_0^2}{2} + x_0[v_1 - v_0] + x_0[v_{-1} - v_0] \right\}.$$

A successful innovation of the neck-and-neck firm makes it a leader, whereas an innovation by the competitor makes it a follower.

The first-order conditions of the problems above yield the following optimal innovation decisions:

$$\begin{aligned} x_1 &= 0 \\ x_0 &= v_1 - v_0 \\ x_{-1} &= v_0 - v_{-1}. \end{aligned} \tag{10}$$

With these values, the BGP value of μ, the share of unleveled sectors, becomes

$$\mu = \frac{2x_0}{2x_0 + x_{-1} + \delta}. \tag{11}$$

Finally, the equilibrium growth rate of this economy is given by

$$g = 2x_0(1 - \mu) \ln \lambda. \tag{12}$$

The growth rate of the economy is determined by innovations of neck-and-neck firms.[10] Interestingly, innovations by followers in unleveled sectors do not contribute to the BGP growth, because their innovations do not push the technology frontier forward; rather, they only help the followers catch up with the frontier. Therefore, increased market concentration (μ)—i.e., a

---

[10] Notice that this result is an artifact of the assumption that the maximum gap between firms is one. In a richer setting where m can take other positive values, leader firms—except for the leader at the largest gap—would also have incentives to innovate and contribute to the aggregate growth of the economy. For an example of such setting, see Akcigit and Ates (2019).

higher share of unleveled sectors in the economy—has a negative impact on economic growth (g).[11]

2.3 Impact of knowledge diffusion, δ

In this section, I discuss some theoretical predictions of the framework introduced above, with a particular focus on the effect of a decline in the intensity of knowledge diffusion on firms' innovation rates and its distributional consequences. The following lemma forms the basis of the main results.

Lemma 1 *The following results hold in the BGP.*

1. *Neck-and-neck firms have higher innovation intensity than laggard firms.*
2. *An increase in knowledge diffusion decreases innovation efforts. The decline is even more drastic for the neck-and-neck firms.*

Proof. *See Akcigit and Ates (2021)*

The first point of Lemma 1 is the well-known escape-competition effect in step-by-step innovation models—namely, the intensification of innovation effort by neck-and-neck firms to get ahead of their competitor and avoid competition. The second result arises because the value of being a leader increases disproportionately as the exogenous risk of losing the position declines. These results lead to the following corollary.

Corollary 1 *In the BGP, a decrease in knowledge diffusion increases the share of unleveled sectors.*

Proof. *See Akcigit and Ates (2021)*

Corollary 1 contrasts two BGP equilibria with different knowledge diffusion rates. As the diffusion intensity decreases, the rate of innovation by neck-and-neck firms rises in response more than that by followers, leading

---

[11] This result does not hinge on the fact that the leader does not innovate. Consider a more general setting with multi-step technology gaps, in which leaders have an incentive to innovate to improve their lead. This incentive weakens as the technological lead widens because the larger lead implies less competitive pressure on the leader. Thus, everything else equal, the overall innovation effort (and aggregate growth) in the economy decreases when average market concentration increases.

to a subsequent increase in the measure of unleveled sectors. This compositional shift is key to the results discussed next.

2.4 Reduction in knowledge diffusion and business dynamism

Next, I discuss the predictions of the model regarding some symptoms that characterize the slowing business dynamism in the US economy.

Prediction 1 *Market concentration rises in response to lower knowledge diffusion.*

Market concentration has been on the rise in the US economy, as documented by Autor et al. (2017a,b) and Grullon et al. (2017). The model generates a similar prediction in response to lower knowledge diffusion. Notice that in the model, markups and profits vanish in leveled industries because of limit pricing, reflecting the intense competition when firms are neck-and-neck. Moreover, sales are equalized. As a result, the aggregate Herfindahl-Hirschman index (HHI) reads as

$$HHI = \mu \times [(100\%)^2 + (0\%)^2] + (1 - \mu) \times [(50\%)^2 + (50\%)^2]$$
$$= 0.5 + 0.5\mu.$$

The HHI, the key measure of market concentration, increases in the measure of unleveled industries (μ), whose BGP value is given by equation (11) and decreases with knowledge diffusion (Corollary 1). Two channels drive this result. First, a lower δ means a smaller frequency at which followers learn from the leaders. Hence, the distribution is pushed toward unleveled sectors. Second, reduced knowledge diffusion increases the return to being the market leader, which incentivizes neck-and-neck firms to innovate relatively more, as they are much closer to capturing the market than a follower. This relatively stronger increase in innovation by neck-and-neck firms also expands the share of unleveled industries. Hence, the market concentration increases with lower knowledge diffusion, i.e.,

$$\frac{d(HHI)}{d\delta} < 0.$$

Prediction 2 *Markups rise in response to lower knowledge diffusion.*

Lower knowledge diffusion helps the model replicate the multi-decade rise in markups, a salient trend in the US economy as documented by a set of recent papers (see, among others, Nekarda and Ramey 2013; De Loecker et al. 2017; Gutiérrez and Philippon 2017; Eggertsson et al. 2018; Hall 2018). In the model, only leaders in unleveled sectors can set positive markups. Therefore, the average markup in this economy is

$$Average\_markup = \mu \times (\lambda - 1) + (1 - \mu) \times 0$$
$$= \mu \times (\lambda - 1).$$

The average markup is proportional to μ, and given Corollary 1, it increases when knowledge diffusion decreases, i.e.,

$$\frac{d(Average\_markup)}{d\delta} < 0.$$

Prediction 3 *Profits rise in response to lower knowledge diffusion.*

Like markups, the profit share in the US economy has been increasing as well. The model generates a consistent prediction, with operating profits as a share of GDP rising in response to lower diffusion. The aggregate profit share is simply

$$Profit / GDP = \mu \times \left(1 - \frac{1}{\lambda}\right). \tag{13}$$

As in the preceding analysis, a reduction in knowledge diffusion pushes up also this ratio:

$$\frac{d(Profit / GDP)}{d\delta} < 0.$$

Prediction 4 *The labor share of output declines in response to lower knowledge diffusion.*

Another prediction of the model consistent with recent trends in the US economy is the decline in the labor share of output (for the empirical evidence, see Karabarbounis and Neiman 2013; Elsby et al. 2013; Lawrence 2015). The labor share in the above economy is

$$Labor\_share = (1 - \mu) \times 1 + \mu \times \frac{1}{\lambda}$$
$$= 1 - \mu \times \left(1 - \frac{1}{\lambda}\right). \tag{14}$$

Notice that the labor share and markups (also, profits) go in opposite directions. Labor is the only input for intermediate production, and when business owners generate some additional windfall as a fraction of the output, it comes at the expense of reduced labor compensation. Consequently, the labor share decreases with lower diffusion rate:

$$\frac{d(Labor\_share\,)}{d\delta} > 0.$$

Prediction 5 *The productivity gap between leaders and followers widens with lower knowledge diffusion.*

Consistent with the evidence in Andrews et al. (2015, 2016), the model generates a widening productivity gap between leaders and followers as knowledge diffusion weakens. The productivity of the market leader relative to the follower is 1 in leveled industries and λ in unleveled industries. Therefore, the average relative productivity can be expressed as

$$Average\_productivity\_gap = \mu \times \lambda + (1 - \mu)$$
$$= 1 + \mu \times (\lambda - 1).$$

Together with Corollary 1, this expression implies that the average productivity gap between the leaders and followers widens when knowledge diffusion slows. Therefore,

$$\frac{d(Average\_productivity\_gap)}{d\delta} < 0.$$

2.5 Discussion of further implications

Akcigit and Ates (2021) review a number of additional characteristics of slowing business dynamism and declining competition in the United States, and the model could well speak to those aspects, too. First, some recent work documents a negative relationship between market concentration and the labor share in an industry (Autor et al. 2017b; Barkai 2017; Eggertsson et al. 2018). Similarly, the labor share is the largest in level industries in the model—i.e., when concentration is the lowest—as neck-and-neck firms do not generate profits. When a level industry becomes unleveled, market concentration rises and the labor share decreases—the leader retains part of its revenue in profits. As such, the model generates the empirical negative association between market concentration and the labor share.

A well-documented observation associated with slowing business dynamism in the United States is the decline in firm entry rate and the share of young firms in economic activity (Decker et al. 2016; Karahan et al. 2016; Gourio et al. 2014). The simple model is silent on these closely tied observations, but we can already develop some intuition on the implications of free entry in this framework. Suppose that we introduce firm entry to the model, with entrants replacing either followers ($m_i = -1$) with probability μ or neck-and-neck firms ($m_i = 0$) with probability $1 - \mu$. This specification would be consistent with the well-established empirical evidence that new firms start small, and only some manage to grow over time to become a leading player in the industry. In this setting, a decline in knowledge diffusion would push up market concentration. Consequently, the probability that an entrant competes against a dominant market leader ($m_i = 1$) increases, which would discourage new firm creation, as entrants are forward-looking agents. In addition, the direct effect of lower δ and the indirect effect of lower firm entry imply that the economic activity by young firms decreases as well.

Two other trends regarding the average growth rate of incumbents indicate a decline in business dynamism concern: (i) Job reallocation has slowed, while (ii) the dispersion of firm growth has decreased (Decker et al. 2016). The model also speaks to the evolution of these variables, but the response of these variables to a decline in knowledge diffusion is ambiguous. Note that two forces drive the changes in these variables: (i) the composition of industries (μ), and (ii) the innovation incentives in each of those industries. First, both followers and neck-and-neck firms increase their investment to innovate in response to lower δ since the value of market leadership increases, and these firms are forward-looking agents. This is the *positive incentive effect*. Yet, a reduction in knowledge diffusion means the share of unleveled sectors—sectors where aggregate investment in innovation is lower—rises. This is the *negative composition effect*. Therefore, the net effect of these forces on firm growth and job reallocation is ambiguous and depends on their relative magnitudes.

The preceding discussion suggests that the theoretical analysis makes ambiguous predictions with respect to some empirical relationships, and a quantitative analysis is necessary to gain further insights. Akcigit and Ates (2023) build a version of the model described here that is versatile enough to conduct a quantitative analysis of the aforementioned empirical trends. First and foremost, it extends the basic model by adding the entry margin. As such, the extended model is where Aghion and Howitt (1992) meets Aghion et al. (2005): creative destruction and firm turnover due to firm entry, as in Aghion and Howitt (1992), complements the strategic interaction aspect of the step-by-step innovation framework. Second, they extend the analysis to transitional dynamics to replicate the experience of the US economy in the past several decades. In addition, the quantitative framework allows the discussion of other potential channels that could have contributed to the observed trends in the data and the assessment of their relative importance. In their analysis, the authors find that the strongest driver of slower business dynamism in the United States has been a decline in the intensity of knowledge diffusion from the frontier firms to laggard ones.

Reduction in knowledge diffusion is able to account for these trends as follows. When knowledge diffusion slows over time, a direct effect is that market leaders are shielded from being copied, which helps them establish stronger market power. When market leaders have a bigger lead over their rivals, the followers get discouraged; hence, they slow. The productivity gap between leaders and followers opens up. The first implication of this widening is that market composition shifts to more concentrated sectors. Second, limit pricing allows stronger leaders (leaders further ahead) to charge higher markups, which also increases the profit share and decreases the labor share of gross domestic product (GDP). Because entrants are forward-looking, they observe the strengthening of incumbents and get discouraged; therefore, entry goes down. Discouraged followers and entrants lower the competitive pressure on the market leader. When leaders face less threat, they relax and experiment less. Hence, overall dynamism and experimentation decrease in the economy. Consequently, with lower innovation investment, productivity growth slows over time, causing the equilibrium interest rate to fall. As such, the model also provides an endogenous mechanism for declining interest rates over time—a widely discussed phenomenon in the United States (Summers 2014).

3 International Trade and Competition

The step-by-step innovation framework also helps shed light on the nature of international technological competition and how competition and innovation interact in open economies. For instance, recent empirical studies find diverging results when analyzing the effect of Chinese import penetration on domestic innovation outcomes. Similarly, an extensive literature explores the effect of trade liberalization on innovation and growth outcomes (Shu and Steinwender 2019). Inherently, the step-by-step innovation model provides an immensely suitable theory to understand the economic mechanisms behind these relationships: Unlike the first-generation Schumpeterian models, it can capture not only the negative effects of competition on innovation, but also potential positive effects via the escape-competition channel. We next discuss a recent application of this framework in an open-economy setting.

3.1 Basic setup

We consider in continuous time the following world economy, which comprises two large open countries. In each country, representative final-good producers operate in perfectly competitive markets and produce the final output combining domestic fixed factor F_c (supplied inelastically) and a measure of intermediate varieties via the following technology:

$$Y_{ct} = \frac{F_c^\beta}{1-\beta} \int_0^1 \left(q_{Ajt}^{\frac{\beta}{1-\beta}} k_{Ajt} + q_{Bjt}^{\frac{\beta}{1-\beta}} k_{Bjt} \right)^{1-\beta} dj,$$

with the parameter β denoting the inverse of the elasticity of substitution across varieties j as well as the share of fixed factor. In this expression, k_{ijt} is the amount of variety j, and q_{ijt} is the associated quality. Note that in this version of the model, intermediate-good firms differ in their product quality, whereas in Section 2 the heterogeneity lay in labor productivity. As we shall see, this structure together with a Cobb-Douglas production function generates isoelastic—as opposed to unit-elastic—demand for intermediate varieties, which in turn leads to scaling of firm-level profits with product quality, providing each intermediate-good firm an incentive to innovate.[12]

Intermediate goods can potentially be produced by infinitely lived incumbent firms from both countries using a linear roundabout production technology with a constant marginal cost η. Importantly, the intermediate varieties are tradable across countries, and for simplicity, we assume away any trade costs.[13] In each product line, one firm from each country engages in Bertrand price competition to capture the market. As we shall

---

[12] Recall that in Section 2 the leader firm optimally chooses to not undertake R&D investment.

[13] The final good is also assumed to be tradable; however, this assumption does not play a role for the dynamics of the model. Instead, it helps ensure trade balance in both economies in a simple and innocuous manner.

see, the firm with a higher product quality has an edge in this competitive environment.

Technological competition and innovation are analogous in nature to the framework in Section 2, except that they pertain to product quality instead of labor productivity.[14] To avoid repetition, we keep their description brief unless otherwise is necessary. Again, the firm with a better technology—product quality, in this case—is the market leader; i.e., firm i in line j is the leader if $q_{ijt} > q_{-ijt}$. Follower and neck-and-neck stages are defined accordingly. Firms can invest in R&D to improve their product quality, with each innovation improving the product quality a multiplicative factor λ. The variable m_{ijt} captures again the technology gap between firm i and $-i$ in line j, reflecting their relative quality levels. We again restrict the maximum gap to be one step.

Setting up the static equilibrium, the final-good production function and the absence of trade costs imply that the final good producers in both countries purchase each variety from the supplier with the higher quality. The final good producers' optimization generates the following (inverse) demand schedule for good j:[15]

$$p_j = F_c^\beta q_j^\beta k_j^\beta. \tag{15}$$

Faced with this demand, the profit maximization problem of the monopolist leader reads as

$$\max_{k_j} (p_j(k_j) - \eta)k_j \quad \textit{subject to equation (15).}$$

The optimal production and price decisions are[16]

$$p_j = \frac{\eta}{1-\beta} \quad \text{and} \quad k_j = \left[\frac{\eta}{1-\beta} \right]^{-\frac{1}{\beta}} F q_j.$$

---

[14] Still, the implications of this setup differ substantially from those in the previous model. For instance, there are additional incentives for innovation: even the market leader tries to innovate, given that equilibrium profits are linear in product quality. For the details of this general setup, please see Akcigit et al. (2018).

[15] We drop the country subscript, because the nation of origin does not matter for the final-good producer. We also remove the time subscript unless it causes confusion.

[16] For the sake of clarity, we maintain the assumption that incumbents play a two-stage game à la Acemoglu et al. (2012), which ensures that the leader can charge the unconstrained monopoly price. Before setting optimal prices in the second stage, firms need to pay an infinitesimally small amount in the first stage. By backward induction, only the firm with the quality advantage enters the game.

Notice that these apply to both domestic sales and exported goods as there are no trade costs. Consequently, the profits of a leading firm is given by

$$\pi_j = \Xi q_j,$$

with $\Xi \equiv \left[\dfrac{\beta-1}{\beta}\right]^{-\frac{1}{\beta}}$. Firms that are not in a leading position do not earn any positive profits. In this setting, the dynamic problems of forward-looking firms are summarized by the following value functions:

$$r_{At} V_{A1t}(q_{jt}) - \dot{V}_{A1t}(q_{jt}) =$$

$$\max_{x_{A1t}} \left\{ \begin{array}{c} 2\Xi q_{jt} - \chi x_{A1t}^2 q_{jt} + x_{A1t}\left[V_{A1t}(\lambda q_{jt}) - V_{A1t}(q_{jt})\right] \\ - x_{B-1t}\left[V_{A0t}(q_{jt}) - V_{A1t}(q_{jt})\right] \end{array} \right\} \qquad (P1)$$

$$r_{At} V_{A0t}(q_{jt}) - \dot{V}_{A0t}(q_{jt}) =$$

$$\max_{x_{A0t}} \left\{ \begin{array}{c} -\chi x_{A0t}^2 q_{jt} + x_{A0t}\left[V_{A1t}(\lambda q_{jt}) - V_{A0t}(q_{jt})\right] \\ - x_{B0t}\left[V_{A-1t}(q_{jt}) - V_{A0t}(q_{jt})\right] \end{array} \right\} \qquad (P2)$$

$$r_{At} V_{A-1t}(q_{jt}) - \dot{V}_{A-1t}(q_{jt}) =$$

$$\max_{x_{A-1t}} \left\{ \begin{array}{c} -\chi x_{A-1t}^2 q_{jt} + x_{A-1t}\left[V_{A0t}(\lambda q_{jt}) - V_{A-1t}(q_{jt})\right] \\ - x_{B1t}\left[V_{A-1t}(\lambda q_{jt}) - V_{A-1t}(q_{jt})\right] \end{array} \right\} \qquad (P3)$$

Equations (P1)–(P3) describe the generic problem of a leader, a neck-and-neck firm, and a follower, respectively. Only the leader earns profits, and it does so by selling to both countries.[17] All firms face a quadratic R&D cost, with x_{ijt} denoting the Poisson flow rate of innovation. When the leader innovates, it improves its quality level, but its position does not change. However, if its rival innovates, it becomes neck-and-neck. In a neck-and-neck sector, an innovation helps the neck-and-neck firm gain a lead over its rival, but if the competitor innovates, the neck-and-neck firm becomes a follower. Finally, an innovation helps the follower catch up with the leader. In case of leader's innovation, the gap remains the same, reflecting spillovers from the

---

[17] Bertrand competition in neck-and-neck sectors pushes their rents down to zero.

frontier firm to the follower, helping the follower remain in the competitive race.

Next, I highlight the forces that international technological competition exerts on incumbents' innovation incentives.

3.2 Dynamic effects of openness and escape-competition effect

In order to emphasize the dynamic strategic behavior of intermediate producers in the face of foreign competition, I focus on a special version of our model with minimal incentives for quality improvements. This assumption does not eliminate all incentives for innovation. Rather, it dampens a particular motive—improving the product quality—to isolate motives that are generated by the competitive race—improving the position relative to the rival. Precisely, we assume that $\lambda = 1 + \varepsilon$, where ε is arbitrarily close to zero, implying that quality improvements from innovations are infinitesimal. Consequently, innovation incentives are driven only by discouragement and escape-competition effects. For convenience, we also take $\chi = 1/2$ and confine our analysis to the BGP. The following proposition argues that, in this environment, firms in neck-and-neck position have the highest innovation intensity.

Proposition 1 *The above assumptions imply that*

1. *the innovation intensity becomes the highest at neck-and-neck position;*
2. *the followers innovate at the same intensity and strictly less than the neck-and-neck firms;*
3. *the leaders do not innovate.*
   Formally, $x_0 > x_{-1} > x_1 = 0$.

Proof. See Appendix B.

Proposition 1 formalizes the fact that the positive effect of foreign competitive pressures on innovation incentives becomes the strongest when firms compete against rivals producing goods of similar quality. This effect is analogous to the one in closed-economy step-by-step models—namely, the *escape-competition* effect—but it gains an international aspect in the context of an open economy. As such, this effect allows the model to capture potential boost from international competition to firms' innovative activity. To be sure, the model still reflects the potential downside of foreign competition: domestic firms that fall behind in the competitive race get discouraged in their innovative effort (*discouragement effect*). Hence, this versatility of the step-by-step innovation framework makes it a very convenient and realistic setting to study the effect of foreign competition on economic growth and analyze industrial policy in open economies. In Akcigit et al. (2018), we do so using a more advanced version of the model, and several interesting implications arise.[18]

First, Akcigit et al. (2018) study a more general setting that features trade costs and allow the productivity gap to widen more than one step. In such a setting, the existence of trade costs modifies the nature of escape-competition effect in significant ways. Raising the cost of imports, they help some domestic firms retain their domestic market, even though their foreign competitor has a better quality. Conversely, it is not enough for a domestic firm to have superior product quality to export; the quality advantage should be large enough to compensate for the additional costs. Accordingly, the "neck-and-neckness" arises at two different stages of international competition, and the innovation effort of a firm intensifies at two different points, for two similar yet distinct reasons: to protect domestic profits when the firm is a technological laggard and to access export markets when the firm is a technology leader. As a result, the innovation effort schedule of a firm as a function of the quality gap relative to its rival has double-peaked shape, and empirical findings provided corroborate this prediction. Notice the difference with respect to the standard model: in the standard setting, competition and innovation effort (escape-competition effect) peak only when the two firms have exactly the same quality, translating to a single-peaked innovation effort schedule. This heterogeneity has subtle implications for policy, as discussed in detail by Akcigit et al. (2018).

The quantitative investigation of this model uncovers intriguing policy implications. First, increased foreign competition reduces the need for R&D subsidies to prop up domestic innovation. As bilateral trade costs decline—i.e., as the world becomes more open—the optimal level of R&D subsidy that a policymaker would set for a given horizon decreases as well. This result also hinges crucially on the escape-competition effect. Lower trade costs imply that more domestic firms face stronger competitive threat, inducing them to innovate more intensively. Given the technology gap in a sector, these stronger incentives push most firms closer to the optimal innovation effort,

---

[18] For excellent surveys of empirical studies on the nexus of foreign competition, innovation, and economic growth, please see the recent reviews by Akcigit and Melitz (2021); Melitz and Redding in Chapter 6 of this volume; and Shu and Steinwender (2019).

reducing the need for R&D subsidies to correct for deficient domestic innovative activity.

Another key policy implication is that it is optimal for the policymaker to slash trade barriers to zero—especially when longer policy horizons are considered and even unilaterally. The optimality of removing unilateral trade barriers unilaterally is a novel finding in the international trade literature and depends crucially on the effect of protectionist policies on market competition and innovation incentives.[19] While trade barriers protect some firms in the short run, helping them retain production and profits, this protection from competitive pressure that foreign rivals could exert reduces the incentives of domestic firms to innovate and improve the competitiveness of their products. Notice that this effect emerges on top of the fact that trade barriers deprive the economy of some superior foreign products through distortions they create in relative prices. This negative dynamic effect of trade barriers on innovation incentives translates into lower productivity growth in the economy over time and becomes the dominant margin in welfare calculations of the policymaker. Therefore, the policymaker chooses optimally to curtail trade barriers even unilaterally.

Finally, the rich dynamics of this model propose a rationale that can reconcile the seemingly contradictory findings of empirical studies that evaluate the effect of import penetration on domestic innovative activity.[20] As discussed, the model implies that stiffer competition encourages some domestic firms to increase their innovation effort and discourages some others, depending on their position in the competitive race. Then, the overall effect of import penetration on domestic innovation outcome would depend on the composition of sectors in an economy—i.e., whether most domestic firms are competitive enough relative to their foreign rivals to begin with. Indeed, Akcigit et al. (2018) corroborate this intuition, showing numerically that overall innovation effort in an economy can decrease or increase in response

---

[19] This result holds even in shorter horizons, as demonstrated by Akcigit et al. (2021), who extend the framework with cross-country heterogeneity in labor productivity, which introduces Ricardian forces of comparative advantage. In this setting, higher trade barriers exert upward pressure on domestic wages, which in turn reduces the competitiveness of the economy, adding an additional force that makes positive trade barriers suboptimal even in the short run.

[20] Bloom et al. (2016) argue that Chinese import competition induced innovative activity in exposed domestic sectors in twelve European countries they analyze (see also Coelli et al. 2016; Gorodnichenko et al. 2010; Iacovone et al. 2011; Iacovone 2012), whereas Autor et al. (2020) find a negative effect on US firms and sectors (see also Hashmi 2013; Hombert and Matray 2015). Yet some other papers, including Aghion et al. (2017), find ambiguous results.

to lower barriers to import. Again, the ultimate response is determined by the initial sectoral composition in terms of competitiveness of domestic firms.

4 Conclusions

Schumpeterian growth theory, with its intuitive and tractable modeling of incentives for innovation, has envisaged long-run productivity growth as an endogenous outcome and fundamentally altered economists' thinking about economic growth. A key margin that affects firms' innovation incentives is the degree of competition among them. The step-by-step innovation framework zeroes in on this margin; and thanks to its realistic yet tractable account of competition and innovation, it has a unique place in the endogenous growth tradition. Distinctively, incumbent firms respond strategically to each other via endogenous innovation decisions and depending on the magnitude of competitive pressure. The fundamental insights this theory offers—importantly, the escape-competition effect, among others—widened the relevance of Schumpeterian growth models greatly and enhanced its applicability to new lines of research. In this chapter, I reviewed two such applications.

In one direction, the step-by-step innovation model sheds light on the causes of slowing business dynamism in the United States (Akcigit and Ates 2021, 2023). A particular mechanism—a decline in knowledge diffusion—seems to have plagued the US economy: through the lens of the model, this decline distorts the competition between market leaders and followers, rigging the game in favor of the former, and leads ultimately to lower innovation incentives for firms in both groups. In another line of research, the step-by-step innovation model enhances our understanding of trade and industrial policies in open economies. Among other things, it helps expose the distortionary dynamic effect of protectionist policies that result in novel policy implications. The key mechanism again emphasizes the significance of competitive pressures—in this case, exerted by foreign rivals—in driving innovative activity by domestic firms.

The two examples highlighted in this chapter illustrate the broad applicability and policy relevance of the step-by-step innovation framework. Yet, a casual examination indicates that this framework has not been utilized to its fullest potential. I contend that its outreach will quickly expand in the years to come, and that, especially with the latest computational techniques and computing power, its quantitative applications will advance further to help us address many other interesting questions at the juncture of competition, innovation, and economic policy.

References

ACEMOGLU, D., AND U. AKCIGIT (2012): "Intellectual Property Rights Policy, Competition and Innovation," *Journal of the European Economic Association*, 10, 1–42.

ACEMOGLU, D., G. GANCIA, AND F. ZILIBOTTI (2012): "Competing Engines of Growth: Innovation and Standardization," *Journal of Economic Theory*, 147, 570–601.

AGHION, P., A. BERGEAUD, M. LEQUIEN, AND M. MELITZ (2017): "The Impact of Exports on Innovation: Theory and Evidence," Harvard University, manuscript.

AGHION, P., N. BLOOM, R. BLUNDELL, R. GRIFFITH, AND P. HOWITT (2005): "Competition and Innovation: An Inverted-U Relationship," *Quarterly Journal of Economics*, 120, 701–728.

AGHION, P., C. HARRIS, P. HOWITT, AND J. VICKERS (2001): "Competition, Imitation and Growth with Step-by-Step Innovation," *Review of Economic Studies*, 68, 467–492.

AGHION, P., C. HARRIS, AND J. VICKERS (1997): "Competition and Growth with Step-by-Step Innovation: An Example," *European Economic Review*, 41, 771–782.

AGHION, P., AND P. HOWITT (1992): "A Model of Growth through Creative Destruction," *Econometrica*, 60, 323–351.

AKCIGIT, U., AND S. T. ATES (2021): "Ten Facts on Declining Business Dynamism and Lessons from Endogenous Growth Theory," *American Economic Journal: Macroeconomics*, 13, 257–298.

——— (2023): "What Happened to U.S. Business Dynamism?," *Journal of Political Economy*, forthcoming.

AKCIGIT, U., S. T. ATES, AND G. IMPULLITTI (2018): "Innovation and Trade Policy in a Globalized World," NBER Working Paper 24543.

AKCIGIT, U., AND M. J. MELITZ (2022): "International Trade and Innovation," in *Handbook of International Economics*, vol. 5, ed. G. Gopinath, E. Helpman, and K. Rogoff, Amsterdam: Elsevier, North Holland.

ANDREWS, D., C. CRISCUOLO, AND P. N. GAL (2015): "Frontier Firms, Technology Diffusion and Public Policy," OECD Productivity Working Paper No. 2.

——— (2016): "The Best versus the Rest: The Global Productivity Slowdown, Divergence across Firms and the Role of Public Policy," OECD Productivity Working Paper No. 5.

AUTOR, D., D. DORN, G. H. HANSON, G. PISANO, AND P. SHU (2020): "Foreign Competition and Domestic Innovation: Evidence from US Patents," *American Economic Review: Insights*, 2, 357–374.

AUTOR, D., D. DORN, L. F. KATZ, C. PATTERSON, AND J. VAN REENEN (2017a): "Concentrating on the Fall of the Labor Share," *American Economic Review*, 107, 180–185.

——— (2017b): "The Fall of the Labor Share and the Rise of Superstar Firms," NBER Working Paper 23396.

BARKAI, S. (2017): "Declining Labor and Capital Shares," manuscript.

BLOOM, N., M. DRACA, AND J. VAN REENEN (2016): "Trade Induced Technical Change? The Impact of Chinese Imports on Innovation, IT and Productivity," *Review of Economic Studies*, 83, 87–117.

BLOOM, N., M. SCHANKERMAN, AND J. VAN REENEN (2013): "Identifying Technology Spillovers and Product Market Rivalry," *Econometrica*, 81, 1347–1393.

BUDD, C., C. HARRIS, AND J. VICKERS (1993): "A Model of the Evolution of Duopoly: Does the Asymmetry between Firms Tend to Increase or Decrease?," *Review of Economic Studies*, 60, 543–573.

CAVENAILE, L., M. A. CELIK, P. ROLDAN-BLANCO, AND X. TIAN (2021a): "Style over Substance? Advertising, Innovation, and Endogenous Market Structure," SSRN Working Paper 3804065.

CAVENAILE, L., M. A. CELIK, AND X. TIAN (2019): "Are Markups Too High? Competition, Strategic Innovation, and Industry Dynamics," SSRN Working Paper 3459775.

——— (2021b): "The Dynamic Effects of Antitrust Policy on Growth and Welfare," *Journal of Monetary Economics*, 121, 42–59.

CHIKIS, C., J. E. GOLDBERG, AND J. D. LÓPEZ-SALIDO (2021): "Do Low Interest Rates Harm Innovation, Competition, and Productivity Growth?," CEPR Discussion Papers 16184.

COELLI, F., A. MOXNES, AND K. H. ULLTVEIT-MOE (2016): "Better, Faster, Stronger: Global Innovation and Trade Liberalization," NBER Working Paper 22647.

DE LOECKER, J., J. EECKHOUT, AND G. UNGER (2017): "The Rise of Market Power and the Macroeconomic Implications," NBER Working Paper 23687.

DECKER, R. A., J. HALTIWANGER, R. S. JARMIN, AND J. MIRANDA (2016): "Where Has All the Skewness Gone? The Decline in High-Growth (Young) Firms in the US," *European Economic Review*, 86, 4–23.

EGGERTSSON, G. B., J. A. ROBBINS, AND E. G. WOLD (2018): "Kaldor and Piketty's Facts: The Rise of Monopoly Power in the United States," NBER Working Paper 24287.

ELSBY, M., B. HOBIJN, AND A. SAHIN (2013): "The Decline of the U.S. Labor Share," Federal Reserve Bank of San Francisco, Working Paper 2013–2027.

FOSTER, L., J. HALTIWANGER, AND C. J. KRIZAN (2000): "Aggregate Productivity Growth: Lessons from Microeconomic Evidence," in *New Developments in Productivity Analysis*, Chicago: University of Chicago Press.

GORODNICHENKO, Y., J. SVEJNAR, AND K. TERRELL (2010): "Globalization and Innovation in Emerging Markets," *American Economic Journal: Macroeconomics*, 2, 194–226.

GOURIO, F., T. MESSER, AND M. SIEMER (2014): "What Is the Economic Impact of the Slowdown in New Business Formation?," *Chicago Fed Letter*, 326.

GROSSMAN, G., AND C. SHAPIRO (1987): "Dynamic R&D Competition," *Economic Journal*, 97, 372–387.

GRULLON, G., Y. LARKIN, AND R. MICHAELY (2017): "Are U.S. Industries Becoming More Concentrated?," manuscript.

GUTIÉRREZ, G., AND T. PHILIPPON (2017): "Declining Competition and Investment in the U.S.," NBER Working Paper 23583.

HALL, R. E. (2018): "New Evidence on Market Power, Profit, Concentration, and the Role of Mega-Firms in the U.S. Economy," Stanford University, manuscript.

HARRIS, C., AND J. VICKERS (1985): "Perfect Equilibrium in a Model of a Race," *Review of Economic Studies*, 52, 193–209.

——— (1987): "Racing with Uncertainty," *Review of Economic Studies*, 54, 1–21.

HASHMI, A. R. (2013): "Competition and Innovation: The Inverted-U Relationship Revisited," *Review of Economics and Statistics*, 95, 1653–1668.

HOMBERT, J., AND A. MATRAY (2015): "Can Innovation Help US Manufacturing Firms Escape Import Competition from China?," CEPR Discussion Papers 10666.

IACOVONE, L. (2012): "The Better You Are the Stronger It Makes You: Evidence on the Asymmetric Impact of Liberalization," *Journal of Development Economics*, 99, 474–485.

IACOVONE, L., W. KELLER, AND F. RAUCH (2011): "Innovation Responses to Import Competition," Princeton University, manuscript.

KARABARBOUNIS, L., AND B. NEIMAN (2013): "The Global Decline of the Labor Share," *Quarterly Journal of Economics*, 129, 61–103.

KARAHAN, F., B. PUGSLEY, AND A. SAHIN (2016): "Demographic Origins of the Startup Deficit," New York Fed, manuscript.

KLETTE, T. J., AND S. KORTUM (2004): "Innovating Firms and Aggregate Innovation," *Journal of Political Economy*, 112, 986–1018.

LAWRENCE, R. Z. (2015): "Recent Declines in Labor's Share in U.S. Income: A Preliminary Neoclassical Account," NBER Working Paper 21296.

LIU, E., A. MIAN, AND A. SUFI (2019): "Low Interest Rates, Market Power, and Productivity Growth," Becker Friedman Institute Working Papers Series 2019–09.

NEKARDA, C. J., AND V. A. RAMEY (2013): "The Cyclical Behavior of the Price-Cost Markup," NBER Working Paper 19099.

OLMSTEAD-RUMSEY, J. (2020): "Market Concentration and the Productivity Slowdown," manuscript.

ROMER, P. M. (1990): "Endogenous Technological Change," *Journal of Political Economy*, 98, S71–102.

SHU, P., AND C. STEINWENDER (2019): "The Impact of Trade Liberalization on Firm Productivity and Innovation," *Innovation Policy and the Economy*, 19, 39–68.

SUMMERS, L. H. (2014): "US Economic Prospects: Secular Stagnation, Hysteresis, and the Zero Lower Bound," *Business Economics*, 49, 65–73.

APPENDIXES

A. Equilibrium

We focus on the balanced growth path (BGP) Markov perfect equilibrium, with equilibrium strategies depending only on the payoff-relevant state variable $m \in \{-1, 0, 1\}$ and all aggregate variables growing at the same rate g while firms' innovation rates remain constant. Henceforth, we will drop the indices $i, j,$ and t when doing so causes no confusion and use only the payoff-relevant state variable m.

1. Equilibrium interest rate:

$$r = g + \rho, \tag{A.1}$$

where g is the BGP growth rate of consumption.

2. Demand schedule for the intermediate good $j \in [0, 1]$:

$$y_{ij} = \frac{Y}{p_{ij}}, \tag{A.2}$$

where p_{ij} is the price of intermediate j charged by the producing monopolist i.

3. Intermediate producer's marginal cost:

$$MC_{ij} = \frac{w}{q_{ij}} \tag{A.3}$$

with w denoting the wage level.

4. Equilibrium intermediate good quantities:

$$y_{ij} = \frac{q_{-ij}}{\omega} \text{ for } q_{ij} \geq q_{-ij} \tag{A.4}$$

and $y_{ij} = 0$ otherwise, with the normalized aggregate wage rate given as $\omega \equiv w/Y$.

5. Optimal production employment of the intermediate producer:

$$l_i = \frac{y_i}{q_i} = \frac{1}{\omega \lambda^{m_i}} \text{ for } m_i \in \{0, 1\}. \tag{A.5}$$

6. Operating profits of an intermediate firm (exclusive of its R&D expenditures):

$$\pi(m_i) = \begin{cases} \left(1 - \dfrac{1}{\lambda}\right)Y & \text{if} \quad m_i = 1 \\ 0 & \text{if} \quad m_i \in \{0, -1\} \end{cases}.$$

7. Markups in leveled ($m_j = 0$) and unleveled ($m_j = 1$) sectors:

$$Markup_j = \frac{p_{ij}}{MC_{ij}} - 1 = \begin{cases} \lambda - 1 & \text{if} \quad m_j = 1 \\ 0 & \text{if} \quad m_j = 0 \end{cases}.$$

8. Aggregate labor share ω (equal to the normalized wage rate in the economy):

$$\omega = 1 - \mu \frac{(\lambda - 1)}{\lambda}. \tag{A.6}$$

9. Stock market value of firms that are in state $m_i \in \{-1, 0, 1\}$, which are denoted by v_{m_i}:

$$\rho v_1 = \max_{x_1} \left\{ \left(1 - \frac{1}{\lambda}\right) + x_1[v_1 - v_1] + (x_{-1} + \delta)[v_0 - v_1] \right\}$$

$$\rho v_{-1} = \max_{x_{-1}} \left\{ -\frac{x_{-1}^2}{2} + (x_{-1} + \delta)[v_0 - v_{-1}] \right\}$$

$$\rho v_0 = \max_{x_0} \left\{ -\frac{x_0^2}{2} + x_0[v_1 - v_0] + x_0[v_{-1} - v_0] \right\}.$$

10. Optimal innovation decisions of leaders, neck-and-neck firms, and followers:

$$x_1 = 0$$
$$x_0 = v_1 - v_0$$
$$x_{-1} = v_0 - v_{-1}. \tag{A.7}$$

11. The law of motion for μ:

$$\dot{\mu} = -\mu(x_{-1} + \delta) + (1 - \mu)2x_0. \tag{A.8}$$

B. Proof of Proposition 1

In this environment firm values can be written as

$$rv_{-1} = -\frac{x_{-1}^2}{2} + x_{-1}[v_0 - v_{-\bar{m}}]$$

$$rv_0 = -\frac{x_0^2}{2} + x_0[v_1 - v_0] + x_0[v_{-1} - v_0]$$

$$rv_1 = 2\Xi - \frac{x_1^2}{2} + x_1[v_1 - v_1] + x_{-1}[v_0 - v_1]$$

Here, $v_m \equiv V_m\, q^{-1}$. Note that, in this setting, the leader does not innovate, i.e., $x_1 = 0$. Now we show $x_0 > x_{-1} > 0$.

1. $v_1 > v_0$: Assume not such that $v_0 \geq = v_1$. Then $[v_1 - v_0] \leq 0$, and $x_0 = 0$. This implies $v_0 = 0 \geq v_1$. But $v_0 = 0$ would mean $rv_1 = 2\Xi - x_{-1}v_1$ and thus $v_1 > 0$, a contradiction. Therefore $x_0 > 0$.

2. $v_0 > v_{-1}$: Assume not such that $v_{-1} \geq v_0$. Then $x_{-1} = 0$ implying that $v_{-1} = 0 \geq v_0$. This is possible only if $x_0 = 0$. But since $v_1 > v_0$ as shown above, $x_0 > 0$, a contradiction. Therefore $x_{-1} > 0$.

3. $[v_1 - v_0] > [v_0 - v_{-1}]$: Assume not such that $[v_0 - v_{-1}] \geq [v_1 - v_0]$. This means $v_0 < 0$ unless $x_0 = 0$. If $v_0 < 0$, it is a contradiction by step 2. If $x_0 = 0$ meaning that $v_0 = 0$ it is a contradiction by step 1. Therefore $[v_1 - v_0] > [v_0 - v_{-1}]$ and $x_0 > x_{-1} > x_1 = 0$.

PART V

The Environment

Green Innovation and Climate Change

CHAPTER 13

Harnessing Creative Destruction to the Tackling of Climate Change

Purpose, Pace, Policy

NICHOLAS STERN

1 Introduction: The Challenge and the Structure of the Argument

1.1 Creative destruction with a compelling purpose

Joseph Schumpeter (1942) gave us the crucial idea of creative destruction and placed it at the heart of our understanding of processes of change in a capitalist economy: he saw it as the key driver of discovery, innovation, investment, and growth. Philippe Aghion and Peter Howitt (e.g., 1998, 2009) gave us an elegant and fruitful way of capturing the idea in formal models, something that had eluded theorists for more than half a century. All those who are trying to understand growth are greatly in their debt. For Schumpeter, the story of creative destruction concerned the forces behind, and the roles of, innovation, investment, and advances in productivity in the overall processes of growth and structural change. The problem I am examining here, the outstanding challenge of this century, is climate change. To tackle climate change effectively, the necessary innovation and investment must drive change with the particular purpose and characteristic of rapidly reducing greenhouse gas emissions and taking them to net zero in order to stabilize global temperatures[1] and keep the increases to an acceptable level. Hence, we must seek to guide and foster the processes of creative destruction for a specific purpose and at real pace. This chapter examines how policy and action can be designed and set to harness creative destruction to deliver decarbonization while also improving living standards in a sustainable way. As Aghion and his collaborators have argued, "only innovation has the potential to improve quality of life while using fewer and fewer of our natural resources and emitting less and less carbon dioxide. Only innovation will enable us to discover new and cleaner sources of energy" (Aghion et al. 2021, chapter 9).

Aghion, Howitt, and collaborators have been working on these issues over a long period of time and developing helpful models that offer real insight (e.g., Acemoglu et al. 2012; Aghion et al. 2014).[2] My own perspective here will build on these and other ideas, particularly concerning economy-wide policy and action to foster innovation and investment.

1.2 Climate change

Greenhouse gases are gases whose molecules oscillate at a frequency that interferes with infrared energy, the form of energy that is reflected from the earth's surface. Carbon dioxide (CO_2) is central among these and is long-lasting; it is released in a number of ways, most importantly by burning fossil fuels. It arises also, together with other greenhouse gases such as methane, from burning or decaying biomass. The greater the concentrations of greenhouse gases in the atmosphere, the more energy is prevented from escaping the atmosphere, and the higher the temperature. Higher temperatures have a profound influence on climate and lives and livelihoods.

To stabilize temperatures we must stabilize concentrations of greenhouse gases, and that means the flow of emissions should be net zero. The earlier net-zero emissions are reached, the lower the temperature at which we stabilize—although, of course, the particular path to net zero is of great importance because it is the sum of emissions over time that increases concen-

---

[1] Stabilizing temperatures requires stabilizing concentrations of greenhouse gases, which requires net-zero emissions. Broadly speaking, the earlier net zero is achieved, the lower the stabilized temperature.

[2] For a summary of key insights from such models, and implications for policy, see Aghion et al. (2014) and Stern and Valero (2021).

trations. This, in broad terms, is the basics of the science.[3] The messages are clear on the importance of the drive to net-zero emissions. Some numbers on paths of emissions associated with different temperature outcomes are illustrated in Section 2 below.

The implication of this simple science is that we must transform our economies and societies rapidly and fundamentally to move to net-zero emissions. An assessment of and decisions concerning how rapidly and how to make this transformation will be influenced by a consideration of the consequences of different patterns of temperature and climate change that can follow from our actions, together with an understanding of the possibilities available to us, and which we would create, for making these changes.

In formulating such an approach, the world has, as embodied in the Paris agreement (UNFCCC, COP21, December 2015), adopted a "guardrail policy"—that is, to keep global average surface temperature increase "well-below 2°C" and make best efforts to hold it to 1.5°C.[4] The importance of the target of 1.5°C has been underscored by both the IPCC report of 2018 (IPCC 2018), which showed that 2°C was much more dangerous than 1.5°C, and the Sixth Assessment Review of the IPCC of August 2021 (IPCC 2021). Both of them clearly indicate the dangers of going beyond 1.5°C and that time is running out if we are to take effective action to give us a reasonable chance of holding to 1.5°C.

1.3 The approach to policy

One could, in principle, identify desirable targets as outcomes from an optimization model that balances climate change risks and costs of emissions reductions. These have been popular in the literature on integrated assessment models (IAMs), building on the early work of Bill Nordhaus (e.g., 1991). In my view, and I have argued this elsewhere (e.g., Stern 2015), building such models in ways that are analytically tractable generally involves losing key elements that shape the challenge of and response to climate change, including damages that can involve the deaths of hundreds of millions or more and the dynamics of innovation and creation of new technologies, particularly in the context of increasing returns to scale. In the face of deep uncertainty (there are many possible catastrophic outcomes of climate change

---

[3] There are relevant nuances, but the basic logic is as described.

[4] Temperature increases are measured relative to the second part of the nineteenth century.

we are not in a position to describe precisely) and extreme uncertainty (catastrophic outcomes we can describe), the world, wisely in my view, has opted for the guardrail approach.

We are now learning that the process of change to net-zero emissions can be one of intense and fruitful discovery and the creation of a much more attractive, less damaging, and more efficient form of development and growth than the dirty, destructive, and wasteful models of the past. In the process of change we can create cities where we can move and breathe, ecosystems that are robust and fruitful. The challenges of climate change and biodiversity loss (see Dasgupta 2021) are closely intertwined.

We can both reduce emissions and raise living standards and well-being across a broad range of dimensions. This is a dynamic story of learning and choices around a new form of growth and development. It is a mistake to portray our decisions in terms of a narrow, largely static, trade-off between output and environment. Much of the economics of climate change has made that mistake (see, e.g., Stern 2015, 2021) and I will refer briefly to this in Part II.

This description of the science, and the fundamental changes in economic development it implies, must guide our overall approach to policy and particularly to innovation, the main focus of this chapter. It is surely clear that we must seek to harness creative destruction for a purpose and must move at pace.

The approach to policy I have tried to pursue over the last decade, and embodied here, is to look at change across the whole economy and all its systems, including energy, transportation, cities, and land use—the main systemic sources of greenhouse gases. This requires us to work to understand the functioning of these systems and how they can be changed. Innovation must concern systems as a whole and not just particular technologies, important though these are. Innovation in institutions, approaches to the political economy, and changing behavior are all part of the agenda for the fostering and management of change. Policy regarding these issues, as with the major systems, must examine carefully the functioning of markets, their failures and, in some cases, absences, the limitations on government, and the implications for the functioning of incentives. There is far more here than just the correcting of one market failure—in particular, the externality associated with greenhouse gases, vitally important though that is.

In looking across the whole economy, and its challenge of change, in this way, I will try to embody the perspectives of someone who has spent long periods in the kitchen of policymaking and providing advice to those who must decide policy. This means marshaling ideas and evidence in real time to make decisions for which time is critical. This is "public economics as if time matters" (Stern 2018), a phrase that was the title of my essay in the issue of the *Journal of Public Economics* celebrating the life of Tony Atkinson, who took a great interest in this subject. We have to take what we can from theories, ideas, and evidence in economics, what we now "think we know," and translate that into advice and guidance for decisions now. Much of the art of economic policymaking lies in how we do this marshaling of ideas and evidence and how we feed this into the world of real politics and decision-making.

1.4 Plan of this chapter

The arguments in relation to the challenge of rapid and fundamental change just described are built as follows. Section 2 offers a very brief description of the basic science and the immense risks of climate change, which is key to understanding the guardrail approach, with its targets. Section 3 sets out the necessary scale and urgency of action and the key areas for action. Section 4 argues that we must recognize the challenge of our starting point and recent history, which has been dramatically influenced by COVID. And Section 5 examines how momentum for action is building, how technology is changing, and the importance of collaboration for effective action.

Sections 1–5, thus, identify the overall nature of the change required. Section 6 examines the investment and innovation necessary for this change. Section 7 discusses how to foster and guide, through policy and action, the innovation and investment that can deliver it. Most of the action for change will be from private producers and households and influenced by markets, but must be fostered by public policy and public and community action. Section 8 offers some concluding remarks.

2 Climate Science

The basic physics of the greenhouse effect and the importance of stabilizing concentrations of greenhouse gases, in order to stabilize temperature and climate, were set out in Section 1.2 above. I describe briefly here some of the potential consequences, the immense risks of unmanaged climate change,

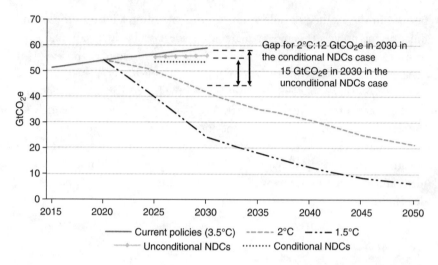

Note: The vertical axis represents emissions in CO₂e; that is, CO_2 plus the effects of other greenhouse gases.

Data source: UNEP (2020).

Figure 13.1. Stylized emissions pathways for 1.5°C and 2°C and the gap to emissions trajectories based on current NDCs

and the paths that could stabilize concentrations in a way that could avoid or reduce the most severe risks. This is what underpins the "guardrail" approach of setting a target or upper limit to temperature increases.

Figure 13.1 illustrates paths of greenhouse gas emissions, in terms of carbon dioxide equivalent (CO_2e), that could stabilize temperatures at 1.5°C and 2.0°C. CO_2e consists of CO_2 plus other greenhouse gases measured in terms of warming equivalent. Emissions of CO_2e from all sources (including land-use change) was estimated at 59.1 gigtonnes of equivalent carbon dioxide ($GtCO_2e$) in 2019, of which 44.3 $GtCO_2$ (i.e., 75 percent) was CO_2 (UNEP 2020). Around 86 percent of CO_2 emissions came from burning fossil fuels (UNEP 2020).

Planned emissions, in terms of the sum of country targets (most countries offer targets or "NDCs," nationally determined contributions, to 2030) proposed in relation to COP21 of the UNFCCC in Paris, are illustrated in Figure 13.1. It can be seen that they show very little in terms of reductions. To get us on a path to 1.5°C, emissions would have to roughly halve in the decade to 2030 and CO_2 emissions would have to go to zero by 2050 (with

CO_2e going to zero a little later). COP26 in Glasgow in November 2021 will discussed (as foreseen in the Paris agreement) how to set targets consistent with the Paris agreement goals of holding warming to well below 2°C and making best efforts to hold warming to 1.5°C. It is clear that major increases in ambition will be necessary to deliver that consistency.

We know that 2°C is much more dangerous than 1.5°C (see Table 13.1). Our current emissions pathway implies that we are headed for temperature increases of more than 3°C (UNEP 2020). As a world, we have not seen an increase of 3°C or more for around 3 million years, and at that time sea levels were 10 to 20 meters higher than now (Dumitru et al. 2019). Those kinds of temperatures would radically change lives and livelihoods across the globe. Many parts of the world could become uninhabitable. Under a business-as-usual scenario, one of the most densely populated regions in the world, the North China Plain, would likely experience deadly heat waves later this century, with "wet-bulb" temperature exceeding the threshold defining what people can tolerate while working outdoors (Kang and Eltahir 2018). Similar deadly heat waves could also occur in other densely populated

Table 13.1. Impacts of 1.5°C and 2°C warming

	1.5°C	2°C	2°C vs. 1.5°C
Extreme heat[1] (proportion of global population exposed to severe heat at least once every 5 years)	14%	37%	2.6x worse
Number of sea-ice-free Arctic summers[2]	At least 1 after ~100 years of stabilized warming	At least 1 after ~10 years of stabilized warming	10x worse
Bioclimatic range loss of >50%[3]	Vertebrate species: 4%	Vertebrate species: 8%	Vertebrate species: 2x worse
	Plant species: 8%	Plant species: 16%	Plant species: 2x worse
	Insect species: 6%	Insect species: 18%	Insect species: 3x worse

[1] Dosio et al. 2018.
[2] IPCC 2018.
[3] Warren et al. 2018.

parts of the world, such as northern India. Hundreds of millions, possibly billions, would have to move,[5] likely resulting in severe and extended conflicts. It is quite possible on current emissions paths that we could see 4°C or 5°C of temperature rise 150 years or so from now—temperatures the world has not seen for tens of millions of years. That would be absolutely devastating.

It is the potential magnitude of risks for 3°, 4°, 5°C—and indeed from 2°C—that has led the world to set the Paris targets and to refocus on 1.5°C. The rest of this chapter is devoted to how we can find and foster new and attractive forms of growth and development that can take us to these targets.

3 Urgency, Scale, and Structure

We saw in Section 2 that, for a reasonable chance of holding temperature rise to 2°C, we must move to a path that cuts emissions by around 30 percent in the decade 2020 to 2030 and by at least 50 percent for 1.5°C. For 1.5°C we must set a target of net zero by 2050 for CO_2. The magnitude of the necessary change is highlighted if we look at likely economic change in terms of growth, investment, and infrastructure during the coming two or three decades.

The world's infrastructure will likely double in the next fifteen to twenty years. A majority of the world's emissions are associated with infrastructure.[6] Key parts of the world, particularly in emerging markets and developing countries, will be going through stages of development with strong investment in energy, transportation, and cities. Many of those investments, particularly in infrastructure, will be planned and set in train in the coming few years. The planning of and investment in infrastructure in this decade will

---

[5] Empirical estimates range substantially, from 50 million to 1 billion migrants associated with the effects of climate change during this century (Ferris 2020). We should remember that we have been forced consistently over the last few decades to bring forward in time our estimates of when serious impacts can occur and revise estimates of their magnitudes upward. And most models do not embody the tipping points that we think may occur at higher temperatures, which could generate dangerous feedback loops (e.g., collapse of the Amazon Rainforest, thawing of permafrost, melting of polar ice sheets).

[6] The existing stock and use of infrastructure is associated with more than 60 percent of the world's greenhouse gas (GHG) emissions (New Climate Economy 2016).

be decisive to our future. If the doubling of infrastructure that is coming in the next decades looks anything like simply adding another lot of infrastructure similar to what we have already, then emissions would likely go on rising to midcentury with the lock-in of fossil-fuel-intensive capital. That would likely put 3°C out of reach and could set us on a path to 4°C or more. The consequences, as we have seen, would be devastating. Therefore, the urgency to design and build differently is intense. And the great scale of the necessary change—including building all our new infrastructure very differently—should be clear.

If the world economy grows at around 3 percent per annum in the next two or three decades, it will roughly double in the next twenty to twenty-five years. Just as for infrastructure, if that "new economy" to be added looks anything like the old, we will be headed for well over 3°C, because emissions would go on rising until midcentury. Similarly, the world's cities will likely double in population over the next four decades or so. Cities are associated with more than two-thirds of emissions from final energy use (UN Habitat, 2021) and the fraction is rising. Again, unless future cities look very different, we will be headed for very dangerous climate change.

The biggest drivers of emissions will be new investment in emerging-market and developing countries, but existing activities across the world will also have to change radically in terms of emissions if we are to drive to net zero. Maintenance and renewal investment, including "retrofitting," must transform our existing activities in energy, transportation, buildings, and so on. Much of this investment will be around existing infrastructure and capital in developed countries. Much of their infrastructure is in strong need of renewal (Bhattacharya et al. 2016), and that renewal and refurbishment should be transformational. It is clear that investment and innovation in these processes in the next one or two decades will be absolutely crucial if we are to get onto a path that can manage dangerous climate change.

Our emphasis in the discussion of investment so far has been on physical capital. But we will have to transform our approach to natural capital too. In the last half century, natural capital—a measure which includes an implied value of our land, forests, oceans, air, and so on—has been reduced by around 40 percent (Dasgupta 2021). The damage to biodiversity and climate is immense. Biodiversity and climate are closely interwoven: a deteriorating climate damages biodiversity and vice versa. But our damage to biodiversity comes from many other factors besides climate change—including via over-exploitation and pollution of various forms.

Investing in natural capital in creative and innovative ways will be crucial to the management of climate and biodiversity. We will need to transform the way we use and look after our land, forests, oceans, and air. For managing climate, we must identify and utilize substantial sources of negative emissions; both restoring degraded land and reforesting will be central to climate action and to the protection and enhancement of biodiversity.

In many ways we can see our land, forests, and oceans as our natural infrastructure. As infrastructure more generally, they enable our lives to function, in large measure via water and its management, via our air, and in many other ways.

The world spends around $700 billion a year (Food and Land Use Coalition 2019) on agricultural subsidies; the consequences are all too often degraded land, poisoned waterways, and destroyed forests. And often it is the richest enterprises that garner the majority of subsidies. Innovation and system change through reformed technologies and accompanying policies could be transformational to both our natural capital and productivity as conventionally measured (Food and Land Use Coalition 2019; Systemiq 2020).

4 The Starting Point: Secular Stagnation and COVID

So far I have emphasized the very damaging nature and structure of our current economic activity and our past activities, particularly via emissions of greenhouse gases, and I have analyzed and described how change must take place over the coming two or three decades. But our ways forward will also be influenced by the world's economic difficulties over the last decade and the crisis of COVID that burst over the world in early 2020. The starting point matters.

In advanced economies, and broadly the world as a whole, the last decade has seen a slowing of growth, in part as a result of a weak recovery from the global financial crisis of 2008–2009. Some of this was related, in some economies, to premature fiscal austerity programs, before growth had been reestablished. Some economists have argued that there are longer-run structural factors at work that led to a strengthened desire to save, such as longer life expectancy and a smaller fraction of the population at working age; see, for instance, Summers (2020) on secular stagnation. This argument is paired with ideas (e.g., Gordon 2012) on the slowing of technical progress and associated diminishing investment opportunities (although see Mokyr et al.

2015 for a different view). This last argument has always seemed unconvincing to me, but it is a subject of some interest and research, and this is not the place to look into it in detail.[7]

However one evaluates these arguments, it is clear that we have seen a world of very low or negative interest rates for many potential borrowers or nations, and it is reasonable to suppose, in Keynesian terms, that we have been living in a world where planned saving exceeds planned investment. This is a key feature of our starting point.

This last decade or so has also been a period where, in many countries, social cohesion has been under stress. Some manifestations, we could argue, were the election of Donald Trump as US president in November 2016, the Brexit vote in the UK in the summer of 2016, and the rise of populism in Turkey, eastern Europe, and Brazil.

This last decade has also seen a rise in international tensions and some moving away from internationalism, particularly under the Trump presidency. Nevertheless, it did see the Paris climate agreement of COP21 in 2015 and the adoption of the Sustainable Development Goals in June 2015. And President Biden has declared a strengthening of internationalism. At the same time, the relationship between the countries with the two biggest economies, the United States and China, is much more tense than a decade ago, and the countries with the two biggest populations, India and China, remain very wary of each other.

All these features were there and problematic before the COVID crisis broke over the world. The COVID pandemic has resulted in tragic human costs worldwide and profound disruptions to the world economy. Many poor countries face severe debt stress as a result of falls in demand, reductions in remittances, and capital flight. They have very little fiscal space to react in a countercyclical manner to a macroeconomic crisis of major proportions.

Of course, COVID is much more than an economic crisis. It has caused loss of life and damage to health of great proportions. It has deepened and widened social inequalities, it has taken many children out of school, and it has created mass unemployment, particularly for young people. Women and girls have been particularly badly affected.

---

[7] Bloom et al. (2020) have argued that the productivity of R&D has declined. They suggest that failure to make adequate investments in innovation is the cause of slowing TFP growth. So theirs is not a Gordon-type argument that this is inevitable, but instead a call to action for more R&D, and R&D in the "right direction" (i.e., green).

The COVID crisis, together with the difficult last decade, forms the starting point for public action. It has been and will be argued here that strong investment and innovation are at the core of a response to the climate crisis. And that investment is required across physical, human, natural, and social capital. Given our description of the difficulties of the starting point, investment and innovation in relation to these forms of capital will be necessary to drive the world out of the COVID crisis. It will be crucial for recovery to tackle both crises together, and with investment and innovation at center stage. Further, the response to both crises must be international. It is a global pandemic and the stress of debt and unemployment are global. The poorer countries are the most vulnerable in relation to both crises. And, climate is quintessentially a problem of a global public good. As I shall argue below, the returns to acting together in response to these world crises have never been greater.

5 Building Momentum; The Growth Story of the Twenty-First Century

Investment and innovation are shaped by expectations. Confidence and a clear sense of direction are crucial to creating the investments and innovation that will drive change, and these in turn boost confidence in the sense of direction.

The understanding that the future is low-carbon has been building strongly across the world—for nations, for communities, and for the private sector—over the last decade, and particularly since Paris COP21 in 2015. And, as I have emphasized, it is striking that this occurred notwithstanding Trump's US presidency of 2017–2020. This understanding has been reinforced by science, technological change, and the law. It has manifested itself in commitments by nations, provinces, cities, communities, and private sector firms, both financial and otherwise. It has been boosted by strong social pressures—in particular, by powerful and informed pressure from the young.

The science, as we argued above in Sections 1 and 2, has become ever more worrying, and the severe consequences of temperature increases above 1°C are already being experienced. The IPCC 1.5°C report of 2018 was a key moment in showing that there are powerful reasons in the science to strengthen our target from "well-below 2°C" to 1.5°C. This has been further underlined by the Sixth Assessment Review of the IPCC (August 2021) (IPCC 2021).

Further, it moved the notion of "net zero" to center stage. Earlier discussions had focused on 80 percent reductions in emissions from 1990 levels by 2050. Net zero is much clearer in relation to the science and can be embraced by all, including individual firms and cities. Indeed, it was remarkable under the 80 percent target how many groups thought they were in the 20 percent.

Technical change has been remarkable in the last decade. There has emerged a whole range of low-emission technologies that are already competitive with fossil-fuel-based technologies without subsidy or a carbon price. In 2020, solar and wind were the cheapest forms of new power generation in countries representing over 70 percent of GDP (Systemiq 2020). And capital costs for renewable electricity continue to fall much faster than those for conventional technologies. By 2030, low-carbon technologies and business models could be competitive in sectors representing over 70 percent of global emissions (today 25 percent) (Systemiq 2020), without carbon tax or subsidy. The pace of the advances we have seen in technology and reductions in cost has been much faster than expected. For example, in its World Energy Output (WEO) reports since 2001, the International Energy Agency (IEA) has consistently projected a much more gradual decline in the levelized cost of electricity from solar photovoltaic (PV) generation than has actually occurred (Ives et al. 2021). A similar gap can be seen between projections and reality for deployment of solar generating capacity (MIT Energy Initiative 2015). A comparable dynamic of rapid decreases in costs and corresponding, dramatic increases in production can be seen between lithium-ion battery prices and manufacture of electric cars (see Figure 13.2).

Commitment to net zero and demand for alignment with the Paris agreement have been associated with a big push worldwide to phase out coal, the most carbon intensive and polluting of fossil fuels. The competitive advantages, even without subsidy or carbon taxes, of round-the-clock (with storage) renewable power in so many parts of the world has led to a real Schumpeterian period of creative destruction. Not surprisingly, there has been strong pushback from vested interests in coal and other fossil fuels. And these are important social and political challenges in making the transition, which policy must manage. These are discussed further in Section 7 below.

The last few years have seen an increasing role for the law. In the UK the Supreme Court ruled in 2018 that government plans for reducing air pollution were too weak and outside the law (ClientEarth 2018). The German highest court ruled in April 2021 that the German government's pace of progress in reducing emissions was illegal, invoking its commitment to Paris

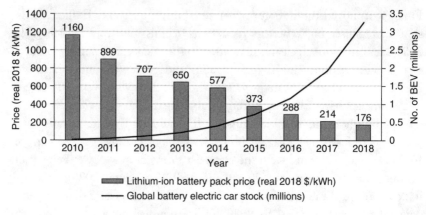

Data sources: Bloomberg NEF (2019); IEA (2020).

Figure 13.2. Lithium-ion battery prices and electric vehicle production

COP21 as part of the reason. In the Netherlands, The Hague District Court ruled that the pace of change of the major oil company, Shell, was too slow (Milieudefensie v. Royal Dutch Shell 2021). Shell was ordered to cut its global carbon emissions by 45 percent compared to 2019 levels by 2030, due to an "unwritten standard of care" that Shell owes to Dutch residents under the Dutch civil code (Grimmitt 2021).

On the finance side, some countries are moving to make mandatory the requirements of the Task Force on Climate-Related Financial Disclosure (TCFD).[8] The UK government has announced its intention to make TCFD-aligned disclosures mandatory across the economy by 2025, with a significant portion of mandatory requirements in place by 2023 (HM Treasury 2020). The TCFD sets out processes and data necessary to reveal climate risks in financial portfolios. The risks include physical risks, transition risks (changing relative prices, regulation, taxation, and so on), and legal risk. There are increasing pressures from shareholders for transition disclosure and risk assessment (Flammer et al. 2021).

Momentum is growing, too, from the understanding that the transition to net-zero emissions can be the growth story of the twenty-first century—full of discovery, innovation, investment, and new forms of growth. The problems of secular stagnation and COVID emphasize the role of new invest-

---

[8] See TCFD (2021) for an overview of the task force and its recommendations.

ment in the shorter term in boosting demand, and indeed, sharpening supply. The Schumpeterian period of innovation for the medium term has already begun. And there is no longer-run high-carbon growth story. It would destroy itself through the very hostile environment it would create.

The realization that this is the new growth story can boost investment and innovation and help create the political commitments necessary to foster and drive change. This does not mean that change is easy. There will be much disruption, dislocation, and opposition (see Section 7). But the rewards are potentially great, over and above the fundamental objective of managing the immense risks of climate change.

The outcome of these developments in expectations, science, law, finance, and understanding about growth possibilities has been a building of momentum. A net-zero commitment is now in place in 124 countries, representing 61 percent of global emissions (Black et al. 2021). Asset managers with $43 trillion in assets under management have committed to supporting the goal of net zero by 2050 or sooner, through the Net Zero Asset Managers initiative (Net Zero Asset Managers Initiative 2021). Of the 2,000 largest publicly traded companies, together representing sales of nearly $14 trillion (Black et al. 2021), 417 have committed to net zero, including Apple, AstraZeneca, Ford Motor Company, HeidelbergCement, Nestlé, and Repsol. Firms are recognizing that employing sustainable business practices need not undermine economic performance, but instead can enhance it (Clark et al. 2015).

It is not surprising that firms that behave more responsibly in relation to climate and the environment do better in relation to conventional measures of performance.[9] The willingness to take irresponsible risks on one dimension may be associated with irresponsible risk-taking on another. Responsible firms attract better employees. For example, Unilever, which has built an environment- and climate-friendly track record, gets around 2 million job applications a year. And we know, as university teachers, from our own students that they seek fulfilling and responsible work. Such firms also are likely to attract patient capital and constructive shareholders. Potential customers may choose to go elsewhere if they see irresponsible firm behavior.

Many players will be involved in carrying through this momentum and creating responses to the immense issues of COVID and climate; the private

---

[9] See Bassetti et al. (2021); Dechezleprêtre et al. (2019); and IEA, Centre for Climate Finance and Investment (2021).

sector, the multilateral development banks, international financial institutions, and the central banks all have crucial roles to play. Working together is of fundamental importance, perhaps now more than at any other time in history.

The returns on collaboration in current circumstances can be expressed in terms of four wins. The first is that we face high unemployment in many countries and we need to expand demand. Expanding demand across countries simultaneously has a much more powerful effect than expanding demand in just one country, because increasing demand in one country spills over to boost employment in others. Second, we have to reset expectations, not only for growth but also for a different kind of growth. If we reset those expectations together, then investors will know that the investments they are considering are of a kind that are going to be in harmony with the movement of demand around the world. A third win is that if there is a shared understanding of the direction of new technologies, then we will create increasing returns to scale in production and discovery. We have already seen that very powerfully in this section, in the way in which costs of solar and wind power have been driven down; the same is happening now with batteries, and electric vehicle costs are going to fall very quickly. The overall scale of technology deployment, achieved by acting together, can generate big returns. The fourth win comes from climate and biodiversity being global public goods. If we emit less greenhouse gas in one country, then all other countries gain from that drop in emissions: similarly protecting and regenerating biodiversity benefits us all.

Having emphasized the building of momentum, however, we must be very clear that the pace of change is nowhere near fast enough. That was evident in the numbers in Figure 13.1 above. The challenge now is to accelerate, but we must recognize that there is momentum that can be accelerated. The momentum feeds innovation, the innovation accelerates action, and momentum builds.

6 Investment and Innovation

6.1 Investment

The first part of this chapter (Sections 1–5) set out the imperative of rapid and fundamental change in our economies, if we are to reduce and manage effectively the immense risk of climate change. It was argued that we have in our hands the possibility of an attractive, new, and sustainable model of growth and development. But if we fail to act with urgency and at scale, the consequences in terms of a hostile climate and environment and loss of lives and livelihoods could be devastating.

Investment and innovation will be the core drivers of change. I examine the scale and nature of investment and innovation necessary in this section. In Section 7 I discuss the policies and actions that can draw through the investment and innovation, and comment briefly on the challenge of finance. Thus we ask what sort of creative destruction we seek and how to make it happen; policy for creative destruction with purpose and pace.

We begin by asking about the necessary scale of investment, drawing on the analysis in Stern (2021). Our overall estimate of the necessary increase in investment is of the order of 2 percentage points of GDP across the world, except for China, and a strong change in the composition of investment. China's investment rate is so high that it does not need to be increased, although the composition should move strongly toward sustainability. The numbers will vary across countries, depending on their circumstances and history of investment, with some emerging-market countries having larger requirements. It would not be correct to ascribe all, or even the majority, of this increased investment to the low-carbon transition. For emerging-market and developing countries, the investment expansion is in large measure to respond to their infrastructure needs at their current stage of development. For example, of India's power needs for 2050, only 20 percent now exists, and similarly for transportation and buildings. The challenge is to bring investment forward and to make it clean. For many rich countries, neglect has put pressure on finding the investment necessary to improve deteriorated infrastructure; this is an opportunity to look for new, cleaner, and more efficient approaches.

The 2 percentage point figure is constructed in Stern (2021) in three complementary (not additive) ways. First, in the context of the decade of faltering growth of investment (see Section 4), these are the kind of increments that could restore overall growth. Second, these figures represent the scale necessary to support the infrastructure investment just described. Third, an examination of the opportunities from new and sustainable technologies, particularly in the power sector, again, point to numbers in the region of 2 percentage points. For more detail, see Stern (2021).

I should note here that I have concentrated on physical capital, and that this is my focus in this chapter. But as I emphasized above, the new approach to growth requires investment in all of physical, human, natural, and social capital. I have discussed numbers in relation to physical capital. Natural capital is crucial, but the scale of the investment is not so large; on the other hand, there is a vital task in preventing wholescale destruction as well as the task of adding to natural capital. Human capital is a somewhat different story. The new forms of investment will need complementary skills. But the big numbers in human capital come from the investments necessary to meet the Sustainable Development Goals for health and education adopted in 2015 for 2030. These are vital investments but raise somewhat different issues. Much of the finance should come from public budgets, and this highlights the importance of domestic resource mobilization.

The investments I describe here, although in very broad terms, are generally investments with high potential returns across a range of outcomes (efficiency, productivity, environment, and so on) in addition to their role in reducing climate risks. And we live in a world, as I have described, where we have a deficiency of planned investment in relation to planned saving. Nevertheless, those investments must be translated from opportunities into real projects and programs. It is here that policy and finance are critical, as I discuss in Section 7.

The necessary investments apply across all geographies and sectors, but they will vary across these dimensions. For developing countries, new infrastructure investment is crucial for development. In richer countries, much of investment will be refurbishment.

Across sectors, the biggest numbers lie in the power sector (see Stern 2021). Emission reductions in other sectors depend crucially on expansion and creation of a net-zero power sector. The future of transport lies in electrification (including, possibly, hydrogen). Similarly, for heating and cooling. The Energy Transitions Commission (ETC) has estimated that, to achieve net zero, the capacity of the power sector must quadruple by 2050 and it should all be net zero by 2040 (see ETC 2021; also IEA 2021).

6.2 Innovation

Strong investment provides creative opportunities for innovation through new capital and new methods; correspondingly a period of weak investment may be less conducive to innovation. But the drive to net zero will require purposive change in the structure of investment toward sustainability across all investment. Thus, in thinking about creative destruction with a purpose, we must both examine innovation across the whole economy and examine the most critical areas for doing things differently. For all of this, pace is of the essence, and this is the case for the world as a whole. This is a challenge for the innovation that is required to decarbonize—which is, looking back, historically unprecedented and, looking forward, of vital significance to our future.

The most important sectors from the perspective of the drive to net zero are: energy, particularly power; transport; and land use. The use of energy and transport occurs in large measure in cities and towns, including in building them. Thus, the big systems at issue are energy, transport, cities, and land, all of which strongly overlap and interconnect.

Innovation will be necessary, too, in building in resilience to major climate change, which is now inevitable. That would include flood and drought resistance, protection against heavy storms, and so on. This is not my main focus in this chapter, but it is a critical part of the challenge of climate change and associated innovation in response. There are many areas where mitigation or emissions reductions, resilience or adaptation, and economic development can be combined with the right kind of investment and innovation. This includes protecting and investing in mangroves, public transport, systems of root intensification for rice, and decentralized solar, to give examples stretching across the whole economy. But there will be many areas where building in resilience does involve direct costs in targeting and strengthening investments, such as in flood barriers and early-warning systems for extreme weather events.

Innovation in systems is an area that has been under-studied in economics. It does appear in studies of economic history and, indeed, in the perspectives of Kondratieff (1925) and Schumpeter (1939), with their emphasis on waves of technological change across the whole economy, occurring with cycles of fifty years or so. For Schumpeter this was a key part of his overall story of innovation. The changes we must make now are on a scale perhaps still larger and faster than Kondratieff and Schumpeter discussed.

In changing systems, it should be clear that action must occur at many points, and we cannot rely on just one policy tool. Thus, for example, we can incentivize the production and purchase of electric vehicles, but at the same time we have to build out the charging infrastructure, which will involve cooperation across a number of areas of cities, energy, connectivity, retail, road, and building design. And we will have to expand and restructure electricity supply to respond to the scale, location, and timing of demand. There will be real challenges to policymaking at all levels—especially with regards to coherence, stability, and integration across the whole system. Policy will also need to foster change in public behavior in parallel with technical change.

Our systems of land use will have to change radically, as will patterns of food consumption. Past systems have led to land degradation, pollution of oceans, water, and air, and destruction of forests. Changing these will similarly involve complex and politically difficult changes. The details in each of these areas are beyond the scope of this chapter, but it should be clear that we will have to tackle the scale, nature, and complexity of such innovation together.

Information technology, artificial intelligence, and data management will play crucial roles in system change. This applies in all of the four systems described. There is some good fortune that great advance in these areas has come at the same time as the need to make fundamental change to tackle climate change. Putting all of this together will involve cooperation, integration, and creativity on a great scale and with some complexity.

The challenges of innovation apply both to the diffusion of existing technologies and to the planning and creation of new technologies. Much is known already about the technologies for renewable electricity and electric vehicles, although technological change is moving quickly and will continue to do so. Similarly for ground- and air-source heating and insulation for buildings. But there will be many obstacles to diffusion and rollout, and much of the encouragement of change and promotion of innovation will be in relation to overcoming some of these obstacles. These include charging facilities for electric vehicles and difficulties in organizing and financing insulation and new forms of heating in buildings. Suppliers, electricity companies, builders, local authorities, and financing facilities will all be involved. How well the details of all this can be managed, and the quality of cooperation, will largely determine the pace and success of the innovations crucial to drive to net zero.

Finally, in this section I should stress the importance of new technologies. Some sectors, such as steel, cement, air, and sea transport, are "hard-to-abate." Technologies for zero carbon are available already for all of these. In some areas, hydrogen (or ammonia) is likely to be important, as will carbon capture. But these technologies are currently expensive. Their costs are falling but new technologies and ways of doing things will be necessary. The work of the Energy Transitions Commission (including ETC 2018) has been very valuable in showing what can be done.

Strong investment in R&D will be crucial. There are technologies that the world as a whole will need, and both collaboration and competition in their development will play their role. A shared sense of direction across the world can also be a powerful factor in taking existing technologies to scale and demonstrating demand for new technologies.

Chris Freeman, an outstanding figure in the study of processes of innovation, and who was steeped in the Schumpeterian tradition, has emphasized the crucial importance of the institutional and value structures in an economy and society that can promote or discourage innovation. These include the incentive structures and organizations created by government and systems of finance and capital markets. A suite of mutually reinforcing policies, regulations, and investments are required to support innovation and its diffusion, taking into consideration all aspects of national innovation systems (Freeman 1987; Edler and Fagerberg 2017; Bloom et al. 2019; Stern and Valero 2021).

Policy will also be important in influencing the "demand side" of the amount and direction of innovation and investment. Changes in behaviors and preferences of consumers, workers, shareholders, and voters are key to driving change in business and policy decisions, and vice versa (Besley and Persson 2020; Aghion et al. 2020). Conversely, resistance or a lack of support from consumers, voters, and businesses (particularly larger firms with strong lobbying power) can be key barriers to change. Indeed, effective implementation of policies that encourage zero-carbon innovation and its diffusion will maximize the chances that clean innovation can benefit from its own path dependencies that will not only accelerate decarbonization but also bring costs down rapidly and help to neutralize resistance to change. And effective communication and participatory decision-making processes at the national and subnational levels will help ensure that the economic (and broader) benefits of decarbonization can be realized and shared, costs distributed fairly, and transitions actively managed (Stern and Valero 2021).

My discussion in this subsection has set out a vital research agenda for a new approach to innovation. It builds on the Schumpeterian tradition and the work of Philippe Aghion and Peter Howitt. It is a challenge that requires research and analysis from the best minds in our subject, and urgently. At the same time, we must make policy now. The tasks are fascinating, as well as of vital importance, and involve many strands of our subject, along with collaboration with other disciplines.

7 Policy for Investment and Innovation

7.1 Market failures, absences, and policy

The challenge is to create policy that can foster investment, innovation, and system and behavior change on the pace and scale necessary. The discussion in Section 6 showed that we will have to use a strong range of complementary mechanisms. Expectations will be crucial on the direction and pace of change, given the commitments that will be necessary by both private and public actors. Hence, institutional structures will be important as well as policy, and the credibility of both will matter. We need a public economics that is genuinely dynamic, involving learning and adjustment, and that can cover systemic change. It is "public economics as if time matters."[10]

There is a problem in the economics profession associated with an inability or unwillingness to move much beyond the static Pigouvian or twentieth-century approach to externalities in analyzing the challenges of climate change. Many discussions of policy suggest that "economic theory says" that policy should be overwhelmingly about a carbon price. A carbon price should indeed be at center stage, but we need so much more in terms of policy and perspectives, and understanding of the issues. However, we must be clear that the suggestion that "theory says" that the carbon price is the most effective route is mistaken for a number of reasons.

The first mistake is that there is a whole collection of market failures and market absences of great relevance beyond the greenhouse gas externality (see Table 13.2 below). The second is that under the temperature target or guardrail approach (see Section 1), the choice of carbon prices is focused on its role, in combination with other policies, in incentivizing paths that achieve the overall target (such as net-zero emissions by midcentury to fit with the temperature target) with as much economic advantage as possible. Such prices are not simply the marginal social cost as in Pigou (see the discussion of the Stern-Stiglitz Commission in Stern, Stiglitz et al. 2017). Third, where the risks of moving too slowly are potentially very large and there are increasing returns to scale and fixed costs in key industries, regulations can help reduce uncertainty and bring down costs (e.g., Weitzman 1974). Fourth,

---

[10] This was the subject of my piece in 2018 in honor of the late Tony Atkinson, an economist of outstanding distinction who had a deep interest in these issues and an extraordinary range of knowledge and skills in our subject and across the social sciences.

many consumers, producers, cities, and countries recognize the obligation to act, and are not blinkered, narrow optimizers with a view of utility focused only on their own consumption. Fifth, much of the challenge of action is how to promote collaboration and act together. This poses a whole set of important questions around institutions and actions for mutual support. This is an immense challenge concerning risk, values, dynamics, and collaboration, and the narrow Pigouvian model, useful though it is, is very far from the whole story.

The required investments, innovations, and change will in large measure be in the private sector, although direct public action, including in key areas of infrastructure, will also be important. Private decision-making is within market structures, and thus how they function will be critical. I begin, therefore, with a discussion of market failures, also of market absences. I will note failures of and limitations on governments as well. My focus is on market failures and absences in relation to innovation.

There are key market failures, central to the processes of investment, innovation, and change, beyond the crucial externality of greenhouse gas emissions. That externality must be the first on the list, but several more must be tackled if we are to create a strong, productive, attractive, effective, and efficient transition. In my view, six are of basic importance: five, in addition to the greenhouse gas externality. These further five are as follows. First, R&D is of special importance here because, as described in Section 6, we must bring through crucial new technologies. In addition to the usual arguments on R&D about the publicness of ideas, we should recognize that the risks of failure are immense, time is of the essence, and the use of the new emissions-reducing ideas itself is a public good.

Second, much of the investment and innovation will be new and will involve systemic change. Capital markets, at the best of times, have their problems in dealing with long-term complexities and large scale, and in this case those issues loom large.

Third, much of the action will take place within and in relation to networks. These include electricity grids, public transport, city structures, reuse and recycling/circular economy, ecosystems, and broadband. Networks, with their strong dependence on mechanisms of interaction, need public action and rules, and sometimes some public ownership, to function well.

Fourth, information will play a critical role in shaping action, and there are likely to be strong asymmetries and problems of moral hazard that require public action to improve the functioning of markets. For consumers it will be important to know the carbon content of the goods they are thinking of buying. Producers will have to understand their options and their supply chains. Investors and potential employees will want to know about the future plans of firms. Regulation in relation to information, and its transparency and reliability, will be of great importance.

Fifth, there is a huge set of issues around what is loosely called co-benefits. More than 8 million deaths across the world in 2018—around 15 percent of total deaths—were linked to air pollution associated with the burning of fossil fuels (Vohra et al. 2021), some of it indoors, some of it outdoors. The burning of fossil fuels is the major source of air pollution, severe damage to ecosystems and biodiversity, and deterioration in water quality and pollution of the oceans.

Different market failures require different policy actions, and many of the market failures interact. Given these interactions, and in the presence of path dependencies in the production, deployment, and diffusion of innovation (Aghion et al. 2014), it is crucial to create an integrated set of policies that together can tackle market failures in a coordinated way, and rapidly shift economies onto a clean innovation path that can benefit from its own patterns of path dependence.

The tackling of some of the problems, including the greenhouse gas externality, should include the right kind of price incentives, and carbon taxes are at the core of policy action. A key insight from the literature on directed technical change (Acemoglu et al. 2012) is that sound policy consists of both carbon taxes and other levers, such as subsidies to "clean" R&D. Regulation and standards will also be important. Regulating out the very wasteful incandescent lightbulbs quickly brought through the far superior LED, and scale brought down costs. Similarly for unleaded petrol. Clear dates beyond which internal combustion engine vehicles cannot be sold are likely to have similar effects. This use of regulation and standards is not necessarily inferior to carbon price, and generally both should be part of a package of policies. We live in a world with strong uncertainties and increasing returns to scale. In this case the clarity that regulation can bring can enable rapid movement to scale and exploit efficiency via economies of scale, when prices alone many not have a strong or clear enough effect. Thus, it is not true that "economics says that the use of prices is more efficient than other tools." That is to appeal to the simplest of economics with complete markets, full information, and diminishing returns to scale, which is not the world we live in.

Table 13.2. Six market imperfections relevant for tackling climate change

Market failure	Description	Policy options
Greenhouse gasses (GHGs)	Negative externality because of the damage that emissions inflict on others	Carbon tax/cap-and-trade/regulation of GHG emissions (standards)
Research, development, and deployment (RD&D)	Supporting innovation and dissemination	Tax breaks, support for demonstration/deployment, publicly funded research
Imperfection in risk/capital markets	Imperfect information assessment of risks; understanding of new projects/technologies	Risk sharing/reduction through guarantees, long-term contracts; convening power for co-financing
Networks	Coordination of multiple supporting networks and systems	Investment in infrastructure to support integration of new technologies in electricity grids, public transport, broadband, recycling; planning of cities
Information	Lack of awareness of technologies, actions, or support	Labeling and information requirements on cars, domestic appliances, products more generally; awareness of options
Co-benefits	Consideration of benefits beyond market rewards	Valuing ecosystems and biodiversity, recognizing impacts on health

Table 13.2 summarizes some key market failures and possible policy actions.

Further, some key markets are absent—for example, long-term carbon markets and markets for new technologies that are yet to be invented. A competitive equilibrium with absent markets is not necessarily efficient. In the context of absent markets, expectations are crucial to investment and innovation. A clear sense of direction, such as from international agreements and the rulings of courts, can be helpful here. Also helpful are structures such as the Climate Change Committee in the UK, established in 2008, which sets out carbon budgets and targets up to fifteen years ahead. This is not the place for detailed discussion—there is a little more on institutions in Section 7.2.

7.2 Institutions and behavior

The remainder of this section raises three broad and important issues for investment and innovation in response to climate change, which cannot pass without emphasis but for which space precludes treatment in any detail.

Credibility is crucial to long-term investment. Government-induced policy risk can be a great deterrent (for a recent empirical study in relation to climate, see Stroebel and Wurgler 2021). Institutional structures can be valuable in embodying the "predictable flexibility" that we need. We cannot set policies in stone, as there is much learning to do, and we must design to learn. At the same time, for investor confidence and as much clarity as possible for innovators, the criteria for policy change should be clear. For example, support for the use of a new technology could be phased out as diffusion occurs and costs fall; these criteria could be set out in advance.

Behaviors of individuals can be conservative, particularly in the face of real and perceived costs of change. Important examples are in home heating and insulation, diet, and a switch to electric vehicles. Helping with understanding of possibilities, with organizing, with costs of change, and with finance will be important strands of public policy.

The economics of institutions and behavior have advanced greatly in the last few decades in economics. They will form a vital part of the economics of climate change, including and particularly in relation to innovation.

7.3 Finance

There is much to be said on finance in relation to innovation and investment. The challenge is to identify the broad thrust, though not all details, of necessary investment and innovation, policies to draw it through, and how to get finance on the right scale, of the right kind, at the right time in place. Even though we currently live in a world where planned investment is deficient in relation to planned saving, that does not mean that the necessary kind of finance is available, particularly at affordable cost.

The management, reduction, and allocation of risk is at center stage of finance. With infrastructure investment and innovation of crucial importance here, development banking will have a vital role to play. These ideas are pursued in, for example, Stern (2015) and Bhattacharya et al. (2016, 2018, 2022).

The bulk of economic growth and infrastructure investment in the coming two or three decades will be in emerging-market and developing countries, in pursuit of development, resilience, and sustainability. These investments will depend on good policies to incentivize investments that manage revenue streams and risk, and on the right kind of finance to reduce and share risk. Much of the investment and finance will be in the private sector, but public international capital flows at reasonably low cost of capital will be crucial. The multilateral development banks and development finance institutions must be center stage and strongly supported by bilateral flows (see, e.g., Bhattacharya et al. 2022).

7.4 Managing change

Radical change, at scale and at pace, involves disruption and dislocation. Consumers will face changes in relative prices. Workers in some industries, such as coal mining or supplying components for internal combustion engines, will see their jobs disappear. Some locations will be strongly affected.

Managing this type of change is often described as offering a "just transition." Where work is lost, it will be important to invest in people and places, to support retraining, and make accessible the great new opportunities that will flow. Some public services that are mobile (such as social security administration) can be relocated to areas badly affected.

For consumers who see price rises or challenges in accessing new technologies, there should be direct support. Some of this could be by allocating some part of carbon tax revenues to poorer groups. Some people—for instance, those living in apartments—will find it more difficult to access electric vehicle charging than richer people living in houses with driveways and garages. Poorer groups may find it more difficult to replace gas boilers with more efficient heat sources. Tackling these distributional issues will be central to a successful transition.

Again, this is not the place to go into these policies in detail, but just to note their importance and that substantial analytical work has taken place and is under way (Burke et al. 2020; Krawchenko and Gordon 2021).

8 A New Story of Development and Growth in the Tradition of Schumpeter, Aghion, and Howitt

In this chapter I have described the imperative of a rapid and strong transition to net-zero emissions if we are to secure a viable future for lives and livelihoods on the planet. We have also seen that this transition to net-zero emissions can be the driver of a new, more efficient, less polluted, more inclusive, and altogether more attractive form of growth. And I have examined public policies and actions that can deliver these new paths, particularly via fostering innovation and investment. We will need new growth perspectives and models, firmly in the tradition of Schumpeter, Chris Freeman, and Aghion-Howitt (Schumpeter 1942; Cole et al. 1973; Aghion and Howitt 2009).

No one model can carry the set of issues I have described in this chapter. We will need a set of models—some focused on particular issues, some overarching, some qualitative, others firmly quantitative. The models will have to, between them and together, embody risk, nonlinearities, instabilities, increasing returns to scale, processes of learning, emergence of new technologies, innovation, complex systems, institutions and behavior, distribution, and relations between richer and poorer communities and countries. We will need all branches of our subject and collaboration with other disciplines.

We will need a special focus on pace and scale. This is not a model where we can set a direction and hope it plays through satisfactorily. We know we have to get to net-zero emissions by 2050 and we have to create and concentrate on paths that can take us there. And we know that even though we already have many of the technologies, there are others that we must both discover and take to scale quickly. We have seen that setting the direction and giving social priority has delivered rapid discovery and cost reductions, even on the back of fairly weak policies. Much faster change is surely possible with still greater clarity and collaboration on direction and much stronger policy.

All of this is in the tradition of Schumpeter, Freeman, Aghion, and Howitt, and must build on their great work. It is a fascinating agenda as well as vitally important. But time is not on our side. We must research and act at the same time.

References

Acemoglu, D., Aghion, P., Bursztyn, L., and Hémous, D. (2012). The environment and directed technical change. *American Economic Review*, 102(1), 131–166.

Aghion, P., Antonin, C., Bunel, S. (2021). *The power of creative destruction: Economic upheaval and the wealth of nations*. Cambridge, MA: Harvard University Press.

Aghion, P., Bénabou, R., Martin, R., and Roulet, A. (2020). Environmental preferences and technological choices: Is market competition clean or dirty? NBER Working Paper 26921.

Aghion, P., Dechezleprêtre, A., Hémous, D., Martin, R., and Van Reenen, J. (2016). Carbon taxes, path dependency, and directed technical change: Evidence from the auto industry. *Journal of Political Economy*, 124, 1–51.

Aghion, P., Hepburn, C., Teytelboym, A., and Zenghelis, D. (2014). Path dependence, innovation and the economics of climate change. The New Climate Economy Working Paper. https://newclimateeconomy.report/workingpapers/workingpaper/path-dependence-innovation-and-the-economics-of-climate-change-2/.

Aghion, P., and Howitt, P. (1998). *Endogenous growth theory*. Cambridge, MA: MIT Press.

Aghion, P., and Howitt, P. (2009). *The economics of growth*. Cambridge, MA: MIT Press.

Bassetti, T., Blasi, S., and Sedita, S. R. (2021). The management of sustainable development: A longitudinal analysis of the effects of environmental performance on economic performance. *Business Strategy and the Environment*, 30, 21–37.

Besley, T., and Persson, T. (2020). Escaping the climate trap? Values, technologies, and politics. Unpublished paper.

Bhattacharya, A., Kharas, H., Plant, M., and Prizzon, A. (2018). The new global agenda and the future of the multilateral development bank system. Brookings Institution.

Bhattacharya, A., Meltzer, J., Oppenheim, J., Qureshi, M.Z., and Stern, N. (2016). Delivering on sustainable infrastructure for better development and better climate. Brookings Institution.

Bhattacharya, A., et al. (2022). Financing a big investment push in emerging markets and developing countries for sustainable, resilient and inclusive recovery and growth. Grantham Research Institute on Climate Change and the Environment, London School of Economics and Political Science, and Brookings Institution.

Black, R., Cullen, K., Fay, B., Hale, T., Lang, J., Mahmood, S., and Smith, S. M. (2021). Taking stock: A global assessment of net zero targets. Energy & Climate Intelligence Unit and Oxford Net Zero.

Bloom, N., Jones, C., Webb, M., and Van Reenen, J. (2020). Are ideas becoming harder to find? *American Economic Review*, 110(4), 1104–1144.

Bloom, N., Van Reenen, J., and Williams, H. (2019). A toolkit of policies to promote innovation. *Journal of Economic Perspectives*, 33(3), 163–184.

Bloomberg NEF (2018). New energy outlook. https://www.csis.org/events/bnefs-new-energy-outlook-2018.

Burke, J., Fankhauser, S., Kazaglis, A., Kessler, L., Khandelwal, N., Bolk, J., O'Boyle, P., and Owen, A. (2020). Distributional impacts of a carbon tax in the UK. Grantham Research Institute on Climate Change and the Environment, and Centre for Climate Change Economics and Policy, London School of Economics and Political Science, and Vivid Economics.

Clark, G. L., Feiner, A., and Viehs, M. (2015). From the stockholder to the stakeholder: How sustainability can drive financial outperformance. SSRN Paper No. 2508281.

ClientEarth (2018). High court ruling on remedies, ClientEarth (no3) vs SSEFRA—Liberty to apply and air pollution plans. https://www.clientearth.org/latest/documents/high-court-ruling-on-remedies-clientearth-no3-vs-ssefra-liberty-to-apply-and-air-pollution-plans/.

Cole, H.S.D., Freeman, C., Jahoda, M., and Pavitt, K.L.R. (eds.) (1973). *Thinking about the future: A critique of "The Limits to Growth."* London: Chatto & Windus for Sussex University Press.

Dasgupta, P. (2021). *The economics of biodiversity: The Dasgupta review.* London: HM Treasury.

Dechezleprêtre, A., Koźluk, T., Kruse, T., Nachtigall, D., and de Serres, A. (2019). Do environmental and economic performance go together? A review of micro-level empirical evidence from the past decade or so. *International Review of Environmental and Resource Economics*, 13(1–2), 1–118.

Dosio, A., Mentaschi, L., Fischer, E. M., and Wyser, K. (2018). Extreme heat waves under 1.5°C and 2°C global warming. *Environmental Research Letters*, 13(5), 054006.

Dumitru, O. A., Austermann, J., Polyak, V. J., et al. (2019). Constraints on global mean sea level during Pliocene warmth. *Nature*, 574, 233–236.

Edler, J., and Fagerberg, J. (2017). Innovation policy: What, why, and how. *Oxford Review of Economic Policy*, 33(1), 2–23.

Energy Transitions Commission (2018). Mission possible: Reaching net-zero carbon emissions from harder-to-abate sectors. https://www.energy-transitions.org/publications/mission-possible/#download-form.

Energy Transitions Commission (2021). Making clean electrification possible: 30 years to electrify the global economy. https://www.energy-transitions.org/publications/making-clean-electricity-possible/

Ferris, E. (2020). Research on climate change and migration: Where are we and where are we going? *Migration Studies*, 8(4), 612–625.

Flammer, C., Toffel, M. W., and Viswanathan, K. (2021). Shareholders are pressing for climate risk disclosures: That's good for everyone. *Harvard*

Business Review. https://hbr.org/2021/04/shareholders-are-pressing-for
-climate-risk-disclosures-thats-good-for-everyone.

Food and Land Use Coalition (2019). Growing better: Ten critical transitions to
transform food and land use. https://www.foodandlandusecoalition.org/wp
-content/uploads/2019/09/FOLU-GrowingBetter-GlobalReport.pdf.

Freeman, C. (1987). *Technology policy and economic performance: Lesson from Japan.*
London: Pinter.

Gordon, R. J. (2012). Is US economic growth over? Faltering innovation confronts
the six headwinds. Centre for Economic Policy Research Policy Insight
No.63.

Grimmitt, M. (2021). Dutch court orders Shell to speed up emissions cuts.
Pinsent Masons, Out-law News, May 28. https://www.pinsentmasons.com
/out-law/news/dutch-court-orders-shell-to-speed-up-emissions-cuts.

HM Treasury (2020). Interim report of the UK's joint government-regulator
TCFD taskforce. https://www.gov.uk/government/publications/uk-joint
-regulator-and-government-tcfd-taskforce-interim-report-and-roadmap.

Intergovernmental Panel on Climate Change (IPCC) (2018). *Global warming of
1.5°C,* ed. V. Masson-Delmotte et al. https://www.ipcc.ch/sr15/.

Intergovernmental Panel on Climate Change (IPCC) (2021). *Climate change 2021:
The physical science basis.* Contribution of Working Group I to the IPCC Sixth
Assessment Report. https://www.ipcc.ch/report/ar6/wg1/.

International Energy Agency (IEA) and Centre for Climate Finance and
Investment (2021a). Clean energy investing: Global comparison of investment
returns. https://www.iea.org/reports/clean-energy-investing-global
-comparison-of-investment-returns.

International Energy Agency (IEA) (2021b). Net zero by 2050: A roadmap for the
global energy sector. https://www.iea.org/reports/net-zero-by-2050.

Ives, M. C., Righetti, L., Schiele, J., De Meyer, K., Hubble-Rose, L., Teng, F.,
Kruitwagen, L., Tillmann-Morris, L., Wang, T., Way, R., and Hepburn, C.
(2021). *A new perspective on decarbonising the global energy system.* Smith
School of Enterprise and the Environment, University of Oxford, Report
No. 21-04.

Kang, S., and Eltahir, E.A.B. (2018). North China Plain threatened by deadly
heatwaves due to climate change and irrigation. *Nature Communications,* 9,
2894.

Kondratieff, N. (1925). The major economic cycles. *Voprosy kon'iunktury,* 1,
28–79.

Krawchenko, T. A., and Gordon, M. (2021). How do we manage a just transition?
A comparative review of national and regional just transition initiatives.
Sustainability, 13, 6070.

Milieudefensie v. Royal Dutch Shell (2021). Hague District Court, judgment of
May 26, 2021. C/09/571932/HA ZA 19-379 (English version).
ECLI:NL:RBDHA:2021:5337. https://uitspraken.rechtspraak.nl
/inziendocument?id=ECLI:NL:RBDHA:2021:5337.

MIT Energy Initiative (2015). "The future of solar energy: An interdisciplinary MIT study." Massachusetts Institute of Technology. https://energy.mit.edu /publication/future-solar-energy/.

Mokyr, J., Vickers, C., and Ziebarth, N. L. (2015). The history of technological anxiety and the future of economic growth: Is this time different? *Journal of Economic Perspectives,* 29(3), 31–50.

Net Zero Asset Managers Initiative (2021). Net Zero Asset Managers initiative announces 41 new signatories, with sector seeing "net zero tipping point," July 6. https://www.netzeroassetmanagers.org/net-zero-asset-managers -initiative-announces-41-new-signatories-with-sector-seeing-net-zero-tipping -point.

New Climate Economy (2016). The sustainable infrastructure imperative. http://newclimateeconomy.report/2016/the-sustainable-infrastructure -opportunity/.

Nordhaus, W. (1991). To slow or not to slow: The economics of the greenhouse effect. *Economic Journal,* 101(407), 920–937.

Schumpeter, J. A. (1939). *Business cycles: A theoretical, historical, and statistical analysis of the capitalist process.* New York: McGraw-Hill Book Co.

Schumpeter, J. A. (1942). *Capitalism, socialism and democracy.* New York: Harper and Brothers.

Stern, N. (2015). *Why are we waiting? The logic, urgency and promise of tackling climate change.* Cambridge, MA: MIT Press.

Stern, N. (2018). Public economics as if time matters: Climate change and the dynamics of policy. *Journal of Public Economics,* 162, 4–17.

Stern, N. (2021). G7 leadership for sustainable resilient and inclusive economic recovery and growth. LSE and Grantham Research Institute Policy Publication, June 7.

Stern, N., Stiglitz, J. E., et al. (2017). Report of the high-level commission on carbon prices. Carbon Pricing Leadership Coalition.

Stern, N., and Valero, A. (2021). Innovation, growth and the transition to net-zero emissions. Chris Freeman Special Issue, *Research Policy,* 50(9).

Stroebel, J., and Wurgler, J. A. (2021). What do you think about climate finance? NBER Working Paper No. 29136.

Summers, L. H. (2020). Accepting the reality of secular stagnation: New approaches are needed to deal with sluggish growth, low interest rates, and an absence of inflation. *Finance & Development,* 57(1).

Systemiq (2020). The Paris effect: How the climate agreement is reshaping the global economy. https://www.systemiq.earth/wp-content/uploads/2020/12 /The-Paris-Effect_SYSTEMIQ_Full-Report_December-2020.pdf.

TCFD (2021). Task Force on Climate-related Financial Disclosures: Overview. https://assets.bbhub.io/company/sites/60/2020/10/TCFD_Booklet_FNL _Digital_March-2020.pdf.

UNEP (UN Environment Program) (2020). *Emissions gap report 2020.* https://www.unep.org/emissions-gap-report-2020.

UN Habitat (2021). Climate Change. https://unhabitat.org/topic/climate-change.

Vohra, K., Vodonos, A., Schwartz, J., Marais, E. A., Sulprizio, M. P., and Mickley, L. J. (2021). Global mortality from outdoor fine particle pollution generated by fossil fuel combustion: Results from GEOS-Chem. *Environmental Research*, 195, 110754.

Warren, R., Price J., and Vanderwal, J. *Science*, 360(6390), 791–795.

Weitzman, M. L. (1974). Prices vs. quantities. *Review of Economic Studies*, 41(4), 477–491.

CHAPTER 14

Science as Civil Society

Implications for a Green Transition

TIMOTHY BESLEY *and* TORSTEN PERSSON

> If facts are the seeds that later produce knowledge and wisdom, then the emotions . . . are the fertile soil in which the seeds must grow.
>
> —Rachel Carson (biologist and writer) in *The Sense of Wonder*

> What you do makes a difference, and you have to decide what kind of difference you want to make.
>
> —Jane Goodall (primatologist and activist)

1 Introduction

In their classic paper (1992), Aghion and Howitt studied the profit motive as a driver of innovation as firms seek a competitive edge. Important as this material driver is, Aghion et al. (2008) emphasize that scientists themselves are often intrinsically motivated. Intrinsic motives may be particularly relevant when the future of the planet is at stake—the innovation process for climate-friendly green goods will likely play a key role in any green transition. In this chapter we present a canonical model of innovation where the motives of scientists matter for the innovation process and—as in Acemoglu et al. (2012) and Aghion et al. (2016, 2019)—there is scope for innovation in both green and brown sectors.

Scientists and their values. In our approach, scientists form a part of civil society. Organizations like the National Academy of Sciences, the Royal Society, and the Royal Swedish Academy of Sciences project views and values that sometimes clash with political authority. Well-known personal examples of such activism in the pollution sphere were set by scientists Rachel Carson and Jane Goodall. They were two of the first to alert the world to ugly pollution and biodynamics more than half a century ago.

Reflecting this kind of engagement, the average scientist does indeed care more about the environment than the public at large. This is illustrated in Figure 14.1, which shows responses to the proposition "It is important to care for the environment" from almost 416,000 participants in several waves of the European Social Survey.[1] The figure shows the difference in shares for each answer between "scientists" and all others, when we adjust for country and survey year. Clearly, the distribution of responses among scientists is shifted to the right relative to that of others—an observation that we take as motivation for our model.[2]

Our model and its antecedents. But even if scientists care about the environment, their actions must make a collective difference to have a societal impact. In our model, we suppose that the psychic payoffs they get from contributing actively to a better world make scientists willing to work for a lower wage in green firms, or demand a wage premium to work in brown firms. This mechanism translates into different innovation costs across sectors and spurs innovation toward a greener future.

---

[1] The ESS respondents in each wave are selected as a representative sample in each of thirty-five European countries. The question on environmental values appeared in all the nine available waves of the survey (every second year between 2002 and 2018). Based on the rich background information about respondents, we classify a particular respondent as a "scientist" whenever she is employed in a STEM profession, according to some thirty occupational (ISCO) codes.

[2] The figure shows the differences in the raw data, but they are more or less exactly the same when we control for country and wave fixed effects. They also hold up when we control for basic demographics (gender and cohort), education, and (household) income. Moreover, similar differences apply if we consider the responses to "Science can solve environmental problems," "It is important to think creatively and have new ideas," and "I am interested in politics" (but not to "I vote for a green party").

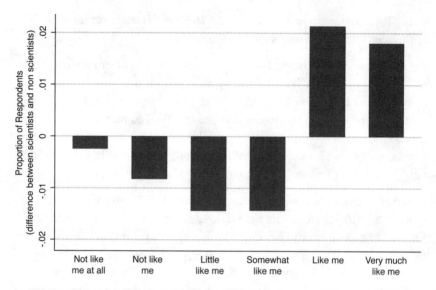

Figure 14.1. Important to care for the environment

But science can be more powerful still, if it encourages consumers to go green. In our model, we use an approach developed in Besley and Persson (2019, 2023). A similar mechanism has been studied by Bezin (2015, 2019). The key idea is that more citizens will change their lifestyle as the quality of goods available for green consumers improves. To see how this might work, consider the decision to drive an electric—rather than a conventional—vehicle. Our approach implies that more people are willing to switch when charging speeds and driving ranges of electric cars are improved. But this requires innovation to target better battery technologies instead of better internal combustion engines. In our simple model, socialization from (cultural or biological) parents decides the future share of green consumers—the socialization process is based on future expected utility, which includes expectations about future technology.

Seen from the other side, when producers / innovators expect more people to change their lifestyle, the expected market share for green (brown) goods goes up (down). This, in turn, increases (reduces) the relative profitability of innovation in green (brown) goods. In the previous paragraph's example, it becomes more profitable to improve battery technologies than combustion engines. While our model—as Bezin's—is about final goods, this mechanism is like the market-size effect on innovation in the existing work on directed innovation in clean versus dirty intermediate goods (Acemoglu et al. 2012; Aghion et al. 2016; Acemoglu et al. 2016).[3]

Together, the green-technology-driven socialization and the green-market-share effect on innovation give rise to a dynamic complementarity. In this setting, science's role in encouraging innovation contributes to more than a technology dynamic; it can also help change the course of society.

Outline of this chapter. This chapter is organized as follows. In Section 2 we lay out a core model where households consume green and brown goods. These are produced by ranges of monopolistically competitive firms that can also invest in innovation to improve product quality. We show how motivation to work in green innovation affects the path of the economy. In Section 3 we extend the model to make the proportions of green and brown consumers endogenous through socialization. Complementarities between jointly evolving culture and technology imply that certain shifts can make society cross a critical juncture where a brown-to-green transition occurs. Science influences this process alongside its influence on technology. Section 4 offers some concluding comments.

2 Core Model

The model—and a number of extensions of it—are fully developed in Besley and Persson (2023), to which the reader is referred for details. We consider two sets of monopolistically competitive firms: one producing varieties of *brown* (polluting) goods, another producing varieties of *green* (nonpolluting) goods. Consumers are of two types with different values (preference maps): green types (environmentalists) chiefly consume green goods, and brown types (materialists) chiefly consume brown goods.

---

[3] Acemoglu and Linn (2004) provide early empirical evidence that a higher expected market share indeed raises innovation (and entry) in the pharmaceutical industry.

Consumers. Each citizen has an exogenous endowment ε of a numeraire good, the consumption of which is x. The numeraire can be transformed into two kinds of goods. A continuum of green goods is indexed by $i \in [0, 1]$, with the quantity, quality, and price on green variety i being $\{y(i), q(i), p(i)\}$. Similarly, a continuum of brown goods is indexed by $j \in [0, 1]$, with a corresponding triple $\{Y(j), Q(j), P(j)\}$. We focus on a case with symmetry within sectors where all brown firms face the same parameters as do all green firms. All firms in a sector thus take the same actions.

A unit mass of citizens/consumers is divided into green, $\tau = 1$, and brown, $\tau = 0$, with μ being the fraction of green. The two consumer types vary according to their consumption values, with green (brown) only valuing green (brown) goods. Preferences are

$$U = x + \frac{1}{1-\sigma}\left(\int_0^1 q(i)^\sigma y(i)^{1-\sigma}\, di\right)^\tau \left(\int_0^1 Q(j)^\sigma Y(j)^{1-\sigma}\, dj\right)^{1-\tau}$$
$$- \theta\tau\int_0^1 \bar{Y}(j)dj \tag{1}$$

with $\sigma < 1$.[4] The last term in (1) represents concerns about the pollution of brown goods, which is related to their aggregate (average) consumption $\bar{Y}$. Thus, we assume that only the green consumers care about the environment.[5] The common budget constraint is

$$R \geq x + \int_0^1 P(j)Y(j)dj + \int_0^1 p(i)y(i)di, \tag{2}$$

where R includes profits, wages (of scientists), and an endowment of the numeraire good.

Maximizing (1) subject to (2), we find that brown (green) consumers buy only brown (green) goods, with the resulting demand functions given by

$$Y = QP^{-\frac{1}{\sigma}} \text{ and } y = qp^{-\frac{1}{\sigma}}. \tag{3}$$

Firms, pricing, and profits. We suppose that each green and brown variety is produced by a monopolist at the same marginal cost χ. Firms care only

---

[4] A simple extension, which would produce qualitatively similar results, would suppose that all consumers have Cobb-Douglas preferences over the two types of goods, with a higher weight on green goods among green consumers. Formally, a weight γ_τ would replace τ in (1), with $\gamma_1 > \gamma_0$.

[5] Again, a difference across consumer types with the green having larger costs than the brown of pollution would do.

about their own profit and are infinitely-lived, run by successive generations of managers, who maximize long-run profits. Firms' profits are distributed to their shareholders (consumers) on an equal per capita basis.

Taking the demand function and marginal cost into account, profits for a typical green-variety firm is $\mu[q^\sigma y^{1-\sigma} - xy]$, whereas that for a brown-variety firm is $(1-\mu)[Q^\sigma Y^{1-\sigma} - \chi Y]$. Profit-maximizing prices have a constant markup over marginal cost:

$$p = P = \frac{\chi}{(1-\sigma)}.$$

Profits per firm are therefore given by

$$\pi(q) = \mu q k \text{ and } \Pi(Q) = (1-\mu)Q_k, \tag{4}$$

where $\kappa = \sigma[\chi/(1-\sigma)]^{1-\frac{1}{\sigma}}$. These profits are scaled by $1-\mu$ and μ, as the market size for each variety of green and brown goods reflects the share of green and brown consumers, respectively.

Innovation. Any existing brown (green) firm can improve the quality of its variety by hiring $N(n)$ inventors/scientists, as in Krusell (1998).[6] The collective action of scientists can work via market allocation if scientists who care about pollution may be more attracted to green sectors.[7] A fraction Ω of the population can train to become inventors/scientists at some (psychic) cost. This cost is w (W) in a green (brown) firm.

We suppose that scientists are part of civil society and are "motivated agents," in the language of Besley and Ghatak (2005). Their willingness to train as scientists is higher if they obtain a green-sector rather than a brown-sector innovation job. Consequently, the psychic costs fulfill $W > w$.

By recruiting scientists, the firm raises its (next-period) product quality to

$$q\left[1 + \left(\frac{n}{q}\right)^\varphi\right] \text{ and } Q\left[1 + \left(\frac{N}{Q}\right)^\varphi\right] \tag{5}$$

---

[6] In his model—unlike this one—inventors work on improving intermediate goods that serve as inputs to produce (a single form of) final goods.

[7] https://www.bloomberg.com/news/articles/2019-08-01/the-oil-industry-s-talent-pipeline -slows-to-a-trickle reports that fossil fuel companies are now having increasing difficulties in attracting new graduates.

because $\varphi < 1$, inventive activity has decreasing returns. The innovation model will allow us to study the growth of technologies in response to changes in environmental values and policy over time. We focus on the case where $(1 - \mu) \int_0^1 N dj + \mu \int_0^1 n di < \Omega$, so the (latent) supply of scientists is ample enough that all of them agree to work for a wage that just compensates for their training cost.

Euler equations and equilibrium growth. Time is infinite, discrete, and indexed by s. The quality levels in each sector are state variables that evolve over time and are indexed by s. Qualities are determined by firms' investments in innovation, which are chosen to maximize the expected discounted sum of profits, using a discount factor denoted by β. We can write the value functions associated with this problem as

$$\tilde{\pi}(q) = \arg \max_{n \geq 0} \left\{ \pi(q) - \omega n + \beta \tilde{\pi} \left(q \left(1 + \left(\frac{n}{q} \right)^\varphi \right) \right) \right\}$$

$$\tilde{\Pi}(Q) = \arg \max_{N \geq 0} \left\{ \Pi(Q)(1 - \mu) - \omega N + \beta \tilde{\pi} \left(Q \left(1 + \left(\frac{N}{Q} \right)^\varphi \right) \right) \right\}.$$

The Euler equations associated with optimal green and brown innovation are

$$\left(\frac{n}{q} \right)^{\varphi - 1} \beta \varphi \sigma \kappa \mu = w \quad \text{and} \quad \left(\frac{N}{Q} \right)^{\varphi - 1} \beta \varphi \sigma \kappa (1 - \mu) = W. \tag{6}$$

Firms thus hire scientists until their expected marginal gain in future profits equals their marginal cost. Having motivated scientists acts much like a subsidy to green innovation and a tax on brown innovation.

The equilibrium growth rates of green and brown product qualities are:

$$\hat{g} = \left[\frac{\beta \varphi \sigma \kappa \mu}{w} \right]^{\frac{\varphi}{1 - \varphi}} \quad \text{and} \quad \hat{G} = \left[\frac{\beta \varphi \sigma \kappa (1 - \mu)}{W} \right]^{\frac{\varphi}{1 - \varphi}}. \tag{7}$$

These depend on the size of the markets for green and brown goods as determined by μ and $(1 - \mu)$, and on the strength of scientists' intrinsic motivations as reflected in W and w. This is the market-size effect in innovation, familiar from the endogenous-growth literature, which we discussed in the introduction.

Green versus brown growth. Scientists in our model act atomistically, but in a value-driven way. Collectively, their values do affect the future path of the economy by encouraging green innovation and discouraging brown innovation. As demand for each variety is increasing in quality, the quality implications mean that brown consumption will not grow as fast as green consumption over time. To see this, note that we can write the relative growth rates as

$$\frac{\hat{g}}{\hat{G}} = \frac{q}{Q} \cdot \left[\frac{\mu}{(1-\mu)} \cdot \frac{W}{w} \right]^{\frac{\varphi}{1-\varphi}}, \tag{8}$$

an expression that is increasing q/Q, W/w, and $\mu(1-\mu)$. These properties illustrate how a society with more motivated scientists experiences greener growth, as does one with a larger share of green consumers or with a higher relative quality of green goods. Market activities thus respond to the values of those who consume and produce the fruits of innovation.

3 Cultural Dynamics

One key feature of the green transition is changing values toward green consumption. However, so far we have taken the share of green consumers—i.e., the value of μ—as fixed. We now use the model of Besley and Persson (2019, 2023) to explore what happens if this share is subject to cultural change. Suppose, therefore, that $\mu \in [0, 1]$ is time dependent, with dynamics determined by a socialization process.

The timing in each period s is as follows:

1. The economy begins current qualities of all green (brown) firms at q_s (Q_s), and a current fraction of green (brown) consumers $\mu_s (1-\mu_s)$.

2. Current production (prices) and consumption maximizes current profits and consumer utility.

3. Parents socialize their children, such that the future fraction of green consumers μ_{s+1} reflects the future "relative fitness" of holding green versus brown values $\Delta (\mu_{s+1})$.

4. To innovate, firms contract with scientists and determine (quality) growth rates $\hat{g}_s + 1$ and $\hat{G}_{s+1}$.

We have already derived the optimal behavior at stages 2 and 4. It remains to specify the outcome of the socialization at stage 3.

Cultural evolution. In the models developed by Besley and Persson (2019, 2023), the dynamics of the green-consumer share follows an equation

$$\mu_{s+1} - \mu_s = \grave{u}2\mu_s(1 - \mu_s)\left[F(\beta\Delta(\mu_{s+1})) - \frac{1}{2}\right], \tag{9}$$

where

$$\Delta(\mu) = \frac{\sigma(\chi)^{1-\frac{1}{\sigma}}}{[1-\sigma]^{\frac{1}{\sigma}}}\left\{q\left[1+\left[\frac{\beta\varphi\sigma\kappa\mu}{w}\right]^{\frac{\varphi}{1-\varphi}}\right]\right.$$
$$\left. -Q\left(\frac{\sigma\chi+(1-\sigma)\theta}{\sigma\chi}\right)\left[1+\left[\frac{\beta\varphi\sigma\kappa(1-\mu)}{W}\right]^{\frac{\varphi}{1-\varphi}}\right]\right\}$$

is the anticipated utility difference between being a green versus a brown consumer in period $s+1$. An equation like (9) can be derived from a variety of microfounded models analogous to those studied in Bisin and Verdier (2001), Tabellini (2008), or Besley and Persson (2019). This reflects an influence on a new generation where (biological or cultural) parents endow their children with values, but the costs and benefits of holding specific values (and thus preferences for consumption) help shape the socialization process. So a world in which it is more attractive to "go green" will see more children becoming green consumers.

It is straightforward to show that $\Delta(\cdot)$ is an increasing function such that a larger expected share of green consumers in the future makes it optimal for more families to go green. This property is driven entirely by the fact that a larger share of green consumers will induce more innovation in the green sector—that is, by the market-size effect in innovation discussed in Section 2.

Putting the innovation and socialization dynamics together, we obtain a dynamic complementarity that drives divergent dynamics, where the path taken depends on the initial conditions: $\{q_0, Q_0, \mu_0\}$.

Convergence to a green steady state? We get a transition to a green steady state with $\mu = 1$ if and only if

$$\frac{q}{Q}\left[\frac{1+\left[\dfrac{\beta\varphi\sigma\kappa\mu}{w}\right]^{\frac{\varphi}{1-\varphi}}}{1+\left[\dfrac{\beta\varphi\sigma\kappa(1-\mu)}{W}\right]^{\frac{\varphi}{1-\varphi}}}\right]>\left(\frac{\sigma\chi+(1-\sigma)\theta}{\sigma\chi}\right). \tag{10}$$

It is natural to think about a starting point where brown firms have a quality advantage—i.e., $q/Q\leq 1$. As the right-hand side expression is a number larger than 1, a *necessary* condition for a green transition is, then, that the green-quality growth rate exceeds the brown-quality growth rate, thus making the expression in square brackets larger than 1.

In our simple model, this is possible *only if* $W>w$—i.e., if scientists are motivated as we discussed above. If equation (10) holds, then we will get rising quality and quantity of green consumption/production, and falling quality and quantity of brown consumption/production. And the latter will bring about a reduction in pollution. The driver of this structural change is that motivated scientists help engineer a green transition based on innovation in the green sector. The rising relative quality of green goods persuades more people to become green consumers, which feeds back to yet stronger incentives for green innovation. And so on ad infinitum.

One way to think about this effect is in terms of a *cultural multiplier* on the relative growth rates due to scientists' motivation. Formally, let $W=\varpi w$ where $\varpi\geq 1$. Differentiating equation (8) yields

$$d\log\left(\frac{\hat{g}}{\hat{G}}\right)\bigg/d\varpi=\frac{\varphi}{1-\varphi}\left[1+\frac{d\mu/d\varpi}{\mu(1-\mu)}\right],$$

where the second term in square brackets is the cultural multiplier. This effect not only makes civil society the driver of a green transition but magnifies the effects of this driver in that transition.

In a situation where (10) does not hold, one could think about events that might bolster ϖ. This could include a stronger slant in science education to learning about the costs of pollution. Another possibility is that civil society could become more organized, increasing the salience of working for green rather than brown firms. A positive shock to ϖ induced by such changes would have the potential to change the trajectory of a society around critical junctures, where $\Delta(\mu)$ is initially close to zero.

One could also get a further complementarity if scientist values were evolving in the same direction as consumer values—formally, ϖ would be positively related to μ. This would further magnify the dynamic effect of shocks to ϖ.

4 Conclusions

This chapter proposes a simple model to illustrate how environmentally minded scientists can help foster a brown-to-green shift in innovation, consumption, and production. We have stressed that motivated science changes the market signals compared to purely profit-driven innovation. Such motivation can serve an important social role in the wake of an externality—like carbon emissions—that needs to be curbed, especially if the benefits of curbing are long-term and global and thus collide with the propensity of elected politicians to focus on short-term and domestic payoffs. We have seen that motivated science may play a further and more subtle role in a green transition—our model stresses the complementarity of innovation and lifestyle changes.

To highlight the implications of motivated science, we have abstracted away from a whole host of other factors. Besley and Persson (2023) discuss a class of political mechanisms including a tax on pollution. They make the more general point that disappointment with conventional politics creates greater climate activism that works directly via the private sector and indirectly via the political sector. Scientists following their values is another expression of this point, which rhymes well with the observation that science has been key in drawing society's attention to the perils of climate change.

Whether or not we think of policy as endogenously determined in the analysis, the role of alternative policy instruments is an important concern. Theory can be a valuable guide as to which policies could be leveraged to promote a green transition, but which policies appear useful depends on the mechanisms highlighted by the theory. The model in this chapter puts the focus directly on the values instilled by the education system both of the general population and in the STEM education of scientists. Indirectly, it suggests that policies that subsidize innovation will have a higher marginal effect on growth in the green sector when scientists have a greater intrinsic motivation for green projects.

Although we have dealt with pollution and climate change, our chapter raises a wider set of issues around the role of science in society. Economists have tended to focus on profit-driven innovation. The Schumpeterian tradition of Aghion and Howitt (1992) pioneered this view, which led us to better appreciate the role of market structure. But science and entrepreneurship also reflect imagination and visions of the future that are not primarily driven by a hunger for economic gain, as in Aghion et al. (2008). It would be dangerous to discount the role of profit-seeking, but leading entrepreneurs are often also visionary leaders whose products can have societal effects beyond the wealth they generate. Such visions could well turn out to be a powerful force in tackling the climate crisis.

References

Acemoglu, Daron, Philippe Aghion, Leonardo Bursztyn, and David Hémous. (2012). "The Environment and Directed Technical Change," *American Economic Review* 102(1), 131–166.

Acemoglu, Daron, Ufuk Akcigit, Douglas Hanley, and William Kerr. (2016). "The Transition to Clean Technology," *Journal of Political Economy* 124(1), 52–104.

Acemoglu, Daron, and Joshua Linn. (2004). "Market Size in Innovation: Theory and Evidence from the Pharmaceutical Industry," *Quarterly Journal of Economics* 119(3), 1049–1090.

Aghion, Philippe, Roland Benabou, Ralf Martin, and Alexandra Roulet. (2019). "Environmental Preferences and Technological Choices: Is Market Competition Clean or Dirty?," unpublished manuscript.

Aghion, Philippe, Antoine Dechezleprêtre, David Hémous, Ralf Martin, and John Van Reenen. (2016). "Carbon Taxes, Path Dependency and Directed Technical Change: Evidence from the Auto Industry," *Journal of Political Economy* 124(1), 1–51.

Aghion, Philippe, Mathias Dewatripont, and Jeremy C. Stein. (2008). "Academic Freedom, Private-Sector Focus, and the Process of Innovation," *RAND Journal of Economics* 39(3), 617–635.

Aghion, Philippe, and Peter Howitt. (1992). "A Model of Growth through Creative Destruction," *Econometrica* 60(2), 323–351.

Besley, Timothy, and Maitreesh Ghatak. (2005). "Competition and Incentives with Motivated Agents," *American Economic Review* 95(3), 616–636.

Besley, Timothy, and Torsten Persson. (2019). "The Dynamics of Environmental Politics and Values," *Journal of the European Economic Association* 17(4), 993–1024.

Besley, Timothy, and Torsten Persson. (2023). "The Political Economics of Green Transitions," *Quarterly Journal of Economics*, forthcoming.

Bezin, Emeline. (2015). "A Cultural Model of Private Provision and the Environment," *Journal of Environmental Economics and Management* 71(3), 109–24.

Bezin, Emeline. (2019). "The Economics of Green Consumption, Cultural Transmission and Sustainable Technological Change," *Journal of Economic Theory* 181, 497–546.

Bisin, Alberto, and Thierry Verdier. (2001). "The Economics of Cultural Transmission and the Dynamics of Preferences," *Journal of Economic Theory* 97(2), 298–319.

Krusell, Per. (1998). "How Is R&D Distributed across Firms? A Theoretical Analysis," unpublished typescript.

Tabellini, Guido. (2008). "The Scope of Cooperation: Values and Incentives," *Quarterly Journal of Economics* 123(3), 905–950.

CHAPTER 15

Climate Policy in Need of Plan B

CHRISTER FUGLESANG *and* JOHN HASSLER

1 Introduction

Climate change due to emissions of greenhouse gases is portrayed by some as an acute threat to our civilization. Emissions of CO_2 and other greenhouse gases strongly affect the climate in a nonlinear way, with tipping points and irreversibilities. Others are skeptical and argue that even though greenhouse gases do affect the balance of incoming energy from the Sun and outgoing energy from Earth to space, the consequences of this for climate as well as the consequences of climate change for human welfare are exaggerated in the media and in political discussion. Unfortunately, science has not yet been able to credibly verify where in this large interval truth lies. Climate policy, or the lack of it, must then be chosen in a situation with very large uncertainty.

Climate change is driven by global aggregate emissions, but there is no single entity that decides their level. Instead, emissions are caused by the decisions of billions of individuals, firms, and other agents. Policies that affect these decisions are decided by hundreds of individual governments with access only to weak and imperfect ways of solving coordination and commitment problems. At the same time, it is clear that cooperation and commitment are necessary to deal with climate change.

These complications must be borne in mind when giving scientific policy advice. Deriving optimal policy in a model where risks can be measured with objective probabilities and policy is chosen by a benevolent central planner is not sufficient if these conditions are not satisfied in reality. The area of climate change is an example of this.

In this chapter we argue in favor of an orderly transition to climate neutrality toward the middle of the current century. The forces of creative destruction are strong and can transform society completely. By using carbon pricing these forces can be used to steer technical change in a direction that makes such a transition possible without large costs if it is allowed to take a few decades. Continued growth and catch-up in the developing countries of the world need not be sacrificed. If climate skeptics are wrong and human welfare is highly sensitive to continued emissions, such a transition will be highly valuable. But if the skeptics are right and we ex post learn that the transition could have been postponed, the cost of this policy mistake is low. Thus, a transition to climate neutrality toward the middle of the century is a good insurance policy. Given that it is not costly, coordination and commitment problems are at least partially mitigated. This is what we will call plan A: transition to climate neutrality toward the middle of the current century using carbon prices.

However, we will also argue that plan A should be complemented by the development of a plan B. This is due to the large uncertainty about how sensitive climate is to emissions and how sensitive human welfare is to climate change. Likely, plan A is sufficient but we cannot rule out that it is not. Due to very high costs and the associated political impossibility, a quick end to the use of fossil fuel is not a viable plan B. Instead, we argue that other solutions need to be sought.

In a choice situation like that of a benevolent central planner choosing policy under commitment to maximize welfare, it can only be good to have more options. However, in the real-world environment where climate policy is determined, this is not necessarily the case. In particular, having access to a plan B may make the outcome worse by leading to less effort in the implementation of plan A. We will investigate this argument in a formal model and show it to be relevant in the case of climate policies. However, we will argue that the argument is likely not strong enough to overturn the benefits of a plan B. Therefore, we will end the chapter by describing one of potentially many possible plan Bs—sunshades in space.

2 Climate Change Uncertainty and Insurance Values

2.1 Uncertainty about climate sensitivity to emissions

Higher concentration of greenhouse gases reduces the outflow of energy from Earth. Given a constant inflow, this creates a surplus in Earth's energy balance that leads to higher ground temperatures. Because a higher temperature increases the outflow, a balanced energy budget will eventually be restored, but at a higher temperature. There are several greenhouse gases, and in principle all gases with molecules having more than two atoms produce greenhouse effects. Carbon dioxide, CO_2, is special in the sense that it is emitted by human activities in quantities that make it the by far largest contributor to the surplus in the global energy budget. Furthermore, it is special in the sense that a substantial share of emissions stay in the atmosphere for thousands of years.[1]

The fundamental principles behind the warming effect of greenhouse gases have been known for centuries, and the effect of a higher atmospheric CO_2 concentration was quantified already in the nineteenth century by Arrhenius (1896). His empirical analysis concluded that a doubling of the CO_2 concentration increases the average temperature at the equator by 5°C and by 6°C at latitude 60 (e.g., in our hometown Stockholm). A few years later, Arrhenius reduced the estimate of this so called *equilibrium climate sensitivity* to a global increase of 4°C (Lapenis 1998). This number is still within the range of uncertainty provided by the sixth IPCC report (IPCC 2021), which states a 90 percent confidence interval between 2°C and 5°C and a best guess of 3°C. These confidence intervals have not changed much since the first IPCC report, which stated an interval between 1.5°C and 4.5°C and a best estimate of 2.5°C (IPCC 1990).[2]

The later reports also provide what is called *likely*, specified as 67 percent, confidence intervals. In the fourth report (IPCC 2007) this is 2°C to 4.5°C with a best guess of 3°C. In the fifth (IPCC 2013), the interval is slightly wider, 1.5°C to 4.5°C, and no best guess is provided. In the sixth report (IPCC 2021) the likely interval is narrowed somewhat to 2.5°C to 4°C and the best guess of 3°C is reintroduced.

---

[1] This is not the case for methane, which is a very potent greenhouse gas and the second largest contributor to the energy budget surplus, but dissolves in the atmosphere in a few decades.
[2] The first report does not provide significance levels for the confidence interval.

These ranges are large and have quite substantial impacts on how much emissions in the future can be allowed, given a particular target for the global mean temperature. This can easily be appreciated, given the finding that advanced Earth models that include a description of the circulation of carbon between the different reservoirs (mainly the atmosphere, the biosphere, and the oceans) produce the result that global warming at a particular point in time is proportional to the historically accumulated amount of emissions up to that point. This finding was first noted by Matthews et al. (2009) and is now incorporated in later IPCC reports. The sixth report (IPCC 2021) states, "This Report reaffirms with high confidence the AR5 finding that there is a near-linear relationship between cumulative anthropogenic CO_2 emissions and the global warming they cause. Each 1000 $GtCO_2$ of cumulative CO_2 emissions is assessed to likely cause a 0.27°C to 0.63°C increase in global surface temperature with a best estimate of 0.45°C." The quantitatively most important uncertainty producing this range is regarding climate's sensitivity to CO_2 concentrations.

Using IPCC's range for the emission sensitivity and the estimate that current accumulated emissions are 2400 $GtCO_2$ (IPCC 2021), we can easily compute that our previous emissions imply a global warming commitment of between 0.65°C and 1.5°C.[3] Suppose now that we set the target to 2°C and hope that the lower value of the climate sensitivity is the correct one. Then, we can emit a further 5000 $GtCO_2$—i.e., twice as much as we have emitted so far in history. If it then turns out that our hopes were in vain, and instead the emission sensitivity is at the upper end of the range, the temperature would rise 4.7°C. These calculations uses the *likely* range, which means a 67 percent likelihood. Using the same argument for the wider 90 percent interval, or including also less likely but possible climate sensitivities, even more striking consequences of making policy errors would result. Below, we will return to the economic consequences of such errors.

2.2 Damage sensitivity to climate change

Climate policy also must take into account the fact that the effects on human welfare of climate change are highly uncertain. Nordhaus and Moffat (2017) and Howard and Sterner (2017) provide metastudies of the global aggregate

---

[3] These estimates are all consistent with the current temperature increase of 1.09°C, since they are based on different assessment of temporary factors affecting the current temperature.

effect of climate change on humans, where effects are monetized and expressed relative to GDP. Used on existing studies, Nordhaus and Moffat (2017) provide an estimated range of damages between −0.1 and 3.4 percent of global GDP for 3°C global warming. The studies underlying Howard and Sterner (2017) have a range from 0 to 12 percent at the same temperature.

Hassler at al. (2018) uses IPCC's likely ranges for the climate sensitivity and the variation in damage sensitivities in Nordhaus and Moffat (2017) to show that uncertainty in terms of the difference in policy implications is very large. In particular, they show that if climate sensitivity and damage sensitivity are at the lower end of the likely ranges, the optimal tax is practically zero at US$1.9/ton CO_2. If both sensitivities are high, it is instead US$72.2/ton CO_2.[4] In both cases, the tax rate should increase at the rate of global GDP growth. The numbers are, of course, conditional on a number of other parameters, such as the rate at which future welfare is discounted. A lower discount rate increases the optimal tax rate but does it approximately proportionally regardless of sensitivities, so that the ratio between the high and the low tax rate is maintained. Reducing the discount rate from 1.5 percent to 0.1 percent, as suggested in the Stern Review, for instance, increases all optimal taxes approximately by a factor of nine.

Hassler et al. (2018) also show that the two types of policy uncertainty, about climate sensitivity and about damage sensitivity, are of similar magnitude in terms of optimal tax implications. A high climate sensitivity and a low damage sensitivity implies an optimal tax of US$10.0 and the converse combination an optimal tax of $12.4/ton CO_2.

2.3 Climate policy under uncertainty

Characterizing optimal policy in situations with risk—i.e., when (objective) probabilities can be assigned to different possible states of the world—has long been standard in economics. Such cost–benefit analysis of risky policy-making is highly useful and practiced in government agencies all over the world, including when dealing with delicate issues such as health, life, and death. The discussion above, where probabilities and probability intervals from IPCC were used, suggests that the same approach could be used when deriving recommendations for climate policy. However, we argue that the

---

[4] Sometimes, optimal taxes and emissions are expressed in mass units of carbon. Since one mass unit of carbon produces 3.66 units of CO_2, conversion is straightforward.

probabilities stated by IPCC are not well suited to being used as input in a model where optimal policy is derived by finding the policy that maximizes expected utility. First, the probabilities cover only a fairly small range of the set of possibilities, failing to assign probabilities to unlikely but possible states of the world. As suggested by Weitzman (2009), such extreme possibilities may be highly relevant for what is good policy. Second, the probabilities stated by IPCC are quite judgmental. This is inevitable in a situation where different models are consistent with observed data while producing highly different predictions for the future. These two arguments make the probabilities stated by IPCC less suitable to use as input in the calculation of expected utility.

A high degree of uncertainty, *ceteris paribus,* increases the value of waiting (Pindyck 1991). One could then make the argument that action should be delayed. However, this conclusion is likely wrong in the case of climate policy. There is no value in waiting in itself. Instead the value arises due to an expected flow of information. By waiting, a more informed and thus better decision can be made. However, based on what we so far have observed, it seems unlikely that the uncertainty about the relevant sensitivities will be much reduced in the near future. Thus, the value of waiting is not high.

Integrated assessment models building on the pathbreaking work by Nordhaus (see KVA 2018 for a summary) describe the interaction between the climate and the economy. They are global and long-run in order to be able to deal with the determinants and consequences of climate change and climate policy. Despite some criticism (see, e.g., Pindyck 2013), we argue that integrated assessment models are highly useful also in situations of large uncertainty about key parameters.

Hassler et al. (2018, 2021a) show the usefulness of integrated assessment models in a simple exercise. They use IPCC's likely range for the climate sensitivity and the damage sensitivity mentioned above and consider the consequences of possible policy mistakes. In a situation with a high degree of uncertainty, policy mistakes are likely. What, then, are the consequences of setting a low carbon tax, hoping for sensitivities at the lower end of the likely range, if this turns out to be the wrong choice? Conversely, what happens if a high tax is set but it turns out that a low tax would have been optimal? The result in the paper is that the consequences of these policy mistakes are highly asymmetric. The consequences of in vain setting a high tax rate are very small compared to the opposite policy mistake. It could have been the case that the costs of policy mistakes are high and symmetric. Then, the problem would be of the *wicked* nature where policy advice is very difficult to give. Instead, the asymmetry points to an ambitious climate policy being a good insurance—fairly cheap also if not needed *ex post*, but good to have in case. This is a quite policy-relevant result that relies on the use of integrated assessment models.

In contrast to Rudik (2020), the result in Hassler et al. (2018, 2021a) is derived in a model without learning. However, as discussed above, learning might not be sufficiently fast to overturn the results. Furthermore, the cost of a transition to climate neutrality depends crucially on how fast the transition is. A fast transition is much more costly, and waiting might lead to such a transition becoming necessary. This strengthens the case for not waiting, but underscores the possibility that policy will ex post turn out to be suboptimal.

A fast transition is costly because the economy is not very flexible in the short run. Hassler et al. (2021b) show that in the short run, a reduction of fossil fuel consumption can basically be done only by reducing production. This is because the production function in the short run requires energy in proportions almost fixed to output. In the longer run, however, the elasticity between energy and other inputs is close to unity, allowing output to grow without energy use increasing. The mechanism behind this is directed technical change—as the price of energy increases, technological effort is redirected toward making production more energy efficient. Hassler et al. (2021b) use aggregate evidence to draw these conclusions. See Aghion et al. (2016) for microeconomic evidence in the same direction. Building on the same ideas, but using a less stylized model where a number of short-run frictions are taken into account, IMF (2020) also shows that a global transition to climate neutrality over three decades based on carbon pricing need not be costly in terms of lost output if complemented by some initial stimulus policy to counteract the initial contractionary effects of carbon prices. The pricing policy should be complemented by subsidies to green technology development. This provides an important complement to make the transition easier, but it is no substitute for pricing. Furthermore, the revenues from pricing emissions are more than sufficient to undo unintended distributional effects (IMF 2020). The fact that, at least in the OECD, the problem of too-low or absent carbon pricing does not apply to transportation fuel (OECD 2016) means that difficulties related to public dissent, such as the French yellow vest movement, may be smaller than sometimes claimed. Of course, many political hurdles must be dealt with before a global agreement on carbon pricing can be achieved. This chapter is not about those hurdles, but we want to note that the recent agreement between the G7 countries to aim for the implementation of a global minimum tax rate on corporate revenues indicates that such agreements are possible.

The conclusion of this section is therefore that an orderly transition to climate neutrality by around 2050 based on carbon pricing is a good insurance policy against the uncertain consequences of using fossil fuel. This is *likely* going to keep climate damages at an acceptable level, and the insurance premium of this policy is not too high. This should therefore be plan A to deal with climate change. A key limitation, however, is captured by the word *likely*. The discussion above has used the *likely* range of uncertainty, described by IPCC as a 67 percent confidence interval. But climate and damage sensitivities may be substantially higher, and plan A might also fail due to a breakdown in international policy cooperation. We therefore argue that we also need to consider the development of a plan B, for unlikely but possible really bad scenarios.

There are arguments against developing a plan B, and the idea is even criticized as being highly dangerous. The arguments behind such claims are usually not formal, an exception being the working paper by Acemoglu and Rafey (2019). IPCC (2014) states that one of the most prominent arguments against developing plan Bs like geoengineering is that they may be seen as a substitute for plan A and reduce the efforts put into implementing it, which may be highly disadvantageous. In Section 3 we will examine this argument in a formal but simple game-theoretic model.

3 The Cost and Benefit of a Climate Plan B

3.1 *An emission abatement game*

In this section we describe a game where agents have a common interest in reducing climate-change damages through emissions abatement. As in reality, a key complication is the free-rider problem, implying that there is an incentive to deviate from the cooperative solution that maximizes joint welfare by emitting more. In order to maintain the cooperative solution, each player has access to a way of reducing the incentive for other players to deviate from the cooperative low-emission solution. However, this requires a costly investment in early phases of the game, and a stronger incentive reduction requires a higher investment. Without any such investments, the incentive to deviate and choose high emission levels will prevail, making the cooperative solution impossible. We do not specify the concrete character of these investments, but it may help to think about them as time-consuming participation in international negotiations as well as building up the capacity to punish other players by, for instance, imposing trade barriers.

The purpose of constructing the model is to analyze the costs and benefits of developing a plan B against climate change. By such a plan we mean the development of a technology that can drastically reduce the negative consequences of climate change. Developing the technology is assumed to have negligible costs, but using it imposes costs on society. These costs stem both from direct technological costs and from the fact that it may have negative side effects. Importantly, we assume that these costs are independent of the amount of climate damages while the direct benefits of executing plan B increase in the amount of climate damages that are mitigated by it. Thus, execution of plan B is beneficial only if climate damages are sufficiently large. As we will see, however, the mere development of the plan has consequences for the game that induces costs on society also in the case when the plan is not executed. Specifically, if the plan is developed, more needs to be invested in maintaining the low-emission cooperative solution in the cases when this is socially preferable over plan B. The existence of a developed plan B also opens up for multiple equilibria where one is plan B despite it not being socially preferable.

Let us now describe the game in more detail with the help of Figure 15.1. The game is a three-stage game with two players, A and B. The *first stage* starts with player A deciding whether or not to develop plan B.[5] It ends with nature choosing the sensitivity of climate damages to emissions. This sensitivity incorporates both the sensitivity of climate to emissions and the sensitivity of damages to climate change. We call this the *damages sensitivity* (to emissions) and label it γ. For simplicity, we assume that it is either strong, γ_s or weak, γ_w. The probability of strong damage sensitivity is $\pi_{\gamma s}$.

In the *second stage*, both players simultaneously decide on investing in the capacity to later punish their opponent for deviations from the low-emissions cooperative solution knowing both γ and whether a plan B has been developed. For players $i \in \{A, B\}$ the punishment capacity is denoted

---

[5] This asymmetry is innocuous because there are no conflicts of interest at this stage.

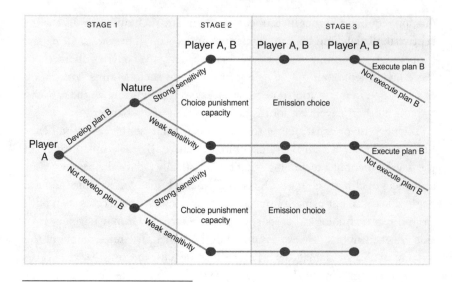

Figure 15.1. Game tree of the emission abatement game

Π_i and building it has costs given by the increasing function $c(\Pi_i)$ with $c(0) = 0$.

In the final, *third stage*, players first choose the amount of emissions simultaneously. For simplicity, we assume that the choice is restricted to either low or high emissions. Choosing high emissions has a private benefit to the player denoted e. High emissions will also increase climate damages for both players, but we will consider the realistic case when these private benefits are larger than the increase in climate damages, holding the actions of the other player fixed. Any player i who chooses high emissions will also face the punishment Π_{-i} determined by the other player in the previous stage. These emission levels will lead to symmetric climate damages for each player (if plan B is not executed) that depend on γ and the aggregate amount of emissions. The damages are denoted $D_{LL}(\gamma)$, $D_{LH}(\gamma)$ and $D_{HH}(\gamma)$ for the three possible aggregate emission levels (both choosing low, one low and one high, and both high). We assume $D_{LL}(\gamma) < D_{LH}(\gamma) < D_{HH}(\gamma)$ and for simplicity that $D_{LH}(\gamma) - D_{LL}(\gamma) = D_{HH}(\gamma) - D_{LH}(\gamma)$. If no plan B was developed in stage 1, this concludes the game. If plan B was developed, any of the agents can decide to execute it. If it is executed, any climate damage is neutralized and replaced by a fixed cost denoted p. Here, there will be no disagreement between the players and the plan will be executed if and only if climate damages are higher than p.

To make the analysis interesting, we assume that $D_{LL}(\gamma_w) < p$ while both $D_{LH}(\gamma_w) > p$ and $D_{LL}(\gamma_s) > p$. Thus, plan B will be executed if it is developed, unless damages sensitivity is weak and the cooperative solution with both players choosing low emissions levels materializes. Furthermore, we assume that $e > D_{LH}(\gamma) - D_{LL}(\gamma)$ so that choosing high emissions is privately optimal (a dominating strategy) if $\Pi_{-i} = 0$.

3.2 Equilibrium

We solve for the equilibrium by backward induction.

3.2.1 Stage 3

Consider first the case in which no plan B has been developed. In stage 3 the game then has the following structure:

Stage 3 game—No plan B developed

		Player B	
		Low	*High*
Player A	*Low*	$-D_{LL}(\gamma), -D_{LL}(\gamma)$	$-D_{LH}(\gamma), e - D_{LH}(\gamma) - \Pi_A$
	High	$e - D_{LH}(\gamma) - \Pi_B, -D_{LH}(\gamma)$	$e - D_{HH}(\gamma) - \Pi_B, e - D_{HH}(\gamma) - \Pi_A$

Under the assumptions given above, cooperation with both players choosing low emission is the only Nash equilibrium if and only if

$$\Pi_{A,B} \geq e - (D_{LH}(\gamma) - D_{LL}(\gamma)) \equiv \bar{\Pi}(\gamma). \tag{1}$$

In words, the punishment must be large enough to deter the value of deviation, which is given by the direct value e and the difference in climate damages under cooperation and deviation.[6] If the punishments chosen by one player is lower than $\bar{\Pi}(\gamma)$, emissions of the other player will be high.

Now consider the case when plan B was developed. The game outcome now depends on whether γ is weak or strong. In the case when $\gamma = \gamma_w$, plan B will be executed if and only if at least one player chooses high emission levels. The game is then as given below.

---

[6] We assume that when indifferent, players choose low emissions.

Stage 3 game—Plan B developed, weak damage sensitivity

		Player B	
		Low	High
Player A	Low	$-D_{LL}(\gamma_w), -D_{LL}(\gamma_w)$	$-p, e-p-\Pi_A$
	High	$e-p-\Pi_B, -p$	$e-p-\Pi_B, e-p-\Pi_A$

The cooperative equilibrium with low emissions then requires

$$\Pi_{A,B} \geq e - (p - D_{LL}(\gamma_w)). \tag{2}$$

Now, because we have assumed that $p < D_{LH}(\gamma_w)$, the temptation to deviate is larger than if plan B was not developed (the right-hand side of equation (2) is larger than the RHS of equation (1)). Thus, punishment must be larger to sustain cooperation.

Furthermore, if player i chooses high emissions, the additional value for the other player, $-i$, of also choosing high will be $e - \Pi_{-i}$ since plan B will be executed whatever the choice of player $-i$. Thus, $\Pi_{-i} = e - (p - D_{LL}(\gamma_w))$ does not rule out the high-emission outcome. To do that, the punishment for deviation must be $\Pi_{A,B} \geq e$.

To limit the number of cases and to stack the case against a plan B, we assume that in the case of multiple equilibria, i.e., when $\Pi_i \in [e - (p - D_{LL}(\gamma_w)), e]$ the high-emissions outcome results.

The final case to consider in stage 3 is when plan B was developed and damage sensitivity is strong. Then, plan B will be executed regardless of emission choices, and the game is now:

Stage 3 game—Plan B developed, strong damage sensitivity

		Player B	
		Low	High
Player A	Low	$-p, -p$	$-p, e-p-\Pi_A$
	High	$e-p-\Pi_B, -p$	$e-p-\Pi_B, e-p-\Pi_A$

Here, the implementation of plan B removes the free-rider problem. Provided $e > \Pi_{-i}$, it is a dominating strategy to choose high emissions, and otherwise emissions are low. Payoffs to players will then be $e - p - \Pi_{-i}$ in the former case and $-p$ in the latter.

This concludes the analysis of stage 3.

3.2.2 Stage 2

Now, consider stage 2, in which the investment in punishment capacity is done simultaneously, given nature's choice of damage sensitivity γ and whether or not plan B has been developed. Without loss of generality, we can restrict the policy space to choosing $\Pi_i \in \{0, \bar{\Pi}(\gamma),\}$ if no plan B is developed, and $\Pi_i \in \{0, e\}$ if it is.

Consider first the case when plan B has not been developed. Incorporating the equilibrium in stage 3 yields the following game structure in stage 2:

Stage 2 game—No plan B developed

		Player B	
		$\Pi_B = 0$	$\Pi_B = \bar{\Pi}(\gamma)$
Player A	$\Pi_A = 0$	$e - D_{HH}(\gamma), e - D_{HH}(\gamma)$	$-D_{LH}(\gamma), e - D_{LH}(\gamma) - c(\bar{\Pi}(\gamma))$
	$\Pi_A = \bar{\Pi}(\gamma)$	$e - D_{LH}(\gamma) - c(\bar{\Pi}(\gamma)),$ $-D_{LH}(\gamma)$	$-D_{LL}(\gamma) - c(\bar{\Pi}(\gamma)),$ $-D_{LL}(\gamma) - c(\bar{\Pi}(\gamma))$

Here, cooperation, i.e., that both players choose to invest in sufficient punishment capacity, is the unique outcome if

$$c(\bar{\Pi}(\gamma)) < D_{LH}(\gamma) - D_{LL}(\gamma). \tag{3}$$

This condition implies that it is worthwhile to take the cost and effort to induce the cooperative low-emissions equilibrium. To make the analysis interesting, we assume this to be the case regardless of the damage sensitivity.

Now, consider the case when plan B has been developed. The game now depends on whether damage sensitivity is weak or strong. Consider first the case of low climate sensitivity. The game is then:

Stage 2 game—Plan B developed, weak damage sensitivity

		Player B	
		$\Pi_B = 0$	$\Pi_B = e$
Player A	$\Pi_A = 0$	$e - p, e - p$	$-p, e - p - c(e)$
	$\Pi_A = e$	$e - p - c(e), -p$	$-D_{LL}(\gamma_w) - c(e), -D_{LL}(\gamma_w) - c(e)$

Here, we see that developing plan B implies that no cooperation where $\Pi_{A,B} = 0$ always is an equilibrium. Additionally, $\Pi_{A,B} = e$ is also an equilibrium if

$$c(e) < p - D_{LL}(\gamma_w). \tag{4}$$

In words, the cost of creating the capacity to punish at a level e, which is $c(e)$, must be lower than the benefit of creating that capacity, which is $p - D_{LL}$ (γ_w). Thus, the development of a plan B makes cooperation more fragile, subject to multiple equilibria. We assume that this multiplicity is resolved by a stochastic mechanism implying that the cooperative low-emissions equilibrium results with a probability π_c.

In addition, because $c(e) > c(\overline{\Pi})$, the cost of implementing the low-emissions equilibrium is higher, and because also $p < D_{LH}(\gamma_w)$, the condition for the existence of the cooperation equilibrium is tighter. Here, we focus on the case when $D_{LL}(\gamma_w) + c(e) < p - e$, so that also when plan B has been developed, it is worth the effort to induce low emissions and no execution of plan B if the damage sensitivity is weak.

Finally, consider the case when damage sensitivity is strong, in which case plan B will always be executed. The game is:

Stage 2 game—Plan B developed, strong damage sensitivity

		Player B	
		$\Pi_B = 0$	$\Pi_B = e$
Player A	$\Pi_A = 0$	$e - p,\ e - p$	$-p,\ e - p - c(e)$
	$\Pi_A = e$	$e - p - c(e),\ -p$	$-p - c(e),\ -p - c(e)$

Here, the only equilibrium is $\Pi_{A,B} = 0$. This concludes the analysis of stage 2.

3.2.3 Stage 1

In stage 1, the decision of whether or not to develop plan B is taken by player A before she knows the realization of the damage sensitivity. If plan B is not developed, the expected payoff is

$$-\underbrace{\left[(1 - \pi_{\gamma_S})(D_{LL}(\gamma_W) + c(\overline{\Pi}(\gamma_W)))\right]}_{A_1} - \underbrace{\left[\pi_{\gamma_S}(D_{LL}(\gamma_S) + c(\overline{\Pi}(\gamma_S)))\right]}_{A_2}.$$

If plan B is developed, the payoff is instead

$$-\underbrace{\left[(1 - \pi_{\gamma_S})(\pi_C(D_{LL}(\gamma_W) + c(e)) + (1 - \pi_C)(p - e))\right]}_{B_1} - \underbrace{\left[\pi_{\gamma_S}(p - e)\right]}_{B_2}.$$

The term A_1 in square brackets is the sum of damages and costs of punishment investments if damage sensitivity is weak and no plan B is developed.

A_1 is smaller than the corresponding term B_1 when plan B was developed for two reasons. First, it takes higher effort to implement the low-emissions equilibrium if plan B is developed $(c(e) > c(\overline{\Pi}(\gamma_W)))$. Second, also when plan B is executed the low-emissions equilibrium is socially preferable when the damage sensitivity is weak, i.e., $(p - e > D_{LL}(\gamma_W) + c(\overline{\Pi}(\gamma_W)))$. When plan B is developed, a possible equilibrium is that neither player invest in punishment capacity and plan B is executed despite being an inferior outcome.

On the other hand, the term A_2 is larger than B_2 because if damage sensitivity is strong, implementing plan B is better than the low-emissions equilibrium.

Note that in this stage of the game, there are no coordination issues. The choice of any of the player coincides with what they jointly would choose.

From the analysis above follows that:

Conclusion 1 *Under the assumptions in this section, there is a $\overline{\pi}_{\gamma_S} > 0$ such that if $\pi_{\gamma_S} \geq \overline{\pi}_{\gamma_S}$, a plan B will be developed in stage 1. This is socially beneficial.*

Here, it is important to note two things. First, if and only if the probability of a high damage sensitivity is sufficiently high, plan B should be developed. Second, the threshold probability is strictly higher than zero. The latter is due to the finding that the existence of a plan B has negative effects on the outcome of the game if plan B is not needed. Specifically, it increases the cost of implementing plan A in case the damage sensitivity is weak and it may be implemented also when not needed from a social perspective. Thus, a plan B should not be developed unless the probability that it is socially beneficial is sufficiently high. This contrasts to the case when there is no coordination game. Then developing a plan B at zero cost can never reduce welfare.

4 Sunshades in Space—A Potential Plan B

We now turn to describing a plan B against climate change—namely, reducing the amount of incoming sunlight to Earth. There are several ways of doing this. Perhaps the best-known method is to inject aerosols into the stratosphere to create a cooling effect similar to the one experienced after large volcanic eruptions. A substantial amount of research has been done on this method, including work by economists (see e.g., Smith 2020; Smith and Wagner 2018; Wagner and Weitzman 2015).

A lesser-known method is to use shades in space. Until recently this was considered impossible due to prohibitively large costs of rocket launches. When launching rockets were the unique privilege of state agencies like NASA, launch costs were on the order of US$10 million per ton. Costs have now come down by almost an order of magnitude. Private initiatives by Elon Musk and others to create more cost-efficient and reusable rockets point to the possibility that costs might be reduced further by a least one, perhaps even two, orders of magnitude. Given this development, Fuglesang and Garcia de Herreros Miciano (2021) recently constructed a concrete proposal for a plan B based on sunshades. We use the remainder of this section to describe the main ideas there.

4.1 Where to place the sunshades

A first question is where the sunshades should be located. One possibility is to have them circulating around Earth like satellites. However, this solution has several disadvantages. One is that options to use this part of space are scarce due to the need for communication and observation satellites. More congestion here obviously increases collision risks. Furthermore, sunshades this close to Earth would be visible, which has potentially negative side effects, and because they are circulating Earth, they would not shade any incoming sunlight when being themselves shaded by Earth.

A much better position is at a so-called Lagrange point where the gravitational forces of Earth and the Sun, together with the centripetal force of rotation around the Sun, balance each other. This occurs at a point approximately 1 percent of the distance from Earth to the Sun or about four times the distance to the Moon. An object placed at the Lagrange point would stay there unless affected by other forces. This location is much less crowded than low-Earth orbits. Furthermore, sunshades placed there would always be in zenith and so far away that they would not be visible to the naked eye.

In reality, however, other forces than the gravitational would affect a sunshade placed at the Lagrange point. In particular, the solar radiation pressure (the force created by photons from the Sun bouncing on the shade) needs to be taken into account. To balance also this force, the shades needs to be placed closer to the Sun so that the increased gravitational force balances the solar radiation pressure. How much closer depends on the mass and the reflectivity of the shade. A lower mass and a higher reflectivity implies that the shade needs to be put closer to the Sun, thus farther away from Earth. A larger distance to Earth has the negative consequence that the shade needs to be larger to decrease the same amount of sunlight reaching Earth.

Reflectivity should be minimized to minimize the total mass of the shades.[7] A higher mass is obviously costly in terms of launch costs. It turns out that to minimize the mass the shades should be put a distance 1.58 percent of the distance to the Sun. This point is actually independent of reflectivity and the share of sunlight to be shaded, although the amount of the mass there increases linearly with both reflectivity and amount of shading. This translates into an optimal areal density (mass per m^2) for the whole sunshade spacecraft, which depends on the reflectivity. Given already existing technologies for solar sails, it is not difficult to create sunshades with a mass equal to that optimum.

4.2 How large an area needs to be shaded?

The size of the sunshades of course depends on how large a cooling effect is required. It is convenient to express the latter in terms of how large a reduction in energy inflow is wanted. The average (over time and space) inflow of energy to Earth from the Sun is 340 W/m^2. The latest IPCC report (IPCC 2021) reports that the greenhouse effect of CO_2 has reduced outflow by 2 W/m^2 compared to 1850. In the same time period the CO_2 concentration has increased by 44 percent, from 286 to 410 ppm. Other greenhouse gases, methane and N_2O in particular, have non-negligible effects (0.5 and 0.2 W/m^2) and also leave the atmosphere much faster. Further, IPCC reports the estimated effect of the energy outflow by a doubling of the CO_2 concentration to be 3.9 W/m^2. As a basis for the calculations, we consider sunshades that are able to shade 1 percent of the inflow and estimate at which level of CO_2 concentration the warming effect then could be mitigated. Arrhenius (1896) showed that the greenhouse effect is approximately logarithmic in the CO_2 concentration. A reduction of the energy outflow by 1 percent of the inflow, i.e., 3.4 W/m^2, would then arise at a CO_2 concentration of 528 ppm. Over the last decade (not including the Corona-year) the CO_2 concentration has increased by 2.4 ppm/year. Reaching 528 ppm, producing a

---

[7] The theoretical optimum would be to have the shades absorb all energy from the Sun and transmit it as infrared radiation toward Earth, where it would be reflected by the atmosphere.

greenhouse effect of 3.4 W/m², would thus take approximately 50 years at the current speed of concentration increase.

If the sunshades were to be placed close to Earth, they would need to cover an area equal to 1 percent of the projected area of the Earth toward the Sun (π times the square of Earth's radius).[8] However, the distance to the Lagrange point is so large that the relevant comparison is the projected area of the Sun. Seen from Earth, it should look as if the shades cover 1 percent of the face of the Sun. Of course, because the distance to the Sun is much larger than the distance to the sunshades, the actual area is much smaller than 1 percent of the Sun's.[9] To shade a share ΔS of the inflow of sunlight, the required sunshade area is equal to

$$\Delta S * (R_{dist})^2 * A_{sun},$$

where is R_{dist} is the distance to the shades relative to the distance to the Sun and A_{sun} is the projected area of the Sun. Using $R_{dist} = 0.0158$ and $A_{sun} = 1.50 * 10^{12}$ km² yields that the sunshades need to be 3.8 million km². This is large—seven times the area of France or more than five times the area of Texas. Certainly, a sunshade in one piece of that size is highly impractical. Instead, the suggestion is to use shades with an individual size about as large as a football field. In the order of 500 million such shades would then need to be constructed.

4.3 How to get the sunshades to their final destination?

The first and foremost challenge when transporting the sunshades to their destination is to lift them up into low orbit at an altitude of about 2000 km, above the crowded space used by communication satellites. Lifting the shades to orbit will be done by reusable rockets. From this orbit, each sunshade will use the solar radiation pressure to reach their final destination, 2.36 million km away from Earth. Thus, the shades need not carry any propellant. The basic principle making this voyage possible is that the solar radiation pressure can be used to reduce the shades' speed around the Sun. The gravitational force of the Sun will then dominate the centrifugal force and the shade starts to fall toward the Sun (see Figure 15.2). The solar radiation pressure

---

[8] Of course, this would be highly impractical since the shaded area would be dark.

[9] Recall that from Earth, it looks like the Moon and the Sun are approximately as large on the sky due to the fact that the Sun is approximately 400 times farther away.

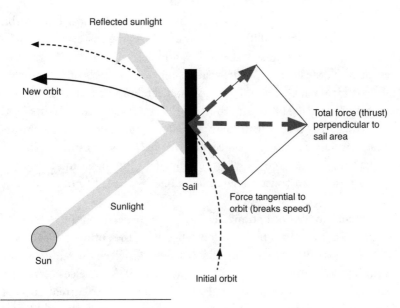

Figure 15.2. Using solar radiation pressure to travel toward Sun

creates a force quite weak relative to that of rockets. Nevertheless, the full journey is calculated to take no more than a few years.

As discussed above, reflectivity should be minimized when the shades are in place at their final destination, since the solar radiation pressure there should be minimized. However, a low reflectivity and the corresponding low solar radiation pressure makes the time to reach to the final destination longer. To circumvent this trade-off, the shades should be constructed with different reflectivities on their two sides. In place, the low-reflectivity side would face the Sun but the other side, with high reflectivity, would be used to propel the travel from Earth. While in place, the solar radiation pressure will be used to maneuver the individual sunshades, pointing them to the Sun and avoiding collisions using swarm technology. Because the Largange point is unstable, the ability to maneuver is also required to keep the sunshades in place.

4.4 Cost estimation and launch plan

The main cost of this plan B in the form of sunshades is to launch the sunshades into low Earth orbit with rockets. When state agencies were the only ones to launch large rockets, the cost of lifting payload to low Earth orbit was in the order of US$10,000/kg. As noted above, the cost has fallen substantially thanks to reusable rocket stages and cost-conscious private companies. SpaceX, the leading private space company, currently offers launches with Falcon Heavy at US$90 million. This rocket takes a payload of 63,800 kg, implying a cost of US$1400/kg. To make the sunshade plan fly, costs need to fall further. It is certainly difficult to make estimates of how much further costs can fall. Here, we use a cost of US$50/kg as an estimate. This is about five times the current cost of the propellant (methane and liquid oxygen) and more than twice the estimate done by the CEO of SpaceX of US$20/kg.

As discussed above, the optimized mass per m^2 depends on the reflectivity of the sunshades. With a sufficiently low reflectivity, the optimum is achieved at an areal density of 8.8 grams/m^2 (8800 kg/km^2). Given the required area of 3.8 million km^2 and using the guesstimate US$50/kg, the cost of lifting the sunshades to low Earth orbit is 1.7 trillion dollars. At current costs of US$1400/kg, the lift cost is US$47 trillion. Manufacturing and additional costs are arguably somewhat easier to estimate and are here set to US$1.3 trillion, making a total of US$3 trillion.

The optimized mass of the sunshades is quite sensitive to the reflectivity that can be achieved. With a less optimistic assumption about the reflectivity, using current technology, the optimized mass of the sunshades is about two and a half times higher. Since the lift and manufacturing costs scale with mass, the costs also increase by approximately a factor 2.5.

Assuming a payload capacity of 100 tons, and the need to lift 34 million tons, 330,000 launches would be required in the optimistic scenario. If this is done over a twenty-year period, 46 rockets need to be launched every day.

4.4.1 Discussion

Are sunshades a reasonable plan B in case plan A against climate change fails? Certainly, this question cannot be affirmatively answered without much more research. However, a few points make us believe that the idea should not be put in the drawer prematurely.

First, the estimates given above do not point to prohibitively high costs. The optimistic calculation of $3 trillion spread globally and over twenty years is of an order of magnitude that is negligible in a possible future situation where climate change threatens the sustainability of our civilization. In fact, it is small enough to be borne by a large country like United States or a group of countries like EU on their own. US GDP is estimated to have been $23 trillion in 2021, and in the EU the corresponding figure is $18 trillion ($22 trillion in international purchasing power). Of this a bit over 20 percent is invested. Thus, both the United States and the EU currently invest more every year than would be invested over a twenty-year period to get the sunshades operative. In fact, even a cost of an order of magnitude larger—due, for example, to very limited technological developments in space technology— appears manageable although probably requiring global cooperation. That the cost is manageable for the EU or the United States individually is an advantage if international climate cooperation breaks down. That it is large enough to deter smaller countries may in fact be an advantage in that competing systems with different aims might be detrimental.

Second, test launches of sunshades propelled by solar radiation pressure could be done soon. The same propulsion technology has already been used in practice in the crowd-funded project Lightsail 2, which in 2019 sent up a satellite in an orbit controlled by a sail propelled by solar radiation pressure. Experimental sunshades using this propulsion technology could be launched very soon at low cost.

Third, the effects on incoming sunlight of the sunshades is easily controllable. Both the total amount of sunlight deflected and its distribution over the globe can be changed basically instantaneously. Thus, the technology does in itself not induce permanent or hard to reverse effects.

Certainly, any solar geoengineering method will have side effects that must be understood (see Irvine et al. 2016 for an overview). However, sunshades in space is in principle much simpler and not as complex as, for instance, stratospheric aerosol injection (SAI) (Irvine 2016). SAI has several side effects whose consequences are as yet not fully understood, that must be carefully studied and understood before it can be implemented in full scale and will require continuous operation for centuries. Sunshades, on the other hand, will stay in place for a very long time and are not very vulnerable to attack by, for instance, terrorists. Nevertheless, research on different alternatives of solar geoengineering should proceed. History suggests that political decisions to bet on only one technology often lead to mistakes. A better strategy is to make final technology choices as late as possible when the development process is not too costly.

5 Policy Conclusions and Suggestions for Future Research

Climate neutrality by 2050 is part of many countries' climate plans. Global climate neutrality by the middle of the century also appears to be a possible outcome in the international game of policy coordination. If realized, such a transition would likely lead to moderate climate damages. If the implementation is based on carbon pricing, it will steer technological change in a way that makes the transition possible without compromising the growth and economic catch-up of developing countries. This should therefore be climate policy plan A.

However, due to large uncertainties, plan A may turn out to be insufficient due to stronger than expected climate sensitivity and less potential for adaptation. International policy coordination may also fail. This creates an argument for a plan B, which realistically cannot be a sudden end to all fossil fuel use. There are theoretically valid arguments against the development of such plans. In this chapter we have characterized some—namely, that they can make it more costly to achieve plan A as well as make it less robust to the possibility of multiple equilibria.

In our analysis, the costs associated with the development of plan B are high only in the state of nature where damage sensitivities are weak, while the benefits arise in the more concerning state with strong damage sensitivities. This limits the strength of the argument against a plan B. Nevertheless, our model is not quantitative, and work of that sort is strongly needed. Arguably, quantitative research that demonstrates that the costs are not exceedingly large should precede any decision to develop different potential plan Bs. However, in contrast to our stylized model, where development is an instantaneous decision, the development takes time. Therefore, we believe that experimentation on different variants of solar radiation management, as well as other forms of geoengineering, should not be postponed.

In this chapter we have discussed neither carbon capture and storage (CCS) of CO_2 from points of emission nor direct air capture (DAC) of CO_2 from the atmosphere. These methods are somewhere in between plan A and B because they (in particular CCS) are likely to be an important part of plan A. In principle, technology might advance so that the latter could form a viable plan B, although costs today are prohibitive.

Finally, we want to stress that whether the sunshade plan or similar ideas actually work is still highly uncertain. Sunshades may have unforeseen side effects and will not remove all negative consequences of CO_2 emissions. In particular, the acidification of the oceans resulting from increased uptake of CO_2 has known, albeit quantitatively uncertain, negative consequences for coral reefs and marine life in general. A way of reducing uncertainty is to develop a portfolio of different potential plan Bs. However, large degrees of uncertainty will remain. This provides a strong argument against using sunshades and similar plans as an alternative plan A. The latter should remain a transition to carbon neutrality by the middle of the current century.

References

Acemoglu, D., and W. Rafey. 2019. "Mirage on the horizon: Geoengineering and carbon taxation without commitment." MIT, manuscript.

Aghion, P., A. Dechezleprêtre, D. Hémous, R. Martin, and J. Van Reenen. 2016. "Carbon taxes, path dependency, and directed technical change: Evidence from the auto industry." *Journal of Political Economy*, 124:1.

Arrhenius, S. 1896. "On the influence of carbonic acid in the air upon the temperature of the ground." *Philosophical Magazine and Journal of Science*, 41:237–276.

Fuglesang, C., and M. Garcia de Herreros Miciano. 2021. "Realistic sunshade system at L1 for global temperature control." *Acta Astronautica*, 186:269–279.

Hassler, J., P. Krusell, and C. Olovsson. 2018. "The consequences of uncertainty: Climate sensitivity and economic sensitivity to the climate." *Annual Review of Economics*, 10:189–205.

Hassler, J., P. Krusell, and C. Olovsson. 2021a. "Suboptimal climate policy." *Journal of the European Economic Association*, 19(6):2895–2928.

Hassler, J., P. Krusell, and C. Olovsson. 2021b. "Directed technical change as a response to natural-resource scarcity." *Journal of Political Economy*, 129:11.

Howard, P., and T. Sterner. 2017. "Few and not so far between: A meta-analysis of climate damage estimates." *Environmental and Resource Economics*, 68:197–225.

IMF. 2020. *World Economic Outlook*, chap. 3, October 2020.

IPCC. 1990. *Climate change: The IPCC scientific assessment, Report prepared for Intergovernmental Panel on Climate Change by Working Group I*. Edited by J. T. Houghton, G. J. Jenkins, and J. J. Ephraums. Cambridge: Cambridge University Press.

IPCC. 2007. *Climate change 2007: The physical science basis. Contribution of Working Group I to the Fourth Assessment Report of the Intergovernmental Panel on Climate Change*. Edited by B. Metz, O. Davidson, P. Bosch, et al. Cambridge: Cambridge University Press.

IPCC. 2013. *Climate change 2013: The physical science basis. Contribution of Working Group I to the Fifth Assessment Report of the Intergovernmental Panel on Climate Change.* Edited by T. F. Stocker, D. Qin, G.-K. Plattner, et al. Cambridge: Cambridge University Press.

IPCC. 2014. *Climate change 2014: Mitigation of climate change, Working Group III Contribution to the Fifth Assessment Report of the Intergovernmental Panel on Climate Change.* Edited by O. Edenhofer, R. Pichs-Madruga, Y. Sokona, et al. Cambridge: Cambridge University Press.

IPCC. 2021. *Climate change 2021: The physical science basis. Contribution of Working Group I to the Sixth Assessment Report of the Intergovernmental Panel on Climate Change.* Edited by V. Masson-Delmotte, P. Zhai, A. Pirani, et al. Cambridge: Cambridge University Press.

Irvine, P., B. Kravitz, M. G. Lawrence, et al. 2016. "An overview of the Earth system science of solar geoengineering." *WIREs Climate Change,* 7:815–833.

KVA. 2018. "Scientific background on the Sveriges Riksbank Prize in Economic Sciences in Memory of Alfred Nobel 2018." Committee for the Prize in Economic Sciences in Memory of Alfred. https://www.nobelprize.org/uploads/2018/10/advanced-economicsciencesprize2018.pdf.

Lapenis, A. G. 1998. "Arrhenius and the Intergovernmental Panel on Climate Change." *EOS,* 79(23):271.

Matthews, H. D., N. P. Gillet, Peter A. Stott, et al. 2009. "The proportionality of global warming to cumulative carbon emissions." *Nature,* 459:829–833.

Nordhaus W., and A. Moffat. 2017. "A survey of global impacts of climate change: Replications, survey methods and a statistical analysis." NBER Working Paper 23646.

OECD. 2016. "Effective carbon rates: Pricing CO_2 through taxes and emissions trading systems." Paris: OECD Publishing.

Pindyck, R. S. 1991. "Irreversibility, uncertainty, and investment." *Journal of Economic Literature,* 29:1110–1148.

Pindyck, R. S. 2013. "Climate change policy: What do the models tell us?" *Journal of Economic Literature,* 51(3):860–872.

Rudik, I. 2020. "Optimal climate policy when damages are unknown." *American Economic Journal: Economic Policy,* 12(2):340–373.

Smith, W. 2020. "The cost of stratospheric aerosol injection through 2100." *Environmental Research Letters,* 15(11).

Smith, W., and G. Wagner. 2018. "Stratospheric aerosol injection tactics and costs in the first 15 years of deployment." *Environmental Research Letters,* 13(12).

Wagner, G., and M. Weitzman. 2015. *Climate shock: The economic consequences of a hotter planet.* Princeton, NJ: Princeton University Press.

Weitzman, M. L. 2009. "On modeling and interpreting the economics of catastrophic climate change." *Review of Economics and Statistics,* 91(1):1–19.

CHAPTER 16

Directed Technical Change and Environmental Economics

ANTOINE DECHEZLEPRÊTRE *and* DAVID HÉMOUS

1 Introduction

While policymakers and climate scientists have long argued that overcoming the challenges brought about by climate change require policies that encourage the development of new technologies that reduce the energy- and emissions-intensity of production and consumption, the economics literature had initially focused on models with exogenous technological change (see, e.g., Nordhaus 1994). In these models, the optimal policy response is a Pigovian tax on greenhouse gas emissions, which progressively increases over time. The growing theoretical literature on directed technical change (DTC) in the environmental context shows that taking into account the endogeneity of innovation can profoundly affect policy recommendations, and the empirical literature has provided ample evidence that innovation indeed responds to economic incentives such as an increase in fuel or energy prices. This chapter presents a short and non-exhaustive review of this literature, which notably builds on Acemoglu, Aghion, Bursztyn and Hémous (2012) (hereafter cited as AABH) and Aghion, Dechezleprêtre, Hémous, Martin, and van Reenen (2016). The review (especially the theoretical part) reproduces in part our recent review in Hémous and Olsen (2021).[1]

---

[1] For other literature reviews, see Popp, Newell, and Jaffe (2010); Fischer and Heutel (2013); Popp (2019); Grubb et al. (2021).

DTC has a long tradition in economics. Hicks (1932) already suggested that an increase in relative prices should induce innovation to economize on the more expensive input, so that labor scarcity with respect to capital should induce labor-saving innovation; and Kennedy (1964) linked the direction of innovation to input cost shares. Early endogenous growth theory models, such as Aghion and Howitt (1992), introduce only one type of innovation, whereas a key feature of DTC growth models is the presence of several types of innovation. The earliest example is Aghion and Howitt (1996), who model separately research and development and analyze researchers' incentives to allocate their effort to one or the other stage of innovation.[2] Closer to the original questions of Hicks (1932) and Kennedy (1964), Acemoglu (1998, 2002) developed the canonical DTC model where innovation can augment either low- or high-skill labor.

Even though growth theorists developed endogenous growth models with DTC in the 1990s, environmental economists did not adopt these until later. Yet a growing empirical literature investigated the impact of energy prices on innovation (Newell, Jaffe, and Stavins 1999; Popp 2002), and on the quantitative side, several papers added induced technical change to computable general equilibrium (CGE) models. Still, these authors did not build on modern growth theory and therefore either ignored knowledge externalities or modeled them in an ad hoc way: for instance, in Nordhaus (2002) and Popp (2004, 2006), technological progress results from the accumulation of an R&D stock similar to capital.[3] Bovenberg and Smulders (1995, 1996) present endogenous growth models in an environmental context but with only one type of innovation.

We focus our review on DTC models in environmental economics that build on modern endogenous growth theory and especially Acemoglu's (1998, 2002) framework. This literature largely focuses on energy and climate-change economics. The main source of difference between these models is whether they consider directed innovation affecting two inputs that are complement or substitute. The complement case (starting with Smulders and de Nooij 2003) is used to study energy or fossil fuel resource-saving innovation as energy and fossil fuel resources are complement to capital or labor. The

---

[2] In their model, research corresponds to the arrival of a new potential line of products, and development corresponds to secondary innovations that introduce one of these products.

[3] See also Goulder and Schneider (1999); Massetti, Carraro, and Nicita (2009); Sue Wing (2003). Gerlagh and Lise (2005) and Grimaud and Rouge (2008) microfound innovation but still impose ad hoc relationships between its social and private values.

substitute case (starting with AABH) focuses on the development of clean technologies that can replace dirty ones, such as renewables versus fossil fuels in electricity production. The substitute case offers policy recommendations that contrast more sharply with the earlier exogenous technical change literature than the complement case—essentially because the complement case naturally leads to an economy featuring a balanced growth path, whereas the substitute case does not. Models with DTC have since been used to study the impact of energy price shocks on innovation in green technology, the determinants of historical energy transitions, and the optimal design of unilateral carbon taxes with endogenous innovation and international trade. On the empirical side, the literature has provided unambiguous evidence that energy and carbon prices are able to redirect innovation activity toward clean technologies, providing strong empirical validation of the basic DTC framework, although many specific questions remain largely unexplored.

Section 2 presents our review of the theoretical literature and a simple original extension of the AABH framework. Section 3 discusses the empirical evidence. We conclude and discuss future research avenues in Section 4.

2 Theoretical Insights from the DTC Literature

In this section, we first review the main lessons from AABH. AABH presents a framework where clean technologies (such as renewables) can substitute for dirty ones (such as fossil fuels) and shows that the optimal policy with endogenous innovation is markedly different from that with exogenous innovation. We then adapt this model to contrast the substitute case with that of two complement inputs, which is adapted to study energy-saving innovation for instance. Section 2.3 presents further applications of the DTC framework. Section 2.4 presents an original extension to the AABH model, where innovations in the dirtier sector can also reduce the emission rate.

2.1 The substitute case: Clean and dirty energy

In AABH, a final good Y_t (the numeraire) is produced with a dirty input Y_{dt} and a clean input Y_{ct}, according to a CES production function:

$$Y_t = \left(Y_{ct}^{\frac{\varepsilon-1}{\varepsilon}} + Y_{dt}^{\frac{\varepsilon-1}{\varepsilon}} \right)^{\frac{\varepsilon}{\varepsilon-1}}. \tag{1}$$

The elasticity of substitution between the two inputs, ε, is greater than 1 so that the two inputs are gross substitutes.[4] This framework is appropriate to study a situation where the clean input can replace the dirty input over time when the latter is not necessary for production. It applies, for instance, to the choice between renewable or nuclear energy and fossil fuels, between electric and fossil fuel vehicles or between bioplastics and traditional plastics. Both Papageorgiou, Saam, and Schulte (2017), using macro data, and Jo (2020), using micro data, estimate elasticities of substitution between clean and dirty energy inputs between 2 and 3; whereas Stöckl and Zerrahn (2020) and Wiskich (2021) find elasticities larger than 3 in electricity production.

Greenhouse gas emissions are proportional to the use of the dirty input: $P_t = \xi Y_{dt}$. This formulation is equivalent to one where emissions are the result of consuming a freely available fossil fuel resource that enters production in a Leontief way with the dirty input. It is also equivalent to the case where the dirty input is an extraction input and Y_{dt} represents the extracted fossil fuel resource. Therefore, AABH focuses on innovations that reduce the effective costs of dirty inputs such as fossil fuel power plants, fossil fuel vehicles, or fossil fuels themselves but that keep the emission intensity of these inputs constant. This ignores innovations aimed at improving energy efficiency or resource productivity ("thermal efficiency"), which we introduce in Section 2.4.

The clean and dirty inputs are each produced using a combination of labor and a sector-specific set of machines indexed by i and of mass one. These machines are distinct for each sector $j \in \{c, d\}$, and their productivity evolves endogenously. The current level of productivity for machine $i \in [0, 1]$ employed in sector $j \in \{c, d\}$ is denoted $A_{ji} > 0$. The production functions for the two sectors are:

$$Y_j = \frac{1}{1-\beta} L_j^\beta \int_0^1 A_{ji}^\beta x_{ji}^{1-\beta}\, di \text{ for } j \in \{c, d\}, \tag{2}$$

where L_j is the mass of workers hired in sector j. Machines are produced monopolistically and their production costs $1 - \beta$ units of the final good.

Innovation is modeled in a quality-ladder fashion (Aghion and Howitt 1992). Time is discrete, and at the beginning of every period, scientists of mass $S = 1$ can work to innovate either in the clean or the dirty sector. Given

---

[4] Aghion and Howitt (2009, chap. 16) look at the perfect substitutes case, $\varepsilon = \infty$, and preempt some of the AABH results.

this choice, each scientist is randomly allocated to one machine in their target sector without congestion (i.e., at most one scientist is allocated to each sector). The probability of a successful innovation in sector j is given by η_j and there are no cross-sectoral spillovers in innovation. An innovation increases the quality of the targeted machine by a factor $1+\gamma$ (without loss of generality we assume $1+\gamma > (1-\beta)^{\frac{\beta-1}{\beta}}$, so that the technological leader charges the unconstrained monopoly price). AABH assumes that the innovator obtains a patent for one period only. As we discuss below, this assumption makes the gap between the private and the social returns of innovation particularly salient, but the insights of AABH generalize to settings where patents last longer.[5] As the supply of R&D resources is fixed, clean R&D fully crowds out dirty R&D. This is not an innocuous assumption, because a policy that aims at increasing clean innovation also depresses dirty innovation and output growth (see Popp 2004).

The aggregate technology in sector j can be defined as $A_j \equiv \int_0^1 A_{ji} di$. The innovation process then leads to the following law of motion for input $j \in \{c, d\}$ technology:

$$A_{jt} = (1 + \gamma \eta_j S_{jt}) A_{jt-1},$$

where S_{jt} is the mass of scientists in sector j, η_j their productivity, and γ the innovation size. This innovation setup features a "building-on-the-shoulders-of-giants" externality typical of Schumpeterian growth models: a successful innovator at time t will not only improve the current technology from $A_{j,t-1}$ to $(1-\gamma)A_{j,t-1}$, but she will also enable future innovators to build on the technology $(1+\gamma)A_{j,t-1}$ instead of having to build on $A_{j,t-1}$. This contrasts with horizontal innovation models where future innovators still need to develop new products "from scratch."

To determine the allocation of scientists, one needs to compute the expected profits realized by innovators in the two sectors. The maximization problems of the clean and dirty input producers give rise to iso-elastic demand functions (with a demand elasticity of $1/\beta$) for the machines. As the monopolists maximize profits given by $\pi_{ji} = p_{ji}x_{ji} - (1-\beta)x_{ji}$, they charge a

---

[5] For simplicity, in sectors without innovation and therefore with no patent, the monopoly rights are attributed at random to an entrepreneur.

markup $1/(1-\beta)$ leading to machine price of 1. The quantity produced by a monopolist and their profits π_{ji} are given by:

$$x_{ji} = p_j^{1/\beta} L_j A_{ji} \quad \text{and} \quad \pi_{ji} = \beta p_j^{1/\beta} L_j A_{ji}. \tag{3}$$

Plugging equation (3) into equation (2) gives the equilibrium quantity of intermediate input j:

$$Y_j = \frac{1}{1-\beta} p_j^{(1-\beta)/\beta} A_j L_j. \tag{4}$$

Because scientists are randomly allocated within a sector, the expected technology obtained by an innovator in sector j is given by $(1-\gamma)A_{j(t-1)}$. From (3), the expected profits of a scientist working for sector j are then given by:

$$\Pi_{jt} = \eta_j(1+\gamma)\beta p_{jt}^{\frac{1}{\beta}} L_{jt} A_{j(t-1)} = \frac{\eta_j \beta p_{jt} Y_{jt}}{1+\gamma \eta_j s_{jt}}, \tag{5}$$

where the second equality uses (4). The ratio of expected profits is then given by:

$$\frac{\Pi_{ct}}{\Pi_{dt}} = \frac{\eta_c(1+\gamma \eta_d s_{dt})}{\eta_d(1+\gamma \eta_c s_{ct})} \frac{p_{ct} Y_{ct}}{p_{dt} Y_{dt}} = \frac{\eta_c}{\eta_d} \underbrace{\left(\frac{p_{ct}}{p_{dt}}\right)^{\frac{1}{\beta}}}_{\text{price effect}} \underbrace{\frac{L_{ct}}{L_{dt}}}_{\text{market size effect}} \underbrace{\frac{A_{ct-1}}{A_{dt-1}}}_{\text{direct productivity effect}}. \tag{6}$$

Scientists will be allocated to the sector with the highest expected profits— namely, to the clean one if this ratio is greater than 1, to the dirty one if it is less than 1, or potentially to both if it is equal to 1. The first equality in (6) shows that scientists target the sector with the largest revenue (adjusted with the productivity of the innovation technology) because profits are proportional to revenues. This is in line with Kennedy's (1964) finding that the relative incentive to innovate combines the innovation possibility frontier (which here is independent of technologies) and the relative factor shares (which here are the revenue shares of the clean and dirty sectors). The second equality decomposes relative revenues between a price effect, a market size effect, and a direct productivity effect.

Labor allocation between the two sectors is endogenous, and equating the marginal product of labor in the two sectors implies that the price ratio is given by

$$p_c/p_d = (A_c/A_d)^{-\beta}. \tag{7}$$

Therefore, the price effect pushes innovation toward the less advanced sector. Demand from the final good producer implies that

$$Y_c / Y_d = (p_c / p_d)^{-\varepsilon}. \tag{8}$$

Combining (4), (7), and (8) gives the labor allocation across the two sectors as:

$$L_c / L_d = (A_c / A_d)^{\sigma - 1} \tag{9}$$

where we define $\sigma = 1 + \beta(\varepsilon - 1)$. Since $\varepsilon > 1$, the $\sigma > 1$ advanced sector attracts relatively more workers. Intuitively, this occurs because the allocation of labor itself depends on relative technologies and relative prices, and this price effect is dominated when the two inputs are substitute. Therefore, the market size effect in (6) pushes innovation toward the more advanced sector.

Using equations (6), (7), and (9), we obtain the relative expected profits from innovation as:

$$\frac{\Pi_{ct}}{\Pi_{dt}} = \frac{\eta_c}{\eta_d} \left(\frac{1 + \gamma \eta_c s_{ct}}{1 + \gamma \eta_d s_{dt}} \right)^{\sigma - 2} \left(\frac{A_{ct-1}}{A_{dt-1}} \right)^{\sigma - 1}. \tag{10}$$

Since the two inputs are substitute $\sigma > 1$, the direct productivity effect and the market size effect dominate the price effect and innovation tends to be directed toward the most advanced sector. This is the first lesson of the framework: there is *path dependence* in innovation in laissez-faire, as societies with a relatively high level of dirty technologies today should expect even more dirty innovations in the future.[6] For sufficiently large or low values of $A_{c(t-1)} / A_{d(t-1)}$, the equilibrium features a corner solution with innovation in only one sector. In particular, for a sufficiently low initial ratio A_{c0} / A_{d0}, all innovation at time 1 occurs in the dirty sector, A_{ct} / A_{dt} further decreases over time, and innovation remains locked in dirty technologies. Intuitively, clean innovations will have a hard time taking off in *laissez-faire*, because an innovation that improves a component in a fossil fuel power plant will have a much larger market than one that improves a component in a solar panel. As a result, while the canonical DTC models of Acemoglu (1998, 2002)

---

[6] For more discussion on path dependence, see the review in Aghion, Hepburn, Teytelboym, and Zenghelis (2019).

focus on a balanced growth path (BGP), AABH focuses on unbalanced trajectories.[7]

Therefore, the production of the dirty inputs and CO_2 emissions grow without bound if fossil fuel technologies are initially ahead. A social planner can avoid such an outcome by implementing clean research subsidies and/or a carbon tax. A clean research subsidy directly multiplies the right-hand side of equation (6), whereas a carbon tax decreases the producer price p_{dt} for given technologies by imposing a wedge between the producer price of the dirty input and its marginal product in final good production. That is, (6) and (10) become

$$\frac{\Pi_{ct}}{\Pi_{dt}} = \frac{(1+q_t)\eta_c p_{ct}^{\frac{1}{\beta}} L_{ct} A_{ct-1}}{\eta_d p_{dt}^{\frac{1}{\beta}} L_{dt} A_{dt-1}}$$

$$= (1+q_t)(1+\tau_t)^\varepsilon \frac{\eta_c}{\eta_d}\left(\frac{1+\gamma\eta_c s_{ct}}{1+\gamma\eta_d s_{dt}}\right)^{\sigma-2}\left(\frac{A_{ct-1}}{A_{dt-1}}\right)^{\sigma-1}, \tag{11}$$

where q_t is a clean research subsidy and τ_t is an (ad valorem) carbon tax.[8]

Provided that the policy intervention is sufficiently large and maintained for a sufficiently long time, the social planner can redirect innovation away from dirty toward clean technologies, ensuring that clean technologies catch up and eventually overtake dirty ones. Once this has been achieved, market forces will favor clean innovation. A temporary intervention is enough to ensure that emissions decline in the long run provided that the two inputs are sufficiently substitute ($\varepsilon > 1/\beta$).[9] Yet such an intervention is not costless: when clean technologies are catching up with dirty ones, productivity growth is low because innovation targets the less productive input. This makes delaying an intervention costly: while the economy remains in laissez-faire, the gap between clean and dirty technologies grows, requiring a longer and there-

---

[7] A BGP can be obtained by introducing (strong) cross-sectoral knowledge spillovers in the innovation function. For instance, if scientists' productivity obeys, $\eta_j (A_{(-j)t}/A_{jt}^{(1-\delta)/2}$, then a BGP can be obtained when $\sigma < 2 - \delta$, while there is still path dependence if $\sigma > 2 - \delta$.

[8] Alsina-Pujols and Hovdahl (2022) show how other instruments, such as limited patent enforcement for dirty innovation, can also redirect innovation toward the clean sector. Nowzohour (2021) analyzes the role of frictions in the reallocation of scientists.

[9] The laissez-faire production of dirty input is decreasing in the clean technology A_c if $\varepsilon > 1/\beta$. Intuitively, when $\varepsilon > 1/\beta$, the two inputs are sufficiently complement that an increase in the clean technology increases demand in the dirty input so much that dirty input production grows through an increase use of machines even if the dirty technology does not grow.

fore costlier intervention later on. This brings us to the second lesson of the framework: taking endogenous technical change into account calls for an *earlier intervention*.[10]

The third lesson from the framework is that *a carbon tax is not enough to obtain the first best*. Formally, AABH considers a social planner who maximizes the intertemporal welfare of a representative agent who cares about consumption and environmental quality. They show that the first best allocation can be decentralized using a Pigovian carbon tax and research subsidies to clean innovation (plus a subsidy to all machines to remove the monopoly distortion). Why is a carbon tax not enough? Innovation in the first best is allocated to the sector with the highest social value, where the ratio of social values is given by:

$$
\frac{SV_{ct}}{SV_{dt}} = \frac{\eta_c(1+\gamma\eta_d s_{dt})\sum_{\tau \geq t} \lambda_{t,\tau} p_{c\tau}^{\frac{1}{\beta}} L_{c\tau} A_{c\tau}}{\eta_d(1+\gamma\eta_c s_{ct})\sum_{\tau \geq t} \lambda_{t,\tau} p_{d\tau}^{\frac{1}{\beta}} L_{d\tau} A_{d\tau}},
\tag{12}
$$

with $\lambda_{t,\tau}$ the discount factor between t and τ. $P_{d\tau}$ is the producer price of the dirty input before any carbon taxation is applied, so a higher social cost of emissions that increases the optimal carbon tax decreases the producer price p_{dt} and raises the relative social value of a clean innovation. Therefore, the social planner allocates innovation according to the discounted benefits that a higher technology brings in every period. In contrast, in the absence of a direct research subsidy, the market allocation depends on the ratio of current profits given by equation (6). With a research subsidy, the market allocation is given by (11), so that a properly chosen research subsidy can reduce the ratio between the private value and social value.

This explains why the market and the social planner would generally not allocate innovation in the same way without the appropriate research subsidy, but AABH's claim is stronger: that the social planner needs to systematically implement research subsidies. In other words, one should expect the ratio of clean to dirty private values of innovation to be lower than that of the social values of innovation. How can that be the case? Essentially it is because the market's "short-termism" affects clean and dirty technologies

---

[10] A similar result is obtained by Gerlagh, Kverndokk, and Rosendahl (2009), who find that endogenous innovation in abatement technology calls for a front-loaded policy.

differently. Assume that dirty technologies are initially more advanced but that the social planner would like to implement an "energy transition" so that clean technologies are expected to dominate in the future (as is arguably the case). Then, in the long run, dirty technologies will have a small market, $\lambda_{t,\tau} p_{d\tau}^{\frac{1}{\beta}} L_{d\tau} A_{d\tau}$ is relatively small for large τ, and a large share of the social benefits of a dirty innovation (say, an improvement in a natural gas power plant) is realized in the short run. The gap between private and social value for a dirty innovation is not that large. In contrast, the market for clean technologies in the future is large, and a large share of the social benefits of a clean innovation (say, an improvement in solar panels) will be realized in the future (here, in the form of even better solar panels), and the gap between the social and private values of a clean innovation is very large.

In AABH the market is particularly myopic because patents last for only one period, but the intuition extends to setups with longer-lived patents (as mentioned in AABH and extensively analyzed in Greaker, Heggedal, and Rosendahl 2018). The reason is that the myopia of the market ultimately stems from the building-on-the-shoulders-of-giants externality, which innovators do not internalize. To show this, consider an extreme case with perpetual patents. In this case, successful innovators must pay royalties to the previous incumbent to compensate them for their profit loss. Then, the ratio of private values of innovation is given by:

$$\frac{\Pi_{ct}}{\Pi_{dt}} = \frac{\eta_c(1+\gamma\eta_d s_{dt})\sum_{\tau\geq t}\lambda_{t,\tau} p_{c\tau}^{\frac{1}{\beta}} L_{c\tau} A_{ct}}{\eta_d(1+\gamma\eta_c s_{ct})\sum_{\tau\geq t}\lambda_{t,\tau} p_{d\tau}^{\frac{1}{\beta}} L_{d\tau} A_{dt}}. \tag{13}$$

While in (12) the sum involves the technology at time τ, $A_{j\tau}$, the sum in (13) is over the technology at the time of invention, t, A_{jt}. This difference reflects the building-on-the-shoulders-of-giants externality that the social planner internalizes: an innovator improves not only the current technology but also all future technologies, because future innovators will build upon her innovation. It is worth pointing out that the inefficiency in the direction of innovation in AABH is therefore intimately linked to the Schumpeterian nature of innovation in their model: in contrast, the optimal policy in a model with horizontal innovation, permanent patents, and DTC need not feature research subsidies on top of Pigovian taxation. In general, finite-lived patents, creative destruction, imitation, and the building-on-the-shoulders-of-giants externality all contribute to make the private value of an innovation short-sighted relative to its social value. In the context of an energy transition, this short-termism of the market leads to too little clean innovation relative to dirty—even with Pigovian taxation, which calls for clean research subsidies.[11]

In summary, three lessons can be drawn from the AABH framework. First, there is path dependence in the development of clean versus dirty technologies, which explains why clean technologies have had a hard time taking off without government support. Second, policy action should be more frontloaded than what a model with exogenous technology would predict. Third, climate change policy should not simply involve Pigovian carbon taxation; instead governments should also use clean research subsidies to boost clean innovation. All these features arise because AABH considers the choice between two substitute inputs and their associated technologies.

To derive quantitative predictions, Acemoglu, Akcigit, Hanley, and Kerr (2016) embed the AABH framework within a firm-dynamics model. They assume that the final good is a Cobb-Douglas aggregate of a mass 1 of intermediates. Each intermediate can be produced with a clean or a dirty input that are perfect substitute, and that each have their own technology evolving on their own ladder. In the spirit of Klette and Kortum (2004), a firm is a collection of leading clean or dirty technologies in different lines. There are two types of innovations: incremental innovations that build on the clean or dirty technology separately, and radical innovation that builds on the leading technology whether it is clean or dirty. This generates cross-sectoral spillovers that mitigate (without eliminating) path dependence in innovation. In addition, the dirty technology input requires the use of an exhaustible resource. This leads to an increase in the resource price over time, which ensures that a transition to clean innovation occurs in laissez-faire. They calibrate the model using firm-level data in the energy sector and patent data. They find that the switch to clean innovation occurs too late to avoid large climate damages in laissez-faire. In contrast, the optimal policy implements a rapid switch from dirty to clean innovation thanks to large clean

---

[11] Gerlagh, Kverndokk, and Rosendahl (2014) make a similar point in a model with clean innovation only. This contrasts the DTC literature covered here with an earlier literature that simply assumed a certain (constant) ratio between private and social values of innovation (Nordhaus 2002; Popp 2004, 2006; Gerlagh and Lise 2005).

research subsidies and a carbon tax. These conclusions are very much in line with AABH.

2.2 The complementarity case: Energy-saving innovation

AABH focuses on the decarbonization of energy production. An alternative way to reduce emissions is to develop energy- or resource-saving innovations. To analyze this case within our framework, assume that the final good is now produced with

$$Y_t = \left(Y_{Pt}^{\frac{\varepsilon-1}{\varepsilon}} + Y_{Et}^{\frac{\varepsilon-1}{\varepsilon}} \right)^{\frac{\varepsilon}{\varepsilon-1}}, \tag{14}$$

where Y_{Pt} denotes a production input, Y_{Et} an energy-services input, and importantly the two inputs are complement: $\varepsilon < 1$. The production input is produced with sector-specific machines and a capital labor aggregate L, while the energy-services input is produced with energy (or a fossil fuel resource) E:

$$Y_P = \frac{L^\beta}{1-\beta} \int_0^1 A_{Pi}^\beta x_{Pi}^{1-\beta} di \quad \text{and} \quad Y_E = \frac{E^\beta}{1-\beta} \int_0^1 A_{Ei}^\beta x_{Ei}^{1-\beta} di. \tag{15}$$

We define aggregate technologies A_{Pt} and A_{Et}. Because the two inputs are complement, an increase in the energy-augmenting technology A_{Et} is energy-saving (or if E is a resource, resource-saving). Theoretical papers have then made different assumptions about the supply of E: Smulders and de Nooij (2003) assume a constant resource flow; Shanker and Stern (2018) assume a perfectly elastically supplied resource; and Di Maria and Valente (2008), André and Smulders (2014), and Hassler, Krusell, and Olovsson (2021) assume that the resource is exhaustible.

This literature derives and analyzes stylized facts on energy consumption and growth. For instance, Hassler et al. (2021) build a quantitative macroeconomic model calibrated to the US economy. Because energy demand is very unresponsive to price changes in the short run, they find an elasticity of substitution between energy and the capital–labor aggregate close to 0. Yet the energy share is relatively stable in the long run. They account for this puzzling pattern through a DTC model. In line with this model, they find that energy-saving technical change took off in the 1970s with the oil shocks. Their model further predicts that resource scarcity (which could result from climate regulation) will lead to only a small increase in the energy share. Interestingly, they argue that the market allocation of innovation is not systematically inefficient. Such a conclusion contrasts sharply with AABH. What drives this difference? In a word, the complementarity between energy and other inputs, which implies that the economy will feature a BGP.

To see this more clearly, let us assume the same innovation technology and market structure as in Section 2.1. Without loss of generality, further assume that L is fixed. The market allocation of innovation then depends on the relative expected profits from labor-augmenting over energy-augmenting innovation, which are given by:

$$\frac{\Pi_{Pt}}{\Pi_{Et}} = \frac{\eta_P(1+\gamma\eta_E s_{Et})}{\eta_E(1+\gamma\eta_P s_{Pt})} \frac{p_{Pt}Y_{Pt}}{p_{Et}Y_{Et}} = \frac{\eta_P}{\eta_E}\left(\frac{p_{Pt}}{p_{Et}}\right)^{\frac{1}{\beta}} \frac{L}{E} \frac{A_{Pt-1}}{A_{Et-1}}$$

$$= \frac{\eta_P(1+\gamma\eta_E s_{Et})}{\eta_E(1+\gamma\eta_P s_{Pt})}\left(\frac{LA_{Pt}}{EA_{Et}}\right)^{\frac{\sigma-1}{\sigma}}. \tag{16}$$

The key difference with the model of Section 2.1 is that because the two inputs are complement ($\sigma < 1$), the price effect now dominates. We can consider, in turn, the three cases for the path of E. If the resource flow is constant, then following the last equality in (16), innovation favors the least advanced sector, so that the economy must converge to a balanced growth path (BGP) where both technologies grow at the same rate and the expected profits are equal ($\Pi_{Pt} = \Pi_{Et}$). Given the first equality, the energy share is constant in the long run and equal to $\eta_P/(\eta_E + \eta_P)$.

A decrease in the resource flow increases the energy price and the energy share, leading to an increase in energy-saving innovation. As a result, if the resource flow decreases over time (because of resource exhaustion or a growing carbon tax), faster growth in energy-saving innovation compensates for it so that the effective amount of energy $A_{Et}E$ grows at the same rate as effective labor $A_{pt}L$.[12] The economy still converges toward a BGP with a constant interior energy share. This is the same logic as in Acemoglu (2003), where labor scarcity leads to labor-augmenting technical change. For the same reason, if the resource price is constant, then innovation in the long run is labor-augmenting.

---

[12] While a tax on energy services Y_E moves innovation toward A_p for any ε, a tax on energy, E, moves innovation toward A_E when $\varepsilon < 1$.

The social planner still allocates scientists according to the ratio of social values, which is given by an equation analogous to (12). In general, the social planner allocation and the market allocation still differ, but they converge toward the same balanced growth path provided that a Pigovian tax corrects for the environmental externality. As a result, research subsidies may still be necessary in the transition, but they become much less critical and need not even be in favor of energy-saving innovations. In fact, in the specific example studied by Hassler et al. (2021), the ratio of social values is always equal to that of private values, and they are not necessary in the transition either (see also Hart 2008). Because the two inputs are complement, the market now favors the least advanced technology adjusting for resource availability, which ensures that the economy moves toward a balanced growth path, in line with the social planner's solution. While public intervention is crucial to engineer a transition from fossil fuels to clean energy, carbon pricing can do the heavy lifting for the development of energy-saving technologies.

As a result of DTC, a very low short-run elasticity between energy and labor-capital is compatible with a higher long-run elasticity. For instance, in the model sketched here, the long-run energy share is fixed at $\eta_p/(\eta_E + \eta_p)$ when the resource flow is constant (and is still close to this value when it decreases over time). In the long run, the economy behaves as if the production function were Cobb-Douglas. In fact, climate models with exogenous technological change often assume such a Cobb-Douglas production function. Are they missing a lot by ignoring the dynamics of technical change? Casey (2019) shows that unfortunately this is the case. He considers a similar setup with a Leontieff production function between energy and the capital–labor aggregate but DTC leading to a unit long-run elasticity and compares it with a Cobb-Douglas economy with exogenous technical change. Both models are calibrated to the US economy. He shows that, following the implementation of a carbon tax, emissions decrease slower in the Leontieff with DTC economy than in the Cobb-Douglas economy, leading to significantly more cumulative emissions and therefore higher damages.

2.3 *Applications to environmental questions*

We now review papers that apply the DTC framework in the context of energy shocks, energy transitions, and carbon leakage.

Energy market shocks. Fried (2018) uses the oil shocks of the 1970s to calibrate a more detailed DTC model. As in Section 2.2, she considers a final good produced with a production input and energy services. Energy services are themselves a CES aggregate of local fossil fuel energy, oil imports, and green energy with an elasticity of substitution greater than 1 (similar to AABH). Innovation can be targeted at the local fossil fuel energy, green energy, or the production input, and she introduces cross-sectoral knowledge spillovers. She compares this economy to one without DTC. She finds that a carbon tax has a large effect on the innovation allocation, so that the carbon tax necessary to cut emissions by 30 percent in 20 years is 19.2 percent smaller in a world with DTC than in a world without DTC.[13]

Acemoglu, Aghion, Barrage, and Hémous (2021) extend AABH to analyze the consequences of the US shale gas revolution on welfare and emissions in the long run. They model electricity as a CES aggregate of clean, natural-gas-based and coal-based electricity (with an elasticity greater than 1). Fossil fuel electricity is produced with a power plant input and the associated resource. Both coal and natural gas generate emissions, but natural gas is much cleaner. Scientists can improve the productivity of fossil fuel power plants or clean power plants. In the short run, the shale gas boom reduces the price of natural gas, electricity production relies more heavily on natural gas and less on coal, and emissions decrease. At the same time, the market for innovations in fossil fuel power plants expands, which leads to a reallocation of innovation away from clean and toward fossil fuel technologies. In line with this prediction, they document that the ratio of green to fossil fuel patents in electricity production has decreased substantially since 2011 (two years after the beginning of the boom). Calibrating their model to the US electricity sector, they predict that because of this innovation response, the shale gas boom will eventually lead to an increase in emissions. They also compute the optimal policy and show that the shale gas boom calls for larger clean research subsidies.[14]

---

[13] Hart (2019) adds energy-saving innovation, physical limits to productivity, and intersectoral knowledge spillovers to an integrated assessment model with AABH features. The optimal policy still features both a carbon tax and clean research subsidies, but the presence of knowledge spillovers reduces the relative importance of research subsidies.

[14] Acemoglu and Rafey (2019) similarly find that progress in geoengineering technology can backfire. When the government cannot commit to its environmental policy, an exogenous im-

Historical energy transitions. A number of papers have used DTC to account for past energy transitions. Stern, Pezzey, and Lu (2020) study the transition from wood to coal that occurred during the Industrial Revolution and perhaps in part caused it. The final good is a CES aggregate of a wood-based input and a fossil-fuel-based input. The two inputs enter the production function symmetrically, but whereas the supply of wood is fixed exogenously, coal is extracted at a constant cost. Similarly to AABH, the two inputs are substitute, so innovation tends to be allocated toward the more abundant input (everything else given). If wood is initially abundant, the economy first relies on the wood-based input and innovates in that sector. Yet without sufficient increasing returns to scale in innovation, output grows less than exponentially. Over time, however, the relative price of coal drops and the relative supply of coal versus wood increases. This eventually redirects innovation toward the coal-based input, at which point economic growth takes off. Gars and Olovsson (2019) use a similar DTC model, where innovation in fossil fuel technologies can ensure higher growth than innovation in wood-powered technologies, to explain the nineteenth-century Great Divergence. They show that when a country starts using fossil fuels, the world fossil fuel price increases, which may discourage other countries from innovating in fossil fuel technologies.

Lemoine (2020) builds a DTC model that generates endogenous energy transitions. Similar to Acemoglu et al. (2021), he models separately the resource used in energy production and the complementary input necessary to produce energy. He models and calibrates historical energy transitions but finds that in the climate change context, research subsidies are still necessary to accelerate the transition to renewables.

Carbon leakage. The previous papers ignored international aspects and studied either the whole world or a country in isolation. Yet given the limited results from international climate negotiations, several countries have been pursuing unilateral climate policies, the effectiveness of which is limited by carbon leakage. Carbon leakage occurs when a reduction in emissions in one country (following the implementation of a carbon policy) is undone by an increase in emissions in the rest of the world. Several papers use DTC models to study whether the innovation response amplifies or mitigates carbon

---

provement in geoengineering technology may decrease future environmental taxes, which decreases current clean innovation and can lead to an increase in emissions.

leakage. Di Maria and Smulders (2004) and Corrado and van der Werf (2008) consider a two-country (North, South), two-goods (energy-intensive, non-energy-intensive) trade model. The North introduces a unilateral carbon tax, so that part of the production of the energy-intensive good moves to the South. In the first paper, innovation occurs endogenously in the North only and the South imitates exogenously. The unilateral carbon tax then increases innovation in the non-energy-intensive good, which amplifies carbon leakage when the goods are complement and mitigates it when they are substitute (because energy-augmenting innovation is energy-saving when the two inputs are complement, and energy-using otherwise). The second paper instead assumes that innovation occurs globally. Then, global innovation is redirected toward the non-energy-intensive good when the two inputs are substitute and to the energy-intensive good when they are complement, always mitigating carbon leakage. Acemoglu, Aghion, and Hémous (2014) and van den Bijgaart (2017) look at the same problem in a two-country version of the AABH model (so with two substitute inputs). Again, a carbon tax in the North leads to a reallocation of part of the production of the dirty input to the South. They take as given the innovation response in the North (contrary to the two previous papers) and respectively find that the imitation and innovation responses in the South amplify carbon leakage.

Hémous (2016) starts from a setup similar to that of Di Maria and Smulders (2004) and Corrado and van der Werf (2008), with trade in an energy-intensive good and a non-energy-intensive good, but he now assumes that the energy-intensive good is itself produced like the final good in AABH as a CES aggregate between a clean input and a dirty input. His model can capture the fact that the emission intensity of the same (energy-intensive) good varies across countries, depending on whether the good is produced with clean or dirty energy. Innovators optimally decide to improve the non-energy-intensive technology, the clean one, or the dirty one. In addition, he assumes that utility is Cobb-Douglas between the energy-intensive and non-energy-intensive goods. The paper contrasts two policies. Like before, a unilateral carbon tax in the North leads to carbon leakage, and the innovation response in the South tends to amplify leakage: as the market for the energy-intensive good expands in the South, innovation there is reallocated toward that sector, and within that sector to dirty technologies (provided that dirty technologies are initially more advanced). In contrast, the North government could implement a green industrial policy, which boosts the development of clean technologies within the energy-intensive sector in the North, and as a result decreases Northern emissions. Importantly, such a policy can also reduce emissions in the South through two channels. First, because innovation in the North is allocated toward clean instead of dirty or non-energy-intensive technologies, the North builds a comparative advantage in that sector. This leads to negative leakage and less dirty innovation in the South (instead the South innovates more in the non-energy-intensive good). Second, if knowledge spillovers are large enough, the South may start innovating in clean instead of dirty technologies in the energy-intensive sector. Therefore, trade acts a double-edged sword: it diminishes the effectiveness of unilateral carbon taxes but also ensures that the appropriate policy can decrease emissions globally.[15]

2.4 Modeling grey innovation

As mentioned before, the baseline AABH model ignores improvements in dirty technologies that reduce the pollution intensity of the dirty good. In contrast, Gans (2012) models innovation in the fossil fuel sector as fossil fuel augmenting. Here, we present a simple extension of AABH that combines both types of dirty innovations. We make two changes to the framework of Section 2.1. First, the dirty input Y_{dt} is now produced competitively using a resource-based input Y_{rt} and a non-resource-based input Y_{pt}:

$$
Y_{dt} = \left(Y_{rt}^{\frac{\theta-1}{\theta}} + Y_{pt}^{\frac{\theta-1}{\theta}} \right)^{\frac{\theta}{\theta-1}},
\tag{17}
$$

where $\theta < 1$ (i.e., the two inputs are complement). The clean resource-based and non-resource-based inputs are all produced competitively according to (2) for $j \in \{c, r, p\}$, and machines are still produced in the same way.[16] Second, we assume that emissions are now proportional to the use of machines in

---

[15] Witajewski-Baltvilks and Fischer (2019) also extend AABH to a two-country model but allow for trade directly in machines (instead of the intermediate inputs), so that innovation incentives depend on market conditions in both countries. When the North is large enough, a unilateral clean research subsidy can redirect innovation toward clean technologies in both countries. In addition, it may induce a climate-skeptic South government to implement its own clean research subsidy for purely economic motives, as long-run growth is higher if both countries innovate in the same sector.

[16] Note that here we are ignoring energy-saving innovations that augment energy productivity in the production of the final good regardless of the source of energy.

the resource-based sector x_{rit}; that is, $P_t = \xi \int_0^1 x_{rit} di$ (implicitly, the use of these machines is associated with the consumption of a fossil fuel in a Leontief way).

In the appendix, we derive that the equilibrium level of pollution is given by:

$$P_t = \xi \left(\frac{A_{dt}}{A_{rt}} \right)^{1-\lambda} \frac{A_{dt}^{\sigma-1}}{A_{ct}^{\sigma-1} + A_{dt}^{\sigma-1}} \left(A_{ct}^{\sigma-1} + A_{dt}^{\sigma-1} \right)^{\frac{1}{\varepsilon-1}} L, \tag{18}$$

with $\lambda \equiv 1 + \beta(\theta - 1)$ defined analogously to σ and the average productivity in sector d defined as $A_{dt} \equiv (A_{rt}^{\lambda-1} + A_{pt}^{\lambda-1})^{\frac{1}{\lambda-1}}$. The first fraction reflects the substitution within the production of the dirty intermediate between the resource-based and the non-resource-based input, as $\theta < 1$, $\lambda < 1$, and this term is decreasing in A_{rt} and increasing in A_{pt}. The second fraction reflects the substitution between the clean and the dirty input; it increases in A_{dt} and decreases in A_{ct}. The third term is the overall productivity in the economy; it reflects a scale effect and increases in all technologies. This equation illustrates well the role of each technology: A_{ct} represents clean alternative to existing fossil-fuel-based technologies (for instance, renewables in energy generation or electric cars in transport); A_{rt} represents resource-saving, and therefore emission-saving, innovations in the production of fossil-fuel-based inputs (for instance, higher thermal efficiency in fossil fuel power plants or higher efficiency in petroleum engines), and A_{pt} represents other improvements in fossil-fuel-based technologies that lead to an increase in the demand for fossil fuels and therefore in emissions (labor-saving innovations in power plants or faster engines in cars).

An increase in clean technologies reduces pollution provided that the clean and dirty inputs are sufficiently substitute: $\varepsilon > 1 + 1/\beta$. The threshold is now different because machines instead of the input are associated with emissions. An increase in the non-resource-based productivity increases emissions. An increase in the resource-saving technology increases or decreases emissions depending on the relative productivity levels. In that sense, they represent "grey innovations."

The innovation technology is the same as in Section 2.1: scientists decide to innovate in clean, resource-based or non-resource-based technologies with a probability of success η_j for $j \in \{c, r, p\}$ depending on the expected profits resulting from their research efforts. Expected profits are still given by (5).

Within the dirty sector, the allocation of innovation between the two inputs now depends on the ratio:

$$\frac{\Pi_{rt}}{\Pi_{pt}} = \frac{\eta_r}{\eta_p} \left(\frac{1+\gamma\eta_r s_{rt}}{1+\gamma\eta_p s_{pt}} \right)^{\lambda-2} \left(\frac{A_{rt-1}}{A_{pt-1}} \right)^{\lambda-1}. \tag{19}$$

Because the resource-based and non-resource-based inputs are complement, $\lambda < 1$, innovation targets the less advanced sector (as in the energy-saving case of Section 2.2), so that should innovation occur in the dirty sector in laissez-faire, it remains balanced between the resource-based and non-resource-based inputs. In contrast, innovation between the clean and the dirty sector still features path dependence and asymptotically only occurs in one of the two sectors (except for a knife-edge case). If the clean sector is initially sufficiently backward relative to the dirty sector, then innovation in laissez-faire occurs in the dirty sector and emissions grow without bound.

Research subsidies can then be used to redirect innovation toward clean or grey technologies. In this context, an interesting question is whether a social planner should aim at making the dirty sector less polluting by focusing on grey innovations or fully switch to clean technologies. A full analysis of the social planner problem is beyond the scope of this chapter, but a first element of response can be found in looking at the growth rates that can be achieved with either strategy. In the long run, innovating in clean technologies leads to a growth rate of $\gamma\eta_c$ and, if the clean and dirty inputs are sufficiently substitute, $\varepsilon > 1 + 1/\beta$, to a decline in emissions. As in AABH, a switch to clean innovation can be achieved through a temporary research subsidy.

Innovation in dirty technologies is balanced between the two sectors in laissez-faire, so that asymptotically the mass of scientists in the resource-saving innovation is $S_{rt} = \eta_p/(\eta_r + \eta_p)$ and the mass of scientists in the resource-using innovation is $S_{pt} = \eta_r/(\eta_r + \eta_p)$, leading to a growth rate of output and emissions given by $\gamma\eta_r\eta_p/(\eta_r + \eta_p)$. Nevertheless, it is possible to ensure a decline in emissions through innovation in the resource-using technology only. From equation (18), note that P_t would decrease over time if the resource-saving technology A_{rt} grows faster than the average dirty productivity A_{dt} (even if clean productivity A_{ct} is constant). Since $\lambda < 1$, the dirty productivity grows asymptotically at the minimum rate of the resource-saving and the resource-using technology. Therefore, a permanent subsidy to resource-saving innovation can guarantee long-run economic growth with declining emissions, but only at the cost of a reduction in long-run economic growth.[17] In the appendix we demonstrate:

Proposition 1 *(i) A temporary subsidy to clean innovation can ensure positive long-run growth at rate $\gamma \eta_c$ with declining emissions when $\varepsilon > 1 + 1/\beta$. (ii) A permanent subsidy to grey innovation can ensure positive long-run growth at a rate approximately equal to $\gamma \eta_r \eta_p / (\eta_r + (1 + (1-\lambda)^{-1}) \eta_p)$ when γ is small while ensuring that emissions decline.*

Therefore, provided that $\varepsilon > 1 + 1/\beta$, a patient social planner would tend to prefer a switch toward green innovation when the clean innovation productivity parameter is relatively high and the resource-based and non-resource-based inputs are less complement. Intuitively, when the production function for the dirty input is closer to Cobb-Douglas, the resource-saving effect of A_{rt} is smaller, requiring us to sacrifice more growth to ensure a decline in emissions. This will be the case in particular when $\eta_c = \eta_r \eta_p / (\eta_r + \eta_p)$; that is, absent environmental concerns, the clean and the dirty technologies would have the same growth potential.

Finally, it is easy to show that a carbon tax (now paid on the use of the machines x_{rit}) redirects innovation within the dirty sector toward the resource-saving technology as in Gans (2012) if innovation occurs in the dirty sector and/or away from the dirty sector and toward clean technologies. Aghion et al. (2016), which we discuss in Section 3, precisely look at the effect of gas prices on clean, grey, and "purely" dirty innovation in the car industry.

3 Empirical Evidence

A large empirical literature has looked for evidence of induced technical change in environmental economics. Popp, Newell, and Jaffe (2010), Popp (2019), and Grubb et al. (2021) provide extensive literature reviews; here,

---

[17] The asymptotic results technically require that there are no physical limits to how high A_{rt} can be, which for some type of innovations may not be realistic (see, e.g., Hart 2019). Nevertheless the analysis is informative as long as we are sufficiently far away from the physical limits. At any rate, the presence of physical limits would reinforce the case for a switch to clean innovation.

we briefly review the earlier literature before focusing on a few recent contributions.

3.1 Energy prices and directed technical change

The closest empirical studies to the theoretical directed technical change literature examine the effect of changing energy prices on innovation. Newell et al. (1999) provide the first example by showing that the energy efficiency of home appliances available for sale changed in response to energy prices between 1958 and 1993. Technical change in air conditioners was biased against energy efficiency in the 1960s when energy prices were low, but this bias reversed after the oil shocks of the 1970s, which led to significant energy price increases.

The early paper by Newell et al. (1999) was a pioneer and a remarkable exception in at least one dimension: the vast majority of the subsequent literature has turned to patent data as an indicator of innovation induced by energy price dynamics. Patent data have a number of attractive features: they are available over long time periods, at a highly technologically disaggregated level—allowing researchers to precisely distinguish between clean and dirty innovations in various sectors—and can be linked with their owners (companies). They also suffer from limitations: in particular, only a small proportion of inventions are patented, and their value is highly heterogeneous. To date, however, no superior indicator has emerged. The literature using detailed product characteristics, such as Newell et al. (1999), is comparably much more limited. This is a remarkable gap in the literature, and an interesting question would be to investigate the extent to which new patents do translate into more energy-efficient products.

In a groundbreaking paper, Popp (2002) uses time-series data on patent applications in the United States from 1970 to 1994 across eleven energy demand or supply technologies, such as solar panels, fuel cells, heat pumps, or waste heat recovery. He then regresses the percentage of all successful domestic patent applications per year in each technology field on the price of energy in the United States in that year. He finds a short-run patents-to-price elasticity of 0.03–0.06 and a larger long-run elasticity of energy efficiency innovation on energy prices of 0.35 (with over half of the effect occurring during the first five years after the price shock). Using a methodology similar to Popp (2002), Crabb and Johnson (2010) find an elasticity for energy-efficient innovation in the US car industry over 1980–1999 of about

0.3 for retail gasoline price. Verdolini and Galeotti (2011) extend this analysis to 17 OECD countries for the period 1979–1998 and confirm Popp's finding with a short-run (one-year) elasticity of 0.04–0.06. Kruse and Wetzel (2016) further confirm this finding for eleven "green" technologies in 26 OECD countries over 1978–2009. In the buildings sector, Costantini, Crespi, and Palma (2017) find taxation on residential energy consumption to induce patent applications for energy-efficient technologies in buildings across 23 OECD countries (1990–2010). Importantly, a consistent finding from this literature is that the innovative response to policy happens quickly: much of the innovative response to higher (fossil-fuel-based) energy prices occurs within five years or less.

Most of the early literature uses macro (sector- or country-level) data, making it difficult to claim causality. For example, in Popp (2002) there is no variation in energy prices across technology fields (average US industry energy prices are used, and thus they vary only through time). This prevents the inclusion of time dummies in the estimated equation, making it impossible to control for macroeconomic shocks potentially correlated with both innovation and the energy price. The more recent literature has provided microeconomic evidence by constructing or observing firm-specific energy prices. In a direct empirical application of the AABH framework, Aghion et al. (2016) focus on the car industry and analyze the effect of gasoline prices on innovation, distinguishing between clean patents (associated with electric, hybrid, and hydrogen engines), dirty patents (associated with combustion engines), and "grey" patents (associated with energy efficiency improvements of combustion engines). To construct firm-specific fuel prices, they take advantage of the fact that innovators in the car industry sell their products across various national markets, and are thus differently exposed to country-specific fuel price variations, depending on their sales distribution (as proxied by the geographical distribution of their patent portfolio). This fuel price is computed as a weighted average of country-level fuel prices, where the firm-specific weights are computed using a firm's patent history pre-sample (as a proxy for firm's market shares).[18] In the spirit of a shift-share instrument, the effect of fuel price on firms' innovation is

---

[18] Because a patent only protects an invention in the country in which it is applied for, whether a firm decides to apply for a patent in a given country or not is indicative of the importance of that country for the firm. Coelli, Moxnes, and Ulltveit-Moe (2022) show empirically that this is a good proxy for market share.

identified by cross-country variations in fuel prices or taxes affecting firms differently according to their exposure to different markets. They estimate a large positive effect of fuel prices on clean innovation with an elasticity close to 1 and a negative effect on dirty innovation with an elasticity close to −0.5.[19] Innovation in fuel efficiency technology (grey innovation, a subset of dirty innovations) is also stimulated, but to a lesser degree, with an elasticity of 0.3. Furthermore, Aghion et al. (2016) find evidence for path dependence in the direction of innovation at the firm level—the propensity to patent in clean is greater when firms have accumulated more clean knowledge on which to build. Through simulations, they show that, in line with AABH, path dependence exacerbates the gap between clean and dirty knowledge in business-as-usual but reduces the increase in fuel prices necessary to induce clean technology to catch up with dirty technology.

Several papers have used the same method as Aghion et al. (2016) to generate energy price variation at the firm level and make further contributions to the empirical DTC literature. Noailly and Smeets (2015) focus on the electricity production sector and study how clean and dirty innovations respond to fuel price (as in Aghion et al. 2016) but also to the market size, where firm-level market size is calculated in an analogous manner (see also Lazkano, Nøstbakken, and Pelli 2017; Lööf, Perez, and Baum 2018). Overall, their results support the DTC hypothesis: increases in renewable market size or fossil fuel prices lead to more renewable innovation, and a larger fossil fuel market leads to more fossil fuel innovation. An increase in fossil fuel price also leads to a large increase in fossil fuel energy-efficiency innovations. Their results also support path dependency.

Having established the empirical existence of directed technical change from price and market size effects, the literature is moving to study other factors driving technical change as well as interaction effects. For instance, Aghion, Bénabou, Martin, and Roulet (2020) extend the setup of Aghion et al. (2016) to study the roles of both consumer value and competition in driving innovation in the car industry. They find that when consumers value the environment more, clean innovation in the car industry increases, particularly when competition is more intense. They estimate that the simultaneous increase in environmental valuation and competition that happened

---

[19] In line with these results, Knittel (2011) finds that there is a trade-off between improving fuel efficiency and other vehicle attributes, and that technical progress has responded to the implementation of regulatory standards.

during 1998–2002 and 2008–2012 had the same effect on innovation as a 40 percent increase in fuel price. Another example is Fredriksson and Sauquet (2017), who find that the innovation effect found by Aghion et al. (2016) is strongest for firms located in countries with French civil law, rather than those with common law, suggesting that the relative "rigidity" of civil law may provide greater certainty regarding future legislation and lessen incumbents' lobbying, increasing the incentive to innovate.

Using different identification strategies, other recent papers have established a causal effect of climate policies on innovation based on microdata. Calel and Dechezleprêtre (2016) examine the influence of the European Union Emissions Trading System (EU ETS), which from 2005 created an EU-wide carbon price for electricity generation and heavy industry. To assess the impact of the EU ETS on low-carbon innovation, they take advantage of the existence of regulatory thresholds at the plant level that determine inclusion in the system. In order to control administrative costs, the EU ETS was designed to cover only large installations with production capacity above a certain threshold: for example, in the steel sector, only plants with a production capacity exceeding 2.5 tonnes per hour are regulated; in the glass sector, installations are included only if their melting capacity exceeds 20 tonnes per day. Firms operating smaller installations are not covered by EU ETS regulations, although the firms themselves might be just as large as those affected by the regulation. Because innovation takes place at the firm level, Calel and Dechezleprêtre (2016) can exploit these installation-level inclusion criteria to compare firms that are located in the same country, operating in the same sector, with similar resources available for research and similar patenting histories, but that have fallen under different regulatory regimes since 2005. This provides an opportunity to apply the sort of quasi-experimental techniques most suited to assessing the causal impacts of environmental policies (List, Millimet, Fredriksson, and McHone 2003; Greenstone and Gayer 2009). The authors follow a matched difference-in-difference strategy where they compare regulated firms with a control group representing what would have happened had the EU ETS not been implemented. They show that the EU ETS increased low-carbon innovation (as measured by patent filings at the European Patent Office) by 30 percent in the matched sample of regulated firms. This result was confirmed by Calel (2020) in a study focusing on the UK. Similar results have been found by studies examining other carbon-pricing instruments. For example, Zhang, Cao, Tang, He, and Li (2019) examine the role of the seven carbon-pricing pilot schemes introduced in China in 2013 on "green" patent applications by regulated firms, and report a significant positive correlation.

3.2 Other environmental policies and induced innovation

Although less directly aimed at testing the validity of the DTC hypothesis, a broader literature has investigated the impact of environmental policy on innovation and is thus worth mentioning here, as these studies collectively reinforce the finding that innovation responds to economic incentives provided by environmental policies, even if the identification strategy is weaker than in microeconomic studies. For example, several early studies used pollution abatement control expenditures (PACE) as a proxy for environmental regulatory stringency. Examples include Lanjouw and Mody (1996), Jaffe and Palmer (1997), and Brunnermeier and Cohen (2003). Each finds a significant correlation within industries over time between PACE and innovative activity, as measured by research and development expenditures or environment-related patent filings.

Renewable energy policies, which require the adoption of renewable energy technologies to generate electricity, have also been shown to incentivize innovation. In a panel of OECD countries, Johnstone, Haščič, and Popp (2010) find that public policies have an effect on innovation in renewable energy, as measured by applications for renewable energy patents submitted to the European Patent Office (EPO). Broad policies (such as renewable energy mandates, which do not target a particular technology) have a larger effect on technologies closer to competing with fossil fuels, in particular wind energy, whereas technologies farther from the market (solar power) require more-targeted subsidies. In one of the largest subsequent studies, covering 19 EU countries over 1980–2007, Nicolli and Vona (2016) show that feed-in tariffs increased patenting in solar photovoltaic technology. Such results, which speak to a form of path dependence within renewables, are consistent with the AABH framework. Dechezleprêtre and Glachant (2014) show that innovation in wind power technology responds positively to policies both at home and abroad. The marginal effect of domestic policies is 12 times greater than that of foreign policies, but the aggregate effect of foreign markets on innovation is larger, because the overall foreign market is typically much larger than the domestic market—suggesting a large overall impact of demand-pull policies on innovation through global value chains.

Finally, a few studies evaluate the effect of international environmental agreements on innovation. A recent example is Dugoua (2020). In this paper, the identification relies on a difference-in-differences strategy, where innovation in particular molecules directly affected by the signing of the agreement is compared to innovation in related but unaffected molecules. She focuses on the Montreal Protocol, which has regulated the use of CFC since 1989, and finds that it led to an increase of 400 percent in patents pertaining to CFC-substitutes relative to similar molecules. Interestingly, she shows that by inducing innovation, the initially modest protocol reduced future abatement costs, leading to a series of increasingly ambitious follow-up agreements. The parallel with climate change, and the AABH framework, is clear: carbon prices and technology development are mutually reinforcing. Carbon prices induce new low-carbon technologies, which in turn can build the case for stronger carbon pricing in the future by lowering the cost of future green technologies.

3.3 Linking innovation market failures to direct technical change

From the empirical literature, there is clear and unambiguous evidence that energy and carbon prices induce innovation in clean technologies (at least, as measured by patents). However, the AABH framework highlights that reaching the first best requires a combination of carbon prices with subsidies to clean R&D because the social value of clean innovation is relatively more back-loaded than that of dirty innovation. From a policy perspective, this raises the question of whether subsidies to clean R&D actually work. Evidence on this issue is—surprisingly—scarce. Pless, Hepburn, and Farrell (2020) report that, of the 1,700 papers on the impact of direct funding for innovation reviewed by the What Works Centre for Local Economic Growth, only 42 use rigorous statistical methods. This emerging literature suggests that direct R&D grants and R&D tax credits have positive effects on firms' innovative activity (Bronzini and Iachini 2014; Bronzini and Piselli 2016; Agrawal, Rosell, and Simcoe 2020; Dechezleprêtre et al. 2016; Ganguli 2017), with heterogeneous effects across types of firms. In addition, grants and tax credits can be complementary for small firms but substitutes for larger firms (Pless 2021).

In the literature that seeks to evaluate R&D support policies, only a couple of studies focus on energy-related innovation. Yet this sector possesses many

features (high capital intensity, long time horizons, little product differentiation, among others) that might make the innovation process specific.
Howell (2017) exploits the fact that the US Department of Energy's Small
Business Innovation Research program allocates R&D grants to small businesses through a grading scheme. Using a regression discontinuity analysis,
she finds that receiving a grant increases patenting, survival rate, and the
probability of subsequently receiving venture capital, with stronger effects
for firms that are likely to be more financially constrained. Within energy
research, Howell (2017) also shows that such R&D subsidies can increase
clean innovation specifically (in hydropower, carbon capture and storage,
building and lighting efficiency, and alternative automotive technologies) but
have no measurable effect on conventional energy technologies (natural gas
and coal), likely because firms developing these technologies are less financially constrained.

A related question is whether there are additional reasons than the one
highlighted in the AABH framework to subsidize clean R&D. As a matter
of fact, recent research has demonstrated that knowledge spillovers are larger
for clean than for dirty technologies. In a comprehensive analysis covering
1.3 million patents filed over sixty years, Dechezleprêtre, Martin, and
Mohnen (2017) show that knowledge spillovers (measured with patent citations) are 40 percent larger for low-carbon than for high-carbon technologies. The higher knowledge spillovers from low-carbon technologies come
primarily from their radical novelty compared with old polluting technologies. New technology fields offer potentially high marginal private returns
to first movers and might thus generate large knowledge spillovers. Comparing the spillovers from low-carbon and high-carbon technologies to a
range of other emerging technologies, such as IT and biotechnologies, Dechezleprêtre et al. (2017) find that the intensity of spillovers from low-carbon
technologies is comparable to that for other emerging technologies, whereas
knowledge spillovers from high-carbon technologies lag behind.

4 Conclusion and Future Avenues

This review highlights that the literature has firmly established that environmental innovations respond strongly to market incentives and that the endogeneity of innovation matters for macroeconomic outcomes. In fact, DTC
theory often provides policy answers that differ from models with exogenous

technology: an environmental policy should be front-loaded to kick-start the green innovation machine; carbon taxes are an important policy tool but not the only one; unilateral environmental policies should not limit themselves to a simple carbon tax; and the development of a bridge technology (such as switching from coal to gas) may backfire if it is not accompanied by further efforts to develop really clean (carbon-free) technologies. Overall, AABH and the unfolding literature provide a strong case for a green innovation policy: climate policy should be designed with innovation at the forefront.

This calls for further integrating DTC in climate change economics. In particular, microfounded DTC should be more systematically incorporated in integrated assessment models. Dietz and Lanz (2019) is a recent example in a detailed multisectoral model with endogenous population dynamics. Kruse-Andersen (2020) also includes population dynamics into a DTC model. Another important avenue is to expand the two-country setups discussed above for more realistic models of international environmental agreements, building on game-theoretic contributions such as Barrett (2006) and Harstad, Lancia, and Russo (2019). Finally, climate change is a problem riddled with uncertainties about climate dynamics and climate damages but also technological prospects. The models reviewed here are all deterministic, but the interaction between technology and uncertainty is a promising avenue for future research.

Empirically, a number of promising research avenues emerge from this review. First, because of data availability, the empirical evidence has mostly focused on patent filings as a measure of innovation output, but more-direct measures of innovation outcomes (e.g., technology cost reductions) are strikingly missing. New and better measures of clean innovation are needed. Understanding the full impact of green innovation policies, through the supply chain (on technology providers or on downstream consumers via cost pass-through), across borders, and via spillovers (knowledge spillovers, product market rivalry), is another promising area, although it faces an inherent trade-off with establishing causality. In this regard, measuring the crowding-out effect of policy-induced clean innovation on other types of innovation is crucial to better understand the welfare effects of climate policy. Third, while the impact of energy and carbon prices on clean innovation is clear, investigation of the impact on incremental versus more radical innovation (which might be needed to reach the recently adopted carbon neutrality targets) appears lacking. More generally, exploration of the heterogeneity of the impact of green innovation policies across technologies, firms, countries, and sectors, depending on their characteristics (financial constraints, competition, knowledge stock), would enrich our understanding of DTC. For example, carbon prices may work less well in certain sectors (e.g., buildings) because of the existence of additional market failures. Finally, an important area for research is that of policy instrument choice, in particular beyond pollution pricing, and evaluating policy interactions and policy mixes (including, most importantly, combinations of pollution pricing instruments with innovation support policies). More empirical research on the impact of R&D support policies specifically targeting energy innovation is also needed.

In a word, theoretical and empirical applications of the DTC framework to the environmental context surely have fine research days ahead.

References

Acemoglu, Daron. 1998. "Why do New Technologies Complement Skills? Directed Technical Change and Wage Inequality." *Quarterly Journal of Economics,* 113(4): 1055–1089.

Acemoglu, Daron. 2002. "Directed Technical Change." *Review of Economic Studies,* 69(4): 871–809.

Acemoglu, Daron. 2003. "Labor- and Capital-Augmenting Technical Change." *Journal of the European Economic Association,* 1(1): 1–37.

Acemoglu, Daron, Philippe Aghion, Lint Barrage, and David Hémous. 2021. "Climate Change, Directed Innovation and Energy Transition: The Long-Run Consequences of the Shale Gas Revolution." Manuscript.

Acemoglu, Daron, Philippe Aghion, Leonardo Bursztyn, and David Hémous. 2012. "The Environment and Directed Technical Change." *American Economic Review,* 102(1): 131–166.

Acemoglu, Daron, Philippe Aghion, and David Hémous. 2014. "The Environment and Directed Technical Change in a North–South Model." *Oxford Review of Economic Policy,* 30(3): 513–530.

Acemoglu, Daron, Ufuk Akcigit, Douglas Hanley, and William Kerr. 2016. "The Transition to Clean Technology." *Journal of Political Economy* 124(1): 52–104.

Acemoglu, Daron, and Will Rafey. 2019. "Mirage on the Horizon: Geoengineering and Carbon Taxation without Commitment." NBER Working Paper 24411.

Aghion, Philippe, Roland Bénabou, Ralf Martin, and Alexandra Roulet. 2020. "Environmental Preferences and Technology Choices: Is Market Competition Clean or Dirty?" NBER Working Paper 26921.

Aghion, Philippe, Antoine Dechezleprêtre, David Hémous, Ralf Martin, and John Van Reenen. 2016. "Carbon Taxes, Path Dependency, and Directed Technical Change: Evidence from the Auto Industry." *Journal of Political Economy,* 214(1): 1–51.

Aghion, Philippe, Cameron Hepburn, Alexander Teytelboym, and Dimitri Zenghelis. 2019. "Chapter Path Dependence, Innovation and the Economics of Climate Change." In *Handbook on Green Growth,* edited by Roger Fouquet, 67–83. Cheltenham, UK: Edward Elgar.

Aghion, Philippe, and Peter Howitt. 1992. "A Model of Growth through Creative Destruction." *Econometrica,* 60(2): 323–351.

Aghion, Philippe, and Peter Howitt. 1996. "Research and Development in the Growth Process." *Journal of Economic Growth,* 1(1): 49–73.

Aghion, Philippe, and Peter Howitt. 2009. *The Economics of Growth.* Cambridge, MA: MIT Press.

Agrawal, Ajay, Carlos Rosell, and Timothy Simcoe. 2020. "Tax Credits and Small Firm R&D Spending." *American Economic Journal: Economic Policy,* 12(2): 1–21.

Alsina-Pujols, Maria, and Isabel Hovdahl. 2022. "Patent Protection and the Transition to Clean Technology." University of Zurich, manuscript.

André, Francisco, and Sjak Smulders. 2014. "Fueling Growth When Oil Peaks: Directed Technological Change and the Limits to Efficiency." *European Economic Review,* 69: 18–39.

Barrett, Scott. 2006. "Climate Treaties and 'Breakthrough' Technologies." *American Economic Review,* 96(2): 22–25.

Bovenberg, A. Lans, and Sjak Smulders. 1995. "Environmental Quality and Pollution-Augmenting Technological Change in a Two-Sector Endogenous Growth Model." *Journal of Public Economics,* 57(3): 369–391.

Bovenberg, A. Lans, and Sjak Smulders. 1996. "Transitional Impacts of Environmental Policy in an Endogenous Growth Model." *International Economic Review,* 37(4): 861–893.

Bronzini, Raffaello, and Eleonora Iachini. 2014. "Are Incentives for R&D Effective? Evidence from a Regression Discontinuity Approach." *American Economic Journal: Economic Policy,* 6(4): 100–134.

Bronzini, Raffaello, and Paolo Piselli. 2016. "The Impact of R&D Subsidies on Firm Innovation." *Research Policy,* 45(2): 442–457.

Brunnermeier, Smita B., and Mark A. Cohen. 2003. "Determinants of Environmental Innovation in US Manufacturing Industries." *Journal of Environmental Economics and Management,* 45(2): 278–293.

Calel, Raphael. 2020. "Adopt or Innovate: Understanding Technological Responses to Cap-and-Trade." *American Economic Journal: Economic Policy,* 12(3): 170–201.

Calel, Raphael, and Antoine Dechezleprêtre. 2016. "Environmental Policy and Directed Technical Change: Evidence from the European Carbon Market." *Review of Economics and Statistics,* 98(1): 173–191.

Casey, Gregory. 2019. "Energy Efficiency and Directed Technical Change: Implications for Climate Change Mitigation." Manuscript.

Coelli, Federica, Andreas Moxnes, and Karen Helene Ulltveit-Moe. 2022. "Better, Faster, Stronger: Global Innovation and Trade Liberalization." *Review of Economics and Statistics,* 104(2): 205–216.

Costantini, Valeria, Francesco Crespi, and Alessandro Palma. 2017. "Character-izing the Policy Mix and Its Impact on Eco-Innovation: A Patent Analysis of Energy-Efficient Technologies." *Research Policy*, 46(4): 799–819.

Crabb, Joseph M., and Daniel K. N. Johnson. 2010. "Fueling Innovation: The Impact of Oil Prices and CAFE Standards on Energy-Efficient Automotive Technology." *Energy Journal*, 31(1).

Dechezleprêtre, Antoine, Elias Einiö, Ralf Martin, Kieu-Trang Nguyen, and John Van Reenen. 2016. "Do Tax Incentives for Research Increase Firm Innovation? An RD Design for R&D." NBER Working Paper 22405.

Dechezleprêtre, Antoine, and Mathieu Glachant. 2014. "Does Foreign Environ-mental Policy Influence Domestic Innovation? Evidence from the Wind Industry." *Environmental and Resource Economics*, 58(3): 391–413.

Dechezleprêtre, A., R. Martin, and M. Mohnen. 2017. "Knowledge Spillovers from Clean and Dirty Technologies: A Patent Citation Analysis." Grantham Research Institute on Climate Change and the Environment Working Paper.

Dietz, Simon, and Bruno Lanz. 2019. "Can a Growing World Be Fed When the Climate Is Changing?" IRENE Working Papers 19-09, IRENE Institute of Economic Research.

Corrado, Di Maria, and Simone Valente. 2008. "Hicks Meets Hotelling: The Direction of Technical Change in Capital-Resource Economies." *Environment and Development Economics*, 13: 691–717.

Dugoua, Eugenie. 2020. "Induced Innovation and International Environmental Agreements: Evidence from the Ozone Regime." LSE/Grantham Research Institute Working Paper.

Fischer, Carolyn, and Garth Heutel. 2013. "Environmental Macroeconomics: Environmental Policy, Business Cycles, and Directed Technical Change." *Annual Review of Resource Economics*, 5: 197–210.

Fredriksson, Per G., and Alexandre Sauquet. 2017. "Does Legal System Matter for Directed Technical Change? Evidence from the Auto Industry." *Applied Economics Letters*, 24(15): 1080–1083.

Fried, Stephi. 2018. "Climate Policy and Innovation: A Quantitative Macroeco-nomic Analysis." *American Economic Journal: Macroeconomics*, 10(1): 90–118.

Ganguli, Ina. 2017. "Saving Soviet Science: The Impact of Grants When Govern-ment R&D Funding Disappears." *American Economic Journal: Applied Economics*, 9(2): 165–201.

Gans, Joshua. 2012. "Innovation and Climate Change Policy." *American Economic Journal: Economic Policy*, 4(4): 125–145.

Gars, Johan, and Conny Olovsson. 2019. "Fuel for Economic Growth?" *Journal of Economic Theory*, 184: 104941.

Gerlagh, Reyer, Snorre Kverndokk, and Knut Einar Rosendahl. 2009. "Optimal Timing of Climate Change Policy: Interaction between Carbon Taxes and Innovation Externalities." *Environmental Resource Economics*, 43: 369–390.

Gerlagh, Reyer, Snorre Kverndokk, and Knut Einar Rosendahl. 2014. "The Optimal Time Path of Clean Energy R&D Policy When Patents Have Finite Lifetime." *Journal of Environmental Economics and Management*, 67: 2–19.

Gerlagh, Reyer, and Wietze Lise. 2005. "Carbon Taxes: A Drop in the Ocean, or a Drop That Erodes the Stone? The Effect of Carbon Taxes on Technological Change." *Ecological Economics*, 54: 241–260.

Goulder, Lawrence H., and Stephen H. Schneider. 1999. "Induced Technological Change and the Attractiveness of CO_2 Abatement Policies." *Resource and Energy Economics*, 21(3–4): 211–253.

Greaker, Mads, Tom-Reiel Heggedal, and Knut Einar Rosendahl. 2018. "Environmental Policy and the Direction of Technical Change." *Scandinavian Journal of Economics*, 120(4): 1100–1138.

Greenstone, Michael, and Ted Gayer. 2009. "Quasi-Experimental and Experimental Approaches to Environmental Economics." *Journal of Environmental Economics and Management*, 57(1): 21–44.

Grimaud, André, and Luc Rouge. 2008. "Environment, Directed Technical Change and Economic Policy." *Environmental and Resource Economics*, 41(4): 439–463.

Grubb, Michael, Paul Drummond, Alexandra Poncia, Will McDowall, David Popp, Sascha Samadi, Cristina Penasco, Kenneth Gillingham, Sjak Smulders, Matthieu Glachant, et al. 2021. "Induced Innovation in Energy Technologies and Systems: A Review of Evidence and Potential Implications for CO_2 Mitigation." *Environmental Research Letters*, 16: 043007.

Harstad, Bard, Francesco Lancia, and Alessia Russo. 2019. "Compliance Technology and Self-Enforcing Agreements." *Journal of the European Economic Association*, 17(1): 1–29.

Hart, Rob. 2008. "The Timing of Taxes on CO_2 Emissions When Technological Change Is Endogenous." *Journal of Environmental Economics and Management*, 55: 194–212.

Hart, Rob. 2019. "To Everything There Is a Season: Carbon Pricing, Research Subsidies, and the Transition to Fossil-Free Energy." *Journal of the Association of Environmental and Resource Economists*, 6(2): 349–389.

Hassler, John, Per Krusell, and Conny Olovsson. 2021. "Directed Technical Change as a Response to Natural-Resource Scarcity." *Journal of Political Economy*, 129(11).

Hémous, David. 2016. "The Dynamic Impact of Unilateral Environmental Policies." *Journal of International Economics*, 103: 80–95.

Hémous, David, and Morten Olsen. 2021. "Directed Technical Change in Labor and Environmental Economics." *Annual Review of Economics*, 13.

Hicks, John. 1932. *The Theory of Wages*. London: Macmillan.

Howell, Sabrina. 2017. "Financing Innovation, Evidence from RD Grants." *American Economic Review*, 107(4).

Jaffe, Adam B., and Karen Palmer. 1997. "Environmental Regulation and Innovation: A Panel Data Study." *Review of Economics and Statistics*, 79(4): 610–619.

Jo, Ara. 2020. "The Elasticity of Substitution between Clean and Dirty Energy with Technological Bias." CER-ETH Working Paper 20/344.

Johnstone, Nick, Ivan Haščič, and David Popp. 2010. "Renewable Energy Policies and Technological Innovation: Evidence Based on Patent Counts." *Environmental and Resource Economics*, 45(1): 133–55.

Kennedy, Charles. 1964. "Induced Bias in Innovation and the Theory of Distribution." *Economic Journal*, 74(295).

Klette, Tor Jakob, and Samuel Kortum. 2004. "Innovating Firms and Aggregate Innovation." *Journal of Political Economy*, 112.

Knittel, Christopher. 2011. "Automobiles on Steroids: Product Attribute Trade-Offs and Technological Progress in the Automobile Sector." *American Economic Review*, 101: 3368–3399.

Kruse, Jürgen, and Heike Wetzel. 2016. "Energy Prices, Technological Knowledge, and Innovation in Green Energy Technologies: A Dynamic Panel Analysis of European Patent Data." *CESifo Economic Studies*, 62(3): 397–425.

Kruse-Andersen, Peter. 2020. "Directed Technical Change, Environmental Sustainability, and Population Growth." Manuscript.

Lanjouw, Jean Olson, and Ashoka Mody. 1996. "Innovation and the International Diffusion of Environmentally Responsive Technology." *Research Policy*, 25(4): 549–571.

Lazkano, Itziar, Linda Nøstbakken, and Martino Pelli. 2017. "From Fossil Fuels to Renewables: The Role of Electricity Storage." *European Economic Review*, 99: 113–129.

Lemoine, Derek. 2020. "Innovation-Led Transitions in Energy Supply." NBER Working Paper 23420.

List, John, Daniel Millimet, Per Fredriksson, and W. Warren McHone. 2003. "Effects of Environmental Regulations on Manufacturing Plant Births: Evidence from a Propensity Score Matching Estimator." *Review of Economics and Statistics*, 85(4): 944–952.

Lööf, Hans, Luis Perez, and Christopher Baum. 2018. "Directed Technical Change in Clean Energy: Evidence from the Solar Industry." Working Paper Series in Economics and Institutions of Innovation 470, Royal Institute of Technology, CESIS—Centre of Excellence for Science and Innovation Studies.

Maria, Corrado Di, and Sjak A. Smulders. 2004. "Trade Pessimists vs. Technology Optimists: Induced Technical Change and Pollution Havens." *B.E. Journal of Economic Analysis and Policy*, 4(2): Article 7.

Massetti, Emanuele, Carlo Carraro, and Lea Nicita. 2009. "How Does Climate Policy Affect Technical Change? An Analysis of the Direction and Pace of Technical Progress in a Climate-Economy Model." *Energy Journal*, 30(2): 7–38.

Newell, Richard G., Adam B. Jaffe, and Robert N. Stavins. 1999. "The Induced Innovation Hypothesis and Energy-Saving Technological Change." *Quarterly Journal of Economics*, 114(3): 941–975.

Nicolli, Francesco, and Francesco Vona. 2016. "Heterogeneous Policies, Heterogeneous Technologies: The Case of Renewable Energy." *Energy Economics*, 56: 190–204.

Noailly, Joëlle, and Roger Smeets. 2015. "Directing Technical Change from Fossil-Fuel to Renewable Energy Innovation: An Application Using Firm-

Level Patent Data." *Journal of Environmental Economics and Management,* 72: 15–37.

Nordhaus, William D. 1994. *Managing the Global Commons: The Economics of Climate Change.* Cambridge, MA: MIT Press.

Nordhaus, William D. 2002. "Modeling Induced Innovation in Climate-Change Policy." In *Technological Change and the Environment,* edited by Arnulf Grübler, Nebojsa Nakicenovic, and William D. Nordhaus, 182–209. Washington, DC: Resources for the Future.

Nowzohour, Laura. 2021. "Can Adjustment Costs in Research Derail the Transition to Green Growth?" https://ideas.repec.org/p/gii/ciesrp/cies_rp_67 .html.

Papageorgiou, Chris, Marianne Saam, and Patrick Schulte. 2017. "Substitution between Clean and Dirty Energy Inputs: A Macroeconomic Perspective." *Review of Economics and Statistics,* 99(2): 281–290.

Pless, Jacquelyn. 2021. "Are 'Complementary Policies' Substitutes? Evidence from R&D Subsidies in the UK." MIT CEEPR Working Paper.

Pless, Jacquelyn, Cameron Hepburn, and Niall Farrell. 2020. "Bringing Rigour to Energy Innovation Policy Evaluation." *Nature Energy,* 5(4): 284–290.

Popp, David. 2002. "Induced Innovation and Energy Prices." *American Economic Review,* 92(1): 160–180.

Popp, David. 2004. "ENTICE: Endogenouse Technological Change in the DICE Model of Global Warming." *Journal of Environmental Economics and Management,* 24(1): 742–768.

Popp, David. 2006. "ENTICE-BR: The Effects of Backstop Technology R&D on Climate Policy Models." *Energy Economics,* 28: 188–222.

Popp, David. 2019. "Environmental Policy and Innovation: A Decade of Research." *International Review of Environmental and Resource Economics,* 13: 265–337.

Popp, David, Richard Newell, and Adam Jaffe. 2010. "Energy, the Environment and Technological Change." In *Handbook of the Economics of Innovation,* edited by Bronwyn Hall and Nathan Rosenberg, 873–937. Amsterdam: Elsevier.

Shanker, Akshay, and David Stern. 2018. "Energy Intensity, Growth and Technical Change." CAMA Working Paper 46/2018.

Smulders, Sjak, and Michiel de Nooij. 2003. "The Impact of Energy Conservation on Technology and Economic Growth." *Resource and Energy Economics,* 25: 59–79.

Stern, David, John Pezzey, and Yingying Lu. 2020. "Directed Technical Change and the British Industrial Revolution." Manuscript.

Stöckl, Fabian, and Alexander Zerrahn. 2020. "Substituting Clean for Dirty Energy: A Bottom-Up Analysis." DIW Berlin Discussion Paper No. 1885.

Sue Wing, Ian. 2003. "Induced Technical Change and the Cost of Climate Policy." MIT Joint Program on the Science and Policy of Global Change.

van den Bijgaart, Inge. 2017. "The Unilateral Implementation of a Sustainable Growth Path with Directed Technical Change." *European Economic Review,* 91: 305–327.

Verdolini, Elena, and Marzio Galeotti. 2011. "At Home and Abroad: An Empirical Analysis of Innovation and Diffusion in Energy Technologies." *Journal of Environmental Economics and Management*, 61(2): 119–134.

Wiskich, Anthony. 2021. "Substitutability between Clean and Dirty Electricity Generation under a Clean Transition." CAMA Working Paper.

Witajewski-Baltvilks, Jan, and Carolyn Fischer. 2019. "Green Innovation and Economic Growth in a North South Model." Resources for the Future Working Paper 19-04.

Zhang, Lu, Cuicui Cao, Fei Tang, Jiaxin He, and Dayuan Li. 2019. "Does China's Emissions Trading System Foster Corporate Green Innovation? Evidence from Regulating Listed Companies." *Technology Analysis & Strategic Management*, 31(2): 199–212.

APPENDIX

This appendix provides mathematical details to the model sketched in Section 2.4.

Deriving equation (18). Equations (3) and (4) now apply to sectors $j \in \{c, r, p\}$. Relative demand for the resource-based and non-resource-based inputs in the dirty sector leads to the relative demand:

$$Y_{rt}/Y_{pt} = (p_{rt}/p_{pt})^{-\theta} \tag{20}$$

and allows us to express the price of the dirty input as:

$$p_{dt} = \left(p_{rt}^{1-\theta} + p_{pt}^{1-\theta}\right)^{\frac{1}{1-\theta}}. \tag{21}$$

Next solving for labor demand in subsectors r and p implies:

$$p_{rt}/p_{pt} = (A_{rt}/A_{pt})^{-\beta}. \tag{22}$$

Plugging this expression together with equation (4) in (20) leads to:

$$L_{rt}/L_{pt} = (A_{rt}/A_{pt})^{\lambda-1}. \tag{23}$$

We define the total labor force working in sector d as $L_{dt} \equiv L_{rt} + L_{pt}$. Using (4) for $j = r, p$, (21), (22), and (23) in (17), we get that Y_{dt} also satisfies (4). As a result, (7), (8), and (9) still apply.

Using (3) and (4) for sector r, we get $P_t/Y_{rt} = \xi(1-\beta)p_{rt}$. Then using (21), (22), (7), and the normalization of the final good price to 1, we get

$$\frac{P_t}{Y_{rt}} = \xi(1-\beta)\frac{(A_{dt}^{\sigma-1}+A_{ct}^{\sigma-1})^{\frac{1}{\sigma-1}}}{A_{rt}^{\beta}}.$$

Using (20) and (22), we further get that:

$$\frac{P_t}{Y_{dt}} = \xi(1-\beta)\frac{(A_{dt}^{\sigma-1}+A_{ct}^{\sigma-1})^{\frac{1}{\varepsilon-1}}}{A_{dt}^{\beta}}\frac{A_{dt}^{1-\lambda}}{A_{rt}^{1-\lambda}}, \tag{24}$$

which is decreasing in A_{rt}. Combining (4), (7), (9), and the labor market clearing condition gives the laissez-faire production of dirty input as

$$Y_d = \frac{A_d^{\varepsilon\beta}L}{(1-\beta)(A_c^{\sigma-1}+A_d^{\sigma-1})^{\frac{\beta\varepsilon-1}{\sigma-1}}}. \tag{25}$$

Similar steps give the final good production as

$$Y_t = (A_{ct}^{\sigma-1}+A_{dt}^{\sigma-1})^{1/(\sigma-1)}\frac{L}{1-\beta}\cdot\lim_{x\to\infty} \tag{26}$$

The ratio of dirty input over final good is then:

$$\frac{Y_{dt}}{Y_t} = \frac{A_{dt}^{\varepsilon\beta}}{(A_{ct}^{\sigma-1}+A_{dt}^{\sigma-1})^{\frac{\varepsilon\beta}{\sigma-1}}}. \tag{27}$$

which decreases in A_{ct} and increases in A_{dt}. Combining these terms together gives (18).

Proof of Proposition 1. Part (i) is already established in the text. Consider a situation where innovation occurs asymptotically in the dirty sector. First note that, asymptotically, we have $g_{A_d} = \min\left(g_{A_r}, g_{A_p}\right)$. From (18), we get that asymptotically

$$P_t : \xi A_{dt}^{2-\lambda}A_{rt}^{\lambda-1}L.$$

Pollution decreases in the long run if $1+g_{A_d}=1+g_{A_p}<\left(1+g_{A_{rt}}\right)^{\frac{1-\lambda}{2-\lambda}}$. From (26), the maximal growth rate of final output achievable through this second strategy is then:

$$g_Y = g_{A_d} = g_{A_p} = \gamma\eta_p s_p^*,$$

where the asymptotic allocation of scientists s_p^* solves

$$(1 + \gamma \eta_p s_p^*)^{2-\lambda} = (1 + \gamma \eta_r (1 - s_p^*))^{1-\lambda}. \tag{28}$$

For γ small, this implies

$$s_p^* = \frac{(1-\lambda)\eta_r}{(2-\lambda)\eta_p + (1-\lambda)\eta_r},$$

leading to the growth rate given in Proposition 1.

PART VI

Development and Political Economy

CHAPTER 17

Creative Destruction, Distance to Frontier, and Economic Development

MICHAEL PETERS *and* FABRIZIO ZILIBOTTI

1 Introduction

Since the groundbreaking work by Aghion and Howitt (1992) the process of creative destruction has been inextricably linked to economic growth and rising living standards. Its broad-spectrum policy implications cover areas such as patent protection and competition policy. The debate over creative destruction, however, has often focused on developed economies. Is creative destruction as important for developing economies?

Acemoglu et al. (2006) argue that developing economies typically rely less on innovation and creative destruction and instead generate most of their growth through the imitation and adoption of technologies already used by firms in more-advanced countries. Throughout the process of convergence, the potential for imitation and technology adoption wanes, and countries must jump-start the process of innovation and select the best firms to continue their process of convergence to the technology frontier.

Yet this path is full of perils. Countries that fail to make their transition into innovation-led growth stop converging. This observation also implies that different policies and institutions may be appropriate (or optimal) at different stages of development. In particular, for countries far away from the technology frontier, economic growth may be aided by government interventions that selectively support specific firms, industries, and geographical areas.

These discriminatory policies, however, often come at a detriment to competition, as they impose implicit or explicit barriers on the entry and growth of new firms. In an environment characterized by large wedges and market failures, the benefits of overcoming credit market and contractual frictions outweigh the cost of reducing creative destruction. However, as an economy approaches the world technology frontier, policies that choke off competition and selection eventually become a burden on further development. As innovation becomes the main source of convergence, countries must introduce economic reforms to liberalize entry and foster creative destruction. Promoting human capital and managerial selection is also crucial for the long-run performance of the country.

Zilibotti (2017) presents empirical evidence from a panel of 43 non-OECD economies in the period 1965–2014 that is consistent with the prediction of the theory. He shows that barriers to entry are relatively less important (and can in some instances even be beneficial) in countries that are very far from the technology frontier. However, as countries come closer to the technology frontier, their growth rate declines faster than in countries promoting creative destruction through low barriers to entry. He also documents that convergence declines over time at a slower rate in countries investing a larger share of their GDP in R&D—an indication of the growing importance of innovation as economies approach the technology frontier.

Vandenbussche et al. (2006) document a similar pattern for human capital. They show that the share of tertiary education in the labor force becomes increasingly important to sustain technological convergence as countries approach the technology frontier. Arguably, this share is a proxy for the quality of managers and entrepreneurs in an economy. These distinct pieces of empirical evidence corroborate the view that while countries at an early stage of economic growth can converge fast to the technology frontier even with little creative destruction, how far the convergence process can go in the long run hinges on the quality, selection, and innovation potential of their firms.

In this chapter we propose a theory consistent with the view that the relative importance of technology adoption versus creative destruction changes over the process of economic development. The novelty of our theory is its focus on firm dynamics, paving the way for the possibility of estimating and testing its prediction using firm-level data rather than aggregate data.

Building blocks. The theory has three building blocks. The first is the celebrated Schumpeterian model of firm dynamics with creative destruction by Klette and Kortum (2004). This model provides a tight link between creative destruction, the process of firm dynamics, and the resulting firm size distribution. Most importantly, it enables us to infer cross-country differences in creative destruction from differences in the size distribution of firms.

The second building block is the idea that firms are heterogeneous in their growth potential; namely, some firms are intrinsically more dynamic than others. We closely follow the analysis of Akcigit et al. (2021), who argue that such heterogeneity is particularly important to understand firm dynamics in developing countries and estimate a related model to firm-level data from India and the United States.[1] Like them, we assume that some entrepreneurs are "transformative" and have the necessary skills to expand, whereas "subsistence entrepreneurs" may simply never grow independently of the environment they operate in.[2] The existence of different firm types highlights the role of creative destruction for the process of selection: if creative destruction is low, subsistence firms are replaced slowly, and in equilibrium a large share of the economy's resources is allocated to firms that do not grow.

The third building block is a process of knowledge diffusion inspired by Acemoglu et al. (2006): countries farther away from the technological frontier can benefit from technology adoption as a substitute for low creative destruction. This ingredient generates a link between cross-country differences in creative destruction and aggregate productivity. In particular, the theory predicts that countries that are far from the technology frontier can grow fast even if firms are not very innovative. However, in the long run, the steady-state distance from the technology frontier at which each country settles hinges on the rate of creative destruction in each country. In turn, this is determined by the quality (e.g., entrepreneurial and managerial human capital) of incumbent and entrant firms and by the extent to which barriers to entry limit churning and creative destruction. These characteristics ultimately pin down the ranking of nations in the stationary productivity distribution of the global economy.

---

[1] A similar structure is also considered in Acemoglu et al. (2018).

[2] Empirical evidence for this dichotomy is presented in Schoar (2010) and Decker et al. (2014). In the context of developing countries, Banerjee et al. (2015) and De Mel et al. (2008) stress the importance of persistent differences in growth potential.

Mechanism of the theory. As in Klette and Kortum (2004), productivity growth stems from both the entry of new firms and the expansion of existing firms. An incumbent firm is indexed by the measure of products for which it owns the best technology. Transformative firms grow by taking over other firms' products and shrink because of creative destruction through both the entry of new firms and the expansion (at their expense) of other incumbent firms. Subsistence firms are by construction stagnant and simply produce in the product market they initially entered until they get replaced.

In our theory, creative destruction is both a cause and a consequence of development. On the one hand, creative destruction is a necessary ingredient for selection and for subsistence firms to exit. It reallocates resources to transformative entrepreneurs who can use such resources more productively. On the other hand, if the majority of entering firms are subsistence producers, creative destruction is bound to be low, as there are simply too few transformative firms to meaningfully affect the process of selection at the aggregate level. Creative destruction, the survival chances of subsistence firms, and the firm size distribution are thus all jointly determined in equilibrium and linked to the level of aggregate productivity.

Estimation. We estimate our model using firm-level data from the United States and India. We assume the United States and India differ in three dimensions: the share of transformative firms, the innovation efficiency of transformative firms, and the cost of entry. We think of these parameters as reduced-form stand-ins for a variety of institutional and technological differences between rich and poor countries. The share of transformative firms in India could, for example, be lower than in the United States if entrepreneurial human capital is relatively scarce or frictions in the labor market reduce the opportunity costs of entrepreneurship for firms with little growth potential. Entry costs could be higher if bureaucratic red tape or other license requirements are more onerous in India. Finally, the expansion incentives for transformative firms could be lower if credit market frictions are more severe or other forms of size-dependent policies reduce the incentives to grow large; see Akcigit et al. (2021).

We show how one can estimate these three parameters directly from three moments of the firm size distribution: the entry rate, the extent of life-cycle growth, and the share of small firms. Our estimation yields three important findings. First, the Indian economy is disadvantaged along all three dimensions: it has higher entry costs, lower incumbent innovation efficiency, and a larger share of subsistence firms. Second, the rate of creative destruction implied by our estimates is much lower in India relative to the United States. Hence, as hypothesized by Acemoglu et al. (2006), the firm-level data exactly show that a relatively backward economy like India has lower creative destruction. Finally, we find that the differences in innovation efficiency (that are related to the human capital of local entrepreneurs) are much larger than differences in entry costs. Consequently, the main reason the United States has higher creative destruction is not that entry is easier but that existing firms innovate and expand at a much faster rate.[3]

Because we can derive closed-form expressions for our calibration targets, our theory concisely highlights which moments in the raw data inform these conclusions. Empirically, Indian firms are small (compared to the United States) and they experience little life-cycle growth. At the same time, entry and exit rates are quite similar. The fact that exit rates are similar, despite the fact that firms are small and hence close to exit threshold, implies that creative destruction in India has to be small. Furthermore, the absence of life-cycle firm growth in India paired with the abundance of very small firms implies that there are not many transformative firms in India and they do not expand efficiently. Finally, to rationalize a common entry rate across countries despite the fact that entrants in the United States face tougher competition from transformative firms implies that entry costs have to also be smaller in the United States.

Policy. We then use our calibrated model to gauge the effectiveness of growth policy in India. We are particularly interested in whether policies that protect firms from competition might be beneficial for innovation and aggregate productivity. When all firms are ex-ante identical, restricting entry necessarily reduces creative destruction and productivity growth. However, when entrepreneurial talent is scarce, there is endogenous selection: large firms are, on average, of better quality and have a higher growth potential than small firms and the average entrant. This raises a case for protecting

---

[3] This finding aligns well with that of recent papers showing that the innovation carried out by incumbent firms is an important engine of productivity growth both in the United States (see Garcia-Macia et al. 2019) and in emerging economies like China and Taiwan (see König et al. 2020). Peters (2020) also finds qualitatively similar results for Indonesia.

and supporting dynamic firms, especially when only a small number of them exist. Easy entry not only replaces good firms with worse firms but also deters innovation investments from dynamic incumbents out of fear of business stealing.

In this scenario, a poor economy has low productivity growth for two reasons. First, most firms are of low quality and are intrinsically stagnant. Second, the few good entrepreneurs are discouraged by the threat of replacement. This argument has two implications, one positive and one normative, that our stylized model spells out. On the one hand, less developed countries have low creative destruction and firms remain small on average. On the other hand, a benevolent government that can identify the good firms could want to protect them from replacement by other (likely worse) firms.

Thus, little creative destruction is in part a symptom of underdevelopment: there are few dynamic firms around. In some circumstances, promoting competition and free entry may not be the optimal policy: it can reduce dynamic selection and the growth and life span of the few existing good firms. In contrast, when there is a large pool of high-skill entrepreneurs, startup firms play an important role in the process and barriers to entry are harmful for growth.

Road map. In the rest of the chapter, we first present some motivating empirical evidence in Section 2. In Section 3 we lay out the model of distance to frontier with firm dynamics and derive the main predictions of the theory. In Sections 4 and 5 we estimate the parameters and perform counterfactual policy experiments. Section 6 concludes.

2 Empirical Evidence

A pervasive feature of economic development is that firms in rich countries look strikingly different from firms in poor countries. Firms in rich countries are larger, they experience growth as they age, and they perform a large share of aggregate economic activity. Figure 17.1a–b proposes a comparison between the United States and India that illustrates this point well. Figure 17.1a shows the firm size distribution. In India, 90 percent of firms have at most four employees, while only a negligible fraction of Indian firms employ more than 100 workers. By contrast, in the United States only one-third of firms have fewer than five employees, while almost 10 percent of them have more than 100 employees. In short, an organization of economic activity in which a sizable share of the labor force works in large corporations is a rich-country phenomenon.

Figure 17.1b (based on Hsieh and Klenow 2014) contrasts the employment life cycle of firms in India and in the United States.[4] Again, the firm life cycle in India is remarkably different from the firm life cycle in the United States. US firms that survive grow as they age. In India, there is very little growth over the life cycle. The evidence in the two panels is intertwined. One of the reasons (and quantitatively a very salient one) there are so many large corporations in the United States is that firms grow as they age. In contrast, Indian firms enter small and neither grow nor exit as they age. These patterns are not unique to the cases of the United States and India. For instance, Bento and Restuccia (2017) document a strong cross-country correlation between income per capita and average firm size.

The patterns in Figure 17.1a–b suggest that there is more creative destruction in rich countries than in poor countries. What are the implications? Is low creative destruction a cause of underdevelopment? Or is it also in part the effect of it? To cast some light on these questions, we now turn to a novel theory that links the process of firm dynamics to differences in aggregate productivity.

3 Theory

We present a simple model that explains why poor countries have (i) lower creative destruction, (ii) smaller firms, and (iii) a higher share of self-employed subsistence firms. The model also accounts for the fact that at the aggregate level, poor countries do not necessarily grow at a slower rate, because they benefit from catch-up growth through the adoption of technologies already in use in other nations. In the steady-state equilibrium of the global economy, all countries grow at the same rate, but there are persistent differences in the

---

[4] Ideally one would want to measure the life cycle using panel data. Because such data are often hard to find in developing countries, many researchers rely on the above cross-sectional age-size relationship. In a stationary environment these two coincide.

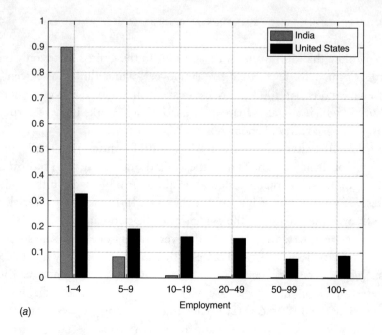

(a)

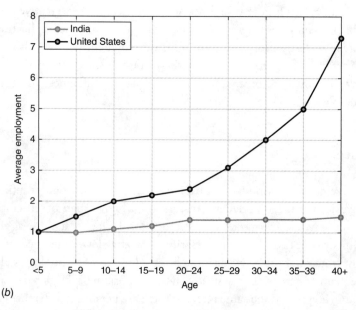

(b)

Notes: (a) Firm size distribution in the United States and India. US data from the Business Dynamics Statistics. India data from the Economic Census, (b) Employment life cycle as reported by Hsieh and Klenow (2014).

Figure 17.1a–b. Firm dynamics in developing countries: India vs. the United States

levels of productivity (i.e., there exists a stationary income distribution) and in the organization of the economy.

Our theory combines elements of Klette and Kortum (2004) and Acemoglu et al. (2006). From Klette and Kortum (2004) we borrow the firm dynamics framework. From Acemoglu et al. (2006) we borrow the idea that countries endogenously specialize in either the adoption of existing knowledge (imitation) or the creation of new ideas, which result in creative destruction. As a result, our theory endogenously generates cross-country differences not only in income per capita but also in the equilibrium distribution of firm size and age–size profile.

Environment. Suppose there are C countries indexed by $c = 1, 2, \ldots, C$. There is no trade, and countries interact only via international technology spillovers described below. The economic structure of each country is similar to that described in Klette and Kortum (2004). A representative household with a unit mass aggregates a continuum one of products in a Cobb-Douglas way:

$$\ln Y_t = \int_0^1 \ln y_{it} di.$$

Each product i is produced using labor and is indexed by its productivity q,

$$y_{it} = q_{it} l_{it}.$$

Firms can produce many products and are thus a collection of multiple product lines.

Static allocation. In equilibrium, each product line i is owned by the monopolist firm that has the highest productivity q_{it}. We assume that each firm can charge a markup μ, which we take as exogenous. This implies that the profits of the monopolist firm producing product i equal

$$\pi_{it} = \frac{\mu - 1}{\mu} p_{it} y_{it} = \frac{\mu - 1}{\mu} Y_t. \tag{1}$$

Total employment in product line i is given by

$$l_i = \frac{y_{it}}{q_{it}} = \frac{1}{\mu} \frac{Y_t}{w_t}.$$

Hence, aggregate output, which we take as the numeraire, is

$$Y_t = \mu L_{Pt} w_t = Q_t L_{Pt}, \tag{2}$$

where $Q_t = \exp\left(\int_{i=0}^{1} \ln q_{it} di\right)$. Given these product-line allocations, we can solve for the firm-level allocations. Firm f with n_f products employs

$$l_f = n_f l_i = n_f \frac{1}{\mu} \frac{Y_t}{w_t} = n_f L_{Pt}$$

workers; that is, employment is proportional to the number of products. Similarly, the total sales of firm f equal $py_f = n_f Y_t$. The number of products n_f thus fully summarizes the state of a firm.

Firm dynamics, entry, and creative destruction. Productivity growth is directly linked to creative destruction and the process of firm dynamics. A firm that introduces a better technology for product i replaces the incumbent monopolist and adds that product to its portfolio. Conversely, the firm that gets replaced declines in size and possibly exits if i was its sole product line.

Creative destruction stems from both incumbents and entrants. At each point in time a mass z of new firms enter and replace randomly selected incumbent monopolists. Each new firm enters with a single product. Importantly, we assume new firms to be heterogeneous in their type, which determines their post-birth innovation potential. A share $1 - \delta$ of them are *subsistence firms*. These firms never innovate after entering the market and simply produce their only initial product until they are replaced. By contrast, a share δ of new entrants are high-type firms led by *transformative entrepreneurs* that have the potential to innovate and grow over time.

Each transformative firm can choose the rate X at which it improves the productivity of a randomly selected product by $\gamma_t > 1$ and replaces an incumbent monopolist. Such expansion activities are costly, and we denote these costs (in units of labor) as

$$c(X, n) = \frac{1}{\phi_x} X^{\zeta} n^{1-\zeta} = \frac{1}{\phi_x} x^{\zeta} n, \tag{3}$$

where $\zeta > 1$ and $x = X / n$ denotes the innovation intensity. The parameter ϕ_x governs the innovation efficiency of transformative entrepreneurs and is a key parameter in our analysis.

Because profits and innovation costs depend only on the number of products n, the value function of a transformative entrepreneur, $V_t^T(n)$, solves the following HJB equation:

$$r_t V_t^T(n) - \dot{V}_t^T(n) = n\pi_t - n\tau_t[V_t^T(n) - V_t^T(n-1)]$$

$$+ \max_x \left\{ nx[V_t^T(n+1) - V_t^T(n)] - \frac{1}{\phi_x} x^\zeta n w_t \right\}, \quad (4)$$

where τ_t denotes the rate of creative destruction at which incumbent monopolists are replaced. The right-hand side of (4) comprises three parts. First, the firm earns the flow profits $n\pi_t$ given in (1). Second, the firm might lose one of its products to other firms, which occurs at the endogenous flow rate $n\tau_t$. Finally, the value function incorporates the option value of expansion: with the flow rate nx, the firm expands into a new market and experiences a capital gain of $V_t(n+1) - V_t(n)$, with the associated costs given by (3).

Along a balanced growth path (BGP), the value function in (4) has a simple solution. In Appendix Section A-1, we establish that $V_t^T(n)$ is given by

$$V_t^T(n) = v_t^T n, \quad \text{where} \quad v_t^T = \frac{\pi_t + (\zeta - 1)\dfrac{1}{\phi_x} x^\zeta w_t}{\rho + \tau}, \quad (5)$$

and the optimal innovation rate x is given by

$$x = \left(\frac{v_t^T}{w_t} \frac{\phi_x}{\zeta} \right)^{1/(\zeta - 1)}. \quad (6)$$

V_t^T in Equation (5) yields the value of each product for a transformative entrepreneur, which includes the discounted value of current profits and the option value of innovation. The appropriate discount rate comprises the time discounting ρ and the rate of creative destruction τ—the higher τ, the shorter the time horizon for each product and, hence, the lower its value. Equation (6) shows that v_t^T determines the incentive for transformative firms to innovate: the higher v_t^T relative to the equilibrium wage, the higher the expansion rate of transformative firms.

Subsistence firms own at most one product. The value of an active subsistence firm is akin to the value of a single product for a transformative firm, except that subsistence firms face an arbitrarily large innovation cost; that is, $\phi_x \to 0$. Hence,

$$v_t^S = \frac{\pi_t}{\rho + \tau}. \quad (7)$$

Equations (5) and (7) highlight an important aspect of our theory: transformative entrepreneurs have a higher private value of owning a product than subsistence firms: $v_t^T > v_t^S$. Because firms capture only a fraction of the social value they create, the gap in the social value of products owned by transformative relative to subsistence firms is even larger. This observation stresses the efficiency-enhancing role of creative destruction originating from transformative firms: in equilibrium, the innovation flow in the economy increases in the share of products owned by transformative firms. Hence, subsistence firms play the role of parasites as argued by La Porta and Shleifer (2009).

Next, consider entry. We assume that entry is subject to a linear technology whereby, if the aggregate entry flow is z, a potential entrant needs to hire $\psi(z)$ workers, where

$$\psi(z) = \frac{1}{\phi_z} z^\chi.$$

Here, $\chi \geq 0$ so that there are decreasing returns to scale to entry at the aggregate level. ϕ_z is an inverse measure of the entry cost. Differences in entry costs across countries could be due to either technological or institutional factors, such as red tape, licenses, and other entry barriers. We assume that new entrants do not know their type and always start with a single product. Therefore, free entry requires that the entry cost equal the expected value of a firm of unknown quality:

$$\frac{1}{\phi_z} z^\chi w_t = \delta v_t^T + (1-\delta) v_t^S = \frac{\pi_t + \delta(\zeta - 1) \dfrac{1}{\phi_x} x^\zeta w_t}{\rho + \tau}. \tag{8}$$

Note that the value of entry is akin to the value of a transformative firm, except that the option value of innovation is discounted by δ.

The rate of creative destruction τ is the key endogenous variable. Its equilibrium expression is pinned down by two endogenous flow rates: z (entry) and x (incumbent innovation). Both of them are constant in a BGP. Because transformative firms innovate only in proportion to the products they possess (recall that x is an innovation *intensity*) and the product space is normalized to unity, the rate of creative destruction is given by

$$\tau = z + \sigma^T x, \tag{9}$$

where σ^T is the endogenous share of products owned by transformative firms. We derive a closed-form expression of σ^T below. Equation (9) highlights that innovative efforts by transformative firms have a multiplier effect. Holding x constant, creative destruction is increasing in the aggregate employment share by transformative firms σ^T. At the same time, we show below that σ^T is increasing in x as transformative firms expand at the expense of subsistence producers.

Aggregate growth and distance to frontier. The product-specific productivity q evolves on a quality ladder. As a new firm innovates and replaces the incumbent producer, quality increases by a factor $\gamma > 1$; that is, the new productivity q'_i is given by $q'_i = \gamma q_i$. We assume that γ varies across countries and over time depending on the position of each country in the international technology ladder. In particular, for a generic country c,

$$\gamma_{ct} = 1 + (Q_{Ft} / Q_{ct})^k, \tag{10}$$

where $\kappa > 0$ is a parameter, Q_c is the aggregate productivity of country c, and Q_F is the aggregate productivity of the frontier economy; that is, the country with the most efficient aggregate technology. For the moment, we simply assume that Q_F grows over time at the constant rate g_F—we later endogenize this. Equation (10) captures a process of knowledge diffusion through international spillovers. The assumption that $\kappa > 0$ incorporates a notion of backwardness and catch-up technology convergence: the further away a country is the technological frontier Q_F, the higher its step size.

Given the rate of creative destruction τ in Equation (9), aggregate productivity growth in country c evolves as follows:

$$g_{ct} = \frac{\dot{Q}_{ct}}{Q_{ct}} = \ln(\gamma_{ct}) \times \tau_c = \ln\left(1 + \left(\frac{Q_{Ft}}{Q_{ct}}\right)^{\kappa}\right) \times \tau_c. \tag{11}$$

Note that the equilibrium converges to a stationary distribution where all countries grow at the common rate g_F. More formally, the steady state is pinned down by the following system of equations for $c = 1, 2, \ldots, C$:

$$g_F = \ln\left(1 + \left(\frac{Q_{Ft}}{Q_{ct}}\right)^{\kappa}\right) \times \tau_c, \tag{12}$$

where Q_F / Q_c is the steady-state productivity gap relative to the technology frontier. Note that, when $c = F$, Equation (12) pins down the growth rate of the world economy: $g_F = \ln(2)\tau_F$. It is at this point clear that the frontier economy is the one with the highest rate of creative destruction. The system of equations in (12) can alternatively be expressed as:

$$Q_c = \left(\exp\left(\frac{\ln(2)\tau_F}{\tau_c} \right) - 1 \right)^{-1/\kappa} Q_F. \tag{13}$$

Equation (13) highlights an important implication of our theory: Along a balanced growth path, countries are ranked on a global productivity ladder, and their rung is fully determined by the rate of creative destruction τ. Countries where creative destruction is large are high up on the ladder and their income per capita is large. Countries with low creative destruction are relatively poor. However, the distribution of income is stationary and all countries grow at the same rate g_F.

The parameter κ determines the speed of convergence. If κ is large, backward countries benefit substantially from their technological backwardness, as the productivity gap translates into a large step size. By contrast, if κ is small, even large differences in productivity do not generate large differences in the step size of creative destruction.

The organization of the economy in the BGP. We now turn to the equilibrium determination of τ in each country. In the BGP, the firm size distribution is stationary in each country, and countries grow at a common constant rate. Both wages w_t and the value functions v_t^T and V_t^S grow at the same constant rate. Within each country, the entry flow z and the innovation intensity x are constant. Because the firm size distribution is stationary, the share of transformative products σ^τ and, hence, the rate of creative destruction τ, are also constant.

To solve for σ^τ, let F^S denote the mass of subsistence firms in the economy. At each point in time, $(1-\delta)\,z$ new subsistence firms are born. Similarly, because all active subsistence firms have just one product, they exit at rate τ. The stationary mass of subsistence firm is then given by

$$F^S = \frac{(1-\delta)z}{\tau}. \tag{14}$$

Note that faster creative destruction reduces the mass of subsistence firms by inducing faster exit. Because subsistence firms produce only a single product, $\sigma^\tau = 1 - F^S$. Equation (9) thus implies that the equilibrium rate of creative destruction τ is determined by the condition

$$\tau = z + \left(1 - \frac{(1-\delta)z}{\tau}\right)x,$$

which solves as

$$\tau = \frac{z+x}{2} + \sqrt{\frac{(z+x)^2}{4} - (1-\delta)zx}. \tag{15}$$

Creative destruction is increasing in both z and x: countries with low entry and low innovation from incumbents have little creative destruction in equilibrium. Moreover, holding z and x constant, τ is increasing in the share of transformative firms δ. Finally, we note that (15) implies that $\tau > x$ as long as $\delta < 1$, $z > 0$, and $x > 0$.

Next, we move to the aggregate resource constraint in the labor market. Individuals can either work as production workers, be hired by potential entrants, or be employed in transformative firms to generate further productivity improvements. Given our set of assumptions, the demand for entry labor is given by $L^E = z\psi(z) = z^{1+\chi}\frac{1}{\phi_z}$. Similarly, the demand for researchers from incumbent firms is $L^R = \frac{1}{\phi_x}x^\zeta \sigma^T$. Recalling that $\sigma^\tau = 1 - F^S$, substituting in the expression of F^S in (14) and normalizing the aggregate labor force to unity yields the following labor market-clearing condition:

$$1 = L^P + z^{1+\chi}\frac{1}{\phi_z} + \frac{1}{\phi_x}x^\zeta\left(1 - \frac{(1-\delta)z}{\tau}\right). \tag{16}$$

Equations (15) and (16) still involve the endogenous variables z and x. In Appendix Section A-2 we fully characterize the equilibrium as the solution of a system of three equations in three unknowns for each country: L^P, z, and x. In particular, using the free entry condition (8), the optimal rate of incumbent innovation (6), and the labor market clearing conditions, we can solve for z and x as functions of the three key structural parameters of the model: the entry costs $1/\phi_z$, the efficiency of incumbent innovation ϕ_x, and the share of high-type firms δ. Given the solutions for x and z we can then use (15) to compute the equilibrium rate of creative destruction τ. Proposition 1 summarizes the characterization of the BGP.

Proposition 1 *There exists a unique BGP equilibrium where the entry flow rate z, the innovation rate of transformative firms x, the rate of creative destruction τ,* *productivity growth g, and the share of production workers L^P are constant and the value functions for subsistence and transformative firms, v_t^S and v_t^T, grow at rate g. In this equilibrium,*

    1. *z* and *x* are consistent with free entry (8) and the incumbents' optimality condition (6);
    2. L^P satisfies the labor market clearing condition (16);
    3. τ is consistent with firms' expansion and entry choices (15);
    4. the value functions v_t^S and v_t^T are given by (7) and (4).

Proof. See Appendix Section A-2.

3.1 Taking stock

Our global economic equilibrium features a stationary productivity distribution across countries owing to international spillovers. Countries with high innovation and creative destruction climb up the global productivity ladder and approach the technological frontier. While progress raises living standards, it also limits the possibilities of further adoption. This is captured by the decline in the step size parameter γ. Thus, as an economy reaches a more advanced stage, its further success hinges on innovation. On average, growth in poor countries is accounted for more by imitation and less by technology adoption: creative destruction events are rare, but each of them shifts the productivity frontier by a larger amount. This description of the aggregate dynamics echoes the theory of Acemoglu et al. (2006).

Figure 17.2 displays the stationary distribution of aggregate productivity Q as a function of the rate of creative destruction. The figure shows three cases corresponding to different values of the parameter κ. The light gray line depicts the case where κ is small and adoption is more difficult. In this case, differences in creative destruction lead to large differences in aggregate productivity because adoption is a poor substitute for creative destruction. In this case, increasing creative destruction from 0.1 or 0.2 (which is roughly the difference between the United States and India that we estimate below) increases aggregate productivity by a factor of 12. By contrast, if adoption is fast (black line), the same difference only leads to a productivity difference by a factor of 4. Hence, in line with Acemoglu et al. (2006), adoption allows poor countries to benefit from technological progress and partially catch up even if they cannot generate a lot of innovation and creative destruction themselves. However, if a country wishes to

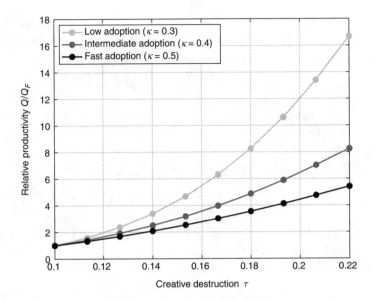

Note: The figure reports the steady-state relationship between τ and Q as implied by equation (13).

Figure 17.2. Creative destruction and aggregate productivity

climb up the technological ladder, it must introduce reforms that foster creative destruction.

3.2 Firm dynamics and firm size distribution

Another important endogenous outcome of the model is the firm size distribution, which is entirely pinned down by the endogenous entry and incumbent innovation flows z and x and by the initial share of transformative firms δ. In this section, we derive closed-form expressions for three moments of the process of firm dynamics that we will use to estimate our theory: the speed of life-cycle growth, shown in Figure 17.1b, the share of small firms shown in Figure 17.1a, and the equilibrium entry rate.[5]

To start with, recall that, given (z, x, δ), we can compute the rate of creative destruction τ (see (15)), the long-run mass of subsistence firms F^{Sub} (see

---

[5] We defer to Appendix Section A-3 for details on the formal derivation.

(14)), and the aggregate share of employment and sales of transformative firms σ^T. Similarly, we can analytically characterize the remaining aspects of the firm size distribution and the process of firm dynamics.

The mass of transformative firms, F^T, is given by $F^T = -\delta \frac{z}{x} \ln\left(1 - \frac{x}{\tau}\right)$. Together with the expression for F^S in (14) this implies that average employment $\bar{\ell}$ and the entry rate er are given, respectively, by

$$\bar{\ell} = \frac{\tau}{z}\frac{1}{1 - \delta\left(1 + \frac{\tau}{x}\ln\left(1 - \frac{x}{\tau}\right)\right)} \quad \text{and} \quad er = \frac{\tau}{1 - \delta\left(1 + \frac{\tau}{x}\ln\left(1 - \frac{x}{\tau}\right)\right)}. \quad (17)$$

Next, we can compute the share of "micro-firms," which we know are pervasive in India (see Figure 17.1). The share of firms with a single product is given by

$$\vartheta(1) = \frac{1}{1 - \delta\left(1 + \frac{\tau}{x}\ln\left(1 - \frac{x}{\tau}\right)\right)}. \quad (18)$$

Note that $\vartheta(1)$ is decreasing in δ if we hold $\frac{x}{\tau}$ constant and decreasing in $\frac{x}{\tau}$ if we hold δ constant. Thus, the large share of tiny producers in India is driven both by the scarcity of transformative entrepreneurs and by the fact that incumbent innovation x is only a small share of creative destruction τ (as opposed to entry z). Equations (17) and (18) also imply that

$$er = \tau \times \vartheta(1). \quad (19)$$

To interpret this equation, note that in a stationary equilibrium the entry rate equals the exit rate. Moreover, the share of exiting firms is simply the share of firms with a single product that experience a creative destruction event. With this in mind, (19) can help us understand why creative destruction is low in India: exit rates at the firm level are not substantially higher than in the United States even though India has a much larger number of small firms close to the exit threshold.

Finally, we can compute the firm's life cycle. Because subsistence firms do not grow and exit at the rate τ, their mass is strictly decreasing with age. In contrast, the life-cycle profile of transformative firms is increasing because these firms can grow. In Appendix Section A-3, we establish that the share of subsistence firms of age a is given by

$$\lambda^{Sub}(a) = \left(1 + \frac{\delta}{1-\delta} \frac{(\tau - x)}{\tau e^{-xa} - x e^{-\tau a}}\right)^{-1}.$$

(20)

$\lambda^{Sub}(a)$ is a decreasing function satisfying $\lambda^{Sub}(0) = 1 - \delta$ and $\lim_{a \to \infty} \lambda^{Sub}(a) = 0$. This equation captures the dynamic selection process by which transformative entrepreneurs replace subsistence entrepreneurs over time. The share of subsistence firms hinges on $\tau - x$. As creative destruction from incumbent firms declines, selection wanes and the share of subsistence firms remains constant over the life cycle at the unconditional level $1 - \delta$. More formally, $\lim_{a \to 0} \lambda^{Sub}(a) = 1 - \delta$.

Another facet of the selection process is the size of transformative firms, conditional on survival:

$$E^T[n|a] = 1 + \frac{x}{(\tau - x)}(1 - e^{-(\tau - x)a}).$$

(21)

The average size of transformative firms is increasing with age and such that $\lim_{a \to \infty} E^T[n|a] = (1 - x/\tau)^{-1}$. The economic significance of old and large superstar firms hinges on x being large relative to τ, but note that because $x < \tau$, the average size does not grow without bounds.

To link the life-cycle profile of transformative firms to the average life-cycle profile in the economy, we must take into account the selection encapsulated in $\lambda^{Sub}(a)$. The average life-cycle profile is given by

$$E[n|a] = \lambda^{Sub}(a) + (1 - \lambda^{Sub}(a))E^T[n|a]$$
$$= 1 + (1 - \lambda^{Sub}(a))\frac{x}{\tau - x}(1 - e^{-(\tau - x)a}).$$

(22)

Equation (22) shows that the slope of the average size profile is the product of the selection term $(1 - \lambda^{Sub}(a))$ times the life-cycle slope of transformative entrepreneurs. A shallow profile of life-cycle growth such as the one noted in Figure 17.1b. for Indian firms is a symptom of weak selection and the slow expansion of transformative firms. In terms of the fundamental parameters, this indicates that India suffers more from the low efficiency of incumbent growth (low ϕ_x) than from large entry barriers (low ϕ_z).

4 Quantitative Analysis

In this section, we take our model to the data. Given the parsimony of the theory, this analysis is necessarily stylized. We view it as the suggestive first step of a more thorough investigation involving data from multiple countries.

Calibration and estimation. We calibrate four parameters exogenously. We assume a discount rate ρ of 0.05 and set the growth rate of the technological frontier g_Q^F to 2 percent. We assume the incumbent innovation cost function to be quadratic. We set $\chi = 0.1$, implying a modest extent of congestion in the entry process.[6]

Then, we estimate the three key parameters ϕ_x, ϕ_z, and δ separately from data for the United States and India. We do so by exactly matching salient moments of the respective firm size distribution and the process of firm dynamics. In particular, we target the entry rate er, the share of small firms $\vartheta(1)$, and the extent of life-cycle growth $E[n|a]$. Our theoretical analysis establishes that these empirical moments uniquely determine z, x, and τ, from which we can ultimately retrieve the structural parameters δ, ϕ_x, and ϕ_z. Finally, given τ for both countries, we use Equation (13) to calibrate the parameter κ to match differences in aggregate productivity between the United States and India from

$$
\frac{Q_{IND}}{Q_{US}} = \left(\frac{\exp\left(\dfrac{g_Q^F}{\tau_{IND}} \right) - 1}{\exp\left(\dfrac{g_Q^F}{\tau_{US}} \right) - 1} \right)^{-1/\kappa}.
$$

Note that κ is calibrated residually and that none of the firm-level moments depend on this parameter.

Results. Table 17.1 reports the data moments, the estimated structural parameters, and the associated equilibrium outcomes x, z, and τ. We target three firm-level data moments. First, we target an 8 percent entry rate for both

---

[6] Congestion is introduced for computational ease: it ensures that the free-entry condition is always binding.

countries, following Akcigit et al. (2021). Second, for the share of small firms $\vartheta(1)$, we target a value of 0.9 for India and a value of 0.4 for the United States based on the data in Figure 17.1a. Note that our target for the United States slightly exceeds the share of firms with one to four employees (which is around 0.32) to adjust for the fact that the smallest size category (which in our theory are firms with a single product) plausibly exceeds four employees in the United States. Third, we measure life-cycle growth by the size of ten-year-old firms relative to new entrants. Because all entrants enter with a single product, this growth rate is given by $E[n|10]$. Figure 17.1b implies a target moment of 2 for the United States, that is, conditional on survival, firms double in size relative to new entrants. The corresponding moment for India is 1.1. These three data moments are sufficient to exactly identify δ, ϕ_x, and ϕ_z for both the United States and India.

Finally, we use differences in aggregate productivity to discipline the adoption parameter κ. As highlighted in Figure 17.2, for given rates of creative destruction in India and the United States, we can infer κ from differences in aggregate productivity. We assume productivity to be eight times larger in the United States than in India. This target gap is smaller than the observed differences in income per capita. However, our model abstracts from other sources of income differences such as physical capital or human capital. This choice has, in any case, no consequence on any of the outcomes of interest.

The first panel of Table 17.1 summarizes the empirical targets. The second panel reports the structural parameters that allow the model to fit those targets. Our model implies that $\delta_{US} > \delta_{IND}$. In the United States, roughly 30 percent of all entering firms are led by transformative entrepreneurs. In India, only 16 percent of entering firms have growth potential, and 84 percent of new entrants are stagnant subsistence firms. This finding is qualitatively in line with the results reported in Akcigit et al. (2021). The next two columns report the cost of incumbent expansion (ϕ_x) and the efficiency of entry (ϕ_z). While both are estimated to be more productive in the United States, the difference is larger for incumbent innovation: $\phi_x^{US}/\phi_x^{IND} > \phi_z^{US}/\phi_z^{IND}$. In other words, not only has the United States a much larger share of transformative firms but also these firms are much more efficient at innovating than the corresponding (transformative) Indian firms.[7]

---

[7] Peters (2020) finds similar patterns between the United States and Indonesia.

Table 17.1. Calibration: Model fit and structural parameter

$$\frac{\tau_{IND}}{\tau_{US}} = \frac{er_{IND}/\vartheta_{IND}(1)}{er_{US}/\vartheta_{US}(1)} \approx \frac{\vartheta_{US}(1)}{\vartheta_{IND}(1)} = \frac{0.4}{0.9} = \frac{0.09}{0.2} \approx 0.45.$$

	Moments				Structural parameters				Equilibrium outcomes		
	er	$\vartheta(1)$	$E[n\|10]$	Q	δ	ϕ_x	ϕ_z	κ	z	x	τ
US	0.08	0.4	2	1	0.29	0.280	0.706	0.42	0.002	0.19	0.2
India	0.08	0.9	1.1	1/8	0.16	0.061	0.533	0.42	0.066	0.061	0.09

Notes: The table reports the targeted moments (the entry rate *er*, the share of small firms $\vartheta(1)$, the life-cycle profile of firms at age ten, $E[n|a]$, and the aggregate productivity Q (relative to the United States), the structural parameters, and the equilibrium outcomes.

Finally, in the last three columns, we report the equilibrium outcomes. First and foremost, creative destruction is much higher in the United States than in India. Equation (19) shows how we can infer this pattern directly from the data, independently from any model parameters.

Intuitively, entry and exit rates vary little across the two countries, but India has roughly twice as many small firms. Thus, creative destruction turns out to be only half as large. Next, the discrepancies in entry costs and incumbent efficiency translate in both a lower entry flow rate z and a lower innovation flow from incumbent firms x. In the United States, innovation from incumbent firms accounts for the vast majority of creative destruction. In India, entry plays a larger role, in relative terms. Empirically, we infer these patterns from the entry rate and the life-cycle growth. Because transformative firms expand at rate x and lose products at rate τ, the steep life-cycle profile in the United States requires x to be large relative to τ. In contrast, in India creative destruction must be large *relative* to the rate at which incumbent firms expand in order to keep firms small on average. This is achieved by having entrants play a relatively more important role.

In Figure 17.3a–b we depict the life-cycle profile of firms in our estimated model. Figure 17.3a displays the average size by age $E[n|a]$ (see (22)) and the life-cycle profile of transformative firms $E^T[n|a]$ (see (21)) for the United States (black lines) and India (gray lines). Firms in the United States grow substantially faster, conditional on survival. In India, the average surviving firm barely doubles its size after as long as thirty years. The dashed lines refer to the transformative firms. Naturally, $E^T[n|a] > E[n|a]$. Interestingly, the (few) transformative firms in India do grow. Quantitatively, in the first five

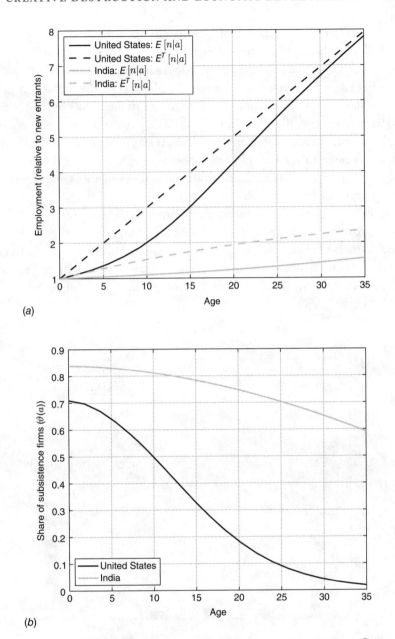

(a)

(b)

Notes: (a) The average life-cycle profile $E[n|a]$ and the life-cycle profile of high-type firms $E^T[n|a]$, (b) The share of subsistence firms by age $\vartheta(a)$. The respective models are parametrized according to the parameters reported in Table 17.1.

Figure 17.3a–b. Life-cycle growth in the US and India

years, good firms in India do not look very different from the average firm in the United States (though they are very different from the transformative US firms). Over time, the average firm looks increasingly similar to a good firm because subsistence firms are more likely to exit. This shake-out process is shown in Figure 17.3b. The share of subsistence firms in the United States is already smaller than in India at birth, but the difference is modest at that point. Thereafter, the process of selection is much faster in the United States. Among thirty-year-old firms, the share of surviving firms is negligible in the United States. In contrast, in India as many as 70 percent of thirty-year-old firms have no growth potential.

In Figure 17.4 we display the resulting firm size distribution, captured by the share of firms with n products. The model qualitatively replicates the salient features of the empirical distribution displayed in Figure 17.1. In India, almost all firms have a single product and the share of firms with more products declines rapidly. In the United States there is also a group of relatively

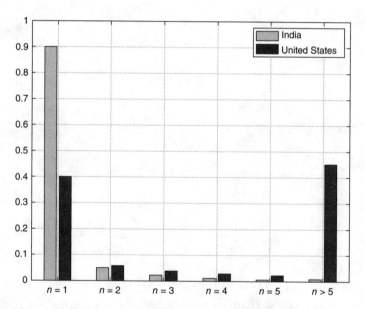

Notes: The figure shows the equilibrium firm size distribution in India and the United States. The respective models are parametrized according to the parameters reported in Table 17.1.

Figure 17.4. Firm size distribution in the US and India: Model

small firms. However, a substantial mass of firms manage to grow large and constitute the right tail of the firm size distribution.

Cross-country differences in productivity, creative destruction, and firm size. Thus far we have focused on the comparison between India and the United States. In this section, we interpret the positive cross-country correlation between aggregate productivity, creative destruction, and average firm size through the lens of our model. We view this as a first step toward a more general analysis that would require data for firm dynamics in multiple countries.

In our theory, creative destruction and aggregate productivity are jointly determined; see Equation (13). All cross-country differences are rooted in differences in entry costs $1/\phi_z$, incumbent innovation efficiency ϕ_x, and the share of transformative entrepreneurs δ. To study the role of each of these parameters, we consider the following exercise. Given the structural parameters (ϕ_x, ϕ_z, δ) in the United States and India, we generate a synthetic cross-section of countries whose structural parameters are convex combinations of these parameters. Hence, a country is characterized by a weight parameter ϖ, and we then set

$$\phi_x(\varpi) = \varpi\phi_x^{US} + (1-\varpi)\phi_x^{IND},$$

and for ϕ_z and δ similarly. Countries with $\varpi \approx 1$ are industrialized countries that are similar to the United States. Countries with $\varpi \approx 0$ are similar to India. Given ϖ, we compute the equilibrium allocation and aggregate productivity. By varying ϖ, we can then trace out a synthetic cross-section of countries and study how creative destruction and properties of the firm-size distribution vary with aggregate productivity.

The results of this exercise are presented in Figure 17.5. We plot creative destruction, the equilibrium entry rate, average firm size, and the rate of life-cycle growth against relative income per capita. Figures 17.5a–b show that creative destruction and aggregate entry and exit are basically dissociated. Even though richer countries have more creative destruction, entry rates are essentially uncorrelated with income per capita. Equation (19) explains why this is the case. A high rate of creative destruction τ is typically associated with a high degree of incumbent innovation x. Thus, the share of small firms $\vartheta(1)$ tends to be small in the stationary equilibrium.

Figures 17.5c–d focus on firm size and the life-cycle profile. The patterns are reminiscent of the empirical findings by Bento and Restuccia (2017) and

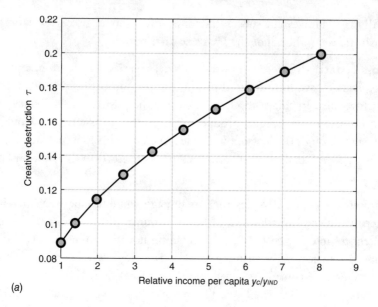

(a)

(b)

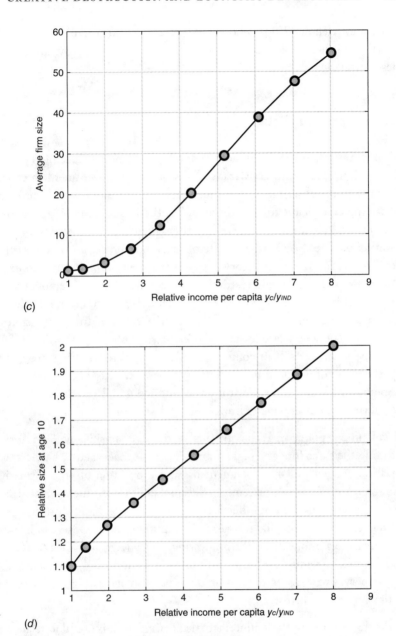

(c)

(d)

Notes: Correlation between aggregate productivity and: (a) Creative destruction, (b) Entry rate, (c) Average firm size, and (d) Life-cycle growth (relative size at age ten).

Figure 17.5a–d. Aggregate productivity, creative destruction, and firm size

Hsieh and Klenow (2014), who show that average firm size and life-cycle growth are systematically larger in richer countries. Our theory rationalizes these correlations.

5 Development Policy

We now return to the discussion of development policy. Acemoglu et al. (2006) argue that at an early stage of development, government interventions that support selected insider firms can be useful to promote development. The empirical evidence discussed in the introduction suggests that entry barriers are less harmful (and, at times, beneficial) for growth in poor countries but become a hurdle to technological convergence as countries come closer to the frontier. Our theory abstracts from credit market and contractual frictions that motivate restrictions on competition in Acemoglu et al. (2006). Yet it allows us to compare the potential gains of different reforms that foster creative destruction. Also, we show that a natural extension of the theory can raise a case for targeted industrial policy.

We perform two sets of counterfactual policy exercises. First, we quantify the effect of different policy reforms on productivity and welfare in an economy like India. Then we study targeted industrial policies that shield transformative entrepreneurs from creative destruction.

Development policy in India. In this section we consider policy reforms affecting the three fundamental parameters in our theory: entry barriers, innovation efficiency of incumbent firms, and proportion of transformative entrepreneurs. Each margin requires different policy instruments. Entry barriers pertain to the area of industrial policy. The second and third margins are related to human capital formation. In addition, the expansion of incumbent firms has implications for innovation policy (e.g., subsidies to R&D) and for policies regulating the growth of incumbent firms—India has a history of pervasive legal restrictions on the expansion of existing firms in order to protect smaller firms.

Before performing the counterfactual experiments, it is useful to relate our analysis to recent empirical studies of economic reforms in India based on a difference-in-difference methodology. Martin et al. (2017) study the effect of policy reforms that reduced small-scale industry promotion in India throughout the early 2000s. Prior to reform, the policy reserved specific production lines for small and medium enterprises. The authors exploit variation in the timing of dereservation and find that districts more exposed to dereservation experienced higher employment and output growth. Aghion et al. (2005, 2008) study an earlier set of reforms dating back to the late 1980s that dismantled the License Raj—a policy comprising both entry barriers and constraints on the expansion of existing firms. The studies document significant differential effects across Indian states that depend on local labor market regulations. The aggregate effects on employment and growth are instead more ambiguous.

We take the estimated model for India and then individually set the entry cost, the efficiency of incumbent growth, and the share of transformative entrepreneurs to the respective values in the United States. We then calculate the equilibrium rate of creative destruction and aggregate productivity for each of the three scenarios.

Figure 17.6a–b summarizes the results. Figure 17.6a displays creative destruction in the India baseline estimated model and in each of the counterfactuals. Creative destruction is higher in all three scenarios, suggesting that entry costs, the low efficiency of incumbent firms, and the small share of transformative entrepreneurs all play a role in explaining low creative destruction in India. Quantitatively, it is incumbent innovation efficiency ϕ_x that plays the most important role. While reducing entry costs or increasing the share of high-type firms increases creative destruction by 10 to 50 percent, creative destruction would almost double if Indian firms had the same capability to expand through innovation as their US counterparts. Figure 17.6b plots the effect on aggregate productivity. We see once again the dominant role of incumbent innovation. While India's productivity would almost double if entry costs were as low as in the United States, productivity would increase by a factor of eight if Indian firms had the same innovation capability as US firms. Note that the effects of increasing the share of high types in India by itself is modest, reflecting the fact that transformative firms in India are substantially less productive than in the United States.

Targeted industrial policy. In the counterfactual experiments of Figure 17.6, barriers to entry are always harmful for growth. However, one might argue that industrial policy has more-refined tools to restrict competition than imposing entry barriers across the board. A benevolent government might have access to some information that allows it to selectively support some firms at the expense of others. Our theory yields a potential rationale of such

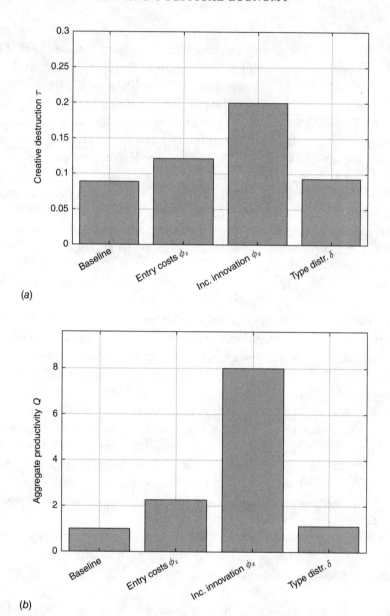

(a)

(b)

Notes: The figure depicts the counterfactual effects of (i) lowering entry costs to the level in the United States, (ii) raising incumbent innovation efficiency to the level of the United States, and (iii) increasing the share of transformative types to the US level. All other parameters are held constant: (a) Respective change in creative destruction τ, (b) Change in aggregate productivity Q.

Figure 17.6a–b. Development policy in India

policies: because transformative firms actually use the products they own as an input to further innovation, the government might want to protect them. And because transformative firms are on average larger and older than subsistence firms, such policy has a flavor of the government protecting old and large producers.

To gauge the potential welfare impact of such policies, we extend our model to allow for *governmental protection*. To capture this idea we augment our model with the assumption that the government can block some successful product innovations that would lead to the replacement of transformative entrepreneurs. More specifically, suppose that the equilibrium degree of creative destruction is τ and that the government can shield transformative products from a share ϱ of such innovations. Then products owned by transformative firms face a business-stealing threat of $(1-\varrho)\tau$, while subsistence producers face a replacement rate of τ.

Such a policy has costs and benefits. On the one hand, it protects better firms from being replaced, thereby increasing the market share of transformative firms. In addition, the reduction in the risk of being replaced encourages transformative firms to invest in innovation and expand. Both of these mechanisms tend to increase aggregate productivity and welfare. On the other hand, such policies also have detrimental effects. First of all, the government intervention mechanically reduces productivity growth by disallowing some product innovations. If F^S denotes the share of products produced by subsistence firms and τ is the rate of attempted creative destruction, the rate of *realized* creative destruction τ^* is given by

$$\tau^* = (F^S + (1-F^S)(1-\varrho))\,\tau. \tag{23}$$

Second, such forms of market protection reduce the expected return of innovation—both for transformative firms and potential entrants—because firms anticipate that a share $(1-F^S)\varrho$ of their innovations will be blocked.

In Appendix Section A-3.1 we show how to extend our theory with this form of industrial policy. Even though this changes the characterization of the value function and the firm size distribution, we can still compute the equilibrium allocations analytically. We can then easily perform policy counterfactuals and study the welfare impact for different choices of the share of protection ϱ.

Figure 17.7a shows the welfare change as a function of ϱ for both the United States and India. We always express welfare relative to the laissez-faire

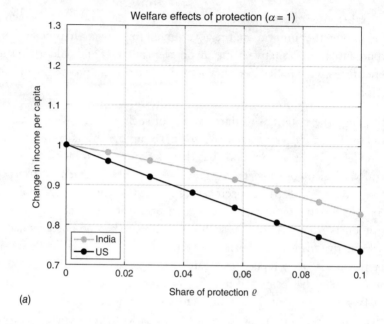

(a)

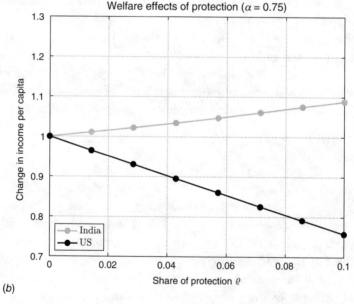

(b)

Notes: The figure depicts the change in welfare as a function of the degree of protection ϱ. We normalize welfare in the baseline ($\varrho=0$) to unity: (*a*) We assume the innovation step size to be the same for transformative and subsistence firms, (*b*) We assume that subsistence firms have a 25 percent smaller step size than transformative firms.

Figure 17.7a–b. The welfare impact of protection policies

equilibrium; that is, $\varrho = 0$. The figure highlights two results. First, protection policies reduce welfare in both countries. Even though the share of transformative firms increases in both economies, the adverse effects of blocking creative destruction dominate these positive selection effects. Second, the consequences of such policies are significantly worse in the United States than in India. The reason is that the US economy already generates a large degree of selection without any governmental protection for transformative firms. Hence, in an advanced economy, industrial policy shields transformative firms from other transformative firms, thereby reducing productivity growth without any significant gain from selection. The situation is different in India, where most firms are subsistence firms and the bulk of overall creative destruction stems from entrants.

The targeted industrial policy just discussed has different lower net costs in India than in the United States but is harmful in both countries. A further extension that can reconcile our theory with the hypothesis of Acemoglu et al. (2006) is that innovation stemming from transformative versus subsistence firms contributes differentially to productivity growth. In particular, we assume that the productivity step size of transformative innovations is γ while that of subsistence firms is only $\alpha\gamma$, where $\alpha \leq 1$. This model nests our benchmark model as a particular case where $\alpha = 1$. As α becomes smaller we approach a limit case in which subsistence firms can simply copy the technology of transformative firms without contributing at all to productivity growth. We refer again to Appendix Section A-3.1 for the details of the formal analysis of this case.

Figure 17.7b shows the results of this case. We assume $\alpha = 0.75$; that is, innovations by subsistence firms contribute 25 percent less to productivity growth than those by transformative firms. The policy has now opposite-sign effects at different stages of development. In the United States the industrial policy still reduces creative destruction, aggregate productivity, and welfare, whereas in India it increases them.

The source of the stark discrepancy is the following. In the United States, only a small share of products are produced by subsistence firms in equilibrium and most of aggregate growth stems from existing firms, which are transformative. The innovation efficiency of subsistence firms has negligible effects on productivity and welfare. Note that the two panels have the same y-axis, indicating that the welfare impact in the United States is insensitive to α.

In India, the share of subsistence firms is large and accounts for a large proportion of the entrants. If the innovations of such firms upon entry is low, their role as "parasites" dominates, and policies protecting the few transformative firms can be beneficial.

6 Conclusions

The positive relationship between aggregate productivity and firm size is a salient feature of economic development. In this chapter we argue that this pattern is the natural implication of a simple model of creative destruction where cross-country income differences are determined by the rate of creative destruction of each economy. Countries where existing firms can grow easily have more creative destruction, are richer, have bigger firms, and weed out less efficient producers quickly. Countries where even the best firms grow slowly have little creative destruction, are relatively poor, and feature many small firms that manage to survive for a long time.

The theory also bears positive and normative implications about the importance of creative destruction at different stages of development. In line with Acemoglu et al. (2006), our theory predicts that growth in poorer economies hinges more on imitation and technology adoption and less on innovation, churning, and creative destruction. The latter accounts for a larger share of productivity growth in more advanced economies.

At the normative level, a calibrated version of the theory suggests that barriers to entry may not be the main culprit for low productivity in developing countries. More important is the shortage of dynamic firms that may reflect the human capital of entrepreneurs and managers, as well as the existence of social norms or explicit legal restrictions that limit the growth of the most productive firms. As an example of the latter, Akcigit et al. (2021) highlight the importance of cross-country differences in the efficiency of managerial delegation.

We study the role of a stylized industrial policy that selectively protects some firms in the economy. In the benchmark estimated model, this type of industrial policy harms creative destruction and growth, but the result can be reversed in poor economies where most entrant firms replace incumbents while generating only small productivity gains and have no expansion potential after entry. In this case, the business-stealing from low-productivity firms can be a major deterrent to innovation from higher-quality incumbent firms. Then, a benevolent government could desire to shield the most dynamic firms from competition. This situation is typical of economies where self-employment and entrepreneurship are last resorts for people on the margins of formal economic activity rather than the choice of the most talented and innovative individuals in society aspiring to success.

The theory presented in this chapter is very stylized. Likewise, the quantification is based on the comparison between only two countries, India and the United States. Future research can build on the insights of this work and carry out more formal estimations using data from many countries. A potential criticism of the theory is that it assigns no role to neck-and-neck competition and escape innovation. Incumbent firms cannot reduce the risk of replacement by improving the product in their current product line. Some of the predictions can change if this realistic feature is incorporated, although we expect the main insights to be robust. The theory also abstracts from distributional effects: creative destruction generates winners and losers, and taking this into consideration is important for normative analysis. We also abstract from frictions and market incompleteness. We hope that these and other limitations can be addressed by future research.

References

Acemoglu, Daron, Philippe Aghion, and Fabrizio Zilibotti. (2006). "Distance to frontier, selection, and economic growth." *Journal of the European Economic Association, 4* (1), 37–74.

Acemoglu, Daron, Ufuk Akcigit, Harun Alp, Nicholas Bloom, and William Kerr. (2018). "Innovation, reallocation, and growth." *American Economic Review, 108* (11), 3450–3491.

Aghion, Philippe, Robin Burgess, Stephen J. Redding, and Fabrizio Zilibotti. (2005). "Entry liberalization and inequality in industrial performance." *Journal of the European Economic Association, 3* (2–3), 291–302.

———. (2008). "The unequal effects of liberalization: Evidence from dismantling the License Raj in India." *American Economic Review, 98* (4), 1397–1412.

Aghion, Philippe, and Peter Howitt. (1992). "A model of growth through creative destruction." *Econometrica, 60* (2), 323–351.

Akcigit, Ufuk, Harun Alp, and Michael Peters. (2021). "Lack of selection and limits to delegation: Firm dynamics in developing countries." *American Economic Review, 111* (1), 231–75.

Banerjee, Abhijit, Emily Breza, Esther Duflo, and Cynthia Kinnan. (2015). "Do credit constraints limit entrepreneurship? Heterogeneity in the returns to microfinance." Working Paper.

Bento, Pedro, and Diego Restuccia. (2017). "Misallocation, establishment size, and productivity." *American Economic Journal: Macroeconomics, 9* (3), 267–303.

de Mel, Suresh, David McKenzie, and Christopher Woodruff. (2008). "Returns to capital in microenterprises: Evidence from a field experiment." *Quarterly Journal of Economics, 123* (4), 1329–1372.

Decker, Ryan, John Haltiwanger, Ron Jarmin, and Javier Miranda. (2014). "The role of entrepreneurship in US job creation and economic dynamism." *Journal of Economic Perspectives, 28* (3), 3–24.

Garcia-Macia, Daniel, Chang-Tai Hsieh, and Peter J. Klenow. (2019). "How destructive is innovation?" *Econometrica, 87* (5), 1507–1541.

Hsieh, Chang-Tai, and Peter Klenow. (2014). "The life cycle of plants in India and Mexico." *Quarterly Journal of Economics, 129* (3), 1035–1084.

Klette, Tor Jakob, and Samuel Kortum. (2004). "Innovating firms and aggregate innovation." *Journal of Political Economy, 112* (5), 986–1018.

König, Michael D., Zheng Song, Kjetil Storesletten, and Fabrizio Zilibotti. (2020). "From imitation to innovation: Where is all that Chinese R&D going?" NBER Working Paper w27404.

Martin, Leslie A., Shanthi Nataraj, and Ann E. Harrison. (2017). "In with the big, out with the small: Removing small-scale reservations in India." *American Economic Review, 107* (2), 354–386.

Peters, Michael. (2020). "Heterogeneous markups, growth, and endogenous misallocation." *Econometrica, 88* (5), 2037–2073.

Porta, Rafael La, and Andrei Shleifer. (2009). "The unofficial economy and economic development." *Brookings Papers on Economic Activity, 39* (2), 275–363.

Schoar, Antoinette. (2010). "The divide between subsistence and transformational entrepreneurship." *Innovation Policy and the Economy, 10*, 57–81.

Vandenbussche, Jerome, Philippe Aghion, and Costas Meghir. (2006). "Growth, distance to frontier and composition of human capital." *Journal of Economic Growth, 11* (2), 97–127.

Zilibotti, Fabrizio. (2017). "Growing and slowing down like China." *Journal of the European Economic Association, 15* (5), 943–998.

APPENDIX

A-1 Optimal Incumbent Innovation and the Value Function

The value function of a high-type firm is given by

$$rV(n) - \dot{V}(n) = \pi n + \max_{x}\{xn(V(n+1) - V(n)) - \phi n x^{\zeta} w_t\} + \tau n(V(n-1) - V(n)).$$

Conjecture that

$$V_t(n) = v_t n.$$

Then

$$rv_t n - \dot{v}_t n = \pi n + n\max_x \left\{ xv_t - \frac{1}{\phi_x} x^\zeta w_t \right\} - \tau n v_t.$$

Hence, homogeneous of degree n. Hence, v_t solves

$$rv_t - \dot{v}_t = \pi + \max_x \left\{ xv_t - \frac{1}{\phi_x} x^\zeta w_t \right\} - \tau v_t.$$

Optimal x solves

$$v_t - \frac{1}{\phi_x} \zeta x^{\zeta-1} w_t = 0$$

so that

$$x = \left(\frac{v_t}{w_t} \frac{\phi_x}{\zeta} \right)^{\frac{1}{\zeta-1}}.$$

Along BGP: $v_t \propto w_t$ so that x is constant. Also

$$\max_x \left\{ xv_t - \frac{1}{\phi_x} x^\zeta w_t \right\} = (\zeta - 1)\frac{1}{\phi_x} x^\zeta w_t.$$

v_t grows at rate g_y. The Euler equation requires $r - g = \rho$. Hence,

$$rv_t - \dot{v}_t = \pi + (\zeta - 1)\frac{1}{\phi_x} x^\zeta w_t - \tau v_t,$$

so that

$$v_t^T = \frac{\pi_t + (\zeta - 1)\dfrac{1}{\phi_x} x^\zeta w_t}{\rho + \tau}.$$

Similarly, the value of a low type is

$$v_t^{Sub} = \frac{\pi_t}{\rho + \tau}.$$

A-2 Steady-State Equilibrium

Using the expression for profits and aggregate output (see (1) and (2)), firms' profits relative to the equilibrium wage are given by

$$\frac{\pi_t}{w_t} = \frac{\mu-1}{\mu}\frac{Y_t}{w_t} = (\mu-1)L_t^P.$$

The free entry condition in (8) thus implies that

$$\frac{1}{\phi_z}z^{\chi} = \frac{\dfrac{\pi_t}{w_t} + \delta(\zeta-1)\dfrac{1}{\phi_x}x^{\zeta}}{\rho+\tau} = \frac{(\mu-1)L_t^P + \delta(\zeta-1)\dfrac{1}{\phi_x}x^{\zeta}}{\rho+\tau}. \qquad \text{(A-1)}$$

Similarly, optimal incumbent innovation is given by (see (6))

$$x = \left(\frac{v_t^T}{w_t}\frac{\phi_x}{\zeta}\right)^{1/(\zeta-1)} = \left(\frac{(\mu-1)L_t^P + (\zeta-1)\dfrac{1}{\phi_x}x^{\zeta}}{\rho+\tau}\frac{\phi_x}{\zeta}\right)^{1/(\zeta-1)}. \qquad \text{(A-2)}$$

Labor market clearing implies that

$$L = L^P + L^E + L^R = L^P + z^{1+\chi}\frac{1}{\phi_z} + \frac{1}{\phi_x}x^{\zeta}\left(1 - \frac{(1-\delta)z}{\tau}\right). \qquad \text{(A-3)}$$

Together with the definition of the rate of creative destruction in (15), equations (A-1), (A-2), and (A-3) are three equations in three unknowns (x, z, L^P). The solution to these equations fully determines the equilibrium.

A-3 The Process of Firm Dynamics and the Firm Size Distribution

Let δ, z, and x be given. Given (δ, x, z) we can solve for: (i) the number of firms and the entry rate, (ii) the rate of life-cycle growth, and (iii) the share of small firms.

The number of firms and the entry rate

The mass of subsistence firms is given in (14). To solve for the mass of transformative firms, we have to solve for the firm size distribution. Let $F_t^T(n)$ denote the mass of transformative firms with n products at time t. For $n > 1$, this mass solves the differential equation

$$\frac{\partial F_t^T(n)}{\partial t} = \tau(n+1)F_t^T(n+1) + x(n-1)F_t^T(n-1) - (\tau+x)nF_t^T(n).$$

Similarly, for $n=1$, it solves the differential equation

$$\frac{\partial F_t^T(1)}{\partial t} = \tau 2 F_t^T(2) + \delta z - (\tau+x)F_t^T(1).$$

In a stationary equilibrium, it is easy to show that the mass of transformative firms is given by

$$F_t^T = -\frac{\delta z}{x}\ln\left(1-\frac{x}{\tau}\right),$$

and the share of transformative firms with n products is

$$\omega_t(n) = \frac{1}{F_t^T}\frac{\delta z}{x}\frac{1}{n}\left(\frac{x}{\tau}\right)^n.$$

The entry rate is therefore given by

$$\text{Entry} - \text{Rate} = \frac{z}{F_t^T + F_t^S} = \frac{z}{\dfrac{(1-\delta)z}{\tau} - \dfrac{\delta z}{x}\ln\left(1-\dfrac{x}{\tau}\right)}. \qquad \text{(A-4)}$$

The rate of life-cycle growth

To calculate the life-cycle growth in our economy, let $\lambda^S(a)$ denote the share of subsistence firms for a cohort of age a. The expected number of products as a function of age is thus given by

$$\begin{aligned}
E[n|a] &= \lambda^S(a)E^S[n|a] + (1-\lambda^S(a))E^T[n|a]\\
&= \lambda^S(a) + (1-\lambda^S(a))E^T[n|a] \qquad \text{(A-5)}
\end{aligned}$$

where $E^S[n|a]$ and $E^T[n|a]$ denote the average number of products as a function of age for subsistence and transformative firms. Of course, $E^S[n|a]=1$. We now compute $E^T[n|a]$ and $\lambda^S(a)$.

Consider first $E^T[n|a]$. For a transformative firm, the setup is the same as in the baseline model of Klette and Kortum (2004). Hence,

$$E^T[n|a] = \frac{1}{1-\gamma(a)} \quad \text{where} \quad \gamma(a) = \frac{x(1-e^{-(\tau-x)a})}{\tau - xe^{-(\tau-x)a}}. \qquad \text{(A-6)}$$

Now consider $\lambda^S(a)$. Because subsistence firms exit at rate τ, the probability of a subsistence firm surviving until age a is given by

$$p^S(a) = e^{-\tau a}.$$

For transformative firms we can again exploit the results from Klette and Kortum (2004). The probability of a transformative firm having zero products at age a is given by

$$p_0^T(a) = \frac{\tau}{x}\gamma(a),$$

where $\gamma(a)$ is given in (A-6). Hence, the share of transformative firms that are still alive at age a is given by

$$p^T(a) \equiv 1 - p_0^T(a) = 1 - \frac{\tau}{x}\gamma(a) = \frac{(\tau - x)e^{-(\tau - x)a}}{\tau - xe^{-(\tau - x)a}}.$$

Given that the initial mass of subsistence (transformative) firms is given by $(1-\delta)$ and δz, we have

$$\lambda^S(a) = \frac{(1-\delta)zp^S(a)}{(1-\delta)zp^S(a) + \delta zp^T(a)} = \frac{1}{1 + \dfrac{\delta}{1-\delta}\dfrac{(\tau - x)e^{xa}}{\tau - xe^{-(\tau - x)a}}}. \qquad \text{(A-7)}$$

The share of small firms

The mass of firms with a single product is given by

$$F_t(1) = F^{Sub} + F_t^T\omega_t(1) = \frac{(1-\delta)z}{\tau} + \frac{\delta z}{x}\frac{x}{\tau} = \frac{z}{\tau}.$$

Hence, the share of firms with a single product is

$$\bar{n}(1) = \frac{z/\tau}{\dfrac{(1-\delta)z}{\tau} - \dfrac{\delta z}{x}\ln\left(1 - \dfrac{x}{\tau}\right)} = \frac{1}{1 - \delta - \delta\dfrac{\tau}{x}\ln\left(1 - \dfrac{x}{\tau}\right)}$$

$$= \frac{1}{1 - \delta\left(1 + \dfrac{\tau}{x}\ln\left(1 - \dfrac{x}{\tau}\right)\right)}. \qquad \text{(A-8)}$$

Note that a higher δ reduces $\varrho(1)$ holding τ constant. In addition, for given x and τ, $\varrho(1)$ does not depend on z.

The firm size distribution

The mass of firms with n products, $F(n)$, is given by

$$F(n) = \begin{cases} \dfrac{z}{\tau} & \text{if } n=1 \\[2ex] \dfrac{\delta z}{x}\dfrac{1}{n}\left(\dfrac{x}{\tau}\right)^n & \text{if } n\geq 2 \end{cases}.$$

Hence, total employment by firms with n products is given by

$$E(n) = nF(n)l = \begin{cases} \dfrac{z}{\tau}l & \text{if } n=1 \\[2ex] \dfrac{\delta z}{x}\left(\dfrac{x}{\tau}\right)^n l & \text{if } n\geq 2 \end{cases},$$

where l denotes aggregate employment per product. Hence, the share of employment in firms with n products is given by

$$q(n) = \dfrac{E(n)}{\displaystyle\sum_{n=1}^{\infty} E(n)}.$$

Note that

$$\sum_{n=1}^{\infty} E(n) = \left(\dfrac{1-\delta}{\tau} + \dfrac{\delta}{\tau-x}\right)zl.$$

Hence,

$$q(n) = \begin{cases} \dfrac{1}{\tau}\dfrac{1}{\left(\dfrac{1-\delta}{\tau} + \dfrac{\delta}{\tau-x}\right)} & \text{if } n=1 \\[4ex] \dfrac{\dfrac{\delta}{x}\left(\dfrac{x}{\tau}\right)^n}{\left(\dfrac{1-\delta}{\tau} + \dfrac{\delta}{\tau-x}\right)} & \text{if } n\geq 2 \end{cases}.$$

A-4 The Model with Industrial Policy

Suppose the government can enact a simple industrial policy of the following form: If a creative destruction event happens on a product produced by a transformative firm, the government can "block" the innovation. While this shields high-type firms, it also has a cost in that the productivity frontier does not evolve.

To incorporate this idea in our model, suppose that a fraction ϱ of all creative destruction for high-type products is blocked. As before, we denote by z and x the flow rates of attempted entry and incumbent expansion and by F^S the share of subsistence products. The aggregate amount of attempted creative destruction is thus still given by

$$\tau = z + (1 - F^S)x. \tag{A-9}$$

However, while subsistence firms are indeed replaced at rate τ, high-type firms are replaced at rate $(1-\varrho)\tau$. The total flow of successful creative destruction is thus given by

$$\tau^* = \tau F^S + \tau(1-\varrho)(1-F^S) = \tau(1-\varrho+\varrho F^S).$$

Given this new structure, the mass of subsistence firms F^S solves the steady-state equation

$$\tau F_t^S = (1 - \delta)z(1 - \tilde{n} + \tilde{n}F^S).$$

Hence,

$$F^S = \frac{(1 - \delta)z(1 - \tilde{n})}{\tau - (1 - \delta)z\tilde{n}}. \tag{A-10}$$

Note that if $\varrho = 0$ we have $F^S = \dfrac{(1-\delta)z}{\tau}$ as before. Note also that if $\varrho = 1$ we have $F^S = 0$. Intuitively: if low-type firms only steal from low-type firm but high-type firms also steal from low-type firms, in the long-run, there will be only high type-firms, and creative destruction will be zero as $\tau^* = \tau F^S = 0$.

Substituting (A-10) in (A-9) yields the rate of attempted creative destruction as

$$\tau = z + \left(1 - \frac{(1 - \delta)z(1 - \tilde{n})}{\tau - (1 - \delta)z\tilde{n}}\right)x.$$

This determines τ as a function of (z, x, δ) and the parameter ϱ. In particular, the solution for τ is

$$\tau = \frac{((1-\delta)\bar{n}+1)z+x}{2} + \sqrt{\frac{\big(((1-\delta)\bar{n}+1)z+x\big)^2}{4} - (x+\bar{n}z)(1-\delta)z}.$$

The rate of actual creative destruction that generates productivity increases τ^* is (given the solution for F^S) given by

$$\tau^* = \frac{(1-\bar{n})\tau^2}{\tau - (1-\bar{n})z\bar{n}}.$$

Hence, given τ we can directly compute τ^*.

Firm size distribution. To compute the firm size distribution, consider first the transformative firms. These firms lose products at rate $\tau^T = (1-\kappa)\,\tau$ and they expand at rate

$$x^T = x(1-\varrho+\varrho F^S),$$

given that a fraction ϱ of all innovations that threaten to replace high-type firms are blocked. Similarly, the entry flow of transformative firms is given by

$$z^T = z(1-\varrho+\varrho F^S).$$

Given (τ^T, x^T, z^T), all the theoretical results by Klette and Kortum (2004) apply. Hence, the number of transformative firms is given by

$$F^T = -\frac{z^T}{x^T}\ln\left(1-\frac{x^T}{\tau^T}\right),$$

and the share of transformative firms with n products is

$$\omega(n) = \frac{1}{F^T}\frac{z^T}{x^T}\frac{1}{n}\left(\frac{x^T}{\tau^T}\right)^n.$$

Aggregate productivity growth. To determine the rate of aggregate productivity growth, we generalize our baseline analysis in the following way (as outlined in the main text): If transformative firms increase the productivity frontier with a step size of γ^T, subsistence firms only generate a step size of $\alpha\gamma^T$, where $0 \le \alpha \le 1$. This implies that productivity growth is given by

$$\frac{\dot{Q}_t}{Q_t} = \ln(\gamma^T)\tau^* + \ln(\alpha)(1-\delta)z(1-\bar{n}+\bar{n}F^S).$$

Note that $\alpha < 1$ so that $\ln(\alpha) < 0$. Hence, given τ^*, productivity growth is decreasing in the extent of low-type innovation $(1 - \delta)z$.

The level of productivity is therefore given by

$$Q = \left(\exp\left(\frac{g_Q - \ln(\alpha)(1 - \delta) z (1 - \tilde{n} + \tilde{n}F^S)}{\tau^*} \right) - 1 \right)^{-1/\kappa} Q_F.$$

Given τ^* and F^S we can solve for Q as a function of parameters.

Value function and optimal entry and innovation. The value function of a high-type firm is given by

$$rV(n) - \dot{V}(n) = \pi n + \max_{x}\{x(1 - \tilde{n} + \tilde{n}F^S)\,n\,(V(n+1) - V(n)) - \phi n x^{\zeta} w_t\}$$
$$+ (1 - \tilde{n})\tau n(V(n-1) - V(n)).$$

Conjecture again that $V_t(n) = v_t n$. Then

$$rv_t n - \dot{v}_t n = \pi n + n\max_{x}\left\{ x(1 - \tilde{n} + \tilde{n}F^S)v_t - \frac{1}{\phi_x}x^{\zeta}w_t \right\} - (1 - \tilde{n})\tau n v_t.$$

This implies that v_t solves

$$rv_t - \dot{v}_t = \pi + \max_{x}\left\{ x(1 - \tilde{n} + \tilde{n}F^S)v_t - \frac{1}{\phi_x}x^{\zeta}w_t \right\} - (1 - \tilde{n})\tau v_t.$$

The optimal rate of incumbent innovation x is given by

$$x = \left(\frac{v_t(1 - \tilde{n} + \tilde{n}F^S)}{w_t} \frac{\phi_x}{\zeta} \right)^{\frac{1}{\zeta - 1}}. \tag{A-11}$$

Because v_t grows at rate $g_y = r - \rho$ along a BGP, the value function for transformative firms is given by

$$v_t^T = \frac{\pi_t + (\zeta - 1)\frac{1}{\phi_x}x^{\zeta}w_t}{\rho + \tau(1 - \tilde{n})}.$$

Note that the policy parameter ϱ appears in two places. First a higher ϱ reduces the discount rate of transformative firms through a lower rate of replacement. Second, ϱ also affects the optimal rate of innovation x and hence the value of transformative firms.

Because the products of subsistence firms are not affected, the value of subsistence firms is given by

$$v_t^S = \frac{\pi_t}{\rho + \tau}$$

as before. Given v_t^S and v_t^T, the free-entry condition is given by

$$\frac{1}{\phi_z} z^\chi = (1 - \tilde{n} + \tilde{n}F^S) \frac{E[V]}{w_t} = (1 - \tilde{n} + \tilde{n}F^S) \left(\delta \frac{v_t^T}{w_t} + (1 - \delta) \frac{v_t^S}{w_t} \right). \qquad \text{(A-12)}$$

Equilibrium. Note that profits are still given by $\pi_t = (\mu - 1)w_t L_t^P$, so that the value functions (relative to the wage) are given by

$$\frac{v_t^T}{w_t} = \frac{(\mu - 1)L_t^P + (\zeta - 1)\dfrac{1}{\phi_x} x^\zeta}{\rho + \tau(1 - \rho)} \quad \text{and} \quad \frac{v_t^S}{w_t} = \frac{(\mu - 1)L_t^P}{\rho + \tau}.$$

Labor market clearing still requires that

$$L_t^P = 1 - z^{1+\chi} \frac{1}{\phi_z} - \frac{1}{\phi_x} x^\zeta (1 - F^S)$$

$$= 1 - z^{1+\chi} \frac{1}{\phi_z} - \frac{1}{\phi_x} x^\zeta \left(1 - \frac{(1 - \delta)z(1 - \tilde{n})}{\tau - (1 - \delta)z\tilde{n}} \right).$$

$$\text{(A-13)}$$

Hence, as before we can use the labor market clearing condition (A-11), the free-entry condition (A-10), and the optimality condition for incumbent expansion (A-9) to compute the equilibrium as a function of parameters.

CHAPTER 18

Socialism, Capitalism, State Capitalism, and Innovation

GÉRARD ROLAND

1 Introduction

Scholars of central planning have emphasized the systemic flaws of socialist economies in satisfying consumer demand, in terms of both diversity and quality of products (horizontal and vertical differentiation). In the final years of the communist regimes in Eastern and Central Europe, communist leaders like Mikhail Gorbachev were themselves frustrated that their socialist economic system was able to have a world-class space program but was intrinsically unable to produce decent TV sets and cars (on the socialist economic system, see Nove 1958; Grossman 1963; Gregory and Stuart 1998; Kornai 1980, 1992; Roland 1989, 1990; and many others). The real, *dynamic* Achilles heel of the socialist centrally planned economy in the Soviet Union and in other communist countries was, however, its inferiority in innovation compared to the capitalist economy. After a spurt of very high growth during the 1930s (during the time of the Great Depression), 1940s, and 1950s, Soviet growth eventually halted in the 1970s and 1980s, leading to a period of "stagnation" (*zastoynyi period*) before the complete collapse of the Soviet communist regime and the socialist economic system around 1990.

The inferiority of the socialist economic system in innovation was not obvious when it was growing fast. The launch of the Sputnik satellite in 1957 created panic in Western countries, leading to huge research expenditures and a more than tripling of the National Science Foundation budget, creating the cohort of "Sputnik professors" in the United States. Observers at the time thought that the Soviet system would outgrow capitalism. Quite telling was the title of the article "Growth versus Choice," by Peter Wiles (1957), a specialist on the Soviet Union in the 1950s. The argument made by Wiles, and many others at the time, was that it was now established that the centrally planned economy had the potential to grow faster than the capitalist economy, but that the latter offered more consumer choice. Even Schumpeter (1942) thought socialism would eventually dominate capitalism, as the "bureaucratization of the world" seemed to him to be an inevitable trend.

At the time, there was limited understanding of the determinants of innovation under socialism. To my knowledge, one of the first to thoroughly analyze innovation in the socialist economy was Gomulka (1971), followed by a large literature on various aspects of growth and innovation in centrally planned economies. Kornai (2013) provides probably the best postmortem analysis on socialism's inferiority in innovation and growth. The understanding gained in the 1970s and 1980s on the fundamental flaws of socialism in relation to innovation has mostly disappeared due to lack of interest from scholars, except for economic historians.

Even now, despite the enormous influence of Aghion and Howitt (1992) on the economics profession, one must acknowledge that innovation and entrepreneurship are by far not at the heart of the economics teaching curriculum, which still mostly emphasizes resource allocation and price theory. This is a pity, because Schumpeter's vision of capitalism is probably more relevant to understanding the dynamics of economic systems like capitalism and socialism, compared to mainstream price theory, which still forms the basics of economics education. The changing views on growth and innovation in the socialist economy compared to the capitalist economy should be a warning sign when confronting the twenty-first century's systemic challenges in the world economy. Similar questions are being raised today about the strength of innovation in China after forty years of miraculous growth generated after China's transition to the market economy. The Chinese economic system, as it has evolved since Mao's death in 1976, is *not* a socialist central planning system, but a (state) capitalist market economy under a communist political regime, a *completely new institutional system* in history.[1] There were signs of panic under the Trump administration that China may become the top innovator in the world due to the huge (and growing) research expenditures in R&D by the communist regime. In 2022 the US Senate passed the *US Innovation and Competition Act*, which includes billions for research in artificial intelligence (AI), quantum computing, robotics, and 5G, on top of money to boost the semiconductor industry. Recalling the first cold war, it is now being asked: Is China capable of overtaking Western countries in innovation or are we seeing a repeat of the misguided 1950s scare?

2 Innovation Issues in the Socialist Economy

We do not have the space in this chapter to survey the vast literature on innovation issues in the socialist economy. Kornai's (2013) crisp and clear analysis shows that centrally planned economies had a very flawed innovation process. He shows that of 87 major breakthrough and revolutionary innovations since 1917 (the year of the October Revolution that later led to the establishment of the socialist economy), *none* originated in socialist economies.

Inventions did take place in the Soviet bloc. The communist regime was not opposed to innovation. It was officially even strongly supportive of science and education. Soviet propaganda was full of talk of the "Scientific-Technological Revolution" (see, e.g., Hoffmann 1978). Scientific education was of very high quality, and there was a very high level of research talent and human capital. Nevertheless, nearly all implemented innovations happened under centralized impulse. The socialist economic system lacked the most relevant features of Schumpeterian innovations. The system simply did not allow for Schumpeterian entrepreneurs who would take risks to implement an innovative idea, either for a product or a process, who would most likely fail, but were driven by the prospect of gigantic rewards in case of success. Because the Schumpeterian entrepreneur is at the heart of capitalism's success, Bolsheviks saw them as a danger to their eschatological dreams of a society of abundance emerging from the success of central planning. Some individuals in socialist economies were able to make worthy inventions. For

---

[1] For a more thorough discussion, see Roland 2019. For a comparison of the evolution of Eastern and Central Europe compared to China, see Roland 2018.

example, the floppy disk was invented by a Hungarian engineer, Marcell Jánosi, but not only was it not produced by socialist industrial leaders, it also was not even supported for patent protection. Obviously, Jánosi was not allowed to produce and market it on his own.

The success of Schumpeterian innovation is related to the freedom of entrepreneurship, the right to retain gigantic rewards in case of success, the incredible decentralization of experimentation (most of which will fail), the competition to be the first to patent an invention, possibilities for quick financing (like venture capital), and, I would add, the social status prestige given to successful entrepreneurs.

The socialist system of innovation involved a multitude of large research institutes hiring talented researchers with very good university educations. Large government funds would finance research projects based on ex ante screening. Researchers could thus explore projects only if they were funded. Successful projects were owned by the government, and successful researchers would be recognized by prizes, salary increases, and promotions. As one can see, this system lacked the fundamental features of Schumpeterian innovation (freedom of entrepreneurship, gigantic rewards, decentralization, competition).

A less obvious but fundamental feature of R&D under central planning was soft budget constraints, an issue explored in a prescient way by Qian and Xu (1998). They set up a model of soft budget constraints, based on Kornai's (1980) original concept and the canonical Dewatripont-Maskin (1995) model, to compare innovation in centralized bureaucracies versus in a decentralized market context. In large bureaucracies, ex ante screening of projects is very strict. The reason is that once a research project has been approved, it suffers from soft budget constraints; that is, the organization will generally prefer to provide additional funding for initially approved projects.[2] Because of the existence of soft budget constraints in centralized organizations, there will be much more ex ante screening, and many potentially successful projects will be denied funding. This will be especially the case for projects that are

---

[2] The fundamental reason for this is the Dewatripont-Maskin application of the sunk-cost argument: When considering to refinance a project or to terminate it, sunk costs are irrelevant and only the cost of refinancing matters relative to the expected outcome of refinancing versus termination. Other reasons may also play a role. Leaders of research institutes may be reluctant to terminate unsuccessful projects because doing so would mean having to acknowledge their mistake in having selected the project in the first place. Similarly, principal investigators may be slow to recognize that their project was flawed in the first place.

very uncertain, in terms of both costs and outcomes. When instead the science is well understood and the projects face less uncertainty, centralization should work relatively well. Centralized bureaucracies will thus perform poorly in terms of radical and disruptive innovations. Instead, under decentralization, there will be less ex ante screening of Schumpeterian entrepreneurs, because they will face hard budget constraints and will as a rule be terminated *ex post* in case of lack of success. The connection between decentralization and hard budget constraints thus favors more radical innovation facing large uncertainties. The Qian-Xu framework delivers insights that can explain innovation flaws not only under socialism but also in very large (private or public) bureaucracies in market economies. The reasoning should also be valid when discussing innovation in China, as we will see below.

A large number of innovations often involve imitation. Firms copy radical innovations that have proved successful, thereby contributing to their diffusion. Kornai (2013) shows that lags in imitation were much higher in the Soviet Union for a number of products such as plastic materials and controlled machine tools. This fact highlights a general problem that central planners faced in the Soviet Union and other socialist economies (see Roland 1989 for a fuller discussion). The political leaders understood the economic importance of innovation and did everything they could to push for the introduction of innovations in the economy. They were able to monitor a few sectors that were of strategic importance, like the space or military programs. Note that these programs also benefited from priority in resource allocation. For the "normal" sectors of the economy, top leaders had a very hard time introducing innovations. These sectors were organized in economic ministries based on their functional specialization (coal, steel, car industry, chemical industry, and so on). "Normal" sectors of the economy were facing both shortages of inputs as well as pressure to achieve quantitative output targets, both being quite complementary. Indeed, the more shortages there were, the more economic ministries were given taut output targets. At the same time, the more ambitious the output plan, the more serious the shortages (excess demand), since they implied the risk that the output plan of a ministry or its enterprises would not be fulfilled, thus jeopardizing bonuses and promotions linked to plan fulfillment. This system tended to reject the introduction of innovations from above. Suppose that a ministry received funds to build a new factory with a new production technology. This generally went along with increases in gross output quotas. The economic ministries were usually reluctant to then close factories with less advanced technology, because it would then be more difficult to fulfill the more ambitious plan. As a result, the introduction of new technologies was rarely associated with the "destruction" of old technologies. Moreover, new technologies involved higher productivity of inputs. Shortage of inputs therefore led to higher risk of not fulfilling the output plan. These were obviously narrow considerations based on plan fulfillment objectives of economic agents in a situation with generalized shortages, but they were part of the bread and butter of real life in the planned economy. As a result, only the top leaders were interested in introducing innovations, making the whole economic system inferior to capitalism in terms of growth potential.

To summarize, innovations under socialism were mostly non-Schumpeterian (military, government initiated), which eventually made socialism economically inferior to capitalism in terms of long-run growth.

3 Innovation in China (Some Pros and Cons)

The current Chinese economic system differs strongly from the socialist economic system that existed in Eastern and Central Europe and also in China until Mao's death. Since 1978, under the impulse of Deng Xiaoping, China introduced market reforms that led to a very successful transition from central planning to a capitalist market economy. This transition was led by the Communist Party of China (CPC) itself, using meritocracy and decentralization to promote miraculous growth for more than forty years (see, e.g., Xu 2013). Some people like to call the Chinese economic system state capitalism, because the state sector, composed of the well-known state-owned enterprises (SOEs), is larger than in other capitalist economies, and also because its political regime is characterized by the omnipresent supervision of the Communist Party in all areas of the economy and society, whose Marxist ideology favors state ownership of the means of production.[3] It would be wrong to deny that the Chinese system is a capitalist system. The private sector is dominant in many sectors of the economy, including urban employment (over 80 percent), agriculture, and the export sector dominated by mixed firms. The Chinese economic system, a capitalist economy under a communist political regime, is a major institutional innovation in world

---

[3] Milanovic (2019) calls it "political capitalism."

history. The European Union calls it a systemic rival. There is a consensus in the United States among both Democrats and Republicans that China is a major threat and competitor. It is, however, honest to say that the system is not well understood, and therefore the nature of the "China threat" is not well understood either. A major question is how long China's high growth rates will last and whether it might overtake the Western democracies in terms of income per capita. To answer that question in a Schumpeterian perspective, one must try to evaluate China's potential for innovation. Because China is a capitalist system, one cannot simply repeat what we know about innovation in the centrally planned economy. On the other hand, because China is ruled by the Communist Party and is a politically centralized system,[4] one may suspect that this may negatively impact the potential for innovation and thus for growth in the long run. As of now, we do not have hard evidence as to whether China's economic system is inferior or not to the United States in terms of innovation potential. This is an area where research is urgently needed. What we do in this section is consider some of China's advantages and disadvantages in terms of its innovation potential. We will try to raise some important questions that research should answer in the future.

First of all, China does have Schumpeterian entrepreneurs. China has 698 billionaires on the international Forbes list and ranks second (the United States still ranks first with 724). They are in all sectors. Among the top ten Chinese on the list for 2021 are five in technology with well-known names (Pony Ma, Colin Huang, Jack Ma, Yiming Zhang, and William Ding). This represents serious progress from 10 to 15 years ago when the top Chinese billionaires were mostly in real estate. There is thus clearly a scaling up, and a snapshot at a point in time may underestimate China's progress in innovation.

Nevertheless, there is a political shadow hanging over China's entrepreneurs. The CPC is eager to keep its leading role in society and in the economy. While private entrepreneurs in China were somewhat mavericks and outcasts in the 1980s and the 1990s, coming from noncommunist families, in contrast to Russia (see, e.g., Djankov et al. 2006a, 2006b), they became better recognized by the CPC as market reforms progressed. Jiang Zemin, China's

---

[4] This political centralization means the "leading role" of the CPC at all levels of the society and economy. It should not be confounded with China's well-known administrative decentralization, giving large autonomy to local officials.

general secretary between 1993 and 2002, introduced the concept of the "Three Represents" whereby the CPC would not only be a Party of Workers and Peasants, but would also admit entrepreneurs within its ranks, and the 2002 Sixteenth Party Congress officially admitted entrepreneurs into the Party. This officialized the existing political connections between entrepreneurs and the CPC. I hold from good sources that Xi Jinping, who came to power in 2012, was not a big fan of that policy because of the potential for corruption in having a select group of entrepreneurs enter the Party. He insisted instead on the fact that the Party should have a leading role in all private enterprises. The dilemma for the CPC is that as the private sector, which is the driving force of growth in China, becomes larger and larger, it also has the potential to use its economic clout to weigh in on the Party's policies, thereby challenging the CPC directly or indirectly. It is in this context that we must understand the Party's "dressing down" of Jack Ma, with the partial dismantling of Ali Baba and prohibition of its IPO.[5] In normal capitalist countries, private firms that become monopolies or even economically very powerful tend to lobby the government and lead to regulatory capture until some grassroots revolt, like in the early twentieth century, imposes important antitrust laws and regulations (see, e.g., Philippon's great 2019 book on the monopolization of the US economy, in contrast to the EU). In China, Xi Jinping has clearly signaled that private firms will not be allowed to become as powerful as in the United States. This may be good for competition policy,[6] but it may also be a disincentive for China's Schumpeterian entrepreneurs.

Second, China has massively improved its education and research system in recent years. This can be seen in PISA rankings where Chinese cities like Beijing and Shanghai and provinces like Jiangsu and Zhejiang became number one in mathematics, science, and reading. Also, Chinese universities are climbing international rankings since they decided to copy the US model of research incentives in a much more radical way than most European universities. Nevertheless, China's talent pool remains more limited than that of the United States, as in practice it attracts only Chinese talent,

---

[5] The recent crackdown on Didi before an IPO can be understood along the same lines.

[6] This would be a too-rosy picture. One should not ignore the fact that many Chinese firms that have mushroomed in recent years have benefited from China's Great Firewall and the prohibition of firms like Google, Amazon, Facebook, and Netflix from entering the Chinese market. Thus, the success of many Chinese high-tech firms happened under very protectionist conditions.

whereas the United States attracts the best talent from all over the world. Moreover, some of the best Chinese researchers still remain in the best US universities where research externalities remain very strong. Finally, it is well recognized that traditional Chinese education encourages very hard work but does not encourage creativity.

Third, a more serious issue is the fact that research inside China operates in an atmosphere of oppression and lack of individual freedom. Xi Jinping bets on a "dual" system where STEM research is completely free but the social sciences are fully under the control of the Party. One may nevertheless wonder how much the lack of total freedom of the mind must have stifling effects on research productivity. We do not have a quantitative answer to that question. It is nevertheless quite fundamental. It is not just about imposing mental pigeonholes on researchers and discouraging interdisciplinary research, it is about creating an atmosphere of possible taboos and fears, in which bureaucrats (political commissars) may discourage creativity and discourage nonconformism. These stifling effects may come on top of China's millennial collectivist culture, which frowns on deviations from conformity (see, e.g., Gorodnichenko and Roland 2017 on the effects of individualism and collectivism on innovation and long-run growth).

Fourth, venture capital is present, but new private firms do not have easy access to quick finance. In AI, a strongly government-supported sector, only 39.2 percent of AI investment is funded by domestic capital (Cui et al. 2020).

On the AI sector itself, which is touted as a big technological success in China because it led to the development of the "social scoring system" for all individuals in China, there are also pros and cons. Beraja et al. (2021) show the positive effect on growth of the Chinese government's policies of collecting large amounts of data on individuals. Access of private firms to government data via AI contracts deliver economies of scope as firms awarded such contracts write more software for both government and private commercial purposes. These growth effects are analogous to those of space and military programs during the cold war. Obviously, these practices involve the violation of citizen privacy and distortions related to crowding-out effects in other sectors. Even in AI, where China now ranks number one in investment per startup, China's academic research still lags behind the United States. Also, 93 percent of AI open-source software packages used in China were developed in US institutions (see the very useful article by Cui et al. 2020).

Fifth, an increasingly big role is played by government in research in China. Government R&D expenditures amounted to 2.4 percent of GDP ($378 billion) on 2020 in China, but they are still smaller than in the United States ($656 billion). It should be noted, however, that there are massive soft budget constraint issues in China preventing creative destruction.[7] SOEs in China suffer in general from soft budget constraints: loss-making enterprises keep being bailed out. A good illustration is the fact that "Third Front" enterprises created under Mao's leadership in the 1970s are in large part still alive. Third Front enterprises were to be located in remote areas, preferably next to mountains or in areas not easily accessible, so that in case foreign forces invaded China,[8] production could continue so as to prevent paralysis of the Chinese economy. The location of those SOEs was thus decided on the basis of military criteria, contrary reasonable economic criteria. Despite a program of closures of small SOEs in the 1990s under Prime Minister Zhu Rongji, most of the largest Third Front SOEs have continued to operate, mostly under loss-making conditions. Soft budget constraints among SOEs in China tend to prevent the "destruction" part in creative destruction.

Sixth, there are now many patents for Chinese products, but they relate mostly to incremental innovations. There is very little evidence so far of disruptive innovations in China, in contrast to Western countries. The logic is very much related to the logic of the Qian and Xu (1998) article discussed above. Soft budget constraints in project funding lead to too-strict and conservative ex ante screening of projects. This is particularly true in all of government-funded R&D in China. Guo et al. (2021) show, for example, that between 1998 and 2018, of new molecular entities discovered in the pharmaceutical industry, none of them were discovered in China; 56 percent were discovered in the United States, and the rest in other advanced market economies.

Seventh, many Chinese innovations are based on imitations and are not at the frontier. Some of these innovations are the result of industrial espionage. Others are the result of the way joint-venture deals were designed in the late 1970s and early 1980s. In order to be allowed to invest in China,

---

[7] On soft budget constraints, see, e.g., Kornai 1980; Dewatripont and Maskin 1995; Qian and Xu 1998; Dewatripont and Roland 2000.

[8] At that time, Chinese leaders feared an invasion by "social-imperialist" Soviet forces. This was extremely paranoid, as Soviet leaders never envisaged invading China.

foreign investors had to engage in joint ventures with Chinese SOEs, and they had to share their technology with their Chinese partners. At the time, this policy was seen as a smart development policy. Now that China is no longer a development economy, this policy has been increasingly criticized as violating intellectual property rights.[9] In any case, all the incremental innovations that are being implemented in China contribute to total factor productivity, but will not necessarily help make China number one in the world in innovation.

Eighth, in the aggregate, many studies find strong R&D misallocation effects on growth (see Hsieh and Klenow 2009; König et al. 2020; Hou 2021; and many others). Many of these misallocation effects are due to soft budget constraints, but macroeconomists have as yet failed to introduce soft budget constraints in their models. In any case, the distortionary effects of R&D on growth, which have been identified by the macroeconomic literature on growth in China, tend to reduce the efficiency of government R&D expenditures in China.

4 Conclusion

To conclude, there is an urgent need to better understand the drivers of innovation in the current Chinese economic system and how they compare to the creative destruction Schumpeterian innovation model in advanced capitalist democracies. Comparative economic analysis will be the most helpful in better understanding this.

If there is one lesson we learned from the history of the twentieth century and the cold war period, it is that there is no a priori need to panic about the innovation progress made in China. We need a rational, evidence-based, comparative analysis of the innovation performance of the Chinese economy relative to the most advanced capitalist economies. We hope that the US Innovation and Competition Act will also contribute to this better understanding.

In any event, as China continues to grow faster than advanced Western economies, even if its innovation performance turns out to be inferior in the

---

[9] Note that economists, in contrast to legal scholars, have never been big fans of intellectual property rights. There are no good economic reasons to scream at China's "violation of intellectual property rights."

long run, China is still poised to become the largest economy in the world. Undoubtedly this will affect geopolitical power relations and create strong international tensions. Even if such tensions will be inevitable in the coming decades, there is no realistic alternative to finding ways to coexist peacefully with China's communist-led capitalist economy in today's globalized world.

References

Aghion, P., and P. Howitt. (1992). "A Model of Creative Destruction." *Econometrica* 60(2): 323–351.

Beraja, M., D. Yang, and N. Yuchtman. (2021). "Data-Intensive Innovation: Evidence from AI Firms in China." NBER Working Paper 27723.

Cui, X., X. Fan, D. Guo, Z. Jin, R. Xiao, and C. Xu. (2020). "China Artificial Intelligence Index 2020." https://opinion.caixin.com/m/2021-02-07/101661472.html.

Dewatripont, M., and E. Maskin. (1995). "Credit and Efficiency in Centralized and Decentralized Economies." *Review of Economic Studies* 62(4): 541–555.

Dewatripont, M., and G. Roland. (2000). "Soft Budget Constraints, Transition and Financial Systems." *Journal of Institutional and Theoretical Economics* 156(1): 245–260.

Djankov, S., Y. Qian, G. Roland, and E. Zhuravskaya. (2006a). "Entrepreneurship in Russia and China Compared." *Journal of the European Economic Association* 4(2–3): 352–365.

Djankov, S., Y. Qian, G. Roland, and E. Zhuravskaya. (2006b). "Who Are China's Entrepreneurs?" *American Economic Review: Papers and Proceedings* 96(2): 348–352.

Gomulka, S. (1971). *Inventive Activity, Diffusion and the Stages of Economic Growth.* Aarhus: Aarhus University Press.

Gorodnichenko, Y., and G. Roland. (2017). "Culture, Institutions, and the Wealth of Nations." *Review of Economics and Statistics* 99(3): 402–416.

Gregory, P., and D. Stuart. (1998). *Comparative Economic Systems.* Cambridge, MA: MIT Press.

Grossman, G. (1963). "Notes for a Theory of the Command Economy." *Soviet Studies* 15(2): 101–123.

Guo, D., H. Huang, K. Jiang, and C. Xu. (2021). "Disruptive Innovations and R&D Ownership Structures." *Public Choice* 187(1–2): 143–163.

Hoffmann, E. (1978). "Review: Soviet Views of the Scientific-Technological Revolution." *World Politics* 30(4): 615–644.

Hou, J. (2021). "Resource Misallocation in the R&D sector: Evidence from China." UC Berkeley, manuscript.

Hsieh, C-T., and P. Klenow. (2009). "Misallocation and Manufacturing TFP in China and India." *Quarterly Journal of Economics* 124(4): 1403–1448.

König, K., K. Storesletten, Z. Song, and F. Zilibotti. (2020). "From Imitation to Innovation: Where Is All That Chinese R&D Going?" Cowles Foundation Discussion Paper No. 2237.

Kornai, J. (1980). *Economics of Shortage*. Amsterdam: North Holland.

Kornai, J. (1992). *The Socialist System: The Political Economy of Socialism*. Princeton, NJ: Princeton University Press.

Kornai, J. (2013). *Dynamism, Rivalry and the Surplus Economy*. Oxford: Oxford University Press.

Milanovic, B. (2019). *Capitalism Alone: The Future of the System That Rules the World*. Cambridge, MA: Belknap Press of Harvard University Press.

Nove, A. (1958). "The Problem of Success Indicators in Soviet Industry." *Economica* 25(1): 1–13.

Philippon, T. (2019). *The Great Reversal: How America Gave up on Free Markets*. Cambridge, MA: Belknap Press of Harvard University Press.

Qian, Y., and C. Xu. (1998). "Innovation and Bureaucracy under Soft and Hard Budget Constraints." *Review of Economic Studies* 65(1): 151–164.

Roland, G. (1989). *Economie Politique du Système Soviétique*. Paris: L'Harmattan.

Roland, G. (1990). "Complexity, Bounded Rationality and Equilibrium in a Soviet-Type Economy." *Journal of Comparative Economics* 14(3): 401–424.

Roland, G. (2018). "The Evolution of Post-Communist Systems." *Economics of Transition* 26(4): 589–614.

Roland, G. (2019). "Coexisting with China in the 21st Century." *Acta Oeconomica* 69(1): 49–70.

Schumpeter, J. (1942). *Socialism, Capitalism and Democracy*. London: Harper and Brothers.

Wiles, P. (1957). "Growth versus Choice." *Economic Journal* 66(262): 244–255.

Xu, C. (2013). "The Fundamental Institutions of China's Reforms and Development." *Journal of Economic Literature* 49(4): 1076–1151.

CHAPTER 19

Lobbying behind the Frontier

MATILDE BOMBARDINI, OLIMPIA CUTINELLI-RENDINA,
and FRANCESCO TREBBI

1 Introduction

This chapter focuses on the political economy of creative destruction. Indeed, political economy considerations are essential to capturing the full extent of the implications of the Schumpeterian approach developed by Philippe Aghion and Peter Howitt (Aghion and Howitt 1992, 2008), to which this book is devoted.

As specified in many chapters of this volume, the process of creative destruction revolves around the clear identification of winners and losers in the unfolding of economic development. Within this framework, antagonist groups of incumbents and challengers are granular and non-atomistic, and therefore they carry the ability not only to affect market outcomes, but also to substantially influence politics.

An important aspect of studying the market–government interactions that arise as a consequence of heightened competitive forces within the Schumpeterian perspective is lobbying activities. This will be the specific subject of analysis of our chapter, particularly focused on US federal lobbying activities. We will then abstract from considerations on revolving doors, campaign donations (Stratmann 2005, Bombardini and Trebbi 2011), strategic advocacy through charitable giving (Bertrand et al. 2018, 2020), or grassroots organizations and umbrella coalitions. Although this omission is clearly a shortcoming of our analysis, we conjecture that the phenomena illustrated

533

below would become even starker in terms of magnitude and direction were these omitted dimensions to be taken into consideration. Conversely, the advantage of employing lobbying expenditures is that they are quantitatively an important channel of political influence. Annual lobbying reports display amounts at least ten times larger than federal campaign contribution totals in dollar terms. A second advantage is that we know the issues targeted by lobbyists, whereas we do not know, for example, the reasons political action committees (PACs) give monetary contributions to politicians. Therefore, we can directly isolate the amount of lobbying expenditures by sector targeting trade policy or other policies (Bombardini and Trebbi 2012) differently from other avenues of political influence studied in the political economy literature.

Our analysis takes its starting point from the important work on the relationship between competition and innovation developed in Aghion et al. (2005), where the phenomenon of a nonlinear relationship between these two equilibrium outcomes was first clearly illustrated. Aghion et al. (2009), furthermore, showed how foreign competition and entry may induce an "escape-competition" effect, stronger for "frontier" firms / sectors that are able to separate from the pack of lower-productivity followers. Within the Schumpeterian framework, firms that are able to innovate and differentiate from the competition will do that when competitive pressures reach certain levels, such as the ones induced by Chinese import penetration following China's accession to the World Trade Organization in 2001.

Empirical validation of this intuition has spurred a lively debate in international trade and productivity studies, not without some nuance. For instance, Autor, Dorn, Hanson, Pisano, and Shu (2016) find a decline in the patenting activity of all publicly traded firms in the United States in industries more exposed to competition from Chinese firms' imports. Positive effects of competition on innovation and productivity are reported for the US case by Hombert and Matray (2018), for the EU by Bloom et al. (2016), and within China itself by Brandt et al. (2017). In addition, Bombardini et al. (2017) and Fieler and Harrison (2018) have also produced supporting evidence highlighting the presence of the innovative push at the top of the productivity distribution (i.e., at the technological frontier).[1]

The main research question at the core of this chapter lies within this debate. If support to Aghion et al. (2009) logic is granted and an escape-

---

[1] For a comprehensive review of this literature, see also Shu and Steinwender (2020).

competition effect (i.e., a positive effect of a foreign competitive shock on domestic innovation) is strong for firms closer to the frontier, then what happens to firms that do not have the know-how to innovate or for whom innovation may not be profitable—those behind the frontier?

The answer, we will show, is this: They lobby the government. Relatedly, this chapter contributes to the extant political economy literature by empirically answering the following complementary questions: Do firms use political influence tools—i.e., lobbying—to curb foreign competition in the event of a negative competitive shock? Which firms tend to lobby more in response to large foreign competition shocks? Did the China shock increase lobbying activity as an avenue to escape competition over the last thirty years in the United States?

A vast literature on special interest politics (Grossman and Helpman 2001; Baumgartner et al. 2009; Drutman 2015) clearly identifies escape-competition objectives, particularly from foreign competition within an international trade context, as one of the goals of lobbying and political influence activities. It is not by chance that one of the first and most influential pieces of research on lobbying within the economics discipline (Grossman and Helpman 1994) was exactly about protection from foreign competition and quid pro quo politics.[2] Several subsequent empirical studies (Gawande 1998; Goldberg and Maggi 1999; Gawande and Bandyopadhyay 2000) have validated and extended this discussion, and today this is an active area of research at the intersection of international trade and political economy.

Employing the most complete US federal lobbying information available (Kim 2018) and state-of-the-art statistical identification approaches to measure the causal effect of heightened competitive pressures from China (Autor et al. 2013) over the period 1999–2017, we report a set of novel empirical findings in line with the Aghion-Howitt logic, yet augmenting it in one important respect: losers from competition engage in nonmarket activities to escape competition more.

---

[2] A quid pro quo approach to lobbying focuses on the payment for policy from a firm to a politician. This is the mechanism at the core of groundbreaking special interest work in economics (Grossman and Helpman 1994). However, original contributions such as Potters and Van Winden (1992), Austen-Smith (1993), Austen-Smith and Wright (1994), and Bennedsen and Feldmann (2002) focus on issues of asymmetry of information and of expertise between firms and politicians. See de Figueiredo and Richter (2014) and Bombardini and Trebbi (2020) for comprehensive discussions of the differences in these interpretations of nonmarket strategies. For the core message of this chapter it will not be necessary to take a stance on whether a quid pro quo or informational mechanism or both are at work.

This chapter shows that in the United States the "China shock" produced an average increase in lobbying activities across all issues (i.e., not only on trade issues, but also on budget, taxes, and all issues pertinent to funding and appropriation of subsidies and trade restrictions) of substantial economic importance. The average increase in imports during the 1999–2017 period is shown to induce an increase in lobbying of approximately 31 percent using industry-level data.

Furthermore, focusing on Compustat firm-level information, it is the firms behind the frontier who increase lobbying after foreign competition increases. The increase in lobbying activities as a consequence of the China shock appears concentrated in the subset of firms below the sample mean for sales, employment, or R&D expenditures. Our results are robust to several modifications of our main variables and time-sampling approaches in the construction of the panel data used in this study.

To summarize, in this chapter we discuss, but do not explicitly formalize, the potential mechanisms behind our findings. A complete formalization is offered in Cutinelli-Rendina (2023), which is also the original reference for the heterogeneity results in this chapter and to which we refer for additional detail. We conjecture here that two different drivers of our findings may be at work simultaneously. First and more directly, in the presence of heightened competition from China, firms that are far from the productivity frontier find it too costly to innovate, and lobbying may be a relatively cheaper tool for them. A second, more subtle, mechanism is that competition improves collective action effort among productivity laggards, as a consequence of the logic of Olson (1965). Innovative frontier firms pull ahead through innovation, leaving behind in the densely contested original product space the pack of firms behind the frontier. Contemporaneously, as result of the heightened competition, the extremely low-productivity firms outright exit the market, due to loss making in the presence of entry from foreign competitors. Therefore, within a sector, there is a simultaneous exit of the very top and of the very bottom productivity firms. The result is to create within the original product space a more concentrated group of medium-/low-productivity firms (those behind the frontier but not the absolute worst ones). In this remaining group, the incentive to free ride in lobbying is lower, and lobbying activities are shown to increase in terms of both per firm spending and total aggregate industry spending.

We believe this chapter offers a contribution to the political economy literature that has recently displayed an increasing interest in lobbying and nonmarket strategies. Examples within economics include Bombardini and Trebbi (2012); Blanes i Vidal et al. (2012); Bertrand et al. (2014); Kang (2016); Bombardini and Trebbi (2020); and Bertrand et al. (2020). An even larger footprint can be found in political science.[3] More importantly, this chapter shows how the intuition of Aghion et al. (2009) produces clear implications beyond markets that may be of vast importance to economic policy.

Our work also connects to another strand of Schumpeterian research, regarding productive and unproductive entrepreneurship. Baumol (1990) may be considered the groundbreaking reference in economics and management studies in this respect.[4] His extensive body of work on unproductive entrepreneurs is a contribution that planted the seed of many subsequent investigations into the misallocation of fixed entrepreneurial resources from productivity-enhancing to rent-seeking activities, as function of time-varying factors (one of which could be foreign competition, as in our instance) in the process of economic development. From Baumol's work we also borrow a more qualitative approach, documenting a few relevant case studies in Section 2.

Relatedly, this chapter directly contributes to the discussion of lobbying efforts exerted by economic losers (Hillman 1982; Cassing and Hillman 1986; Baldwin and Baldwin 1996; Brainard and Verdier 1997; Baldwin and Robert-Nicoud 2007). This specific literature focuses on groups sustaining concentrated losses as the result of some form of foreign competition and documents their nonmarket response. The papers in this area are clear that the response through activation of political ties may then take the form of information about the political consequences of the policy or direct electoral support, both of which are likely also at play within our context.[5]

In complementary work, Akcigit et al. (2023) (in addition to the chapter in this volume by the same authors) explore a similar aspect of the Schumpeterian framework: incumbent firms' protection of their positional rents. They provide empirical evidence of this regularity based on detailed data on political connections and effort to innovate in a representative sample of Italian firms. Within the framework postulated by Akcigit et al. (2023), incumbents attempt to "ring fence" their rents through political protection. As incumbents may happen to be the relatively lower-productivity firms in the

---

[3] See Drutman (2015) and de Figueiredo and Richter (2014) for recent reviews.

[4] For a qualitative discussion, see Litan and Hathaway (2017).

[5] See also Bombardini and Trebbi (2011) for a discussion of these channels.

Italian context, this logic perfectly conforms to the one we study in this chapter, and the focus on a country other than the United States provides external validity to our empirical findings and ultimately to the Aghion-Howitt logic.

Finally, this chapter connects to a political economy literature emphasizing different modes of interactions with the political environment for industries at different distances from the technological frontier. Aghion et al. (2007) is an example with reference to the differential role of democratic institutions and innovation for industries closer to the world technological frontier, where openness and entry characteristically associated to liberal democracy matter more. Acemoglu et al. (2005) emphasize the role of economic losers in slowing down the process of institutional evolution. The evidence in this chapter obviously points to lobbying as one such mechanism through which this may manifest.

The chapter is organized as follows. Section 2 presents a series of motivating case studies to frame the subsequent empirical analysis. Section 3 describes the data and the construction of the variables used in our main tests. Section 4 presents our empirical strategy and approach to inference. Section 5 reports our main results on both the average effect of the competition shock and heterogeneity by high- and low-productivity firms. Section 6 concludes.

2 Case Studies

Before discussing our data and empirical strategy in a more targeted statistical analysis of the US case, we begin our analysis by providing a modicum of qualitative evidence motivating our broader interest in the phenomenon of lobbying behind the frontier. This section is therefore aimed at briefly illustrating different forms of lobbying and political influence by economic laggards, which are indeed pervasive in both high- and low-income countries, framing more broadly the phenomenon investigated in this study.

2.1 Zombie firms

To illustrate the reasons non-frontier firms may revert to nonmarket strategies when exposed to adverse market shocks, a particularly stark case can be made through the example of zombie firms. The OECD (McGowan et al. 2017) defines zombie companies as "old firms that have persistent problems

meeting their interest payments"; they are essentially incumbent firms surviving in the market solely due to the forbearance of their creditors. Furthermore, the OECD study attributes to the presence of such zombies a
major and increasingly heavier drag on total factor productivity in high-
income countries since the mid-2000s.

Related to our work, observers have directly linked the mechanics of the
zombie firms phenomenon to special interest politics and "lobbying by economic losers." In commenting on the OECD report cited above, for instance,
The Economist magazine reports that "governments tend to back existing
firms, since they have the power to lobby; small start-ups don't get a hearing."[6]
"Which companies are most likely to get protected? The obvious answer is
incumbent groups that possess lobbying clout."[7] These are essentially the
mechanisms that we analyze.

In the persistent Japanese crisis Caballero et al. (2008) have shown con-
vincingly that zombie banks (i.e., insolvent financial institutions) have played
a prominent role in depressing growth. The authors trace their survival back
to mechanisms common to zombies in other industries: close ties with the
government, and regulatory incentives to issue bad loans. *Macmillan Dictionary* defines a zombie bank as "a bank that is worth less than nothing, but
continues to operate because its debt is supported by the government."[8] The
role of the government is explicit.

It is important to further clarify here that zombie companies may gain
political access not just through outright quid pro quo politics and bribes,
but because these firms represent sizable voter blocs, valuable to politicians
in future elections (Stratmann 1992; Bradford 2003; Bombardini and Trebbi
2011). For example, in the UK during both the Brexit and the COVID-19
crises, the prevalence of the zombie phenomenon (supported by outright
government-backed credit guarantees) was often remarked upon and rationalized by market observers, at least in part, as a politically motivated move.[9]

---

[6] Buttonwood, "Attack of the zombie firms," *The Economist,* January 12, 2017.

[7] Buttonwood, "Industrial policies mean cosseting losers as well as picking winners," *The Economist,* January 19, 2017.

[8] See also Admati (2017).

[9] Alex Morales, "One in five U.K. firms can barely cover debt-interest payments," Bloomberg,
September 10, 2020; Jonathan Ford, "Zombies are the least of Britain's small business problems," *Financial Times,* July 19, 2020.

2.2 Senescent industries

In the United States, the 1980s and 1990s brought simultaneously a stark decline in manufacturing production and increased lobbying for protection from international competition. These facts stimulated a vast literature on the political economy of senescent and declining industry trade protection, most clearly encapsulated by the theoretical discussions in Cassing and Hillman (1986), Braillard and Verdier (1994), Brainard and Verdier (1997), and Baldwin and Robert-Nicoud (2007). All these contributions draw attention to both the persistence of tariffs over time in Western economies (for example, through the various rounds of GATT negotiations) and the declining productivity dynamics within manufacturing sectors (shoes, apparel, steel production, shipbuilding, etc.), highlighting the shift away from costly technological innovation toward political influence activities. This theme is central to the point that much of the debate among contributors was about the exact technology of lobbying and the degree of sensitivity of political response functions to sector employment (Brainard and Verdier 1997). Brainard and Verdier, for example, state that "the empirical evidence that declining industries receive a disproportionate share of protection" in countries such as the US would be "better explained by a bias in the political process than by pure economic differences."[10]

In fact, the "Buy American" provisions implemented by both of the two most recent US administrations have strong roots in lobbying efforts by declining industries, such as steel, an industry that has been in steady decline since the early 1960s in the United States[11] Federal lobbying by the steel industry has substantially increased, from $4.8 million in 2000 to $12.18 million in 2018, for instance, while production has remained roughly constant over the same period.[12] Figure 19.1 reports the complete available time series of aggregate US lobbying spending for steel producers, as available from the Center for Responsive Politics, which employs the same data as Kim

---

[10] Brainard and Verdier (1997), 223.

[11] Brody Mullins and Kristina Peterson, "Bill's 'buy America' provision sets up potential clash for GOP, Donald Trump," *Wall Street Journal,* December 2, 2016; Yuka Hayashi, "Biden's 'buy American' plan eyed warily by other countries," *Wall Street Journal,* January 24, 2021.

[12] See William Mauldin, "Big Steel, a Tariff Winner, Steps Up Its Spending in Washington," *Wall Street Journal,* February 12, 2019.

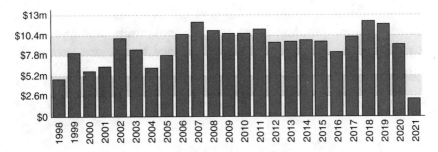

Figure 19.1. US steel producers' total federal lobbying (by year)

(2018).[13] This speaks directly to the statistical analysis in the following sections of this chapter.

2.3 *China's state-owned enterprises*

The case of Chinese state-owned enterprises (SOEs) is perhaps one of the most emblematic examples of unproductive firms in low-income countries using government connections to shield them from market competition. SOEs in China are an important political element of the Chinese Communist Party (CCP) patronage architecture, as they are used as tools to solidify factional ties and to allocate rents to political cadres.[14]

Brandt et al. (2020) report that "SOE priority status has survived decades of underperformance. During 1978–2007, the state sector 'contributed essentially zero to aggregate growth in total factor productivity' (Zhu 2012). Additional evidence confirms the deleterious impact of state ownership on growth, profitability, and structural change."

Maybe more worryingly, the economic role of such political connections in enabling bad companies to expand (particularly through acquisition via "politically connected investors" or using a "protective umbrella," to use the Chinese terms) has been increasing between 2000 and 2020, as recent analysis has shown (see, e.g., Bai et al. 2020). In China the costs in terms of

---

[13]Available at https://www.opensecrets.org/federal-lobbying/industries/summary?id=N14; last accessed June 2021.
[14]For a related discussion, see Bai et al. (2020).

economic performance are clear. Bai et al. (2020) report that "capital productivity of firms owned by the directly connected private owners are on average 40 percent lower than those firms owned by unconnected private
owners." Productivity gains from reforms associated with the screening out
of large numbers of unproductive SOEs between 1998 and 2007 (Hsieh and
Song 2015; Berkowitz et al. 2017) also appear reversed in recent times.

3 Data

Our baseline measure of political activity will be the sum of annual expenses
in lobbying at the firm level for US firms over the period 1999–2017. Thanks
to the legal framework built in the US Lobby Disclosure Act of 1995 and
amended and strengthened by the Honest Leadership and Open Government Act of 2007, there exists an exhaustive and public database where all
active federal lobbyists are supposed to register, declare their activities and
issues petitioned, and report payments received from clients—the firms under
analysis in our paper. Although the primary data is available from the Senate
Office of Public Records (SOPR), Kim (2018) offers a much cleaner organization of this data, supplementing information about each firm and its
industry, linking lobbying reports to unique identifiers, enabling the cross-
reference of the SOPR data set to other important firm-level databases
(such as the gvkey identifier for the Compustat database or the bvdid for
the Orbis data—more on this below), and correcting faulty or incomplete
entries.

From the Kim (2018) database, we collect information on: (1) the name
(and gvkey if relevant) of the firm paying for lobbying services; (2) the amount
spent by the client for these lobbying services; (3) the issue lobbied (out of a
predefined list of 76 issues listed in the lobbying reports); and (4) the firm's
industry. The data is available from 1998, and we collect all the entries until
2017. We start our analysis in 1999 to be sure all the firms lobbying at the
federal level are actually registered.

To give a sense of the magnitudes involved, total US federal lobbying
spending averaged $3–$3.5 billion per year for the past ten years, starting
from $1.5 billion in 1998, with about 12,000 registered lobbyists oper-
ating across all federal agencies each year.

Because we are looking to study both the intensive and the extensive
margin of the lobbying response to an increase in foreign competition, we

cross-reference the lobbying data set to Compustat data and keep all the firms in industries that have received imports from China, even if they never see any lobbying activity. Compustat is a standard repository of balance-sheet-level information for publicly traded and large corporations and a routine reference data set for research in financial economics. It has to be noted that the focus on Compustat data per se induces a strong element of selection in our analysis. Compustat firms are typically large and complex organizations and are representative only of the right tail of the size distribution of all US firms. It is also known that such large business entities may be more prone to lobbying activities, due to the inherent fixed costs of government interaction and the retention of specialized advocacy personnel, as illustrated, for example, in Kerr et al. (2014). Even though it is less than representative, we believe Compustat is actually an appropriate sample for our analysis because it identifies the sample of firms for which lobbying decisions are actionable in practice.

Trade data between China and the United States is obtained from the UN Comtrade Database for the period 1999–2017 (Comtrade 2020). This data gives the value of the bilateral trade at the six-digit HS level, which we map into six-digit NAICS codes using the Schott (2008) concordance tables. When an HS code is mapped into multiple NAICS codes, we report the corresponding value of imports to all the industries.

We use measures of sales, employment, and R&D expenses from Compustat North America. The number of patent applications comes from the USTPO database (Graham et al. 2013). Missing a common identifier between our database and the USPTO one, we use a fuzzy matching on names to link patent applications to their filing firms.

4 Empirical Strategy

Our empirical strategy is organized around two main reduced-form equations. We first estimate the impact of changes in industry exposure to import competition on lobbying expenditures at the firm level. The main empirical model we estimate is in first differences:

$$\Delta Lobby_{i,j,t} = \alpha_\tau + B_1 \Delta Imp_{j,t} + \gamma X_{j,t} + \varepsilon_{i,j,t} \tag{1}$$

where $\Delta Lobby_{i,j,\tau}$ is the relative change in lobbying expenditures of firm i, in industry j over time period τ and is defined as $\Delta Lobby_{i,j,\tau} = log(Lobby_{i,j,t}) -$

$log(Lobby_{i,j,t-1})$. All null lobbying expenses are replaced by 1. ΔImp is the relative change in imports and is defined analogously. $X_{j,t}$ are industry characteristics controlling for the factor intensity at the beginning of the period. In particular, we control for the industry level of investment, capital over the value-added, employment, and wage bill. For robustness we also use the difference in imports over a period divided by the average of the two periods (Davis et al. 2006), i.e.:

$$\Delta Imp_{j,t} = \frac{Imp_{j,t} - Imp_{j,t-1}}{0.5 Imp_{j,t} + 0.5 Imp_{j,t-1}}. \tag{2}$$

The explicit focus on first differences within firm i in our empirical analysis is driven by the need to focus on identifying variations not driven by firm-specific fixed observed or unobserved characteristics, such as the firm's size or industry of operation. These extraneous dimensions may cloud the analysis; it is well established that very large firms able to overcome the fixed costs involved in initiating federal lobbying activities or firms in regulated industries (such as utilities, pharmaceuticals, or banking) lobby considerably more.[15]

An important question about our regression is whether firms react to observed trade or expected trade when they set their lobbying expenses for the period. Our strategy studies more directly the first alternative. Considering, however, that firms' expectations about imports depend heavily on actual flows, our time structure also provides indirect evidence on the relationship between expected change in imports and lobbying behaviors.

The second main specification will extend equation (1) to a heterogeneity analysis, allowing us to focus on firms behind the frontier through a split sample approach.

In our analysis of equation (1), standard errors are clustered at the industry-period level. We define five periods of time: 1999–2002, 2002–2006, 2006–2010, 2010–2014, and 2014–2017. We also explored "long" differences over the two periods 1999–2010 and 2010–2017 to assess robustness of our findings.

All of the firms identified in Compustat appear during their registration period. However, we make an effort to go beyond the register and include firms before / after their presence in the register. To this goal, we use the USPTO database to assess whether the firm existed before (after) its entry

---

[15] See Kerr et al. (2014) for evidence and an extensive discussion.

(exit) in the register/Compustat. Missing years between two years with information are filled with zero expenses in lobbying, as the firm is shown to exist but it is not lobbying.

The main concern about estimating our baseline regression (1) as an OLS is that we could capture the increase in the US demand, and not a supply shock from China. Following Autor et al. (2013), we instrument US imports change from China by the change in imports of eight other countries, during the same period. These countries are Australia, Denmark, Finland, Germany, Japan, New Zealand, Spain, and Switzerland. We refer to this new variable as $\Delta OImp$ and define it in the following way: $\Delta OImp = log(OImp_t) - log(OImp_{t-1})$, where $OImp$ denotes the total imports from these eight countries. Autor et al. (2013) provide a discussion and evidence in support of the validity of this identifying assumption, which is that the demand import shocks of these eight developed economies are orthogonal one to another.

The main threat to our identification strategy is that firms might lobby to gain a comparative advantage over Chinese firms in the eight other developed countries. This would be a direct violation of our exclusion restriction. In a robustness exercise, we remove from our data all the lobbying bills referring to trade issues. This approach removes the bills focusing on the threat of foreign competition, but it also removes the bills focusing on comparative productivity of US exports. Our results are qualitatively the same as in the baseline case.

We do not discuss this identification strategy further, in the interest of space, just noting here that our approach is, by now, fairly standard in this literature. We refer the reader interested in the debate about the econometrics of the China shock and its recent developments to Autor, Dorn, and Hanson (2016).

4.1 Other sampling and data considerations

As we have now specified all main variables of interests, we present here a brief discussion of the summary statistics in Table 19.1, to provide some context to readers not familiar with lobbying data.

Our data set is composed of 3,212 individual firms, of which 1,142 also appear at least once in the SOPR data set with strictly positive lobbying expenses. Average lobbying expenses, considering all the observations and including firms that do not lobby, are $217,000. The total lobbying expenses in our data set goes from around $240 million in 1999 to $300 million in 2017. These are figures congruent with the ones reported in Bertrand et al.

Table 19.1. Summary statistics

	Mean	Median	Min	Max	Sd	Count
			All firms			
Lobby exp.	216,702	0	0	32,680,098	1,257,910	13,036
Δ Lobby exp.	.301	0	−13.98	15.7	3.6	8,719
			Lobbying firms			
Lobby exp.	545,984	18	0	32,680,098	1,951,251	5,174
Δ LogLobbying	.670	0	−13.98	15.7	5.4	3,921
			Import changes			
Δ LogImports	.623	.502	−5.37	6.647	.930	1,029
Δ LogOtherImports	.592	.513	−5.09	7.66	.79	1,029

(2014). Furthermore, the order of magnitudes surpasses by far campaign contributions, as illustrated in Bombardini and Trebbi (2020). We conjecture here that adding other political tools to our analysis would only increase, both in direction and in magnitude, the effects that we report below based on lobbying expenditures alone. This rationale is based on a reduction in attenuation due to measurement error.

Firms are spread across 241 industries, and we observe in the data a positive average and median change in imports over industries and periods. The same can be said about lobbying expenses. Focusing on firms that lobby at least once, we can observe that the mean difference in lobbying expenses is very close in magnitude to the equivalent measure for imports.

Trade and tariff issues together account for 9 percent of all the lobbying expenses in our data set and receive the second largest amount of money for federal lobbying, right after the taxes issue. We decide not to focus solely on the expenses that officially target trade laws, because other laws (such as product regulations or public subsidies) might indirectly raise new barriers to foreign entry, even if they don't necessarily fall under the trade issue umbrella.

5   Main Results

This section reports our main empirical findings for this chapter. We begin by studying firms' responses in terms of their lobbying activity as the result of heightened foreign competition over the entire period of analysis 1999–2017.

Table 19.2 presents the estimation results for our baseline model in equation (1). The coefficients on the difference in imports are all positive and significant across specifications. Column 1 shows that there is a positive and statistically significant correlation between the change in imports and the change in lobbying expenses at the firm level. Column 2 presents the corresponding instrumental variable (IV) estimate based on the China shock in eight countries. In columns 3 and 5, respectively, we control first for the period, and then for both the period and the industry fixed characteristics. Recalling that our analysis already operates in first differences, the latter are to be interpreted as controls for time trends in a linear specification. The effect of the China shock remains significant across all specifications and the order of magnitude of the estimated coefficient is stable, indicating that omitted dimensions may not be a prominent concern in terms of misspecification in our analysis.

We note that the coefficients tend to be larger in the IV specifications (even columns in Table 19.2) than in the OLS one (odd columns) in terms of magnitudes. This may be linked to a plausible reverse causality issue in the OLS specification, due to the fact that lobbying expenses could have had a negative impact on Chinese imports to the United States, by stifling them as predicated by our analysis, thus naturally biasing OLS coefficients downward.

In terms of quantitative interpretation of our estimates, these effects appear economically meaningful. Given an average difference in log imports during this period of 0.62, the coefficient of 0.43 from column 6, which represents

Table 19.2. The average effect of competition on lobbying

Dependent variable: Δ Lobby

	(1)	(2)	(3)	(4)	(5)	(6)
Δ Imports	0.175**	0.404***	0.137+	0.335*	0.131+	0.431**
	(0.072)	(0.121)	(0.090)	(0.178)	(0.088)	(0.217)
First-stage F-stat		40.84		20.95		12.37
Observations	8574	8574	8574	8574	8562	8562
Model	OLS	2SLS	OLS	2SLS	OLS	2SLS
Period controls	No	No	Yes	Yes	Yes	Yes
Industry controls	No	No	No	No	Yes	Yes

Notes: *** 1%, ** 5%, * 10% significance. Standard errors in parentheses, clustered at the industry-period level. The outcome is the log of (1+Lobbying Expenditures). Odd columns report OLS coefficients and even columns report 2SLS coefficients.

the causal effect of the China shock in our more conservative specification, implies that lobbying expenditures as a consequence of the industry-level foreign competition shock increase, on average, by 31 percent each period.

5.1 Who lobbies?

In this section we show that viewing the question of the relationship between competition and lobbying through a Schumpeterian prism allows us to further interpret the heterogeneity of the response that we detect in the data.

As a premise, an important part of the lobbying literature focuses on how firms within an industry organize against foreign competition. Beginning from the pathbreaking theoretical model in Grossman and Helpman (1994), various papers have studied empirically how local firms within an industry organize for protection in an international trade context. Examples include Goldberg and Maggi (1999), Gawande and Bandyopadhyay (2000), and Stoyanov (2009). Our baseline result in Table 19.2, stating that firms facing an increasing competition from foreign firms tend to increase their lobbying activity, appears in line with the "protection for sale" line of thought.

However, extant related research also emphasizes that within-industry heterogeneity in lobbying activities is relevant (Bombardini 2008; Bombardini and Trebbi 2012; Kim 2017), and in this section we exploit such within-industry heterogeneity. Such margin of heterogeneity is immediately suggested by the Aghion-Howitt framework. Recall that Aghion et al. (2005) predicts that competitors in a same industry will mainly innovate to escape competition when they are "neck-and-neck." When firms are technologically very far one from another, the laggard firm will be discouraged and will not attempt to catch up through investment in innovation. Extreme laggards may outright exit the market, and other non-frontier firms facing productive international competitors may stop innovating. In fact, we know that the massive decrease in patenting in the United States caused by the China shock can be traced back to the relatively smaller and less innovative firms (Autor, Dorn, Hanson, Pisano, and Shu 2016).

In this environment non-frontier firms may resort to nonmarket strategies to preserve their profits. The hypothesis here is that when innovation over the technological frontier becomes too expensive, some firms turn to lobbying, which has become relatively cheaper, rather than innovation. It is non-frontier firms that attempt to escape from competition through lobbying the government.

In order to test this hypothesis, we separate our sample within industries according to measures of size and productivity. Our measures of size are sales, employment, and R&D expenditures, while our measures of productivity are sales per employee, R&D expenses per employee, and the number of patent applications filed, all variables considered at the beginning of the period τ. We split the sample according to the industry mean for all variables, except for patents, where we form one group with firms that did not file a patent application with the USPTO in the year starting the period, and one group with firms that did file at least one patent application. Because our sample of firms is composed by the firms in Compustat, we can only focus on frontier firms and firms just behind the frontier. Our results should be understood as focusing on a subset of the very large firms, and not on all firms in an industry.

Tables 19.3 and 19.4 present our main results for size and productivity heterogeneity, respectively. We will discuss these estimates jointly, as a synoptic reading of the findings provides a better sense of their robustness.

The intuition behind the findings in Tables 19.3 and 19.4 is similar across all specifications: it is always and only the firms below the industry mean that increase their lobbying expenses following the adverse competitive shock due to Chinese import penetration. In essence, the finding is that firms behind the frontier are the ones responding to heightened competition through lobbying. Indeed, these firms' response is so strong that we detect the entire industry average lobbying activity increasing in Table 19.2.

Table 19.3. Heterogeneity: Lobbying from behind the frontier

Dependent variable: Δ Lobby						
	$< Ind$ mean	$\geq Ind$ mean	$< Ind$ mean	$\geq Ind$ mean	$< Ind$ mean	$\geq Ind$ mean
	(1)	*(2)*	*(3)*	*(4)*	*(5)*	*(6)*
	Sales		*Employment*		*R&D exp.*	
$\Delta Imports$	0.822***	−0.265	0.626***	−0.206	1.092***	−0.181
	(0.274)	(0.482)	(0.216)	(0.516)	(0.361)	(0.526)
First-stage F-stat	7.87	21.47	8.64	16.88	6.77	19.94
Observations	5615	1628	6678	1632	4634	1319
Period, industry FE	Yes	Yes	Yes	Yes	Yes	Yes

Notes: *** 1%, ** 5%, * 10% significance. Standard errors in parentheses, clustered at the industry-period level. The outcome is the log of (1+Lobbying Expenditures). All specifications report 2SLS coefficients and include industry and period fixed effects.

Table 19.4. Heterogeneity: Measures scaled by employment levels

Dependent variable: Δ Lobby

	< Ind mean	≥ Ind mean	< Ind mean	≥ Ind mean	No	Yes
	(1)	(2)	(3)	(4)	(5)	(6)
	Sales / Emp		R&D / Emp		Patents	
Δ Imports	0.803***	0.200	1.281***	−0.099	1.662***	0.012
	(0.309)	(0.382)	(0.392)	(0.348)	(0.316)	(0.349)
First-stage F-stat	8.85	13.23	8.17	8.63	12.17	11.20
Observations	3879	2770	3689	1813	5481	3180
Period, industry FE	Yes	Yes	Yes	Yes	Yes	Yes

Notes: *** 1%, ** 5%, * 10% significance. Standard errors in parentheses, clustered at the industry-period level. The outcome is the log of (1+Lobbying Expenditures). All specifications report 2SLS coefficients and include industry and period fixed effects.

Especially for the measures of sales and R&D expenses (in levels and per employee) the magnitude of the effect of the China shock on lobbying activity for non-frontier firms is much larger than in the baseline regression of Table 19.2. Coefficient estimates hover around 0.80–1.28, twice as large at the estimate (0.43) reported in column 6 of Table 19.2.

Differently, we notice that for frontier firms, the coefficient is negative in four out of six specifications, even if they are always not statistically distinguishable from zero. These firms are most likely responding to increased competition by innovating and moving into products that cannot be easily challenged by foreign competitors.

5.2 Discussion of the mechanisms

The findings in Section 5.1 can be rationalized using a model where lobbying and innovation are instruments available to firms facing increases in competition. Cutinelli-Rendina (2023) explicates a stylized model based on Fieler and Harrison (2018), where firms face a nested CES demand and choose between producing two versions of a variety: a more differentiated version or a less differentiated one. All less differentiated varieties in a sector share the same "nest," whereas each more differentiated variety has its own nest. Less differentiated varieties have a higher price elasticity of demand, but lower fixed costs. Firms choosing more differentiation can then impose a higher markup and reap higher profits in their nest. Differentiation is here intuitively interpreted as innovation.

Firm i also has the possibility to invest individually an amount λ_i to lobby for industry protection. The lobbying efforts of all the firms at the sector level are imperfect substitutes and are aggregated following the technology:

$$\Lambda = (\Sigma_i \lambda_i^\rho)^{\frac{1}{\rho}}.$$

The marginal cost of foreign competitors is then increased by $F(\Lambda)$, where F is the lobbying success function satisfying simple assumptions (the function must be differentiable, increasing, and concave—all standard assumptions in politico-economic models of special interest politics). Although this black-box approach to the special interest politics dimension of the model may feel reductive, we highlight here that the literature in quid pro quo lobbying tends to successfully achieve good empirical fit with such theoretical simplifications.[16]

Similarly, as in Fieler and Harrison (2018), a competition shock decreasing the marginal cost of (foreign) competitors is going to have two impacts on the production decisions of the firms sharing the less differentiated nest: differentiation and exit will both increase. Intuitively, this is because the markup of firms that remain less differentiated will decrease. The novelty here is the introduction of the lobbying option and the prediction that lobbying will increase at the sector level, even if some firms leave the nest where lobbying takes place. Differentiation on the part of high-productivity firms and exit of the least productive set of firms explain the concentration of the lobbying activity among fewer actors.

Two mechanisms drive the increase in lobbying at the sector level: the first, and more intuitive, is that firms for which differentiation is too expensive will naturally increase their lobbying efforts in proportion to the threat of competition. The second mechanism is more subtle and linked to an improved collective action coordination in the undiversified "nest." With a reduced number of firms in the nest (some moving out to a new nest, and others outright exiting the market due to loss making), there is more concentration and less free-riding per standard Olson (1965) logic, increasing incrementally each individual firm's lobbying effort for the stayers.[17] These combined

---

[16] Examples include Bombardini and Trebbi (2011), Kang (2016), and Huneeus and Kim (2018).

[17] This second element is reminiscent of effects also discussed in Baldwin and Robert-Nicoud (2008).

two mechanisms induce sector-level increases in lobbying under standard parameterizations.[18]

While there might be other, more complex reasons the change in lobbying due to import competition may be most pronounced in relatively less productive/smaller firms (for example, due to the differential mobilization of voting blocs of employees or other electoral channels), we believe that the two mechanisms highlighted in this section are likely deserving of attention due to their simplicity and plausibility.

6 Conclusions

Competition may stimulate innovation among high-performance firms, especially in the presence of persistent shocks, as in the case of entry of Chinese exporters post China's WTO accession in the early 2000s.

However, the work of Aghion and Howitt clearly postulates the emergence of both winners and losers (Aghion et al. 2009), with the latter group facing a different set of incentives than high-performance winning firms in the former group.

It turns out that these two groups take on completely different strategies in responding to foreign competition. While high-productivity firms may respond via innovation, in this chapter we show that the response to the China shock from US firms behind the productivity frontier comes in the form of a nonmarket activity: they lobby the US government more. Less productive firms focus on maintaining or erecting new barriers to entry in the form of regulation, carve-outs, and domestic subsidies rather than innovation and diversification.

In the data we report economically meaningful responses in terms of lobbying to import penetration from China by employing the state-of-the-art China shock identification strategy of Autor et al. (2013) and therefore causally linking increases in within sector competition and lobbying effort of domestic firms.

The postulated rationale behind the nonmarket response of non-frontier firms is because innovation is relatively more costly for those behind the frontier, but also because collective action becomes easier in the aftermath of a

---

[18] See analysis in Cutinelli-Rendina (2023).

competitive shock. Extremely unproductive firms exit and highly productive firms break away from the industry pack, leaving the remaining set of actors in a more concentrated environment where lobbying is easier and there is less free riding.

The "lobbying behind the technological frontier" phenomenon that we have uncovered in this chapter appears a logical extension of the Schumpeterian framework developed by Philippe Aghion and Peter Howitt over the last three decades and one of the many important political economy offshoots of their oeuvre. To provide further perspective, this chapter also offers a brief discussion of a few salient case studies focused on the political efforts of economic laggards.

Future work should extend our systematic statistical analysis to cases outside the United States, where nonmarket strategies of firms might be as effective as in Washington, DC, if not more. The case of Brussels and European Union lobbying comes to mind.

References

Acemoglu, D., Johnson, S., and Robinson, J. A. (2005). Institutions as a fundamental cause of long-run growth. *Handbook of Economic Growth 1*, 385–472.

Admati, A. R. (2017). *It takes a village to maintain a dangerous financial system*. Oxford: Oxford University Press.

Aghion, P., Alesina, A. F., and Trebbi, F. (2007). Democracy, technology, and growth. NBER Working Paper 13180.

Aghion, P., Bloom, N., Blundell, R., Griffith, R. and Howitt, P. (2005). Competition and innovation: An inverted-U relationship. *Quarterly Journal of Economics 120*(2), 701–728.

Aghion, P., Blundell, R., Griffith, R., Howitt, P. and Prantl, S. (2009). The effects of entry on incumbent innovation and productivity. *Review of Economics and Statistics 91*(1), 20–32.

Aghion, P., and Howitt, P. (1992). A model of growth through creative destruction. *Econometrica 60*(2), 323–351.

Aghion, P., and Howitt, P. W. (2008). *The economics of growth*. Cambridge, MA: MIT Press.

Akcigit, U., Baslandze, S., and Lotti, F. (2023). Connecting to power: Political connections, innovation, and firm dynamics. *Econometrica 91*(2), 529–564.

Austen-Smith, D. (1993). Information and influence: Lobbying for agendas and votes. *American Journal of Political Science 37*(3), 799–833.

Austen-Smith, D., and Wright, J. R. (1994). Counteractive lobbying. *American Journal of Political Science 38*(1), 25–44.

Autor, D., Dorn, D., and Hanson, G. H. (2013). The China syndrome: Local labor market effects of import competition in the United States. *American Economic Review 103*(6), 2121–2168.

Autor, D. H., Dorn, D., and Hanson, G. H. (2016). The China shock: Learning from labor-market adjustment to large changes in trade. *Annual Review of Economics 8*, 205–240.

Autor, D., Dorn, D., Hanson, G. H., Pisano, G., and Shu, P. (2016). Foreign competition and domestic innovation: Evidence from US patents. NBER Working Paper 22879.

Bai, C.-E., Hsieh, C.-T., Song, Z. M., and Wang, X. (2020). Special deals from special investors: The rise of state-connected private owners in China. NBER Working Paper 28170.

Baldwin, R. E., and Baldwin, R. E. (1996). Alternate approaches to the political economy of endogenous trade liberalization. *European Economic Review 40*(3–5), 775–782.

Baldwin, R. E., and Robert-Nicoud, F. (2007). Entry and asymmetric lobbying: Why governments pick losers. *Journal of the European Economic Association 5*(5), 1064–1093.

Baldwin, R. E., and Robert-Nicoud, F. (2008). Trade and growth with heterogeneous firms. *Journal of International Economics 74*(1), 21–34.

Baumgartner, F. R., Berry, J. M., Hojnacki, M., Leech, B. L., and Kimball, D. C. (2009). *Lobbying and policy change: Who wins, who loses, and why.* Chicago: University of Chicago Press.

Baumol, W. (1990). Entrepreneurship productive, unproductive, and destructive. *Journal of Political Economy 98*(3), 893–921.

Bennedsen, M., and Feldmann, S. E. (2002). Lobbying legislatures. *Journal of political Economy 110*(4), 919–946.

Berkowitz, D., Ma, H., and Nishioka, S. (2017). Recasting the iron rice bowl: The reform of China's state-owned enterprises. *Review of Economics and Statistics 99*(4), 735–747.

Bertrand, M., Bombardini, M., Fisman, R., Hackinen, B., and Trebbi, F. (2018). Hall of mirrors: Corporate philanthropy and strategic advocacy. NBER Working Paper 25329.

Bertrand, M., Bombardini, M., Fisman, R., and Trebbi, F. (2020). Tax-exempt lobbying: Corporate philanthropy as a tool for political influence. *American Economic Review 110*(7), 2065–2102.

Bertrand, M., Bombardini, M., and Trebbi, F. (2014). Is it whom you know or what you know? An empirical assessment of the lobbying process. *American Economic Review 104*(12), 3885–3920.

Blanes i Vidal, J., Draca, M., and Fons-Rosen, C. (2012). Revolving door lobbyists. *American Economic Review 102*(7), 3731.

Bloom, N., Draca, M., and Van Reenen, J. (2016). Trade induced technical change? The impact of Chinese imports on innovation, IT and productivity. *Review of Economic Studies 83*(1), 87–117.

Bombardini, M. (2008). Firm heterogeneity and lobby participation. *Journal of International Economics 75*(2), 329–348.

Bombardini, M., Li, B., and Wang, R. (2017). Import competition and innovation: Evidence from China. University of British Columbia, manuscript.

Bombardini, M., and Trebbi, F. (2011). Votes or money? Theory and evidence from the US Congress. *Journal of Public Economics 95*(7), 587–611.

Bombardini, M., and Trebbi, F. (2012). Competition and political organization: Together or alone in lobbying for trade policy? *Journal of International Economics 87*(1), 18–26.

Bombardini, M., and Trebbi, F. (2020). Empirical models of lobbying. *Annual Review of Economics 12*(1).

Bradford, S. (2003). Protection and jobs: Explaining the structure of trade barriers across industries. *Journal of International Economics 61*(1), 19–39.

Braillard, S. L., and Verdier, T. (1994). Lobbying and adjustment in declining industries. *European Economic Review 38*(3–4), 586–595.

Brainard, S. L., and Verdier, T. (1997). The political economy of declining industries: Senescent industry collapse revisited. *Journal of International Economics 42*(1–2), 221–237.

Brandt, L., Rawski, T. G., et al. (2020). China's great boom as a historical process. IZA Institute of Labor Economics Discussion Paper No. 13940.

Brandt, L., Van Biesebroeck, J., Wang, L., and Zhang, Y. (2017). WTO accession and performance of Chinese manufacturing firms. *American Economic Review 107*(9), 2784–2820.

Caballero, R. J., Hoshi, T., and Kashyap, A. K. (2008). Zombie lending and depressed restructuring in Japan. *American Economic Review 98*(5), 1943–1977.

Cassing, J. H., and Hillman, A. L. (1986). Shifting comparative advantage and senescent industry collapse. *American Economic Review 76*(3), 516–523.

Comtrade, U. (2020). International trade statistics database. United Nations Comtrade Database.

Cutinelli-Rendina, O. (2023). Lobbying or innovation: Who does what against foreign competition. Paris School of Economics Working Paper No. 2023-08. https://hal.science/PJSE_WP/halshs-03970033v1.

Davis, S. J., Faberman, R. J., and Haltiwanger, J. (2006). The flow approach to labor markets: New data sources and micro-macro links. *Journal of Economic Perspectives 20*(3), 3–26.

de Figueiredo, J. M., and Richter, B. K. (2014). Advancing the empirical research on lobbying. *Annual Review of Political Science 17*, 163–185.

Drutman, L. (2015). *The business of America is lobbying: How corporations became politicized and politics became more corporate.* Oxford: Oxford University Press.

Fieler, A. C., and Harrison, A. (2018). Escaping import competition in China. NBER Working Paper 24527.

Gawande, K. (1998). Stigler–Olson lobbying behavior in protectionist industries: Evidence from the lobbying power function. *Journal of Economic Behavior & Organization 35*(4), 477–499.

Gawande, K., and Bandyopadhyay, U. (2000). Is protection for sale? Evidence on the Grossman-Helpman theory of endogenous protection. *Review of Economics and Statistics 82*(1), 139–152.

Goldberg, P. K., and Maggi, G. (1999). Protection for sale: An empirical investigation. *American Economic Review 89*(5), 1135–1155.

Graham, S. J., Hancock, G., Marco, A. C., and Myers, A. F. (2013). The USPTO trademark case files dataset: Descriptions, lessons, and insights. *Journal of Economics & Management Strategy 22*(4), 669–705.

Grossman, G. M., and Helpman, E. (1994). Protection for sale. *American Economic Review 84*(4), 833–850.

Grossman, G. M., and Helpman, E. (2001). *Special interest politics.* Cambridge, MA: MIT Press.

Hillman, A. L. (1982). Declining industries and political-support protectionist motives. *American Economic Review 72*(5), 1180–1187.

Hombert, J., and Matray, A. (2018). Can innovation help US manufacturing firms escape import competition from China? *Journal of Finance 73*(5), 2003–2039.

Hsieh, C.-T., and Song, Z. M. (2015). Grasp the large, let go of the small: The transformation of the state sector in China. NBER Working Paper 21006.

Huneeus, F., and Kim, I. S. (2018). The effects of firms' lobbying on resource misallocation. MIT Political Science Department Research Paper No. 2018-23.

Kang, K. (2016). Policy influence and private returns from lobbying in the energy sector. *Review of Economic Studies 83*(1), 269–305.

Kerr, W. R., Lincoln, W. F., and Mishra, P. (2014). The dynamics of firm lobbying. *American Economic Journal: Economic Policy 6*(4), 343–79.

Kim, I. S. (2017). Political cleavages within industry: Firm-level lobbying for trade liberalization. *American Political Science Review 111*(1), 1.

Kim, I. S. (2018). Lobbyview: Firm-level lobbying & congressional bills database. Unpublished manuscript, MIT, Cambridge, MA. http://web.mit.edu/insong/www/pdf/lobbyview.pdf.

Litan, R. E., and Hathaway, I. (2017). Is America encouraging the wrong kind of entrepreneurship? *Harvard Business Review 13.*

McGowan, M. A., Andrews, D., and Millot, V. (2017). The walking dead? Zombie firms and productivity performance in OECD countries. OECD Economics Department Working Paper No. 1372.

Olson, M. (1965). *The logic of collective action.* Cambridge, MA: Harvard University Press.

Potters, J., and Van Winden, F. (1992). Lobbying and asymmetric information. *Public Choice 74*(3), 269–292.

Schott, P. K. (2008). The relative sophistication of Chinese exports. *Economic Policy 23*(53), 6–49.

Shu, P., and Steinwender, C. (2020). How free trade changes domestic firms' ability to innovate. *LSE Business Review* (January 29, blog).

Stoyanov, A. (2009). Trade policy of a free trade agreement in the presence of foreign lobbying. *Journal of International Economics* 77(1), 37–49.

Stratmann, T. (1992). Are contributors rational? Untangling strategies of political action committees. *Journal of Political Economy* 100(3), 647–664.

Stratmann, T. (2005). Some talk: Money in politics—A (partial) review of the literature. *Public Choice 124*, 135–156.

Zhu, X. (2012). Understanding China's growth: Past, present, and future. *Journal of Economic Perspectives 26*(4): 103–124.

CHAPTER 20

Barriers to Creative Destruction

Large Firms and Nonproductive Strategies

SALOMÉ BASLANDZE

1 Introduction

The Schumpeterian notion of creative destruction (Schumpeter 1942), first formally introduced in growth theory by Philippe Aghion and Peter Howitt (Aghion and Howitt 1992), opens up the possibility for conflict in the growth process between entrant firms with new technology and incumbent firms with old technology. Incumbents resolve this conflict in different ways. Some firms may try to win the market with productive strategies, such as innovation; others may rely on nonproductive strategies that retain a firm's existing market position without innovating.

Productive, innovation-based strategies let firms gain a competitive advantage with new or better-quality product offerings or more efficient ways of producing existing goods. These strategies create value for society by moving the technology frontier and advancing aggregate productivity growth. Nonproductive strategies, such as the leveraging of political connections, nonproductive patenting, and anticompetitive acquisitions, are often intended to increase a firm's competitive advantage by blocking creative destruction and reallocating resources away from other firms. The focus of this chapter is on the firms' choices between these strategies. The allocation of firms' efforts between productive and nonproductive strategies ultimately determines an economy's growth and aggregate welfare (Baumol 1990; Murphy et al. 1991).

Theoretical efforts have recognized that vested incumbents are incentivized to do what they can to slow down the process of creative destruction. A long-standing theoretical literature in industrial organization has explored entry deterrence resulting from various forms of strategic investments by incumbents (Salop 1979; Dixit 1980; Gilbert and Newbery 1982; Tirole 1988).[1] Krusell and Rios-Rull (1996) and Mukoyama and Popov (2014) showed that, in environments where firms can influence entry policies, incumbents make an effort to prevent the adoption of new technologies, ultimately hindering aggregate growth. In recent work, Glode and Ordoñez (2021) theoretically show that technological advancement may increase the fruitfulness of rent-seeking activity, thus raising the possibility that the use of nonproductive strategies might be on the rise.

Empirically, what are these nonproductive strategies that preserve firms' market positions by slowing creative destruction? What are the characteristics of firms that use these strategies, how prevalent are these strategies, and what are the aggregate implications?

Though there is available much anecdotal evidence and casual observations, detailed evidence using micro-level data sets is needed to learn about the nature and extent of nonproductive strategies among firms. Identification and the precise analysis of these strategies can inform policy recommendations and help policymakers identify institutions that might be amenable to strategic manipulation.

This chapter focuses on three types of nonproductive strategies for which micro-level evidence is growing: political connections, nonproductive patenting, and anticompetitive acquisitions. I review recent evidence based on new granular microdata and discuss its aggregate implications.

In different contexts, empirical data shows that as firms gain market share, they rely less on productive, innovation-based strategies, but increasingly use nonproductive strategies that maintain the firm's position in the market by discouraging competition. This evidence can be easily understood through the lens of two classic effects in the economics literature: *Arrow's replacement* effect (Arrow 1962) and the "preserving-the-market" effect as in Gilbert and Newbery (1982). While market leaders have lower incentives for innovation

---

[1] See Wilson (1992) for a review of different types of strategic models of entry deterrence, Segal and Whinston (2007) for a more recent discussion of antitrust in innovative industries, and Cabral and Polak (2012) for the analysis of dominant firms and entrants' innovation incentives.

due to own replacement, they have greater incentives to protect their larger rents with the use of nonproductive strategies. It is essential to evaluate both static and dynamic effects of nonproductive strategies to understand the aggregate implications of this evidence. Statically, some of these strategies may create value, for example, by lowering certain market frictions or with static gains from reallocation. Still, dynamically, the losses due to hindered innovation and slowed creative destruction may outweigh the static benefits.

Macroeconomic quantitative structural evaluations of the empirical evidence are needed, especially in light of recent trends on increasing market power, slower business dynamism, and stagnating productivity growth (Decker et al. 2016; Gutiérrez and Philippon 2017; Autor et al. 2020; De Loecker et al. 2020; Akcigit and Ates 2021). Important contributions in this direction are discussed.

The following three sections will review recent studies that leverage novel granular data sets to study political connections, nonproductive patenting, and anticompetitive acquisitions. In each section after providing the micro evidence and theoretical intuition, I discuss existing quantitative macro studies that quantify related strategies and consider potential policy implications. In Section 5, I conclude by highlighting areas for future research.

2 Large Firms, Political Connections, and Creative Destruction

2.1 Italy

How do political connections help firms? What are the aggregate implications of political connections for the economy? It is challenging to answer these questions jointly because of the lack of systematic data on firms' political connections at a large scale. Recently Akcigit et al. (2023) drew upon multiple administrative data sources to compile a data set that offers direct measures of firms' political connections. The data set gives a view of Italy's entire private sector over multiple decades. The wealth of systematic microdata provides important lessons for the macro outcomes: the widespread connections of large incumbents set back incumbents' innovation efforts, create barriers to creative destruction, and, as a result, are detrimental for aggregate dynamics. I will discuss the findings of this study in more detail next.

Data, measurement, and institutional context. Observing the connections between firms and politicians is difficult—many relationships are hard to track, and exchanges of favors are not often recorded with receipts. Researchers have made considerable progress by findings ingenious ways to proxy for political connections in various empirical contexts (see Akcigit et al. 2022 for an extensive literature review). The approach taken in Akcigit et al. (2023) detects firms' political connections from documented formal employment relationships between firms and local politicians. In Italy, local politicians serving at the municipal, provincial, or regional level can simultaneously hold employment in the private sector. By matching the entire employer–employee data set from social security records with an administrative registry of local politicians in Italy, employment-based political connections at the firm level can be tracked systematically.

In the matched data set, a firm is defined as politically connected during a given year if the firm employs at least one local politician in that year. Local politicians in Italy hold various levels of legislative and executive positions: they are the members of local government councils and can also hold high-ranking positions, such as mayors or provincial or regional presidents. The data also includes politicians' party affiliations, which sorts politicians according to the relative power they have from being in the minority or majority party or a coalition. This heterogeneity in political power allows Akcigit et al. (2023) to define different levels of political connections. For example, a firm has a majority-level or high-ranking connection if the firm employs a politician who belongs to the majority party or holds a high-ranking position, respectively.

This firm-level data is then matched with firms' financial information and patent data, allowing the evaluation of firm performance along multiple dimensions. The data set spans the years 1985–2014 and tracks more than four million distinct firms and 500,000 local politicians over that time. The above-described matching process identified 449,000 firm-year observations of political connections for 112,000 unique firms. On average and across all industries, 5 percent of firms are connected, but these firms account for a third of Italy's overall employment.

How important are connections with local politicians? Clearly, political connections identified from local politicians' employment capture just a subset of many possible links between firms and bureaucrats. For example, the data do not include politicians at the national level. However, these higher-level connections with national politicians would likely leave a paper trail in the form of connections with local politicians. In addition, the decentralization of Italy's government, with 8,110 municipalities, 103 provinces, and 20 regions, means that local politicians hold substantial power, and connections with local politicians may go a long way in helping firms "grease the wheels of commerce." Among other functions, local politicians administer most of the bureaucratic procedures that firms must deal with, oversee the issuance of permits and licenses, and provide local public goods and services.

Italy provides a particularly good context for the study of the micro and macro aspects of political connections. In addition to the unique opportunity offered by the granularity of available data that directly indicates political connections, the resulting insights can be linked to important macroeconomic trends in Italy over recent decades. Declining productivity growth and stalling business dynamism have troubled many advanced economies in the past decades; the Italian experience has been particularly difficult. To illustrate this point, Figure 20.1a plots the three-year moving average growth rate of GDP per capita in Italy. Figure 20.1b plots the share of large firms (with more than one hundred employees) that are connected with high-ranking politicians. As the growth rate entered a stark decline, the economy also saw a significant increase in the extent of large incumbents' political connections. These figures are merely suggestive, however—using detailed microdata analysis and theoretical insights from the economics of creative destruction and growth, Akcigit et al. (2023) try to get a richer understanding of the link between political connections and negative aggregate market dynamics.

Delving into microdata. The analysis starts by exploring the firm-level data to gain insight into the possible channels through which political connections affect firms and the aggregate economy. Political connections represent nonproductive strategies if the firms use their connections for private gains without innovating or advancing productivity. Connections do not necessarily have to be unproductive. For example, firms might call in favors from bureaucrats to bend certain regulations that hinder the entry and adoption of new innovative products or services. A look into the firm's innovation, growth, and productivity dynamics around the time when firms acquired political connections can help to distinguish between the productive and nonproductive nature of those connections.

First off, the study measures innovative activity and political connections for firms with different market shares. Firms are ranked based on their

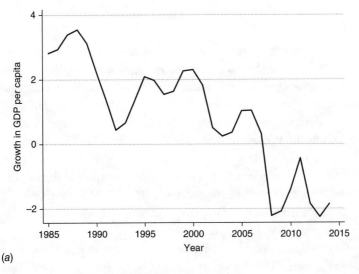

(a)

Source: Author's own calculation using Italian Statistical Office data.

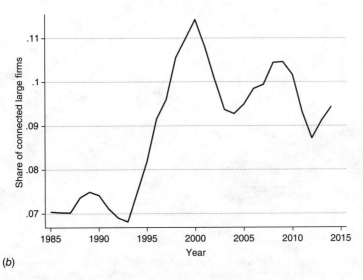

(b)

Reformatted from Akcigit, Baslandze, and Lotti (2023), Appendix, figure A.1.

Notes: (a) Plots a 3-year moving average of GDP per capita growth in Italy over time, (b) Is taken from Akcigit et al. (2018) and plots the average share of large firms across Italian industries that are connected with high-rank politicians. A large firm is defined as a firm with more than 100 workers. The firm is connected with a high-rank politician if it employs at least one worker who at the same time serves as a mayor, region/province president, vice mayor or vice president, or president/ vice president of a local government council.

Figure 20.1a–b. Declining growth and rising connections of large firms in Italy

employment shares in their respective industries and regions over time. Figure 20.2 then plots for each rank the average intensity of innovation—the number of patent applications per one hundred white-collar workers, and the average intensity of connections—the number of employed politicians per one hundred white-collar workers. Both are adjusted for industry, region, and year fixed effects. We see that firms with larger market share tend to innovate less intensely while having relatively more political connections than smaller firms. These patterns hold for various proxies for firm innovation, connectedness, and definitions of market share. If these connections were productive, we would see the opposite trend, with connections and innovation efforts going hand in hand.

Further evidence points to the nonproductive use of political connections by market leaders. Although connections lead to growth in firm size, these

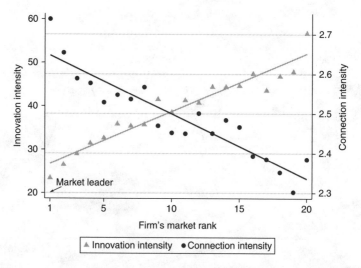

Notes: Figure is reproduced from Akcigit et al. (2018). On the x-axis, firms are ranked based on the employment share in their industry × region in a year. Market leaders have the rank of 1. Gray triangles depict the average innovation intensity measured as the number of patent applications, normalized by firm size (100 white-collar workers). Black circles denote connection intensity measured as the number of politicians employed in a firm, again normalized by firm size. Both outcome variables are adjusted for industry, region, and year fixed effects. The gray and black lines depict regression lines from regressing connection and innovation intensities on market rank, controlling for industry, region, and year fixed effects.

Reformatted from Akcigit, Baslandze, and Lotti (2023), figure 5.

Figure 20.2. Intensity of innovation and political connections over firm's market rank

connections do not lead to increased productivity. Using firm-level OLS and fixed-effect regressions and conditioning on other firm-level controls, the study shows that moving from having no connections to having connections is associated with a 1–4 percentage point increase in employment and value-added growth. Productivity does not increase, however, and even decreases slightly, as measured by labor productivity or total factor productivity (TFP). The growth in firm size is temporary, and it is larger for firms connected with majority-party politicians. Firm-level connections are also associated with longer survival in the market and greater profits, but are not associated with indicators of innovative activity, like increased expenses on intangibles or expanded patent filings.

Although instructive, these firm-level correlations may be driven by other factors, making it hard to determine causality. The study exploits random variation caused by closely contested local elections to move forward with causal identification. The margins for these elections were so close that the outcome can be considered as effectively decided "by chance." The study's regression discontinuity design (RDD) compares the postelection performance of firms that, at the time of the election, employed politicians whose party entered the majority or minority as a result of the election. This design allows the comparison of ex ante identical firms who were randomly assigned to having more or less political advantage by the result of a close election. Indeed, balancing tests shown in the article support this assumption of randomization—winning and losing firms are in fact ex ante similar on many dimensions. However, the postelection outcomes of these firms differ. As before, firms connected with winning politicians tend to grow in size while showing no improvement in productivity, relative to firms connected with losing politicians.

Although this RDD analysis provides local treatment estimates that are specific to the narrow context of marginal elections, it is a credible identification exercise. Combined with the firm-level estimates on the entire sample of firms discussed above, these exercises suggest that firms rely on political connections mainly for nonproductive reasons, and that this behavior is particularly prevalent among large market leaders.

Macro implications and channels. The effects of nonproductive strategies exploited by existing incumbents go beyond private gains and can have dire consequences for aggregate firm and productivity dynamics. To see this, let us first turn to the theory of creative destruction to which this volume is devoted. Akcigit et al. (2023) develop a simple theory of innovation, creative destruction, and growth, in which firms choose both innovation and political connections. To model political connections, the study adopts the most "innocuous" approach and introduces wedges to the firms' cost (e.g., Restuccia and Rogerson 2008; Hsieh and Klenow 2009; Garicano et al. 2016) to represent market frictions smoothed by political connections.

What do these wedges stand for in the data? Akcigit et al. (2023) find that government regulations and bureaucracy are the most relevant channels through which political connections transmit into poor economic performance in Italy. In their day-to-day operations, firms deal with various forms of regulations and bureaucracy (e.g., obtaining permits and licenses, complying with environmental/safety regulations), and face administrative burdens that local bureaucrats handle. However, the Italian bureaucracy ranks consistently in the bottom among the OECD countries in terms of the Government Effectiveness Index,[2] and the quality of bureaucracy in Italy also has deteriorated over time (Gratton et al. 2021). Consistent with this, incumbents in industries facing the largest burden of bureaucracy and regulations are more likely to be politically connected than incumbent firms in lightly regulated industries. The connected incumbents in highly regulated industries also benefit the most from their political connections. Hence, regulations and dysfunctional bureaucracy are a mediating channel through which political connections affect firm dynamics and growth.

The modeling choices are guided by empirical evidence. The model is consistent with the micro evidence discussed above and grants insight into the macro implications of the micro behavior. As in the standard framework of Aghion and Howitt (1992), it is entrants, not incumbents, who have incentives for innovation; and large incumbents are incentivized to forge political connections: for them, the gains from reducing market frictions outweigh the costs of forming connections.

The model helps illuminate the aggregate implications of political connections. The key is to understand how creative destruction works. In standard models, creative destruction occurs when entrepreneurial innovators improve on the technology held by incumbent firms, and the better technology is supposed to outcompete old technology. Experience and empirical evidence suggest that this is not often the case, however, and

---

[2] The Worldwide Governance Indicators project by the World Bank, 1996–2020.

political connections help explain why. Incumbent firms tend to be larger and tend to have more political connections, so they face fewer market frictions. The unequal distribution of market frictions puts entrants at a disadvantage, effectively raising the bar for replacement through innovation. As a result, although connections are modeled as "innocuous," the nonproductive use and uneven distribution of political connections leads to an aggregate decline in creative destruction, innovation, and ultimately growth.

Macroeconomic data was used to verify the aggregate implications of this model. Political connections are, in fact, linked with worsened industry dynamics across different markets. Creative destruction and reallocation are less intense in markets in which a large share of incumbents have rich political connections.

2.2 Other contexts

Although results of this study pertain to the empirical setting of Italy, there are no obvious reasons to think the findings and intuition from the model are specific to the Italian experience. I briefly review other recent evidence about political connections in the context of creative destruction (for a review of different aspects, see Akcigit et al. 2023).

Across countries, Comin and Hobijn (2009) show that lobbying dampens the adoption of new technologies, especially when incumbents in the adopting country are invested in old technologies that are close predecessors to new technologies. In a related strand of works, incumbent firms have been shown to leverage their political connections against foreign competition. Bombardini et al. (Chapter 19, this book) discuss evidence that lobbying was used to deter foreign competition in response to the import shock in the United States. This lobbying was particularly pronounced among firms behind the technology frontier, again indicating that innovation and political connections go in opposite directions.

Gutiérrez and Philippon (2019) find that the elasticity of entry to an industry's median Tobin's Q has declined over time in the United States. That is, firms enter less into industries where existing firms have larger market values. The authors' analysis shows that an increase in regulations and lobbying expenditures by firms in high-Q industries is likely a significant driver of this decline in "free entry" since 2000. Consistent with this, Bessen (2016) also argues that political influence, in the form of lobbying and campaign contributions, and regulations are important factors in explaining rising corporate profits, especially since 2000.

3 Large Firms, Patenting, and Creative Destruction

Incumbent firms rely on a range of other strategies to maintain their market positions. One of them is patenting. As one of the widely used forms of intellectual property protection, patents were introduced to reward and promote innovation and technological progress. As a result, patents have traditionally been associated with innovation. But is this still the case? Do patents still signal technological progress, or do we witness the rise of nonproductive patenting that solely serves the role of protection?

Figure 20.3 plots aggregate trends in patenting and TFP growth in the United States. Figure 20.3a shows the total number of patent applications in the United States. Figure 20.3b shows a smooth 10-year trend in aggregate TFP growth. While patenting has surged beginning with the 1980s, TFP growth has been stalling. If patents signal innovation, why are these innovations not reflected in aggregate statistics? It could be the case that we witness the changing nature of the innovation process—"low-hanging fruits" have all been grabbed, and "ideas are harder to find" (Jones 2009; Gordon 2016; Bloom et al. 2020). In this case, more patents would need to fuel the same increase in productivity. However, it could also be the case that more patents filed today are nonproductive, and so are meant to reduce creative destruction but not to find their ways in actual innovations in the economy.

Indeed, concerns over strategic patenting and the accumulation of patent thickets have grown over time (Cohen et al. 2000; Jaffe and Lerner 2004; Akcigit and Ates 2023). Nonetheless, the challenge in identifying whether a patent is nonproductive—that is, not underlying any real innovation in the market—lies in the fact that it is hard to track innovations, and patents are often our only way to proxy them. Rich microdata and new ways of measuring innovation and patent content are needed to understand the nature of patenting and firms' nonproductive strategies.

A study by Argente et al. (2020) tries to disentangle productive from nonproductive patents to learn about firms' strategies. Argente et al. (2020) focus on the empirical context of the consumer product goods (CPG) sector, where rich micro-level data can be used to identify firms' innovations in the

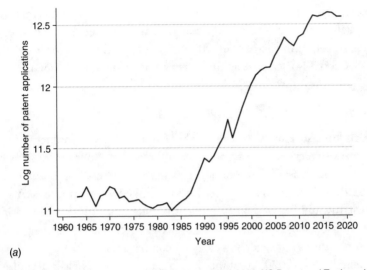

(a)

Data source: US Patent Statistics Chart Calendar Years 1963–2020, US Patent and Trademark Office.

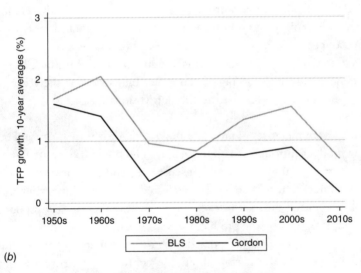

(b)

Data sources: US Bureau of Labor Statistics (BLS); Gordon (2015, 54–59).

Notes: (a) Plots the log number of patent applications in the USPTO, (b) Plots annualized 10-year TFP growth series from BLS Multifactor Productivity data and Gordon (2015). "2010s" represents the average for 2010–2014 for the Gordon series and 2010–2019 for BLS.

Figure 20.3a–b. The US trends in patenting and TFP growth

market and link them with firms' patents. The study finds that patent filings of market leaders are often nonproductive: they hinder the process of creative destruction in the market while failing to lead to new or better products. Section 3.1 discusses the findings of this study in more detail.

3.1 Consumer product goods sector

Data and measurement. A data set that can identify nonproductive patents must meet two criteria. First, concrete information about innovations must be present, such as evidence of new products or process improvements; and second, these innovations must be able to be linked to patent filings. A simple idea then would be to identify productive patents as those reflected in the innovations in the market and nonproductive patents as those not associated with innovations but deterring entry by competitors.

Argente et al. (2020) combines a rich data set that Nielsen Retail Measurement Services (RMS) collects from retail point-of-sale systems with data from the US Patent and Trademark Office (USPTO) to meet these two criteria. Point-of-sale data sets from grocery, drug, and general-merchandise retailers are gaining in popularity for firm-level micro and macro studies (Hottman et al. 2016; Argente et al. 2018). This data set's main advantages are its granular information on firms' product portfolios in the CPG sector and its near-universal coverage of an entire industry over the years 2006–2015. This information is used to develop various measures of product innovation by firms.

The relevant measures of product innovation take the quantity and quality of new product introductions into account. Detailed product attributes and hedonic price regressions are then used to develop an index of the novelty embedded in each new product. The preferred measure of innovation is, then, a quality-adjusted product introduction—the number of new products introduced, weighted by the products' novelty indices.

These products are then matched with patent filings by the introducing firms. To gather information about the content of a firm's patents and products, texts of patent applications and product descriptions from RMS and Wikipedia are compiled. Textual analysis is then applied to match the firm's patents with the closest product categories (a set of similar products) that the firm produces. Because this data offers no measure of process innovations, patents that are likely related to process improvements are excluded.

This procedure yields firm-level data that includes measures of firms' product innovation in various product categories and firms' patenting activity related to products in those categories. The data set covers 35,000 firms in the CPG sector. These firms hold a total of one million patents; a third of these are relevant to the products included in RMS. Not surprisingly, the majority of product innovations in the data do not match to patents; hence, these innovations would not be evidenced by patenting statistics.

Delving into microdata. With this rich data set at hand, the study next relates firms' patenting activity to their product innovation. First off, the data show that firms filing patents tend to introduce more and better products, primarily within one or two years after a patent is issued. Hence, patents do capture product innovation in the market, on average.

However, the study documents an important heterogeneity in the patents-to-products relationship, and this is the key to understanding firms' use of nonproductive strategies. We observe a disconnect between patenting and product innovation for firms as we move up the firm size distribution. Figure 20.4 is reproduced from Argente et al. (2020). Figure 20.4a shows the average quality-adjusted product introduction rate for firms in different firm size (sales) percentiles in various product categories. As a firm's market share within a product category grows, its product innovation rate in that category declines, with the market leader contributing proportionately least to the aggregate innovation introduced in the market.

Crucially, this relaxation in innovative efforts is accompanied by a disproportionate increase in patenting activity. Market leaders issue more patents per each new product introduced, even when conditioned on the relative innovativeness embedded in new products. Figure 20.4b shows how the number of patent applications per quality-adjusted innovation increases with firm size within a narrowly defined product category. The article calculates the patents-to-innovation elasticity by firm size and finds that it declines as a firm's market share in a product category increases.

By itself, this trend in the increase in patenting without accompanying product innovation would not be worrying if, instead of new products, larger firms used their patents for other productive reasons, such as process and method improvements, patent sale and licensing, or experimentation and delayed product development. However, the data show that these alternative uses of patents do not account for the observed declining patents-to-innovation relationship with firm size.

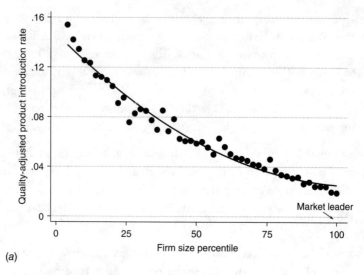

(a)

Extracted and reformatted from Argente et al. (2020), figure 3.

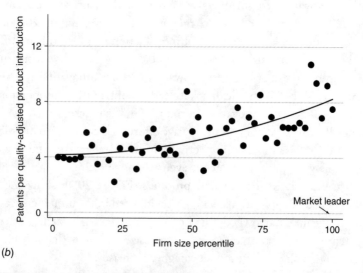

(b)

Reformatted from Argente et al. (2020), figure 4, right.

Notes: (a) Depicts the average quality-adjusted product introduction rate for firms in different size (sales) percentiles in the product category in a year, (b) Depicts the ratio of patent applications over quality-adjusted new products across the firm size percentile.

Figure 20.4a–b. Product innovation and patenting over firm size

Instead, the data suggest that the market leaders' increased patenting is largely nonproductive and limits the entry of other competitors. Fewer products are introduced by other firms in a product category where large incumbents file more patents. The same is not true if patent filers are the smaller firms. Consistent with this, conditional on quantity and quality of product introduction, large firms' patents carry a greater revenue premium; that is, market leaders tend to monetize their patents more effectively.

The study further documents that patents of market leaders are quite different from patents of smaller firms. Large firms' patent applications are textually more similar to their existing patents, are involved in litigations more often, and accumulate lower citations from other firms. This is consistent with the finding in Akcigit and Kerr (2018) that for the entire sample of patenting firms, large firms switch from doing radical and exploratory patenting to incremental and exploitative patenting, measured by the number of citations and share of self-citations to firms' patents.

A theory of creative destruction with nonproductive patenting. A small extension of the theory of growth and creative destruction provides a natural intuition for the observed facts and helps us quantify the private value of a patent. In the model where innovation and patenting decisions are different choices, we see that the link between innovation and patenting gets weaker for bigger firms. It is this disconnect that, through the lens of the model, identifies the extent of nonproductive patenting in the data.

The model combines two classic intuitions from the literature. Similar to the classic *Arrow effect* (Arrow 1962), the model implies that market leaders benefit less from innovating and commercializing their products as innovations cannibalize the firms' own rents. This effect is also at the heart of the basic Schumpeterian model of Aghion and Howitt (1992) and is prominently featured in subsequent works (e.g., Akcigit and Kerr 2018). The present model extends this intuition by highlighting one of the strategies that market leaders use instead of innovating: strategic patenting. The benefits from lower creative destruction obtained by means of patent protection are larger for market leaders simply because they have more to lose. As a result, market leaders file patents without innovating, leading to nonproductive patenting aimed solely at preventing creative destruction. This intuition is similar to the preemption idea from classic work by Gilbert and Newbery (1982).

Combining these two opposite effects, the model provides a unified way to account for the reduced product innovation and increased patenting by market leaders observed in the data. The model is used to quantitatively decompose the private value of a patent and show its implications for creative destruction in the consumer goods sector.

Note that this model does not speak to the virtues of the patent system as a whole. The model is silent about the ex ante incentives that the patent system provides for innovation. An evaluation of the welfare implications of the patent system requires a comprehensive quantitative analysis of the trade-off between ex ante innovation incentives, knowledge diffusion from patents, and the strategic misuse of patents that twist the competition.[3]

3.2 Other contexts and policy implications

Argente et al. (2020) illustrates that many patents held by large firms do not lead to actual innovations in the market and solely serve as an impediment to creative destruction and reallocation. The study focuses only on the CPG sector because of the unique opportunity presented by detailed scanner data sets. However, such data sets do not reflect process innovations or innovations outside consumer goods sector. Although the model's intuitions are generalizable, new data and methods are needed to detect nonproductive patenting in other contexts and evaluate whether empirical findings for the CPG sector are extendable to other settings. This section briefly reviews related micro evidence in other contexts and discusses aggregate implications and policy.

Due to data limitations, there is little empirical evidence about whether patents translate into actual innovations in the market. However, there is more evidence about whether patents deter follow-on research or product introduction. Galasso and Schankerman (2014) show that when patent right is invalidated, the focal patent receives more follow-on citations from future patents. The authors look at patent invalidation decisions by the US Court of Appeals. The case for each patent goes to a panel of randomly assigned judges who have different tendencies to be lenient about

---

[3] See Nicholas (2013) for an excellent survey of the creative and destructive roles of patents, and Abrams et al. (2019) for the review of the studies on different uses of patents.

interpreting a patent as valid. Analyzing the subsequent citation patterns of 1,258 "lucky" and "unlucky" patents, Galasso and Schankerman (2014) find that patent invalidation leads to a roughly 50 percent increase in follow-on citations by other firms. This estimate is mainly driven by invalidated patents of large firms.

These effects are very heterogeneous across different patent technology classes. For example, the effects are absent for patents related to human genomics. Indeed, a study by Sampat and Williams (2019) do not find that the patent grant harms subsequent research and product development in human genes technology. In another study, Cockburn and MacGarvie (2011) find that entry in software products declines when there are more patents relevant to that market. Similarly, exploiting patent-publication paired data, Murray and Stern (2007) show a reduction in subsequent patent citations after patent rights are formally granted.

Argente et al. (2020) show that market leaders' patents are often not linked to innovation, in addition to their anticompetitive effects. This behavior might offer a partial explanation for the recent decline in the diffusion of knowledge from leaders to laggards. Akcigit and Ates (2023) (see also Chapter 12 in this book) build an endogenous growth model that incorporates various channels that could explain salient macroeconomic changes in the United States over recent decades. A decline in the rate of knowledge diffusion from frontier to laggard firms is likely the most significant contributor to reduced business dynamism. This channel is likely to operate in other countries, too; Andrews et al. (2016) document an increasing gap between frontier and laggard firms in the OECD.

If tools originally meant to promote innovation are effectively stifling innovation today, perhaps policy could intervene. Patent reforms are a continual subject of policy discussions (Jaffe and Lerner 2004), and they should be, given the importance of incentives that patent law creates. To combat the rise in nonproductive patenting, the USPTO must apply more scrutiny to patent filings, especially those filed by large firms. With the help of textual analysis and machine learning tools, patent applications that are too similar to their predecessors could be singled out and their necessity and applicability could be scrutinized. In current patent law, patented inventions are not required to be applied in practice. Perhaps the adoption of some form of *bona fide* use from trademark law could discourage nonproductive patenting.

4 Mergers and Acquisitions

Acquiring competitors is yet another strategy that incumbent firms may use to stymie creative destruction. An increase in market dominance and a reduction in competition are often cited as the motives for many merger and acquisition (M&A) deals. How prevalent these motives are and how much they reduce creative destruction in the economy is ultimately an empirical question. Section 4.1 reviews recent empirical studies on anticompetitive acquisitions. Section 4.2 reviews studies supporting contrasting motives for merger—those driven by efficiency considerations due to synergies between firms.[4] Section 5, the conclusion, discusses recent quantitative models that incorporate both these channels and study antitrust policies in a dynamic environment with innovation.[5]

4.1 Empirical evidence

Anticompetitive acquisitions

A growing body of empirical evidence points toward increasing anticompetitive acquisitions in the United States. Anticompetitive acquisitions aiming to increase incumbents' market power and to reduce creative destruction often act through targeting *current* competitors or preempting nascent and *potential* competitors.

In the case of *current* competitors' acquisitions, the growing body of empirical work finds evidence that these strategies lead to higher prices for consumers. For example, analyzing international acquisitions in the beer and spirits industry, Alviarez et al. (2020) show that markups increase after multinational "big giants" acquire "local stars." The study estimates that the price index is 30 percent higher in countries that allow acquisitions relative to the United States and the EU that force brand divestitures. Similarly, Dafny et al. (2012) estimate the effects of a merger of two healthcare insurers on health insurance premiums in the United States. To identify the causal effect of the industry concentration on premiums, the authors exploit

---

[4] Andrade et al. (2001) offer an excellent review of these and other motives for M&As. Kaplan (2000) offers a compilation of in-depth analyses of specific M&A cases in various industries.
[5] See Nocke (2021) for a rich survey of recent theoretical studies on merger policy.

the heterogeneous increase in industry concentration across markets due to premerger differences in local market shares held by merging firms. Using rich data on all of the health plans offered by a sample of employers over time, the authors estimate that the merger resulted in about 7 percentage points increase in a premium. Similarly, Miller and Weinberg (2017) show that the merger of two big companies in the beer industry drastically increased beer prices by helping price coordination in a more concentrated market.

The above studies provide evidence for anticompetitive acquisitions after firms purchase or merge with current competitors. Detecting preemption is more challenging: *potential* competitors are harder to detect. Incumbents may purchase targets whose ideas are too nascent so that targets do not yet show up in the data as being important competitors. Several studies aim to detect these preemptions using new data and approaches.

A recent study by Cunningham et al. (2021) makes a big step in this direction. The study shows that incumbents in the pharmaceutical industry preempt future competition by acquiring targets and discontinuing their innovative drug developments. The authors collect data on the development of 16,000 drugs and combine them with information on company acquisitions, which enables them to determine potentially overlapping and competing projects based on the same therapeutic class and the mechanism of action of the drugs. By comparing projects acquired by overlapping incumbents to those acquired by nonoverlapping incumbents, the study estimates that acquired projects are 23.4 percent less likely to have continued development activity. These project terminations also do not seem to be driven by project delays, slower speed of project development, potential project selection, or optimal capital redeployment stories. Instead, evidence in this study supports the "killer acquisition" theory, whereby incumbents strategically neutralize potential competitors at their nascency.

Interestingly, all these acquisitions go under the radar of the competition authorities: killer acquisitions bunch just below the Federal Trade Commission (FTC) acquisition thresholds. This is not surprising, given that these acquisitions target small but high-potential firms. This highlights limitations of the existing FTC thresholds, which focus on *current* market shares. On aggregate, the authors estimate that if these killer acquisitions were disallowed, the drug project development would continue for 4.3 percent more drugs in a year.

Preemption of competition is also found to be an important reason for M&As by Grimpe and Hussinger (2008), who provide suggestive evidence for this motive in technology markets. First, using data from the European Patent Office, the authors construct a measure of the potential preemptive power of firms' patents. Next, they show that acquirers pay more for targets whose patents are technologically related to their own patents, especially if the targets' patents are better at blocking entry.

Synergies

Alongside this evidence on anticompetitive acquisitions, economic theory suggests that M&As often create efficiency gains from production or technological synergies between merging firms. A rich empirical literature explores this possibility. Hoberg and Phillips (2010) pin down the importance of product market synergies in M&A deals. To measure relatedness and asset complementarities between firms, the authors analyze texts of product descriptions from 10,000 reports filed with the US Securities and Exchange Commission (SEC). Firms using similar language to describe products are considered to be close in the product market. The results show that firms are more likely to merge and generate higher returns if they are close in the product market space. At the same time, targets distinct from the acquirer's rivals generate even higher returns, indicating that acquirers seek to differentiate their products in a competitive landscape.

The importance of technological synergies for M&A transactions is explored by Bena and Li (2014), who analyze the patents of M&A participants over the period 1984–2006. Supporting the idea of technological synergies, the authors find that technological overlap between firms (shared technology classes and cross-citations between firms' patents) increases the likelihood of merger transaction. Furthermore, using a quasi experiment comparing withdrawn bids (due to reasons that are exogenous to innovation) with successful deals, the study shows that premerger technological overlap between merging firms increases postmerger innovation output. Consistent with this, Phillips and Zhdanov (2013) suggest that an option of being bought out by large firms incentivizes smaller firms to be more, and large firms to be less, R&D intensive. Similarly, Gans and Stern (2000) show that the market for ideas (with low licensing or acquisition cost) might incentivize incumbent firms to reduce R&D because of the expectation of buying innovations from smaller firms.

4.2 Aggregate implications

While extant literature has primarily focused on evaluating a *static* trade-off between synergies and higher market concentration, growing evidence on anticompetitive acquisitions preempting creative destruction suggests we should shift our attention to the *dynamic* implications of these strategies. This dynamic view should take into consideration incumbents' and entrants' innovation incentives and implications for long-term productivity and growth.

A recent study by Cavenaile et al. (2021) considers these dynamic aspects. The authors present a general equilibrium growth model with innovation and M&A activities to quantify the long-run welfare implications of antitrust policy. The model incorporates potential synergies from M&As, current reduction in market concentration, and, importantly, the effect on future innovation incentives. The authors show that strengthening the current antitrust policies would be beneficial in the long run. These long-run effects are an order of magnitude larger than more standard, static effects. With stricter antitrust, large incumbents increase their innovation efforts, too: when firms cannot rely on nonproductive strategies, they have to switch back to productive, innovation-driven strategies. Consistent with the evidence from Cunningham et al. (2021), the authors point out that the FTC's current HHI measures of competition often fail to account for anticompetitive acquisitions, because HHI measures are static, and many acquisitions target the currently small but high-potential firms.

Mermelstein et al. (2020) also study optimal antitrust policy in a dynamic setting. In the model, firms can decrease their marginal costs either internally, through their own investments, or externally, by buying out other firms. Merger creates efficiency gains through scale economies. In addition to the standard static trade-off between efficiency gains and static market power, an antitrust authority now also considers dynamic implications for post-merger investment as well as investment incentives for other firms. A general lesson is that optimal merger policy is very different in an environment with dynamic concerns. The study also highlights that existing antitrust policies influence firms' (premerger) investment decisions: consistent with empirical work reviewed above (Gans and Stern 2000; Hoberg and Phillips 2010), knowing that merger policy is lax, small firms now invest more, relative to large firms, hoping to be bought out. This investment-for-buyout behavior is not efficient and justifies a stricter antitrust.

5 Conclusion

The process of creative destruction, while moving technological progress ahead, creates losers and winners along the way. It is this conflict that incentivizes the vested incumbents to find ways to resist the power of creative destruction. This chapter was devoted to reviewing recent micro-level evidence on incumbents' use of nonproductive strategies of political connections, nonproductive patenting, and anticompetitive acquisitions. The theory of creative destruction and growth then was used to shed light on the aggregate implications of these strategies.

Two directions for future research loom large. First, novel granular data sets and techniques are needed to identify other nonproductive strategies that incumbent firms use in different contexts. Uncovering these strategies will highlight institutional features and policies (or lack of them) that make these strategies possible. Second, to quantitatively evaluate how the micro-level evidence on nonproductive strategies aggregates to macro-level outcomes, we need to estimate rich microfounded structural models of the macroeconomy. It is of pressing importance to evaluate how much the strategies employed by market leaders contribute to the much-discussed recent trends of increasing market power and industry concentration, slower business dynamism, decreasing investment, and stagnating productivity growth.

References

Abrams, David S., Ufuk Akcigit, Gokhan Oz, and Jeremy G. Pearce. (2019). "The Patent Troll: Benign Middleman or Stick-Up Artist?" NBER Working Paper 25713.

Aghion, Philippe, and Peter Howitt. (1992). "A Model of Growth through Creative Destruction." *Econometrica, 60* (2), 323–351.

Akcigit, Ufuk, and Sina T. Ates. (2021). "Ten Facts on Declining Business Dynamism and Lessons from Endogenous Growth Theory." *American Economic Journal: Macroeconomics, 13* (1), 257–298.

———. (2023). "What Happened to U.S. Business Dynamism?" *Journal of Political Economy,* forthcoming.

Akcigit, Ufuk, Salomé Baslandze, and Francesca Lotti. (2023). "Connecting to Power: Political Connections, Innovation, and Firm Dynamics." *Econometrica, 91* (2): 529–564.

Akcigit, Ufuk, and William R. Kerr. (2018). "Growth through Heterogeneous Innovations." *Journal of Political Economy, 126* (4), 1374–1443.

Alviarez, Vanessa, Keith Head, and Thierry Mayer. (2020). "Global Giants and Local Stars: How Changes in Brand Ownership Affect Competition." CEPII Research Center Working Paper 2020–13.

Andrade, Gregor, Mark Mitchell, and Erik Stafford. (2001). "New Evidence and Perspectives on Mergers." *Journal of Economic Perspectives, 15* (2), 103–120.

Andrews, Dan, Chiara Criscuolo, and Peter N. Gal. (2016). "The Best versus the Rest: The Global Productivity Slowdown, Divergence across Firms and the Role of Public Policy." OECD Productivity Working Paper No. 5.

Argente, David, Salomé Baslandze, Douglas Hanley, and Sara Moreira. (2020). "Patents to Products: Product Innovation and Firm Dynamics." CEPR Discussion Paper 14692.

Argente, David, Munseob Lee, and Sara Moreira. (2018). "How Do Firms Grow? The Life Cycle of Products Matters." Society for Economic Dynamics 2018 Meeting Paper 1174.

Arrow, Kenneth. (1962). "Economic Welfare and the Allocation of Resources for Invention." In *The Rate and Direction of Inventive Activity: Economic and Social Factors*, NBER, 609–626.

Autor, David, David Dorn, Lawrence F. Katz, Christina Patterson, and John Van Reenen. (2020). "The Fall of the Labor Share and the Rise of Superstar Firms." *Quarterly Journal of Economics, 135* (2), 645–709.

Baumol, William J. (1990). "Entrepreneurship: Productive, Unproductive, and Destructive." *Journal of Political Economy, 98* (5, Part 1), 893–921.

Bena, Jan, and Kai Li. (2014). "Corporate Innovations and Mergers and Acquisitions." *Journal of Finance, 69* (5), 1923–1960.

Bessen, James E. (2016). "Accounting for Rising Corporate Profits: Intangibles or Regulatory Rents?" Boston University School of Law, Law and Economics Research Paper No. 16–18.

Bloom, Nicholas, Charles I. Jones, John Van Reenen, and Michael Webb. (2020). "Are Ideas Getting Harder to Find?" *American Economic Review, 110* (4), 1104–1144.

Bombardini, Matilde, Olimpia Cutinelli-Rendina, and Francesco Trebbi. (2021). "Lobbying behind the Frontier." NBER Working Paper 29120.

Cabral, Luis M. B., and Ben Polak. (2012). "Standing on the Shoulders of Babies: Dominant Firms and Incentives to Innovate." NYU Working Paper No. 2451/31642.

Cavenaile, Laurent, Murat Alp Celik, and Xu Tian. (2021). "The Dynamic Effects of Antitrust Policy on Growth and Welfare." *Journal of Monetary Economics, 121*, 42–59.

Cockburn, Iain, and Megan J. MacGarvie. (2011). "Entry and Patenting in the Software Industry." *Management Science, 57*, 915–933.

Cohen, Wesley M., Richard R. Nelson, and John P. Walsh. (2000). "Protecting Their Intellectual Assets: Appropriability Conditions and Why U.S. Manufacturing Firms Patent (or Not)." NBER Working Paper 7552.

Comin, Diego, and Bart Hobijn. (2009). "Lobbies and Technology Diffusion." *Review of Economics and Statistics, 91* (2), 229–244.

Cunningham, Colleen, Florian Ederer, and Song Ma. (2021). "Killer Acquisitions." *Journal of Political Economy, 129* (3), 649–702.

Dafny, Leemore, Mark Duggan, and Subramaniam Ramanarayanan. (2012). "Paying a Premium on Your Premium? Consolidation in the US Health Insurance Industry." *American Economic Review, 102* (2), 1161–1185.

Decker, Ryan, John Haltiwanger, Ron Jarmin, and Javier Miranda. (2016). "Where Has All the Skewness Gone? The Decline in High-Growth (Young) Firms in the U.S." *European Economic Review, 86* (C), 4–23.

Dixit, Avinash. (1980). "The Role of Investment in Entry-Deterrence." *Economic Journal, 90* (357), 95–106.

Galasso, Alberto, and Mark Schankerman. (2014). "Patents and Cumulative Innovation: Causal Evidence from the Courts." *Quarterly Journal of Economics, 130* (1), 317–369.

Gans, Joshua S., and Scott Stern. (2000). "Incumbency and R&D Incentives: Licensing the Gale of Creative Destruction." *Journal of Economics & Management Strategy, 9* (4), 485–511.

Garicano, Luis, Claire Lelarge, and John Van Reenen. (2016). "Firm Size Distortions and the Productivity Distribution: Evidence from France." *American Economic Review, 106* (11), 3439–3479.

Gilbert, Richard, and David Newbery. (1982). "Preemptive Patenting and the Persistence of Monopoly Power." *American Economic Review, 72*, 514–526.

Glode, Vincent, and Guillermo Ordoñez. (2021). "Technological Progress and Rent Seeking." SSRN, Jacobs Levy Equity Management Center for Quantitative Financial Research Paper.

Gordon, Robert J. (2015). "Secular Stagnation: A Supply-Side View." *American Economic Review, 105* (5), 54–59.

———. (2016). *The Rise and Fall of American Growth: The U.S. Standard of Living since the Civil War.* Princeton, NJ: Princeton University Press.

Gratton, Gabriele, Luigi Guiso, Claudio Michelacci, and Massimo Morelli. (2021). "From Weber to Kafka: Political Instability and the Overproduction of Laws." *American Economic Review, 111* (9), 2964–3003.

Grimpe, Christoph, and Katrin Hussinger. (2008). "Pre-empting Technology Competition through Firm Acquisitions." *Economics Letters, 100* (2), 189–191.

Gutiérrez, Germán, and Thomas Philippon. (2017). "Declining Competition and Investment in the U.S." NBER Working Paper 23583.

———. (2019). "The Failure of Free Entry." Technical Report, NBER Working Paper 26001.

Hoberg, Gerard, and Gordon Phillips. (2010). "Product Market Synergies and Competition in Mergers and Acquisitions: A Text-Based Analysis." *Review of Financial Studies, 23* (10), 3773–3811.

Hottman, Colin J., Stephen J. Redding, and David E. Weinstein. (2016). "Quantifying the Sources of Firm Heterogeneity." *Quarterly Journal of Economics, 131* (3), 1291–1364.

Hsieh, Chang-Tai, and Peter J. Klenow. (2009). "Misallocation and Manufacturing TFP in China and India." *Quarterly Journal of Economics, 124* (4), 1403–1448.

Jaffe, Adam, and Josh Lerner. (2004). *Innovation and Its Discontents: How Our Broken Patent System Is Endangering Innovation and Progress, and What to Do about It.* Princeton, NJ: Princeton University Press.

Jones, Benjamin F. (2009). "The Burden of Knowledge and the 'Death of the Renaissance Man': Is Innovation Getting Harder?" *Review of Economic Studies, 76* (1), 283–317.

Kaplan, Steven. (2000). *Mergers and Productivity.* Chicago: University of Chicago Press.

Krusell, Per, and Jose-Victor Rios-Rull. (1996). "Vested Interests in a Positive Theory of Stagnation and Growth." *Review of Economic Studies, 63* (2), 301–329.

Loecker, Jan De, Jan Eeckhout, and Gabriel Unger. (2020). "The Rise of Market Power and the Macroeconomic Implications." *Quarterly Journal of Economics, 135* (2), 561–644.

Mermelstein, Ben, Volker Nocke, Mark A. Satterthwaite, and Michael D. Whinston. (2020). "Internal versus External Growth in Industries with Scale Economies: A Computational Model of Optimal Merger Policy." *Journal of Political Economy, 128* (1), 301–341.

Miller, Nathan H., and Matthew C. Weinberg. (2017). "Understanding the Price Effects of the MillerCoors Joint Venture." *Econometrica, 85* (6), 1763–1791.

Mukoyama, Toshihiko, and Latchezar Popov. (2014). "The Political Economy of Entry Barriers." *Review of Economic Dynamics, 17* (3), 383–416.

Murphy, Kevin M., Andrei Shleifer, and Robert W. Vishny. (1991). "The Allocation of Talent: Implications for Growth." *Quarterly Journal of Economics, 106* (2), 503–530.

Murray, Fiona, and Scott Stern. (2007). "Do Formal Intellectual Property Rights Hinder the Free Flow of Scientific Knowledge? An Empirical Test of the Anti-Commons Hypothesis." *Journal of Economic Behavior & Organization, 63* (4), 648–687.

Nicholas, Tom. (2013). "Are Patents Creative or Destructive?" Harvard Business School Working Paper 14-036.

Nocke, Volker. (2021). "Horizontal Merger Policy: New Work on an Old Problem." Chapter prepared for *Advances in Economics and Econometrics: Twelfth World Congress,* Econometric Society Monograph.

Phillips, Gordon M., and Alexei Zhdanov. (2013). "R&D and the Incentives from Merger and Acquisition Activity." *Review of Financial Studies, 26* (1), 34–78.

Restuccia, Diego, and Richard Rogerson. (2008). "Policy Distortions and Aggregate Productivity with Heterogeneous Establishments." *Review of Economic Dynamics, 11* (4), 707–720.

Salop, Steven C. (1979). "Strategic Entry Deterrence." *American Economic Review, 69* (2), 335–338.

Sampat, Bhaven, and Heidi L. Williams. (2019). "How Do Patents Affect Follow-On Innovation? Evidence from the Human Genome." *American Economic Review, 109* (1), 203–236.

Schumpeter, Joseph A. (1942). *Capitalism, Socialism and Democracy.* London: Harper and Brothers.

Segal, Ilya, and Michael D. Whinston. (2007). "Antitrust in Innovative Industries." *American Economic Review, 97* (5), 1703–1730.

Tirole, Jean. (1988). *The Theory of Industrial Organization.* Cambridge, MA: MIT Press.

Wilson, Robert. (1992). "Chapter 10 Strategic Models of Entry Deterrence." In *Handbook of Game Theory with Economic Applications,* edited by Robert J. Auman and Serfgui Hart, 305–329. Amsterdam: Elsevier.

PART VII

Finance

CHAPTER 21

Finance and Growth

Firm Heterogeneity and Creative Destruction

ŞEBNEM KALEMLI-ÖZCAN *and* FELIPE SAFFIE

1 Introduction

There is an extensive literature on the interplay of finance and growth. The comprehensive review of Levine (2005) shows that countries with better-functioning banks and markets grow faster. Levine (2005) points to several channels underlying this relationship: better allocation of capital, better financial intermediation, better monitoring of investments, and higher quality of investment. The review by Aghion et al. (2018) adds to this list the importance of finance in Schumpeterian models of innovation-led growth, especially when firms are subject to financial frictions.

Finance is at the heart of any innovation-based growth model. Entrepreneurs have to collateralize their ideas in order to seek funding to finance R&D (Mann 2018; Hochberg et al. 2018), whereas the payoff to innovation is often back-loaded, requiring continuous financing well before generating cash inflows. Because of the forward-looking nature of innovation, interest rate fluctuations play a key role in innovation decisions today and can potentially affect the path of aggregate productivity well into the future. Moreover, because firm heterogeneity is key in models of innovation-led growth (Akcigit and Kerr 2018; Acemoglu et al. 2018), the allocative role of the financial system also plays a central role in selecting the set of active firms. Aghion et al. (2018) show how to incorporate financial frictions in a simple version of Aghion and Howitt (1992), but they call for more effort in modeling finance within the new generation of innovation-led growth with firm dynamics that are uniquely suited to face the richness of the micro data.

In a globalized world, the channels described in Levine (2005) have become more complex. Financial intermediaries operate on a global scale, making financial conditions largely exogenous to firms, financial institutions, and policy makers in financially integrated economies (Rey 2013). Moreover, the field of international finance has seen an explosion in the availability of detailed micro data linking financial and real choices at the firm level in several countries. The potential exogeneity of financial flows and the availability of micro data make international finance the ideal field for studying the intersection of finance and growth. This field is an ideal laboratory to understand how finance shapes firms' decisions that might affect the process of creative destruction. In fact, sudden stop episodes provide large exogenous financial variation with a precise timing.[1]

Financial crises cast a long shadow on output (Cerra and Saxena 2008; Reinhart and Rogoff 2009) and aggregate productivity (Meza and Quintin 2007; Pratap and Urrutia 2012; Hardy and Sever 2021). This persistence is indicative of dynamic distortions in productivity growth that can cause economic scarring and output hysteresis. Firm-level evidence points to granular productivity losses caused by financial factors (Hallward-Driemeier and Rijkers 2013; Duval et al. 2020; Manaresi and Pierri 2019; De Ridder 2022; Besley et al. 2020). Moreover, finance shows rich heterogeneity at the firm level.[2] For example, work by Rey (2013), Coimbra and Rey (2017), Kalemli-Özcan (2019), and Di Giovanni et al. (2017) provides evidence that larger banks lend more and larger firms borrow more. Moreover, small firms are relatively more innovative but, at the same time, small and young firms are also more financially constrained (Akcigit and Kerr 2018; Gopinath et al. 2017; Dinlersoz et al. 2019). In this chapter we review some of this empirical evidence and we provide new evidence based on micro data from several countries to understand how financial crises trigger selection in the entry and exit margins.

---

[1] A sudden stop is a typical financial crisis in small open economies. It is characterized by sharp capital outflows and strong reversals of the current account.

[2] Other financial channels include the role of ownership and risk taking in innovation (Aghion et al. 2013, Penciakova 2018), the development of venture capital (Ates, Greenwood, et al. 2018; Akcigit et al. 2019), or how to collateralize intangible assets (Amable et al. 2010; Mann 2018).

Despite abundant empirical evidence and the suitability of the creative destruction framework to model firm heterogeneity, there have been few bridges unifying the innovation-led growth models with the international business cycle quantitative literature. In fact, most of the Schumpeterian models that explore the interlinks between finance and growth are continuous time models solved along a nonstochastic balanced growth path. The key obstacle when integrating innovation-based models with firm dynamics based on Klette and Kortum (2004) into stochastic models of crises is the limitations of discrete time. Despite recent advances in numerical solutions for continuous time business cycle models (Brunnermeier and Sannikov 2016; Achdou et al. 2022), the dynamic stochastic general equilibrium (DSGE) literature has been mainly developed in discrete time. In fact, the main goal of the quantitative DSGE literature is to relate to the time series properties of the data, and the nature of data is discrete (Fernández-Villaverde and Guerrón-Quintana 2021).

To overcome this challenge, we use a simplified version of the solution developed by Ates and Saffie (2021) to provide a tractable path that allows creative destruction and firm dynamics to be integrated into the workhorse quantitative models of international finance (Mendoza 1991, 2010). This mapping preserves the richness and tractability of Klette and Kortum (2004), allowing the models to speak directly to firm–product data not only during tranquil times but also during crises. This class of models generates the hysteresis documented by the empirical literature and provides a testable microfoundation for the channels that generate the economic scarring. Moreover, the framework can be extended to capture firm heterogeneity and financial frictions that can be directly contrasted to granular and aggregate data.

2 Financial Crises and Productivity

In most countries there was a large increase in corporate debt prior to the global financial crisis, most prominently in southern European countries (Kalemli-Özcan et al. 2018). Simultaneously, investment to GDP also declined most for this set of countries. Moreover, not only do high-debt countries, pre-crisis, decrease investment most post-crisis; the investment stays sluggish in these countries for a long time (Kalemli-Özcan et al. 2018). We can see the negative effect in investment even three years after the financial crisis. As documented by Kalemli-Özcan et al. (2018), periphery countries where firms had high leverage before the crisis, had experienced the largest drop in investment and took longest to recover. This hysteresis and lack of recovery is pervasive not only in investment dynamics; GDP also shows persistent negative effects after financial crisis (Cerra and Saxena 2008). Therefore, financial crises are characterized by a lack of the so-called *Solow recovery*.

Two natural questions are: Why do firms accumulate debt during boom? and What does this imply for TFP? Firm heterogeneity in accessing finance plays a key role, with implications for aggregate productivity when all firms face a lower interest rate during booms. A decrease in real interest rate increases desired capital for all firms. However, while large firms with high net worth can borrow and invest, facing lower returns to capital, smaller firms with low net worth cannot borrow and invest and hence face higher returns to capital. This type of dispersion in returns to capital across firms within a narrowly defined four-digit sector leads to a decline in aggregate productivity of that sector.

Is there any evidence for such size-dependent constraints? The answer is yes, as shown in Gopinath et al. (2017), where small firms are much more constrained relative to large firms because large firms are more leveraged.

To dig deeper into the selection effect before and after the crisis, in Table 21.1 we run a regression at the firm level, where we regress entry into a certain sector (panel A) and exit from a certain sector (panel B) on firm productivity and firm productivity interacted with the foreign finance in that sector. We did this before and after the 2008 crisis.

As shown in Table 21.1, our results are striking. Financial crisis trigger selection in terms of entry and exit and this is more powerful in sectors with more foreign finance.

3 Creative Destruction and Aggregate Risk

3.1 A simple model of creative destruction

The first step to study the interaction between financial crises and growth is to combine dynamic models featuring aggregate risk and endogenous technical change. Because of the tractability and simplicity of the Romer (1990)

Table 21.1. Selection and productivity during crises

Panel A	Entry Rate-Sector			
	(1)	*(2)*	*(3)*	*(4)*
	Before crisis	*After crisis*	*Before crisis*	*After crisis*
Firm TFP	−0.0004**	0.0007**	−0.0004*	0.0005**
	(0.0002)	(0.0003)	(0.0002)	(0.0002)
Firm TFP x Foreign finance			−0.0004	0.0014**
			(0.0007)	(0.0006)
Foreign finance			−0.0001	−0.0053
			(0.0034)	(0.0033)

Panel B	Exit Rate-Sector			
	(1)	*(2)*	*(3)*	*(4)*
	Before crisis	*After crisis*	*Before crisis*	*After crisis*
Firm TFP	−0.0004	−0.0017**	−0.0001	−0.0011*
	(0.0005)	(0.0008)	(0.0004)	(0.0006)
Firm TFP x Foreign finance			−0.0013	−0.0034**
			(0.0010)	(0.0016)
Foreign finance			0.0088	0.0270***
			(0.0060)	(0.0076)
Observations	1926409	1219387	1907641	1211350
R-squared	0.562	0.808	0.571	0.811
FirmFE	Yes	Yes	Yes	Yes
Country × sectorFE	Yes	Yes	Yes	Yes
YearFE	Yes	Yes	Yes	Yes

Notes: "Firm TFP" is a firm-level variable estimated via: $\log y_{it} = d_t(s) + \beta^l(s) \log l_{it} + \beta^k(s) \log k_{it} + \log Z_{it} + \varepsilon_{it}$, where i is firm, s is sector, $d_t(s)$ is a time-fixed effect for the given sector, y_{it} denotes nominal value added divided by the two-digit output price deflator, l_{it} denotes the wage bill divided by the same output price deflator, and k_{it} denotes the (book) value of fixed assets divided by the aggregate price of investment goods. $\beta^l(s)$ denotes the elasticity of value added with respect to labor, and $\beta^k(s)$ denotes the elasticity of value added with respect to capital. These elasticities vary at 24 industries defined by their two-digit industry classification. Our estimation uses the methodology developed in Wooldridge (2009) and hence we refer the reader to his paper for details of the estimation process. Given our estimated elasticities $\hat{\beta}^\ell(s)$ and $\hat{\beta}^k(s)$, we then calculate firm (log) productivity as $\log Z_{it} = \log y_{it} - \hat{\beta}^\ell(s) \log \ell_{it} - \hat{\beta}^k(s) \log k_{it}$. "Foreign finance" is a sector level variable, referring to sectoral FDI and foreign ownership, and comes from Akcigit, Ates, and Kalemli-Özcan (2018).

$^*p < 0.1$; $^{**}p < 0.05$; $^{***}p < 0.001$

framework, the literature extending DSGE models to feature endogenous productivity has focused on this non-Schumpeterian framework when developing quantitative tools. In fact, Barlevy (2004) shows that the cost of business cycles is amplified when stationary shocks affect the number of varieties in a Romer (1990) product space. Comin and Gertler (2006) study the ability of endogenous growth to generate low-frequency cycles in an otherwise standard close economy real business cycle (RBC) model.[3]

Closer to our purposes, Queralto (2020) and Guerron-Quintana and Jinnai (2019) combine Comin and Gertler (2006) with the financial crisis model of Gertler and Karadi (2011) to document that crises can generate hysteresis in productivity by affecting the creation of new varieties. In these models, a financial crisis increases the cost of developing new varieties and decreases the discounted value of future profits, therefore permanently decreasing the number of available products with respect to a counterfactual economy that was able to avoid the crisis. Because in the Romer (1990) framework there is no post-entry dynamics and every homogeneous product line is unaffected by other firms' expansion decisions, these models could not be contrasted with the richness of the micro financial data documented in Section 2.[4]

The main challenge when mapping creative destruction models with firm dynamics in the spirit of the Klette and Kortum (2004) extension of Aghion and Howitt (1992) is that the DSGE literature has been built in discrete time, whereas creative destruction models take advantage of the tractability of continuous time. To better understand the convenience of continuous time, let's consider the problem of an incumbent firm in Klette and Kortum (2004). An incumbent firm with n products optimally chooses innovation effort (L units of labor) to generate an innovation on a new product line with a Poisson arrival rate X.[5] The cost function is given by:

$$X = \xi n^{1-\gamma} L^\gamma = n\xi \left[\frac{L}{n}\right]^\gamma \Rightarrow x = \xi l^\gamma, \tag{1}$$

---

[3] This framework has been extended beyond a closed economy to study cross-country spillovers (Gavazzoni and Santacreu 2020; Comin et al. 2014), and it has been used to study sovereign default crises (Gornemann 2014) and exchange rate fluctuations (Gornemann et al. 2020).

[4] Aghion, Akcigit, and Howitt (2015) provide an excellent discussion of the tractability and limitations of the Romer (1990) framework when compared to the Schumpeterian paradigm.

[5] Because there is a continuum of products, and innovation is undirected, the event of landing on a product line already owned by the firm has zero probability.

where small cases represent values normalized by the number of product lines. Then, an incumbent maximizes firm value according to the following value function:

$$rV_n - \dot{V} = n\pi - n\Delta[V_{n-1} - V_n] + n\left[\max_x \left\{ x(V_{n+1} - V_n) - w\left(\frac{x}{\xi}\right)^{\frac{1}{\gamma}} \right\} \right], \quad (2)$$

where V_n is the value of a firm with n products, π are the per product profits, $\dot{V}$ represents the instantaneous change on the value, Δ is the endogenous creative destruction rate, and w is the wage.[6] Note that a firm with n products experiences only three possible outcomes: (i) neither winning nor losing a product, (ii) winning a new product, or (iii) losing an existing product. Because of continuous time, those are the only relevant outcomes to consider. In any instant, the probability of winning and losing multiple products lines is practically nil. This convenience is lost when combining Klette and Kortum (2004) into a classical DSGE framework—in discrete time, in every period a firm could lose or win multiple products. Ates and Saffie (2021) develop a mapping to discrete time that keeps the tractability of the original framework to study the long-run productivity effect of financial crises. In particular, they assume that expansion and destruction probabilities are governed by binomial processes. Therefore, a firm with n products that optimally chooses an innovation rate x will win k new products with probability:

$$B(k, n, x) = \binom{n}{k} x^k (1 - x)^{n-k}, \quad (3)$$

and lose $\tilde{k}$ products when facing the aggregate creative destruction rate Δ according to:

$$B(\tilde{k}, n, \Delta) = \binom{n}{\tilde{k}} \Delta^{\tilde{k}} (1 - \Delta)^{n-\tilde{k}}. \quad (4)$$

---

[6] Because of the log-log structure in production and the Bertrand monopolistic competition assumption, profits are independent of the product-specific productivity and depend only on the relative productivity between the leader and the closest follower.

Because we want to study aggregate financial crises, we also introduce aggregate risk to the economy, denoting the stochastic history by s^t. Then, the discrete time problem of an incumbent becomes:

$$V_n(s^t) = \max_{x_n(s^t)} n \left[\pi(s^t) - w(s^t) \left(\frac{x_n(s^t)}{\xi} \right)^{\frac{1}{\gamma}} \right]$$

$$+ E_t \left[m(s^{t+1}) \sum_{\tilde{k}=0}^{n} B(\tilde{k}, n, \Delta(s^t)) \sum_{k=0}^{n} B(k, n, x_n(s^t)) V_{n-\tilde{k}+k}(s^{t+1}) \, \Big| \, s_t \right],$$ (5)

where $m(s^{t+1})$ denotes the stochastic discount factor of the household that owns the firms.[7] Note that because firms are atomistic, we can assume that the two binomial processes are independent and, therefore, separable. The combination of the two binomial processes characterizes the probability distribution of a firm with n products to transition in only one period to any number of products in $[0, 2n]$ instead. Besides being able to capture all potential firm-level transitions, this framework also preserves the proportionality of the value function that has made the Klette and Kortum (2004) model so popular in the creative destruction literature. In fact, we can guess and verify that $V_n(s^t) = nV_1(s^t)$. This means that every firm invests the same amount per product. By replacing the guess, factoring the future value of a product, and using the properties of the binomial distribution, equation (5) simplifies to:

$$V_1(s^t) = \max_{x(s^t)} \pi(s^t) - w(s^t) \left(\frac{x(s^t)}{\xi} \right)^{\frac{1}{\gamma}}$$

$$+ E_t[m(s^{t+1}) \, (1 - \Delta(s^t) + x(s^t)) V_1(s^{t+1}) \, | \, s_t].$$ (6)

The optimal innovation effort per product line is therefore independent of the total number of products that the firm has:

$$x^*(s^t) = \Gamma_0 \left[\frac{E_t[m(s^{t+1}) V_1(s^{t+1}) \, | \, s_t]}{w(s^t)} \right]^{\frac{\gamma}{\gamma-1}},$$ (7)

---

[7] The innovation investment at time t materializes in product transitions at time $t+1$. Entry of new firms also takes one period to materialize.

where Γ_0 is a constant. To model entry of new firms, define $M(s^t)$ as the mass of new entrepreneurs trying to start a business. We assume that when $M(s^t)$ entrepreneurs pay κ unit of labor each to enter, only $M(s^t)^v$ with $v<1$ become next period's mono-product firms, we get the following entry rate:

$$M^*(s^t) = \Gamma_1 \left[\frac{E_t[m(s^{t+1})V_1(s^{t+1})\,|\,s_t]}{w(s^t)} \right]^{\frac{1}{v-1}}, \qquad (8)$$

where Γ_1 is a constant. Combining the innovation from entrants and incumbents, we get the aggregate creative destruction rate:

$$\Delta(s^t) = M^*(s^t) + x^*(s^t).$$

To link these innovation decisions to productivity growth, we need more structure on the production side of the economy. For simplicity, we assume that intermediate varieties are produced according to the following production function:

$$y_i(s^t) = q_i(s^t)l_i(s^t), \qquad (9)$$

where $q_i(s^t)$ is the efficiency in the production of product line i, and $l_i(s^t)$ represents the labor used in production.[8] Furthermore, we assume that innovations by incumbents or entrants on a given product line increase the product-level technology by a factor of $(1+\sigma)$ with $\sigma>0$ being the step size. These products are aggregated by a final good producer with the following technology:

$$\ln Y(s^t) = z(s^t) + \int_0^1 \ln y_i(s^t)di, \qquad (10)$$

where $Y(s^t)$ is the unique final good and $z(s^t)$ is an aggregate efficiency shock. Following Aghion and Howitt (1992), if we assume Bertrand monopolistic competition, then we can show that profits and labor per product are independent of the product-specific efficiency $q_i(s^t)$; in particular:

$$\pi(s^t) = \frac{\sigma}{1+\sigma} Y(s^t) \qquad (11)$$

$$l(s^t) = \frac{Y(s^t)}{w(s^t)(1+\sigma)}. \qquad (12)$$

---

[8] Any technology with constant marginal cost would lead similar tractability. For example, a Cobb-Douglas aggregation of capital and labor.

Moreover, replacing equation (9) in equation (10) we obtain:

$$Y(s^t) = e^{z(s^t)} A(s^t) l(s^t), \tag{13}$$

where $A(s^t)$ is the endogenous productivity level defined by:

$$A(s^t) = e^{\int_0^1 \ln q_i(s^t) di}. \tag{14}$$

Endogenous productivity growth is generated by creative destruction such that:

$$\ln A(s^t, s_{t+1}) - \ln (A(s^t)) = \Delta(s^t) \ln (1 + \sigma)$$

$$\text{or} \quad \frac{A(s^t, s_{t+1})}{A(s^t)} = 1 + g(s^t, s_{t+1}) = (1 + \sigma)^{\Delta(s^t)}, \tag{15}$$

where $g(s^t, s_{t+1})$ is the growth rate of the endogenous productivity index. When a shock triggers fluctuations in $\Delta(s^t)$, equation (15) provides a mapping to productivity growth generating hysteresis in the productivity index from equation (14) and, therefore, in every growing variable.

Note that the stochastic framework retains the tractability of its continuous time counterpart, allowing for a stochastic analysis beyond the balanced growth path. A corollary of the linearity of the value function in the number of products is that the size distribution is not needed when solving the model. Nevertheless, the size distribution is a well-defined object that can be used to estimate the parameters of the model and validate entry, exit, and size transitions at the firm level. Because there is a continuum of products, we can use the law of large numbers to track the distribution of firms. In particular, denote by $\Omega_n(s^t)$ the mass of firms with n products. The law of motion of this distribution is characterized by a system of dynamic equations that depend only on the innovation rate of incumbents and the mass of entrants:

$$\Omega_1(s^t) = M^*(s^{t-1}) + \sum_{n=1}^{\infty} \Omega_n(s^{t-1}) \sum_{k=0}^{1} B(k, n, x^*(s^{t-1})) B((k+n-1, n, \Delta(s^{t-1}))$$

$$\Omega_{\tilde{n}>1}(s^t) = \sum_{n=\mathbb{I}+\left(\frac{\tilde{n}}{2}\right)}^{\tilde{n}} \left\{ \Omega_n(s^{t-1}) \sum_{k=\tilde{n}-n}^{n} B(k, n, x^*(s^{t-1})) B(k-(\tilde{n}-n), n, \Delta(s^{t-1})) \right\}$$

$$+ \sum_{n=\tilde{n}+1}^{\infty} \left\{ \Omega_n(s^{t-1}) \sum_{k=0}^{\tilde{n}} B(k, n, x^*(s^{t-1})) B(k-(\tilde{n}-n), n, \Delta(s^{t-1})) \right\},$$

where $I^+(a)$ refers to the integer closest to a such that $I^+(a) \geq a$.[9] The first equation has two terms: the first one tracks the entry of new firms with one product, and the second term tracks firms that used to have more than one product and contracted to exactly one product. The second line shows an analogous law of motion for categories of firms with more than one product, where the first component is firms that started with fewer than $\tilde{n}$ products and had net gains that left them at $\tilde{n}$, and the second term reflects firms that were above $\tilde{n}$ and experienced net losses that left them exactly at $\tilde{n}$.[10]

Having shown the tractability of the mapping between continuous-time creative destruction models and their discrete-time counterpart, we proceed to introducing financial crises into this simple framework.

3.2 Financial crises and aggregate productivity

The simplest way to introduce aggregate risk and financial crises is to follow the framework of Mendoza (1991) used by Neumeyer and Perri (2005) and Uribe and Yue (2006) to study the effects of interest rate shocks in small open economies. Equation (10) introduced an aggregate efficiency shock. We will use the problem of the household to introduce our second aggregate shock. Without loss of generality, we assume logarithmic utility and a fixed supply of hours normalized to unity. In particular, the representative household solves the following problem:

$$\max_{C(s^t), B(s^t)} \sum_{t=0}^{\infty} \beta^t E\left[\ln C(s^t) \mid s_0\right] \quad \text{subject to:}$$

$$C(s^t) \leq w(s^t) + B(s^{t-1}) R(s^{t-1}) + T(s^t) - B(s^t)$$
$$- \frac{\psi}{2} Y(s^t) \left(\frac{B(s^t)}{Y(s^t)} - \bar{b}(1+\bar{g})\right)^2,$$

where C is consumption of the only final good in the economy, B represents holding of the noncontingent bonds, and T are lump sum transfers from the profits of the intermediate good producers. The interest rate follows an AR(1);

---

[9] A firm with n products can become a firm with $n' \in (0, 2n)$ in one period, so at most it can double its size in one period.

[10] The condition that ensures that the mass of products is always equal to one is given by $\sum_{n=1}^{\infty} n\Omega_n(s^t) = 1$.

this is the second shock of the model. The last term in the borrowing constraint is a bond-holding cost used to eliminate nonstationary debt dynamics in small open economies, forcing the debt-to-output ratio to converge to $\bar{b}(1 + \bar{g})$ in the long run (Schmitt-Grohà and Uribe 2003); the parameter ψ is typically set to a small number that does not influence the dynamic properties of the model.[11] The stochastic discount factor of the household is given by:

$$m(s^{t+1}) = \beta \frac{C(s^t)}{C(s^{t+1})}. \tag{16}$$

In this simple model, the key determinant of the stochastic discount factor is the interest rate shock. In fact, as borrowing becomes more expensive, it is more taxing to stabilize consumption. Under a pure aggregate efficiency shock, borrowing can always be used to partially smooth consumption. A financial crisis is typically modeled as an increase in the interest rate coupled with a negative aggregate demand shock. To understand the effect of these crises in aggregate productivity, we need to understand how these shocks affect creative destruction—in particular, how their effect propagates in equations (7) and (8). Three objects determine this pass-through: (i) the stochastic discount factor, (ii) the next period value of a product line, and (iii) the current wage. Combining equations (13) and (12) we get:

$$w(s^t) = \frac{e^{z(s^t)} A(s^t)}{1 + \sigma}. \tag{17}$$

Therefore, when aggregate efficiency is low, aggregate output (equation (10)) and profits (equation (11)) decrease, but so does the wage (equation (17)). Therefore, given the high persistence of productivity shocks, as a first-order effect we expect the ratio of next period value of a product line and this period wage to be fairly stable in response to aggregate efficiency shocks. Moreover, as we discussed earlier, the stochastic discount factor is typically stable under pure aggregate efficiency shocks. Therefore, in this simple framework, aggregate efficiency shocks do not generate significant changes in creative destruction rate and therefore do not trigger significant hysteresis in productivity.[12] This is not the case for pure financial shocks. In fact, even

---

[11] The final good is the only tradable good. The model features endogenous trade and current account imbalances.

[12] Changes in preferences and the inclusion of other frictions can generate some pass-though, but the main economic force behind this stability is always present.

though interest rate shocks trigger only negligible effects in current profits and wages (Mendoza 1991), they generate wide swings on the stochastic discount factor, ultimately shaping the response of the rate of creative destruction. Thus, stationary interest rate shocks generate hysteresis in aggregate productivity. Therefore, models of creative destruction can rationalize why financial crises cast large shadows (Cerra and Saxena 2008; Reinhart and Rogoff 2009). These models also provide an endogenous connection between high interest rates and low productivity, a correlation typically assumed in the financial crises literature (Neumeyer and Perri 2005; Uribe and Yue 2006; Mendoza 2010).

3.3 Firm heterogeneity and model performance

The exposition so far has not levered all the power of the creative destruction framework. The literature of creative destruction has included rich heterogeneity that shapes macro dynamics and policy design (Acemoglu et al. 2018). This richness can be carried to the discrete-time DSGE literature, and it is just as important when studying financial crises. The tractability of the framework allows for heterogeneity beyond size and productivity. For instance, Ates and Saffie (2021) consider two types of firms that differ on the productivity advantage that they generate when they innovate in a given product, allowing for dynamic selection effects during crises. In fact, the model is able to replicate the firm-level dynamics exhibited in Chile during the 1998 financial crisis triggered by the Russian default. During the crisis, fewer firms enter but a larger fraction of the firms are high type. Selection also implies that high-type incumbents are less likely to exit during the crisis. This microfounded composition channel that shapes the productivity effect of a financial crisis cannot be modeled outside the creative destruction framework and was therefore absent in the DSGE literature based on Romer (1990). From a quantitative perspective, creative destruction is economically significant. Ignoring selection and firm dynamics overestimates the consumption equivalent welfare cost of the crisis by 60 percent.

For Ates and Saffie (2021), a financial crisis is a large exogenous shock to the interest rate. Newer-generation models of financial crises are based on Mendoza (2010), where an occasionally binding borrowing constraint triggers a financial crisis after a bad combination of shocks. These models can nest regular business cycles and large financial crises in a single framework. Benguria et al. (2022) show how creative destruction can be incorporated in these richer models of crises, further allowing for heterogeneous innovations, endogenous real exchange rate fluctuations, and exporting entry and exit at the intermediate product level consistent with Akcigit, Ates, and Impullitti (2018)—thereby showing that DSGE models with creative destruction can display rich firm heterogeneity and elaborated financial crises. We will use their results to illustrate the quantitative behavior of this class of models.

First, from a microeconomics perspective, the model generates well-defined size distributions. Because of data limitations, models of creative destruction have typically identified plants or patents with products when validating the size distribution (Akcigit and Kerr 2018). Benguria et al. (2022) have access to novel data for the portfolio of domestic and exporting products of Chilean manufacturing firms. Therefore, they use for the first time product-level data to validate their firm dynamic model. Figure 21.1 shows the (nontargeted) performance of the model in terms of the ergodic distribution. Panels a and b show that the model can replicate the product portfolio of exporters and non-exporter firms, and panel c shows that the model also mimics the overall firm-size distribution in terms of workers. Moreover, the model replicates firm-level product–portfolio dynamics during the Chilean sudden stop of 1998. Therefore, the creative destruction DSGE framework allows aggregate models to be estimated and validated using granular data.

Second, Figure 21.2 uses their financial crisis results to illustrate how these models can generate hysteresis and how firm heterogeneity shapes the response of endogenous productivity. Panel a shows the dynamics of GDP in the model on a window of four years around a sudden stop (SS) and compares it with the twenty-year trend that preceded the financial crisis. The model generates a boom before the crisis and persistent hysteresis in GDP even four years after the event. Panel b shows the source of this hysteresis. In fact, the productivity index deviates from its trend due to the slowdown in creative destruction during the crisis. The model in Benguria et al. (2022) features semi-endogenous growth so there is a convergence in productivity levels in the long-run.[13] Even under semi-endogenous growth, productivity is below its pre-crisis trend for thirty years. Third, the counterfactual analysis in panel b shows the role of heterogeneity when studying financial crises. The decrease in incumbents' efforts to enter the domestic market at the

---

[13] The foreign market grows exogenously and acts as an attractor for the small open economy.

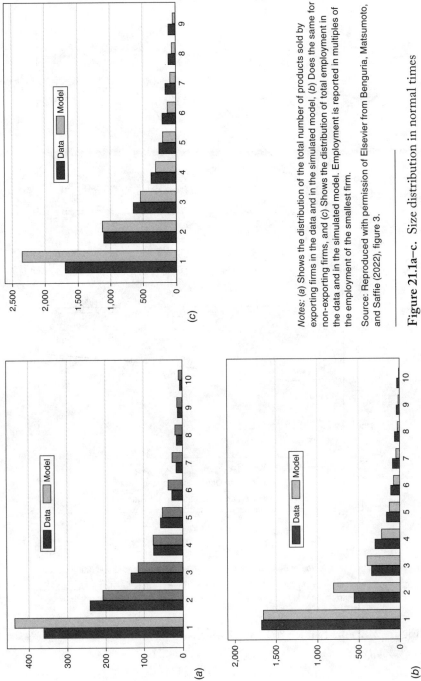

Notes: (a) Shows the distribution of the total number of products sold by exporting firms in the data and in the simulated model, (b) Does the same for non-exporting firms, and (c) Shows the distribution of total employment in the data and in the simulated model. Employment is reported in multiples of the employment of the smallest firm.

Source: Reproduced with permission of Elsevier from Benguria, Matsumoto, and Saffie (2022), figure 3.

Figure 21.1a–c. Size distribution in normal times

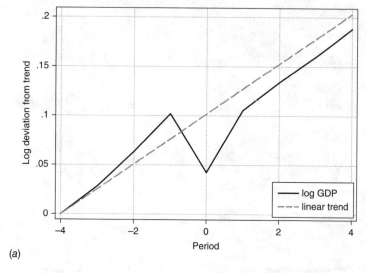

(a)

Reproduced with permission of Elsevier from Benguria, Matsumoto, and Saffie (2022), figure 8(b).

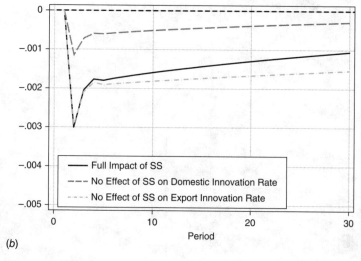

(b)

Reproduced with permission of Elsevier from Benguria, Matsumoto, and Saffie (2022), figure 9.

Notes: (a) Shows the path of GDP (in log deviation from trend) and its trend, (b) Uses alternative economies to illustrate the role of exporting and domestic innovation by incumbent firms.

Figure 21.2a–b. Sudden stops and hysteresis

product level drives the productivity drop in impact, whereas the effort of incumbents to start exporting their domestic products drives the recovery from the crisis.

In a nutshell, creative destruction can be incorporated into DSGE models without compromising the richness of its connection to granular data. Moreover, models of financial crises provide new avenues for studying the importance of firm heterogeneity when studying productivity dynamics.

3.4 Firm-level financial frictions

So far we have not deviated from the tractability of the Klette and Kortum (2004) model where the linearity of the value function on the number of products allows the researcher to abstract from the size distribution when solving the model. Nevertheless, size does matter for both innovation and finance. On the one hand, Akcigit and Kerr (2018) show that small firms are more productive and more intensive in R&D investment. Therefore, they introduce decreasing returns to scale in the production function of ideas depicted in equation (1). On the other hand, Gopinath et al. (2017) show that small firms are more financially constrained than large firms. They propose a size-based borrowing constraint at the firm level to capture this restriction. Both of these changes break the linearity of the value function. Although the literature has documented that financial frictions shape the business cycle properties of R&D, productivity, and the desirability of stabilization policies (e.g., Aghion et al. 2010, 2012; Aghion, Hemous, and Kharroubi 2014), firm-dynamic models with financial constraints and aggregate risk (e.g., Khan and Thomas 2013) have largely ignored the Schumpeterian forces of creative destruction. Because incorporating these firm-level frictions in quantitative models of firm dynamics and creative destruction with aggregate risk has been an elusive challenge, we conclude this chapter showing how the firm-level problem can be defined and solved using numerical methods.[14]

The incumbent problem in equation (5) can be modified to accommodate firm-level financial constraints and a cost advantage in innovation for small

---

[14] Schmitz (2021) solves a problem similar to the one depicted in this subsection. He simplifies the problem by assuming away the inter-temporal investment-saving decision at the firm level and assuming that incumbents can win or lose only one product per period.

firms. In particular, an incumbent firm chooses innovation intensity and debt holdings to solve the following recursive problem:

$$
V(S) = \max_{x(S),d'(S)} n\left[\pi(S) - w(S)\left(\frac{x(S)}{\xi}\right)^{\frac{1}{\gamma}} n^{\chi}\right] - (1+r)d + d'(S)
$$

$$
+ E_t\left[m(S')\sum_{\tilde{k}=0}^{n} B\left(\tilde{k}, n, \Delta\left(S\right)\right)\sum_{k=0}^{n} B\left(k, n, x(S)\right)V_{n-\tilde{k}+k}(S')\mid S\right]
$$
(18)

subject to:

$$
n\pi(s^t) - (1+r)\,d - nw\left(S\right)\left(x(S)\right)^{\xi}n^{\chi} \le d'(S) \le F(n),
$$
(19)

where $S = (r, z, d, n, \Phi(n, d))$ denotes the relevant state variables, including the joint distribution of debt and number of products $\Phi(n, d)$. Constraint (19) shows that the firm has to borrow to finance innovation effort if operational cash flows plus savings are not sufficient to cover the innovation cost. The constraint also shows that borrowing is limited and that the limit is a function of the size of the firm.[15] Note that the decreasing returns in the production of innovation ($\chi \in (0, 1)$) and the size-dependent borrowing constraint allow the model to encompass the findings of Akcigit and Kerr (2018) and Gopinath et al. (2017). These features also break the linearity of the value function such that size now matters: n firms each with one product and d debt stock each will make different decisions per product line than one firm with n products and $n * d$ total debt. The distribution $\Phi(n, d)$ is therefore needed to solve the model, because firms need to predict not only future wages but also aggregate growth and aggregate creative destruction. Therefore, to solve this problem, techniques akin to Krusell and Smith (1998) must be implemented.[16]

This framework is a promising avenue for studying how capital inflows might shift innovation toward larger and less-productive firms and away from small and more-productive firms, slowing down aggregate productivity growth. It can also be used to understand how precautionary motives generate resource-hoarding incentives among innovative firms. In fact, antici-

---

[15] In this model, a size constraint can also be interpreted as an earning-based constraint consistent with the evidence in Lian and Ma (2021) and Drechsel et al. (2023).

[16] A comparison of numerical methods can be found in Terry (2017).

pating a potential financial crisis, firms can postpone innovation to build a financial buffer.

4 Conclusion

Since the very beginning, finance was at the heart of Schumpeter's economic framework. Soon after the formalization of his growth theory by Grossman and Helpman (1991) and Aghion and Howitt (1992), the empirical literature showed that Schumpeter was right (King and Levine 1993) and that finance and growth cannot be studied in isolation. Innovation requires financing for an idea that has yet to produce value; therefore, saving and borrowing are essential for innovation. Moreover, innovation is forward looking in nature, and, thus, subject to the inter-temporal pounding of interest rates. This relationship is particularly important during financial crises, when capital is scarce and the future looks grim.

Recent developments in the empirical literature have used financial crises as quasi natural experiments to understand how finance can shape firm dynamics and creative destruction. Financial crises cast long shadows in output and productivity that last for decades. Because young and small firms are important drivers of productivity enhancement (Akcigit and Kerr 2018) and they are also more financially vulnerable (Gopinath et al. 2017), when liquidity is scarce we are likely to see sizable distortions to creative destruction.

As discussed by Aghion et al. (2018), the literature has struggled to jointly model financial frictions in Schumpeterian models of firm dynamics (Klette and Kortum 2004); therefore, quantitative models have lagged behind the richness of the recent empirical analysis linking finance and productivity. This chapter proposed a path forward that allows macro models with financial crises to incorporate rich creative destruction features and match firm dynamics. The key is to provide a tractable discrete-time framework that can be incorporated into large DSGE models (Ates and Saffie 2021). This framework not only can provide a micro foundation for the large shadows cast by financial crises, but it also can use granular data when estimating and validating DSGE models. Because the DSGE literature has been dominated by discrete-time models (Fernández-Villaverde and Guerrón-Quintana 2021), we propose a discrete-time version of the creative destruction literature. An interesting future avenue for research would be to use continuous-time DSGE models (Achdou et al. 2022) to nest models of creative destruction.[17]

The framework presented in this chapter can be used beyond the study of financial crises. For instance, monetary policy surprises also have persistent effects in output (Brunnermeier et al. 2021), and they trigger real effects through financial channels (Aghion, Hemous, and Kharroubi 2014; Aghion et al. 2019) especially in small and medium-sized firms (Caglio et al. 2021). Therefore, a rich creative destruction framework is likely to help us understand the long-run consequences of monetary policy and its optimal design. Some studies have used models based on Romer (1990) to study the financial channel of monetary policy (Moran and Queralto 2018; Garga and Singh 2021), contrasting their findings with aggregate VAR dynamics. Future research could consider using the Schumpeterian framework of creative destruction and firm dynamics to understand the role of heterogeneity and speak not just to the aggregate data but also to the granular evidence in the literature.

References

Acemoglu, D., U. Akcigit, H. Alp, N. Bloom, and W. Kerr. (2018). Innovation, reallocation, and growth. *American Economic Review*, 108(11):3450–3491.

Achdou, Y., J. Han, J.-M. Lasry, P.-L. Lions, and B. Moll. (2022). Income and wealth distribution in macroeconomics: A continuous-time approach. *Review of Economic Studies*, 89(1):45–86.

Aghion, P., U. Akcigit, and P. Howitt. (2014). What do we learn from Schumpeterian growth theory? In *Handbook of economic growth*, vol. 2, ed. P. Aghion and S. Durlauf, 515–563. Elsevier.

Aghion, P., U. Akcigit, and P. Howitt. (2015). Lessons from Schumpeterian growth theory. *American Economic Review*, 105(5):94–99.

Aghion, P., G.-M. Angeletos, A. Banerjee, and K. Manova. (2010). Volatility and growth: Credit constraints and the composition of investment. *Journal of Monetary Economics*, 57(3):246–265.

Aghion, P., P. Askenazy, N. Berman, G. Cette, and L. Eymard. (2012). Credit constraints and the cyclicality of R&D investment: Evidence from France. *Journal of the European Economic Association*, 10(5):1001–1024.

---

[17] This avenue is largely unexplored because the applications of continuous-time DSGE models have been mostly focused on heterogeneous household models with nominal frictions.

Aghion, P., E. Farhi, and E. Kharroubi. (2019). Monetary policy, product market competition and growth. *Economica*, 86(343):431–470.

Aghion, P., D. Hemous, and E. Kharroubi. (2014). Cyclical fiscal policy, credit constraints, and industry growth. *Journal of Monetary Economics*, 62:41–58.

Aghion, P., and P. Howitt. (1992). A model of growth through creative destruction. *Econometrica*, 60(2):323–351.

Aghion, P., P. Howitt, and R. Levine. (2018). Financial development and innovation-led growth. In *Handbook of finance and development*, ed. T. Beck and R. Levine. Edward Elgar.

Aghion, P., J. Van Reenen, and L. Zingales. (2013). Innovation and institutional ownership. *American Economic Review*, 103(1):277–304.

Akcigit, U., S. T. Ates, and G. Impullitti. (2018). Innovation and trade policy in a globalized world. NBER Working Paper 24543.

Akcigit, U., E. Dinlersoz, J. Greenwood, and V. Penciakova. (2019). Synergizing ventures. NBER Working Paper 26196.

Akcigit, U., and W. R. Kerr. (2018). Growth through heterogeneous innovations. *Journal of Political Economy*, 126(4):1374–1443.

Amable, B., J.-B. Chatelain, and K. Ralf. (2010). Patents as collateral. *Journal of Economic Dynamics and Control*, 34(6):1092–1104.

Ates, S. T, and J. Greenwood, et al. (2018). Beyond cash: venture capital, firm dynamics, and economic growth. Federal Reserve Board of Governors, unpublished paper.

Ates, S. T., and F. E. Saffie. (2021). Fewer but better: Sudden stops, firm entry, and financial selection. *American Economic Journal: Macroeconomics*, 13(3):304–356.

Barlevy, G. (2004). The cost of business cycles under endogenous growth. *American Economic Review*, 94(4):964–990.

Benguria, F., H. Matsumoto, and F. Saffie. (2022). Productivity and trade dynamics in sudden stops. *Journal of International Economics*, 139:103631.

Besley, T. J., I. A. Roland, and J. Van Reenen. (2020). The aggregate consequences of default risk: Evidence from firm-level data. NBER Working Paper 26686.

Brunnermeier, M., D. Palia, K. A. Sastry, and C. A. Sims. (2021). Feedbacks: Financial markets and economic activity. *American Economic Review*, 111(6):1845–1879.

Brunnermeier, M. K., and Y. Sannikov. (2016). Macro, money, and finance: A continuous-time approach. In *Handbook of Macroeconomics*, 2:1497–1545. Elsevier.

Caglio, C. R., R. M. Darst, and E. Kalemli-Özcan. (2021). Risk-taking and monetary policy transmission: Evidence from loans to SMEs and large firms. NBER Working Paper 28685.

Cerra, V., and S. C. Saxena. (2008). Growth dynamics: The myth of economic recovery. *American Economic Review*, 98(1):439–457.

Coimbra, N., and H. Rey. (2017). Financial cycles with heterogeneous intermediaries. NBER Working Paper 23245.

Comin, D., and M. Gertler. (2006). Medium-term business cycles. *American Economic Review,* 96(3):523–551.

Comin, D., N. Loayza, F. Pasha, and L. Serven. (2014). Medium term business cycles in developing countries. *American Economic Journal: Macroeconomics,* 6(4):209–245.

De Ridder, M. (2022). Intangibles investment and the persistent effect of financial crises on output. POID Working Paper 64. https://poid.lse.ac.uk /PUBLICATIONS/abstract.asp?index=9810.

Di Giovanni, J., S. Kalemli-Özcan, M. F. Ulu, and Y. S. Baskaya. (2017). International spillovers and local credit cycles. NBER Working Paper 23149.

Dinlersoz, E., S. Kalemli-Özcan, H. Hyatt, and V. Penciakova. (2019). Leverage over the firm life cycle, firm growth, and aggregate fluctuations. FRB Atlanta Working Paper No. 2019-18.

Drechsel T., et al. (2023). Earnings-based borrowing constraints and macroeconomic fluctuations. *American Economic Journal* (forthcoming) https://www .aeaweb.org/articles?id=10.1257/mac.20210099&from=f.

Duval, R., G. H. Hong, and Y. Timmer. (2020). Financial frictions and the great productivity slowdown. *Review of Financial Studies,* 33(2):475–503.

Fernández-Villaverde, J., and P. A. Guerrón-Quintana. (2021). Estimating DSGE models: Recent advances and future challenges. *Annual Review of Economics,* 13:229–252.

Garga, V., and S. R. Singh. (2021). Output hysteresis and optimal monetary policy. *Journal of Monetary Economics,* 117:871–886.

Gavazzoni, F., and A. M. Santacreu. (2020). International R&D spillovers and asset prices. *Journal of Financial Economics,* 136(2):330–354.

Gertler, M., and P. Karadi. (2011). A model of unconventional monetary policy. *Journal of Monetary Economics,* 58(1):17–34.

Gopinath, G., S. Kalemli-Özcan, L. Karabarbounis, and C. Villegas-Sanchez. (2017). Capital allocation and productivity in south Europe. *Quarterly Journal of Economics,* 132(4):1915–1967.

Gornemann, N. (2014). Sovereign default, private investment, and economic growth. Job market paper.

Gornemann, N., P. Guerron-Quintana, and F. Saffie. (2020). Exchange rates and endogenous productivity. FRB International Finance Discussion Paper No. 1301.

Grossman, G. M., and E. Helpman. (1991). Quality ladders in the theory of growth. *Review of Economic Studies,* 58(1):43–61.

Guerron-Quintana, P. A., and R. Jinnai. (2019). Financial frictions, trends, and the great recession. *Quantitative Economics,* 10(2):735–773.

Hallward-Driemeier, M., and B. Rijkers. (2013). Do crises catalyze creative destruction? Firm-level evidence from Indonesia. *Review of Economics and Statistics,* 95(1):1788–1810.

Hardy, B., and C. Sever. (2021). Financial crises and innovation. *European Economic Review,* 138:103856.

Hochberg, Y. V., C. J. Serrano, and R. H. Ziedonis. (2018). Patent collateral, investor commitment, and the market for venture lending. *Journal of Financial Economics*, 130(1):74–94.

Kalemli-Özcan, S. (2019). US monetary policy and international risk spillovers. NBER Working Paper 26297.

Kalemli-Özcan, S., L. Laeven, and D. Moreno. (2018). Debt overhang, rollover risk, and corporate investment: Evidence from the European crisis. NBER Working Paper 24555.

Khan, A., and J. K. Thomas. (2013). Credit shocks and aggregate fluctuations in an economy with production heterogeneity. *Journal of Political Economy*, 121(6):1055–1107.

King, R. G., and R. Levine. (1993). Finance and growth: Schumpeter might be right. *Quarterly Journal of Economics*, 108(3):717–737.

Klette, T. J., and S. Kortum. (2004). Innovating firms and aggregate innovation. *Journal of Political Economy*, 112(5):986–1018.

Krusell, P., and A. A. Smith Jr. (1998). Income and wealth heterogeneity in the macroeconomy. *Journal of Political Economy*, 106(5):867–896.

Levine, R. (2005). Finance and growth: Theory and evidence. In *Handbook of Economic Growth*, vol. 1, ed. P. Aghion and S. Durlauf, 865–893. Elsevier.

Lian, C., and Y. Ma. (2021). Anatomy of corporate borrowing constraints. *Quarterly Journal of Economics*, 136(1):229–291.

Manaresi, F., and M. N. Pierri. (2019). Credit supply and productivity growth. IMF Working Paper 2019-107.

Mann, W. (2018). Creditor rights and innovation: Evidence from patent collateral. *Journal of Financial Economics*, 130(1):25–47.

Mendoza, E. G. (1991). Real business cycles in a small open economy. *American Economic Review*, 81(4):797–818.

Mendoza, E. G. (2010). Sudden stops, financial crises, and leverage. *American Economic Review*, 100(5):1941–1966.

Meza, F., and E. Quintin. (2007). Factor utilization and the real impact of financial crises. *B.E. Journal of Macroeconomics*, 7(1).

Moran, P., and A. Queralto. (2018). Innovation, productivity, and monetary policy. *Journal of Monetary Economics*, 93:24–41.

Neumeyer, P. A., and F. Perri. (2005). Business cycles in emerging economies: The role of interest rates. *Journal of Monetary Economics*, 52(2):345–380.

Penciakova, V. (2018). Diversification and risky innovation among US firms. FRB Atlanta, Google Scholar.

Pratap, S., and C. Urrutia. (2012). Financial frictions and total factor productivity: Accounting for the real effects of financial crises. *Review of Economic Dynamics*, 15(3):336–358.

Queralto, A. (2020). A model of slow recoveries from financial crises. *Journal of Monetary Economics*, 114:1–25.

Reinhart, C. M., and K. S. Rogoff. (2009). The aftermath of financial crises. *American Economic Review*, 99(2):466–472.

Rey, H. (2013). Dilemma not trilemma: The global cycle and monetary policy independence. *Jackson Hole Symposium Proceedings*.

Romer, P. M. (1990). Endogenous technological change. *Journal of Political Economy*, 98(5, Part 2):S71–S102.

Schmitt-Grohé, S., and M. Uribe. (2003). Closing small open economy models. *Journal of International Economics*, 61(1):163–185.

Schmitz, T. (2021). Endogenous growth, firm heterogeneity and the long-run impact of financial crises. *European Economic Review*, 132:103637.

Terry, S. J. (2017). Alternative methods for solving heterogeneous firm models. *Journal of Money, Credit and Banking*, 49(6):1081–1111.

Uribe, M., and V. Z. Yue. (2006). Country spreads and emerging countries: Who drives whom? *Journal of International Economics*, 69(1):6–36.

CHAPTER 22

Creative Destruction, Finance, and Firm Dynamics

MURAT ALP CELIK

1 Introduction

New ideas are the engine of sustained economic growth, and the creative destruction that ensues in their wake is one of the primary drivers of firm and industry dynamics. Sometimes these new ideas manifest as small yet continuous improvements in how we combine inputs into outputs in a more efficient manner. At other times, innovations can disrupt entire industries, or better yet, lead to the generation of completely new ones. At the firm level, a new invention can help a firm outshine its competitors; and at the country level, technology is what separates developed countries from developing ones, with all the implications it carries for living standards. Given these observations, it is not possible to overemphasize the importance of new ideas for social welfare and progress.

The processes through which these new ideas are generated and embedded in economic activity, however, are by no means simple or free of problems. From the very possibility of an idea's generation to its eventual use in production, there are several steps the idea must go through, each laden with various inefficiencies. Identifying and alleviating these inefficiencies has been a significant research area for economists since the pathbreaking contribution of Philippe Aghion and Peter Howitt (Aghion and Howitt 1992), and one of the pillars of endogenous growth theory. In this chapter I will seek

611

to provide a broad overview of these various inefficiencies and highlight areas that require more scrutiny in future research, with a particular emphasis on how finance and firm dynamics affect the discovery of new ideas, and the creative destruction they cause.

To tally the major steps of the generation of economic growth through new ideas, it helps to imagine a hypothetical idea, and contemplate its life cycle and the associated problems:

- Ideas come into existence only as a result of the mental effort of those who conceive them. However, those with the ability, training, and resources to come up with new ideas are scarce. Can financial frictions and other distortions faced by individuals affect the size and the quality of the pool of innovators?

- The generation of an idea is insufficient for it to affect economic growth. It must be incarnated in a service or product, or enhance a process. This can require considerable investment and funding, which the owner of an idea might not possess due to financial frictions. Can financial frictions faced by firms affect the efficiency and speed at which ideas are integrated into production?

- Ideas might not always occur to, or be owned by, their best users. Sometimes the owners might not have the funds or the infrastructure to commercialize the ideas. At other times, the technological fit between ideas and their owners might be too low, due to the serendipitous nature of innovation. Some firms might also want to acquire innovations developed by other firms, instead of relying on in-house research and development (R&D). A market for ideas exists to resolve the inefficiencies in the ownership of ideas, where they can be reallocated through licensing agreements, patent sales, or wholesale acquisition of one firm by another. What are the inefficiencies inherent in these markets, and how important are they?

In the remainder of this chapter, I will focus on each step in this extensive, yet inevitably incomplete, list. Section 2 scrutinizes the role of financial frictions on the selection of inventors. Section 3 focuses on the impact of financial frictions faced by firms on their discovery and commercialization of new ideas, and presents a new endogenous growth model with collateral constraints. Section 4 considers the various inefficiencies in the market for ideas and mergers and acquisitions (M&A) between innovative firms. Section 5 concludes.

2 The Selection of Inventors and Financial Frictions

Every idea has an innovator. However, not every person has the chance to become an innovator. Inventors of patents, scientists who produce break-through research, and entrepreneurs who implement new business ideas constitute a small and selected population. This selection is influenced to a great degree by financial considerations, be it the availability of parental resources, funds to acquire necessary training, or the capital needed to finance new prototypes or startups. These bottlenecks can influence both the quality and the quantity of ideas a society can come up with.

Allocation of talent—assigning the right people to the right jobs—can have a first-order effect on the productivity of a society. The susceptibility of the allocation mechanism to be distorted away from the socially optimal outcome by private expenditures might create significant welfare losses in the presence of high levels of inequality in private resources. The losses are especially magnified if the best and the brightest of a society are not allocated to the professions where their social contribution would be the greatest. Scientists and inventors, as producers of new knowledge and inventions, are certainly among the professions where this effect might be the greatest, since they produce public goods that everyone can benefit from.

Consider the example of Albert Einstein. As a scientist and inventor, he produced more than 300 scientific papers and 50 patented inventions. His groundbreaking contributions in the field of physics have birthed a paradigm shift, and led to the discovery of countless new ideas and inventions. However, he did not become such a prolific innovator in a vacuum. His father, Hermann Einstein, was a rich salesman and engineer, and owned his own company, which manufactured electrical equipment based on direct current. Thanks to his parental background, Albert Einstein was able to receive education in various high-quality schools in Germany, Italy, and Switzerland, including his alma mater, ETH Zurich. How would the world look today if Einstein had not been able to receive the necessary education to be a scientist and an inventor, and became a factory worker instead? Better yet, how do we know if we are not missing out on potential Einsteins right now?

Over the past decade, several papers have investigated which people become inventors, and which inventors turn out to be the most prolific, using data from a variety of sources. Using inventor, patent, and census data from the United States, Celik (2023) finds that individuals from richer backgrounds are much more likely to become inventors, but this is not true for those from more educated backgrounds. At the same time, conditional on becoming an inventor, those from more educated backgrounds turn out to be much more prolific inventors, as measured using a wide array of inventor productivity metrics, whereas those from richer backgrounds exhibit no such aptitude. Interestingly, this high predictive power of family background is despite the use of surname-level information from two to three generations ago, implying that social mobility is quite low when it comes to what determines a person's likelihood to become an inventor. Using social security data from the United States, Bell, Chetty, Jaravel, Petkova, and Van Reenen (2019) also find that individuals from higher-income families are more likely to become inventors. Aghion, Akcigit, Hyytinen, and Toivanen (2018) use a richer data set from Finland, where individuals are directly linked to their parents and, in the case of men, IQ test results. They also show that parental income has a significant predictive power for who becomes an inventor, even when controlling for IQ test scores, but the positive correlation becomes economically insignificant once the education of the individual (i.e., having a PhD) is controlled for. Akcigit, Grigsby, and Nicholas (2017) report that the same holds even during the "golden age of innovation" in the United States in the 1940s, showing that these patterns are not a recent phenomenon specific to the more recent data on inventors (1976+).

The documented positive correlation between who becomes an inventor and the income of their family, by itself, is not a direct cause for concern. If the unobserved ability has any intergenerational persistence—be it through nature or nurture—the observed correlation pattern would emerge even if the allocation of talent in innovation were perfectly meritocratic, as the parents of talented individuals would have a higher probability to be talented themselves compared to the population mean. A problem arises, however, if observable characteristics that predict performance as an inventor do not coincide with those that predict selection into the pool of inventors, as documented in Celik (2023). In the United States, those from more educated backgrounds are found to be more prolific inventors by a considerable margin, but they are not the ones who have an advantage in becoming inventors. On the other hand, some individuals from richer families who become inventors turn out to be quite mediocre after they make it into the profession. These correlation patterns suggest that the rich might have an advantage in giving their children a leg up in the competition to become an inventor.

A closer look at the data suggests pathways through which higher parental resources can help guarantee a higher probability to become an inventor, irrespective of talent. NSF National Survey of College Graduates (2003) reveals that two-thirds of the inventors in the United States have a graduate degree, of which half are PhDs. As seen in Aghion et al. (2018), even in Finland, which boasts a publicly funded education system, higher parental resources predict a higher probability of receiving a PhD. In the United States, the competition for receiving a prestigious degree is much fiercer. Parents spend considerable time and resources to improve the likelihood that their children will obtain the best credentials possible. The most direct way they can help is to pay the tuition and living expenses for prestigious colleges, which can be as high as 3–4 times the net wage of the median worker. But much more extravagant options exist as well. In a 2018 lawsuit, the New York–based private college counseling firm Ivy Coach was revealed to charge a client $1.5 million to help their child with applications to boarding school and college. Other families are known to found charitable nongovernmental organizations and install their child as the manager in an effort to give a boost to the noncurricular activities part of the child's school application. In such a high-stakes environment, it is difficult for talented individuals from poor families to compete on equal footing; they often have to brood over more ordinary problems such as whether they will be able to pay back their student loans after graduation even if they are admitted to their desired programs, or whether they should simply skip college and join the workforce instead.

To quantify the effects of the misallocation of talent in innovation due to differences in parental resources and to analyze potential policy changes that can alleviate the inefficiency, Celik (2023) develops an endogenous growth model with a rich household side in the vein of heterogeneous agents models such as Aiyagari (1994). The households are heterogeneous in wealth, education, and unobserved innate ability that is persistent across generations. Parents invest in the education of their offspring and leave bequests. The training necessary to become an inventor is scarce; hence, individuals compete against each other in a tournament setting to receive it. Factors that improve inventor productivity, such as innate ability and education, increase the probability of receiving this training, but so does private credentialing spending, which is unproductive by itself. Thus, through excessive spending on credentialing, individuals who inherit generous bequests can become inventors even if they are of mediocre talent, preventing more talented individuals from poorer backgrounds from becoming inventors. This is individually rational but socially inefficient, as it reduces the quality of the inventor pool used in generating productivity-improving innovations that drive economic growth in the absence of intervention. The estimated model suggests that shutting down the channel for unproductive credentialing spending would achieve an increase of 21 basis points in long-run growth, and a 6 percent increase in consumption-equivalent welfare, through allocating the most talented individuals to the professions where their contribution will be the greatest.

Finding policies that can alleviate misallocation of talent in a decentralized economy is tougher. While changes in college admission standards could in theory reduce the friction, it is unlikely to completely counteract the advantages conferred to individuals who originate from rich families over the "missing Einsteins" from underprivileged backgrounds. The mismatch between talent and wealth lies at the heart of the problem—if the talented and the wealthy coincided perfectly, a near-perfect allocation of talent would arise despite the unproductive spending on the credentialing rat-race. Motivated by this observation, Celik (2023) considers progressive taxation of bequests and inter vivos transfers coupled with lump-sum transfers, and finds that this policy could achieve one-quarter of the previously mentioned gain in long-run growth at 5 basis points. Increasing the amount of scholarships available for tuition and living expenses for talented applicants could be another, more targeted policy. Any potential policy, however, has to compete with alternative policies that could prove equally worthwhile in boosting innovation and economic growth. Akcigit, Pearce, and Prato (2020) study the optimal allocation of funds between R&D subsidies and public investment in higher education using Danish micro-data. They find that a combined policy works best, and that education policy would be more effective in societies with high income inequality, for which the United States would be an example.

3 Financing the Discovery and Development of Ideas

Coming up with an idea does not enhance productivity by itself. It must first be implemented and commercialized, and made a part of the system of production. It must be refined by follow-up research and development efforts so that the idea can manifest as a new product or service, or improve existing production processes. All of these can require a substantial amount of funds, which might be hard to come by, especially for small or young firms. As a result, financial frictions can potentially reduce or delay the incorporation of new ideas into the economy.

There exists an extensive literature that studies the effects of financial frictions on firm investment and dynamics. Prominent papers include Kiyotaki and Moore (1997), Jeong and Townsend (2007), Buera (2009), Amaral and Quintin (2010), Buera, Kaboski, and Shin (2011), Buera and Shin (2013), Midrigan and Xu (2014), Moll (2014), and Cole, Greenwood, and Sanchez (2016). Despite the extensive literature, the interactions of financial frictions and innovation have received comparatively less attention on the theory front compared to firms' investment in tangible assets, such as land, plants, machinery, vehicles, and so on. Financing for innovation is quite different from that for tangible assets. Innovation is oftentimes a very risky process that can fail to generate any value, which would make any potential investor anxious to begin with. Even when successful, the resultant ideas can be patented, but patents are much harder to value and transfer than tangible assets, making them less effective as collateral to finance future investment. All these factors separate the financing of innovation from more tangible types of investment available to firms. In the rest of this section, I will develop a simple model to highlight these differences, and discuss their implications.

3.1 A simple model of innovation under financial frictions

3.1.1 Overview

Time is continuous and denoted by $t \geq 0$. At any point in time, there is a mass $M_t > 0$ of firms that own a mass $N_t > 0$ of product lines. Individual firms own a collection of product lines. Each product line allows a firm to use physical capital as an input to produce the final good. Production exhibits decreasing returns to scale. The final good is sold in a competitive market. Firms are subject to financial frictions. The amount of physical capital a firm can use depends on the equity of a firm, which is modeled as a collateral constraint. Firms can add new product lines to their portfolio through successful innovation. Firms increase their chance of success in innovation through R&D investment. R&D expenses reduce a firm's equity, which in turn tightens the collateral constraint. Firms can also lose product lines due to obsolescence or creative destruction by competing firms. Accumulation of product lines over time results in endogenous long-run growth.

3.1.2 Production

Consider a firm indexed by $j \in [0, M_t]$ that owns $n_{j,t} \in \mathbb{N}^+$ product lines at time t. Let these product lines be indexed by $i \in \{1, 2, \ldots, n_{j,t}\}$. At time t and for each product line i, the firm can use physical capital $k_{i,t}$ to produce the final good $y_{i,t}$ according to the technology

$$y_{i,t} = z k_{i,t}^\alpha \tag{1}$$

with $z > 0$ and $\alpha \in (0,1)$. The final good is sold in a competitive market, and its price is normalized to one. Each unit of physical capital has the cost flow $R_t = r_t + \delta$, where r_t is the real interest rate, and $\delta > 0$ is the depreciation rate of physical capital. At time t, the total output of firm i is given by $y_{j,t} = \sum_{i=1}^{n_{jt}} y_{i,t}$, and the total output in the economy is therefore:

$$Y_t = \int_{j=0}^{M_t} y_{j,t}\, dj = \int_{j=0}^{M_t} \left(\sum_{i=1}^{n_{j,t}} z k_{i,t}^\alpha \right) dj. \tag{2}$$

3.1.3 Innovation, creative destruction, obsolescence, and firm exit

Over time, firms can add new product lines to their portfolio through successful innovation, or lose them to obsolescence. Each product line owned by the firm grants the firm the ability to invest resources into R&D to generate a Poisson arrival rate of successful innovation $x_{i,t} > 0$. To generate this arrival rate, the firm incurs an R&D cost flow in terms of the final good given by the cost function

$$C(x_{i,t}) = \chi x_{i,t}^\phi \tag{3}$$

where $\chi > 0$ is a scale parameter and $\phi > 1$ determines the convexity. On the other hand, each product line owned by the firm can be lost to obsolescence at the exogenous Poisson arrival rate $\tau^0 > 0$, or endogenous creative destruction by other firms $\tau_t^{cd} \geq 0$, resulting in a total rate of $\tau_t = \tau^o + \tau_t^{cd}$. Taken together, at any time t, a firm j with $n_{j,t}$ product lines adds a new product line to its portfolio at the rate $x_{j,t} = \sum_{i=1}^{n_{j,t}} x_{i,t}$, and loses one of its existing product lines at the rate $\tau_t n_{j,t}$. The number of product lines of a firm grows or shrinks over time according to these two forces. If a firm loses its last product line, it exits the economy. Finally, assume that $\Upsilon \in (0,1)$ fraction of successful product line creations are destructive, and the remaining $1-\Upsilon$ fraction create a new product line without destroying existing ones.

3.1.4 Financial frictions and firm equity

In this section, financial frictions are introduced into the model. Denote the total capital used by firm j at time t as $k_{j,t} = \sum_{i=1}^{n_{j,t}} k_{i,t}$. Denote the equity of firm j at time t as $a_{j,t}$. At any time t, firm j faces the collateral constraint given by

$$k_{j,t} \le \lambda a_{j,t} \tag{4}$$

where $\lambda \ge 1$ is a parameter that governs the maximum leverage $k_{j,t}/a_{j,t}$ a firm can have. The proposed specification of the collateral constraint is a common one that is used in Moll (2014), among others. By varying λ from unity to infinity, one can trace out all degrees of capital market efficiency from no capital markets to perfect capital markets. Due to this collateral constraint, firms with sufficiently low equity might produce less output than they otherwise would.

Financial frictions make it necessary to keep track of a firm's equity as a state variable. The equity of a firm evolves according to the ordinary differential equation:

$$\dot{a}_{j,t} = y_{j,t} - (r_t + \delta)k_{j,t} + r_t a_{j,t} - \sum_{i=1}^{n_{j,t}} C(x_{i,t}). \tag{5}$$

The first term is the revenue flow from production. The second term is the cost of using physical capital. The third term is the rent flow from equity. The last term is the cost of R&D. In cases where $k_{j,t} < a_{j,t}$, the firm is lending to other firms in the economy. In cases where $k_{j,t} > a_{j,t}$, the firm is leveraged, and borrowing from others. It is imposed that a firm's equity cannot go below zero.

3.1.5 Firm entry

At any point in time, there is a continuum of entrepreneurs of measure one who can potentially found a new firm. New firms start with a single product line, and an initial amount of equity $\underline{a} > 0$ must be invested into the firm. In order to generate a Poisson arrival rate e_t of successful firm creation, an entrepreneur must incur an R&D cost flow in terms of the final good given by

$$C_e(e_t) = v\left(\frac{e_t}{M_t}\right)^\epsilon, \tag{6}$$

where $v > 0$ is a scale parameter and $\epsilon > 1$ governs the convexity. Recall that M_t is the measure of firms in the economy at time t. An increase in M_t lowers the cost of new firm creation. A common feature in endogenous growth models, this term is interpreted as knowledge spillovers from incumbent firms to the entrants, and ensures the existence of a balanced growth path equilibrium.[1]

3.1.6 Static profit maximization of incumbent firms

The static profit maximization problem of the incumbent firm j at time t is stated as:

$$\Pi\left(n_{j,t}, a_{j,t}\right) = \max_{\{k_{i,t}\}_{i=1}^{n_{j,t}}} \left\{\sum_{i=1}^{n_{j,t}}\left(zk_{i,t}^\alpha - (r_t + \delta)k_{i,t}\right)\right\} \tag{7}$$
$$\text{subject to } \sum_{i=1}^{n_{j,t}}k_{i,t} \le \lambda a_{j,t}$$

The first thing to notice is that the first-order conditions with respect to $k_{i,t}$ for any i are identical, which implies $k_{i,j} = k_{j,t}/n_{j,t}$ for all i; i.e., the total capital used by the firm is split equally across all product lines. If the collateral constraint does not bind, optimality equates the marginal product of capital to its cost, which delivers:

$$k_{i,t} = \left(\frac{r_t + \delta}{\alpha z}\right)^{\frac{1}{\alpha-1}} \equiv k_t^*. \tag{8}$$

The constraint binds when $\dfrac{a_{j,t}}{n_{j,t}} < \dfrac{k_t^*}{\lambda}$; or in words, when the equity per product line is insufficiently low to finance operating at the firm's efficient scale. In such cases, the firm levers up to the maximum extent possible,

---

[1] Alternatively, one could assume the mass of entrepreneurs to grow proportionally with the mass of incumbent firms to obtain isomorphic results. One could interpret this as spinoffs from incumbent firms.

which delivers $k_{i,t} = \lambda \dfrac{a_{j,t}}{n_{j,t}} < k_t^*$. Note that, regardless of whether the con-

straint binds or not, the optimal profit flow satisfies:

$$\Pi\left(n_{j,t}, a_{j,t}\right) = n_{j,t}\Pi\left(1, \frac{a_{j,t}}{n_{j,t}}\right). \tag{9}$$

3.1.7 Dynamic profit maximization of incumbent firms

Given the solution to the static problem, the incumbent firm must choose its innovation policies to maximize the value of the firm. Since the static profit flow depends on the number of product lines and equity, these are also state variables in the dynamic problem. Define $V(n,a)$ as the value of an incumbent firm that owns n product lines and has an equity of a. Then the dynamic profit maximization problem of this firm at time t is stated as:

$$\begin{aligned}
r_t V(n, a) = \max_{\{x_i\}_{i=1}^n} \Big\{ &\Pi(n, a) + r_t a - \sum_{i=1}^n C(x_i) \\
&+ V_a(n, a)\left(\Pi(n, a) + r_t a - \sum_{i=1}^n C(x_i)\right) \\
&+ \left(\sum_{i=1}^n x_i\right)[V(n+1, a) - V(n, a)] \\
&+ n\tau_t[V(n-1, a) - V(n, a)]\Big\},
\end{aligned} \tag{10}$$

where some subscripts are suppressed for clarity. The first three terms are the static profit, equity rent, and R&D cost flows, respectively. The fourth term captures the influence of the change in equity a on firm value. The fifth term accounts for the change in firm value conditional on adding a new product line as a result of successful innovation, whereas the sixth term accounts for the same conditional on losing a product line to obsolescence.

Similar to the static problem, the first-order conditions with respect to x_i for all i are identical, so it can be asserted that $x_i = x$ for all i. The first-order condition with respect to this joint x then becomes:

$$(1 + V_a(n, a))C'(x) = [V(n+1, a) - V(n, a)]. \tag{11}$$

The left-hand side is the marginal cost of innovation, and the right-hand side is the marginal benefit. In a model without financial frictions, the term $V_a(n, a)$

would not exist. Its presence captures the fact that investing resources into R&D also reduces equity, which may decrease static profits $\Pi(n, a)$ whenever the collateral constraint binds. This increases the effective cost of R&D for financially constrained firms. The policy function for x is given by:

$$\hat{x}(n, a) = \left(\frac{V(n+1, a) - V(n, a)}{\chi\phi(1 + V_a(n, a))} \right)^{\frac{1}{\phi-1}}. \tag{12}$$

3.1.8 Entrepreneurs' new firm creation problem

Given the mass M of firms active in the economy, define the value of being an entrepreneur as $W(M)$. The dynamic new firm creation problem of the entrepreneurs at time t is stated as:

$$r_t W(M) - W'(M)g_{M,t} = \max_e \{-C_e(e_t) + e(V(1, \underline{a}) - \underline{a})\}, \tag{13}$$

where $g_{M,t}$ is the growth rate of the mass of firms M_t at time t. The first term in the maximization is the R&D cost needed to found a new firm. The second term is the expected flow value from founding one. If the entrepreneur is successful, it founds a new firm with a single product line, and must invest into the firm an initial amount of equity $\underline{a} > 0$. The optimal policy for e is therefore:

$$\hat{e}(M) = M \left(\frac{V(1, \underline{a}) - \underline{a}}{v\epsilon} \right)^{\frac{1}{\epsilon-1}}. \tag{14}$$

3.1.9 Interpreting the model results and its implications

The proposed model combines an endogenous growth model with a financial frictions framework that uses collateral constraints, which leads to some interactions that the two models would not generate in isolation. I will discuss these interactions in the same order as the model is solved.

First, the static profit flow of a firm would depend only on the number of product lines $n_{j,t}$ without a collateral constraint. Its introduction reduces the profit flow of the firm when the constraint binds, resulting in a profit stream that depends on both the number of product lines, $n_{j,t}$, and the equity per product line, $a_{j,t}/n_{j,t}$, since the maximum capital that can be used in each product line is $k_{i,t} = \lambda \dfrac{a_{j,t}}{n_{j,t}}$. Statically, this resulting inefficiency is the same as that found in standard models with financial frictions: To maximize static output, a social planner would distribute capital equally across all product lines, since they all share a common productivity z; i.e., $k_{i,t} = K_t / N_t$, $\forall i$. Any dispersion away from this allocation reduces the level of output. Different from standard models with financial frictions, the dispersion also affects the dynamic decisions of the incumbent firms and entrepreneurs, which I will discuss next.[2]

Consider the dynamic innovation decision of the incumbent firms, and the associated first order condition given in equation (11). If the collateral constraint is removed, the first-order condition would simply read:

$$C'(x) = [V(n+1) - V(n)] \tag{15}$$

instead of

$$(1 + V_a(n, a))C'(x) = [V(n+1, a) - V(n, a)]. \tag{16}$$

The first difference is seen on the marginal benefit side. Since the static profit flow depends not only on the number of product lines n, but also on whether there is enough equity a to rent a sufficient amount of physical capital, firms with different amounts of equity per product line a/n face a different marginal benefit from expanding into a new product line, despite the fact that its productivity is homogeneous at z for all firms and their product lines. Consequently, although the social value of expansion into a new product line is the same, firms face different private marginal benefits due to the dispersion in a/n across firms. This constitutes a dynamic inefficiency, where firms can under- or over-invest in expansion compared to what a social planner would choose. To provide a real-world example, consider a firm with very low equity per product line a/n compared to the economy average. From a dynamic efficiency point of view, we would want this firm to invest into expansion as much as any other firm. However, since this firm's a/n is low, the new product line would be worth much less in private, as the firm does not have the funds to spare to finance production. This reduces innovation

---

[2] Note that the dispersion of a/n in the basic model owes only to the randomness in gaining new product lines conditional on successful innovation, and losing them due to creative destruction. In reality, firms face additional volatility in earnings unrelated to innovation. The model can be extended to capture these additional channels that generate further dispersion in a/n, such as assuming that the productivity constant $z > 0$ follows a Markov process as in Ocampo-Diaz and Herreno (2021), introducing capital depreciation shocks as in Jungherr, Meier, Reinelt, and Schott (2020), or other Poisson events that represent unexpected cash inflows and outflows in general.

by highly financially constrained firms, whereas financially unconstrained firms might invest too much in innovation, as their private benefit might even exceed the social benefit a planner would consider. Taken together, these results suggest that financial frictions can decrease both overall spending on innovation (private benefits < public benefits), and misallocate innovation spending across product lines and firms, given a fixed amount of spending (public benefit is homogeneous, but private benefits are dispersed due to the cross-firm dispersion in a/n).

The second difference is seen on the marginal cost side. In the absence of financial frictions, the term $V_a(n, a)C'(x)$ would not be present. This term captures the fact that investment in R&D steals away resources that could be used to finance production. Each dollar spent on expanding into new product lines reduces the equity of the firm, and if the collateral constraint is binding, this reduces firm value because, going forward, the firm will need to rent less capital than it otherwise would. This extra term is less troublesome for firms that already have enough equity to finance their production. But for highly constrained firms with a low a/n, the private cost they face is also higher than it should be. In other words, the dispersion in a/n across firms creates a dispersion in the private marginal cost of innovation that wouldn't exist in a model without a collateral constraint. This means the innovation incentives of firms with low equity per product line are hurt on both accounts: their private benefits from expansion are lower than socially optimal, and their private cost to do so is higher than socially optimal. The dispersion in a/n can therefore also depress overall innovation, and misallocate it across firms due to the dispersion in private marginal costs.[3]

Finally, the financial frictions also affect the entrepreneurs' decisions to found new businesses. In a model without the collateral constraint, the new firm would simply be worth $V(1)$. In the current model, it is worth $V(1, \underline{a}) - \underline{a}$. To the extent the initial equity per product line $\underline{a}$ is lower than k^*/λ, the

---

[3] It also bears mentioning that the model with financial frictions can generate underinvestment in innovation compared to the first-best under no financial frictions even in the absence of dispersion in a/n when the total amount of funds available is sufficiently low. In such a scenario, the constraint would bind for all firms simultaneously, and all firms would underinvest. The dispersion in a/n causes further underinvestment in total innovation as a result of misallocating the limited amount of funds available. This is akin to how a positive average markup with no markup dispersion still generates a reduction in output, whereas dispersion in markups generates misallocation of inputs and further depresses total output in models with imperfect competition in the product market.

initial profit flow will suffer until the firm can build up its equity. Further-more, the need to finance both R&D and future production using equity also depresses the equilibrium value of the firm value function $V(n,a)$ itself due to a lower option value arising from the possibility of future expansion. Consequently, the inequality $V(1, \underline{a}) - \underline{a} < V(1)$ holds for any finite value of $\lambda > 0$.[4] Overall, the financial frictions reduce the initial value of new businesses and lower new business entry and, consequently, lower both business dynamism and economic growth.

3.2 Relating the results to the existing literature on financial frictions

How do the results obtained from the proposed model mesh with and compare against what we already know from earlier work on financial frictions? What new insights do we obtain by endogenizing productivity growth? Are there any lessons from the existing literature that do not hold anymore?

To answer these questions, it helps to remember how firm productivity is modeled in the existing literature on financial frictions and firm investment. In general, there are two approaches. One is to draw a firm's productivity from a fixed distribution, such as the Pareto distribution, after which it either never evolves or is redrawn from the same distribution with some probability, as in Buera and Shin (2013). Another approach is to assume that the firm's productivity evolves according to an exogenously specified Markov process (as in Moll 2014), which is commonly chosen to be a first-order autoregressive process (AR(1)). Some papers, such as Midrigan and Xu (2014), combine the two approaches, where the productivity of a firm has both a permanent component and a persistent yet stochastic one (finite-state Markov process).

---

[4] To see why this is the case, first note that $V(1,a) - a \leq V(1)$ is true for any a. The subtraction of a eliminates the rent flow ra, and the cash flows on both sides become static profit flow minus R&D cost. As shown in Section 3.1.6, $\Pi(n,a) \leq \Pi(n)$, since $\Pi(n)$ is the value where firm can pick the optimal k^* without any constraints. For any finite value of $\lambda > 0$ and any a, there exists $n \in \mathbb{N}^+$ such that $\frac{a}{n} < \frac{k^*}{\lambda}$, i.e., the constraint binds, and we have $\Pi(n,a) < \Pi(n)$. The probability that a firm can reach n product lines over a finite period of time T is always strictly positive under positive R&D spending, which $C'(0) = 0$ guarantees. Because the constraint strictly binds over a positive measure of future histories given any finite $\lambda > 0$, we conclude $V(1, \underline{a}) - \underline{a} < V(1)$. As one eliminates financial frictions by taking the limit $\lambda \to \infty$, the left-hand side converges to the right-hand side.

The common factor in all approaches is that the evolution of a firm's productivity is exogenous, and it cannot be influenced by the firms or the government. There can be heterogeneity in firm investment in capital, entry, and exit based on firm productivities; government policy can influence these investments and change the selection of firms; and consequently, total factor productivity and total output can change. However, there is no feedback in the reverse direction, and therefore no effect of financial frictions on the evolution of productivity and the resultant firm dynamics. The simple model outlined above shows that (i) financial frictions can cause dynamic underinvestment in innovation as well as misallocation of innovation spending across firms, which leads to a permanent drop in the growth rate of output and firm entry, as opposed to the static level effect present in existing models; and (ii) the need to spend resources on innovation itself reduces firm equity, and tightens the financial constraint of the firm, creating a feedback loop between a firm's investment in intangible and tangible capital. Because the welfare impact of even a small change in the growth rate of output tends to be substantial under common preferences, existing studies might be underestimating the negative impact of financial frictions at the aggregate level in the long run.

Another point of deviation is the rate at which firms can reach their efficient scale, if ever. A key lesson from the existing literature on financial frictions and firm investment is that, over time, firms can "save themselves out of the constraint." Consider a model where a firm draws a permanent productivity level from an exogenous distribution. Then, there exists a level of equity a^* with which the firm can attain its efficient scale k^*. Firms may start out with insufficient equity, but over time they can build up their equity so that the constraint no longer binds. In such a world, from the firm's perspective, financial constraints are a transitory problem, and at the aggregate level they are a problem only to the extent that existing firms are replaced by new firms with insufficient equity. The same lesson holds for models with a highly persistent Markov process for productivity.

By comparison, the efficient scale of a firm in the proposed model with endogenous growth is ever-increasing conditional on firm survival. It is not permanent, and there is no mean-reversion as would be the case for an AR(1) process. There is a permanent race between equity and the number of product lines. A firm that has high success in innovation finds itself routinely underfunded, as n grows ahead of a, and the financial constraint tightens.[5] A firm that is not successful in innovation or loses its product lines to creative destruction can attain its efficient scale, but receives a lackluster return on its excess equity, and is less profitable. Consequently, financial frictions become a permanent problem for all firms, rather than a transitory one, influencing their output and investment decisions throughout the firm's life cycle. At the aggregate level, older firms that had some time to build up their equity might still have binding collateral constraints if they had a growth spurt, amplifying the traditional static negative effect on total factor productivity and output in existing models.

To sum up, financial frictions, which were already recognized as a significant problem for aggregate productivity, might be even more detrimental for welfare if we take into account the endogenous firm investment in productivity. A quantitative investigation of how much the addition of the innovation margin matters seems to be a worthwhile research avenue.

3.3 Policy implications, further considerations, and alternative solutions

The proposed model demonstrates that even in a simple setting with firms that are ex ante homogeneous in their productive and innovative efficiency (same z, χ, and ϕ), financial frictions in the form of a collateral constraint can generate significant dynamic inefficiencies in the form of lower overall innovation, misallocation of R&D inputs across firms, and lower firm entry and business dynamism. Financially constrained firms operate below their efficient scale and invest less in innovation.

Directly tackling this problem would necessitate micro-management of firms' capital allocation or their equity levels, which cannot be easily accomplished in a decentralized economy. A less direct solution would be to address the underinvestment problem in innovation by differential R&D subsidies to firms contingent on observables that are correlated with their ability to fund their operations and research. In most countries, a significant portion of subsidies to research and development are not state-contingent—in other words, "one-size-fits-all" policies are predominant. However, we know that small and young firms face a higher difficulty in financing their operations and research because they did not have the time to build up their

---

[5] This problem is further magnified if firms are heterogeneous in their innovative efficiency χ, which is discussed in Section 3.3.

equity and "save themselves out of the constraint." Firms also differ in their access to equity finance, where publicly listed firms can ameliorate the problem by directly issuing new shares rather than relying on debt financing. It should then be possible to design R&D policies that favor more financially constrained firms by favoring smaller and younger private firms over well-established firms with easy access to debt and equity financing. While imperfect, such policies can still be welfare-enhancing.

It should also be kept in mind that the simple model abstracts away from many features, such as heterogeneity in firms' efficiency in innovation. If some firms were to be more efficient in innovation, they would be able to come up with more product lines during the same span of time, and that would further exacerbate the problem they face, as building up equity internally would be even harder, and their equity per product line would be lower. Their buildup of internal equity would simply not catch up to the speed at which they innovate. Another simplifying assumption is that all firms face the same collateral constraint. Taking the model seriously, this would mean that all firms would lever up to the maximum amount allowed when the constraint is binding. However, firms' leverage ratios show great variation for private firms, as found in Dinlersoz, Kalemli-Ozcan, Hyatt, and Penciakova (2018). Not only do small and young private firms have little equity; they also may face tighter limits on their possible leverage ratios, once again exacerbating the inefficiency.

Fortunately, there are also alternative solutions to circumvent or alleviate the negative effects of financial constraints on firm innovation. One method is to go public, so that the firm can use equity financing, as discussed before. However, going public has its costs, and the reduced concentration in firm ownership can aggravate the potential agency frictions between the owners and the managers, making corporate governance a potential concern. In particular, a manager might choose a suboptimal rate of innovation compared to what the firm's shareholders (or the society) prefer. Aghion, Van Reenen, and Zingales (2013) find that the presence of institutional owners among shareholders plays a key role in promoting innovation by better alignment of manager incentives. Celik and Tian (2023) find that managerial compensation structure is the key mechanism through which institutional ownership affects firm innovation. Institutional investors reduce the manager's influence over the determination of his contract, which results in a package richer in stock options, incentivizing a higher innovation rate, which is better for shareholders and society alike. Despite this alleviating effect, the agency frictions are found to remain substantial. Eliminating them can increase growth by 51 percent and welfare by 7.1 percent.

Another potential solution is venture capital (VC) and angel investors. The importance of VC in the US economy has surged over the past fifty years, from roughly $300 million in 1970 to $54 billion in 2015 (using 2009 dollars). Only a tiny fraction of firms have access to VC, and many of the selected companies become superstar firms, including household names such as Apple, Microsoft, Google, and Amazon. Greenwood, Han, and Sanchez (2022) investigate the relationship between venture capital and growth using an endogenous growth model incorporating dynamic contracts between entrepreneurs and venture capitalists, and find that VC significantly boosts innovation, productivity, employment growth, and welfare. Ates (2018) develops a dynamic general equilibrium model that incorporates an explicit VC market with search frictions, featuring endogenous selection and operational knowledge transfer between the VCs and the firms, and finds that one-third of the VCs' positive impact on economic growth arises from the operational knowledge channel. Akcigit, Dinlersoz, Greenwood, and Penciakova (2022) examine the VC market both empirically and theoretically, and find that the presence of venture capital, the degree of assortative matching between VCs and firms, and the taxation of VC-backed startups matter significantly for productivity growth.

Finally, if a firm does not have the resources to properly commercialize its new ideas, there are various methods through which ideas can be reallocated across firm boundaries, such as licensing and patent sales. In more extreme cases, a firm can choose to completely acquire another firm in order to obtain both the target's patent portfolio and its existing assets and employees, who possess the necessary familiarity with the ideas embedded in these patents. This reallocation of ideas through patent sales and mergers and acquisitions is the topic of Section 4.

4 Acquisition and Reallocation of Ideas and Synergistic Mergers

The generation of ideas can be a serendipitous process. New ideas may not always occur to their best potential users. In some cases this might simply be due to the innovator not having sufficient funds to translate it into a new service or product. At other times it might be an issue of technological fit.

The incarnation of an idea requires a vision or an application, and the know-how to implement it, which are often possessed by those who work in areas related to the end-use of an idea. Firms often develop ideas that are not close to their primary business activity, in which case transferring the idea to another firm with a better technological fit can generate positive value. This necessitates a market for ideas, where economic agents can buy and sell innovations, which has the potential to allocate ideas more efficiently.

A glimpse at the patent assignment data from the United States Patent and Trademark Office (USPTO) reveals that this is definitely not a rare phenomenon. Among all patents registered between 1976 and 2006 in the United States, 16 percent are sold at least once, and this number goes up to 20 percent for domestic patents. These high ratios are observed despite the fact that they do not include technology transfers through licensing agreements, or wholesale transfer of patents as a result of mergers and acquisitions. On the whole, these numbers suggest an active market for ideas in the United States.

Some natural questions to ask are how efficient the market for ideas is, and what the macroeconomic impact would be if its efficiency could be further improved. Akcigit, Celik, and Greenwood (2016) conduct an empirical analysis of patent sale micro-data in the United States, and develop a search-theoretic model of the market of ideas with endogenous growth, which is aimed to answer these questions.

The empirical findings lend credence to the story of technological fit: Patents are found to contribute more to a firm's stock market value if they are technologically closer to the owning firm—i.e., the technological distance between the patent and the firm's previously invented stock of patents, as captured by the citation frequencies between different technology classes, is lower. This finding indicates that incorporating ideas that are technologically closer to a firm's field of expertise yields higher benefits as captured by firm value. Consistent with this finding, firms are found to be more likely to sell a patent to another firm if it is technologically distant. Conditional on a patent sale, it is also true that the patents are technologically closer to their buyers than their sellers, indicating that patent sales improve the technological fit between ideas and their owners on average.

The market for ideas, however, is not without its problems. For economic progress, both the possibility and the speed of exchange are important. Buying and selling intellectual property is a difficult activity, because each patent represents a unique idea. It is not always readily apparent who the potential buyers and the competing sellers are, especially in situations where firms desire to keep their business strategies secret. Information asymmetry between the inventor of an idea and the potential buyers can also lead to further frictions where the buyers need to spend time and resources to assess the true value and technological fit of an idea. As a result of all these complications, the market for patents is found to be substantially illiquid, where the sale of a patent takes 5.5 years on average, with a large standard deviation of 4.6 years.

Akcigit, Celik, and Greenwood (2016) estimate their structural model to fit the above-mentioned facts and gauge the efficiency of the market for ideas. Its contribution to growth and welfare is found to be significant even under conservative assumptions. The calculations indicate that if the market for ideas were shut down, long-run growth would go down by 6 basis points, with a 1.18 percent consumption-equivalent welfare loss, despite the fact that the shutdown triggers increased in-house R&D to compensate. The gains from a more efficient market for ideas are found to be much more substantial. Allowing the sellers to find the perfect buyers through directed search increases growth by 11 basis points, and welfare by 2 percent. Increasing the contact rate to its maximum value—i.e., removing the huge delay in patent sales by increasing the matching efficiency—boosts growth by 94 basis points, which translates to a tremendous 14 percent gain in consumption-equivalent welfare. These findings suggest that there is significant room for improvement in the efficiency of the market for ideas, although the exact methods to do so remain elusive.

The market for ideas interacts closely with firm finance. The simple model in Section 3 highlighted how financially constrained firms might not be able to exploit their new products to their fullest extent even if technological fit was not an issue. Chiu, Meh, and Wright (2017) develop a theoretical model where this idea is taken to the extreme: Inventors can conduct R&D and come up with new inventions, but they lack the ability to commercialize them. Instead, they must sell their ideas to entrepreneurs who can use them in production. Entrepreneurs, on the other hand, must have cash on hand in order to buy an idea, which implies that financial frictions can hinder the efficiency of the market for ideas. A quantitative investigation of the magnitude of this effect might be a fruitful research avenue.

The interaction can also be in the opposite direction: Even though patents are harder to appraise and transfer than tangible assets, they can still be used as collateral, even if highly discounted due to the illiquidity of the market for ideas. Previously invented ideas can therefore act as collateral and relax the financial constraints a firm faces. Akcigit, Celik, Itenberg, and Ordonez (2016) document that around 10 percent of patents granted by the USPTO between the years 1980 and 2006 were pledged as collateral to secure credit at least once. This pledging intensity, on the other hand, is found to be quite heterogeneous across patent technology classes. Looking at the problem from a lender's point of view, the value of a patent as collateral hinges on the ease with which it can be liquidated in the case of a default. Liquidation, in turn, is easier if the patent market for the technology is more active. Consistent with this line of reasoning, it is found that the pledging intensity is higher in technology classes with a more active secondary market for patents, as captured by the number of potential buyers and the rate at which patents are bought and sold. This has further implications for the direction of technical change, as financial frictions are less severe in industries with more active patent markets, which is associated with higher firm entry and investment.

As mentioned before, another way ideas can be transferred between firms is the wholesale acquisition of one firm by another, instead of buying the patents piecemeal. Mergers and acquisitions are observed very frequently in industries such as health care and information and communication technologies, where startups consider a profitable acquisition as a successful end goal. Even among large public companies that engage in innovation, M&A is quite common: among publicly listed US firms that had at least one patent between the years 1980 and 2006, the annual probability of being acquired by another such firm is 1.91 percent. However, this market for wholesale acquisition of ideas through M&A is as ridden with frictions as the market for patents, if not more so, as acquirers find it challenging to assess the value of innovative targets under asymmetric information.

There are three aspects to consider: First, even if one ignores the additional difficulties inherent in appraising the intellectual property of target firms, finding a good target for M&A and conducting due diligence along more standard dimensions is a long and arduous process. David (2021) develops a search and matching model of mergers and acquisitions in general equilibrium, and uses it to evaluate the implications of merger activity for aggregate economic outcomes. In this framework, firms are heterogeneous in terms of their productivity, which is persistent outside M&A, but change endogenously according to a synergistic merger technology in the case of an acquisition. It is found that the efficiency of the M&A market contributes significantly to the level of aggregate output and consumption.

The second and third aspects to consider are the difficulties in the evaluation of intellectual property under information frictions, and how the activity in the M&A market affects the endogenous decisions of firms to innovate. Celik, Tian, and Wang (2022) develop and estimate a structural model of acquiring innovative firms under information frictions, featuring endogenous merger, innovation, and offer composition decisions. Different from David (2021), the information asymmetry is explicitly modeled, where acquirers face adverse selection risk due to the private information of the targets regarding the value of their own innovation. To quantify and discipline the effect of information frictions on M&A between innovative firms, Celik, Tian, and Wang (2022) rely on three empirical observations that shed more light on the interaction: First, the takeover exposure of firms is found to follow an inverted-U shape rather than an increasing relation in firm innovation stock, as more-innovative firms are more challenging to appraise, and the high adverse selection risk manifests as partial market failure. Consistent with this observation, more-innovative targets are more likely to turn down bids, indicating more cautious offers by acquirers due to the possibility of "lemons" accepting them, as in Akerlof (1978). Finally, in order to partly mitigate the adverse selection risk, acquirers can choose to make an offer that consists of more equity compared to cash so that the target shareholders also have some skin in the game. It is observed that the equity share of offers increases with target innovativeness, consistent with the theory. The model matches these regularities to gauge the magnitude of information frictions via indirect inference.

The quantitative results suggest that the information frictions in M&A are substantial. Specifically, it is estimated that due diligence by the acquirers helps reveal only 30 percent of the private information possessed by the targets, and thus, acquirers face severe adverse selection risk in purchasing innovative targets, creating substantial barriers to trade. Eliminating the information frictions is predicted to increase capitalized expected gain from M&A by around 60 percent. A more efficient M&A market also has an indirect effect on firm innovation, increasing average R&D intensity by 10 percent. The average productivity level increases due to an increase in both quality and quantity of M&A, as well as innovation, which results in a permanent 3 percent increase in output and social welfare.

There is, of course, also the "dark side" of M&A. While the above-mentioned papers focus on the synergy gains of M&A from reallocating ideas across firm boundaries, they do so under the assumption of perfect competition. In reality, a firm might want to acquire another for anticompetitive reasons, such as reducing current competition to increase its current market share, markups, and profits; or reducing future competition by buying out innovative rivals while they are still small—the "killer acquisitions" as in Cunningham, Ederer, and Ma (2021). Consequently, the antitrust authorities have to weigh the potential synergy gains from mergers against their anticompetitive impact on static product market competition, as well as dynamic competition in innovation. Cavenaile, Celik, and Tian (2021) build a unified framework that combines and generalizes the Schumpeterian step-by-step innovation framework with static oligopolistic competition models such as Atkeson and Burstein (2008) or Autor, Dorn, Katz, Patterson, and Van Reenen (2020), and dynamic industry equilibrium models as in Ericson and Pakes (1995), to study the effectiveness and the macroeconomic impact of antitrust enforcement in the United States. It is found that the existing antitrust policies do indeed promote growth and welfare, and that more stringent policies can boost these gains substantially. Interestingly, the dynamic effects of antitrust enforcement on growth and welfare are found to be an order of magnitude more important than the traditionally studied impact on static allocative efficiency through the reduction of markups and market concentration. The primary benefits of increased antitrust enforcement come through the reduction of the rate at which anticompetitive mergers occur, in which large superstars preemptively acquire innovative firms that can be potential rivals in the future. These anticompetitive mergers ensure the dominance of the incumbent firms, which reduce their innovation drastically after the acquisition, since they do not face intense dynamic competition anymore. These results highlight the importance of considering the dynamic effects in the regulation of industries: without taking innovation into account, evaluation would be constrained to the static analyses of the 1970s, which culminated in the seemingly out-of-date HHI-based antitrust policy guidelines followed by the Department of Justice and the Federal Trade Commission. New guidelines that directly target anticompetitive acquisitions and pay more attention to dynamic competition in innovation compared to static product market competition are likely to yield substantial gains in growth and welfare.

5 Conclusion

As the previous sections demonstrate, there are numerous bottlenecks in the process through which new ideas are discovered, reallocated, implemented, and utilized to eventually culminate in higher growth and welfare. The identification of these bottlenecks and their policy implications has been a very active research area in the past three decades, which owes its existence to the voluminous pathbreaking contributions on creative destruction, endogenous growth, and firm dynamics by Philippe Aghion and Peter Howitt. Our work as economists, however, is far from complete. Many important questions still remain unanswered, and direct solutions to most of the highlighted inefficiencies are yet to be found. It is likely to remain an active field of research in the foreseeable future.

Beyond the intellectual value of gaining a better understanding of these economic processes, the real-world application of the insights obtained can have far-reaching consequences. Slight changes in the rate of economic growth can deliver tremendous improvements in living standards over long periods of time, and therefore, the benefits to resolving the various inefficiencies that plague the process of innovation can justify large investments in time and resources.

It should be noted that many laws, regulations, and government policies that influence technological progress across the world were designed before the advent of the growing literature on endogenous growth and creative destruction. As is the case for antitrust regulation, many such policies are predicated on earlier economic models in which the long-run dynamics are lacking or altogether absent. The duty therefore falls to us to make the policymakers and the broader public aware of the advances in our understanding, and refine the policy implications that arise as a consequence. It is my hope that this combined volume will succeed in contributing toward this goal.

References

AGHION, P., U. AKCIGIT, A. HYYTINEN, AND O. TOIVANEN (2018): "The Social Origins of Inventors," NBER Working Paper 24110.

AGHION, P., AND P. HOWITT (1992): "A Model of Growth through Creative Destruction," *Econometrica*, 60(2), 323–351.

AGHION, P., J. VAN REENEN, AND L. ZINGALES (2013): "Innovation and Institutional Ownership," *American Economic Review*, 103(1), 277–304.

AIYAGARI, S. R. (1994): "Uninsured Idiosyncratic Risk and Aggregate Saving," *Quarterly Journal of Economics*, 109(3), 659–684.

AKCIGIT, U., M. A. CELIK, AND J. GREENWOOD (2016): "Buy, Keep, or Sell: Economic Growth and the Market for Ideas," *Econometrica*, 84(3), 943–984.

AKCIGIT, U., M. A. CELIK, O. ITENBERG, AND G. ORDONEZ (2016): "Patents as Collateral and Directed Technical Change," Working Paper.

AKCIGIT, U., E. DINLERSOZ, J. GREENWOOD, AND V. PENCIAKOVA (2022): "Synergizing Ventures," *Journal of Economic Dynamics and Control*, 143, 104427.

AKCIGIT, U., J. GRIGSBY, AND T. NICHOLAS (2017): "The Rise of American Ingenuity: Innovation and Inventors of the Golden Age," NBER Working Paper 23047.

AKCIGIT, U., J. G. PEARCE, AND M. PRATO (2020): "Tapping into Talent: Coupling Education and Innovation Policies for Economic Growth," NBER Working Paper 27862.

AKERLOF, G. A. (1978): "The Market for 'Lemons': Quality Uncertainty and the Market Mechanism," in *Uncertainty in Economics*, ed. P. Diamond and M. Rothschild, 235–251. Elsevier.

AMARAL, P. S., AND E. QUINTIN (2010): "Limited Enforcement, Financial Intermediation, and Economic Development: A Quantitative Assessment," *International Economic Review*, 51(3), 785–811.

ATES, S. T. (2018): "Beyond Cash: Venture Capital, Firm Dynamics, and Economic Growth," Working Paper.

ATKESON, A., AND A. BURSTEIN (2008): "Pricing-to-Market, Trade Costs, and International Relative Prices," *American Economic Review*, 98(5), 1998–2031.

AUTOR, D., D. DORN, L. F. KATZ, C. PATTERSON, AND J. VAN REENEN (2020): "The Fall of the Labor Share and the Rise of Superstar Firms," *Quarterly Journal of Economics*, 135(2), 645–709.

BELL, A., R. CHETTY, X. JARAVEL, N. PETKOVA, AND J. VAN REENEN (2019): "Who Becomes an Inventor in America? The Importance of Exposure to Innovation," *Quarterly Journal of Economics*, 134(2), 647–713.

BUERA, F. J. (2009): "A Dynamic Model of Entrepreneurship with Borrowing Constraints: Theory and Evidence," *Annals of Finance*, 5(3), 443–464.

BUERA, F. J., J. P. KABOSKI, AND Y. SHIN (2011): "Finance and Development: A Tale of Two Sectors," *American Economic Review*, 101(5), 1964–2002.

BUERA, F. J., AND Y. SHIN (2013): "Financial Frictions and the Persistence of History: A Quantitative Exploration," *Journal of Political Economy*, 121(2), 221–272.

CAVENAILE, L., M. A. CELIK, AND X. TIAN (2021): "The Dynamic Effects of Antitrust Policy on Growth and Welfare," *Journal of Monetary Economics*, 121, 42–59.

CELIK, M. A. (2023): "Does the Cream Always Rise to the Top? The Misallocation of Talent in Innovation," *Journal of Monetary Economics*, 133, 105–128.

CELIK, M. A., AND X. TIAN (2023): "Agency Frictions, Managerial Compensation, and Disruptive Innovations," *Review of Economic Dynamics,* forthcoming.

CELIK, M. A., X. TIAN, AND W. WANG (2022): "Acquiring Innovation under Information Frictions," *Review of Financial Studies,* 35(10): 4474–4517.

CHIU, J., C. MEH, AND R. WRIGHT (2017): "Innovation and Growth with Financial, and Other, Frictions," *International Economic Review,* 58(1), 95–125.

COLE, H. L., J. GREENWOOD, AND J. M. SANCHEZ (2016): "Why Doesn't Technology Flow from Rich to Poor Countries?," *Econometrica,* 84(4), 1477–1521.

CUNNINGHAM, C., F. EDERER, AND S. MA (2021): "Killer Acquisitions," *Journal of Political Economy,* 129(3), 649–702.

DAVID, J. M. (2021): "The Aggregate Implications of Mergers and Acquisitions," *Review of Economic Studies,* 88(4), 1796–1830.

DINLERSOZ, E., S. KALEMLI-OZCAN, H. HYATT, AND V. PENCIAKOVA (2018): "Leverage over the Life Cycle and Implications for Firm Growth and Shock Responsiveness," NBER Working Paper 25226.

ERICSON, R., AND A. PAKES (1995): "Markov-Perfect Industry Dynamics: A Framework for Empirical Work," *Review of Economic Studies,* 62(1), 53–82.

GREENWOOD, J., P. HAN, AND J. M. SANCHEZ (2022): "Financing Ventures," *International Economic Review,* 63(3), 1021–1053.

JEONG, H., AND R. M. TOWNSEND (2007): "Sources of TFP Growth: Occupational Choice and Financial Deepening," *Economic Theory,* 32(1), 179–221.

JUNGHERR, J., M. MEIER, T. REINELT, AND I. SCHOTT (2020): "Corporate Debt Maturity Matters for Monetary Policy," Working Paper.

KIYOTAKI, N., AND J. MOORE (1997): "Credit Cycles," *Journal of Political Economy,* 105(2), 211–248.

MIDRIGAN, V., AND D. Y. XU (2014): "Finance and Misallocation: Evidence from Plant-Level Data," *American Economic Review,* 104(2), 422–58.

MOLL, B. (2014): "Productivity Losses from Financial Frictions: Can Self-Financing Undo Capital Misallocation?," *American Economic Review,* 104(10), 3186–3221.

NATIONAL SURVEY OF COLLEGE GRADUATES (2003): *National Center for Science and Engineering Statistics,* https://www.nsf.gov/statistics/srvygrads/survey2003/grads_2003.pdf.

OCAMPO-DIAZ, S., AND J. HERRENO (2021): "Self-Employment and Development," Working Paper.

PART VIII

Taxation

CHAPTER 23

Taxation, Innovation, and Economic Growth

CHARLES I. JONES

1 Introduction

Growth research for the past thirty-five years has brought three central concepts to fruition: the nonrivalry of ideas, creative destruction, and the role of misallocation in driving TFP and income differences. Philippe Aghion and Peter Howitt have been the driving force for the second of these, creative destruction. And this volume is a testimony to how deep and far-reaching this concept has been, giving rise to children and grandchildren and great grandchildren.

Two of my own recent papers are part of this long list of descendants. Jones and Kim (2018) builds on Gabaix (2009) to study top income inequality. As emphasized by Gabaix (2009), Pareto distributions emerge when exponential growth occurs for an exponentially distributed amount of time. That is, we need some force that constrains the exponential growth; otherwise the distribution will simply fan out forever. Creative destruction is a natural constraining force. An entrepreneur comes up with a great idea and then sells a product based on that idea to an exponentially growing market. This occurs until a new innovator comes up with a better idea: creative destruction keeps fortunes from growing too far apart. An implication is that the dynamic competition of creative destruction can simultaneously spur economic growth and constrain top income inequality.

A completely different application is Jones and Tonetti (2020), which studies the economics of data. Because data is nonrival (or "infinitely usable"), just like ideas, efficiency suggests that data should be used broadly: we want machine learning algorithms trained to spot cancer or drive trucks to be trained on as much data as possible. However, firms that are developing these algorithms have an incentive to keep this data private. Broad use would increase competition and the risk of creative destruction. Institutions related to data use and ownership may therefore play an important role.

When Aghion and Howitt (1992) were first putting their paper together, I'm sure they had no idea how far-reaching their paper would become. It is a pleasure for all of us to witness—and partake in—the opening of so many doors to interesting and significant research questions.

What I will do in this chapter is explore further one of those many doors: the interaction between taxation and economic growth. In Section 2, I begin by reviewing some of the key pieces of empirical evidence related to taxation and growth. In Section 3, I turn to some insights uncovered by growth theory. Finally, I conclude in Section 4 with what I see as a key question for future research. Specifically, how large is the overall degree of increasing returns associated with the nonrivalry of ideas?

2 Evidence on Taxation and Growth

2.1 Aggregate evidence

An excellent starting point for understanding the evidence on taxation and growth is a set of graphs first presented by Stokey and Rebelo (1995). They made the surprising point that even though there have been large changes in taxation over the twentieth century, average growth rates in the United States were remarkably stable.

Figure 23.1 shows a ten-year moving average of the growth rate of GDP per person in the United States. In particular, it shows that the average growth rate of around 2 percent per year is stable going back all the way to 1880. There are decades where growth is a little faster or a little slower, but over the long time series, the stability of average growth rates is a fact that stands out.

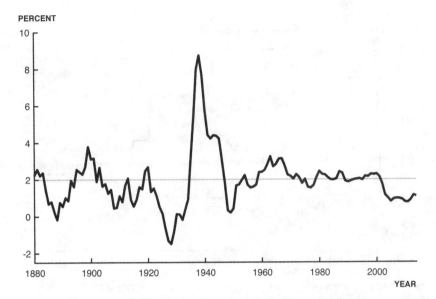

Notes: The growth rate is a 10-year centered moving average of annual growth in US GDP per person. Data before 1929 is from Barro and Ursúa (2010); later data is from the US National Income and Product Accounts.

Data sources: Barro-Ursúa Macroeconomic Data (2010); US National Income and Product Accounts

Figure 23.1. US economic growth in GDP per person

Figure 23.2 shows two time series related to taxation in the United States. The second line in this figure is total US government revenues as a share of GDP. The series begins at 10 percent in 1929, but was presumably low in the preceding decades as well. It then rises throughout the next fifty years before stabilizing between 25 and 30 percent. The main point of Stokey and Rebelo (1995) was that this huge change in taxation occurred with seemingly very little effect on rates of economic growth; any theory of economic growth needs to be consistent with this fact.

But of course the fact itself is perhaps more complicated than it first appears. For example, the first line in Figure 23.2 shows the top marginal tax rate for federal personal income taxation. This rate rises sharply in the first part of the sample, from a low of 7 percent to a high of 94 percent! But after reaching this peak at the end of World War II, the top marginal rate declines to below 40 percent by the late 1980s.

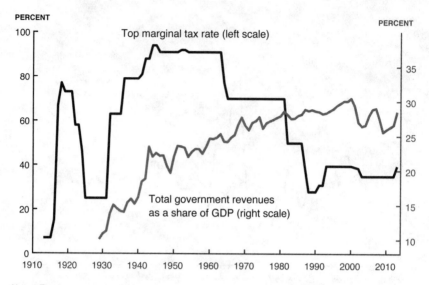

PERCENT

Top marginal tax rate (left scale)

Total government revenues
as a share of GDP (right scale)

Notes: Total government revenues is based on the FRED series "W021RC1A027NBEA." The top
marginal tax rate is for federal taxation from TaxFoundation2013.

Data sources: Federal Reserve Economic Data (FRED); Tax Foundation (2013)

Figure 23.2. Taxation in the United States

It is tempting to conclude from this evidence that taxes do not affect economic growth. After all, there have been large changes in the tax system over the past 100+ years while growth rates have been remarkably stable. Perhaps innovators are only motivated by "higher concerns" and do not respond to taxes?

But this view is far too simplistic. After all, many other things are changing throughout this period, so the "other things equal" criterion needed for such a conclusion is most certainly not met. In part, the higher tax revenue goes to fund all levels of education, the US space program, DARPA, the NIH, the National Science Foundation, and various other forms of basic research. Moreover, the United States does not grow only because of ideas invented in the United States but instead benefits from ideas created throughout the world. How do ideas from Europe, Japan, and China change this picture?

Hsieh, Hurst, Jones, and Klenow (2019) emphasize another important change in the past half century: an improvement in the allocation of talent. In 1960 more than 90 percent of doctors, lawyers, and managers were white men. By 2010 this fraction had fallen to 60 percent. A natural interpretation of this evidence is that labor market and human capital barriers prevented talented women and minorities in the early years from pursuing their comparative advantage. Declines in these barriers over the past fifty years have improved the allocation of talent. They estimate that declining barriers explain as much as 40 percent of the increase in income per person since 1960.

Finally, Atkeson, Burstein, and Chatzikonstantinou (2019) and Jones (2022) show that transition dynamics in many idea-driven growth models can be particularly long, with half-lives potentially reaching a century or more. If that view is correct, then empirical work is made more complicated: To what extent do innovations and policy changes from the 1940s and 1960s impact economic growth today?

It should now be clear why it is very hard to interpret aggregate evidence like that shown in Figures 23.1 and 23.2. There are too many other things changing at the same time that are impossible to control for. The aggregate evidence on growth and taxes is ultimately not compelling and perhaps cannot be. For this reason, our best evidence comes from microeconomic studies.

2.2 Microeconomic evidence

Perhaps not surprisingly, the most compelling evidence on taxation, innovation, and growth comes from looking at how researchers and entrepreneurs are affected by specific policy changes. This evidence suggests that innovators, far from being romantic dreamers immune to economic considerations, respond quite strongly to economic incentives and taxes.

Some of the most interesting recent research looks at the geographic mobility of top innovators when taxes change. Akcigit, Baslandze, and Stantcheva (2016) use panel data on inventors from the United States and European Patent Offices to study the international mobility of superstar inventors (those in the top 5 percent of the distribution) with respect to top tax rates. In particular, they estimate the elasticity of the number of inventors to the "keep rate" $1 - \tau$, sometimes also called the "net of tax rate." For domestic star inventors the elasticity is small, at 0.03, whereas for foreign star inventors the elasticity is much larger, around 1.0.

Moretti and Wilson (2017) conduct a related exercise but look across US states rather than internationally. Average personal income tax rates at the 99th percentile of the income distribution vary considerably across states; for example, in 2010 the value was 8.1 percent in California but zero percent in Texas, Florida, Washington, and six other states. They find remarkably large long-run elasticities of 1.8 for personal income taxes and 1.9 for the state corporate income tax.

These mobility studies do an excellent job of highlighting that taxes matter for the behavior of inventors. Far from being "pie in the sky" scientists divorced from mundane factors, these researchers change their behavior in response to economic incentives.

However, these mobility studies suffer from an important limitation insofar as we care about how the quantity of innovation itself responds to taxes. It is possible that researchers move geographically in response to taxes but do not change the quantity of innovation that they produce. Maybe all the innovators leave California for Texas and Florida but the aggregate amount of innovation is unchanged.

Akcigit, Grigsby, Nicholas, and Stantcheva (2021) follow individual inventors over time in the United States to estimate the effect of taxation on inventive effort itself. In regressions including inventor fixed-effects as well as a host of other controls, they find an elasticity of patent counts with respect to the keep rate at the 90th percentile of the income distribution of 0.8 and an elasticity of total citations around 1.0, both with standard errors of less than 0.2. Given that the public economics literature typically considers elasticities for top income earners (not just inventors) in a broad range from 0.1 to 0.5, these elasticities are remarkably high. Clearly more research on this topic will be needed to draw firm conclusions. But to the best of our knowledge and based on the latest estimates, inventive effort appears to be quite sensitive to taxation.

3 Theory

A rich literature studies optimal top income taxation. The main trade-off in this literature is between redistribution and the "size of the pie." Behind the veil of ignorance, there is a strong incentive to provide insurance to people who will be unlucky to be born with low ability on some dimension. But pushing against this is the fact that we want talented people to have the right incentives to work hard. Mirrlees (1971), Diamond (1998), and Saez (2001) are classic papers in this literature, providing a nuanced analysis of the optimal top tax rate. More recently, this literature has been extended in many useful directions. Several papers incorporate the accumulation of human and physical capital, the imperfect substitutability of different types of labor, and general externalities (see Rothschild and Scheuer 2013, 2014; Badel and Huggett 2017; Lockwood, Nathanson, and Weyl 2017; and Sachs, Tsyvinski, and Werquin 2020).

Jaimovich and Rebelo (2017) study the growth consequences of taxation in a Romer (1990) setup. They are motivated by the puzzle discussed earlier: If long-run growth rates are sensitive to tax policy, then why do we see so little evidence of this in time series and cross-sectional evidence? They argue that talent heterogeneity may be the explanation. The most talented researchers will engage in innovation for almost any tax rate. When taxes are on the order of 30 percent, the marginal researcher has relatively low talent, so changing the talent cutoff may have small effects on growth.

Building on this broad literature, I have a recent paper (Jones 2020) that considers optimal income taxation when economic growth is driven by the discovery of ideas by a relatively small number of researchers. Whereas Jaimovich and Rebelo (2017) study the extensive margin of who becomes an inventor, Jones (2020) instead focuses on the standard intensive effort margin. To understand the point of that paper, it is helpful to review the "traditional" approach to taxation in growth models.

Suppose output Y is produced using capital K, regular workers L, and high-income earners ("managers") M. Let the production function be given by

$$Y = K^\alpha M^\theta L^{1-\alpha-\theta}. \tag{1}$$

Top income taxation distorts the effort by the managers and therefore reduces GDP in this economy. Obviously, one key parameter in determining the magnitude of this effect is the elasticity of top earners' effort to taxes, which is what I discussed in Section 2. But another crucial parameter influencing the "size of the pie" effect is θ: How important are top earners to the overall success of the economy?

Empirically, the share of income that is taxed at the top marginal rate in the United States is around 10 percent. Given that θ will determine the share of GDP paid to managers, it is plausible that $\theta \approx 0.10$ in a setting like this. The modest share of GDP paid to top earners constrains the effect of taxes on GDP. By contrast, if somehow θ were much larger, the effect of taxes on GDP would be correspondingly larger and that would imply that optimal top tax rates would be lower.

Modern growth theory based on Romer (1990) and Aghion and Howitt (1992) incorporates an additional key factor of production: ideas. The discovery of new ideas is at the heart of economic growth and responsible for the remarkable rise in living standards in much of the world over the past two centuries. This leads to a production function such as

$$Y = A^\gamma K^\alpha M^\theta L^{1-\alpha-\theta}, \tag{2}$$

where A denotes the stock of ideas that have been discovered.

Importantly, notice that the stock of ideas enters the production function *outside* of the constant returns to scale piece, so that production now exhibits increasing returns to scale. This was the key contribution of Romer (1990): because ideas are nonrival or "infinitely usable," production is characterized by increasing returns. If we want to double production using the traditional inputs, we can do that by *replicating* the entire setup: we build an identical factory, populate it with identical equipment and materials, and hire an identical workforce. Notice that this replication works *using the existing, unchanged stock of ideas*. That is, whatever blueprint we were using in the first factory—say the design of a fantastic new cancer drug—we can use that same blueprint in the new factory as well. Because the idea is nonrival, it does not need to be rediscovered for the new factory. There are constant returns to traditional inputs and therefore increasing returns to those inputs and ideas taken together. If we double the traditional inputs and the stock of ideas, we will more than double production.

This is important for the theory of taxation because it opens the door to a new parameter, γ, which is not constrained by constant returns to scale. Notice that in the traditional production function in equation (1), the importance of managers (θ) has to "compete" with capital and labor. Since capital and labor already make up a large share of factor payments, the managerial share θ is almost forced to be small. But because ideas enter *outside* the constant returns, the parameter γ suffers from no such constraint.

Top income taxation affects GDP through the managers via θ but also through the innovators via the stock of ideas and γ. While θ is relatively small, the parameter γ is potentially large and therefore top income taxation can have much larger effects. For example, $\theta \approx 0.10$, but plausible estimates of γ include values such as ¼, ½, or even 2! Jones (2020) shows that this consideration can substantially reduce welfare-maximizing top tax rates. Because of uncertainty about various parameters, that paper does not provide a single value as an answer. But a robust finding is that optimal top tax rates can be reduced substantially by considering the distortions associated with innovation.

The economics of the problem is also worth appreciating. From modern growth theory—and especially the literature emerging from Aghion and Howitt (1992)—we've learned that long-run growth comes from a relatively small number of entrepreneurs and innovators creating new ideas that raise everyone's standard of living. Distorting the effort of these entrepreneurs and innovators, then, could be extremely costly. Put differently, we can raise the living standards of poor people by taxing the rich and transferring the proceeds. Alternatively, we can raise the living standards of poor people by creating new ideas. Historically and around the world, the latter has been overwhelmingly responsible for improvements in living standards.

3.1 Key research question: How important are ideas?

This analysis suggests a key question for future research: How important are ideas, and in particular, how large is χ, the degree of increasing returns associated with the nonrivalry of ideas?

This question pertains to essentially every model of growth driven by innovation, dating all the way back to Romer (1990) and Aghion and Howitt (1992). Put differently, if we double the number of researchers in the United States or in the world, by how much does that raise living standards and economic growth twenty-five years from now?

These are difficult questions to answer, in part because ideas and researchers are hard to measure, and in part because it is difficult to estimate production functions in economics because of identification problems.

There are some papers that have made progress on this question, however. Ngai and Samaniego (2011) allow different industries to have different parameters in their idea production functions. Ideas may be more or less important in different sectors, and the knowledge spillovers associated with ideas may be different as well. This can lead some sectors, like information technology or agriculture, to exhibit rapid rates of TFP growth, while others, such as construction and services, exhibit lower rates of TFP growth, at least as measured by our imperfect statistics. Akcigit and Kerr (2018), Bloom, Jones, Van Reenen, and Webb (2020), and Sampson (2020) also push in this direction, but there is clearly scope for much more work here.

Other papers look at exogenous shocks to migration patterns to try to estimate the degree of increasing returns. Arkolakis, Lee, and Peters (2020) use European immigration to the United States between 1880 and 1920 and estimate a range of values of 0.7 to 1.3. Peters (2019) uses the pseudo-random settlement of East Germans into West Germany after World War II and finds a value of 0.89. A difficulty with interpreting these numbers as the overall degree of increasing returns is that cross-sectional estimates include reallocations from one region to another that may wash out in the aggregate. But these studies are clearly a valuable addition to the literature, and they offer the intriguing possibility that the degree of increasing returns may be quite large. (For comparison, in much of my work, I've often focused on values closer to ⅓, but emphasizing a great deal of uncertainty surrounding this value.)

The overall degree of increasing returns associated with the nonrivalry of ideas is a fundamental concept in modern growth theory. Its magnitude matters for virtually every question of interest to growth economists, and estimating this value should be a top priority in future research.

4 Conclusion

The area studying taxation, innovation, and economic growth is just one of the many subfields of economics that has gained tremendously from the Schumpeterian creative destruction perspective emphasized in the foundational work by Philippe Aghion and Peter Howitt. One mark of a truly great idea is the number of doors it opens for future research, and by that measure, Aghion and Howitt (1992) is surely one of the most important papers ever written in the growth literature.

References

Aghion, Philippe, and Peter Howitt. (1992). "A Model of Growth through Creative Destruction." *Econometrica, 60* (2), 323–351.

Akcigit, Ufuk, Salome Baslandze, and Stefanie Stantcheva. (2016). "Taxation and the International Mobility of Inventors." *American Economic Review, 106* (10), 2930–2981.

Akcigit, Ufuk, John Grigsby, Tom Nicholas, and Stefanie Stantcheva. (2021). "Taxation and Innovation in the 20th Century." *Quarterly Journal of Economics, 137* (1), 329–385.

Akcigit, Ufuk, and William R. Kerr. (2018). "Growth through Heterogeneous Innovations." *Journal of Political Economy, 126* (4), 1374–1443.

Arkolakis, Costas, Sun Kyoung Lee, and Michael Peters. (2020). "European Immigrants and the United States' Rise to the Technological Frontier." Technical Report, Yale University.

Atkeson, Andrew, Ariel Burstein, and Manolis Chatzikonstantinou. (2019). "Transitional Dynamics in Aggregate Models of Innovative Investment." *Annual Review of Economics, 11* (1), 273–301.

Badel, Alejandro, and Mark Huggett. (2017). "The Sufficient Statistic Approach: Predicting the Top of the Laffer Curve." *Journal of Monetary Economics, 87* (C), 1–12.

Barro, Robert J., and José F. Ursua. (2010). "Barro-Ursua Macroeconomic Data." https://scholar.harvard.edu/barro/publications/barro-ursua-macroeconomic -data.

Bloom, Nicholas, Charles I. Jones, John Van Reenen, and Michael Webb. (2020). "Are Ideas Getting Harder to Find?" *American Economic Review, 110* (4), 1104–1144.

Diamond, Peter A. (1998). "Optimal Income Taxation: An Example with a U-Shaped Pattern of Optimal Marginal Tax Rates." *American Economic Review, 88* (1), 83–95.

Gabaix, Xavier. (2009). "Power Laws in Economics and Finance." *Annual Review of Economics, 1* (1), 255–294.

Hsieh, Chang-Tai, Erik Hurst, Charles I. Jones, and Peter J. Klenow. (2019). "The Allocation of Talent and U.S. Economic Growth." *Econometrica, 87* (5), 1439–1474.

Jaimovich, Nir, and Sergio Rebelo. (2017). "Nonlinear Effects of Taxation on Growth." *Journal of Political Economy, 125* (1), 265–291.

Jones, Charles I. (2020). "Taxing Top Incomes in a World of Ideas." Technical Report, Stanford University, December.

Jones, Charles I. (2022). "The Past and Future of Economic Growth: A Semi-Endogenous Perspective." *Annual Review of Economics, 14,* 125–152.

Jones, Charles I., and Jihee Kim. (2018). "A Schumpeterian Model of Top Income Inequality." *Journal of Political Economy, 126* (5), 1785–1826.

Jones, Charles I., and Christopher Tonetti. (2020). "Nonrivalry and the Economics of Data." *American Economic Review, 110* (9), 2819–2858.

Lockwood, Benjamin, Charles Nathanson, and E. Glen Weyl. (2017). "Taxation and the Allocation of Talent." *Journal of Political Economy, 125* (5), 1635–1682.

Mirrlees, James A. (1971). "An Exploration in the Theory of Optimum Income Taxation." *Review of Economic Studies, 38,* 175–208.

Moretti, Enrico, and Daniel J. Wilson. (2017). "The Effect of State Taxes on the Geographical Location of Top Earners: Evidence from Star Scientists." *American Economic Review, 107* (7), 1858–1903.

Ngai, Rachel, and Roberto Samaniego. (2011). "Accounting for Research and Productivity Growth across Industries." *Review of Economic Dynamics, 14* (3), 475–495.

Peters, Michael. (2019). "Market Size and Spatial Growth—Evidence from Germanys Post-War Population Expulsions." Yale University, manuscript.

Romer, Paul M. (1990). "Endogenous Technological Change." *Journal of Political Economy, 98* (5), S71–S102.

Rothschild, Casey, and Florian Scheuer. (2013). "Redistributive Taxation in the Roy Model." *Quarterly Journal of Economics, 128* (2), 623–668.

Rothschild, Casey, and Florian Scheuer. (2014). "A Theory of Income Taxation under Multidimensional Skill Heterogeneity." NBER Working Paper 19822.

Sachs, Dominik, Aleh Tsyvinski, and Nicolas Werquin. (2020). "Nonlinear Tax Incidence and Optimal Taxation in General Equilibrium." *Econometrica, 88* (2), 469–493.

Saez, Emmanuel. (2001). "Using Elasticities to Derive Optimal Tax Rates." *Review of Economic Studies, 68,* 205–229.

Sampson, Thomas. (2020). "Technology Gaps, Trade and Income." LSE manuscript.

Stokey, Nancy L., and Sergio Rebelo. (1995). "Growth Effects of Flat-Rate Taxes." *Journal of Political Economy, 103,* 519–550.

Tax Foundation. (2013). "U.S. Federal Individual Income Tax Rates History, 1862–2013." https://taxfoundation.org/us-federal-individual-income-tax-rates-history/.

CHAPTER 24

The Effects of Taxes on Innovation

Theory and Empirical Evidence

STEFANIE STANTCHEVA

1 Introduction

Income taxes are typically set to raise revenues and redistribute income at the lowest possible efficiency costs, which result from the distortions in individual behaviors that taxes entail. Individuals can respond along many margins, such as labor supply, tax avoidance and evasion, and geographic mobility. But one margin that taxes may affect—innovation—is less frequently considered. Conceptually, taxes reduce the expected net returns to innovation inputs and can reduce innovation. Much like other margins of responses to taxes, this efficiency cost must be taken into account.

Innovation is done by a relatively small number of people, but it is nevertheless likely to have widespread benefits. First, it is generally considered to be the source of technological progress and the main driver of economic growth in the long run (Aghion and Howitt 1992; Romer 1994; Jones 1995). As Akcigit et al. (2022) show, US states with the most innovations also witnessed the fastest growth between 1900 and 2000. Earlier work has found that innovation is also associated with social mobility (Aghion et al. 2019) and well-being (Aghion et al. 2016).

It may sometimes appear that innovation is a mysterious process conjured up by scientists who have little concern for taxation or financial incentives in general. Pathbreaking superstar inventors from history, such as Thomas Edison, Alexander Graham Bell, and Nikola Tesla, all strove for intellectual achievement more than did rational economic agents who follow financial incentives. Yet innovation is also dependent on investments. While inventors may have different motivations, such as social recognition or the love of discovery, they also face an economic reality. How strongly innovation responds to taxes is an empirical question that has been the subject of a growing body of recent work.

In this chapter, I study how to account for innovation when setting personal income and capital taxation. I distinguish between two cases: one in which the government can set a differentiated tax on inventors and one in which the government is constrained to set the same tax on all agents. I begin with a model that flexibly accounts for the spillovers generated by innovation and the nonpecuniary benefits inventors receive from innovation. Thanks to the framework of Saez and Stantcheva (2018), the problem can be turned into an equivalent static model, which allows for an easier derivation of formulas expressed in terms of estimable sufficient statistics.[1] The second part of this chapter discusses the empirical evidence on the effects of taxes on the quantity, quality, and location of innovation, as well as tax avoidance and income shifting done through innovation.

2 Model

I start by presenting a simple way to think about optimal labor and capital income taxes when there is innovation that generates spillovers. Many of the assumptions can easily be relaxed, and I will discuss some of these extensions below. There are two key elements in the model. The first is that innovation generates spillovers onto other agents in the economy (Akcigit et al. 2021; Bloom et al. 2013; Jones and Williams 1998). The second is that innovators receive both pecuniary and nonpecuniary benefits from innovation (Putney and Putney 1962; Stuart and Ding 2006).

---

[1] The model does not cover targeted tax policies such as R&D tax credits, local tax incentives for innovating firms, or subsidies for specific types of research, although these are discussed conceptually and in the empirical parts.

2.1 Setting

Innovation spillovers. Innovators in the economy, indexed by i, exert effort and invest capital to produce innovation output. Innovation generates spillovers on other agents in the economy. To model these in a simple, reduced-form way, I assume that the labor and capital incomes of other agents are directly affected by innovation. Thus, if a socially valuable innovation is produced for which the private return to the innovator, in the form of either capital or labor income, is below its social return, other agents in the economy will benefit from higher incomes.

More precisely, if an inventor produces an innovation that yields an income value of y_i, they receive $z_i = \eta_i \cdot y_i$ with $0 < \eta_i$ as a private income. Hence, the reward to the innovator can differ from their actual innovation value, and the gap between the two is the spillover $\pi_i := (\eta_i - 1)y_i$. If $\eta_i > 1$, the innovator receives an additional rent above and beyond the social value of innovation, and the spillover on others is negative. This could occur, for instance, if the monopoly power or business-stealing effects are large relative to the net value of the innovation. In contrast, if $\eta_i < 1$, the innovator's reward is below the value of the innovation and they create a positive spillover on others. Similarly, for a given capital stock (wealth) $\tilde{k}_i$ and (heterogeneous) return on capital r_i, the innovator receives income $r_i k_i = \eta_i r_i \tilde{k}_i$. Denote the gap between the private and social returns on capital by $b_i := (\eta_i - 1)r_i\tilde{k}_i$. The inventor can influence the share of the spillover that goes to them by exerting effort or paying a cost. This will be called "rent-seeking" because it is about increasing one's private return without increasing the total social return.

The average spillover from innovation in the economy must come at the expense or benefit of some agents. Suppose that there are N agents in total in the economy. For simplicity, I assume that all agents bear the average spillover uniformly.[2] Thus, the government can fully tax or rebate back the average (negative or positive) spillover to everyone using a lump-sum tax or transfer.

Innovators face increasing and convex costs of producing innovation income and of capturing a higher share of their innovation output for

---

[2] This assumption can be relaxed; see Piketty et al. (2014).

themselves, $h_i(z_i)$ and $v_i(\eta)$. Furthermore, they also have a net utility from holding wealth (the capital stock k_i) equal to $a_i(k_i)$. This could be a net benefit, if innovators enjoy having wealth for prestige and social reasons, or it could be negative if it takes a lot of effort to manage a larger stock of capital.

Innovators' nonpecuniary benefits. The justification for this formulation of "wealth-in-the-utility" comes from Saez and Stantcheva (2018). It essentially captures the fact that the benefits from capital income are not merely seen in the form of future consumption. This formulation is empirically justified. In practice, it is very difficult to rationalize the massive wealth holdings observed in the data through a consumption motive only: Bill Gates and Elon Musk probably do not plan to "consume" all of their wealth. Furthermore, models without wealth in the utility have difficulty reconciling the dispersion in labor income with the dispersion in capital and wealth holdings. It is likely that inequality in capital and wealth comes not only from differences in labor income only, but also from differences in discount rates and returns, as well as heterogeneous values from holding wealth. Finally, there are also more technical reasons, since the neoclassical model of Chamley-Judd (Chamley 1986; Judd 1985) has difficulty accommodating heterogeneity across respondents and generates infinite elasticities of capital income to the net-of-tax return in the steady state.

There are several ways to microfound this wealth-in-the-utility specification: social benefits and prestige from having wealth (or owning a successful, innovative business), a bequest motive, philanthropy and moral recognition, or "services" from having wealth. Importantly, these benefits go above and beyond the future consumption stream that wealth provides. Saez and Stantcheva (2018) provide an application of the wealth-in-utility model to entrepreneurship.

Dynamics and static equivalent. Time is continuous, infinite horizon, and each individual has a discount rate δ_i that captures pure discounting, as well as a (heterogeneous) probability of death. The per-period utility payoff of each innovator is thus:

$$u_i(c_i(t),\, k_i(t),\, z_i(t),\, \eta_i(t)) = c_i(t) + a_i(k_i(t)) - h_i(z_i(t)) - v_i(\eta_i(t)). \tag{1}$$

The individual index i can capture any arbitrary heterogeneity in the preferences for work and wealth, as well as in the discount rate δ_i. The discounted utility of i from an allocation $\{c_i(t), k_i(t), z_i(t), \eta_i(t)\}_{t \geq 0}$ is:[3]

$$V_i\left(\{c_i(t), k_i(t), z_i(t), \eta_i(t)\}_{t \geq 0}\right)$$
$$= \delta_i \bullet \int_0^{\infty} [c_i(t) + a_i(k_i(t)) - h_i(z_i(t)) - v_i(\eta_i(t))]e^{-\delta_i t} dt. \tag{2}$$

At time 0, initial wealth of innovator i is k_i^{init}. For any given time-invariant tax schedule $T(z, rk)$ based on labor and capital incomes, the budget constraint of individual i is:

$$\frac{dk_i(t)}{dt} = r_i k_i(t) + z_i(t) - T(z_i(t), r_i k_i(t)) - c_i(t). \tag{3}$$

$T_L'(z, rk) \equiv \partial T(z, rk)/\partial \eta y$ denotes the marginal tax with respect to labor income and $T_K'(z, rk) \equiv \partial T(z, rk)/\partial rk$ denotes the marginal tax with respect to capital income.

The Hamiltonian of individual i at time t, with co-state $\lambda_i(t)$ on the budget constraint, is:

$$H_i(c_i(t), z_i(t), k_i(t), \eta_i(t), \lambda_i(t)) = c_i(t) + a_i(k_i(t)) - h_i(z_i(t)) - v_i(\eta_i(t))$$
$$+ \lambda_i(t) \bullet [r_i k_i(t) + z_i(t)$$
$$- T(z_i(t), r_i k_i(t)) - c_i(t)].$$

Taking the first order conditions, the choice $(c_i(t), k_i(t), z_i(t), \eta_i(t))$ is such that:

$$\lambda_i(t) = 1 \tag{4}$$

$$h_i'(z_i(t)) = (1 - T_L'(z_i(t), r_i k_i(t))) \tag{5}$$

$$a_i'(k_i(t)) = \delta_i - r[1 - T_K'(z_i(t), r_i k_i(t))] \tag{6}$$

$$v_i'(\eta_i(t)) = (1 - T_K'(z_i(t), r_i k_i(t)))r_i(t)\tilde{k}_i(t) + (1 - T_L'(z_i(t), r_i k_i(t)))y_i(t) \tag{7}$$

$$c_i(t) = rk_i(t) + z_i(t) - T(z_i(t), r_i k_i(t)) \tag{8}$$

In this model, $(c_i(t), k_i(t), z_i(t), \eta_i(t))$ jumps immediately to its steady-state value (c_i, k_i, z_i, η_i) characterized by

$$h_i'(z_i) = (1 - T_L'), a_i'(k_i) = \delta_i - r_i(1 - T_K'), v_i'(\eta_i)$$
$$= (1 - T_K')r_i\tilde{k}_i + (1v - T_L')y_i, c_i = r_i k_i + \eta_i y_i - T(z_i, r_i k_i).$$

---

[3] The utility is normalized by the discount rate δ_i so that an extra unit of consumption in perpetuity increases utility by one unit uniformly across all individuals.

This is achieved by a Dirac quantum jump in consumption at instant $t = 0$, so as to bring the wealth level from the initial k_i^{init} to the steady state value k_i. Because of this immediate adjustment and the lack of transition dynamics, we have that:

$$V_i\left(\{c_i(t), k_i(t), z_i(t), \eta_i(t)\}_{t \geq 0}\right) = \left[c_i + a_i(k_i) - b_i(z_i) - v_i(\eta_i)\right] + \delta_i \bullet (k_i^{init} - k_i),$$

where the last term $(k_i^{init} - k_i)$ represents the utility cost of going from wealth k_i^{init} to wealth k_i at instant 0, achieved by the quantum Dirac jump in consumption.

The dynamic model captured by (2) is therefore equivalent to a static model. Put differently, the optimal choice (c_i, k_i, z_i, η_i) from the dynamic problem also maximizes the static utility equivalent:[4]

$$U_i(c_i, k_i, z_i, \eta_i) = c_i + a_i(k_i) - b_i(z_i) - v_i(\eta_i) + \delta_i \bullet (k_i^{init} - k_i), \qquad (9)$$

subject to the static budget constraint $c_i = r_i k_i + z_i - T(z_i, r_i k_i)$.

In the rest of this chapter I will use the static equivalent U_i from equation (9), keeping in mind that it is equivalent to the original discounted utility V_i from equation (2).

2.2 Optimal tax formulas

Having specified the setting and converted the dynamic problem into an equivalent static problem, we can consider the optimal tax rates in two cases. In the first case, the government is able to set a differentiated tax regime for innovators. In this case, the tax rates derived here apply specifically to innovators' capital and labor income. In the second case, the government is unable to distinguish between innovators and other agents. Thus, the tax

---

[4] The key assumption that drives this result is the linearity of utility in consumption, which precludes any consumption smoothing motive and, hence, avoids any transitional dynamics. While this assumption is not always appealing, Saez and Stantcheva (2018) provide a justification of why it may be quite relevant when thinking of top income taxation, and show that it can be relaxed without affecting the core qualitative findings. Intuitively, the faster the transitional dynamics are (i.e., the faster capital income responds to taxes), the closer the simpler model with linear utility comes to a full-fledged model with concave utility. Furthermore, Saez and Stantcheva (2018) argue that it is morally and politically unappealing for the government to exploit sluggish short-run responses, and that the long-run elasticity that applies after agents have made short-run adjustments is more relevant for sound fiscal policy.

rates apply to all agents in the economy, regardless of whether or not they engage in innovation.

In either case, the government sets the time invariant tax system $T(z, rk)$, subject to budget-balance, to maximize its social objective:

$$SWF = \int_i \omega_i \cdot U_i(c_i, k_i, z_i, \eta_i)di, \tag{10}$$

where $\omega_i \geq 0$ is the Pareto weight on individual i. We denote by $g_i = \omega_i \cdot U_{ic}$ the social marginal welfare weight on individual i. With utility linear in consumption, we have $g_i = \omega_i$. Without loss of generality, the weights can be normalized to sum to one over the population so that $\int_i \omega_i di = 1$.

2.2.1 Optimal capital and labor income taxation of inventors

I start by studying the optimal linear taxes at rates τ_K and τ_L on capital and labor income of inventors. Suppose that there is a mass one of innovators in the economy. Denote by $\bar{r}_i \equiv r_i \cdot (1 - \tau_K)$ the net-of-tax (social) return on capital. The individual maximizing choices are such that

$$a_i'(k_i) = \delta_i - \bar{r}_i \tag{11}$$

$$h_i'(z_i) = [1 - \tau_L] \tag{12}$$

$$v'(\eta_i) = (1 - \tau_L)z_i/\eta_i + \bar{r}_i k_i/\eta_i \tag{13}$$

so that k_i depends positively on $\bar{r}_i$, while z_i depends positively on $1 - \tau_L$. In addition, η_i depends positively on both net-of-tax rates. For budget balance, tax revenues are rebated lump-sum.

Let $\pi^m(1 - \tau_L) := \int_{i=0}^{1} \pi_i di$ be the average income spillover of innovators and $b^m(\bar{r}) := \int_{i=0}^{1} b_i di$ the average capital return spillover, which are both functions of the net-of-tax rates. Let also $z^m(1 - \tau_L) = \int_{i=0}^{1} z_i di$ be the aggregate labor income of inventors that depends on $1 - \tau_L$, and let $rk^m(\bar{r}) = \int_{i=0}^{1} r_i k_i di$ be the aggregate capital income of innovators, which depends on $\bar{r}$. By the assumption that the spillover hits all agents in the economy uniformly and that the government can rebate or tax it lump-sum, the transfer to each individual (innovators and non-innovators) is $G = \tau_K \cdot rk^m(\bar{r}) + \tau_L \cdot z^m(1 - \tau_L) - [b^m + \pi^m]$.

The government chooses τ_K and τ_L to maximize social welfare SWF in equation (10), with $c_i = (1 - \tau_K) \cdot r_i k_i + (1 - \tau_L) \cdot z_i + \tau_K \cdot rk^m + \tau_L \cdot z^m - [b^m + \pi^m]$ and $U_i(c_i, k_i, z_i, \eta_i) = c_i + a_i(k_i) - h_i(z_i) - v_i(\eta_i) + \delta_i \cdot (k_i^{init} - k_i).$[5]

Let the elasticity of aggregate innovator capital income rk^m with respect to the net-of-tax capital rate $1 - \tau_K$ be denoted by e_K and the elasticity of their aggregate labor income by z^m with respect to the net of tax rate $1 - \tau_L$ be e_L. Because there are no income effects, we have $e_L > 0$ and $e_K > 0$. Similarly, define $e_b = \dfrac{d \log(b^m)}{d \log(1 - \tau_K)}$ to be the elasticity of the spillover with respect to the net-of-tax capital income tax rate and $e_\pi = \dfrac{d \log(\pi^m)}{d \log(1 - \tau)}$ the elasticity of the spillover with respect to the net-of-tax labor income rate. Taking the derivative of the government objective with respect to the capital tax rate τ_K and applying the envelope theorem for the agents' choices yields:

$$\frac{dSWF}{d\tau_K} = rk^m \cdot \left[\int_i g_i \cdot \left(1 - \frac{r_i k_i}{rk^m} \right) di - \frac{\tau_K}{1 - \tau_K} \cdot e_K + e_b \frac{b^m}{rk^m} \frac{1}{1 - \tau_K} \right].$$

At the optimal τ_K, we have $dSWF/d\tau_K = 0$, leading to the following proposition.

Proposition 1 *Optimal linear capital and labor income taxes on innovators. The optimal linear capital tax on innovators is given by:*

$$\tau_K = \frac{1 - \bar{g}_K + e_b(b^m / rk^m)}{1 - \bar{g}_K + e_K} \quad \text{with} \quad \bar{g}_K = \frac{\int_i g_i \cdot r_i k_i}{\int_i r_i k_i}$$

$$\text{and} \quad e_K = \frac{(1 - \tau_K)}{rk^m} \cdot \frac{drk^m}{d(1 - \tau_K)} > 0. \tag{14}$$

The optimal labor tax on innovators, obtained through similar derivations, is given by:

---

[5] The government thus sets tax rates on innovators to maximize overall social welfare. This can be done in this setting without consideration of what other taxes are in place on (non-innovating) agents, because the only interaction for the purpose of taxes of the innovating and non-innovating agents is through the spillover, which will be taken into account in the tax revenues. Two critical assumptions for being able to look at the tax rates on innovators separately from the tax rates on other agents are that the government can rebate or tax the spillover lump-sum and that agents do not have income effects. Other agents' spillovers on innovators do not interact with the choice of the optimal tax rates on innovators either.

$$\tau_L = \frac{1 - \overline{g}_L + e_\pi (\pi^m / z^m)}{1 - \overline{g}_L + e_L} \quad \text{with} \quad \overline{g}_L = \frac{\int_i g_i \cdot z_i}{\int_i z_i} \tag{15}$$

$$\text{and} \quad e_L = \frac{1 - \tau_L}{z^m} \cdot \frac{dz^m}{d(1 - \tau_L)} > 0.$$

The optimal capital tax rate on innovators. Consider first the optimal capital tax. It depends on the social preferences embodied in the social welfare weights g_i. These can take many forms and lead to interesting tax results. In a nutshell, as long as wealth is concentrated among individuals with lower social marginal welfare weights (such that g_i is decreasing in k_i), we have $\overline{g}_K < 1$ and, absent the spillover, the optimal capital tax is strictly positive. The optimal capital tax rate will be lower (i) the higher the social welfare weight put on inventors relative to other agents, and (ii) the higher the weight of the wealthier inventors overall relative to the average person in the economy. On the other hand, if inventors have very unequal levels of capital income and society puts more weight on the entrepreneurs who start out with little capital, the optimal capital tax rate will be higher in order to redistribute toward the lower-income innovators (and lower-income agents overall).

The optimal capital tax rate also depends on the elasticity of capital income to taxes, which captures the efficiency costs of taxing capital. The higher this elasticity, the lower the optimal capital tax rate should be. Imagine, for instance, that capital is highly mobile or easy to hide from tax authorities (as we will review in the empirical sections below). Then it may be difficult, from a feasibility standpoint, to heavily tax the capital of innovators.

Finally, the optimal tax rate depends on the strength and responsiveness of the innovation spillover to taxes. This term is a Pigouvian correction for the externality induced by the capital investment of inventors. The higher the positive spillover on other agents (i.e., the less the innovator's private return relative to the social return), the lower the capital tax rate should be set. Furthermore, if the (positive) spillover is also highly elastic to taxes, then the tax rate should be lower too. In fact, if the spillover on others is very large and positive, that optimal tax could be negative (i.e., a capital subsidy).

Contrary to the often-cited Chamley-Judd result, the optimal capital tax is not generically zero. It will be zero only in a few specific cases. The first is if $\overline{g}_K = 1$ and $e_b = 0$, which means that there are no redistributive concerns for capital income or capital income is perfectly equally distributed (i.e., g_i is uncorrelated with k_i) and that there are either no spillovers ($b^m = 0$) or that the spillovers are inelastic to taxes ($e_b = 0$). A second case is if capital is infinitely elastic to taxes: i.e., if $e_K = \infty$.

The optimal labor tax rate on innovators. The labor income tax rate is driven by the same considerations as the capital tax rate: the social welfare weight on inventors relative to the weight on non-inventors, the elasticity of inventors' labor income to taxes, and the strength and elasticity of the spillover from inventors' effort. Imagine that inventors only care about the thrill of the discovery and about adding to society. This would imply that their elasticity to taxes is close to zero. On the contrary, one may imagine that there is nothing special about the payoff of inventors relative to many other high-skilled professions, and that their labor supply elasticity is thus comparable to that of non-inventors.

The revenue maximizing tax rates on innovation are the ones that arise when zero weight is placed on innovators per se ($\overline{g}_K = 0$ and $\overline{g}_L = 0$) and are given by:

$$\tau_K^R = \frac{1 + e_b(b^m / rk^m)}{1 + e_K} \quad \text{and} \quad \tau_L^R = \frac{1 + e_\pi(\pi^m / z^m)}{1 + e_L}. \tag{16}$$

Generalization. These formulas, expressed in terms of sufficient statistics, are more general and hold beyond the specific model presented. In particular, individual utilities can have arbitrary heterogeneity. However, it is important to bear in mind that all elasticities can depend on the tax system. Thus, evaluating large tax reforms or finding the optimum that is very different from the status quo (at which elasticities are empirically estimated) would require a way of estimating elasticities structurally.

The model only considered intensive-margin responses on the choice of labor effort, capital investments, and rent-appropriation of inventors. Individual inventors can also respond to taxes by switching between the corporate and noncorporate sector, by changing occupation altogether, by hiding their income, or by moving to another country. The observed macro-level elasticities in the formulas will be the combination of all these micro-level responses. For a discussion of the possible channels through which general tax policy and targeted incentives (such as R&D tax credits) can shape innovation, see Akcigit and Stantcheva (2020).

The general rule on how to think about these margins of responses is as follows: Tax base externalities (say, to another taxed occupation or the noncorporate sector) would lead to additional terms in the formulas above (see Piketty et al. 2014). Migration responses or outright evasion (i.e., any shift of income toward tax bases that are *de facto* taxed at a zero rate) would appear in the elasticities, but would not change the actual formulas.

2.2.2 Optimal top labor tax and capital tax rates

Suppose now that the government cannot distinguish between innovators and non-innovators. In this section, I derive the optimal labor and capital income tax rates that apply above a given threshold (i.e., the "top" tax rates). This is without loss of generality, as it nests the case of the optimal overall linear capital and labor income tax rates, by simply setting the top tax thresholds to zero.

Suppose that there is a mass one of top earners who have labor income higher than $\bar{z}$ and capital income higher than $\bar{k}$. Among these top earners, there are innovators as well as other professionals. These top earners may all generate different levels of positive, negative, or zero spillovers. When considering the top tax rates, the government has to take into account the composition of top earners and their average spillovers and responses to taxes.

The government sets linear tax rates τ_L and τ_K in the top tax brackets. Redefine our variables introduced above to signify averages across top earners. For instance, let $z^m := \int_{i: z_i \geq \bar{z}} z_i di$ be the average labor income of top bracket taxpayers and $\pi(1 - \tau) := \int_{i: z_i \geq \bar{z}} \pi_i di$ their average spillover, which are both functions of the top net-of-tax rate. Similarly, redefine the elasticities introduced above to be elasticities with respect to the net-of-tax top rates of the variables pertaining to top earners. Furthermore, introduce the Pareto parameters $a_L = z^m / (z^m - \bar{z})$ and $a_K = rk^m / (rk^m - r\bar{k}^m)$ that capture the thickness of the top tail of the distributions. Suppose again that the average spillover generated in the top bracket comes at the equal expense of all agents in the economy. Finally, let $\bar{g}_K^{top} = \dfrac{\int_{i: k_i \leq \bar{k}} r_i k_i g_i}{\int_i g_i rk^m}$ be the capital income-weighted average marginal social welfare weight on top earners relative to the average weight in the economy, and define $\bar{g}_L^{top} = \dfrac{\int_{i: z_i \leq \bar{z}} z_i g_i}{\int_i g_i z^m}$ similarly.

Similar derivations as above yield to the optimal linear tax rates in the top brackets above a given capital income and labor income threshold.

Proposition 2 *Optimal top capital and labor income tax rates. The optimal capital and labor income tax rates on agents (inventors and non-inventors) earning income above thresholds $\bar{z}$ and $\bar{rk}$ are given by:*

$$\tau_K^{top} = \frac{1 - \bar{g}_K^{top} + a_K \cdot b^m / (rk^m) \cdot e_b}{1 - \bar{g}_K^{top} + a_K^{top} \cdot e_K^{top}} \tag{17}$$

$$\tau_L^{top} = \frac{1 - \bar{g}_L^{top} + a_L \cdot \pi^m / z^m \cdot e_\pi}{1 - \bar{g}_L^{top} + a_L \cdot e_L^{top}}. \tag{18}$$

Note that because capital income is so concentrated, a fully nonlinear tax system would converge quickly to the top linear capital tax rate and this rate has wide applicability. This is not true to the same extent with the labor income tax.

Discussion. The broad factors shaping top capital and labor income taxes are similar to the ones affecting the optimal tax rate on innovators. The most important distinction is that the parameters of optimal tax rates for innovators reflect the *composition* of top earners.

For instance, imagine that society believes that inventors are "deserving" top earners because they have positive spillovers on others, but that other high-earning professions are not as deserving. The higher the share of inventors among top earners, the higher the social welfare weight on all top earners will be, leading to lower optimal top tax rates. Similarly, if inventors have large positive externalities, the more represented they are among top earners and the lower top tax rates should be. Interestingly, voters' perceptions of the composition of top earners are not always in line with reality, as shown in Stantcheva (2020) by using large-scale survey evidence. Respondents tend to underestimate the share of managers, executives, doctors, and finance professionals in the top 1 percent: for instance, the perceived share of executives and managers (10 percent) is three times lower than the actual share (31 percent). On the contrary, respondents tend to overestimate the share of scientists (5 percent perceived vs. 2 percent actual), and that of media, arts, and sports professionals (9 percent perceived vs. 2 percent actual). Importantly, respondents tend to overestimate the share of entrepreneurs (10 percent perceived vs. 2 percent actual).

In practice, if tax rates cannot be differentiated by inventors and non-inventors, given that a very small share of inventors are among top earners, spillovers would have to be very large and positive in order to warrant a lower top tax rate on all top earners. This is the consequence of having a blunt tool that cannot be differentiated.

2.2.3 The choice of instruments

The above formulas give the optimal tax rates on either inventors or all top earners, taking into account the effects of taxation on innovation. They do not explicitly try to foster innovation. If the goal is to stimulate innovation, general taxation policy may not be the best tool, because it is not targeted at all. A specific incentive for inventors (Section 2.2.1) may be a less blunt tool.

Regarding targeted policies, the first issue is whether subsidies on inputs (such as R&D tax credits or subsidies) are more efficient than lower tax rates (which can be viewed as subsidies on the output). Akcigit et al. (2021) show that the answer depends on what information the government has. Their analysis is for innovative firms but would apply similarly to individual innovators.

If the government cannot observe firms' research productivity and is trying to screen good firms from bad ones, uniform tax or subsidy rates are not optimal. Instead, it is efficiency-enhancing to have R&D subsidy rates that are decreasing in the amount of R&D, and profit taxes that are declining in profits. This finding is driven by the high complementary of R&D investments and firms' research productivities in the data: higher-productivity firms generate disproportionately more innovation from a given R&D investment. Since higher-productivity firms have a comparative advantage at innovation, it is better to incentivize R&D investments less for lower-productivity firms. Otherwise, it becomes excessively attractive for high-productivity firms to pretend to be low-productivity ones. A higher incentive for R&D for higher research productivity firms is provided with a lower marginal profit tax at higher profit levels and a lower R&D marginal subsidy rate at higher R&D levels. Intuitively, higher-productivity firms are able to generate more profits from the same research investments, and an allocation with a lower marginal profit tax and a lower marginal R&D subsidy is more attractive to high-productivity firms than to low-productivity firms.

Furthermore, it turns out that the most important feature is the non-linearity in the R&D subsidy: making the profit tax linear (and lower) only generates a small welfare loss. The intuition is that a constant profit tax that is more generous than it should be for low-profit firms, and at about the right level for high-profit firms, does reasonably well because the loss from being too generous to low-profit firms is small (because taxing their low profit levels does not yield much revenue to start with). Thus, linear corporate income taxes—common in practice—can be very close to optimal for innovating firms if combined with the right nonlinear R&D subsidy.

The second important issue with targeted incentives for innovation is whether there are supply-side constraints. For instance, any increase in tax incentives may end up pushing up costs of R&D (e.g., wages of researchers) if the supply of inventors is limited (Van Reenen 2021; Akcigit et al. 2020). Akcigit et al. (2020) show that the strength of R&D incentives can be multiplied when coupled with higher education policy targeting credit-constrained talented people. In highly unequal societies, human capital policies are likely to be more effective than R&D incentives. Furthermore, these two types of policies act at different horizons, with human capital policies affecting longer-run outcomes more strongly. Overall, Van Reenen (2021) and Akcigit et al. (2020) suggest that human capital policies may have large returns, and they may be important complements to any tax incentives for innovation.

I now turn to the empirical evidence on the effects of taxes on innovation. To my knowledge, there is no direct estimate of the elasticities of *income* specific to inventors that we would need to calibrate the formulas in Section 2.2.1. However, I will point to all the pieces of information that we do have, which all contribute to the elasticity of inventors' taxable incomes. The formulas in Section 2.2.2 require estimates of taxable income and rent elasticities for all top earners. For taxable income elasticities, see Saez et al. (2012). For estimates of rent elasticities among executives and CEOs, see Piketty et al. (2014).

3 Historical Evidence

I start with historical, long-term evidence. Historical data is an invaluable resource in the study of major questions, such as the effects of taxes on growth, as it permits leveraging the abundant tax variation that has happened over time.

Akcigit et al. (2022) provide long-run historical evidence on the impact of both personal and corporate income taxation at both the individual inventor level and the state level over the twentieth century. They leverage four historical data sets: a panel data set based on inventors from digitized patent data since 1920, which lets them track inventors and their innovations, citations, place of residence, and technological fields, and the firms (if any) to which they assign their patents; a new data set on historical state-level corporate income taxes; a database on personal income tax rates from Bakija (2006); and additional innovation-related outcomes, such as patent values from Kogan et al. (2017), and state-level value added, manufacturing share, average weekly earnings, establishment size, and total payroll from Allen (2004) and Haines et al. (2010).

As in the model above, the macro-level responses (here, at the state level) are an aggregate of the micro-level responses (of each individual inventor), although the authors consider a wider range of possible adjustment margins to taxes, such as cross-state mobility and reallocation between the corporate and noncorporate sectors. They also distinguish between inventors who work for companies ("corporate" inventors) and individual "garage" inventors operating outside the boundaries of firms that may react differently, based on different incentives and motivations.

Using several distinct and complementary strategies to identify the impact of taxes on innovation, the authors find that at the macro state level, personal and corporate income taxes have significant negative effects on the quantity of innovation, as captured by the number of patents, and on the number of inventors working in the state. The elasticities for personal net-of-tax rates are between 0.8 to 1.8.[6] The quality of innovation, as proxied by the forward citations received by patents, is similarly responsive, and hence,

---

[6] The corresponding elasticities for the corporate tax rate are 1.3 to 2.8.

average quality is not meaningfully affected by taxation. The authors also find that there is a shift in the composition of patents from noncorporate to corporate if the corporate tax rate declines.

At the individual inventor level, personal income taxes significantly negatively impact inventors' likelihood of having any patent and the number of their patents. There is, again, only a small effect on the quality of the average patent, but a larger effect on "home-run" patents with many citations. The elasticity of patents to the personal income net-of-tax rate is around 0.8, and the elasticity of citations is around 1.[7]

The authors also find significant mobility responses to taxes. The elasticity to the net-of-tax personal income tax rate of the number of inventors residing in a state is between 0.10 and 0.15 for inventors from that state and 1.0 to 1.5 for out-of-state inventors. On average, the mobility elasticity is 0.34. Noncorporate inventors are elastic to both corporate and personal income taxes when choosing which state to live and work in. More precisely, their elasticity with respect to net-of-tax personal rates is 0.72 or 0.6 with respect to the net-of-tax corporate rate. The authors estimate that the large macro-level elasticities to personal net-of-tax rates come from both mobility and innovation output responses. Overall, the elasticities of inventors to taxes are comparable, but somewhat larger, than those of other high-skilled agents. The macro-level elasticities of patents are also consistent with other macro estimates for employment or output.

We can relate these estimates to the optimal tax on inventors formula in Section 2.2.1. To calibrate these formulas, we would need to convert the elasticities of innovation into elasticities of income of inventors, using estimates of how inventor income changes with innovation quantity and quality.

4 Quantity and Quality of Innovation

In modern-day data, there is abundant evidence regarding the effect of tax incentives on innovation. Most studies focus on the effects of direct tax breaks for innovation, such as R&D tax credits, with very few papers considering the indirect effects of general corporate taxation. On the latter topic,

---

[7] Interestingly, corporate income taxes affect only the innovation output of corporate inventors, not that of noncorporate inventors. The elasticity of patents of corporate inventors with respect to the net-of-tax corporate rate is 0.49 and that of their citations is 0.46.

Schwellnus and Arnold (2008) report a negative effect of corporate taxation on productivity and investment for firms in manufacturing and services across many countries. Atanassov and Liu (2020) study US publicly traded firms in the period 1998–2006 and find that corporate tax cuts lead to higher innovation output, as measured by the number of patents (quantity) and citations per patent (a measure of patent quality), especially for firms that are financially constrained, have smaller collateral assets and weaker corporate governance, and more frequently use tax avoidance strategies. In a study of European multinational enterprise groups (MNEs), Karkinsky and Riedel (2012) estimate that for the period 1995–2003, a 1 percentage point increase in the tax rate on royalty income leads to a −3.5 percent to −3.8 percent decrease in the number of patents in a given country.

On R&D-specific incentives, most of the key papers find significant effects. Reviewing the US innovation tax policy in the 1980s, Hall (1993) finds an elasticity of R&D spending to R&D tax credits of around 1. These findings appear to hold across OECD countries overall, for which Hall and Van Reenen (2000) find that a dollar in tax credit for R&D stimulates a dollar of additional R&D. Bloom et al. (2002) study the effectiveness of R&D tax credits in OECD countries from 1979 through 1994. They find that reducing the cost of R&D by 10 percent leads to a 1 percent increase in R&D in the short run and an almost 10 percent increase in the long run.

Romero-Jordán et al. (2014) use EESE survey data for 1995–2015 to study the impact of two Spanish tax incentives for R&D. They estimate that tax credits exert a positive and significant effect on private R&D investments, but only for large firms. Public grants act very differently: They contribute to R&D investment by alleviating firms' financial constraints through a signaling effect, which in turn simplifies access to external debt for firms that obtain the grants.

Dechezleprêtre et al. (2016) exploit a change in the UK R&D tax regime in 2008 that raised the size threshold for a more generous "SME" tax regime. The authors find that this led to an economically and statistically significant increase in R&D investment and patenting. Furthermore, they find no evidence of a decrease in the quality of patents, which supports the idea that R&D tax credits do not merely cause relabeling of existing spending. Concerning effectiveness, they estimate that the policy stimulated £1.7 of R&D for every £1 of subsidy, and that in its absence R&D would be around 10 percent lower over the period 2006–2011. Their findings are supported by Guceri and Liu (2019), who estimate an elasticity of −1.6 and £1.3 of R&D

for every pound of forgone corporate tax revenue in the UK for the same period.

Chen et al. (2021) leverage China's InnoCom program, which provided large tax cuts for companies investing in R&D over a predetermined threshold. They find that this tax incentive significantly increased R&D investment over the period 2008–2011. However, they also show that expense relabeling reduces the effective R&D investment by a quarter.

Several papers focus on innovation tax policy across US states. Wilson (2009) examines R&D tax incentives across US states between 1981 and 2004 and estimates that, on average, a 1 percentage point increase in a state's effective R&D tax credit rate leads to a long-run increase in R&D spending of 3–4 percent inside the state and a decrease of 3–4 percent in R&D spending outside of it. A possible interpretation of this high elasticity is that there is ample cross-state R&D and business shifting. Rao (2016) studies the impact of the US federal R&D tax credit over the period 1981–1991 and estimates that a 10 percent reduction in the user cost of R&D leads to a 19.8 percent short-run increase in the research intensity ratio, measured as the ratio of R&D spending to sales. It is specifically R&D deemed as qualified for the federal tax credit that increases the most. Long-run estimates suggest that the average firm faces adjustment costs when scaling up R&D and increases spending over time. Most of the increase in R&D spending seems to be accounted for by additional spending on wages and research supplies.

5 Mobility of Inventors

Taxes can also influence the location choices of innovators. Moretti and Wilson (2017) focus on a select group of scientists' responses to changes in personal and business tax differentials across states. They uncover large, stable, and precisely estimated effects of personal and corporate taxes on the scientists' migration patterns. The long-run elasticity of mobility relative to taxes is 1.8 for personal income taxes, 1.9 for state corporate income tax, and −1.7 for the investment tax credit. While there are many other factors that matter for where innovative individuals and innovative companies decide to locate, there are enough firms and workers on the margin that state taxes matter. Moretti and Wilson (2014) examine the effect of R&D tax credits on the number of these so-called star inventors in the biotech sector. They estimate that a 10 percent decline in the user cost of capital induced by an increase in R&D tax incentives raises the number of star scientists by 22 percent. An important question about differential R&D tax credits across US states is whether the total effect is zero-sum at the federal level. This same question was asked above regarding state personal and corporate income taxes by Akcigit et al. (2022), who found that the corporate tax was more likely to generate cross-state business shifting without actual gains in innovation at the federal level.

The impact of top tax rates on the international mobility of inventors is studied by Akcigit et al. (2016). The authors also focus on what they term "superstar inventors," those with the most and highest-cited patents since 1977. Using panel data on inventors from the US and European Patent Offices, the authors track inventors across countries and over time. Superstar inventors' location choices are significantly affected by top tax rates: the elasticity to the net-of-tax rate of the number of domestic superstar inventors is around 0.03, while that of foreign superstar inventors is around 1.

It is important to bear in mind that these are the partial effects of taxation, holding all else constant. But tax revenues are used to fund amenities that may also be valuable. Akcigit et al. (2016) find that inventors are less elastic to taxes if they work in a field that is particularly successful in a given location. Akcigit et al. (2022) also find that elasticities to taxes are dampened when there are "agglomeration effects"—namely, when there are more people working in the same field in a given location.

6 Income Shifting and Tax Avoidance through Innovation

Individuals and firms engaging in innovation can also respond to taxes by misreporting their innovative activity and the resulting income. Furthermore, innovation may in itself be a channel of tax avoidance and tax sheltering of income.

Blair-Stanek (2015) considers different ways in which a US company can engage in tax avoidance practices. First, intellectual property (IP) rights could be sold to the subsidiary at a price that is below market ("transfer pricing"), either bundled with a "service" related to the IP or on their own. In this way, the true value of the patent could be hidden from tax authorities.

The reason tax-induced manipulation of transfer prices is possible lies in the difficulty of finding comparable IP transactions between unrelated parties to accurately price these transactions.

Alternatively, a company can license patent rights to a subsidiary in a tax haven. By doing so, future profits will be subjected to the low tax rate of the country of the subsidiary, whereas the legal ownership remains in the United States. US legal ownership can be attractive if it offers greater protection for IP rights. In the context of the US taxation, this practice may often be more advantageous than the outright sale of IP to the subsidiary for an artificially low price. Lastly, another possibility consists of a cost sharing agreement (CSA), where the US company will provide the IP for an artificially low price while the subsidiary will contribute to the funding for the IP improvement. This kind of agreement will guarantee that profits coming from outside the US will not be subject to US taxation. Multinational companies are more likely to engage in CSAs if their domestic intangible assets are more valuable and if the nature of the IP development makes it easy to understate the fair market value of the IP (De Simone and Sansing 2019).

In a meta-analysis of international corporate tax avoidance, Beer et al. (2020) confirm that the separation between the country of ownership and the country where R&D is conducted is an important way for firms to reduce their tax burdens. Dischinger and Riedel (2011) also argue that the relocation choice of IP is driven by the incentive to save taxes through the relocation of highly profitable intangible assets to low-tax countries and confirm this on European MNEs over the period 1995–2005.

Cheng et al. (2021) find a positive correlation between patents and tax planning using Compustat and USPTO data for 1987–2012. Firms with more domestic patents shift more income outside the US as compared to firms with fewer patents, suggesting that income shifting through patents may be a significant way to avoid tax obligations. Gao et al. (2016) use the same data for the period 1987–2010 and find a strong connection between patenting activity and tax avoidance. Furthermore, the magnitude of tax avoidance is more pronounced for innovative firms headquartered in states offering R&D tax credits.

Dudar and Voget (2016) calculate the tax elasticity of patent and trademark location choices for the period 1996–2012. The elasticity of patent location ranges between −0.05 and −0.85 and the elasticity of trademark locations falls between −0.77 and −3.14. Thus, this study not only supports the hypothesis of IP driving tax erosion, it also highlights that differences between various types of intangible assets should not be neglected. Trademarks are more mobile within a company group than patents are.

Skeie et al. (2017) estimate the effect of taxes on multinational companies' choice of patent location. They distinguish between nonshifted patents, for which the country of the applicant is the same as the country of the inventor, and shifted patents, for which these countries differ. Using the OECD-PATSTAT and OECD-Orbis database for the period 2004–2010, they show that a 5 percentage points cut in the preferential tax rate on patent income correlates with a 6 percent increase in patent applications. However, higher-tax rate countries that have stricter anti-avoidance rules also have a greater volume of nonshifted patents, suggesting that fewer patents may be shifted out of them than out of similar countries with less strict rules. Similar conclusions are reached by Baumann et al. (2020). They combine PATSTAT and Amadeus data for the period 1990–2006 and find that, even though the general tendency for firms is to match high-value patents to low-tax countries, this inclination is lower if controlled foreign corporation rules are enforced.

7 Patent Boxes: Preferential Tax Treatment of Innovation

An important tax reduction policy for innovation consists of so-called patent boxes. They offer a reduced tax rate—either through a separate tax schedule or special deductions—on income arising from licensing or using intellectual property (Merrill 2016). Differing from other existing tax incentives for R&D, IP boxes provide a back-end tax reduction for successful innovations. Hall (2020) emphasizes that they not only target the activities receiving a reward through the patent, they also promote patent assertion and provide an additional incentive to renew patents that might otherwise be abandoned. At the same time, they may also encourage "patent trolling" by protecting the income of firms specializing in patent litigation and enforcement. Patent boxes can affect the full chain of decision-making of firms, as do direct subsidies of innovation inputs. Thus, Brannon and Hanlon (2015) find that profitable survey respondents in the biotech and pharmaceutical industries would allocate more income, R&D, and manufacturing to the United States if an innovation box system were to be adopted.

It has been argued that patent boxes encourage tax shifting by firms because the profits from intangible assets and IP are difficult to disentangle from other profits. They may affect the location of profits without truly affecting the location of R&D activities. The extent to which such shifting actually happens depends on the conditions set in the patent box.

First, there are some restrictions to patent boxes, following the directives of the so-called nexus approach promoted by the OECD (Faulhaber 2017), whose rationale can be summarized as follows: Countries are permitted to provide benefits under patent boxes only as long as there is a nexus between certain qualifying R&D expenditures and the income receiving advantageous tax treatment. In particular, the latter must be commensurate to the amount of R&D undertaken by the taxpayer receiving benefits. Even though this rule does not eliminate the income-shifting problem, it significantly constrains it.

A further solution that has been implemented to mitigate tax avoidance is the "addback statute." Suppose a company has a patent held by one of its subsidiaries in a tax haven. With the enactment of this statute, the company must add back the royalty from the patent to the taxable income in the company's state. Clearly, any enforcement policy that de facto increases the tax rate of companies comes with a cost. Li et al. (2021) study the effects of the addback statute and find a statistically and economically significant decrease of 5 percent in the number of citations received by patents and of 4.77 percentage points for the number of patents filed by relevant firms after three years. Furthermore, Martins (2018) contends that implementation of the nexus approach in 2016 to the Portuguese IP box significantly increased tax and accounting complexity.

Mohnen et al. (2017) analyze the Dutch innovation box policy, which requires that the tax advantage must be linked to the firm's own and, therefore, local R&D activity. Using difference-in-difference and matching evidence, they find that firms that take advantage of this policy instrument tend to have higher R&D activities, but the extra R&D generated is not sufficient to justify the tax losses. Nevertheless, their estimate is not far off from those obtained for tax credits of different kinds in several countries.

IP box regimes can also differ in how they define IP income. Some regimes apply to income derived from patents that already existed prior to the box and acquired after its implementation, while others only apply to newly created IP. Boxes can also apply to all revenues generated from IP or, instead, to income (revenues minus costs). Therefore, when studying firms' responses, such specificities matter. Ohrn (2016) merges data on IP box regimes from Evers et al. (2015) and international payment flows and R&D from the US Bureau of Economic Analysis (BEA) and finds that R&D spending responds only to IP boxes that apply to newly developed R&D or to revenues rather than income. Furthermore, US payments to foreign affiliates for the use of IP rise only in innovation box regimes that apply to income derived from existing or acquired R&D.

Finally, Faulhaber (2017) suggests that the introduction of patent box regimes exerts competitive—and not necessarily efficient—pressure on neighboring countries. They cite the case of Spain, which modified its patent box regulation following the implementation of patent boxes in other countries, such as Malta and Cyprus. In the latter, the patent boxes were advantageous and did not require that the R&D take place in their jurisdictions.

8 Conclusion

In this chapter I derived optimal formulas for the taxes on labor and capital incomes, taking into account the spillovers from innovation. Inventors can engage in productive effort and saving, but also in rent-seeking by trying to capture a larger share of the total social surplus from innovation. The formulas derived are in terms of sufficient statistics that can, in principle, be estimated in the data.

Ultimately, if the goal is to foster innovation, then general taxes, such as income and capital taxes that cannot be differentiated for innovators and non-innovators, are blunt tools. The spirit of this chapter, instead, is to show that the efficiency costs from reduced innovation may need be taken into account when setting taxes and to pinpoint the factors on which the magnitudes of these costs depend. For instance, if innovators make up a significant share of top earners or if spillovers from innovation are very large, optimal tax rates may be meaningfully different when innovation is taken into account than when it is not. If the goal is to stimulate innovation, direct research incentives allow for better targeting (see Akcigit et al. 2021).

The second part of this chapter reviewed some of the evidence to date on the effects of taxes on innovation. In recent years, significant progress has been made on these issues thanks to the creative use of patent and inventor data, historical data, and administrative data. Future work could shed more light on the elasticities of innovators' incomes to taxation and on the specific ways in which they adjust to tax changes.

References

Aghion, Philippe, Ufuk Akcigit, Antonin Bergeaud, Richard Blundell, and David Hemous. (2019). "Innovation and Top Income Inequality." *Review of Economic Studies, 86* (1), 1–45.

Aghion, Philippe, Ufuk Akcigit, Angus Deaton, and Alexandra Roulet. (2016). "Creative Destruction and Subjective Well-Being." *American Economic Review, 106* (12), 3869–3897.

Aghion, Philippe, and Peter Howitt. (1992). "A Model of Growth through Creative Destruction." *Econometrica, 60* (2), 323–351.

Akcigit, Ufuk, Salome Baslandze, and Stefanie Stantcheva. (2016). "Taxation and the International Mobility of Inventors." *American Economic Review, 106* (10), 2930–2981.

Akcigit, Ufuk, John Grigsby, Tom Nicholas, and Stefanie Stantcheva. (2022). "Taxation and Innovation in the 20th Century." *Quarterly Journal of Economics, 137* (1), 329–385.

Akcigit, Ufuk, Douglas Hanley, and Stefanie Stantcheva. (2021). "Optimal Taxation and R&D Policies." *Econometrica, 90* (2), 645–684.

Akcigit, Ufuk, Jeremy G. Pearce, and Marta Prato. (2020). "Tapping into Talent: Coupling Education and Innovation Policies for Economic Growth." NBER Working Paper 27862.

Akcigit, Ufuk, and Stefanie Stantcheva. (2020). "Taxation and Innovation: What Do We Know?" NBER Working Paper 27109.

Allen, Samuel K. (2004). "The Economics and Politics of Workers' Compensation: 1930–2000." PhD dissertation, University of Arizona.

Atanassov, Julian, and Xiaoding Liu. (2020). "Can Corporate Income Tax Cuts Stimulate Innovation?" *Journal of Financial and Quantitative Analysis, 55* (5), 1415–1465.

Bakija, Jon. (2006). "Documentation for a Comprehensive Historical U.S. Federal and State Income Tax Calculator Program." Williams College Working Paper.

Baumann, Martina, Tobias Boehm, Bodo Knoll, and Nadine Riedel. (2020). "Corporate Taxes, Patent Shifting, and Anti-Avoidance Rules: Empirical Evidence." *Public Finance Review, 48* (4), 467–504.

Beer, Sebastian, Ruud De Mooij, and Li Liu. (2020). "International Corporate Tax Avoidance: A Review of the Channels, Magnitudes, and Blind Spots." *Journal of Economic Surveys, 34* (3), 660–688.

Blair-Stanek, Andrew. (2015). "Intellectual Property Law Solutions to Tax Avoidance." *UCLA Law Review, 62* (1), 2–73.

Bloom, Nicholas, Rachel Griffith, and John Van Reenen. (2002). "Do R&D Tax Credits Work? Evidence from a Panel of Countries 1979–1997." *Journal of Public Economics, 85* (1), 1–31.

Bloom, Nicholas, Mark Schankerman, and John Van Reenen. (2013). "Identifying Technology Spillovers and Product Market Rivalry." *Econometrica, 81* (4), 1347–1393.

Brannon, Ike, and Michelle Hanlon. (2015). "How a Patent Box Would Affect the US Biopharmaceutical Sector." *Tax Notes, 146* (5), 635–639.

Chamley, Christophe. (1986). "Optimal Taxation of Capital Income in General Equilibrium with Infinite Lives." *Econometrica, 80* (3), 607–622.

Chen, Zhao, Zhikuo Liu, Juan Carlos Suárez Serrato, and Daniel Yi Xu. (2021). "Notching R&D Investment with Corporate Income Tax Cuts in China." *American Economic Review, 111* (7), 2065–2100.

Cheng, C. S. Agnes, Peng Guo, Chia-Hsiang Weng, and Qiang Wu. (2021). "Innovation and Corporate Tax Planning: The Distinct Effects of Patents and R&D." *Contemporary Accounting Research, 38* (1), 621–653.

De Simone, Lisa, and Richard C. Sansing. (2019). "Income Shifting Using a Cost-Sharing Arrangement." *Journal of the American Taxation Association, 41* (1), 123–136.

Dechezleprêtre, Antoine, Elias Einiö, Ralf Martin, Kieu-Trang Nguyen, and John Van Reenen. (2016). "Do Tax Incentives for Research Increase Firm Innovation? An RD Design for R&D." NBER Working Paper 22405.

Dischinger, Matthias, and Nadine Riedel. (2011). "Corporate Taxes and the Location of Intangible Assets within Multinational Firms." *Journal of Public Economics, 95* (7–8), 691–707.

Dudar, Olena, and Johannes Voget. (2016). "Corporate Taxation and Location of Intangible Assets: Patents vs. Trademarks." ZEW-Centre for European Economic Research Discussion Paper 16-015.

Evers, Lisa, Helen Miller, and Christoph Spengel. (2015). "Intellectual Property Box Regimes: Effective Tax Rates and Tax Policy Considerations." *International Tax and Public Finance, 22* (3), 502–530.

Faulhaber, Lilian V. (2017). "The Luxembourg Effect: Patent Boxes and the Limits of International Cooperation." *Minnesota Law Review, 101* (4), 1641–1702.

Gao, Lei, Leo L. Yang, and Joseph H. Zhang. (2016). "Corporate Patents, R&D Success, and Tax Avoidance." *Review of Quantitative Finance and Accounting, 47* (4), 1063–1096.

Guceri, Irem, and Li Liu. (2019). "Effectiveness of Fiscal Incentives for R&D: Quasi-Experimental Evidence." *American Economic Journal: Economic Policy, 11* (1), 266–291.

Haines, Michael R. (2010). "Historical, Demographic, Economic, and Social Data: The United States, 1790–2002." Inter-university Consortium for Political and Social Research 2896.

Hall, Bronwyn H. (1993). "R&D Tax Policy during the 1980s: Success or Failure?" *Tax Policy and the Economy, 7,* 1–35.

Hall, Bronwyn. (2020). "Tax Policy for Innovation." NBER Working Paper 25773.

Hall, Bronwyn, and John Van Reenen. (2000). "How Effective Are Fiscal Incentives for R&D? A Review of the Evidence." *Research Policy, 29* (4–5), 449–469.

Jones, Charles I. (1995). "R & D-Based Models of Economic Growth." *Journal of Political Economy, 103* (4), 759–784.

Jones, Charles I., and John C. Williams. (1998). "Measuring the Social Return to R&D." *Quarterly Journal of Economics, 113* (4), 1119–1135.

Judd, Kenneth L. (1985). "Redistributive Taxation in a Simple Perfect Foresight Model." *Journal of Public Economics, 28* (1), 59–83.

Karkinsky, Tom, and Nadine Riedel. (2012). "Corporate Taxation and the Choice of Patent Location within Multinational Firms." *Journal of International Economics, 88* (1), 176–185.

Kogan, Leonid, Dimitris Papanikolaou, Amit Seru, and Noah Stoffman. (2017). "Technological Innovation, Resource Allocation, and Growth." *Quarterly Journal of Economics, 132* (2), 665–712.

Li, Qin, Mark (Shuai) Ma, and Terry Shevlin. (2021). "The Effect of Tax Avoidance Crackdown on Corporate Innovation." *Journal of Accounting and Economics, 71* (2), 101382.

Martins, António. (2018). "The Portuguese Intellectual Property Box: Issues in Designing Investment Incentives." *Journal of International Trade Law & Policy, 17* (3), 86–102.

Merrill, Peter. (2016). "Innovation Boxes: BEPS and Beyond." *National Tax Journal, 69* (4), 847–862.

Mohnen, Pierre, Arthur Vankan, and Bart Verspagen. (2017). "Evaluating the Innovation Box Tax Policy Instrument in the Netherlands, 2007–13." *Oxford Review of Economic Policy, 33* (1), 141–156.

Moretti, Enrico, and Daniel Wilson. (2014). "State Incentives for Innovation, Star Scientists and Jobs: Evidence from Biotech." *Journal of Urban Economics, 79* (C), 20–38.

Moretti, Enrico, and Daniel Wilson. (2017). "The Effect of State Taxes on the Geographical Location of Top Earners: Evidence from Star Scientists." *American Economic Review, 107* (7), 1858–1903.

Ohrn, Eric. (2016). "The Effect of IP Box Regimes on International IP Payments and Foreign Research and Development." Technical Report, Grinnell College, manuscript.

Piketty, Thomas, Emmanuel Saez, and Stefanie Stantcheva. (2014). "Optimal Taxation of Top Labor Incomes: A Tale of Three Elasticities." *American Economic Journal: Economic Policy, 6* (1), 230–271.

Putney, Snell, and Gladys J. Putney. (1962). "Radical Innovation and Prestige." *American Sociological Review, 27* (4), 548–551.

Rao, Nirupama. (2016). "Do Tax Credits Stimulate R&D Spending? The Effect of the R&D Tax Credit in Its First Decade." *Journal of Public Economics, 140*, 1–12.

Romer, Paul M. (1994). "The Origins of Endogenous Growth." *Journal of Economic Perspectives, 8* (1), 3–22.

Romero-Jordán, Desiderio, María Jesús Delgado-Rodríguez, Inmaculada Alvarez-Ayuso, and Sonia de Lucas-Santos. (2014). "Assessment of the Public Tools Used to Promote R&D Investment in Spanish SMEs." *Small Business Economics, 43* (4), 959–976.

Saez, Emmanuel, Joel Slemrod, and Seth Giertz. (2012). "The Elasticity of Taxable Income with Respect to Marginal Tax Rates: A Critical Review." *Journal of Economic Literature, 50* (1), 3–50.

Saez, Emmanuel, and Stefanie Stantcheva. (2018). "A Simpler Theory of Optimal Capital Taxation." *Journal of Public Economics, 162,* 120–142.

Schwellnus, Cyrille, and Jens Matthias Arnold. (2008). "Do Corporate Taxes Reduce Productivity and Investment at the Firm Level? Cross-Country Evidence from the Amadeus Dataset." OECD Economics Department Working Paper.

Skeie, Øystein Bieltvedt, Åsa Johansson, Carlo Menon, and Stéphane Sorbe. (2017). "Innovation, Patent Location and Tax Planning by Multinationals." OECD Economics Department Working Paper.

Stantcheva, Stefanie. (2020). "Understanding Economic Policies: What Do People Know and Learn?" Harvard University Working Paper.

Stuart, Toby E., and Waverly W. Ding. (2006). "When Do Scientists Become Entrepreneurs? The Social Structural Antecedents of Commercial Activity in the Academic Life Sciences." *American Journal of Sociology, 112* (1), 97–144.

Van Reenen, John. (2021). "Innovation and Human Capital Policy." NBER Working Paper 28713.

Wilson, Daniel J. (2009). "Beggar Thy Neighbor? The In-State, Out-of-State, and Aggregate Effects of R&D Tax Credits." *Review of Economics and Statistics, 91* (2), 431–436.

PART IX

Science

CHAPTER 25

Of Academics and Creative Destruction

Startup Advantage in the Process of Innovation

JULIAN KOLEV, ALEXIS HAUGHEY, FIONA MURRAY,
and SCOTT STERN

Introduction

Innovation serves as an essential engine of modern economies, most prominently as a driver of long-term productivity and growth. Economists have long sought to understand the drivers of innovation as a window into the differential growth rates of nations, regions, and firms. The pathbreaking contributions of our colleagues Phillipe Aghion and Peter Howitt provide foundational insight into the drivers of innovation, and in particular the roles that incentives and competition play in shaping innovative investment and effort by different organizations.

The first economic question that arises when considering the rate of innovation is whether (and which) organizations have adequate incentives to undertake the costly investments needed to drive innovation. In "A Model of Growth through Creative Destruction," Aghion and Howitt (1992; hereafter cited as AH) provide the critical building blocks necessary for addressing this challenge by clarifying precisely how firm-level incentives for investment are shaped by the prospect of creative destruction. Specifically, AH highlight the fact that incentives for innovation whose outcome offers a superior alternative to that currently available in the market reside with entrepreneurs rather than incumbent firms (due to the "replacement effect"), but these incentives are themselves shaped by the prospect of subsequent follow-on innovation that will in turn overtake the (transitory) market power of a successful startup. In other words, AH offer a general equilibrium framework in which (a) startup firms play a distinctive and outsized economic role in the process of economic growth, and (b) innovation incentives for new entrants reflect a balance between potential market power for a single period versus the degree to which incentives are provided for subsequent entrants to innovate in future periods.

While AH provide critical insight into the incentives of startup ventures to engage in the process of innovation, their framework abstracts away from the incentives provided to the agents undertaking that research. This is the question that is addressed in the (complementary) theoretical framework of Aghion, Dewatripont, and Stein (2008; hereafter cited as ADS). Similar to AH, ADS consider a multi-period model of innovation where incentives for a company to innovate in a given period are shaped by expected returns in some future period. However, relative to AH, ADS emphasize that a successful innovation may involve a long research line with multiple stages, and they examine the challenges facing an organization contracting with researchers at each stage of this line. A critical insight from ADS is that when researchers have a preference to maintain a degree of control over project choices, it is optimal to cede the control over early-stage projects to researchers (similar to the incentives of academia); by contrast, private funders (i.e., investors) will optimally assert control over project direction as the innovation gets closer to the marketplace.

A natural question that arises is how the two perspectives of ADS and AH are related to one another. On the one hand, AH suggest that startups play a particularly important role in driving creative destruction. On the other hand, ADS suggest that a for-profit firm (whether incumbent or startup) is likely to be involved in the late (but perhaps not early) stages of commercialization of a multistage innovation process. However, neither model directly addresses how the process of creative destruction (in the market) is related to the incentives (within organizations) required to invest in a multistage innovation process. The purpose of this chapter is to explore the connection between these two perspectives.

Our analysis suggests that startups play a special role in the process of commercializing innovations, linking early-stage scientific research to the broader economy-wide impact of creative destruction. This linkage is particularly important given the increasing reliance on science-driven startups in addressing a range of pressing societal challenges. Our analysis reflects and extends the durable and far-reaching implications of the Aghion and Howitt creative destruction framework for understanding the relationships among innovation, institutions, and economic growth.

Building on a more in-depth discussion contrasting AH and ADS, our analysis begins with a set of short case studies illuminating the process by which foundational scientific research is transferred from academia into the private sector. In each case, though there is no requirement that a startup venture be involved in the process of commercialization, we illustrate that a critical step in the handoff from academia to industry takes place through entrepreneurship and startup venture formation. This motivates our more formal analysis, where we extend the ADS model to specify the conditions under which startup ventures will optimally bridge the gap between universities and large firms. We identify two distinct drivers of "startup advantage": first, academic startup founders may have access to private information about the value of specific high-risk research lines. Startups are, therefore, willing to pursue these ideas at an earlier stage in the innovation process described in the ADS model. Second, startups do not experience the cannibalization effect described in AH, whereby successful innovation by an incumbent comes at the expense of their own preexisting competitive advantage. Because of this difference, startups are in a position to pursue more disruptive research lines in which incumbents would normally underinvest or lack interest. Taken together, these two channels form the foundation of "startup advantage," whereby new ventures are uniquely positioned to develop and extend research lines that are distinct from the innovations targeted by incumbents.

Our theoretical analysis generates two central hypotheses. First, startup innovation will be more valuable and ultimately more impactful than that of *either* universities or large firms, and second, startups will generate innovations that are more radical and disruptive than those of incumbent firms. We provide descriptive statistics consistent with these hypotheses using a sample of patents generated in the vicinity of the top 25 research universities in the United States from 2000 to 2015.[1] We find strong evidence for

---

[1] We thank Mercedes Delagado for sharing patent data on these 25 research-intensive universities.

startup advantage in both average forward citations and the rate of outlier patents (in the top 5 percent of the citation distribution), supporting our first hypothesis. We also find that startup patents score higher in terms of originality and generality relative to patents from established firms (but not significantly different from university patents), which is consistent with our second hypothesis. Finally, we show direct evidence for creative destruction by tracking the development of startups over time: they play an increasingly prominent role in their regional innovation ecosystems. Overall, our findings suggest that startup innovation is qualitatively different from the innovation in other organizational settings: there is a clear "startup advantage" in the quality and impact of startup patents relative to established firms.

Related Literature and Motivation

A tale of two theoretical frameworks

The foundation of our analysis is grounded in endogenous growth theory, where resources dedicated to research and innovation generate improvements in productivity and thus in output quality. In AH, firms compete to develop an innovation that consists of a new intermediate good. This new intermediate good results in more efficient production of a consumption good, in turn driving growth in the economy. The innovating firm is able to attain an immediate (transitory) monopoly until the next innovation occurs. In this framework, there is a natural tendency toward creative destruction, driven by the Arrow replacement effect (Arrow 1962): incumbent firms have less incentive to innovate than new entrants, because incumbents would cannibalize their existing profits.[2] The AH results highlight the distinction between startups and incumbents within the private sector of the economy: even though both types of firms seek to maximize profit, they pursue meaningfully different kinds of innovation.

The model of creative destruction presented in AH sits in some creative tension with ADS. The ADS framework models a multistage (rather than single-stage) research line whereby the optimal organization type for inno-

---

[2] As discussed by Schumpeter (1942), it is possible for the tendency toward creative destruction to be overturned if incumbents have access to more effective means of innovation—for instance, owing to returns to scale or superior access to funding or scientific talent. We are able to directly assess this possibility in our empirical analysis.

vation is determined by a wage differential between academia and the private sector. This wage differential is driven by the disutility suffered by the researcher when she is "focused" or forced to perform her non-preferred strategy to advance a research line (Stern 2004). As a result of this wage differential, high-freedom organizational forms (i.e., academia) are optimal early in the research line, whereas high-focus organizational forms (i.e., the private sector) take over once the expected value of success from focused effort exceeds the lost utility from the lack of researcher freedom. In this framework, the key insight is that different organizational forms generate different incentives for researchers, and are therefore better suited to different stages of the innovation process.[3] The ADS model emphasizes the contrast between academia and the private sector, but assumes that all private-sector organizations are identical. It therefore serves as both a counterpoint and a complement to the AH framework, which highlights the differences between startups and incumbent firms but does not consider academia as a source of innovation.

Bringing together AH and ADS, it becomes apparent that a comprehensive understanding of the innovation process and the ecosystems in which innovation takes place must grapple with both differences between organizational forms (public and private) as well as heterogeneity among private-sector firms. A natural question arises when combining these theoretical frameworks: When a research line transitions from academia to the private sector (as depicted by ADS), will it be transferred to an incumbent firm or to a startup venture (as depicted by AH)? More broadly, what is the role of startups in moving innovation from ideas to impact, what is their contribution to the development of multistage research lines, and when does startup advantage arise?

Motivating examples: Global health and climate security

Startup ventures are an increasingly important organizational form in the commercialization of university technologies in critical areas such as global health, climate security, and infrastructure. Below we examine three high-profile technologies originating from universities: mRNA vaccines, nuclear

---

[3] These differences are further accentuated by other aspects of the innovation ecosystem, most prominently the degree of openness: increasing open access to research inputs has a disproportionate positive impact on researchers operating under academic freedom (Murray et al. 2016).

fusion, and low-carbon manufacturing. Within each example, we explore the organizational choices made by founders to create startup companies even under conditions where it is not immediately apparent why a new entrant would be the optimal organization to develop the next stages of these innovations. A deep analysis of these cases provides us with key motivating insights into the conditions that drive startup venture innovation, guiding our formal modeling and shaping our empirical analysis of these phenomena.

Global health: mRNA vaccines. The global health crisis initiated by the COVID-19 pandemic is a clear illustration of the critical role of startups in the innovation process. Both of the early successes in vaccine development were completed by startups—Moderna in the United States and BioNTech (in collaboration with Pfizer)[4] in Germany. These ventures became household names in late 2020, but both were founded approximately a decade previously with the express goal of building on important research lines undertaken in a range of different academic research laboratories around the world (most notably at the University of Pennsylvania, Philadelphia). In each case, the new ventures were continuing research lines that had been long in the making. The first demonstration of mRNA coding for "therapeutic proteins" in a mammalian setting took place in 1990, and the problem of delivery *in vivo* into cell lines was overcome only in the mid- to late-2000s (and even then, only in lab-based experiments in research mice). The founder-entrepreneurs of BioNTech and Moderna had specific private beliefs (and insights) into the potential value of mRNA vaccines, and were therefore willing to create new ventures and find investors who were also willing to develop a novel and untested technology. In contrast, incumbent pharmaceutical firms perceived mRNA vaccines to be relatively risky, and chose to remain uninvolved in the early stages of research, only later forming partnerships with the two companies. Specifically, Moderna's first vaccine-related licensing agreement was with Merck in 2015,[5] and BioNTech became involved with Pfizer only through a research collaboration for influenza signed

---

[4] We emphasize the role of BioNTech rather than Pfizer because BioNTech was heavily involved in the mRNA research that ultimately generated its COVID-19 vaccine, whereas it was only in 2018 that Pfizer joined BioNTech's efforts to develop mRNA vaccines (focusing specifically on influenza), and its COVID-related contributions focused on providing support with clinical trials, logistics, and manufacturing.

[5] See https://investors.modernatx.com/news/default.aspx for details.

in 2018.[6] Both partnerships focused more on later-stage clinical trials and commercialization, with the startup partner responsible for the initial vaccine development.[7] By highlighting the critical role of startup-developed technologies, COVID-19 has provided a timely window into the essential role of startup ventures in crisis innovation (Johnson and Murray 2021).

Climate security: Nuclear fusion. Beyond global health and life sciences (where the role of startup ventures is well known), startups have also made significant contributions to innovation in longer-term challenges, such as climate security, based either on unique (private) information and beliefs of the founding researchers or on the fact that incumbents underinvest due to their high switching costs and significant inertia. We illustrate these points by contrasting two recent climate security startups—one in energy and the other in manufacturing, both Boston-based and both with funding from The Engine (a venture capital fund built by MIT but now independent, whose emphasis is on investments in startup ventures applying novel and complex science and technology to missions of global significance).

Commonwealth Fusion Systems (CFS) was founded in 2018 by MIT post-doctoral researcher Robert Mumgaard, then at the MIT Plasma Science and Fusion Center, and offers a critical example of the value of private information in generating a startup advantage. The venture uses only recently (commercially) available high-temperature superconductors to create magnets that enable a new approach to fusion system design. If successful at full scale, the approach will provide the first net-energy-producing fusion reactor ready for widespread deployment. CFS builds upon long research lines that date back to the 1950s: fusion energy research has been funded by governments around the world for decades prior to the founding of CFS. Despite this long history, incumbent energy providers (and even many academics) have always considered fusion power to be "twenty years away," suggesting a research line of extensive duration and considerable resource requirements likely only to be taken on by a large industry incumbent with substantial resources. In addition, from 2008 onward, US government funding for fusion research was shifting toward a single massive-scale fusion project based in

---

[6] See https://biontech.de/sites/default/files/2019-08/20180816_BioNTech-Signs-Collaboration -Agreement-with-Pfizer.pdf for details.

[7] Interestingly, the cases of Moderna and BioNTech's competing COVID vaccines offer a valuable contrast in commercialization strategies: Moderna chose to pursue commercialization of its mRNA vaccine through an integrated approach, whereas BioNTech chose to partner with Pfizer for clinical trials, marketing, and distribution.

France known as ITER.[8] Nonetheless, by 2015 Mumgaard, along with Professor Dennis White and others at MIT, believed that the new improvements in superconducting magnets, combined with new reactor designs, meant that there was finally an innovation path to commercial deployment of fusion power.

Importantly, the private information and resulting beliefs held by the CFS founders were central to their willingness to pursue this research line from academia into a private-sector venture. At the time of founding, it would have been extremely difficult (and costly) for large incumbent energy companies to test these beliefs and to pursue the project internally; in contrast, startup investors were able to share funding risks across a large syndicate (which included Italian energy incumbent ENI) and allocate funding conditional on key technical milestones. As a result, CFS provides a canonical example of settings where private information about the risk of a particular research approach is central to advantages that a startup venture has in the further development of a promising research line, particularly when academic funding is increasingly limited. Moreover, it does so in a context in which incumbent risks of cannibalization are likely very low, given the extremely long deployment timelines and the complementarity of zero-carbon electricity generation with existing power transmission infrastructure.

Climate security: Low-carbon manufacturing. New ventures also play a role in contexts where cannibalization, rather than private information, is the dominant difference between startup ventures and incumbents. As a case in point, the new venture Sublime Systems is currently commercializing a novel process for low-carbon cement, in an industry where established incumbents have traditionally underinvested in research lines when faced with high switching costs and potential cannibalization. Sublime founder Dr. Leah Ellis developed a new approach to reducing cement kiln emissions by up to 50 percent (with few, if any, significant changes to the properties or chemistry of the resulting cement). A significant contributor to climate challenges, cement production today creates approximately 8 percent of global CO_2 emissions (Lehne and Preston 2018). Nonetheless, cement production has been subject to very little innovation, with its production dominated by a small number of large established firms (Lehne and Preston 2018) using a traditional process that uses lime, silica, and alumina simply mixed under high

---

[8] For more details, see https://www.iter.org/.

temperatures. The innovation under development by Sublime Systems (and initiated at Dalhousie University and then MIT) uses an electrochemical method that electrifies Portland cement manufacturing and in doing so produces concentrated CO_2 that is easily captured.[9] While novel as a research line applied to cement, electrochemistry is an extremely well-established branch of chemistry (founded by, among others, Alessandro Volta at the turn of the nineteenth century) that has been used as the basis for industrial processes since the extraction of aluminum (by Héroult and Hall in 1886) and ammonia (via the Haber process). The lack of incumbent interest in alternative research lines suggests a clear case of incumbent risks of cannibalization rather than any private information about the risks of a new approach. As such, Sublime Systems provides a clear contrast to Commonwealth Fusion: its entry into the cement industry highlights a setting in which startup ventures play an essential role in the innovation process due to their greater willingness to cannibalize existing industry products.

Motivating trends: AUTM licensing

Examining trends in university patenting license provides further evidence of the growing startup advantage in commercializing university technologies. According to the data from Association of University Technology Managers (AUTM 2020), illustrated in Figure 25.1, there is significant growth in the proportion of startup licenses granted by the top-25 research universities in our sample, rising from 17 percent in 2001 to 29 percent in 2019. This rise in startup licensing is accompanied by a corresponding decline in the share of licenses to large incumbent firms, which fell from 37 percent to 26 percent during the same period. The proportion of licenses to small, non-startup firms remained relatively unchanged. Importantly, the increasing share of startup licenses comes on top of an 80 percent rise in the overall rate of university licensing during the same time period, resulting in a threefold increase in the raw number of licenses to startup ventures. As startups displace the role of large firms,[10] it becomes even more important to understand how

---

[9] For the full details of Dr. Ellis's process for the electrification of cement manufacturing, see Ellis et al. (2020).

[10] The trends in university licensing stand in significant contrast to the trend of the rising roles of incumbents in patent activity, as demonstrated in Figure 25.3 of our own analysis as well as recent work on declining business dynamism (Akcigit and Ates 2021). This contrast is likely due to the differences between university licensing and corporate patenting, where the former

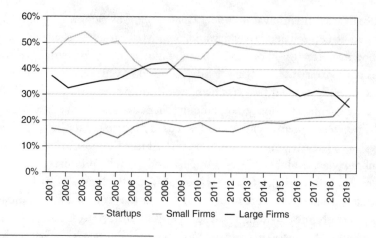

Figure 25.1. Proportion of university licenses by firm type

startup ventures contribute to the larger innovation ecosystem via their unique role in the innovation process.

Theory and predictions

The role of academic startups in the process of innovation

Startups play a distinctive role in driving innovation during the transition from early-stage research in academia to the private sector. However, as discussed above, there is a gap in the theoretical literature in terms of explaining how and why startups might be able to pursue innovations that are either infeasible or suboptimal in other institutional contexts. To bridge this gap, we first synthesize the core structure and insights from the models of innovation in AH and ADS, and then turn to the potential role for startups in the context of a theoretical framework that combines the insights of the above models.

---

tends toward basic research and the development of new technologies, while the latter is more often associated with applied research, incremental innovation, and patent thickets.

Our starting point is the ADS model, which emphasizes how the distinctive allocation of decision rights—most notably, over whether researchers have the ability to choose their own research direction (i.e., "academic freedom")—influences the organization of research between academia and the private sector. The ADS model focuses on a multistage research process: at each of k stages of a given research line, a decision-maker chooses whether to attempt to move research to the next "stage" of the line (or perhaps explore an alternative direction). If the decision-maker chooses to attempt to advance the research line, a single researcher exerts effort (for which she has to be paid a wage w), and success in moving the project to the next stage occurs with probability p. If all k stages of a research line are executed successfully, the result is a final output with value V; otherwise, the research line returns no value.

The key insight of ADS arises from considering the impact of the allocation of control rights over whether to pursue the given research line; in other words, the identity of the decision-maker is the crucial distinction between the organizational forms of academia and the private sector. On the one hand, if a private-sector manager maintains control, their primary interest will be in projects that have a chance of (eventually) producing commercial value, and so they will always direct the researcher to pursue the next stage of the commercially oriented research line (ADS refers to this as the "practical" research direction). However, if the control over research direction is allocated to the researcher, as it would be in academia, she *might* (with probability α) choose the practical strategy (this research might be of intrinsic interest to her), but with probability $1 - \alpha$, the researcher would choose an alternative research direction to pursue her own interests. In other words, while the manager and researcher have partially overlapping preferences in terms of research direction, the manager must maintain control over the research direction if they want to ensure the highest probability of attempting to move the innovation to the next research stage.

Of course, this structure raises the immediate question of why the manager would *ever* allocate the rights to the research direction to the researcher (since the researcher may divert the project from the practical direction). Building on the empirical evidence in Stern (2004), ADS assume that the researcher values the ability to maintain academic freedom and so would "pay" z in order to maintain control rights over their research direction. As such, if the reservation wage of a researcher who is given academic freedom is R (in other words, this is the wage she would have to be paid to exert effort while also getting to choose her own research direction), then the manager will have to offer at least $R + (1 - \alpha)z$ to hire the researcher to pursue the research line under the manager's control.

The presence of a compensating differential for academic freedom induces a tradeoff in how to allocate the decision rights for the research project. Most notably, for any given research stage i (assuming that it is worthwhile to pursue this research stage regardless of how the decision rights are allocated), the relative cost-effectiveness of allocating the decision rights to the researcher is increasing in z, the preference for academic freedom, and α, the probability that the researcher would choose the practical strategy anyway.

With the above assumptions, the ADS model is able to determine, at every stage of the innovation process, both whether the research line is feasible and what allocation of decision rights is optimal. If we define Π_{i+1} to be the value of successfully completing research stage i and moving to stage $i+1$ (i.e., the research exerts effort in the practical direction and is indeed successful), then as illustrated in Figure 25.2, the *minimum* value of the project for which academia is viable is $\Pi_{i+1} > \dfrac{R}{\alpha p}$ and the *minimum* value for which a project is viable in the private sector is $\Pi_{i+1} > \dfrac{R + (1 - \alpha)z}{p}$.

While project viability is an important constraint on the model's parameters, the primary focus of ADS is on the optimal choice between pursuing the research line in academia or in the private sector. Figure 25.2 illustrates this tradeoff as being determined by the combination of the research line's expected value Π_{i+1} and the researcher's disutility z if she lacks control over the research line's direction. Because $z = 0$ implies that the researcher does not place any value on academic freedom, the control rights for research direction will be allocated to the firm. However, as the relative value placed on academic freedom increases, the manager has increased incentive to forego the wage premium $(1 - \alpha)z$ required to maintain control, and instead prefers to cede control of the research direction of the project to the researcher. Of course, the shifting of decision rights to the researcher makes it less likely that the project will be successful in moving to the next stage of the research line: with probability $1 - \alpha$, the researcher will ultimately choose the alternative rather than the practical path. Concretely, this means that the research line will optimally occur in academia if $z > p\Pi_{i+1}$, whereas the private sector will be the optimal organizational form in all other cases. Thus,

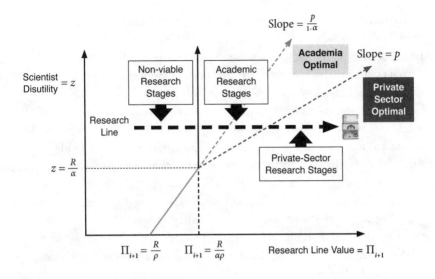

Figure 25.2. Research lines in the Aghion-Dewatripont-Stein (ADS) framework

for very high values of z, the researcher is allocated control (with the corresponding decline in the probability of success of a commercial project).

The central insight of ADS arises from the fact that, for a multistage research line, the $i+1^{\text{th}}$ stage of a research line is always more valuable (from the perspective of its prospective financial return) than the ith stage of that research line (i.e., $\Pi_{i+1} > \Pi_i$). Since the commercial value of the research line is realized only by successfully traversing all k stages, the value function is increasing when any progress occurs that allows research to be conducted closer to the end of the line. In Figure 25.2, from the perspective of a given research line, this is equivalent to a shift along the x-axis for a given level of z. Crucially, this has the consequence that, for any research project that is feasible (i.e., $\Pi_1 > \dfrac{R}{p}$), research will either be conducted in the private sector, or, if $\Pi_1 > \dfrac{R}{\alpha p}$ and $Z > \dfrac{R}{\alpha}$, will first be conducted in an academic environment (freedom for researchers) and then, as long as z is not too high relative to the value of the research line, transition at a discrete point toward a more commercial environment (in which the decision rights are allocated to the manager).

The ADS framework offers an important conceptual contribution and testable theoretical predictions regarding the allocation of decision rights between a more commercially focused versus more academically focused research environment. However, the baseline ADS model does not specify the distinct role played by startup firms (relative to incumbents). Specifically, building on the motivating examples from the previous section, the ADS model does not provide a rationale for why "academic" startups (firms founded in and around leading academic research environments) seem to play such a distinctive role in the innovation process. In technology transfer, this phenomenon is termed "the valley of death"—referring to the gap in interest from either industry or academia at intermediate stages of the research process. We argue that overcoming this "valley of death" is the key role of startups in transferring technologies from academia to the private sector.

We therefore extend the ADS model to consider three (non-mutually-exclusive) factors—equity incentives, private information, and cannibalization—that might be associated with a role for academic startups, and then draw out the potential empirical implications of those factors for academic startup innovation (compared to university and established-firm innovation).

Perhaps the simplest potential explanation for the role of academic startups in the process of innovation is that, at some point in the research process, it is important to provide financial incentives for researchers to pursue the practical path. And, indeed, it may be the case that the prospect of significant financial gain might motivate individuals to exit an academic institution or large established firm to found or join a startup company. However, as long as there is ex ante symmetric information between the (presumably capital-constrained) researchers and private funders, there is no reason that any monetary incentive that would be required to induce effort on the part of the researcher could not be offered within an established company. More subtly, if an equity-oriented research contract depends on achieving success to the next stage of the research line, then the purpose of such incentives should be to encourage researchers to choose the practical direction. Within the ADS framework, such an incentive contract must be preferred by both the manager and the researcher, relative to simply allocating decision rights to the manager. However, as long as the researcher is even slightly more risk-averse than the manager (which seems like a reasonable assumption), then the researcher would prefer to be guaranteed an upfront wage payment (including a premium for ceding control over research direction), and the manager would prefer to guarantee that the researcher will pursue the practical strategy. In other words, though academic startup founders do receive equity incentives as part of the founding process, equity incentives on their own do not provide a sufficient rationale for academic startups as a distinctive institutional form in the process of innovation.[11]

A more promising potential driver of academic startups may lie in the fact that the research process itself not only requires effort and choice but also yields private information to researchers. Specifically, for a research project conducted within the academic sector, the researchers themselves are able to observe private signals about the potential value of the overall project or the likelihood of success. For example, in a case such as Commonwealth Fusion Systems, the researchers are uniquely informed about both the nature of the technical breakthrough they have developed within the university, and also the challenges they are likely to confront in the overall process of innovation. From the perspective of the ADS model, the researchers themselves might receive a private signal of the value of p for future stages of the project, and so know whether continued effort is likely to ultimately yield a successful innovation. For example, one could consider an extreme case where researchers were able to observe whether $p = 1$ for all future stages of the project (in other words, the project is guaranteed to succeed if subsequent research is directed toward the practical path). Of course, the researcher could disclose their information about that signal to the manager; however, under the baseline ADS model, the researcher's wage following disclosure would simply be equal to $R + (1 - \alpha)z$, as the manager would capture the surplus of the successful project. By contrast, if the researcher were compensated using equity, or chose to found a separate organization to commercialize the innovation, she could capture the some or all of the value of the research line's output, V, net of any wage costs for commercialization in future periods. More formally, in cases where researchers receive private information regarding the probability of success p of their research line, and this probability is sufficiently high relative to ex ante expectations, then an organizational form that offers the researcher either partial or full ownership of the research line's payoffs through equity-based compensation would dominate both academic institutions and established firms.

---

[11] For an in-depth discussion of the incentive structures most conducive to motivating innovation, see Manso (2011).

Shifting from theory to theoretical predictions, we would anticipate that academic startups are more likely in the case where the academic researcher receives private information about the underlying value or potential of success of the research line. This ability of researchers to select the most promising projects on the basis of private information implies that high-risk, high-reward research lines will preferentially flow into startups rather than incumbent firms. This same selection effect, in combination with the tendency of research lines to increase in value as they advance from stage to stage, also implies that startup innovation will also be more novel and more impactful than university innovation. We formalize these insights in the following hypothesis:

Hypothesis. *Vision: Relative to both universities and established firms, startups will be associated with innovation that is more original and more impactful over time.*

Our third potential driver of startup advantage is based on the foundations of creative destruction, as presented by AH. Specifically, we would expect there to be differences in the perceived value of a research line when comparing the perspective of a startup to that of an established firm. An established firm that brings a new product or service to market would tend to cannibalize at least some of its existing offerings, so its marginal benefit of successfully completing the research line would be lower in proportion to the degree of cannibalization. By contrast, startups have no preexisting products or services to cannibalize, and would therefore obtain a greater marginal benefit from completing the same research line. Within our theoretical framework, we formalize this idea as the case where $V^{startup} > V^{incumbent}$. Importantly, because of the recursive nature of multistage research lines, this implies that $\Pi_{i+1}^{startup} > \Pi_{i+1}^{incumbent}$ for all stages i of the research line. The degree of cannibalization leading to this discrepancy in perceived value would be greater for highly novel and disruptive technologies, since they would likely be substitutes for existing products and services offered by incumbents, as in the example of the cement-production technologies developed by Sublime Systems.[12] By contrast, the case where innovations would tend to complement incumbents' existing offerings is captured by having $V^{incumbent} > V^{startup}$. Indeed, the case where the research line's output is more valuable to incumbents than to startups is discussed at length by Gilbert and

---

[12] We would also expect that academic researchers may care about the nonmonetary impact of their inventions, particularly by placing more weight on the broader social value of a potential invention.

Newbery (1982), who focus on the decline in industry profits if a monopolist allows a new entrant to join the market. Importantly, this would apply only to innovations that would share the market with existing products (i.e., incremental technologies), rather than innovations that would replace the incumbent's offerings (i.e., radical technologies) as described in Arrow (1962) and AH. This distinction between incremental and radical technologies is further explored by Gans and Stern (2003), who highlight the importance of complementary assets and functional "markets for ideas" as key drivers of whether startups are likely to cooperate with incumbents or seek to undermine them as they develop new technologies.

In both of the above cases, any difference in the perceived value of a completed research line would flow back to earlier research stages, based on the private-sector institution developing the research line. By introducing AH's creative destruction into our framework, we generate a second hypothesis in the context of academic innovation ecosystems: we would expect to see more radical and disruptive innovations pursued by startups, while more incremental innovations are pursued by established firms.

Hypothesis. *Creative Destruction: Relative to established firms, startups will be associated with innovation that is more radical and more impactful over time.*

Setting, Methods, and Data

The goal of our empirical analysis is to test the above hypotheses by documenting the unique characteristics of startup patents, and to contrast them with patenting activities performed within academic research institutions and private-sector organizations. In this section, we describe our empirical setting of top-research-university ecosystems, define key variables, and characterize our empirical strategy.

Empirical setting

Our empirical setting targets the regional ecosystems around the 25 top research universities in the United States, as defined by Delgado and Murray (2022). Specifically, these are the universities that were listed as assignees on the largest number of patents granted in the 2011–2015 time period. While this sample is selected partially for convenience, it is worth noting that these universities make up approximately 50 percent of all academic patenting during our sample period. In addition, they account for approximately

40 percent of all university patent licensing as captured by AUTM records, reflecting the strong emphasis on both innovation and commercialization for the universities in our chosen sample.

In addition to the geographic focus above, we also target the time period 2000–2015 for our analysis, again coinciding with the sample period of Delgado and Murray (2022). This time period also overlaps with the decline of large firms and the rise of small firms and startups in university licensing, as described in our analysis of AUTM licensing data above. The termination of the sample period in 2015 is necessary in order to have sufficient time to collect forward citations following patent publication. Moreover, the 2000–2015 time period also overlaps with the longer-term expansion in patenting (Lerner and Seru 2021), and the increasing importance of agglomeration economies that tend to be co-located with major research universities (Carlino and Kerr 2015). In light of these trends, our empirical setting offers insight into a narrow but crucially important aspect of the innovation ecosystem.

Data sources and key variables

The primary data source for our analysis is the PatentsView database, which tracks all patents granted by the US Patent and Trademark Office from 1976 to the present. This database includes a wide range of patent-level measures, including filing and grant dates, primary technology classes based on the Cooperative Patent Classification (CPC) system, and forward and backward patent-to-patent citations. PatentsView also disambiguates patent assignees and their locations, as well as the locations of inventors listed on each patent. We supplement this data set in a number of important ways: first, using the data set constructed by Delgado and Murray (2022), we identify the patents granted to the 25 top US universities by patent count, based on the 2011–2015 time period. Second, we merge in nonpublic administrative data from the USPTO to identify patents processed under small-entity or micro-entity status, as reflected by patent fees. Finally, using the precise latitude and longitude of each of the universities in our sample, we are able to identify the full population of granted patents that have at least one assignee and at least one inventor within a ten-mile radius.[13]

---

[13] For our regression analysis, we also merge in county-year covariates, including population, income per capita, unemployment rate, labor force participation, and the total number of patents granted within the county for each calendar year.

Using the data described above, we proceed to construct the central variables of our analysis. Our primary explanatory variable is *Organization-Type*, a patent-level categorical variable which takes the values of "University," "Startup," or "Incumbent." University patents are directly identified by Delgado and Murray (2022). Startup patents are defined as those processed under small-entity or micro-entity status (indicating that they have no more than 500 employees), and patents where all assignees are at most five years old in terms of their "patent age," or years from their first patent filing.[14] Finally, incumbent patents are those that were processed under normal (i.e., undiscounted) patent fees, and where all assignees are at least ten years old in terms of patent age. Any patents that do not meet these definitions are excluded from our analysis, in order to highlight the differences between these groups. For example, a patent that results from a collaboration between a startup and an incumbent would not be classified under either category. In extended analysis, we also introduce an additional category for *OrganizationType:* the "Scale-Up," which we define as a former startup that continues to generate patents but has either stopped qualifying for small-entity or micro-entity status, or is now older than five years in "patent age." We use this measure to capture the degree of creative destruction within our sample, as we track the displacement of incumbents by both startups and scale-ups.

Our outcome variables focus on capturing the differences in the type of patents being produced by the organizations described above. Our first set of outcomes track the number of forward citations (i.e., citations from future patents) that accrue after a given patent is published. In order to capture the dynamic aspects of forward citations, and to effectively compare patents of different vintages, we divide forward citations into three distinct time periods relative to the original grant date: 0–5 years, 6–10 years, and 11–15 years. The last of these categories, in combination with the fact that we track patent citations through the end of 2020, means that we are limited to patents granted no later than 2005 when we analyze the full range of forward citation dynamics. In addition to average citation counts, we also track outlier patents. For this outcome measure, we calculate the 95th percentile of forward citations (at both five- and ten-year horizons) for each combination of grant year and CPC class (e.g., grant year 2004 and CPC

---

[14] We calculate "patent age" based on the gap between filing dates for each assignee's patents. However, because our outcome measures are often based on citations, we group patents by grant year in our figures and regression analysis.

class A01). We then generate indicators for whether each patent exceeds these percentiles, thereby falling in the top 5 percent of all patents for its year and technology.

Moving beyond citation rates, our final set of outcome measures seeks to capture the nature of innovation by different organizational types by looking at the distribution of citations across patent classes. To do so, we replicate the patent-level measures of *originality* and *generality* first developed by Hall, Jaffe, and Trajtenberg (2001). The *originality* measure tracks the dispersion of backward patent-to-patent citations across technology classes, and aims to capture more novel and groundbreaking patents. Similarly, *generality* tracks the dispersion of forward patent-to-patent citations across technology classes, and aims to capture how basic or fundamental a patent is. For this latter measure, we once again limit the time horizon of forward citations to facilitate comparisons across patents of different vintages, calculating generality on the basis of both five-year and ten-year forward citations.

Methods

Using the variables described above, our methodology is simple and straightforward: we calculate averages and standard errors for our outcome variables across organizational types, and plot the results across a series of bar graphs. This approach does not offer causal identification: we are not able to estimate a counterfactual for how a given innovation would have differed if it had been developed under a different organizational form. However, the strength of this approach is that it highlights the stark differences in patented innovations across universities, startups, and incumbents in terms of their respective contributions to their regional innovation ecosystems. In extended analysis presented in the appendix, we replicate the comparisons in our figures using a multiple-regression framework that controls for a broad range of covariates including fixed effects for county, grant year, and technology, and a range of additional covariates. While the regression-based methods are also only able to capture correlation rather than causation, the breadth of control variables allows us to rule out alternative explanations like startups and incumbents working in different technological fields or operating in different geographic locations. Overall, our methods aim to highlight the differences among patents emerging from universities, startups, and incumbents, while focusing on locations and time periods where all three groups would be important contributors to the innovation ecosystem.

Results

Our main results begin with Figure 25.3, which depicts the relative numbers of patents granted to each type of organization in our sample during the 2000–2005 time period. We observe that while universities and startups both generate similar numbers of patents, the majority of inventions in our sample are generated by incumbent firms. This is not a surprising pattern: our sample includes major innovation ecosystems such as Silicon Valley, Seattle, and Boston, where many large corporations have extensive research and development facilities. Having established this baseline, we proceed to examine whether there is a difference in the type of inventions being produced by the organizations in our sample.

Forward citations

The primary empirical test of our analysis is to compare the value of the average invention generated within each of our organizational forms. We do so through the measure of average forward citations, which we depict in Figure 25.4. By restricting our analysis to the 2000–2005 cohort, we are able to track forward citations at horizons of 0–5, 6–10, and 11–15 years from the grant date of the original patent. We find that across all time periods, startup

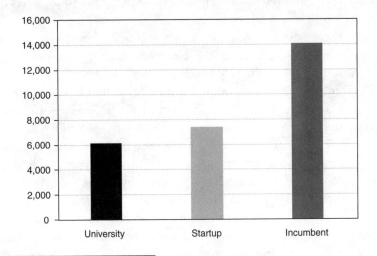

Figure 25.3. Total granted patents (2000–2005)

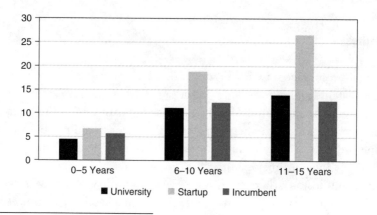

Figure 25.4. Startup advantage: Forward citations

patents generate more forward citations on average than those of either universities or incumbent firms. Even more importantly, this "startup advantage" increases over time: startup patents receive 20 percent more citations from 0–5 years, 50 percent more citations from 6–10 years, and 100 percent more citations from 11–15 years. We replicate these patterns using a multiple-regression framework in Table 25.A1 of the Appendix, which includes a broad range of fixed effects and covariates. Our findings indicate that startup inventions are more valuable and more impactful than inventions emerging from other organizational forms, and that this advantage only increases over longer forward-citation horizons.

In addition to the average value of patents produced by different organizations, we are also interested in the rate of outlier inventions. For this analysis, we turn to Figure 25.5, which presents the rates of patents in the top 5 percent of their grant-year and technology cohort based on forward citations. It is worth noting that all of the rates in Figure 25.5 exceed 5 percent, reflecting the fact that inventions generated within the ecosystems of top research universities tend to be more valuable than the broader patent population. Turning to a comparison across organizational types, we find that startup patents are approximately 40 percent more likely to be "outlier inventions" in the top 5 percent of the citation distribution. This is true whether we look at five-year or ten-year forward citation horizons. Further, startup patents are more likely to be outliers when compared not only against incumbents but also against university inventions. This latter finding is particularly surprising, as the top research universities in our sample are generally viewed as generating highly influential and valuable research. In extended

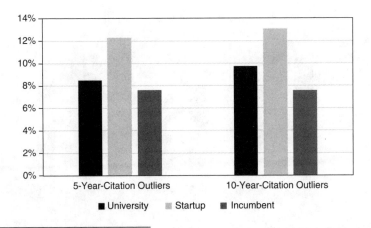

Figure 25.5. Rate of top 5 percent outlier patents

analysis depicted in Figure 25.A1 of the Appendix, we also show that the best patents generated by startups are far more impactful than the best patents generated by either universities or incumbents, and that this advantage is even more pronounced at longer forward-citation horizons. Overall, these results offer strong evidence for the existence of a "startup advantage" in terms of the value of the inventions they generate: not only are startup patents more cited on average, but they also are more likely to be outliers that have an out-size contribution to future innovation, and over longer horizons than inventions from either incumbents or universities.

Originality and generality

Beyond exploring the value of inventions through the analysis of forward citation rates, we would also expect to find differences in the type of innovations generated by startups. For this analysis, we explore the measures of originality and generality, which are calculated based on the dispersion of backward and forward citations, respectively, across patent classes. Figure 25.6 presents our findings: for both originality and generality, we find that startup and university inventions are nearly identical, and that both exceed the inventions of incumbents in these measures. As these measures are both based on Herfindahl calculations, they always range between zero and one; in our sample, both measures also have a standard deviation of approximately 0.28. In light of this, startup inventions are more original by approximately half a standard deviation relative to incumbent innovations, and more general

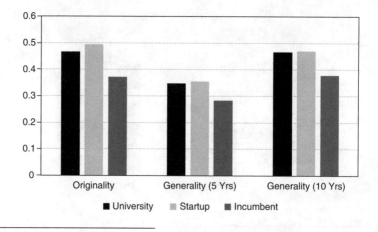

Figure 25.6. Patent originality and patent generality

by approximately one-third of a standard deviation for both five- and ten-year forward citation horizons. We find a similar pattern of results with slightly smaller differences when implementing multiple-regression estimators in Table 25.A2 of the Appendix. Overall, our results in this section suggest that startup innovation is quite similar to the inventions generated by university researchers, and that both of these organizations generate patents with greater originality and greater generality than those of incumbents.

Assignee dynamics and "scale-ups"

Having highlighted in the previous sections a number of significant differences between startup inventions and those of universities and incumbents, we now turn to the question of dynamics: What happens as the startups we track increase in size and age to become more like the incumbent firms against which they are compared? For this analysis, we introduce the category of "Scale-Up" organizations, which are former startups that are now older than five years in "patent age," or whose patents no longer qualify for small-entity patent fees. We present our main findings in Figure 25.7, which tracks this expanded set of four organizational types in terms of their citation-weighted patent output over time. We find that scale-ups, which are ruled out by definition in the first year of our sample, grow in importance over time and end up overtaking incumbents in terms of citation-weighted patents by

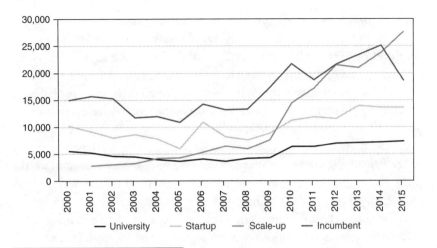

Figure 25.7. Patent Count Dynamics with Scale-Ups

the end of our sample period in 2015. Other organizational types also experience meaningful growth over this same time period, reflecting the overall increase in innovation occurring in these ecosystems. However, the greater level of growth demonstrated by scale-ups indicates that a significant amount of creative destruction is being driven by the former startups identified in our sample. Interestingly, in extended analysis presented in Figure 25.A2 of the appendix, we find that forward citations for these organizational types are approximately equal, and are significantly higher than those for either universities or incumbents. This suggests that the "startup advantage" we identified earlier carries over as startups become scale-ups, and raises the possibility that this higher level of patent value may be an important driver of creative destruction.

Discussion and Conclusions

In this chapter we present theory and evidence for the unique role of startups in the innovation ecosystem. We begin with vignettes of prominent startups: Moderna, BioNTech, Commonwealth Fusion, and Sublime Systems demonstrate the tendency for startups to pursue novel, high-upside technologies, while Sublime Systems offers an example of a startup aiming to displace existing technologies in an industry dominated by powerful incumbents.

We also present evidence from university licensing that startups have taken an increasing share of the technology transfer ecosystem since 2000, reaching nearly 30 percent of all licenses in 2019 while displacing large firms. Next, combining and extending the insights of AH and ADS, we argue that there are two specific channels through which theory predicts startups will have an advantage in multistage research lines. First, startups will have private information on the value of their ideas, and this asymmetry is likely to be highest in novel and high-upside technologies, leading them to be developed internally rather than transferred to an outside party. Second, startups do not face the threat of cannibalization, and are more likely to pursue disruptive technologies that would undermine the competitive advantages of existing incumbents.

We evaluate the above predictions using a data set of all patents granted within the regional innovation ecosystems centered on the top 25 US research universities from 2000 to 2015. Our results suggest that there is a clear startup advantage in terms of both the average and the right tail of innovation value, as measured by forward citations, relative to both academic and incumbent patents. We then show that startup inventions are both more original and more general than those of other institutions, and conclude by highlighting how former startups, or scale-ups, have overtaken preexisting incumbents in their citation-weighted inventions in the space of just fifteen years. Taken together, our findings highlight that startups produce inventions that are both more valuable and more disruptive and novel than those pursued by either private-sector incumbents or academic institutions.

Limitations and generalizability

While our findings shed light on the significant differences between startup and incumbent innovation, there are several limitations worth noting when considering their appropriate interpretation. First and foremost, our analysis does not offer identification of causal effects: we can only document the trends and patterns that exist within the innovation ecosystems covered by our sample. Thus, rather than attempting to estimate what would have happened if a startup technology were counterfactually developed by an incumbent, we instead show that fundamentally different types of inventions are being pursued within these distinct organizational types. We do not attempt to distinguish between interpretations based on the causal impact of different organizational types from those based on selection effects applied to research lines, innovators, or funding sources. Indeed, we expect these to differ significantly across our organizational types, and seek to document the combined impact of all of these factors. For example, our findings of a "startup advantage" are likely to be driven in part by a selection effect: whether due to private information, credit constraints, or other factors, startups tend to pursue a smaller number of high-impact innovations, while incumbents develop a larger number of innovations that are, on average, lower in terms of forward citations, originality, and generality. We do not attempt to separate the impact of such selection from the potential for startups to positively impact the technologies they pursue, but we do show evidence in Figure 25.A1 of the appendix that the "best" (i.e., 95th-percentile) startup inventions are more highly cited than the "best" incumbent innovations. This difference implies that at least some of the startup advantage that we document is a fundamental difference in the innovative process, rather than startups selecting only innovations in the right tail of a similar distribution as the one available to incumbents.

Despite these limitations, our regression analysis does include fixed effects for locations, calendar years, and technology classes, and subsample analyses indicate that our results are likely to generalize across a broad range of geographies, time periods, and economic sectors. Further, while our sample focuses on university ecosystems with exceptionally high rates of innovation, our broader examination of AUTM data suggests that other ecosystems are likely to experience similar patterns. Overall, we expect the startup advantages in citations, originality, and generality to hold in any setting where startups represent a meaningful portion of the innovation ecosystem.

Policy implications

By clarifying the unique contribution of startups to their innovation ecosystems, our work suggests a number of policies that would be appropriate when seeking to support and enhance innovation. A prominent issue in innovation policy has been the challenge of increasingly long gaps between the initiation of a research line and its ultimate commercialization, which can lead to significant underinvestment relative to shorter-term research (Budish, Roin, and Williams 2015). How can policymakers ensure that the maximal number of socially valuable lines are kept alive? Our findings suggest that long-horizon funding for basic research can be a critical driver of startup creation, which in turn generates the startup advantages described in our empirical analysis. Specifically, university technology transfer should focus on the potential for long-term value creation and optionality rather than short-term revenue goals.

Breaking down our two channels of startup advantage, we first turn to the concept of "vision" and the ability of startups to pursue high-risk, high-payoff outcomes where they have private information. Given that most research lines depend at least in part on the unique insights of researchers, what type of institutions and policies encourage pursuit of individual vision? We propose the following: First, institutions that provide training and support for not only research but also commercialization and scaling would be most likely to generate the benefits of the "vision" channel. Second, this support would be complementary to sources of patient and independent capital to help provide critical "tests" for unique contrarian visions.

Our second channel focuses on creative destruction: Given that the pursuit of research lines from initial idea to ultimate commercialization depends on market incentives, how do we ensure the pursuit of socially valuable innovations that may disrupt existing incumbents? Again, our analysis suggests a number of potentially valuable policy interventions. First, in light of the prominence of startups in university licensing and technology transfer, interventions targeted at universities, with an emphasis on educating innovators on the path from "idea to impact" (Frølund, Murray, and Riedel 2018). Second, policymakers can seek to offer signals (and incentives) for research directions that are valuable even in the face of powerful incumbents. Indeed, the incumbents themselves might also be spurred to greater levels of innovation by the rise in competition (Aghion et al. 2005). Closely related to this is the idea of a proactive and pro-innovation competition policy: reducing entry barriers and limiting the power of incumbents to isolate themselves from competition would increase the tendency for innovative entry and subsequent startup advantage. Taken together, these policy interventions are likely to promote higher rates of startup formation and invention, and would either take advantage of or actively increase the startup advantages that we document, and would offer a significant enhancement of the broader innovation ecosystem.

References

Aghion, P., Bloom, N., Blundell, R., Griffith, R., and Howitt, P. (2005). Competition and innovation: An inverted-U relationship. *Quarterly Journal of Economics, 120*(2), 701–728.

Aghion, P., Dewatripont, M., and Stein, J. C. (2008). Academic freedom, private-sector focus, and the process of innovation. *RAND Journal of Economics, 39*(3), 617–635.

Aghion, P., and Howitt, P. (1992). A model of growth through creative destruction. *Econometrica, 60,* 323–351.

Akcigit, U., and Ates, S. T. (2021). Ten facts on declining business dynamism and lessons from endogenous growth theory. *American Economic Journal: Macroeconomics, 13*(1), 257–298.

Arrow, K. (1962). Economic welfare and the allocation of resources for invention. In NBER, *The Rate and Direction of Inventive Activity: Economic and Social Factors,* 609–626. Princeton University Press.

AUTM. (2020). US 2020 Licensing Activity Survey. Edited by Grant Allard, John Miner, Dustin Ritter, Paul Stark, and Ashley Stevens. https://autm.net/surveys-and-tools/surveys/licensing-survey/2020-licensing-survey.

Budish, E., Roin, B. N., and Williams, H. (2015). Do firms underinvest in long-term research? Evidence from cancer clinical trials. *American Economic Review, 105*(7), 2044–2085.

Carlino, G., and Kerr, W. R. (2015). Agglomeration and innovation. In *Handbook of regional and urban economics,* vol. 5, edited by Gilles Duranton, J. Vernon Henderson, and William C. Strange, 349–404.

Delgado, M., and Murray, F. (2022). *Mapping the regions, organizations and individuals that drive inclusion in the innovation economy* (NBER no. c14571), vol. 1 of *Entrepreneurship and innovation policy and the economy.* University of Chicago Press.

Ellis, L. D., Badel, A. F., Chiang, M. L., Park, R. J. Y., and Chiang, Y. M. (2020). Toward electrochemical synthesis of cement—An electrolyzer-based process for decarbonating $CaCO_3$ while producing useful gas streams. *Proceedings of the National Academy of Sciences, 117*(23), 12584–12591.

Frølund, L., Murray, F., and Riedel, M. (2018). Developing successful strategic partnerships with universities. *MIT Sloan Management Review, 59*(2), 71–79.

Gans, J. S., and Stern, S. (2003). The product market and the market for "ideas": Commercialization strategies for technology entrepreneurs. *Research Policy, 32*(2), 333–350.

Gilbert, R. J., and Newbery, D. M. (1982). Preemptive patenting and the persistence of monopoly. *American Economic Review, 72*(3), 514–526.

Hall, B. H., Jaffe, A. B., and Trajtenberg, M. (2001). The NBER patent citation data file: Lessons, insights and methodological tools. NBER Working Paper 8498.

Johnson, E., and Murray, F. (2021). What a crisis teaches us about innovation. *MIT Sloan Management Review, 62*(2), 58–65.

Lehne, J., and Preston, F. (2018). Making concrete change: Innovation in low-carbon cement and concrete. Chatham House Report, Energy Environment and Resources Department: London, 1–66.

Lerner, J., and Seru, A. (2021). The use and misuse of patent data: Issues for finance and beyond. *Review of Financial Studies, 35*(6), 2667–2704.

Manso, G. (2011). Motivating innovation. *Journal of Finance, 66*(5), 1823–1860.

Murray, F., Aghion, P., Dewatripont, M., Kolev, J., and Stern, S. (2016). Of mice and academics: Examining the effect of openness on innovation. *American Economic Journal: Economic Policy, 8*(1), 212–252.

Schumpeter, J.A. (1942). *Capitalism, socialism and democracy.* McGraw-Hill.

Stern, S. (2004). Do scientists pay to be scientists? *Management Science, 50*(6), 835–853.

APPENDIX

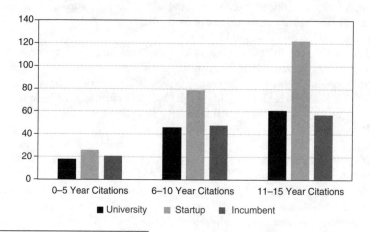

Figure 25.A1. 95th percentile of the forward citation distribution

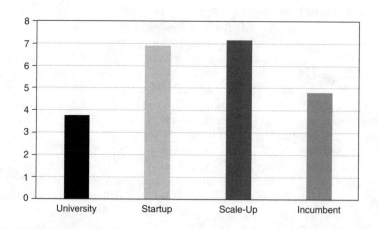

Figure 25.A2. Forward citations with scale-up patents (average five-year citations by assignee category)

Table 25.A1. Forward citations

Variables	(1)	(2)	(3)
	DV = Forward citations		
	0–5 Years	6–10 Years	11–15 Years
Patent category (base = incumbent)			
Startup patent	1.580***	1.974***	2.444***
	(0.129)	(0.214)	(0.391)
University patent	1.345***	1.477***	1.578***
	(0.122)	(0.168)	(0.196)
Additional controls			
Application and grant timing	Y	Y	Y
County covariates	Y	Y	Y
Grant year FEs	Y	Y	Y
County FEs	Y	Y	Y
NBER technology category FEs	Y	Y	Y
Patent cohorts	2000–2005	2000–2005	2000–2005
Observations	27,637	27,637	27,637
Number of counties	22	22	22
R-squared	0.105	0.128	0.160

Notes: Poisson specifications; coefficients reported as incidence rate ratios. Robust standard errors clustered by county in parentheses.

*** $p < 0.01$; ** $p < 0.05$; * $p < 0.1$

Table 25.A2. Originality and generality

Variables	(1)	(2)	(3)
	DV = Originality	DV = 5-Yr Generality	DV = 10-Yr Generality
Patent category (base = incumbent)			
Startup patent	0.063***	0.057***	0.061***
	(0.016)	(0.011)	(0.013)
University patent	0.091***	0.078***	0.084***
	(0.015)	(0.011)	(0.016)
Additional controls			
Application and grant timing	Y	Y	Y
County covariates	Y	Y	Y
Grant year FEs	Y	Y	Y
County FEs	Y	Y	Y
NBER technology category FEs	Y	Y	Y
Number of relevant citations (10 bins)	Y	Y	Y
Patent cohorts	2000–2005	2000–2005	2000–2005
Mean of DV	0.425	0.316	0.423
St. dev. of DV	0.283	0.284	0.277
Observations	26,477	21,949	25,398
Number of counties	22	22	22
R-squared	0.306	0.392	0.299

Notes: OLS specifications; robust standard errors clustered by county in parentheses.

*** $p < 0.01$; ** $p < 0.05$; * $p < 0.1$

CHAPTER 26

Creative Destruction or Destructive Creation?

A Prelude to the Industrial Revolution

JOEL MOKYR

Introduction

The Industrial Revolution was the mother of all creative destruction. Before 1750, of course, there was plenty of technological progress, and some of it destroyed jobs—one thinks of the scribes and copyists displaced by the printing press. Yet it is clear that innovation before the Industrial Revolution was not powerful enough to make much of a dent in the very low rates of economic growth before 1800, and hence its power to be a major disruptor was equally limited. The Industrial Revolution changed all that. It did not invent invention per se, but as Alfred North Whitehead famously wrote, it invented the *method* of invention—not only by realizing the potential of science as a "storehouse of ideas" but also by coming up with the "imaginative designs" needed to bridge the gap between a scientific idea and production (Whitehead [1925] 1953, 96–97). Creative destruction required original thinkers and the freedom to be a nonconformist, but it equally needed competent artisans to carry out the new designs. Invention led to creative destruction, but also, as I shall argue below, to destructive creation, the price of progress.

Growth before the Industrial Revolution could of course be equally destructive. Much of it had the nature of "Smithian growth"—essentially the gains from trade and specialization and the realization of comparative advantage. Trade and the realization that certain crops could be transplanted from area to area (resulting from the "Columbian exchange") led to the prosperity of Britain and the Netherlands on the eve of the Industrial Revolution and to a host of new products being made available (see Nunn and Qian 2010 for an excellent survey), at a price. The horrid destruction that these voyages inflicted on non-European populations—some of it accidental through the spread of infectious disease, some of it intentional through the slave trade and slave-operated plantations—dwarfed any destruction that the technological creativity of the Industrial Revolution inflicted on the populations of European economies.

In what follows, I look at the sources of creative destruction during the Industrial Revolution. In previous work (Kelly et al. 2014, 2021; Mokyr 2021) my collaborators and I have pointed to the origins of Britain's technological precocity in the eighteenth century. Aghion, Antonin, and Bunel (2021) touch upon the topic in their book: "The Industrial Revolution was an illustration of three fundamental principles of the paradigm of creative destruction, namely cumulative innovation . . . institutions [that] . . . foster innovation, and competition" (39). There is little to disagree with in this statement, as long as we add one more element: mechanical competence.

Looking at the statement in Aghion et al. (2021), it seems perhaps intuitively obvious that institutions would play a role in this transformation. But some of the most influential scholars in economic history have taken a skeptical view.[1] At the most basic level, the issue is quite simple: the literature that stresses institutions as a driver of economic growth focus on market-driven Smithian growth, which needed peace, freedom, mobility, and a rule of law to thrive. The problem is that such growth runs into mercilessly sharp diminishing returns and cannot support sustained and continuous economic growth (Mokyr 2018). Neither can capital accumulation. Only the expansion of useful knowledge can do that, even though

---

[1] McCloskey (2010, 296–345; 2016) launches what is probably the most effective criticism of institutions as a factor in triggering economic growth. For a reply, see Greif and Mokyr (2016).

there, too, it is often thought that opportunities are exhausted at various points.[2] It is far from clear what institutions foster and support creative destruction. Do such institutions thrive primarily in a free-market and low-regulation environment in which competitive firms are free to experiment and in which "thinking outside the box" is not just tolerated but encouraged? Or do they need government funding and support of innovative firms and projects, as Mazzucato has insisted and others have contested (Mazzucato 2015; McCloskey and Mingardi 2020). Is it even possible that authoritarian and repressive regimes, such as the Soviet Union or contemporary China, are capable of sustained creativity and innovation notwithstanding the absence of freedom? Is their creativity doomed if individual freedom and dissent are severely curbed?

The institutions that foster creative destruction are above all required to do two things: provide incentives for the inventors and entrepreneurs, and make sure that they have the technical and financial wherewithal to carry out their designs. Yet, as many scholars starting from Greif (2005) and McCloskey (2021) have argued, institutions depend on a cultural underpinning that ensures that they will be effective. If society postulates rules that nobody takes seriously because they conflict with their deep beliefs or values, those rules will be hard to enforce unless applied with considerable coercive power. The institutions that drove technological progress in the eighteenth century rested on a set of cultural beliefs we tend to group under the umbrella term "the Enlightenment," the central cultural development of the eighteenth century. Specifically, they rested on those elements in Enlightenment thought that addressed matters of material progress and the solution of technological issues through expanded useful knowledge. We thus speak of a "medical enlightenment" (Porter 1982), an "agricultural enlightenment" (Jones 2016), and an "industrial enlightenment" (Mokyr 2009). Culture (what people believe and think they know) and institutions (the rules and customs that determine their incentives) coevolve and affect one another in many complex ways (for a survey, see Alesina and Giuliano 2015). In the era of the Industrial Revolution, the central cultural tenet that drove creative destruction was a firm belief in progress.

---

[2] The most extensive exposition of this argument is Gordon (2016). For a recent quantitative examination, see Bloom et al. (2020).

Institutions and the Industrial Revolution

The literature that links institutions to the Industrial Revolution has expanded quite a bit in recent years as a result of the influential work of Douglass North and other members of the neo-institutional school (Mokyr 2008; Kapás 2012). They can be roughly divided into two groups: those that focus on general political changes in Britain in the century before the advent of the Industrial Revolution, and those that focus on more specific institutions that affected incentives directly. The literature on the role of politics was launched in a groundbreaking paper by North and Weingast (1989), which argued that the Glorious Revolution and the subsequent Bill of Rights, above all, shaped the English (and soon after the British) polity in a way that was conducive to economic development. They maintained that the system that emerged after the Glorious Revolution and the Bill of Rights in 1689 was one in which the British had made the government guarantee to its citizens that it would not tax them without Parliament's consent. In other words, it "pre-committed" to be constrained by Parliament. Pincus and Robinson (2014) argue that the Glorious Revolution once and for all determined the *de facto* rules by which political power was exercised: the emergence of parliamentary sovereignty meant that policy was henceforth set by political parties and thus ministers, and that the Whigs set an agenda of "economic modernization."

The difficulty with this approach is that it explains a polity that is more amenable to create "inclusive institutions," encourage trade, rationalize government, and set up more effective organizations, such as the Bank of England. It is not one that is specifically friendly to creative destruction. It took another seventy years after the Bill of Rights for the wave of inventions we associate with the Industrial Revolution to start in earnest in the 1760s.

The best way to think of the "general institutions" argument is this: In the seventeenth century, and specifically after the Glorious Revolution, England (and then Britain) "solved" the problem of *meta-institutions*. If institutions are the rules by which the economy operates, the higher-level question arises: What are the rules by which society makes the rules? The answer is that the rules are set by meta-institutions and that the effectiveness of society to set these rules depends on the legitimacy of the meta-institutions. In Britain the question was resolved peacefully and Parliament became "the place where absolute despotic power, which must in all governments reside somewhere, is entrusted," as Blackstone noted in 1765. While there was no guarantee that this would be *necessarily* good for economic growth, eighteenth-century developments drove it in that direction. Moreover, in many countries, struggles over meta-institutions led to bloody revolutions, which then degenerated into military dictatorships and wars, as well as a reactionary backlash. Britain (excepting Ireland) was spared violent insurrections and upheaval even if a conservative backlash to what was happening in France did lead to a temporary political setback in the 1790s.

One important advantage was that Britain's Parliament was on the whole friendly to innovation and hostile to Luddite movements and other forms of resistance to technological progress. Almost everywhere in Europe innovation was resisted by vested interests and workers concerned about the effect of creative destruction on their employment and skills. In Britain, by and large, the government was not sympathetic to these movements and supported the industrialists, with force when needed. Parliament also created a mechanism for enclosures, which sped up the reorganization of agriculture. Remarkably, violent resistance to eighteenth-century parliamentary enclosures was minimal.

Specific institutions have been suggested as important contributions to the Industrial Revolution. Of those, the most intuitive and seemingly persuasive is the English patent law, which was passed in 1624 and was widely regarded at the time as a great advantage to Britain.[3] Modern economists, including Aghion et al. (2021), have tended to agree (North and Thomas 1973, 156; Aghion et al. 2021, 37). Other contemporaries strongly disagreed.[4] A recent summary (Bottomley 2014, 293) concludes that the patent system "made a signal contribution to technological development during the Industrial Revolution." But a closer examination of patents in the Industrial Revolution raises some legitimate concerns about the magnitude (if not the

---

[3] Johann Wolfgang von Goethe felt that the clever Englishman transforms an invention through the patent system into a "real possession, and thereby avoids all annoying disputes concerning the honor due," and sighed that "one may well ask why are they in every respect in advance of us" (cited in Klemm 1964, 173). Adam Smith ([1757] 1978, 83, 472) admitted that the patent system was the one monopoly (or "priviledge" as he called it) he could live with, because it left the decision on the merit of an invention to the market rather than to officials. Smith thought, somewhat unrealistically, that if an "invention was good and such as is profitable to mankind, [the inventor] will probably make a fortune by it."

[4] Charles Babbage, never one to mince words, denounced the patent law as a "system of vicious and fraudulent legislation" that deprived the inventor of the fruits of his genius and put the most productive citizens of society in a position of "legalized banditti" and as "a fraudulent lottery which gives its blanks to genius and its prizes to knaves" (Babbage 1830, 333, 321).

direction) of the effect. As a prime causal factor, however, it runs into a number of logical problems. First, the number of patents taken out is very small and shows no trend before the middle of the eighteenth century, when it suddenly surges upward. In other words, for more than a century, the system laid dormant; its sudden spike must have been driven by something else. Second, the Netherlands did have a system of patents awarded by both the estates general and the provincial estates from the late 1580s on, awarding a peak number of 119 patents in the 1620s. Yet in the eighteenth century, the number dwindled to insignificance (Davids 2008, 400–416).[5] Third, only a relatively small percentage of significant inventions were patented, as Moser (2005, 2021) has shown in detail. This was even true for the United States, where patenting was quite cheap relative to Britain.

There were many reasons for this low patenting rate besides the exorbitant cost. For some inventions, secrecy and first-mover advantage were better ways to secure a flow of rents. Some were awarded prizes and pensions for having materially contributed to the welfare of the nation. For others the high costs in Britain were a serious obstacle. In a land of budding liberalism, the antipathy to monopolies often led to infringement suits being lost.[6] The bureaucratic complexity of filing for a patent was well-described in novels of the time, such as Dickens's satire of the "Great Circumlocution Office" in *Little Dorrit*. Others refused to patent as a matter of principle, because they felt that it would somehow deprive their fellow humans of the blessings of their invention, or were motivated by nonpecuniary incentives.[7]

The other seemingly unique institution that has been suggested as a possible factor in the Industrial Revolution is the English Poor Law. Beginning in the sixteenth century with the dismantlement of Church institutions, the English state gradually displaced the Church and voluntary associations as the main provider of poor relief. The "Old Poor Law" of 1601 formalized this system. It was modified repeatedly but remained in force in its basic outlines

---

[5] France, too, had an institution that rewarded inventors, although it was entirely controlled by the state and one could dispute whether to call it a patent system (Hilaire-Pérez 1991).

[6] British judges (especially before 1830) were often hostile to patentees, considering them monopolists. One justice expressed a standard eighteenth-century view of patents by noting that "on the whole there was a great deal of oppression of the lower orders of men from Patents, by those who were more opulent" (cited by Robinson 1972, 137).

[7] "When one loves science," wrote Claude Berthollet, the inventor of the critically important chlorine bleaching process, to James Watt, "one has little need for fortune which would only risk one's happiness."

until 1834. In a groundbreaking paper, Solar (1995) suggested a variety of ways in which the Poor Law contributed to British economic development and industrialization.[8] One ingenious mechanism was suggested by Greif and Sasson (2011), who argue that the Poor Law provided a safety net that encouraged people to take more risks and display more entrepreneurial behavior. Essentially, it provided a risk-sharing mechanism that led to more risk-taking. In a similar vein, Greif and Iyigun (2013) argue that the Old Poor Law helped foster social order and prevented riots. A somewhat different angle on the effect of the Poor Law is provided by Kelly and Ó Gráda (2014), who demonstrate that the Poor Law was associated with the disappearance of the Malthusian "positive check" in England. The significance of this development on long-term economic growth was substantial, as the Malthusian negative feedback mechanism was one way in which the "iron law" kept wages and incomes low. By redistributing resources to the very poor, England's Poor Laws helped create a more secure and healthy working class.

Finally, a little-recognized institutional advantage of Britain was that it enjoyed a great deal of market integration. Many ancien régime continental states had barriers toward internal trade: in Germany and Italy, of course, political fragmentation paired to mercantilist regulations prevented free movement of goods and labor. But in France too, seemingly unified, internal tariffs hampered the free flow of goods, and were one of the early items that the French Revolution targeted for abolition (Dincecco 2010). The French Revolution and subsequent upheavals (with their inevitable high costs) were necessary to eliminate an advantage that Britain had enjoyed since the Middle Ages. This institutional advantage was magnified by coastal shipping and an improving highway and canal system. At first blush, integration may seem to have benefited Smithian rather than Schumpeterian growth, but regional specialization meant that the returns to investing in human capital in the regions that had a comparative advantage in high-skill production would increase (Kelly et al. 2021). Other connections from market integration and better transport to technological progress have been analyzed in detail in

---

[8] Solar argues that poor relief functioned as health and/or employment insurance that was relatively free of moral hazard and adverse selection. Insurance made people more willing to work for wages in place of owner/tenant farming, which allowed a more efficient allocation of labor to the most productive farms. A large, stable pool of wage workers with no ties to a specific plot of land provided firms with flexibility in hiring and firing, further boosting the efficient allocation of labor.

Szostak (1991). Here, too, institutions mattered: Britain was a highly taxed country, but by eschewing internal tariffs the British were able to benefit from growing regional specialization and gains from (internal) trade.

Institutions and the roots of British leadership

In a series of papers, Kelly, Mokyr, and Ó Gráda (2014, 2020, 2021), as well as in other papers (Mokyr 2008, 2021), we have argued that one underestimated driving cause of British leadership was, after all, a form of human capital, but one that was not much correlated with schooling and literacy. All the inventors and all the entrepreneurs of the world cannot bring about an Industrial Revolution (or any other form of creative destruction) unless there are skilled artisans and engineers who can read their blueprints, install and repair the equipment, provide the correct materials and fuels, and scale up their models. The abundant supply of such people in Britain was not self-evident, and, indeed, it needs to be explained. The evidence for this superiority seems unassailable. Contemporaries, both in Britain and on the Continent, loudly sang the praises of British artisans.[9] Moreover, for much of the eighteenth and nineteenth centuries, British technicians and mechanics swarmed all over the Continent, installing, operating, and maintaining advanced equipment in economies that wanted to compete with Britain, were able to get their hands on British equipment, but could not find local engineers and other experts that could deal with the equipment (Henderson 1954; Bensimon 2011).

The success of the Industrial Revolution in the eighteenth century must be explained in part by the growth in artisanal skill in the preceding centuries. What mattered here was not just average skills, but above all the high-level capabilities and sophistication of the ones in the upper tail. Some examples of these great engineers on the eve of the Industrial Revolution are well-known, such as John T. Desaguliers (1683–1744), who combined

---

[9] Detailed evidence is presented elsewhere (e.g., Mokyr 2009, 107–108; Kelly, Mokyr, and Ó Gráda 2020). One telling example is the widely cited statement by none else but Jean Baptiste Say, the inventor of Say's law and Adam Smith's most eminent follower in France. He noted in 1803 that "the enormous wealth of Britain is less owing to her own advances in scientific acquirements, high as she ranks in that department, as to the wonderful practical skills of her adventurers in the useful application of knowledge and the superiority of her workmen" (Say [1803] 1821, 1:32–33).

scientific work with engineering.[10] Outside Britain, some famous and not so famous artisans illustrate the continuous progress of craftsmanship and mechanical competence, nowhere more than in clock- and instrument-making.[11] Scattered but consistent evidence indicates that between the invention of the printing press and the Industrial Revolution, European artisans were becoming more skilled.[12] If in 1500 Europeans still had to sail around Africa to acquire Indian textiles and Chinese pottery, by 1750 they were able to make their own. In most other areas, they had advanced far beyond anyone else.

To understand the roots of this critical development, we have to realize that artisans were produced by other artisans through apprenticeship. Engineering schools were rare in this era; the first ones were founded in France in the 1740s. But practically every artisan was trained through apprenticeship.[13] The contract between master and apprentice was a complex transaction, because the master provided not only training but often also room and board. In exchange, apprentices paid an upfront fee and promised to work for the master as a servant after completing the training. For obvious reasons, this very incomplete contract provided lots of possibilities for opportunistic behavior on both sides.

The solutions to this incomplete contract problem bring the focus back to institutions. In much of Europe, guilds still played a central role in enforcing and policing various aspects of apprenticeship. As guilds were becoming

---

[10] Desaguliers, the son of Huguenot refugees, was a tireless experimenter and practical instrument maker as well as one of Newton's most devoted acolytes. He was one of many who worked on ventilation and heating issues, and redesigned chimneys and air heaters. He designed new types of water wheels and steam engines and constructed improved versions of various instruments, including a pyrometer, a barometer, a crane, and various pumps (Fara 2004; Carpenter 2011).

[11] The Renaissance produced some remarkable artisans in Western Europe, such as the Dutchman Cornelis Drebbel, the Cremona engineer (who worked in Spain) Janello Torriani, the French potter Bernard Palissy, and the English clockmaker Thomas Tompion.

[12] Relying on scattered evidence, Epstein (2008, 71) has suggested that considerable productivity growth was due to the anonymous improvements and experimentation carried out by Europe's craftsmen, from the woolen industry to printing and clock making. Kelly and Ó Gráda (2017) show that in the seventeenth century, the English watch industry experienced a decline in the real price of watches by an average of 1.3 percent per year between 1685 and 1810, the result of an increasingly finer division of labor and learning by doing. Another example is the small-arms industry. Hoffman (2015) showed the secular decline in the prices of firearms due to the growth in total factor productivity, estimating a rise in total factor productivity of pistols at 1.1 percent per year from 1556 to 1706, relative to a low-tech product such as spades.

[13] Some of the following is discussed in much greater detail in De la Croix, Doepke, and Mokyr (2018) and Mokyr (2019).

increasingly rigid and restrictive, this made it more difficult to train the nimble minds and dexterous fingers that Britain became famous for.[14] In Britain, enforcement was more or less independent of guilds. Instead, it was based on reputation mechanisms that made many contracts self-enforcing, as pointed out by Jane Humphries in a pathbreaking paper (Humphries 2003). Yet contracts were enforced in "the shadow of the law," and as a *pis aller* both sides had the option to go to court. Going to a formal court of law such as a Justice of the Peace was possible, but given the cost and uncertainty of the outcome and the long duration of lawsuits, it was rarely resorted to, even if some courts, such as the Lord Mayor's Court in London, employed speedier and less costly arbitration and more balanced reconciliation procedures (Wallis 2012, 793). Above all, Britain in the eighteenth century can be described as a *civil economy* in which artisans and merchants depended on their reputations for business, a world in which most people were able to bring about a cooperative equilibrium that allowed markets to function reasonably smoothly—including the market for artisanal training. Opportunistic or other forms of bad behavior might taint someone as "not being a gentleman" and not being trustworthy, which would be costly at many levels. Knowing this, the equilibrium path would be one of cooperation; and part of that made the apprentice-master relation work better.[15]

In this regard, if we want to understand the institutions that fostered creative destruction, we should recognize not just the importance of formal third-party contract enforcement but also the significance of "private-order" institutions, which were an integral part of the way society operated. Britain in the eighteenth century has been dubbed an "Associational Society" by its leading historian (Clark 2000). Membership in clubs, societies, academies, and various other spontaneous private-order organizations became a dominant feature of middle-class England. Many of these associations, of course, had little to do with the dissemination of useful knowledge. They were

---

[14] Highly skilled artisans needed to be able to adapt to the needs of different, if often related, occupations (Cookson 2018, 106, 126). The most telling evidence for this agility was that a full one-third of the list of innovators compiled by Anton Howes made inventions that were quite different from their specialized training and skill, and invented in a range of seemingly unrelated fields (Howes 2017, 36). High-level skills did not yet imply high levels of specialization. As Howes put it, "mechanical training could be applied to anything, from textile machinery to agricultural machinery to coachbuilding" (24).

[15] Humphries (2010, 282–284) recounts a number of cases in which disputes between master and apprentice were resolved by social and reputational pressures, many of them supported by the need of the master to maintain his social relations with the parents.

social gatherings, eating and (mostly) drinking clubs, sports and musical organizations, and so on. The significance of these associations was not so much in what they did, but in the creation of networks underlying the civil economy, in which economic agents met and exchanged information. These networks ensured that most members would behave in an "honorable" manner and thus minimized the need for third-party (that is, the state) enforcement of contracts.

The result was that Britain, thanks largely to its greater supply of high-skilled craftsmen, took the lead in the Industrial Revolution. Yet its leadership was almost entirely due to its superiority in *tacit* knowledge.[16] The nature of the Industrial Revolution and its aftermath was in slowly switching from tacit knowledge as the center of gravity to more formal knowledge, created by mathematicians, physicists, chemists, medical doctors, and people schooled in "engineering science."

In other words, while Britain seems to have enjoyed a comparative advantage in tacit knowledge and the "knacks" of the trade, the European Continent had a comparative advantage in formal and codified knowledge. The most extensive technical book on coal and collieries was written by a French physician, Jean-François C. Morand (1768–1779). While England had the most developed and sophisticated copper-smelting industry in eighteenth-century Europe, economic historians depend on Continental sources for its description (Harris 1974, 97). Perhaps the largest compilation of technical descriptions of manufacturing and related activities was contained in the enormous collection (80 volumes) of industrial handbooks published by the French Académie before the Revolution—namely, the massive *Description des Arts et Métiers* published between 1761 and 1788, including 13,000 pages and 1804 plates.[17] The great encyclopedia of d'Alembert and Diderot, too, contained a great deal of technical descriptions. Even in civil engineering, where British superiority was among the most pronounced, French texts

---

[16] In 1752 the French Academician and industrial consultant Mignot de Montigny wrote, "The arts never pass in written form from one nation to another, only the eyes and practice can train men in this work" (cited by Harris 1998, 550).

[17] The chief editor was Henri-Louis Duhamel du Monceau, a distinguished botanist and naval architect and one of the most remarkable figures of the French Enlightenment, who personified the practical side of Enlightenment science. "His hallmark was neither style nor wit. It was usefulness" (Gillispie 1980, 338).

dominated.[18] The English produced and engineered; the French wrote about it. The historical dynamic, however, worked against the British as technology began to rely more and more on formal science.

Destruction creation

The unprecedented progress that Enlightenment *philosophes* had hoped for exacted a high price. The Industrial Revolution was responsible for the unprecedented growth of the new industrial towns, of which Manchester and Glasgow were the best examples. Even non-Marxist historians have agreed that the creation of an industrial and urban wage-labor class, whether one uses the term "proletariat" or not, was a decisive factor directing the evolution of Victorian society. The emergence of an urban working class in congested, unhealthy, and disagreeable industrial towns was described with alarming detail by contemporaries. Of those, Friedrich Engels's famous book *The Condition of the Working Class in England in 1844* has received the most fame or notoriety, but his descriptions are consistent with (and to some extent derived from) those of other contemporary observers of life in the new industrial towns, such as Peter Gaskell, William Alison, and James Kay-Shuttleworth. No document laid this fact out more clearly than Edwin Chadwick's justly celebrated *Report on the Sanitary Condition*, first published in 1842, which described in great detail the environmental impact of the Industrial Revolution in urban areas.[19]

Modern research has put formidable quantitative muscle in this anecdotal skeleton. Huck (1995) showed in detail the appalling levels of infant mortality in British industrial towns and sees them as evidence of stagnant living standards in these cities, in which a worse physical environment offset higher wages. In two remarkable papers, Walker Hanlon and Brian Beach have shown how the heavy use of coal, touted by many as the most striking

---

[18] Among the notable engineering texts were "the best contemporary account of the steam engine" written by Gaspard de Prony (1794), the widely read and translated *Essay sur la Composition des Machines* published in 1808 by Agustín de Betancourt and José Maria Lanz, and J.P.N. Hachette's *Traité élémentaire des machines* (1811). See Cardwell (1994, 205).

[19] Chadwick was no socialist, but he described what he saw: "The familiarity with the sickness and death constantly present in the crowded and unwholesome districts, appears to re-act as another concurrent cause in aggravation of the wretchedness and vice in which they are plunged. Seeing the apparent uncertainty of the morrow, the inhabitants really take no heed of it, and abandon themselves with the recklessness and avidity of common soldiers in a war to whatever gross enjoyment comes within their reach" ([1843] 1965, 198).

feature of the Industrial Revolution, led to major environmental effects on the life of the people living in the new industrial cities, as measured through its effects on life expectancy.[20] Moreover, they show that the use of coal slowed down city growth, and that had there been more regulation, growth would have been faster (Beach and Hanlon 2018; Hanlon 2020). The Industrial Revolution took place in an institutional environment that had changed dramatically from a mercantilist world of regulation and control to a liberal world that was as close to laissez-faire as any economy is likely to get. Yet the patent market failures that were obvious in the new industrial urban centers pointed to the inevitable demise of the relatively purist laissez-faire policies of the first half of the nineteenth century.

Another striking example of industrial pollution is the Leblanc soda-making process, a French invention (1785) that, as in many other cases, was first deployed on an industrial scale in Britain, in this case primarily by an Irish-born entrepreneur named James Muspratt at St. Helens in Lancashire. The invention was a major technological breakthrough, as soda was an important material in a host of chemical industries. Reed (2013) refers to the name of the waste product of the Leblanc process, *galligu*, as "a wonderfully onomatopoeic word to describe a black, evil-smelling, viscous material." A ton of soda implied about 1.75 tons of galligu. Galligu was not just malodorous; it was also quite toxic, containing arsenic and other heavy metals, and leached into the groundwater. Most was deposited on wasteland adjoining the works, scarring the landscape and polluting the surrounding land, air, and water, some of which is still unusable today. It has been estimated that by the 1870s the annual amount of this waste produced in Britain was close to 500,000 tons. People living close to the works complained vociferously about the "nuisance" created by this pollution. In addition, releasing hydrogen chloride from tall chimneys without any amelioration proved a constant scourge for landowners and people living close by the works who were affected by the debilitating effects of the gas, as well as for manufacturers fighting the legal redress for the alleged damage in-

---

[20] Beach and Hanlon (2018) estimate that raising local industrial coal use by 1 SD from the mean increased infant mortality by roughly 6–8 percent and under-five mortality by 8–15 percent. In terms of life expectancy, given mortality patterns in the 1851–60 decade, the impact of a 1 SD increase in local industrial coal use on under-five mortality is associated with a reduction in life expectancy at birth of 0.84–1.58 years or 2.19–4.11 percent. In the most heavily polluted cities, such as Sheffield, Manchester, or Birmingham, where coal use was more than two standard deviations above the national mean, the effects were quite large, which could explain Huck's (1995) findings.

flicted. Soda-making was the driver behind the first environmental legislation, the Alkali Acts of 1863 and 1868.

The destruction wrought by the Industrial Revolution was, perhaps inevitably, most devastating to specific human capital. The mechanization of skilled tasks destroyed the value of workers' skills and abilities, famously leading to considerable resentment that drove many machine-breaking riots. The Luddite riots in the Midlands between 1812 and 1816 are widely cited, but they were only the tip on the iceberg. Much of the displacement took place in the wool industry, which for centuries had been the mainstay of the British textile industry; it suffered not only from technological change but also from increasing competition from cotton textiles, which were growing at a much faster rate. Scribbling mills (which prepared the raw fleece for carding) and gig mills (which brought up the nap on woolen fabrics) threatened traditional skills. Here creation was truly destructive: Benjamin Gott, a Leeds wool manufacturer, built a new factory in Leeds named Bean Ing, which was a paragon of modern technology and rational management.[21] But this new age of large mills threatened to become the workers' worst nightmare, wiping out their livelihood and way of life. In the "West Country" of England (Gloucestershire, Wiltshire, Somerset) the highly specialized wool industry, mostly consisting of small independent producers, could not survive mechanization (Randall 1991, 40, 45). Deindustrialization ensued, but not before some serious rioting occurred.

Historians have been more sensitive to the nonpecuniary costs of the Industrial Revolution than have economists, who have tended to dismiss the resistance as a form of rent-seeking. In an eloquent passage, Randall (1991, 48) points to what he calls the "amorality of the factory system." In the old system, customs protected the worker's rights and dignity. The factory steamrollered customs, replacing a "moral economy" with the amoral (though not immoral) economy of pure, impersonal relations. For the economist, a more prosaic way of defining the issue is to point out that the factory reduced the choice set between leisure and income to a single point; in contrast, self-employed cottage industry workers could optimize over a continuous choice set. Yet this captures only one aspect of the costs of creative destruction.

---

[21] A classic text on the Leeds wool industry is an eloquent description of what creative destruction can look like: "The boldness of Gott's conception of a factory in 1792 is perhaps without parallel . . . Bean Ing sprang out of nothing; it was an ideal, a dream of the new age of industrialization, materialized forthwith in bricks and iron, in steam and machinery" (Crump 1931, 255).

The most famous example of destructive creation during the Industrial Revolution was the fate of the handloom weaver (Bythell 1969). Handloom weavers have often served as an example of the costs of laissez-faire economy subject to exogenous shocks.[22] Hobsbawm tersely suggests that the weavers "starved progressively in a vain attempt to compete with the new machines" (Hobsbawm 1969, 93). The mechanization of weaving, first in cotton and then in other textiles, clearly threatened and eventually eliminated this occupation, which had been one of the largest single occupations in Britain.[23] The story is far less clear-cut than the pessimist accounts of Thompson and Hobsbawm indicate, yet at the end of the day there is no question that even in the most optimistic accounts, handloom weavers have been dubbed "the leading example of technological unemployment during English industrialization" (Hartwell 1969, xi). Lyons (1989) has argued that even though the plight was real enough, it was a matter of one generation that could not readily adapt, but that the offspring of the weavers found employment in a rapidly growing economy. Moreover, the ranks of weavers had swollen considerably in the "golden age" decades when spinning had been mechanized but power looms were still few and imperfect. Free entry into the industry meant that during periods of boom, the growth in the numbers of weavers kept wages in check, but that when conditions turned down as power looms became more common after 1820, many were driven to exit the industry. However, as Bythell (1969, 58–61) notes, the picture is muddled by the fact that for many handloom weavers, the work was part-time, even casual employment. Moreover, in his view, the transition occurred with remarkable speed and ease, and what was notable was the speed with which handloom weavers disappeared, rather than the "protraction of their agony" (Bythell 1969, 268). The conclusions are, of course, debatable (Perkin 1971). The abruptness that Bythell underlines meant that a whole generation did not have the time needed to adapt; technological unemployment was less of a

---

[22] In the words of the most influential social historian of the Industrial Revolution of his generation, "In the weavers' history we have a paradigm case of the operation of a repressive and exploitative system upon a section of workers without trade union defences. Government not only intervened actively against their political organizations . . . it also inflicted upon the weavers the negative dogma of the freedom of capital as intransigently as it was to do upon the victims of the Irish Famine" (Thompson 1963, 312).

[23] As late as 1834 the Select Committee appointed to look into the weavers' plight estimated that 800,000 or more people were wholly dependent on the loom (*British Parliamentary Papers*, 1834–1835, 3). Bythell (1969, 57) estimates the number of weavers only in cotton at 200,000–250,000.

threat when the decline in the demand for labor in the affected industry was slow and gradual.

Another sector of the economy that was disrupted by destructive creation was framework knitters. Known as "stockingers," they were located in the east Midlands, half of them in Nottinghamshire. Certainly by the 1830s they had fallen on very hard times and had to make their children join the work in a desperate attempt to survive.[24] The decline of this trade and the associated economy were factors in the 1810 Nottinghamshire riots, which had been thought to be moderate compared to the Luddite riots in Lancashire and the West Riding of Yorkshire (Roberts 2017). The transformation of the British economy, amplified by the shocks of the Napoleonic Wars, caused a contraction of what social historians have called the "makeshift economy," the "patchy, desperate and sometimes failing strategies of the poor to make ends meet" (King and Tomkins 2003). It may well be that the precariousness of the economic status of framework knitters in the Midlands pushed them into rioting. What is obvious is that the British authorities had little sympathy for these victims of destructive creation. In Hobsbawm's eloquent words, industrialization first increased the numbers of handloom weavers and framework knitters until the end of the Wars. "Thereafter it destroyed them by slow strangulation . . . skilled craftsmen were degraded in to sweated out-workers . . . pre-industrial traditions could not could not keep their head above the inevitably rising level of industrial society" (Hobsbawm 1969, 90–91).

A very different but striking example of the destructiveness of the Industrial Revolution is provided by a social historian, Emma Griffin (2018). One of the costs of the Industrial Revolution, she believes, is the disruption of the allocation of resources *within* the family, at the micro-micro

---

[24] In a special section dealing with the hosiery trade, the Royal Commission on Children in Factories of 1833 commission (*British Parliamentary Papers*, 1833) reported that "the long and extreme depreciation in the value of the stocking maker's labour . . . [had caused] "hopeless poverty producing fearful demoralization" (579). A local witness before the same Commission, describing the state of framework knitters, maintained that "the condition of these persons [children between the ages of six and eighteen] is very low and depressed . . . the general appearance both of men and women and children employed in this branch of manufactures, their habits of work and subsistence are more destructive of health, comfort, cleanliness and general state of well-being than any [other] state of employment." Another added, "They are, many of them, unhealthy and dyspeptic; . . . I can tell a stockinger well by his appearance; there is a paleness and certain degree of emaciation and thinness about them . . . hopeless poverty is producing fearful demoralisation" (535, 557).

level. Industrialization raised male incomes, "but at the same time it changed patterns of behaviour that had historically helped to ensure that children received the food they needed." High wages, she feels, "went hand in hand with the erosion of age-old social pressures upon men to provide for their families, resulting in the divergence between male wages and family living standards" (Griffin 2018, 102–103). While Huck and Hanlon document the cost to the urban working class in terms of disease and pollution, Griffin stresses the grinding misery of the rural poor. Searching close to 350 autobiographies for references to hunger and similar terms, she finds that in rural households, dependents were most likely to suffer from occasional hunger. Yet in industrial regions, too, childhood deprivation was common. Griffin's argument is that the Industrial Revolution was both an economic and a cultural event. "Wages formed the bedrock of well-being within families, but a complex series of social and cultural norms were needed in order to turn those wages into well-being." Men whose real wages were increasing had a greater propensity "of reneging on their responsibility to provide with the consequence that children's living standards lagged behind the male wage" (Griffin 2018, 106). Strikingly, infant mortality—a standard metric of living standards—stayed stubbornly high in England until the closing years of the nineteenth century.

Conclusions

How dangerous is destructive creation? It is no accident that economic historians speak of "technological *progress*" but "institutional *change*." Technology, like all forms of knowledge, is on the whole cumulative: we know (most of) what previous generations knew, but we know more. Especially since the invention of the printing press and other ways of reproducing knowledge, it is rare for knowledge to be lost or forgotten. Institutions, on the other hand, tend to follow no monotonic time path. Even though there have been periods of noticeable improvements toward inclusive and open societies in which human rights and individual freedoms were respected, more often than not they were followed by periods in which autocratic and repressive regimes took over. The corridors to open and inclusive societies are narrow and full of dead ends (Acemoglu and Robinson 2018). Technology and institutions, however, affect one another in subtle ways.

The Industrial Revolution provides an example of how technological progress and institutions interacted. As we saw, the institutional environment affected the rate of technological progress. But the reverse effect was there as well. The rise of the factory and polluted and congested industrial urban centers made liberalism in its purer forms unsustainable. Child labor laws, the regulation of urban amenities, and concern about public health and consumer safety all came to the fore during the Industrial Revolution. Urban poverty may not have been all that much worse than rural poverty, but it was more visible and salient. Regulation and growing state control followed, and in the end the twentieth century produced the welfare state, often through "a winding road"—as one might expect from a highly nonlinear historical dynamic of coevolution (Boyer 2019).

Perhaps one of the dimensions that economic historians of technology have left out from their discussion is that technology is about more than just the control of natural forces by humans; it also determines the tools by which humans influence, control, and manipulate one another. Any regime relies on instruments to exercise power and help create obedience: Josef Goebbels's radio and Xi Jinping's surveillance cams and facial recognition algorithms are just two examples of how autocratic regimes harness the cutting-edge technology of their age to suppress human rights and liberty. Perhaps, then, that threatens to become the worst enemy of progress, and the ultimate form of destructive creation. Will the inventiveness and ingenuity that have made humanity so much richer than any generation in the past also create the capabilities by which malevolent rulers will control their citizens through lies and terror?

References

Acemoglu, Daron and James Robinson. 2018. *The Narrow Corridor: States, Societies, and the Fate of Liberty.* New York: Penguin Books.

Aghion, Philippe, Céline Antonin, and Simon Bunel. 2021. *The Power of Creative Destruction: Economic Upheaval and the Wealth of Nations.* Cambridge, MA: Harvard University Press.

Alesina, Alberto, and Paola Giuliano. 2015. "Culture and Institutions." *Journal of Economic Literature* 53 (4): 898–944.

Babbage, Charles. 1830. "Reflections on the Decline of Science in Britain and on Some of Its Causes." *Quarterly Review* (London), 43 (May/October), 307–342; repr. New York: Augustus Kelley, 1970.

Beach, Brian, and Walker Hanlon. 2018. "Coal Smoke and Mortality in an Early Industrial Economy." *Economic Journal* 128 (615): 2652–2675.

Bensimon, Fabrice. 2011. "British Workers in France, 1815–1848." *Past and Present* 213 (1): 147–189.

Bloom, Nicholas, Charles I. Jones, John Van Reenen, and Michael Webb. 2020. "Are Ideas Getting Harder to Find?" *American Economic Review* 110 (4): 1104–1144.

Bottomley, Sean. 2014. *The British Patent System during the Industrial Revolution, 1700–1852.* Cambridge: Cambridge University Press.

Boyer, George. 2019. *The Winding Road to the Welfare State: Economic Insecurity and Social Welfare Policy in Britain.* Princeton, NJ: Princeton University Press.

British Parliamentary Papers. 1833. Vol. 20 (450) ("Royal Commission on Employment of Children in Factories. First Report and Minutes of Evidence.").

British Parliamentary Papers. 1834–1835. Vol. 10 (556) ("Select Committee on Handloom Weavers' Petitions").

Bythell, Duncan. 1969. *The Handloom Weavers.* London: Cambridge University Press.

Cardwell, Donald S. L. 1994. *The Fontana History of Technology.* London: Fontana Press.

Carpenter, Audrey T. 2011. *John Theophilus Desaguliers.* London: Continuum.

Chadwick, Edwin. [1843] 1965. *Report on the Sanitary Condition of the Labouring Population of Great Britain,* ed. M. W. Flinn. London: Her Majesty's Stationery Office / Edinburgh: Edinburgh University Press.

Clark, Peter. 2000. *British Clubs and Societies, 1580–1800: The Origins of an Associational World.* Oxford: Clarendon Press.

Cookson, Gillian. 2018. *The Age of Machinery: Engineering in the Industrial Revolution, 1770–1850.* London: Boydell and Brewer.

Crump, W. B. 1931. "The History of Gott's Mills." In *The Leeds Woolen Industry, 1780–1820,* ed. W. B. Crum, 254–271. Leeds: Thoresby Society.

Davids, K. 2008. *The Rise and Decline of Dutch Technological Leadership.* 2 vols. Leiden: Brill.

De la Croix, David, Matthias Doepke, and Joel Mokyr. 2018. "Clans, Guilds, and Markets: Apprenticeship Institutions and Growth in the Pre-Industrial Economy." *Quarterly Journal of Economics* 133 (1): 1–70.

Dincecco, Mark. 2010. "Fragmented Authority from Ancien Régime to Modernity: A Quantitative Analysis." *Journal of Institutional Economics* 6 (3): 305–328.

Epstein, Stephan R. 2008. "Craft Guilds, the Theory of the Firm, and the European Economy, 1400–1800." In *Guilds, Innovation and the European Economy, 1400–1800,* ed. S. R. Epstein and Maarten Prak, 52–80. Cambridge: Cambridge University Press.

Fara, Patricia. 2004. "Desaguliers, John Theophilus (1683–1744)." In *Oxford Dictionary of National Biography.* Oxford: Oxford University Press.

Gillispie, Charles Coulston. 1980. *Science and Polity in France: The End of the Old Regime.* Princeton, NJ: Princeton University Press.

Gordon, Robert J. 2016. *The Rise and Fall of American Growth: The US Standard of Living since the Civil War*. Princeton, NJ: Princeton University Press.

Greif, Avner. [1994] 2005. *Institutions and the Path to the Modern Economy: Lessons from Medieval Trade*. Cambridge: Cambridge University Press.

Greif, Avner, and Murat Iyigun. 2013. "What Did the Old Poor Law Really Accomplish? A Redux." Unpublished working paper.

Greif, Avner, and Joel Mokyr. 2016. "Institutions and Economic History: A Critique of Professor McCloskey." *Journal of Institutional Economics* 12 (1): 29–41.

Greif, Avner, and Diego Sasson. 2011. "Risk, Institutions and Growth: Why England and Not China?" IZA Discussion Paper 5598.

Griffin, Emma. 2018. "Diets, Hunger and Living Standards during the British Industrial Revolution." *Past and Present* 239 (1): 71–111.

Hanlon, Walker. 2020. "Coal Smoke, City Growth, and the Costs of the Industrial Revolution." *Economic Journal* 130 (626): 462–488.

Harris, J. R. 1974. "The Rise of Coal Technology." *Scientific American* (August): 92–97.

Harris, J. R. 1998. *Industrial Espionage and Technology Transfer: Britain and France in the Eighteenth Century*. Aldershot: Ashgate.

Hartwell, R. Max. 1969. "Introduction." In Bythell (1969).

Henderson, W. O. 1954. *Britain and Industrial Europe, 1750–1870: Studies in British Influence on the Industrial Revolution in Western Europe*. Liverpool: Liverpool University Press.

Hilaire-Pérez, Liliane. 1991. "Invention and the State in Eighteenth-Century France." *Technology and Culture* 32 (4): 911–931.

Hobsbawm, Eric. 1969. *Industry and Empire*. Harmondsworth: Penguin Books.

Hoffman, Philip T. 2015. *Why Did Europe Conquer the World?* Princeton, NJ: Princeton University Press.

Howes, Anton. 2017. "The Relevance of Skills to Innovation during the British Industrial Revolution, 1547–1851." Unpublished working paper.

Huck, Paul. 1995. "Infant Mortality and Living Standards of English Workers during the Industrial Revolution." *Journal of Economic History* 55 (3): 528–550.

Humphries, Jane. 2003. "English Apprenticeships: A Neglected Factor in the First Industrial Revolution." In *The Economic Future in Historical Perspective*, ed. P. A. David and M. Thomas, 73–102. Oxford: Oxford University Press.

Humphries, Jane. 2010. *Childhood and Child Labour in the British Industrial Revolution*. Cambridge: Cambridge University Press.

Jones, Peter M. 2016. *Agricultural Enlightenment: Knowledge, Technology, and Nature*. Oxford: Oxford University Press.

Kapás, Judit. 2012. "Which Institutions Caused the British Industrial Revolution?" In *Institutions and the Industrial Revolution*, ed. J. Kapás and P. Czeglédi, 35–59. Debrecen: University of Debrecen.

Kelly, Morgan, Joel Mokyr, and Cormac Ó Gráda. 2014. "Precocious Albion: A New Interpretation of the British Industrial Revolution." *Annual Review of Economics* 6: 363–391.

Kelly, Morgan, Joel Mokyr, and Cormac Ó Gráda. 2020. "Could Artisans Have Caused the Industrial Revolution?" In *Reinventing the Economic History of Industrialization,* ed. Kristine Bruland, Anne Gerritsen, Pat Hudson, and Giorgio Riello, 25–43. Montreal: McGill-Queen's University Press.

Kelly, Morgan, Joel Mokyr, and Cormac Ó Gráda. 2021. "The Mechanics of the Industrial Revolution." Unpublished paper.

Kelly, Morgan, and Cormac Ó Gráda. 2014. "Living Standards and Mortality since the Middle Ages." *Economic History Review* 67 (2): 358–381.

Kelly, Morgan, and Cormac Ó Gráda. 2017. "Adam Smith, Watch Prices, and the Industrial Revolution." *Quarterly Journal of Economics* 131 (4): 1727–1752.

King, Steven, and Alannah Tomkins. 2003. *The Poor in England 1700–1850: An Economy of Makeshifts.* Manchester: Manchester University Press.

Klemm, Friedrich. 1964. *A History of Western Technology.* Cambridge, MA: MIT Press.

Lyons, John S. 1989. "Family Response to Economic Decline: Handloom Weavers in Early Nineteenth-Century Lancashire." *Research in Economic History* 12: 45–91.

Mazzucato, Mariana. 2015. *The Entrepreneurial State: Debunking Public vs. Private Sector Myths.* Rev. ed. New York: Public Affairs.

McCloskey, Deirdre N. 2010. *Bourgeois Dignity: Why Economics Can't Explain the Modern World.* Chicago: University of Chicago Press.

McCloskey, Deirdre. 2021. "How Growth Happens." Paper presented to the Cato Institute Conference, unpublished.

McCloskey, Deirdre N., and Alberto Mingardi. 2020. *The Myth of the Entrepreneurial State.* Great Barrington, MA: American Institute for Economic Research.

Mokyr, Joel. 2008. "The Institutional Origins of the Industrial Revolution." In *Institutions and Economic Performance,* ed. Elhanan Helpman, 64–119. Cambridge, MA: Harvard University Press.

Mokyr, Joel. 2009. *The Enlightened Economy.* New York: Yale University Press.

Mokyr, Joel. 2018. "The Past and the Future of Innovation: Some Lessons from Economic History." *Explorations in Economic History* 69: 13–26.

Mokyr, Joel. 2019. "The Economics of Apprenticeship." In *Apprenticeship in Early Modern Europe,* ed. Maarten Prak and Patrick Wallis, 20–43. Cambridge: Cambridge University Press.

Mokyr, Joel. 2021. "'The Holy Land of Industrialism': Rethinking the Industrial Revolution." *Journal of the British Academy* 9.

Morand, Jean-François-Clément. [1769–1778] 2012. *L'art d'exploiter les mines de charbon de terre: Du charbon de terre et de ses mines.* Repr., Paris: Hachette Livres.

Moser, Petra. 2005. "How Do Patent Laws Influence Innovation? Evidence from Nineteenth-Century World Fairs." *American Economic Review* 95 (4): 1214–1236.

Moser, Petra. 2021. *Pirates and Patents: An Economic History of Innovation in Europe and the United States*. Unpublished book manuscript.

North, Douglass C., and Robert Thomas. 1973. *The Rise of the Western World: A New Economic History*. Cambridge: Cambridge University Press.

North, Douglass C., and Barry Weingast. 1989. "Constitutions and Commitment: Evolution of Institutions Governing Public Choice in Seventeenth Century England." *Journal of Economic History* 49 (4): 803–32.

Nunn, Nathan, and Nancy Qian. 2010. "The Columbian Exchange: A History of Disease, Food, and Ideas." *Journal of Economic Perspectives* 24 (2): 163–188.

Perkin, Harold. 1971. "Review of *The Handloom Weavers*." *Journal of Social History* 4 (3): 290–293.

Pincus, Steven C. A., and James A. Robinson. 2014. "What Really Happened during the Glorious Revolution?" In *Economic Institutions, Rights, Growth, and Sustainability: The Legacy of Douglass North*, ed. Itai Sened and Sebastian Galiani. Cambridge: Cambridge University Press.

Porter, Roy. 1982. "Was There a Medical Enlightenment?" *British Journal for Eighteenth Century Studies* 5: 49–63.

Randall, Adrian. 1991. *Before the Luddites*. Cambridge: Cambridge University Press.

Reed, Peter. 2013. "Galligu: An Environmental Legacy of the Leblanc Alkali Industry, 1814–1920." *Royal Society of Chemistry Environmental Chemistry Group, E.C.G. Bulletin*, February, https://www.envchemgroup.com/galligu-an-environmental-legacy-of-the-leblanc-alkali-industry-1814-1920.html.

Roberts, Matthew. 2017. "Rural Luddism and the Makeshift Economy of the Nottinghamshire Framework Knitters." *Social History* 42 (3): 365–398.

Robinson, Eric. 1972. "James Watt and the Law of Patents." *Technology and Culture* 13 (2): 115–139.

Say, Jean-Baptiste. [1803] 1821. *A Treatise on Political Economy*. 4th ed. Boston: Wells and Lilly.

Smith, Adam. [1757] 1978. *Lectures on Jurisprudence*. Oxford: Clarendon Press.

Solar, P. M. 1995. "Poor Relief and English Economic Development before the Industrial Revolution." *Economic History Review*, n.s., 48 (1): 1–22.

Szostak, Rick. 1991. *The Role of Transportation in the Industrial Revolution*. Montreal: McGill's-Queen's University Press.

Thompson, E. P. 1963. *The Making of the English Working Class*. New York: Vintage Books.

Wallis, Patrick. 2012. "Labor, Law, and Training in Early Modern London: Apprenticeship and the City's Institutions." *Journal of British Studies* 51 (4): 791–819.

Whitehead, Alfred North. 1925. *Science and the Modern World*. New York: Macmillan.

Conclusion

The Promise of the Creative Destruction Paradigm

PHILIPPE AGHION *and* PETER HOWITT

1 Introduction

We met by chance in 1987 at MIT, where we had neighboring offices during the academic year 1987–1988.[1] Right away we began working together. Putting an IO model of repeated patent races into a macro framework, we created a growth model that was based on Schumpeter's celebrated idea of creative destruction.

It soon became clear to us that this new framework was capable of shedding light on the interaction of growth with other economic aspects such as competition and trade, unemployment, convergence, business cycles, technological waves, exhaustible resources, learning by doing, the organization of research, and so on. A theoretical exploration of some of these aspects led to our first book, *Endogenous Growth Theory.*[2]

But how to reconcile theory with data? In 1998 we started collaborating with Richard Blundell, Rachel Griffith, and Nick Bloom on the relation-

---

[1] Philippe Aghion was starting at MIT as an assistant professor and Peter Howitt was visiting MIT from the University of Western Ontario.

[2] See Aghion and Howitt (1998). For other textbook surveys of growth theory from Solow to the Schumpeterian model, see also Grossman and Helpman (1991), Barro and Sala-i-Martin (1995), Acemoglu (2009), and Aghion and Howitt (2009).

ship between competition and innovation-led growth.[3] We then realized that Schumpeterian theory was the first aggregate growth theory with a micro-structure rich enough, and with room for enough heterogeneity, to be tested using large micro data sets, instead of being limited to the aggregate data contained in the Penn World Tables, or in Madison's historical data set.

The work that younger researchers have done since then has shown that the theory is even richer and more fruitful than we could have imagined, in many different dimensions.[4] The contributors to this volume have brought these different dimensions together masterfully, shedding further light on growth and competition, international trade, politics, the environment, un-employment, the productivity slowdown, finance, firm dynamics, inequality, secular stagnation, monetary policy, and economic development. In these concluding remarks we will briefly comment on some of the multiple achieve-ments of the Schumpeterian paradigm.

This chapter is organized as follows. In Section 2 we introduce the Schum-peterian growth paradigm, and then we show how this paradigm can be used to elucidate enigmas in recent growth history. In Section 3 we illus-trate how the Schumpeterian paradigm can be tested using rich micro data, focusing on the relationship between product market competition and in-novation-led growth. In Section 4 we use the paradigm to question some common wisdoms on growth policymaking. Finally, Section 5 concludes.

2 The Paradigm of Creative Destruction and Some Growth Enigmas

The paradigm revolves around three main ideas. The first idea is that long-term growth results from cumulative innovation, where each new innovator builds upon previous innovations. In particular, institutions that favor the diffusion and codification of knowledge contribute to making innovation cu-mulative; that is, they make it unnecessary to climb the same mountain over and over like Sisyphus. The second idea is that innovation is motivated by the prospect of innovation rents. Institutions that secure those rents, in

---

[3] This collaboration built on previous work on growth with step-by-step innovation, in particular Aghion, Harris, and Vickers (1997); and Aghion, Harris, Howitt, and Vickers (2001).

[4] Here we refer the reader to Aghion, Akcigit, and Howitt (2014); and to Ufuk Akcigit's mas-terful introduction to this volume.

particular by protecting intellectual property rights, encourage entrepreneurs to invest more in innovation. The third idea is creative destruction: new innovations render previous innovations obsolete. In other words, there is a permanent conflict between the old and the new.

At the heart of this new growth paradigm lies the following contradiction. On the one hand, innovation rents are needed to motivate innovation investments. On the other hand, yesterday's innovators are tempted to use their innovation rents to prevent subsequent innovations because they don't want themselves to suffer from creative destruction.

Regulating capitalism is primarily about how to manage this contradiction. Interestingly, even as he saw creative destruction as a potential driving force of growth, Schumpeter himself was quite pessimistic about the future of capitalism, as he anticipated that previous innovators would turn into entrenched conglomerates that would successfully impede new innovations. Even though to some extent recent economic history seems to support Schumpeter's worries, we believe that it is possible to manage the above contradiction so as to "save capitalism from the capitalists," to use the title of Rajan and Zingales's latest book.[5] In that sense we are more like "Gramscian optimists" advocating an "optimism of the will."

We judge paradigms mainly by their ability to shed light on important phenomena and enigmas. The Schumpeterian paradigm penetrates key enigmas in the history of economic growth that growth models without creative destruction could not explain.[6] We shall focus on three enigmas: the growth takeoff, secular stagnation, and the middle-income trap.

The transition from stagnation to growth. Why didn't growth take off until the beginning of the nineteenth century? Why did everything start in Europe, and more specifically in the United Kingdom—and not in China, which had pioneered inventions such as the wheel or the compass long before the Industrial Revolution? The Schumpeterian paradigm with its three components—cumulative innovation, innovation rents, and creative destruction—helps answer these questions, and here Joel Mokyr's enormous contribution takes center stage (see Mokyr 2002; Mokyr and Voth 2010). First, cumulative innovation was favored in Europe by the decreasing cost of printing, by the publication of encyclopedias that helped codify the knowl-

---

[5] See Rajan and Zingales (2004).
[6] In particular, Solow (1956) and Romer (1990).

edge and know-how available at the time, by the emergence of affordable postal services, and by the free circulation of ideas between inventors and between countries. Second, it was supported by the emergence of institutions that protected intellectual property rights, following the Glorious Revolution in England, and subsequently the French Revolution and Napoleon. Third, creative destruction was facilitated in Europe by competition among nations. This competition enabled innovation and creative destruction to take place despite the presence in each country of forces resisting new innovation. By contrast, in China the only innovations that were allowed were those handpicked by the emperor, which in turn explains why the Chinese economy stagnated throughout the nineteenth century and well into the twentieth century while Europe and then the United States were taking off.

Secular stagnation. Why, after a boost between 1995 and 2005, has US productivity growth fallen since 2005? Why has productivity growth fallen despite the information technology and artificial intelligence revolutions? And why have firms' markups increased over the same period? Different candidate explanations for the growth decline have been explored—including, for example, the view that new ideas may be harder to get, or the fact that growth is mismeasured—and there is good evidence supporting these two claims. Yet two attempts using the Schumpeterian paradigm have been particularly successful at explaining both the decline in growth and the increase in rents. These two attempts explore different dimensions of cross-firm heterogeneity.

The first attempt, by Akcigit and Ates (2021), uses an extension of the paradigm, outlined in Section 3, where in each sector of the economy there is a technological leader and a technological laggard, where the leader innovates at the frontier and the laggard tries to catch up, and where the laggard must first catch up to the leader before it can surpass it. The authors argue that over the past years it has become harder for the laggards to catch up with the leaders, one reason being that the leaders have become better at preventing the diffusion of their knowledge, by, for example, acquiring patents for defensive purposes. The result is that innovation by laggards has been discouraged, hence the growth decline, whereas leaders' rents have increased.

The second attempt, by Aghion, Bergeaud, et al. (2019), explores another extension of the paradigm where there are two types of firms in the economy: superstar firms and non-superstar firms. The superstar firms have accumulated social capital and know-how or developed networks that other firms cannot emulate. The argument then is that the IT revolution has enabled super-star firms to control a larger fraction of sectors in the economy. This explains the surge in productivity growth between 1995 and 2005. It also explains the surge in rents, as superstar firms tend to have higher markups than other firms. The flipside is that as they became hegemonic, superstar firms ended up discouraging innovation and entry by non-superstar firms, hence the observed decline in growth and entry since the early 2000s.

The middle-income trap. After emerging from the Korean War in the late 1950s with a very low per capita GDP, South Korea experienced a very high growth rate, especially between 1960 and 1997, but then growth declined dramatically. This "middle-income trap" phenomenon is easily explained using a straight extension of the Schumpeterian growth paradigm, where firms in any country can choose between technological catch-up toward the frontier productivity level in their sectors, and frontier innovation to improve upon the current frontier technology in their sector.[7] In less advanced countries, where most firms are far below the technological frontier, catching up is the main source of growth because firms make a substantial technological leap whenever they catch up with the frontier. By contrast, in more advanced countries, where most firms are initially close to the frontier in their sectors, frontier innovation becomes the main source of growth. The explanation for the middle-income trap phenomenon is that some countries failed to make the transition from institutions and policies that favor catch-up growth toward institutions that favor frontier innovation. In particular, we shall argue in Section 3 that competition enhances productivity growth more in countries that are close to the world technological frontier than in countries that are far below the technological frontier. But why did South Korea fail to toughen its competition policy as it moved closer to the world productivity frontier? The reason is that the catch-up growth period favors the emergence of large conglomerates, which then use their accumulated wealth to pressure politicians and judges to prevent the implementation of new—e.g., more pro-competitive—rules and policies in order to preserve their rents. In South Korea, the conglomerates are called *chaebols*.

---

[7] See Acemoglu, Aghion, and Zilibotti (2006).

Whether we discuss the growth takeoff, or the recent growth decline, or the middle-income trap, we come across the same basic contradiction between the need for innovation rents and the use of those rents by incumbent firms to prevent subsequent innovation. As mentioned above, Schumpeter's belief was that capitalism is doomed because he thought it would be impossible to prevent incumbent firms from barring new innovations, either directly or by exploiting political connections with government authorities. However, the above discussions also suggest that Schumpeter's pessimism might have been somewhat excessive.

Thus, when discussing the growth takeoff, we saw that the competition among nations could force individual countries to accept new innovations. Similarly, our discussion on secular stagnation suggested that more appropriate competition policies in the United States would limit the scope for defensive patenting by leaders in the various sectors, or would limit the power of superstar firms to expand and thereby control most sectors of the economy, and would encourage innovation by laggards and/or non-superstar firms, thereby fostering aggregate productivity growth. Finally, our analysis of middle-income traps called for curbing the lobbying power of incumbent firms in order to hasten the transition toward institutions and policies that favor frontier innovation. Interestingly, the Asian financial crisis of 1997 and 1998 led to the bankruptcy of some *chaebols*, such as Daewoo, and weakened those *chaebols* that managed to survive. And because it limited the influence of chaebols, the crisis opened the Korean economy to competition, which in turn stimulated productivity growth, patenting, and entry by non-*chaebol* firms in all industries, thereby fostering aggregate productivity growth in South Korea.[8]

3 Taking the Paradigm to Micro Data: Competition and Innovation

An empirical study using UK firm-level data by Blundell et al. (1995, 1999) found a positive correlation between product market competition and innovation/growth. This, in turn, challenged the Schumpeterian paradigm: to

---

[8] See Aghion, Guriev, and Jo (2019); and chapter 7 of Aghion, Antonin, and Bunel (2021).

the extent that competition should reduce the ex post rents from innovation, competition should also reduce the incentives to innovate.

How, if at all, could we reconcile theory and evidence? Should we throw the model in the garbage bin and start again from scratch? Or should we simply ignore the empirical challenges and proceed as before?

We decided to go for a third way: namely, to look more closely at our growth model and try to identify the assumption or assumptions that generate this counterfactual prediction of a negative relationship between competition and growth.

And we finally identified the culprit: in our initial model, the firms that innovate are only the currently inactive firms, not the currently active firms (i.e., not the current technological leaders). Thus, an innovating firm in our model would move from zero profit (pre-innovation) to a positive profit (post-innovation). No wonder, then, that competition would discourage innovation: competition reduces the post-innovation profit, which here is equal to the net profit from innovation.

However, in reality one finds at least two types of firms in most sectors of the economy, and these two types of firms do not react in the same way to increased competition. You first have what we call "leaders"—firms that are close to the current technological frontier in their sector. These firms are currently active, and they make substantial profits even before innovating this period, and they increase their profits by innovating at the frontier. Second, you have what we call the "laggard firms"—firms far below the current technological frontier. These firms make initially low profits, and to increase their profits they first need to catch up with the current technology frontier.

To try to understand why these two types of firms react differently to competition, imagine for a moment that what you are looking at are not firms but students in a classroom. Among them you have the top students and the bottom of the class. And suppose that you are opening the class to an additional student who turns out to be a very good student. This is how one would represent an increase in competition in this context. How will the students react to this new student joining the classroom? The answer is that letting the new student in will encourage the other top students to work harder in order to remain the best, whereas it will further discourage students at the bottom of the class, as those will find it even harder to catch up.

Quite strikingly, firms react like classroom students: namely, faced with a higher degree of competition in their sector, firms that are close to the technology frontier will innovate more in order to *escape competition*, whereas firms that are far from the technological frontier and try to catch up will be *discouraged* by the higher degree of competition, and as a result innovate less: these latter firms behave like in the basic Schumpeterian model.

Overall, the effect of competition on innovation and productivity growth is an inverted-U, which synthetizes the positive *escape-competition effect* and the negative *discouragement effect*. The prediction of opposite reactions of frontier versus non-frontier firms to competition, and of an inverted-U overall, were tested and confirmed in joint work with Richard Blundell, Nick Bloom, and Rachel Griffith using the same kind of firm-level data as in the empirical studies I mentioned above.

The prediction that more intense competition enhances innovation in "frontier" firms but may discourage it in "non-frontier" firms was tested by Aghion, Blundell, et al. (2009) using again panel data of UK firms. One important implication is that competition should be more growth-enhancing in countries that are closer to the world technology frontier, because in these countries more firms are close to the technology frontier in their sectors. We made use of this prediction when discussing the middle-income trap in Section 2.

Another prediction from our enriched model with leaders and laggards is that there is complementarity between patent protection and product market competition in fostering innovation. Intuitively, competition reduces the profit flow of non-innovating frontier firms, whereas patent protection is likely to enhance the profit flow of an innovating frontier firm. Both contribute to raising the net profit gain of an innovating frontier firm; in other words, both types of policies tend to enhance the escape-competition effect.

Our prediction of a complementarity between competition and patent protection was tested by Aghion, Howitt, and Prantl (2015) using OECD country-industry panel data.

A third prediction is that trade liberalization, and in particular import competition on firms' output markets, should have a more positive effect on innovation for firms close to the technological frontier in their sectors than for firms far below the frontier. This prediction is confirmed in recent work by Aghion, Bergeaud, Lequien, et al. (2021) using comprehensive firm-level panel data from France. We refer the reader to the trade survey by Melitz and Redding in this volume.

This extended framework with leaders and laggards and catch-up versus frontier innovation has been used repeatedly in recent years. We already mentioned the explanation in Akcigit and Ates (2021) for the growth decline:

namely, that over the past years it has become harder for the laggards to catch up with the leaders, so that innovation by laggards has been discouraged. Using the same model, Liu, Mian, and Sufi (2022) argue that the growth decline is explained by the fall in interest rates, which increases the value to leaders of a bigger technological lead. This in turn encourages leaders to innovate more while making it harder for laggards to catch up.

In the end, this dialogue between theory and empirics turned out to be mutually enriching. On the one hand, our empirical colleagues realized that the relationship between competition and growth was more involved and subtle than what they thought based on their initial studies. On the other hand, we understood how to enrich our model so as to bring out not one but two basic effects of competition on innovation and growth, to identify conditions under which one or the other effect dominates, and why when aggregating across all firms / sectors we obtain the inverted-U relationship that Scherer (1965) had anticipated but could not explain.

But more importantly, this collaboration inaugurated a whole new way of doing growth theory: namely, by submitting ourselves to a constant back and forth between the model and the data. In our inverted-U paper (Aghion, Bloom, Blundell, et al. 2005) we used micro data to test the additional predictions of various extensions of our basic model in order to finally converge on a model of competition and growth that fits the data.

Since the inverted-U paper came out, the Schumpeterian growth literature has been considerably enriched. First with the model by Klette and Kortum (2004), which introduced entry, exit, and firm dynamics into the creative destruction framework.[9] In particular, the model could account for important stylized facts such as that (i) the firm size distribution is highly skewed; (ii) firm size and firm age are highly correlated; and (iii) small firms exit more frequently than large firms. All these are facts that non-Schumpeterian models could not account for.

Then, to a large extent under the leadership of Ufuk Akcigit and Pete Klenow, the literature underwent a dramatic boost with a whole new wave of Schumpeterian growth models that were confronted to the data using both regression analyses *and* highly sophisticated calibration techniques. This in turn made it possible to go much further than simply testing predictions.

---

[9] We refer the reader to the pioneering work by John Haltiwanger and his co-authors on firm dynamics and job creation and destruction in the United States. In particular, see Haltiwanger, Jarmin, and Miranda (2013).

For example, using these new techniques one could assess the relative importance of small versus large firms, of creative destruction versus increased variety, of basic versus applied research, or of good rents stemming from innovation versus bad rents stemming from political connections; one could also quantify the effects of industrial policies focused on incumbent firms, or the extent to which productivity growth is mismeasured due to creative destruction, or the effects of labor market regulations on aggregate innovation.[10]

These are just few illustrations of all that the Schumpeterian approach can deliver as we keep extending the paradigm in multiple directions, and each time by maintaining the dialogue between the model and the data through increasingly sophisticated techniques.

4 Identifying Misguided Policy Recommendations

The paradigm of creative destruction not only sheds light on various aspects of the growth process; it also provides new glasses to look at policy design and by doing so it allows us to identify erroneous reasonings and to question flawed policy recommendations. In this section we shall question three such wisdoms. First, the claim that we should tax robots. Second, the idea that negative growth is the best way to fight climate change. Third, the view that there is a tradeoff between becoming more innovative and becoming more inclusive or protective: choosing the former would imply renouncing the latter and vice-versa.

Should we tax robots? A dominant view of automation is that it increases aggregate unemployment by substituting capital for labor. The fear that machines would lead to mass unemployment goes back to 1589 when William Lee introduced his knitting machine; most famous is the Luddite movement in 1811–1812 to fight manufacturers' use of machines for producing cotton and wood textiles; and in the 1930s economists starting with J. M. Keynes expressed concern about the danger of mass "technological unemployment."

More recently, the IT and AI revolutions revived the fear that technological progress would make labor increasingly redundant, and the idea has

---

[10] Three pioneering papers in this new wave are Akcigit and Kerr (2010, 2018); Acemoglu, Akcigit, et al. (2018); and Garcia-Macia, Klenow, and Hsieh (2019).

been put forward by economic scholars, and also policymakers, that robots should be taxed in order to protect aggregate employment. A dominant view, indeed, sees robotization and other forms of automation as primarily destroying jobs, even if this may ultimately result in new job creations taking advantage of the lower equilibrium wage induced by the job destruction. Hence the policy recommendation that robots should be taxed in order to protect aggregate employment and also wages.

However, there is an alternative view: namely, that automating firms become more productive, which enables them to lower their quality-adjusted prices and therefore to increase the market for their products possibly partly by stealing business from other firms—domestic or foreign—that did not automate. This productivity effect may more than offset the direct substitution effect of automation (i.e., the replacement of workers by machines), in which case automation will result in higher labor demand by the automating firms.

In Aghion, Antonin, et al. (2022) we consider various measures of industrial capital, including the "industrial automation" measure in Acemoglu and Restrepo (2022), and then we show that an increase in any of these measures results in higher firm-level employment. Taxing robots would reduce firms' incentives to become more productive through automation, hence to increase their market worldwide and therefore their labor demand. The end result of taxing robots may then be to reduce aggregate domestic employment.

Negative growth or green innovation? To fight climate change, some scholars or politicians have advocated negative growth. They find support for their view by looking at the relationship between growth and CO_2 emissions or temperature over the past centuries: as a matter of fact, temperature and aggregate CO_2 emissions worldwide started to increase precisely at the time of the growth takeoff in the nineteenth century. And in China and India, CO_2 emissions initiated their accelerated rise precisely when these two countries engaged on high-growth paths. However, we know what negative growth looks like since the lockdowns we experienced two years ago. In France, during the first lockdown between March and May 2020, domestic GDP went down by 35 percent, whereas CO_2 emissions were reduced by only 8 percent. Fighting climate change through negative growth would be like imposing such a lockdown forever, and we know how psychologically damaging that two-month lockdown was, particularly for the young.

A more promising route, and in fact the only way to reconcile climate with sustained growth and prosperity, is green innovation: to discover cleaner sources of energy, cleaner products, and cleaner production technologies.

But then comes the question: Why can't we rely on firms alone to generate green innovation? The reason is that those incumbent firms that innovated in dirty technologies in the past tend to continue to innovate in dirty technologies in the future.[11] In Acemoglu et al. (2012) we refer to this phenomenon as "path-dependence" in the direction of incumbent firms' innovation.

A first implication of path-dependence is that creative destruction should help: indeed, new entrants are not subject to path-dependence because they were not around in the past by definition. In other words, in an economy where incumbent firms innovated mainly in dirty technologies in the past, by its very nature creative destruction favors greener innovation.

A second implication is that outside intervention is needed to redirect incumbent firms' innovation toward clean technologies. The good news is that there are multiple channels and instruments that can be activated for that purpose. Some channels rely primarily on state intervention: carbon taxes and tariffs, subsidies to green innovation, industrial policy. But other channels also involve civil society: social norms and how much citizens value the environment, consumers' information about the CO_2 content of firms' production and inputs, shareholders' concern for corporate social responsibility, and so on.

In the end, the key to successfully fighting climate change lies with creative destruction and with the triangle between firms, the state, and civil society. Thus, in countries with higher concern of civil society for the environment, more intense competition policy implemented by the state will induce firms to innovate greener in order to escape competition from potential rivals.[12]

Do we have to choose between innovation and inclusion? Should we follow US capitalism, more innovative, or German/Scandinavian capitalism, which is more inclusive and protective? Are we bound to an "either/or" choice between these two forms of capitalism?

---

[11] See Aghion, Dechezleprêtre, et al. (2016).
[12] See Aghion, Bénabou, et al. (2023).

What makes us depart from the "either/or" view is, first, the strong belief that capitalism cannot be fully dynamic unless it is inclusive; it cannot be fully innovative if vested interests prevent the emergence of new talents.

Moreover, there are policies that can help move capitalism both toward more innovativeness *and* toward more protection or inclusiveness. Here we shall focus on two such policies—namely, competition policy and education.

Competition policy. In Section 2 we argued that by increasing the number of product lines controlled by superstars, the IT revolution ended up reducing innovation and growth in the overall economy in the long run. And an inadequate competition policy in the United States favored this evolution: in the absence of regulations on mergers and acquisitions the superstar firms could grow and expand without limit, thereby discouraging entry and innovation by non-superstar firms in the economy. Reforming competition policy so as to better take into account the effect of mergers and acquisitions on future innovation and entry[13] should both foster innovation-led growth and make growth more inclusive by allowing new innovative entrepreneurs to enter the market.[14]

Education. Recent studies have pointed to the fact that parental income and/or parental education affects an individual's probability to become an innovator. This in turn leads a "lost Einsteins" phenomenon (see Bell et al., 2019): highly talented children who could have become innovators, had they been born to wealthy or well-educated parents, fail to innovate if born to low-educated families. The reason is that more-educated parents transmit knowledge and aspirations to their children, both of which are needed to become an innovator. An interesting example is Finland. In 1970 Finland reformed its education system to make it more inclusive. As it turns out, parental income or education does not affect the probability of becoming an inventor for those individuals who started school after the reform, but it affects the probability of becoming an inventor for individuals who experienced the pre-reform schooling system. This in turn suggests that investing in a more inclusive and high-quality education system should both stimulate innovation-led growth *and* make growth more inclusive, simply by en-

---

[13] Such reform is advocated by Richard Gilbert in his recent book *Innovation Matters: Competition Policy for the High-Technology Economy*, 2021, MIT Press.

[14] That entrant innovation should foster social mobility is shown in Aghion, Akcigit, et al. (2019).

abling more talented individuals to become innovators—that is, by reducing the number of "lost Einsteins."

Overall, we are not condemned to choosing between innovation and inclusion. We can activate forces that will make our economies both more innovative and more inclusive by constantly favoring the entry of new innovative firms and the emergence of new talents.

5 Conclusion

We are deeply indebted to Ufuk Akcigit and John Van Reenen for having organized and managed this volume under extremely trying circumstances. We would also like to pay tribute to the memory of Emmanuel Fahri, whose vision and generosity gave birth to this volume project. Schumpeterian theory has come a long way in the past thirty-five years, largely thanks to the editors and the contributors to this volume. Our greatest hope is that the deeper understanding of capitalism that these stellar researchers have provided will lead to a more humane, harmonious, and productive experience of capitalism in the twenty-first century. Finally we owe special thanks to Ian Malcolm for his invaluable help and encouragements.

References

Acemoglu, Daron. 2009. *Introduction to Modern Economic Growth.* Princeton University Press.

Acemoglu, Daron, Philippe Aghion, Leonardo Bursztyn, and David Hemous. 2012. "The Environment and Directed Technical Change." *American Economic Review,* 102(1), 131–166.

Acemoglu, Daron, Philippe Aghion, and Fabrizio Zilibotti. 2006. "Distance to Frontier, Selection, and Economic Growth." *Journal of the European Economic Association,* 4(1), 37–74.

Acemoglu, Daron, Ufuk Akcigit, Harun Alp, Nicholas Bloom, and William Kerr. 2018. "Innovation, Reallocation, and Growth." *American Economic Review,* 108(11), 3450–3491.

Acemoglu, Daron, and Pascual Restrepo. 2022. "Demographics and Automation." *Review of Economic Studies,* 89(1), 1–44.

Aghion, Philippe, Ufuk Akcigit, Antonin Bergeaud, Richard Blundell, and David Hemous. 2019. "Innovation and Top Income Inequality." *Review of Economic Studies,* 86(1), 1–45.

Aghion, Philippe, Ufuk Akcigit, and Peter Howitt. 2014. "What Do We Learn from Schumpeterian Growth Theory?" In *Handbook of Economic Growth*, vol. 2, ed. Philippe Aghion and Steven Durlauf, 515–563. Elsevier.

Aghion, Philippe, Celine Antonin, and Simon Bunel. 2021. *The Power of Creative Destruction: Economic Upheaval and the Wealth of Nations.* Harvard University Press.

Aghion, Philippe, Celine Antonin, Simon Bunel, and Xavier Jaravel. 2022. "What Are the Labor and Product Market Effects of Automation? New Evidence from France." CEPR Discussion Paper DP14443.

Aghion, Philippe, Roland Bénabou, Ralf Martin, and Alexandra Roulet. 2023. "Environmental Preferences and Technological Choices: Is Market Competition Clean or Dirty?" *American Economic Review: Insights* (forthcoming).

Aghion, Philippe, Antonin Bergeaud, Timo Boppart, Peter J. Klenow, and Huiyu Li. 2019. "A Theory of Falling Growth and Rising Rents." NBER Working Paper 26448.

Aghion, Philippe, Antonin Bergeaud, Matthieu Lequien, Marc Melitz, and Thomas Zuber. 2021. "Opposing Firm-Level Responses to the China Shock: Horizontal Competition versus Vertical Relationships?" NBER Working Paper 29196.

Aghion, Philippe, Nicholas Bloom, Richard Blundell, Rachel Griffith, and Peter Howitt. 2005. "Competition and Innovation: An Inverted-U Relationship." *Quarterly Journal of Economics*, 120(2), 701–728.

Aghion, Philippe, Richard Blundell, Rachel Griffith, Peter Howitt, and Susanne Prantl. 2009. "The Effects of Entry on Incumbent Innovation and Productivity." *Review of Economics and Statistics*, 91(1), 20–32.

Aghion, Philippe, Antoine Dechezleprêtre, David Hemous, Ralf Martin, and John Van Reenen. 2016. "Carbon Taxes, Path Dependency, and Directed Technical Change: Evidence from the Auto Industry." *Journal of Political Economy*, 124(1), 1–51.

Aghion, Philippe, Sergei Guriev, and Kangchul Jo. 2019. "Chaebols and Firm Dynamics in Korea." CEPR Discussion Paper 13825.

Aghion, Philippe, Christopher Harris, Peter Howitt, and John Vickers. 2001. "Competition, Imitation and Growth with Step-by-Step Innovation." *Review of Economic Studies*, 68(3), 467–492.

Aghion, Philippe, Christopher Harris, and John Vickers. 1997. "Competition and Growth with Step-by-Step Innovation: An Example." *European Economic Review*, 41(3–5), 771–782.

Aghion, Philippe, and Peter Howitt. 1998. *Endogenous Growth Theory.* MIT Press.

Aghion, Philippe, and Peter Howitt. 2009. *The Economics of Growth.* MIT Press.

Aghion, Philippe, Peter Howitt, and Susanne Prantl. 2015. "Patent Rights, Product Market Reforms, and Innovation." *Journal of Economic Growth*, 20(3), 223–262.

Akcigit, Ufuk, and Sina T. Ates. 2021. "Ten Facts on Declining Business Dynamism and Lessons from Endogenous Growth Theory." *American Economic Journal: Macroeconomics*, 13(1), 257–298.

Akcigit, Ufuk, and William R. Kerr. 2010. "Growth through Heterogeneous Innovations." NBER Working Paper 16443.

Akcigit, Ufuk, and William R. Kerr. 2018. "Growth through Heterogeneous Innovations." *Journal of Political Economy,* 126(4), 1374–1443.

Barro, Robert J., and Xavier Sala-i-Martin. 1995. *Economic Growth.* McGraw Hill.

Bell, Alex, Raj Chetty, Xavier Jaravel, Neviana Petkova, and John Van Reenen. 2019. "Who Becomes an Inventor in America? The Importance of Exposure to Innovation." *Quarterly Journal of Economics,* 134(2), 647–713.

Blundell, Richard, Rachel Griffith, and John Van Reenen. 1995. "Dynamic Count Data Models of Technological Innovation." *Economic Journal,* 105(429), 333–344.

Blundell, Richard, Rachel Griffith, and John Van Reenen. 1999. "Market Share, Market Value and Innovation in a Panel of British Manufacturing Firms." *Review of Economic Studies,* 66(3), 529–554.

Garcia-Macia, Daniel, Chang-Tai Hsieh, and Peter J. Klenow. 2019. "How Destructive Is Innovation?" *Econometrica,* 87(5), 1507–1541.

Grossman, Gene, and Elhanan Helpman. 1991. *Innovation and Growth in the Global Economy.* MIT Press.

Haltiwanger, John, Ron S. Jarmin, and Javier Miranda. 2013. "Who Creates Jobs? Small versus Large versus Young." *Review of Economics and Statistics,* 95(2), 347–361.

Klette, Tor Jacob, and Samuel Kortum. 2004. "Innovating Firms and Aggregate Innovation." *Journal of Political Economy,* 112(5), 986–1018.

Liu, Ernest, Atif Mian, and Amir Sufi. 2022. "Low Interest Rates, Market Power, and Productivity Growth." *Econometrica,* 90(1), 193–221.

Mokyr, Joel. 2002. *The Gifts of Athena: Historical Origins of the Knowledge Economy.* Princeton University Press.

Mokyr, Joel, and Hans-Joachim Voth. 2010. "Understanding Growth in Europe, 1700–1870: Theory and Evidence." In *The Cambridge Economic History of Modern Europe,* vol. 1, ed. Stephen Broadberry and Kevin H. O'Rourke, 7–40. Cambridge University Press.

Rajan, Raghuram, and Luigi Zingales. 2004. *Saving Capitalism from the Capitalists: Unleashing the Power of Financial Markets to Create Wealth and Spread Opportunity.* Princeton University Press.

Romer, Paul. 1990. "Endogenous Technical Change." *Journal of Political Economy,* 98(5), 71–102.

Scherer, Frederic M. 1965. "Firm Size, Market Structure, Opportunity, and the Output of Patented Inventions." *American Economic Review,* 55(5), 1097–1125.

Solow, Robert. 1956. "A Contribution to the Theory of Economic Growth." *Quarterly Journal of Economics,* 70(1), 65–94.

Index

Figures and tables are denoted by *f* or *t* following the page number. Footnotes are denoted by n following the page number.